Blackstone's Statutes
Family Law

Blackstone's Statutes
Family Law

2006–2007

Fifteenth Edition

Edited by

Mika Oldham

MA, PhD

Fellow of Jesus College, Cambridge

OXFORD

UNIVERSITY PRESS

OXFORD
UNIVERSITY PRESS

Great Clarendon Street, Oxford OX2 6DP

Oxford University Press is a department of the University of Oxford.
It furthers the University's objective of excellence in research, scholarship,
and education by publishing worldwide in

Oxford New York

Auckland Cape Town Dar es Salaam Hong Kong Karachi
Kuala Lumpur Madrid Melbourne Mexico City Nairobi
New Delhi Shanghai Taipei Toronto

With offices in

Argentina Austria Brazil Chile Czech Republic France Greece
Guatemala Hungary Italy Japan Poland Portugal Singapore
South Korea Switzerland Thailand Turkey Ukraine Vietnam

Oxford is a registered trade mark of Oxford University Press
in the UK and in certain other countries

Published in the United States
by Oxford University Press Inc., New York

This selection © Mika Oldham 2007

The moral rights of the author have been asserted
Database right Oxford University Press (maker)

Crown copyright material is reproduced under Class Licence
Number C01P0000148 with the permission of OPSI
and the Queen's Printer for Scotland

First published by Blackstone Press

First edition 1990	Sixth edition 1997	Eleventh edition 1999
Second edition 1992	Seventh edition 1998	Twelfth edition 2003
Third edition 1994	Eighth edition 2002	Thirteenth edition 2004
Fourth edition 1995	Ninth edition 2000	Fourteenth edition 2005
Fifth edition 1996	Tenth edition 2001	Fifteenth edition 2007

British Library Cataloguing in Publication Data

Data available

Typeset by Newgen Imaging Systems (P) Ltd., Chennai, India
Printed in Great Britain
on acid-free paper by
CPI Bath

ISBN 0–19–928823–2   978–0–19–928823–6

1 3 5 7 9 10 8 6 4 2

CHRONOLOGICAL CONTENTS

ALPHABETICAL CONTENTS

PREFACE

The most important changes to the statutes this year are those introduced by the Children and Adoption Act 2006, which amends the Children Act 1989 and the Criminal Justice Act 2003 in order to strengthen the powers of the courts to enforce contact orders. Other changes to existing enactments are effected by primary legislation, including the Mental Capacity Act 2005, the Constitutional Reform Act 2005 and the Equality Act 2006, and by secondary legislation.

As with earlier editions, statutes are included in chronological order and amendments incorporated directly into the relevant text. In line with usual teaching convention, statutes are treated as fully in force once Royal Assent is received. My thanks to the staff at OUP for their constant friendliness and willingness to help. I would also like to express my gratitude to colleagues in other institutions whose helpful comments have assisted in the preparation of this edition. As always, any further comments or suggestions would be welcome.

Mika Oldham
June 2006

Wills Act 1837

(7 Will. 4 & 1 Vict., c. 26)

3 All property may be disposed of by will

It shall be lawful for every person to devise, bequeath, or dispose of, by his will executed in manner herein-after required, all real estate and all personal estate which he shall be entitled to, either at law or in equity, at the time of his death, and which if not so devised, bequeathed, or disposed of would devolve upon his executor or administrator; and the power hereby given shall extend to all contingent, executory, or other future interests in any real or personal estate, whether the testator may or may not be ascertained as the person or one of the persons in whom the same respectively may become vested, and whether he may be entitled thereto under the instrument by which the same respectively were created or under any disposition thereof by deed or will; and also to all rights of entry for conditions broken, and other rights of entry; and also to such of the same estates, interests, and rights respectively, and other real and personal estate, as the testator may be entitled to at the time of his death, notwithstanding that he may become entitled to the same subsequently to the execution of his will.

7 No will of a person under age valid

No will made by any person under the age of eighteen years shall be valid.

9 Signing and attestation of wills

No will shall be valid unless—

> (a) it is in writing, and signed by the testator, or by some other person in his presence and by his direction; and
>
> (b) it appears that the testator intended by his signature to give effect to the will; and
>
> (c) the signature is made or acknowledged by the testator in the presence of two or more witnesses present at the same time; and
>
> (d) each witness either—
>> (i) attests and signs the will; or
>>
>> (ii) acknowledges his signature,
>>
>> in the presence of the testator (but not necessarily in the presence of any other witness),

but no form of attestation shall be necessary.

. . .

18 Wills to be revoked by marriage, except in certain cases

(1) Subject to subsections (2) to (4) below, a will shall be revoked by the testator's marriage.

(2) A disposition in a will in exercise of a power of appointment shall take effect notwithstanding the testator's subsequent marriage unless the property so appointed would in default of appointment pass to his personal representatives.

(3) Where it appears from a will that at the time it was made the testator was expecting to be married to a particular person and that he intended that the will should not be revoked by the marriage, the will shall not be revoked by his marriage to that person.

(4) Where it appears from a will that at the time it was made the testator was expecting to be married to a particular person and that he intended that a disposition in the will should not be revoked by his marriage to that person,—

> (a) that disposition shall take effect notwithstanding the marriage; and
>
> (b) any other disposition in the will shall take effect also, unless it appears from the will that the testator intended the disposition to be revoked by the marriage.

18A   Effect of dissolution or annulment of marriage on wills

(1) Where, after a testator has made a will, a decree of a court of civil jurisdiction in England and Wales dissolves or annuls his marriage or his marriage is dissolved or annulled and the divorce or annulment is entitled to recognition in England and Wales by virtue of Part II of the Family Law Act 1986,—

(a) provisions of the will appointing executors or trustees or conferring a power of appointment, if they appoint or confer the power on the former spouse, shall take effect as if the former spouse had died on the date on which the marriage is dissolved or annulled, and

(b) any property which, or an interest in which, is devised or bequeathed to the former spouse shall pass as if the former spouse had died on that date,

except in so far as a contrary intention appears by the will.

(2) Subsection (1)(b) above is without prejudice to any right of the former spouse to apply for financial provision under the Inheritance (Provision for Family and Dependants) Act 1975.

18B   Will to be revoked by civil partnership

(1) Subject to subsections (2) to (6), a will is revoked by the formation of a civil partnership between the testator and another person.

(2) A disposition in a will in exercise of a power of appointment takes effect despite the formation of a subsequent civil partnership between the testator and another person unless the property so appointed would in default of appointment pass to the testator's personal representatives.

(3) If it appears from a will—

(a) that at the time it was made the testator was expecting to form a civil partnership with a particular person, and

(b) that he intended that the will should not be revoked by the formation of the civil partnership,

the will is not revoked by its formation.

(4) Subsections (5) and (6) apply if it appears from a will—

(a) that at the time it was made the testator was expecting to form a civil partnership with a particular person, and

(b) that he intended that a disposition in the will should not be revoked by the formation of the civil partnership.

(5) The disposition takes effect despite the formation of the civil partnership.

(6) Any other disposition in the will also takes effect, unless it appears from the will that the testator intended the disposition to be revoked by the formation of the civil partnership.

18C   Effect of dissolution or annulment of civil partnership on wills

(1) This section applies if, after a testator has made a will—

(a) a court of civil jurisdiction in England and Wales dissolves his civil partnership or makes a nullity order in respect of it, or

(b) his civil partnership is dissolved or annulled and the dissolution or annulment is entitled to recognition in England and Wales by virtue of Chapter 3 of Part 5 of the Civil Partnership Act 2004.

(2) Except in so far as a contrary intention appears by the will—

(a) provisions of the will appointing executors or trustees or conferring a power of appointment, if they appoint or confer the power on the former civil partner, take effect as if the former civil partner had died on the date on which the civil partnership is dissolved or annulled, and

(b) any property which, or an interest in which, is devised or bequeathed to the former civil partner shall pass as if the former civil partner had died on that date.

(3) Subsection (2)(b) does not affect any right of the former civil partner to apply for financial provision under the Inheritance (Provision for Family and Dependants) Act 1975.

...

33 Gifts to children or other issue who leave issue living at the testator's death shall not lapse

(1) Where—

(a) a will contains a devise or bequest to a child or remoter descendant of the testator; and

(b) the intended beneficiary dies before the testator, leaving issue; and

(c) issue of the intended beneficiary are living at the testator's death,

then, unless a contrary intention appears by the will, the devise or bequest shall take effect as a devise or bequest to the issue living at the testator's death.

(2) Where—

(a) a will contains a devise or bequest to a class of persons consisting of children or remoter descendants of the testator; and

(b) a member of the class dies before the testator, leaving issue; and

(c) issue of that member are living at the testator's death,

then, unless a contrary intention appears by the will, the devise or bequest shall take effect as if the class included the issue of its deceased member living at the testator's death.

(3) Issue shall take under this section through all degrees, according to their stock, in equal shares if more than one, any gift or share which their parent would have taken and so that no issue shall take whose parent is living at the testator's death and so capable of taking.

(4) For the purposes of this section—

(a) the illegitimacy of any person is to be disregarded; and

(b) a person conceived before the testator's death and born living thereafter is to be taken to have been living at the testator's death.

...

Evidence Amendment Act 1853
(16 & 17 Vict., c. 83)

1 Husbands and wives of parties to be admissible witnesses

On the trial of any issue joined, or of any matter or question, or on any inquiry arising in any suit, action, or other proceeding in any court of justice, or before any person having by law or by consent of parties authority to hear, receive, and examine evidence, the husbands and wives of the parties thereto, and of the persons in whose behalf any such suit, action, or other proceeding may be brought or instituted, or opposed or defended, shall, except as hereinafter excepted, be competent and compellable to give evidence, either viva voce or by deposition, according to the practice of the court, on behalf of either or any of the parties to the said suit, action, or other proceeding.

2 Saving as to criminal cases

Nothing herein shall render any husband competent or compellable to give evidence for or against his wife, or any wife competent or compellable to give evidence for or against her husband, in any criminal proceeding.

Married Women's Property Act 1882
(45 & 46 Vict., c. 75)

11 Moneys payable under policy of assurance not to form part of estate of the insured

A married woman may effect a policy upon her own life or the life of her husband for her own benefit; and the same and all benefit thereof shall enure accordingly.

A policy of assurance effected by any man on his own life, and expressed to be for the benefit of his wife, or of his children, or of his wife and children, or any of them, or by any woman on her own life, and expressed to be for the benefit of her husband, or of her children, or of her husband and children, or any of them, shall create a trust in favour of the objects therein named, and the moneys payable under any such policy shall not, so long as any object of the trust remains unperformed, form part of the estate of the insured, or be subject to his or her debts: Provided, that if it shall be proved that the policy was effected and the premiums paid with intent to defraud the creditors of the insured, they shall be entitled to receive, out of the moneys payable under the policy, a sum equal to the premiums so paid. The insured may, by the policy, or by any memorandum under his or her hand, appoint a trustee or trustees of the moneys payable under the policy, and from time to time appoint a new trustee or new trustees thereof, and may make provision for the appointment of a new trustee or new trustees thereof, and for the investment of the moneys payable under any such policy. In default of any such appointment of a trustee, such policy, immediately on its being effected, shall vest in the insured and his or her legal personal representatives, in trust for the purposes aforesaid. The receipt of a trustee or trustees duly appointed, or in default of any such appointment, or in default of notice to the insurance office, the receipt of the legal personal representatives of the insured shall be a discharge to the office for the sum secured by the policy, or for the value thereof, in whole or in part.

17   Questions between husband and wife as to property to be decided in a summary way
In any question between husband and wife as to the title to or possession of property, either party may apply by summons or otherwise in a summary way to the High Court or such county court as may be prescribed and the court may, on such an application (which may be heard in private), make such order with respect to the property as it thinks fit.

In this section 'prescribed' means prescribed by rules of court and rules made for the purposes of this section may confer jurisdiction on county courts whatever the situation or value of the property in dispute.

Law of Property Act 1925
(15 & 16 Geo. 5, c. 20)

37   Rights of husband and wife
A husband and wife shall, for all purposes of acquisition of any interest in property, under a disposition made or coming into operation after the commencement of this Act, be treated as two persons.

53   Instruments required to be in writing
   (1) Subject to the provisions hereinafter contained with respect to the creation of interests in land by parol—
   (a) no interest in land can be created or disposed of except by writing signed by the person creating or conveying the same, or by his agent thereunto lawfully authorised in writing, or by will, or by operation of law;
   (b) a declaration of trust respecting any land or any interest therein must be manifested and proved by some writing signed by some person who is able to declare such trust or by his will;
   (c) a disposition of an equitable interest or trust subsisting at the time of the disposition, must be in writing signed by the person disposing of the same, or by his agent thereunto lawfully authorised in writing or by will.
   (2) This section does not affect the creation or operation of resulting, implied or constructive trusts.

184   Presumption of survivorship in regard to claims to property

In all cases where, after the commencement of this Act, two or more persons have died in circumstances rendering it uncertain which of them survived the other or others, such deaths shall (subject to any order of the court), for all purposes affecting the title to property, be presumed to have occurred in order of seniority, and accordingly the younger shall be deemed to have survived the elder.

Administration of Estates Act 1925
(15 & 16 Geo. 5, c. 23)

PART IV   DISTRIBUTION OF RESIDUARY ESTATE

46   Succession to real and personal estate on intestacy

(1) The residuary estate of an intestate shall be distributed in the manner or be held on the trusts mentioned in this section, namely:—

    (i)   If the intestate leaves a spouse or civil partner, then in accordance with the following Table:

TABLE

If the intestate—	
(1) leaves— (a) no issue, and (b) no parent, or brother or sister of the whole blood, or issue of a brother or sister of the whole blood	the residuary estate shall be held in trust for the surviving spouse or civil partner absolutely.
(2) leaves issue (whether or not persons mentioned in sub-paragraph (b) above also survive)	the surviving spouse or civil partner shall take the personal chattels absolutely and, in addition, the residuary estate of the intestate (other than the personal chattels) shall stand charged with the payment of a fixed net sum, free of death duties and costs, to the surviving spouse or civil partner with interest thereon from the date of the death at such rate as the Lord Chancellor may specify by order until paid or appropriated, and, subject to providing for that sum and the interest thereon, the residuary estate (other than the personal chattels) shall be held— (a) as to one half upon trust for the surviving spouse or civil partner during his or her life, and, subject to such life interest, on the statutory trusts for the issue of the intestate, and (b) as to the other half, on the statutory trusts for the issue of the intestate.
(3) leaves one or more of the following, that is to say, a parent, a brother or sister of the whole blood or issue of a brother or sister of the whole blood, but leaves no issue.	the surviving spouse or civil partner shall take the personal chattels absolutely and, in addition, the residuary estate of the intestate (other than the personal chattels) shall stand charged with the payment of a fixed net sum, free of death duties and costs, to the surviving spouse or civil partner with interest thereon from the date of the death at such rate as the Lord Chancellor may specify by order until paid or appropriated, and, subject to providing for that sum and the interest thereon, the residuary estate (other than the personal chattels) shall be held—

TABLE (*cont.*)

> (a) as to one half in trust for the surviving spouse or civil partner absolutely, and
> (b) as to the other half—
>> (i) where the intestate leaves one parent or both parents (whether or not brothers or sisters of the intestate or their issue also survive) in trust for the parent absolutely or, as the case may be, for the two parents in equal shares absolutely
>> (ii) where the intestate leaves no parent, on the statutory trusts for the brothers and sisters of the whole blood of the intestate.

(ii) If the intestate leaves issue but no spouse or civil partner, the residuary estate of the intestate shall be held on the statutory trusts for the issue of the intestate;

(iii) If the intestate leaves no spouse or civil partner and no issue but both parents, then the residuary estate of the intestate shall be held in trust for the father and mother in equal shares absolutely;

(iv) If the intestate leaves no spouse or civil partner and no issue but one parent, then the residuary estate of the intestate shall be held in trust for the surviving father or mother absolutely;

(v) If the intestate leaves no spouse or civil partner and no issue and no parent, then the residuary estate of the intestate shall be held in trust for the following persons living at the death of the intestate, and in the following ordr and manner, namely:—

First, on the statutory trusts for the brothers and sisters of the whole blood of the intestate; but if no person takes an absolutely vested interest under such trusts; then

Secondly, on the statutory trusts for the brothers and sisters of the half blood of the intestate; but if no person takes an absolutely vested interest under such trusts; then

Thirdly, for the grandparents of the intestate and, if more than one survive the intestate, in equal shares; but if there is no member of this class; then

Fourthly, on the statutory trusts for the uncles and aunts of the intestate (being brothers or sisters of the whole blood of a parent of the intestate); but if no person takes an absolutely vested interest under such trusts; then

Fifthly, on the statutory trusts for the uncles and aunts of the intestate (being brothers or sisters of the half blood of a parent of the intestate);

(vi) In default of any person taking an absolute interest under the foregoing provisions, the residuary estate of the intestate shall belong to the Crown or to the Duchy of Lancaster or to the Duke of Cornwall for the time being, as the case may be, as bona vacantia, and in lieu of any right to escheat.

The Crown or the said Duchy or the said Duke may (without prejudice to the powers reserved by section nine of the Civil List Act 1910, or any other powers), out of the whole or any part of the property devolving on them respectively, provide, in accordance with the existing practice, for dependants, whether kindred or not, of the intestate, and other persons for whom the intestate might reasonably have been expected to make provision.

(1A) The power to make orders under subsection (1) above shall be exercisable by statutory instrument subject to annulment in pursuance of a resolution of either House of Parliament; and such order may be varied or revoked by a subsequent order made under the power.

(2) A spouse or civil partner shall for all purposes of distribution or division under the foregoing provisions of this section be treated as two persons.

(2A) Where the intestate's spouse or civil partner survived the intestate but died before the end of the period of 28 days beginning with the day on which the intestate died, this section shall have effect as respects the intestate as if the spouse or civil partner had not survived the intestate.

(3) Where the intestate and the intestate's spouse or civil partner have died in circumstances rendering it uncertain which of them survived the other and the intestate's spouse or civil partner is by virtue of section one hundred and eighty four of the Law of Property Act 1925 deemed to have survived the intestate, this section shall, nevertheless, have effect as respects the intestate as if the spouse or civil partner had not survived the intestate.

(4) The interest payable on the fixed net sum payable to a surviving spouse or civil partner shall be primarily payable out of income.

47 Statutory trusts in favour of issue and other classes of relatives of intestate

(1) Where under this Part of this Act the residuary estate of an intestate, or any part thereof, is directed to be held on the statutory trusts for the issue of the intestate, the same shall be held upon the following trusts, namely:—

  (i) In trust, in equal shares if more than one, for all or any of the children or child of the intestate, living at the death of the intestate, who attain the age of eighteen years or marry under that age or form a civil partnership under that age, and for all or any of the issue living at the death of the intestate who attain the age eighteen years or marry, or form a civil partnership, under that age of any child of the intestate who predeceases the intestate, such issue to take through all degrees, according to their stocks, in equal shares if more than one, the share which their parent would have taken if living at the death of the intestate, and so that no issue shall take whose parent is living at the death of the intestate and so capable of taking;

  (ii) The statutory power of advancement, and the statutory provisions which relate to maintenance and accumulation of surplus income, shall apply, but when an infant marries, or forms a civil partnership, such infant shall be entitled to give valid receipts for the income of the infant's share or interest;

  …

  (iv) The personal representatives may permit any infant contingently interested to have the use and enjoyment of any personal chattels in such manner and subject to such conditions (if any) as the personal representatives may consider reasonable, and without being liable to account for any consequential loss.

(2) If the trusts in favour of the issue of the intestate fail by reason of no child or other issue attaining an absolutely vested interest—

  (a) the residuary estate of the intestate and the income thereof and all statutory accumulations, if any, of the income thereof, or so much thereof as may not have been paid or applied under any power affecting the same, shall go, devolve and be held under the provisions of this Part of this Act as if the intestate had died without leaving issue living at the death of the intestate;

  (b) References in this Part of this Act to the intestate 'leaving no issue' shall be construed as 'leaving no issue who attain an absolutely vested interest';

  (c) References in this Part of this Act to the intestate 'leaving issue' or 'leaving a child or other issue' shall be construed as 'leaving issue who attain an absolutely vested interest.'

(3) Where under this Part of this Act the residuary estate of an intestate or any part thereof is directed to be held on the statutory trusts for any class of relatives of the intestate, other than issue of the intestate, the same shall be held on trusts corresponding to the statutory trusts for the issue of the intestate (other than the provision for bringing any money or property into account) as if such trusts (other than as aforesaid) were repeated with the

substitution of references to the members or member of that class for references to the children or child of the intestate.

(4) References in paragraph (i) of subsection (1) of the last foregoing section to the intestate leaving, or not leaving, a member of the class consisting of brothers or sisters of the whole blood of the intestate and issue of brothers or sisters of the whole blood of the intestate shall be construed as references to the intestate leaving, or not leaving, a member of that class who attains an absolutely vested interest.

. . .

48 Powers of personal representative in respect of interests of surviving spouse

(2) The personal representatives may raise—

(a) the fixed net sum or any part thereof and the interest thereon payable to the surviving spouse or civil partner of the intestate on the security of the whole or any part of the residuary estate of the intestate (other than the personal chattels), so far as that estate may be sufficient for the purpose or the said sum and interest may not have been satisfied by an appropriation under the statutory power available in that behalf; and

(b) in like manner the capital sum, if any, required for the purchase or redemption of the life interest of the surviving spouse or civil partner of the intestate, or any part thereof not satisfied by the application for that purpose of any part of the residuary estate of the intestate;

and in either case the amount, if any, properly required for the payment of the costs of the transaction.

49 Application to cases of partial intestacy

(1) Where any person dies leaving a will effectively disposing of part of his property, this Part of this Act shall have effect as respects the part of his property not so disposed of subject to the provisions contained in the will and subject to the following modifications:—

(a) the personal representative shall, subject to his rights and powers for the purposes of administration, be a trustee for the persons entitled under this Part of this Act in respect of the part of the estate not expressly disposed of unless it appears by the will that the personal representative is intended to take such part beneficially.

(4) The references in subsection (3) of section forty-seven A of this Act to property are references to property comprised in the residuary estate and, accordingly, where a will of the deceased creates a life interest in property in possession, and the remaining interest in that property forms part of the residuary estate, the said references are references to that remaining interest (which, until the life interest determines, is property not in possession).

. . .

Children and Young Persons Act 1933
(23 Geo. 5, c. 12)

PART I   PREVENTION OF CRUELTY AND EXPOSURE TO MORAL AND PHYSICAL DANGER

Offences

1   Cruelty to persons under sixteen

(1) If any person who has attained the age of sixteen years and has responsibility for any child or young person under that age, wilfully assaults, ill-treats, neglects, abandons, or

exposes him, or causes or procures him to be assaulted, ill-treated, neglected, abandoned, or exposed, in a manner likely to cause him unnecessary suffering or injury to health (including injury to or loss of sight, or hearing, or limb, or organ of the body, and any mental derangement), that person shall be guilty of a misdemeanour, and shall be liable—

    (a) on conviction on indictment, to a fine, or alternatively, or in addition thereto, to imprisonment for any term not exceeding ten years;

    (b) on summary conviction, to a fine not exceeding the prescribed sum, or alternatively, or in addition thereto, to imprisonment for any term not exceeding six months.

  (2) For the purposes of this section—

    (a) a parent or other person legally liable to maintain a child or young person, or the legal guardian of a child or young person, shall be deemed to have neglected him in a manner likely to cause injury to his health if he has failed to provide adequate food, clothing, medical aid or lodging for him, or if, having been unable otherwise to provide such food, clothing, medical aid or lodging, he has failed to take steps to procure it to be provided under the enactments applicable in that behalf;

    (b) where it is proved that the death of an infant under three years of age was caused by suffocation (not being suffocation caused by disease or the presence of any foreign body in the throat or air passages of the infant) while the infant was in bed with some other person who has attained the age of sixteen years, that other person shall, if he was, when he went to bed, under the influence of drink, be deemed to have neglected the infant in a manner likely to cause injury to its health.

  (3) A person may be convicted of an offence under this section—

    (a) notwithstanding that actual suffering or injury to health, or the likelihood of actual suffering or injury to health, was obviated by the action of another person;

    (b) notwithstanding the death of the child or young person in question.

. . .

17   Interpretation of Part I

  (1) For the purposes of this Part of this Act, the following shall be presumed to have responsibility for a child or young person—

    (a) any person who—

      (i)   has parental responsibility for him (within the meaning of the Children Act 1989); or

      (ii) is otherwise legally liable to maintain him; and

    (b) any person who has care of him.

  (2) A person who is presumed to be responsible for a child or young person by virtue of subsection (1)(a) shall not be taken to have ceased to be responsible for him by reason only that he does not have care of him.

. . .

Principles to be observed by all courts in dealing with children and young persons

44   General considerations

  (1) Every court in dealing with a child or young person who is brought before it, either as an offender or otherwise, shall have regard to the welfare of the child or young person and shall in a proper case take steps for removing him from undesirable surroundings, and for securing that proper provision is made for his education and training.

Law Reform (Married Women and Tortfeasors) Act 1935
(25 & 26 Geo. 5, c. 30)

PART I   CAPACITY, PROPERTY, AND LIABILITIES OF MARRIED WOMEN: AND LIABILITIES OF HUSBANDS

1   Capacity of married women

Subject to the provisions of this Part of this Act, a married woman shall—

    (a) be capable of acquiring, holding and disposing of, any property; and

    (b) be capable of rendering herself, and being rendered, liable in respect of any tort, contract, debt, or obligation; and

    (c) be capable of suing and being sued, either in tort or in contract or otherwise;

    (d) be subject to the law relating to bankruptcy and to the enforcement of judgments and orders,

in all respects as if she were a feme sole.

2   Property of married women

(1) Subject to the provisions of this Part of this Act all property which—

    (a) immediately before the passing of this Act was the separate property of a married woman or held for her separate use in equity; or

    (b) belongs at the time of her marriage to a woman married after the passing of this Act; or

    (c) after the passing of this Act is acquired by or devolves upon a married woman,

shall belong to her in all respects as if she were a feme sole and may be disposed of accordingly.

3   Abolition of husband's liability for wife's torts and ante-nuptial contracts, debts and obligations

Subject to the provisions of this Part of this Act, the husband of a married woman shall not, by reason only of his being her husband, be liable—

    (a) in respect of any tort committed by her whether before or after the marriage, or in respect of any contract entered into, or debt or obligation incurred, by her before the marriage; or

    (b) to be sued, or made a party to any legal proceeding brought, in respect of any such tort, contract, debt, or obligation.

National Assistance Act 1948
(11 & 12 Geo. 6, c. 29)

PART IV   GENERAL AND SUPPLEMENTARY

Recovery of expenses

42   Liability to maintain wife or husband, and children

(1) For the purposes of this Act—

    (a) a man shall be liable to maintain his wife and his children, and

    (b) a woman shall be liable to maintain her husband and her children.

(2) Any reference in subsection (1) of this section to a person's children shall be construed in accordance with section 1 of the Family Law Reform Act 1987.

43   Recovery of cost of assistance from persons liable for maintenance

(1) Where assistance is given or applied for by reference to the requirements of any person (in this section referred to as a person assisted), the local authority concerned may

make a complaint to the court against any other person who for the purposes of this Act is liable to maintain the person assisted.

(2) On a complaint under this section the court shall have regard to all the circumstances and in particular to the resources of the defendant, and may order the defendant to pay such sum, weekly or otherwise, as the court may consider appropriate.

...

(5) Payments under subsection (2) of this section shall be made—

    (a) to the local authority concerned, in respect of the cost of assistance, whether given before or after the making of the order, or

    (b) to the applicant for assistance or any other person being a person assisted, or

    (c) to such other person as appears to the court expedient in the interests of the person assisted,

or as to part in one such manner and as to part in another, as may be provided by the order.

(6) An order under this section shall be enforceable as a magistrates' court maintenance order within the meaning of section 150(1) of the Magistrates' Courts Act 1980.

Marriage Act 1949
(12 & 13 Geo. 6, c. 76)

PART I   RESTRICTIONS ON MARRIAGE

1   Marriages within prohibited degrees

(1) A marriage solemnized between a person and any person mentioned the list in Part 1 of Schedule 1 shall be void.

(2) Subject to subsection (3) of this section, a marriage solemnized between a person and any person mentioned in the list in Part 2 of Schedule 1 shall be void.

(3) Any such marriage as is mentioned in subsection (2) of this section shall not be void by reason only of affinity if both the parties to the marriage have attained the age of twenty-one at the time of the marriage and the younger party has not at any time before attaining the age of eighteen been a child of the family in relation to the other party.

(4) Subject to subsection (5) of this section, a marriage solemnized between a person and any person mentioned in the list in Part 3 of Schedule 1 shall be void.

(5) Any such marriage as is mentioned in subsection (4) of this section shall not be void by reason only of affinity if both the parties to the marriage have attained the age of twenty-one at the time of the marriage and the marriage is solemnized—

    (a) in the case of a marriage between a person and the parent of a former spouse of that person, after the death of both the former spouse and the former spouse's other parent;

    (b) in the case of a marriage between a person and the parent of a former civil partner of that person, after the death of both the former civil partner and the former civil partner's other parent;

    (c) in the case of a marriage between a person and the former spouse of a child of that person, after the death of both the child and the child's other parent;

    (d) in the case of a marriage between a person and the former civil partner of a child of that person, after the death of both the child and the child's other parent.

2   Marriages of persons under sixteen

A marriage solemnized between persons either of whom is under the age of sixteen shall be void.

3   Marriages of persons under eighteen

(1) Where the marriage of a child, not being a widower or widow, is intended to be solemnized on the authority of a certificate issued by a superintendent registrar under Part III

of this Act, whether by licence or without licence, the consent of the appropriate persons shall be required. Provided that—

> (a) if the superintendent registrar is satisfied that the consent of any person whose consent is so required cannot be obtained by reason of absence or inaccessibility or by reason of his being under any disability, the necessity for the consent of that person shall be dispensed with, if there is any other person whose consent is also required; and if the consent of no other person is required, the Registrar General may dispense with the necessity of obtaining any consent, or the court may, on application being made, consent to the marriage, and the consent of the court so given shall have the same effect as if it had been given by the person whose consent cannot be so obtained;
>
> (b) if any person whose consent is required refuses his consent, the court may, on application being made, consent to the marriage, and the consent of the court so given shall have the same effect as if it had been given by the person whose consent is refused.

(1A) The appropriate persons are—

> (a) if none of paragraphs (b) to (h) apply, each of the following—
>> (i) any parent of the child who has parental responsibility for him; and
>> (ii) any guardian of the child;
>
> (b) where a special guardianship order is in force with respect to a child, each of the child's special guardians, unless any of paragraphs (c) to (g) applies;
>
> (c) where a care order has effect with respect to the child, the local authority designated in the order, and each parent, guardian or special guardian (in so far as their parental responsibility has not been restricted under section 33(3) of the Children Act 1989), unless paragraph (e) applies;
>
> (d) where a residence order has effect with respect to the child, the persons with whom the child lives, or is to live, as a result of the order, unless paragraph (e) applies;
>
> (e) where an adoption agency is authorised to place the child for adoption under section 19 of the Adoption and Children Act 2002, that agency or, where a care order has effect with respect to the child, the local authority designated in the order;
>
> (f) where a placement order is in force with respect to the child, the appropriate local authority;
>
> (g) where a child has been placed for adoption with prospective adopters, the prospective adopters (in so far as their parental responsibility has not been restricted under section 25(4) of the Adoption and Children Act 2002), in addition to those persons specified in paragraph (e) or (f);
>
> (h) where none of paragraphs (b) to (g) apply but a residence order was in force with respect to the child immediately before he reached the age of sixteen, the persons with whom he lived, or was to live, as a result of the order.

(1B) In this section—

'guardian of a child', 'parental responsibility', 'residence order', 'special guardian', 'special guardianship order' and 'care order' have the same meaning as in the Children Act 1989;

'adoption agency', 'placed for adoption', 'placement order' and 'local authority' have the same meaning as in the Adoption and Children Act 2002;

'appropriate local authority' means the local authority authorised by the placement order to place the child for adoption.

(2) Subsection (1) shall apply to marriages intended to be solemnized on the authority of a common licence, with the substitution of references to the ecclesiastical authority by whom the licence was granted for references to the superintendent registrar, and with the substitution of a reference to the Master of the Faculties for the reference to the Registrar General.

(3) Where the marriage of a child not being a widower or widow, is intended to be solemnized after the publication of banns of matrimony then, if any person whose consent to the marriage would have been required under this section in the case of a marriage intended to be solemnized otherwise than after the publication of the banns, openly and publicly declares or causes to be declared, in the church or chapel in which the banns are published, at the time of the publication, his dissent from the intended marriage, the publication of banns shall be void.

(4) A clergyman shall not be liable to ecclesiastical censure for solemnizing the marriage of a child after the publication of banns without the consent of the parents or guardians of the child unless he had notice of the dissent of any person who is entitled to give notice of dissent under the last foregoing subsection.

(5) For the purposes of this section, 'the court' means the High Court, the county court of the district in which any applicant or respondent resides, or a court of summary jurisdiction acting in the local justice area which includes the place in which any applicant or respondent resides, and rules of court may be made for enabling applications under this section—

(a) if made to the High Court, to be heard in chambers;

(b) if made to the county court, to be heard and determined by the registrar subject to appeal to the judge;

(c) if made to a court of summary jurisdiction, to be heard and determined otherwise than in open court,

and shall provide that, where an application is made in consequence of a refusal to give consent, notice of the application shall be served on the person who has refused consent.

(6) Nothing in this section shall dispense with the necessity of obtaining the consent of the High Court to the marriage of a ward of court.

4 Hours for solemnization of marriages

A marriage may be solemnized at any time between the hours of eight in the forenoon and six in the afternoon.

PART II MARRIAGE ACCORDING TO RITES OF THE CHURCH OF ENGLAND

Preliminary

5 Methods of authorising marriages

A marriage according to the rites of the Church of England may be solemnized—

(a) after the publication of banns of matrimony;

(b) on the authority of a special licence of marriage granted by the Archbishop of Canterbury or any other person by virtue of the Ecclesiastical Licences Act 1533 (in this Act referred to as a 'special licence');

(c) on the authority of a licence of marriage (other than a special licence) granted by an ecclesiastical authority having power to grant such a licence (in this Act referred to as a 'common licence'); or

(d) on the authority of certificates issued by a superintendent registrar under Part III of this Act,

except that paragraph (a) of this section shall not apply in relation to the solemnization of any marriage mentioned in subsection (2) of section 1 of this Act.

5A Marriages between certain persons related by affinity

No clergyman shall be obliged—

(a) to solemnize a marriage which, apart from the Marriage (Prohibited Degrees of Relationship) Act 1986, would have been void by reason of the relationship of the persons to be married; or

(b) to permit such a marriage to be solemnized in the church or chapel of which he is the minister.

5B Marriages involving person of acquired gender

(1) A clergyman is not obliged to solemnise the marriage of a person if the clergyman reasonably believes that the person's gender has become the acquired gender under the Gender Recognition Act 2004.

(2) A clerk in Holy Orders of the Church in Wales is not obliged to permit the marriage of a person to be solemnised in the church or chapel of which the clerk is the minister if the clerk reasonably believes that the person's gender has become the acquired gender under that Act.

Marriage by banns

6 Place of publication of banns

(1) Subject to the provisions of this Act, where a marriage is intended to be solemnized after the publication of banns of matrimony, the banns shall be published—

    (a) if the persons to be married reside in the same parish, in the parish church of that parish;

    (b) if the persons to be married do not reside in the same parish, in the parish church of each parish in which one of them resides:

Provided that if either of the persons to be married resides in a chapelry or in a district specified in a licence granted under section twenty of this Act, the banns may be published in an authorised chapel of that chapelry or district instead of in the parish church of the parish in which that person resides.

. . .

(4) Banns of matrimony may be published in any parish church or authorised chapel which is the usual place of worship of the persons to be married or of one of them although neither of those persons resides in the parish or chapelry to which the church or chapel belongs;

Provided that the publication of the banns by virtue of this subsection shall be in addition to and not in substitution for the publication of banns required by subsection (1) of this section.

7 Time and manner of publication of banns

(1) Subject to the provisions of section nine of this Act, banns of matrimony shall be published on three Sundays preceding the solemnization of the marriage during morning service or, if there is no morning service on a Sunday on which the banns are to be published, during evening service.

(2) Banns of matrimony shall be published in an audible manner and in accordance with the form of words prescribed by the rubric prefixed to the office of matrimony in the Book of Common Prayer, and all the other rules prescribed by the said rubric concerning the publication of banns and the solemnization of matrimony shall, so far as they are consistent with the provisions of this Part of this Act, be duly observed.

(3) The parochial chuch council of a parish shall provide for every church and chapel in the parish in which marriages may be solemnized, a register book of banns made of durable materials and marked in the manner directed by section fifty-four of this Act for the register book of marriages, and all banns shall be published from the said register book of banns by the officiating clergyman, and not from loose papers, and after each publication the entry in the register book shall be signed by the officiating clergyman, or by some person under his direction.

. . .

8 Notice to clergyman before publication of banns

No clergyman shall be obliged to publish banns of matrimony unless the persons to be married, at least seven days before the date on which they wish the banns to be published for the first time, deliver or cause to be delivered to him a notice in writing, dated on the day on which it is so delivered, stating the christian name and surname and the place of residence of each of them, and the period during which each of them has resided at his or her place of residence.

9 Persons by whom banns may be published

(1) Subject to the provisions of this section and of section fourteen of this Act, it shall not be lawful for any person other than a clergyman to publish banns of matrimony.

(2) Where on any Sunday in any church or other building in which banns of matrimony may be published a clergyman does not officiate at the service at which it is usual in that church or building to publish banns, the banns may be published—

    (a) by a clergyman at some other service at which banns of matrimony may be published; or

    (b) by a layman during the course of a public reading authorised by the bishop of the diocese of a portion or portions of the service of morning or evening prayer, the public reading being at the hour when the service at which it is usual to publish banns is commonly held or at such other hour as the bishop may authorise:

Provided that banns shall not be published by a layman unless the incumbent or minister in charge of the said church or building, or some other clergyman nominated in that behalf by the bishop, has made or authorised to be made the requisite entry in the register book of banns of the said church or building.

(3) Where a layman publishes banns of matrimony by virtue of this section the layman shall sign the register book of banns provided under section seven of this Act and for that purpose shall be deemed to be the officiating clergyman within the meaning of that section.

10 Publication of banns commenced in one church and completed in another

(1) Where the publication of banns of matrimony has been duly commenced in any church, the publication may be completed in the same church or in any other church which, by virtue of the Union of Benefices Measure 1923 or the New Parishes Measure 1943, has at the time of the completion taken the place of the first-mentioned church for the purpose of publication of banns of matrimony either generally or in relation to the parties to the intended marriage.

. . .

11 Certificates of publication of banns

(1) Where a marriage is intended to be solemnized after the publication of banns of matrimony and the persons to be married do not reside in the same parish or other ecclesiastical district, a clergyman shall not solemnize the marriage in the parish or district in which one of those persons resides unless there is produced to him a certificate that the banns have been published in accordance with the provisions of this Part of this Act in the parish or other ecclesiastical district in which the other person resides.

(2) Where a marriage is intended to be solemnized in a church or chapel of a parish or other ecclesiatical district in which neither of the persons to be married resides, after the publication of banns therein by virtue of subsection (4) of section six of this Act, a clergyman shall not solemnize the marriage unless there is produced to him—

    (a) if the persons to be married reside in the same parish or other ecclesiastical district, a certificate that the banns have been published in accordance with the provisions of this Part of this Act in that parish or district; or

    (b) if the persons to be married do not reside in the same parish or other ecclesiastical district, certificates that the banns have been published as aforesaid in each parish or district in which one of them resides.

. . .

(4) Any certificate required under this section shall be signed by the incumbent or minister in charge of the building in which the banns were published or by a clergyman nominated in that behalf by the bishop of the diocese.

12 Solemnization of marriage after publication of banns

(1) Subject to the provisions of this Part of this Act, where banns of matrimony have been published, the marriage shall be solemnized in the church or chapel or, as the case may be, one of the churches or chapels in which the banns have been published.

(2) Where a marriage is not solemnized within three months after the completion of the publication of the banns, that publication shall be void and no clergyman shall solemnize the marriage on the authority thereof.

Marriage by common licence

15   Places in which marriages may be solemnized by common licence

(1) Subject to the provisions of this Part of this Act, a common licence shall not be granted for the solemnization of a marriage in any church or chapel other than—

> (a) the parish church of the parish, or an authorised chapel of the ecclesiastical district, in which one of the persons to be married has had his or her usual place of residence for fifteen days immediately before the grant of the licence; or
> (b) a parish church or authorised chapel which is the usual place of worship of the persons to be married or of one of them.

(2) For the purposes of this section, any parish in which there is no parish church or chapel belonging thereto or no church or chapel in which divine service is usually solemnized every Sunday, and any extra-parochial place which has no authorised chapel, shall be deemed to belong to any adjoining parish or chapelry.

16   Provisions as to common licences

(1) A common licence shall not be granted unless one of the persons to be married has sworn before a person having authority to grant such a licence—

> (a) that he or she believes that there is no impediment of kindred or alliance or any other lawful cause, nor any suit commenced in any court, to bar or hinder the solemnizing of the marriage in accordance with the licence;
> (b) that one of the persons to be married has had his or her usual place of residence in the parish or other ecclesiastical district in which the marriage is to be solemnized for fifteen days immediately before the grant of the licence or that the parish church or authorised chapel in which the marriage is to be solemnized is the usual place of worship of those persons or of one of them;
> (c) where one of the persons to be married is a child and is not a widower or widow, that the consent of the person or persons whose consent to the marriage is required under section three of this Act has been obtained, that the necessity of obtaining any such consent has been dispensed with under that section, that the court has consented to the marriage under that section, or that there is no person whose consent to the marriage is so required.

(1A) A common licence shall not be granted for the solemnization of a marriage mentioned in subsection (2) of section 1 of this Act unless—

> (a) the person having authority to grant the licence is satisfied by the production of evidence that both the persons to be married have attained the age of twenty-one; and
> (b) he has received a declaration in writing made by each of those persons specifying their affinal relationship and declaring that the younger of those persons has not at any time before attaining the age of eighteen been a child of the family in relation to the other.

(1B) In the case of a marriage mentioned in subsection (4) of section 1 of this Act which by virtue of subsection (5) of that section is valid only if at the time of the marriage both the parties to the marriage have attained the age of twenty-one and the death has taken place of two other persons related to those parties in the manner mentioned in the said subsection (5), a common licence shall not be granted for the solemnization of the marriage unless the person having authority to grant the licence is satisfied by the production of evidence—

> (a) that both the parties to the marriage have attained the age of twenty-one; and
> (b) that both those other persons are dead.

(2) Subject to subsection (2A) of this section, if any caveat is entered against the grant of a common licence, the caveat having been duly signed by or on behalf of the person by whom

it is entered and stating his place of residence and the ground of objection on which the caveat is founded, no licence shall be granted until the caveat or a copy thereof is transmitted to the ecclesiastical judge out of whose office the licence is to issue, and the judge has certified to the registrar of the diocese that he has examined into the matter of the caveat and is satisfied that it ought not to obstruct the grant of the licence, or until the caveat is withdrawn by the person who entered it.

(2A) Where in the case of a marriage mentioned in subsection (2) of section 1 of this Act a caveat is entered under subsection (2) of this section on the ground that the persons to be married have not both attained the age of twenty-one or that one of those persons has at any time before attaining the age of eighteen been a child of the family in relation to the other, then, notwithstanding that the caveat is withdrawn by the person who entered it, no licence shall be issued unless the judge has certified that he has examined into that ground of objection and is satisfied that the ground ought not to obstruct the grant of the licence.

(2B) In the case of a marriage mentioned in subsection (2) of section 1 of this Act, one of the persons to be married may apply to the ecclesiastical judge out of whose office the licence is to issue for a declaration that, both those persons having attained the age of twenty-one and the younger of those persons not having at any time before attaining the age of eighteen been a child of the family in relation to the other, there is no impediment of affinity to the solemnization of the marriage; and where any such declaration is obtained the common licence may be granted notwithstanding that no declaration has been made under the said subsection (1A).

(3) Where a marriage is not solemnized within three months after the grant of a common licence, the licence shall be void and no clergyman shall solemnize the marriage on the authority thereof.

...

Marriage under superintendent registrar's certificate

17 Marriage under superintendent registrar's certificate

A marriage according to the rites of the Church of England may be solemnized on the authority of certificates of a superintendent registrar in force under Part III of this Act in any church or chapel in which banns of matrimony may be published or in the case of a marriage in pursuance of section 26(1)(dd) of this Act the place specified in the notices of marriage and certificates as the place where the marriage is to be solemnized.

Provided that a marriage shall not be solemnized as aforesaid in any such church or chapel without the consent of the minister thereof or wherever the marriage is solemnized by any person other than a clergyman.

...

Miscellaneous provisions

22 Witnesses

All marriages solemnized according to the rites of the Church of England shall be solemnized in the presence of two or more witnesses in addition to the clergyman by whom the marriage is solemnized.

24 Proof of residence not necessary to validity of marriage by banns or common licence

(1) Where any marriage has been solemnized after the publication of banns of matrimony, it shall not be necessary in support of the marriage to give any proof of the residence of the parties or either of them in any parish or other ecclesiastical district in which the banns were published, and no evidence shall be given to prove the contrary in any proceedings touching the validity of the marriage.

(2) Where any marriage has been solemnized on the authority of a common licence, it shall not be necessary in support of the marriage to give any proof that the usual place of

residence of one of the parties was for fifteen days immediately before the grant of the licence in the parish or other ecclesiastical district in which the marriage was solemnized, and no evidence shall be given to prove the contrary in any proceedings touching the validity of the marriage.

25 Void marriages

If any persons knowingly and wilfully intermarry according to the rites of the Church of England (otherwise than by special licence)—

    (a) Except in the case of a marriage in pursuance of section 26(1)(dd) of this Act, in any place other than a church or other building in which banns may be published;

    (b) without banns having been duly published, a common licence having been obtained, or certificates having been duly issued under Part III of this Act by a superintendent registrar to whom due notice of marriage has been given; or

    (c) on the authority of a publication of banns which is void by virtue of subsection (3) of section three or subsection (2) of section twelve of this Act, on the authority of a common licence which is void by virtue of subsection (3) of section sixteen of this Act, or on the authority of certificates of a superintendent registrar which are void by virtue of subsection (2) of section thirty-three of this Act;

    (d) in the case of a marriage on the authority of certificates of a superintendent registrar, in any place other than the church building or other place specified in the notices of marriage and certificates as the place where the marriage is to be solemnized,

or if they knowingly and wilfully consent to or acquiesce in the solemnization of the marriage by any person who is not in Holy Orders, the marriage shall be void.

PART III   MARRIAGE UNDER SUPERINTENDENT REGISTRAR'S CERTIFICATE

Issue of certificates

26 Marriages which may be solemnized on authority of superintendent registrar's certificate

    (1) Subject to the provisions of this Part of this Act, the following marriages may be solemnized on the authority of two certificates of a superintendent registrar—

    (a) a marriage in a registered building according to such form and ceremony as the persons to be married see fit to adopt;

    (b) a marriage in the office of a superintendent registrar;

    (bb) a marriage on approved premises;

    (c) a marriage according to the usages of the Society of Friends (commonly called Quakers);

    (d) a marriage between two persons professing the Jewish religion according to the usages of the Jews;

    (dd) the marriage (other than a marriage in pursuance of paragraph (c) or (d) above) of a person who is house-bound or is a detained person at the place where he or she usually resides;

    (e) a marriage according to the rites of the Church of England in any church or chapel in which banns of matrimony may be published.

27 Notice of marriage

    (1) Where a marriage is intended to be solemnized on the authority of certificates of a superintendent registrar, notice of marriage in the prescribed form shall be given—

    (a) if the persons to be married have resided in the same registration district for the period of seven days immediately before the giving of the notice, by each of those persons to the superintendent registrar of that district;

(b) if the persons to be married have not resided in the same registration district for the said period of seven days as aforesaid, by either of those persons to the superintendent registrar of the registration district in which he or she resided for that period.

(3) A notice of marriage shall state the name and surname, occupation, place of residences and nationality of each of the persons to be married, whether either of them has previously been married or formed a civil partnership and, if so, how the marriage or civil partnership ended and in the case of a marriage intended to be solemnized at a person's residence in pursuance of section 26(1)(dd) of this Act, which residence is to be the place of solemnization of the marriage and, in any other case, the church or other building or premises in or on which the marriage is to be solemnized and—

(a) shall state the period, not being less than seven days, during which each of the persons to be married has resided in his or her place of residence;

(4) The superintendent registrar shall file all notices of marriage and keep them with the records of his office, and shall subject to section 27A of this Act also forthwith enter the particulars given in every such notice, together with the date of the notice and the name of the person by whom the notice was given, in a book (in this Act referred to as 'the marriage notice book') furnished to him for that purpose by the Registrar General, and the marriage notice book shall be open for inspection free of charge at all reasonable hours.

(5) If the persons to be married wish to be married in the presence of a registrar in a registered building for which an authorised person has been appointed, they shall, at the time when notice of marriage is given to the superintendent registrar under this section, give notice to him that they require a registrar to be present at the marriage.

. . .

27A Additional information required in certain cases

(1) This section applies in relation to any marriage intended to be solemnized at a person's residence in pursuance of section 26(1)(dd) of this Act, and in the following provisions of this section that person is referred to as 'the relevant person'.

(2) Where the relevant person is not a detained person, each notice of marriage required by section 27 of this Act shall be accompanied by a medical statement relating to that person made not more than fourteen days before the date on which the notice is given.

(3) Where the relevant person is a detained person, each notice of marriage required by section 27 of this Act shall be accompanied by a statement made in the prescribed form by the responsible authority not more than twenty-one days before the date on which notice of the marriage is given under section 27:—

(a) identifying the establishment where the person is detained; and

(b) stating that the responsible authority has no objection to that establishment being specified in the notice of marriage as the place where that marriage is to be solemnized.

(4) Each person who gives notice of the marriage to the superintendent registrar in accordance with section 27 of this Act shall give the superintendent registrar the prescribed particulars, in the prescribed form, of the person by or before whom the marriage is intended to be solemnized.

(5) The superintendent registrar shall not enter the particulars given in the marriage notice book until he has received the statement and the particulars required by subsections (2) or (3) and (4) of this section.

(6) The fact that a superintendent registrar has received a statement under subsection (2) or (as the case may be) (3) of this section shall be entered in the marriage notice book together with the particulars given in the notice of marriage and any such statement together with the form received under subsection (4) of this section shall be filed and kept with the records of the office of the superintendent registrar or, where notice of marriage is required to be given to two superintendent registrars, of each of them.

(7) In this section:—

'medical statement', in relation to any person, means a statement made in the prescribed form by a registered medical practitioner that in his opinion at the time the statement is made:—

(a) by reason of illness or disability, he or she ought not to move or be moved from the place where he or she is at the time, and

(b) it is likely that it will be the case for at least the following three months that by reason of the illness or disability he or she ought not to move or be moved from that place; and

'registered medical practitioner' has the meaning given by Schedule 1 to the Interpretation Act 1978; and

'responsible authority' means:—

(a) if the person is detained in a hospital (within the meaning of Part II of section 145(1) of that Act); or

(b) if the person is detained in a prison or other place to which the Prison Act 1952 applies, the governor or other officer for the time being in charge of that prison or other place.

27B   Provisions relating to section 1(3) marriages

(1) This section applies in relation to any marriage mentioned in subsection (2) of section 1 of this Act which is intended to be solemnized on the authority of certificates of a superintendent registrar.

(2) The superintendent registrar shall not enter notice of the marriage in the marriage notice book unless—

(a) he is satisfied by the production of evidence that both the persons to be married have attained the age of twenty-one; and

(b) he has received a declaration made in the prescribed form by each of those persons, each declaration having been signed and attested in the prescribed manner, specifying their affinal relationship and declaring that the younger of those persons has not at any time before attaining the age of eighteen been a child of the family in relation to the other.

(3) The fact that a superintendent registrar has received a declaration under subsection (2) of this section shall be entered in the marriage notice book together with the particulars given in the notice of marriage and any such declaration shall be filed and kept with the records of the office of the superintendent registrar or, where notice of marriage is required to be given to two superintendent registrars, of each of them.

(4) Where the superintendent registrar receives from some person other than the persons to be married a written statement signed by that person which alleges that the declaration made under subsection (2) of this section is false in a material particular, the superintendent registrar shall not issue a certificate unless a declaration is obtained from the High Court under subsection (5) of this section.

(5) Either of the persons to be married may, whether or not any statement has been received by the superintendent registrar under subsection (4) of this section, apply to the High Court for a declaration that, both those persons having attained the age of twenty-one and the younger of those persons not having at any time before attaining the age of eighteen been a child of the family in relation to the other, there is no impediment of affinity to the solemnization of the marriage; and where such a declaration is obtained the superintendent registrar may enter notice of the marriage in the marriage notice book and may issue a certificate whether or not any declaration has been made under subsection (2) of this section.

(6) Section 29 of this Act shall not apply in relation to a marriage to which this section applies, except so far as a caveat against the issue of a certificate for the marriage is entered under that section on a ground other than the relationship of the persons to be married.

27C Provisions relating to section 1(5) marriages

In the case of a marriage mentioned in subsection (4) of section 1 of this Act which by virtue of subsection (5) of that section is valid only if at the time of the marriage both the parties to the marriage have attained the age of twenty-one and the death has taken place of two other persons related to those parties in the manner mentioned in the said subsection (5), the superintendent registrar shall not enter notice of the marriage in the marriage notice book unless satisfied by the production of evidence—

   (a) that both the parties to the marriage have attained the age of twenty-one, and

   (b) that both those persons are dead.

28 Declaration to accompany notice of marriage

   (1) No certificate for marriage shall be issued by a superintendent registrar unless the notice of marriage is accompanied by a solemn declaration in writing, in the body or at the foot of the notice, made and signed at the time of the giving of the notice by the person by whom the notice is given and attested as mentioned in subsection (2) of this section—

   (a) that he or she believes that there is no impediment of kindred or alliance or other lawful hindrance to the marriage;

   (b) that the persons to be married have for the period of seven days immediately before the giving of the notice had their usual places of residence within the registration district or registration districts in which notice is given;

   (c) where one of the persons to be married is a child and is not a widower or widow, that the consent of the person or persons whose consent to the marriage is required under section three of this Act has been obtained, that the necessity of obtaining any such consent has been dispensed with under that section, that the court has consented to the marriage under that section, or that there is no person whose consent to the marriage is so required.

   (2) Any such declaration as aforesaid shall be signed by the person giving the notice of marriage in the presence of the superintendent registrar to whom the notice is given or his deputy, or in the presence of a registrar of births and deaths or of marriages for the registration district in which the person giving the notice resides or his deputy, and that superintendent registrar, deputy superintendent registrar, registrar or deputy registrar, as the case may be, shall attest the declaration by adding thereto his name, description and place of residence.

28A Power to require evidence

   (1) A superintendent registrar to whom a notice of marriage is given under section 27, or any other person attesting a declaration accompanying such a notice, may require the person giving the notice to provide him with specified evidence—

   (a) relating to that person; or

   (b) if the superintendent registrar considers that the circumstances are exceptional, relating to each of the persons to be married.

   (2) Such a requirement may be imposed at any time—

   (a) on or after the giving of the notice of marriage; but

   (b) before the superintendent registrar issues his certificate under section 31.

   (3) 'Specified evidence', in relation to a person, means such evidence as may be specified in guidance issued by the Registrar General—

   (a) of the person's name and surname,

   (b) of the person's age,

   (c) as to whether the person has previously been married or formed a civil partnership and, if so, as to the ending of the marriage or civil partnership, and

   (d) of the person's nationality.

29 Caveat against issue of certificate or licence

   (1) Any person may enter a caveat with the superintendent registrar against the issue of a certificate for the marriage of any person named therein.

(2) If any caveat is entered as aforesaid, the caveat having been signed by or on behalf of the person by whom it was entered and stating his place of residence and the ground of objection on which the caveat is founded, no certificate shall be issued until the super-intendent registrar has examined into the matter of the caveat and is satisfied that it ought not to obstruct the issue of the certificate, or until the caveat has been withdrawn by the person who entered it; and if the superintendent registrar is doubtful whether to issue a certificate he may refer the matter of the caveat to the Registrar General.

(3) Where a superintendent registrar refuses, by reason of any such caveat as aforesaid, to issue a certificate, the person applying therefore may appeal to the Registrar General who shall either confirm the refusal or direct that a certificate shall be issued.

(4) Any person who enters a caveat against the issue of a certificate on grounds which the Registrar General declares to be frivolous and to be such that they ought not to obstruct the issue of the certificate, shall be liable for the costs of the proceedings before the Registrar General and for damages recoverable by the person against whose marriage the caveat was entered.

(5) For the purpose of enabling any person to recover any such costs and damages as aforesaid, a copy of the declaration of the Registrar General purporting to be sealed with the seal of the General Register Office shall be evidence that the Registrar General has declared the caveat to have been entered on grounds which are frivolous and such that they ought not to obstruct the issue of the certificate.

30   Forbidding of issue of certificate

Any person whose consent to a marriage intended to be solemnized on the authority of certificates of a superintendent registrar is required under section three of this Act may forbid the issue of such a certificate by writing, at any time before the issue of the certificate, the word 'forbidden' opposite to the entry of the notice of marriage in the marriage notice book, and by subscribing thereto his name and place of residence and the capacity, in relation to either of the persons to be married, in which he forbids the issue of the certificate; and where the issue of a certificate has been so forbidden, the notice of marriage and all proceedings thereon shall be void:

Provided that where, by virtue of paragraph (b) of the proviso to subsection (1) of the said section three, the court has consented to a marriage and the consent of the court has the same effect as if it had been given by a person whose consent has been refused, that person shall not be entitled to forbid the issue of a certificate for that marriage under this section, and the notice of marriage and the proceedings thereon shall not be void by virtue of this section.

31   Marriage under certificate without licence

(1) Where a marriage is intended to be solemnized on the authority of certificates of a superintendent registrar, the superintendent registrar to whom notice of marriage has been given shall suspend or affix in some conspicuous place in his office, for 15 successive days next after the day on which the notice was entered in the marriage book, the notice of marriage, or an exact copy signed by him of the particulars thereof as entered in the marriage notice book.

(2) At the expiration of the said period of 15 days the superintendent registrar, on the request of the person by whom the notice of marriage was given, shall issue a certificate in the prescribed form unless—

> (a) the superintendent registrar is not satisfied that there is no lawful impediment to the issue of the certificate; or
> (b) the issue of the certificate has been forbidden under the last foregoing section by any person authorised in that behalf.

. . .

(4) No marriage shall be solemnized on the production of certificates of a superintendent registrar until after the expiration of the waiting period in relation to each notice of marriage.

. . .

(4A) 'The waiting period', in relation to a notice of marriage, means—

    (a) the period of 15 days, or

    (b) such shorter period as may be determined by the Registrar General under sub-section (5A) or by a superintendent registrar under any provision of regulations made under subsection (5D),

after the day on which the notice of marriage was entered in the marriage notice book.

. . .

(5A) If, on an application made to the Registrar General, he is satisfied that there are compelling reasons for reducing the 15 day period because of the exceptional circumstances of the case, he may reduce that period to such shorter period as he considers appropriate.

(5B) 'The 15 day period' means the period of 15 days mentioned in subsections (1) and (2).

(5C) If the Registrar General reduces the 15 day period in a particular case, the reference to 15 days in section 75(3)(a) is to be treated, in relation to that case, as a reference to the reduced period.

. . .

31A Appeal on refusal under section 31(2)(a)

(1) If, relying on section 31(2)(a), a superintendent registrar refuses to issue a certificate, the person applying for it may appeal to the Registrar General.

(2) On such an appeal, the Registrar General must—

    (a) confirm the refusal; or

    (b) direct that a certificate be issued.

(3) If—

    (a) relying on section 31(2)(a), a superintendent registrar refuses to issue a certificate as a result of a representation made to him, and

    (b) on an appeal against the refusal, the Registrar General declares the representation to have been frivolous and to be such that it ought not to obstruct the issue of a certificate,

the person making the representation is liable for the costs of the proceedings before the Registrar General and for damages recoverable by the applicant for the certificate.

(4) For the purpose of enabling a person to recover any such costs and damages, a copy of the declaration of the Registrar General purporting to be sealed with the seal of the General Register Office is evidence that the Registrar General has declared the representation to have been frivolous and to be such that it ought not to obstruct the issue of a certificate.

33 Period of validity of certificate

(1) A marriage may be solemnized on the authority of certificates of a superintendent registrar at any time within the period which is the applicable period in relation to that marriage.

(2) If the marriage is not solemnized within the applicable period—

    (a) the notices of marriage and the certificates are void; and

    (b) no person may solemnize the marriage on the authority of those certificates.

(3) The applicable period, in relation to a marriage, is the period beginning with the day on which the notice of marriage was entered in the marriage notice book and ending—

    (a) in the case of a marriage which is to be solemnized in pursuance of section 26(1)(dd), 37 or 38, on the expiry of three months; and

    (b) in the case of any other marriage, on the expiry of twelve months.

(4) If the notices of marriage given by each person to be married are not given on the same date, the applicable period is to be calculated by reference to the earlier of the two dates.

34 Marriages normally to be solemnized in registration district in which one party resides

Subject to section 35, a superintendent registrar may not issue a certificate for the solemnization of a marriage elsewhere than within a registration district in which one of the persons to be married has resided for seven days immediately before the giving of the notice of marriage.

35 Marriages in registration district in which neither party resides

(1) A superintendent registrar may issue a certificate for the solemnization of a marriage in a registered building which is not within a registration district in which either of the persons to be married resides, where the person giving the notice of marriage declares by endorsement thereon in the prescribed form—

    (a) that the persons to be married desire the marriage to be solemnized, according to a specified form, rite or ceremony, being a form, rite or ceremony of a body or denomination of christians or other persons meeting for religious worship to which one of them professes to belong;

    (b) that, to the best of his or her belief, there is not within the registration district in which one of them resides any registered building in which marriage is solemnized according to that form, rite or ceremony;

    (c) the registration district nearest to the residence of that person in which there is a registered building in which marriage may be so solemnized; and

    (d) the registered building in that district in which the marriage is intended to be solemnized;

and where any such certificate is issued in respect of each of the persons to be married, the marriage may be solemnized in the registered building stated in the notice.

(2) A superintendent registrar may issue a certificate for the solemnization of a marriage in a registered building which is the usual place of worship of the persons to be married, or of one of them, notwithstanding that the building is not within a registration district in which either of those persons resides.

(2A) A superintendent registrar may issue a certificate for the solemnization of a marriage in the office of another superintendent registrar, notwithstanding that the office is not within a registration district in which either of the persons to be married resides.

(2B) A superintendent registrar may issue a certificate for the solemnization of a marriage on approved premises, notwithstanding that the premises are not within a registration district in which either of the persons to be married resides.

(3) A superintendent registrar may issue a certificate for the solemnization of a marriage in any parish church or authorised chapel which is the usual place of worship of the persons to be married, or of one of them, notwithstanding that the church or chapel is not within a registration district in which either of those persons resides.

(4) A superintendent registrar may issue a certificate for the solemnization of a marriage according to the usages of the Society of Friends or in accordance with the usages of persons professing the Jewish religion, notwithstanding that the building or place in which the marriage is to be solemnized is not within a registration district in which either of the persons to be married resides.

(5) Where a marriage is intended to be solemnized on the authority of certificates of a superintendent registrar issued under subsection (2) or subsection (3) of this section, each notice of marriage given to the superintendent registrar and each certificate issued by the superintendent registrar shall state, in addition to the description of the registered building or, as the case may be, the parish church or authorised chapel, in which the marriage is to be solemnized, that it is the usual place of worship of the persons to be married or of one of them and, in the latter case, shall state the name of the person whose usual place of worship it is.

. . . .

39A Marriage of former civil partners one of whom has changed sex

  (1) This section applies if—

    (a) a court—

      (i) makes final a nullity order which annuls a civil partnership on the ground that an interim gender recognition certificate has been issued to one of the civil partners, or

      (ii) . . . .

and, on doing so, issues a full gender recognition certificate (under section 5A(1) of the Gender Recognition Act 2004) to that civil partner, and

(b) the former civil partners wish to marry each other in England or Wales in accordance with this Part without being delayed by the waiting period.

(2) For the purposes of this section the relevant period is the period—

(a) beginning with the issue of the full gender recognition certificate, and

(b) ending at the end of 1 month from the day on which it is issued.

(3) If either of the former civil partners—

(a) gives notice of marriage in accordance with this Part during the relevant period, and

(b) on doing so, makes an election under this section,

this Act applies with the modifications set out in subsections (4) to (6).

(4) In section 31 (marriage under certificates)—

(a) omit subsections (1), (4), (4A) and (5A) to (5I), and

(b) in subsection (2), for 'At the expiration of the said period of 15 days', substitute 'As soon as notice of marriage has been given,'.

(5) For section 33(3) (period of validity of certificate: applicable period) substitute—

'(3) The applicable period, in relation to a marriage, is the period of 1 month beginning with the day on which the notice of marriage was entered in the marriage notice book.'

(6) In section 75 (offences relating to solemnization of marriages), omit subsections (2)(d), (2A) and (3)(a).

(7) . . . .

(8) In subsection (1)(b), 'the waiting period' has the meaning given by section 31(4A).'

Marriages in registered buildings

41 Registration of buildings

(1) Any proprietor or trustee of a building, which has been certified by law as a place of religious worship may apply to the superintendent registrar of the registration district in which the building is situated for the building to be registered for the solemnization of marriages therein.

(2) Any person making such an application as aforesaid shall deliver to the superintendent registrar a certificate, signed in duplicate by at least twenty householders and dated not earlier than one month before the making of the application, stating that the building is being used by them as their usual place of public religious worship and that they desire that the building should be registered as aforesaid, and both certificates shall be countersigned by the proprietor or trustee by whom they are delivered.

(3) The superintendent registrar shall send both certificates delivered to him under the last foregoing subsection to the Registrar General who shall register the building in a book to be kept for that purpose in the General Register Office.

(4) The Registrar General shall endorse on both certificates sent to him as aforesaid the date of the registration, and shall keep one certificate with the records of the General Register Office and shall return the other certificate to the superintendent registrar who shall keep it with the records of his office.

(5) On the return of the certificate under the last foregoing subsection, the superintendent registrar shall—

(a) enter the date of the registration of the building in a book to be provided for that purpose by the Registrar General;

(b) give a certificate of the registration signed by him, on durable materials, to the proprietor or trustee by whom the certificates delivered to him under subsection (2) of this section were countersigned; and

(c) give public notice of the registration of the building by advertisement in some newspaper circulating in the county in which the building is situated and in the London Gazette.

...

42   Cancellation of registration and substitution of another building

(1) Where, on an application made by or through the superintendent registrar of the registration district in which the building is situated, it is shown to the satisfaction of the Registrar General that a registered building is no longer used for the purpose of public religious worship by the congregation on whose behalf it was registered, he shall cause the registration to be cancelled.

(3) Where the Registrar General cancels the registration of any building, under this section, he shall inform the superintendent registrar who shall enter that fact and the date thereof in the book provided for the registration of buildings, and shall certify and publish the cancellation, in the manner provided by subsection (5) of the last foregoing section in the case of the registration of a building.

(5) Where the registration of any building has been cancelled under this section, it shall not be lawful to solemnize any marriage in the disused building, unless the building has been registered again in accordance with the provisions of this Part of this Act.

43   Appointment of authorised persons

(1) For the purpose of enabling marriages to be solemnized in a registered building without the presence of a registrar, the trustees or governing body of that building may authorise a person to be present at the solemnization of marriages in that building and, where a person is so authorised in respect of any registered building, the trustees or governing body of that building shall within the prescribed time and in the prescribed manner, certify the name and address of the person so authorised to the Registrar General and to the superintendent registrar of the registration district in which the building is situated.

Provided that, in relation to a building which becomes registered after the thirtyfirst day of December, nineteen hundred and fifty-eight, the power conferred by this subsection to authorise a person to be present as aforesaid shall not be exercisable before the expiration of one year from the date of registration of the building or, where the congregation on whose behalf the building is registered previously used for the purpose of public religious worship another building of which the registration has been cancelled not earlier than one month before the date of registration aforesaid, one year from the date of registration of that other building.

(2) Any person whose name and address have been certified as aforesaid is in this Act referred to as an 'authorised person.'

(3) Nothing in this section shall be taken to relate to or have any reference to marriages solemnized according to the usages of the Society of Friends or of persons professing the Jewish religion.

44   Solemnization of marriage in registered building

(1) Subject to the provisions of this section, where the notices of marriage and certificates issued by a superintendent registrar state that a marriage between the persons named therein is intended to be solemnized in a registered building, the marriage may be solemnized in that building according to such form and ceremony as those persons may see fit to adopt:

Provided that no marriage shall be solemnized in any registered building without the consent of the minister or of one of the trustees, owners, deacons, or managers thereof, or in the case of a registered building of the Roman Catholic Church, without the consent of the officiating minister thereof.

(2) Subject to the provisions of this section, a marriage solemnized in a registered building shall be solemnized with open doors in the presence of two or more witnesses and in the presence of either—

(a) a registrar of the registration district in which the registered building is situated, or

(b) an authorised person whose name and address have been certified in accordance with the last foregoing section by the trustees or governing body of that registered building or of some other registered building in the same registration district.

(3) Where a marriage is solemnized in a registered building each of the persons contracting the marriage shall, in some part of the ceremony and in the presence of the witnesses and the registrar or authorised person, make the following declaration:—

'I do solemnly declare that I know not of any lawful impediment why I, *AB*, may not be joined in matrimony to *CD*'

and each of them shall say to the other:—

'I call upon these persons here present to witness that I, *AB*, do take thee, *CD*, to be my lawful wedded wife [*or* husband]':

(3A) As an alternative to the declaration set out in subsection (3) of this section the persons contracting the marriage may make the requisite declaration either—

(a) by saying 'I declare that I know of no legal reason why I [*name*] may not be joined in marriage to [*name*]'; or

(b) by replying 'I am' to the question put to them successively 'Are you [*name*] free lawfully to marry [*name*]?'

and as an alternative to the words of contract set out in that subsection the persons to be married may say to each other 'I [*name*] take you [*or* thee] [*name*] to be my wedded wife [*or* husband]'.

. . .

Marriages in register offices

45 Solemnization of marriage in register office

(1) Where a marriage is intended to be solemnized on the authority of certificates of a superintendent registrar, the persons to be married may state in the notices of marriage that they wish to be married in the office of the superintendent registrar or one of the superintendent registrars, as the case may be, to whom notice of marriage is given, and where any such notices have been given and the certificates have been issued accordingly, the marriage may be solemnized in the said office, with open doors in the presence of the superintendent registrar and a registrar of the registration district of that superintendent registrar and in the presence of two witnesses, and the persons to be married shall make the declarations and use the form of words set out in subsection (3) or (3A) of the last foregoing section in the case of marriages in registered buildings.

(2) No religious service shall be used at any marriage solemnized in the office of a superintendent registrar.

45A Solemnization of certain marriages

(1) This section applies to marriages solemnized, otherwise than according to the rites of the Church of England, in pursuance of section 26(1)(dd) of this Act at the place where a person usually resides.

(2) The marriage may be solemnized according to a relevant form, rite or ceremony in the presence of a registrar of the registration district in which the place where the marriage is solemnized is situated and of two witnesses and each of the persons contracting the marriage shall make the declaration and use the form of words set out in subsection (3) or (3A) of section 44 of this Act in the case of marriages in registered buildings.

(3) Where the marriage is not solemnized in pursuance of subsection (2) of this section it shall be solemnized in the presence of the superintendent registrar and a registrar of the registration district in which the place where the marriage is solemnized is situated and in the presence of two witnesses, and the persons to be married shall make the declarations and use the form of words set out in subsection (3) or (3A) of section 44 of this Act in the case of marriages in registered buildings.

(4) No religious service shall be used at any marriage solemnized in the presence of a superintendent registrar.

(5) In subsection (2) of this section a 'relevant form, rite or ceremony' means a form, rite or ceremony of a body of persons who meet for religious worship in any registered building being a form, rite or ceremony in accordance with which members of that body are married in any such registered building.

46   Register office marriage followed by religious ceremony

(1) If the parties to a marriage solemnized in the presence of a superintendent registrar desire to add the religious ceremony ordained or used by the church or persuasion of which they are members, they may present themselves, after giving notice of their intention so to do, to the clergyman or minister of the church or persuasion of which they are members, and the clergyman or minister, upon the production of a certificate of their marriage before the superintendent registrar and upon the payment of the customary fees (if any), may, if he sees fit, read or celebrate in the church or chapel of which he is the regular minister the marriage service of the church or persuasion to which he belongs or nominate some other minister to do so.

(2) Nothing in the reading or celebration of a marriage service under this section shall supersede or invalidate any marriage previously solemnized in the presence of a superintendent registrar, and the reading or celebration shall not be entered as a marriage in any marriage register book kept under Part IV of this Act.

(3) No person who is not entitled to solemnize marriages according to the rites of the Church of England shall by virtue of this section be entitled to read or celebrate the marriage service in any church or chapel of the Church of England.

Marriages on approved premises

46A   Approval of premises

(1) The Chancellor of the Exchequer may by regulations make provision for and in connection with the approval by local authorities of premises for the solemnization of marriages in pursuance of section 26(1)(bb) of this Act.
...

46B   Solemnization of marriage on approved premises

(1) Any marriage on approved premises in pursuance of section 26(1)(bb) of this Act shall be solemnized in the presence of—
>   (a) two witnesses, and
>   (b) the superintendent registrar and a registrar of the registration district in which the premises are situated.

(2) Without prejudice to the width of section 46A(2)(e) of this Act, the Chancellor of the Exchequer shall exercise his power to provide for the imposition of conditions as there mentioned so as to secure that members of the public are permitted to attend any marriage solemnized on approved premises in pursuance of section 26(1)(bb) of this Act.

(3) Each of the persons contracting such a marriage shall make the declaration and use the form of words set out in section 44(3) or (3A) of this Act in the case of marriages in registered buildings.

(4) No religious service shall be used at a marriage on approved premises in pursuance of section 26(1)(bb) of this Act.

Marriages according to usages of Society of Friends

47   Marriages according to usages of Society of Friends

(1) No person who is not a member of the Society of Friends shall be married according to the usages of that Society unless he or she is authorised to be so married under or in pursuance of a general rule of the said Society in England.

(2) A marriage solemnized according to the said usages shall not be valid unless either—
>   (a) each person giving notice of marriage declares, either verbally or, if so required, in writing, that each of the parties to the marriage is either a member of the Society of Friends or is in profession with or of the persuasion of that Society; or

(b) there is produced to the superintendent registrar, at the time when notice of marriage is given, a certificate purporting to be signed by a registering officer of the Society of Friends in England to the effect that any party to the marriage who is not a member of the Society of Friends or in profession with or of the persuasion of that Society, is authorised to be married according to the said usages under or in pursuance of a general rule of the said Society in England.

(3) Any such certificate as aforesaid shall be for all purposes conclusive evidence that any person to whom it relates is authorised to be married according to the usages of the said Society, and the entry of the marriage in a marriage register book under Part IV of this Act, or a certified copy thereof made under the said Part IV, shall be conclusive evidence of the production of such a certificate.

(4) A copy of any general rule of the Society of Friends purporting to be signed by the recording clerk for the time being of the said Society in London shall be admitted as evidence of the general rule in all proceedings touching the validity of any marriage solemnized according to the usages of the said Society.

Miscellaneous provisions

48   Proof of certain matters not necessary to validity of marriages

(1) Where any marriage has been solemnized under the provisions of this Part of this Act, it shall not be necessary in support of the marriage to give any proof—

(a) that before the marriage either of the parties thereto resided, or resided for any period, in the registration district stated in the notices of marriage to be that of his or her place of residence;

(b) that any person whose consent to the marriage was required by section three of this Act had given his consent;

(c) that the registered building in which the marriage was solemnized had been certified as required by law as a place of religious worship;

(d) that that building was the usual place of worship of either of the parties to the marriage; or

(e) that the facts stated in a declaration made under subsection (1) of section thirty-five of this Act were correct:

nor shall any evidence be given to prove the contrary in any proceedings touching the validity of the marriage.

(2) A marriage solemnized in accordance with the provisions of this Part of this Act in a registered building which has not been certified as required by law as a place of religious worship shall be as valid as if the building had been so certified.

49   Void marriages

If any persons knowingly and wilfully intermarry under the provisions of this Part of this Act—

(a) without having given due notice of marriage to the superintendent registrar;

(b) without a certificate for marriage having been duly issued, in respect of each of the persons to be married, by the superintendent registrar to whom notice of marriage was given;

(d) on the authority of certificates which are void by virtue of subsection (2) of section thirty-three of this Act;

(e) in any place other than the church, chapel, registered building, office or other place specified in the notices of marriage and certificates of the superintendent registrar;

(ee) in the case of a marriage purporting to be in pursuance of section 26(1)(bb) of this Act, on any premises that at the time the marriage is solemnized are not approved premises;

(f) in the case of a marriage in a registered building (not being a marriage in the presence of an authorised person), in the absence of a registrar of the registration district in which the registered building is situated;

(g) in the case of a marriage in the office of a superintendent registrar, in the absence of the superintendent registrar or of a registrar of the registration district of that superintendent registrar;

(gg) in the case of a marriage on approved premises, in the absence of the superintendent registrar of the registration district in which the premises are situated or in the absence of a registrar of that district; or

(h) in the case of a marriage to which section 45A of this Act applies, in the absence of any superintendent registrar or registrar whose presence at that marriage is required by that section;

the marriage shall be void.

50 Person to whom certificate to be delivered

(1) Where a marriage is intended to be solemnized on the authority of certificates of a superintendent registrar, the certificates shall be delivered to the following person, that is to say:—

(a) if the marriage is to be solemnized in a registered building or at a person's residence in the presence of a registrar, that registrar;

(b) if the marriage is to be solemnized in a registered building without the presence of a registrar, the authorised person in whose presence the marriage is to be solemnized;

(c) if the marriage is to be solemnized in the office of a superintendent registrar, the registrar in whose presence the marriage is to be solemnized;

(cc) if the marriage is to be solemnized on approved premises, the registrar in whose presence the marriage is to be solemnized;

(d) if the marriage is to be solemnized according to the usages of the Society of Friends, the registering officer of that Society for the place where the marriage is to be solemnized;

(e) if the marriage is to be solemnized according to the usages of persons professing the Jewish religion, the officer of a synagogue by whom the marriage is required to be registered under Part IV of this Act;

(f) if the marriage is to be solemnized according to the rites of the Church of England, the officiating clergyman.

. . .

(3) Where a marriage is solemnized in a registered building without the presence of a registrar, the certificates shall be kept in the prescribed custody and shall be produced with the marriage register books kept by the authorised person under Part IV of this Act as and when required by the Registrar General.

. . .

52 Provision for marriages in Welsh language

The Registrar General shall furnish to every registrar in Wales and in every place in which the Welsh language is commonly used a true and exact translation into the Welsh language of the declarations and forms of words required to be used under section forty-four of this Act, and the said translation may be used in any place in which the Welsh language is commonly used in the same manner as is prescribed by the said section forty-four for the use of the declarations and forms of words in the English language.

PART IV   REGISTRATION OF MARRIAGES

53 Persons by whom marriages are to be registered

Subject to the provisions of Part V of this Act, a marriage shall be registered in accordance with the provisions of this Part of this Act by the following person, that is to say,—

(a) in the case of a marriage solemnized according to the rites of the Church of England, by the clergyman by whom the marriage is solemnized;

(b) in the case of a marriage solemnized according to the usages of the Society of Friends, by the registering officer of that Society appointed for the district in which the marriage is solemnized;

(c) in the case of a marriage solemnized according to the usages of persons professing the Jewish religion, by the secretary of the synagogue of which the husband is a member;

(d) in the case of a marriage solemnized in a registered building or at a person's residence in the presence of a registrar, by that registrar;

(e) in the case of a marriage solemnized in a registered building without the presence of a registrar, by the authorised person in whose presence the marriage is solemnized;

(f) in the case of a marriage solemnized in the office of a superintendent registrar by the registrar in whose presence the marriage is solemnized;

(g) in the case of a marriage solemnized on approved premises in pursuance of section 26(1)(bb) of this Act, by the registrar in whose presence the marriage is solemnized.

55   Manner of registration of marriages

(1) Every person who is required under this Part of this Act to register a marriage shall, immediately after the solemnization of the marriage, or, in the case of a marriage according to the usages of the Society of Friends, as soon as conveniently may be after the solemnization of the marriage, register in duplicate in two marriage register books the particulars relating to the marriage in the prescribed form:

. . .

56   Power to ask for particulars of marriage

Every person who is required under this Part of this Act to register a marriage may ask the parties to the marriage the particulars relating to the marriage which are required to be entered in the marriage register book.

. . .

63   Searches in register books

(1) Every incumbent, registering officer of the Society of Friends, secretary of a synagogue and registrar by whom a marriage register book is kept shall at all reasonable hours allow searches to be made in any marriage register book in his keeping, and shall give a copy certified under his hand of any entry in such a book, on payment of the following fee, that is to say—

(b) Certified copy of entry issued under that subsection

(i)   when application is made at the time of registering or to a registrar the sum of £3.50,

(ii)   in any other case, the sum of £6.50.

(2) The last foregoing subsection shall apply in the case of a registered building for which an authorised person has been appointed with the substitution for the reference to the incumbent of a reference to the person having the custody of a marriage register book in accordance with regulations made under section seventyfour of this Act.

64   Searches of indexes kept by superintendent registrars

(1) Every superintendent registrar shall cause indexes of the marriage register books in his office to be made and to be kept with the other records of his office, and the Registrar General shall supply to every superintendent registrar suitable forms for the making of such indexes.

(2) Any person shall be entitled at any time when the register office is required to be open for the transaction of public business to search the said indexes, and to have a certified copy of an entry in the said marriage register books under the hand of the superintendent registrar, on payment to the superintendent registrar of the following fee, that is to say:

(a) for every general search, the sum of £[18.00],

(c) for every certified copy, the sum of £[6.50].

65   Searches of indexes kept by Registrar General

(1) The Registrar General shall cause indexes of all certified copies of entries in marriage register books sent to him under this Part of this Act to be made and kept in the General Register Office.

(2) Any person shall be entitled to search the said indexes at any time when the General Register Office is open for that purpose, and to have a certified copy of any entry in the said certified copies of marriage register books, on payment to the Registrar General or to such other person as may be appointed to act on his behalf of the following fee, that is to say:—

  (a) for every general search, the sum of £[18.00],

  (c) for every certified copy, the sum of £[6.50].

(3) The Registrar General shall cause all certified copies of entries given in the General Register Office to be sealed or stamped with the seal of that Office; and any certified copy of an entry purporting to be sealed or stamped with the said seal shall be received as evidence of the marriage to which it relates without any further or other proof of the entry, and no certified copy purporting to have been given in the said Office shall be of any force or effect unless it is sealed or stamped as aforesaid.

67   Interpretation of Part IV

In this Part of this Act, except where the context otherwise requires, the following expressions have the meanings hereby respectively assigned to them, that is to say:—

'general search' means a search conducted during any number of successive hours not exceeding six, without the object of the search being specified;

'particular search' means a search of the indexes covering a period not exceeding five years for a specified entry;

'registering officer of the Society of Friends' means a person whom the recording clerk of the Society of Friends certifies in writing under his hand to the Registrar General to be a registering officer in England of that Society;

'secretary of a synagogue' means—

  (a) a person whom the President of the London Committee of Deputies of the British Jews certifies in writing to the Registrar General to be the secretary of a synagogue in England of persons professing the Jewish religion;

  (b) the person whom twenty householders professing the Jewish religion and being members of the West London Synagogue of British Jews certify in writing to the Registrar General to be the secretary of that Synagogue;

  (c) the person whom twenty householders professing the Jewish religion and being members of the Liberal Jewish Synagogue, St. John's Wood, certify in writing to the Registrar General to be the secretary of that Synagogue;

  (d) a person whom the secretary of either the West London Synagogue of British Jews or the Liberal Jewish Synagogue, St. John's Wood, certifies in writing to be the secretary of some other synagogue of not less than twenty householders professing the Jewish religion, being a synagogue which is connected with the said West London Synagogue or with the said Liberal Jewish Synagogue, St. John's Wood, as the case may be, and has been established for not less than one year.

'superintendent registrar' means—

  (a) in the case of a marriage registered by a clergyman, the superintendent registrar of the registration district in which is situated the church or chapel of which the incumbent keeps the marriage register book in which the marriage is registered;

  (b) in the case of a marriage registered by a registering officer of the Society of Friends, the superintendent registrar of the registration district which is assigned by the Registrar General to that registering officer;

  (c) in the case of a marriage registered by the secretary of a synagogue, the superintendent registrar of the registration district which is assigned by the Registrar General to that secretary;

(d) in the case of a marriage registered by an authorised person, the superintendent registrar of the registration district in which the registered building in which the marriage was solemnized is situated;

(e) in the case of a marriage registered by a registrar, the superintendent registrar of the registration district within which that registrar was appointed to act.

...

PART VI   GENERAL

72   Supplementary provisions as to marriages in usual places of worship

(1) For the purposes of the following provisions of this Act, that is to say, subsection (4) of section six, paragraph (b) of subsection (1) of section fifteen and subsection (3) of section thirty-five, no parish church or authorised chapel shall be deemed to be the usual place of worship of any person unless he is enrolled on the church electoral roll of the area in which that church or chapel is situated, and where any person is enrolled on the church electoral roll of an area in which he does not reside that enrolment shall be sufficient evidence that his usual place of worship is a parish church or authorised chapel in that area.

(2) Persons intending to be married shall have the like but no greater right of having their banns published and marriage solemnized by virtue of the said provisions in a parish church or authorised chapel which is the usual place of worship of one or both of them as they have of having their banns published and marriage solemnized in the parish church or public chapel of the parish or chapelry in which they or one of them resides.

(3) Where any marriage has been solemnized by virtue of the said provisions it shall not be necessary in support of the marriage to give any proof of the actual enrolment of the parties or of one of them on the church electoral roll of the area in which the parish church or authorised chapel in which the marriage was solemnized was situated, nor shall any evidence be given to prove the contrary in any proceedings touching the validity of the marriage.

...

75   Offences relating to solemnization of marriages

(1) Any person who knowingly and wilfully—

(a) solemnizes a marriage at any other time than between the hours of eight in the forenoon and six in the afternoon (not being a marriage by special licence, a marriage according to the usages of the Society of Friends or a marriage between two persons professing the Jewish religion according to the usages of the Jews);

(b) solemnizes a marriage according to the rites of the Church of England without banns of matrimony having been duly published (not being a marriage solemnized on the authority of a special licence, a common licence, or certificates of a superintendent registrar);

(c) solemnizes a marriage according to the said rites (not being a marriage by special licence or a marriage in pursuance of section 26(1)(dd) of this Act) in any place other than a church or other building in which banns may be published;

(d) solemnizes a marriage according to the said rites falsely pretending to be in Holy Orders;

shall be guilty of felony and shall be liable to imprisonment for a term not exceeding fourteen years.

(2) Any person who knowingly and wilfully—

(a) solemnizes a marriage (not being a marriage by special licence, a marriage according to the usages of the Society of Friends or a marriage between two persons professing the Jewish religion according to the usages of the Jews) in any place other than—

(i) a church or other building in which marriages may be solemnized according to the rites of the Church of England, or

(ii) the registered building, office, approved premises or person's residence specified as the place where the marriage was to be solemnized in the notices of marriage and certificates required under Part III of this Act;

(aa) solemnizes a marriage purporting to be in pursuance of section 26(1)(bb) of this Act on premises that are not approved premises;

(b) solemnizes a marriage in any such registered building as aforesaid (not being a marriage in the presence of an authorised person) in the absence of a registrar of the district in which the registered building is situated;

(bb) solemnizes a marriage in pursuance of section 26(1)(dd) of this Act, otherwise than according to the rites of the Church of England, in the absence of a registrar of the registration district in which the place where the marriage is solemnized is situated;

(c) solemnizes a marriage in the office of a superintendent registrar in the absence of a registrar of the district in which the office is situated;

(cc) solemnizes a marriage on approved premises in pursuance of section 26(1)(bb) of this Act in the absence of a registrar of the district in which the premises are situated;

(d) solemnizes a marriage on the authority of certificates of a superintendent registrar before the expiry of the waiting period in relation to each notice of marriage; or

(e) solemnizes a marriage on the authority of certificates of a superintendent registrar after the expiration of the period which is, in relation to that marriage, the applicable period for the purposes of section 33 of this Act;

shall be guilty of felony and shall be liable to imprisonment for a term not exceeding five years.

(2A) In subsection (2)(d) 'the waiting period' has the same meaning as in section 31(4A).

(3) A superintendent registrar who knowingly and wilfully—

(a) issues any certificate for marriage before the expiry of 15 days from the day on which the notice of marriage was entered in the marriage notice book;

(b) issues any certificate for marriage after the expiration of the period which is, in relation to that marriage, the applicable period for the purposes of section 33 of this Act;

(c) issues any certificate the issue of which has been forbidden under section thirty of this Act by any person entitled to forbid the issue of such a certificate; or

(d) solemnizes or permits to be solemnized in his office or, in the case of a marriage in pursuance of section 26(1)(bb) or (dd) of this Act, in any other place, any marriage which is void by virtue of any of the provisions of Part III of this Act;

shall be guilty of felony and shall be liable to imprisonment for a term not exceeding five years.

(4) No prosecution under this section shall be commenced after the expiration of three years from the commission of the offence.

. . .

76   Offences relating to registration of marriages

(1) Any person who refuses or without reasonable cause omits to register any marriage which he is required by this Act to register, and any person having the custody of a marriage register book or a certified copy of a marriage register book or part thereof who carelessly loses or injures the said book or copy or carelessly allows the said book or copy to be injured while in his keeping, shall be liable on summary conviction to a fine not exceeding level 3 on the standard scale.

(3) Any registrar who knowingly and wilfully registers any marriage which is void by virtue of any of the provisions of Part III of this Act shall be guilty of felony and shall be liable to imprisonment for a term not exceeding five years.

(6) No prosecution under subsection (3) of this section shall be commenced after the expiration of three years from the commission of the offence.

77 Offences by authorised persons

Any authorised person who refuses or fails to comply with the provisions of this Act or of any regulations made under section 74 thereof shall be guilty of an offence against this Act, and, unless the offence is one for which a specific penalty is provided under the foregoing provisions of this Part of this Act, shall be liable, on summary conviction, to a fine not exceeding the prescribed sum or, on conviction on indictment, to imprisonment for a term not exceeding two years or to a fine, and shall upon conviction cease to be an authorised person.

78 Interpretation

(1) In this Act, except where the context otherwise requires, the following expressions have the meanings hereby respectively assigned to them, that is to say—

'approved premises' means premises approved in accordance with regulations under section 46A of this Act as premises on which marriages may be solemnized in pursuance of section 26(1)(bb) of this Act;

'authorised chapel' means—

(a) in relation to a chapelry, a chapel of the chapelry in which banns of matrimony could lawfully be published immediately before the passing of the Marriage Act 1823, or in which banns may be published and marriages may be solemnized by virtue of section two of the Marriages Confirmation Act 1825, or of an authorisation given under section three of the Marriage Act 1823;

(b) in relation to an extra-parochial place, a church or chapel of that place in which banns may be published and marriages may be solemnized by virtue of section two of the Marriages Confirmation Act 1825, or of an authorisation given under section three of the Marriage Act 1823, or section twenty-one of this Act;

(c) in relation to a district specified in a licence granted under section twenty of this Act, the chapel in which banns may be published and marriages may be solemnized by virtue of that licence;

'authorised person' has the meaning assigned to it by section 43 of this Act;

'brother' includes a brother of the half blood;

'child', except where used to express a relationship, means a person under the age of eighteen;

'child of the family' in relation to any person, means a child who has lived in the same household as that person and been treated by that person as a child of the family;

'clergyman' means a clerk in Holy Orders of the Church of England;

'common licence' has the meaning assigned to it by section 5 of this Act;

'ecclesiastical district,' in relation to a district other than a parish, means a district specified in a licence granted under section 20 of this Act, a chapelry or an extra-parochial place;

'marriage notice book' has the meaning assigned to it by section 27 of this Act;

'parish' means an ecclesiastical parish and includes a district constituted under the Church Building Acts 1818 to 1884, notwithstanding that the district has not become a new parish by virtue of section fourteen of the New Parishes Act 1856 or section five of the New Parishes Measure 1943, being a district to which Acts of Parliament relating to the publication of banns of matrimony and the solemnization of marriages were applied by the said Church Building Acts as if the district had been an ancient parish, and the expression 'parish church' shall be construed accordingly;

'prescribed' means prescribed by regulations made under section 24 of this Act;

'registered building' means a building registered under Part III of this Act;

'registrar' means a registrar of marriages;

'Registrar General' means the Registrar General of Births, Deaths and Marriages in England;

'registration district' means the district of a superintendent registrar;

'sister' includes a sister of the half blood;

'special licence' has the meaning assigned to it by section 5 of this Act;

'superintendent registrar' means a superintendent registrar of births, deaths and marriages;

'trustees or governing body,' in relation to Roman Catholic registered buildings, includes a bishop or vicar general of the diocese.

(2) Any reference in this Act to the Church of England shall, unless the context otherwise requires, be construed as including a reference to the Church in Wales.

(3) For the purposes of this Act a person is house-bound if—

(a) each notice of his or her marriage given in accordance with section 27 of this Act is accompanied by a medical statement (within the meaning of section 27A(7) of this Act) made, not more than fourteen days before the date on which that notice was given, in relation to that person; and

(b) he or she is not a detained person.

(4) For the purposes of this Act a person is a detained person if he or she is for the time being detained—

(a) otherwise than by virtue of section 2, 4, 5, 35, 36 or 136 of the Mental Health Act 1983 (short term detentions), as a patient in a hospital; or

(b) in a prison or other place to which the Prison Act 1952 applies, and in paragraph (a) above 'patient' and 'hospital' have the same meanings as in Part II of the Mental Health Act 1983.

(5) For the purposes of this Act a person who is house-bound or is a detained person shall be taken, if he or she would not otherwise be, to be resident and usually resident at the place where he or she is for the time being.

SCHEDULE 1   KINDRED AND AFFINITY

PART 1   PROHIBITED DEGREES: KINDRED

1. (1) The list referred to in section 1(1) is—

Adoptive child	Grandchild
Adoptive parent	Parent
Child	Parent's sibling
Former adoptive child	Sibling
Former adoptive parent	Sibling's child
Grandparent	

(2) In the list 'sibling' means a brother, sister, half-brother or half-sister.

PART 2   DEGREES OF AFFINITY REFERRED TO IN SECTION 1(2) AND (3)

2. The list referred to in section 1(2) is as follows—

Child of former civil partner	Former spouse of grandparent
Child of former spouse	Former spouse of parent
Former civil partner of grandparent	Grandchild of former civil partner
Former civil partner of parent	Grandchild of former spouse

PART 3   DEGREES OF AFFINITY REFERRED TO IN SECTION 1(4) AND (5)

3. The list referred to in section 1(4) is as follows—

Parent of former spouse	Former spouse of child
Parent of former civil partner	Former civil partner of child.

Maintenance Orders Act 1950
(14 Geo. 6, c. 37)

PART II   ENFORCEMENT

16   Application of Part II

(1) Any order to which this section applies (in this Part of this Act referred to as a maintenance order) made by a court in any part of the United Kingdom may, if registered in accordance with the provisions of this Part of this Act in a court in another part of the United Kingdom, be enforced in accordance with those provisions in that other part of the United Kingdom.

(2) This section applies to the following orders, that is to say—

　　(a) an order for alimony, maintenance or other payments made or deemed to be made by a court in England under any of the following enactments:—

　　　　(i)　sections 15 to 17, 19 to 22, 30, 34 and 35 of the Matrimonial Causes Act 1965, and sections 22, 22A, 23 and 27 of the Matrimonial Causes Act 1973 (as that Act had effect immediately before the passing of the Family Law Act 1996), and section 14 or 17 of the Matrimonial and Family Proceedings Act 1984;

　　　　(ii)　Part I of the Domestic Proceedings and Magistrates' Courts Act 1978;

　　　　(iii)　Schedule 1 to the Children Act 1989;

　　　　(v)　paragraph 23 of Schedule 2 to the Children Act 1989 or section forty-three of the National Assistance Act 1948;

　　　　(vi)　section 18 of the Supplementary Benefits Act 1976;

　　　　(viii)　section 106 of the Social Security Administration Act 1992.

　　　　(ix)　Part 1, 8 or 9 of Schedule 5 to the Civil Partnership Act 2004, Schedule 6 to that Act or paragraph 5 or 9 of Schedule 7 to that Act;

. . .

17   Procedure for registration of maintenance orders

(1) An application for the registration of a maintenance order under this Part of this Act shall be made in the prescribed manner to the appropriate authority, that is to say—

　　(a) where the maintenance order was made by a court of summary jurisdiction in England, a justice or justices acting in the same local justice area as the court which made the order;

　　(b) where the maintenance order was made by a court of summary jurisdiction in Northern Ireland, a resident magistrate acting for the same petty sessions district as the court which made the order;

　　(c) in every other case, the prescribed officer of the court which made the order.

(2) If upon application made as aforesaid by or on behalf of the person entitled to payments under a maintenance order it appears that the person liable to make those payments resides in another part of the United Kingdom, and that it is convenient that the order should be enforceable there, the appropriate authority shall cause a certified copy of the order to be sent to the prescribed officer of a court in that part of the United Kingdom in accordance with the provisions of the next following subsection.

(3) The court to whose officer the certified copy of a maintenance order is sent under this section shall be—

　　(a) where the maintenance order was made by a superior court, the Senior Courts, the Court of Session or the Court of Judicature, as the case may be;

　　(b) in any other case, a court of summary jurisdiction acting for the place in England or Northern Ireland in which the defendant appears to be, or, as the case may be, the sheriff court in Scotland within the jurisdiction of which he appears to be.

(4) Where the prescribed officer of any court receives a certified copy of a maintenance order sent to him under this section, he shall cause the order to be registered in that court in the prescribed manner, and shall give notice of the registration in the prescribed manner to the prescribed officer of the court which made the order.

(5) The officer to whom any notice is given under the last foregoing subsection shall cause particulars of the notice to be registered in his court in the prescribed manner.

(6) Where the sums payable under a maintenance order, being an order made by a court of summary jurisdiction in England or Northern Ireland, are payable to or through an officer of any court, that officer shall, if the person entitled to the payments so requests, make an application on behalf of that person for the registration of the order under this Part of this Act; but the person at whose request the application is made shall have the same liability for costs properly incurred in or about the application as if the application had been made by him.

(7) An order which is for the time being registered under this Part of this Act in any court shall not be registered thereunder in any other court.

18   Enforcement of registered orders

(1) Subject to the provisions of this section, a maintenance order registered under this Part of this Act in a court in any part of the United Kingdom may be enforced in that part of the United Kingdom in all respects as if it had been made by that court and as if that court had had jurisdiction to make it; and proceedings for or with respect to the enforcement of any such order may be taken accordingly.

(1A) A maintenance order registered under this Part of this Act in a court of summary jurisdiction in England or Northern Ireland shall not carry interest; but where a maintenance order so registered is registered in the High Court under Part I of the Maintenance Orders Act 1958 or section 36 of the Civil Jurisdiction and Judgments Act 1982, this subsection shall not prevent any sum for whose payment the order provides from carrying interest in accordance with section 2A of the said Act of 1958 or section 11A of the Maintenance and Affiliation Orders Act (Northern Ireland) 1966.

(1B) A maintenance order made in Scotland which is registered under this Part of this Act in the Senior Courts or the Court of Judicature shall, if interest is by the law of Scotland recoverable under the order, carry the like interest in accordance with subsection (1) of this section.

(2) Every maintenance order registered under this Part of this Act in a magistrates' court in England and Wales shall, subject to the modifications of sections 76 and 93 of the Magistrates' Courts Act 1980 specified in subsections (2ZA) and (2ZB) of this section, be enforceable as a magistrates' court maintenance order within the meaning of section 150(1) of the Magistrates' Courts Act 1980.

(2ZA) Section 76 (enforcement of sums adjudged to be paid) shall have effect as if for subsections (4) to (6) there were substituted the following subsections—

'(4) Where proceedings are brought for the enforcement of a magistrates' court maintenance order under this section, the court may vary the order by exercising one of its powers under subsection (5) below.

(5) The powers of the court are—

(a) the power to order that payments under the order be made directly to the designated officer for the court or for any other magistrates' court;

(b) the power to order that payments under the order be made to the designated officer for the court or for any other magistrates' court, by such method of payment falling within section 59(6) above (standing order, etc.) as may be specified;

(c) the power to make an attachment of earnings order under the Attachment of Earnings Act 1971 to secure payments under the order.

(6) In deciding which of the powers under subsection (5) above it is to exercise, the court shall have regard to any representations made by the debtor (within the meaning of section 59 above).

(7) Subsection (4) of section 59 above (power of court to require debtor to open account) shall apply for the purposes of subsection (5) above as it applies for the purposes of that section but as if for paragraph (a) there were substituted—

"(a) the court proposes to exercise its power under paragraph (b) of section 76(5) below, and".'

(2ZB) In section 93 (complaint for arrears), subsection (6) (court not to impose imprisonment in certain circumstances) shall have effect as if for paragraph (b) there were substituted—

'(b) if the court is of the opinion that it is appropriate—

(i) to make an attachment of earnings order; or

(ii) to exercise its power under paragraph (b) of section 76(5) above.'

(2A) Any person under an obligation to make payments under a maintenance order registered under this Part of this Act in a court of summary jurisdiction in England or Northern Ireland shall give notice of any change of address to the proper officer of the court; and any person who without reasonable excuse fails to give such a notice shall be liable on summary conviction to a fine not exceeding level 2 on the standard scale.

(2B) In subsection (2A) of this section 'proper officer' means—

(a) in relation to a court of summary jurisdiction in England and Wales, the designated officer for the court; and

(b) in relation to a court of summary jurisdiction in Northern Ireland, the clerk of the court.

(3A) Notwithstanding subsection (1) above, no court in England in which a maintenance order is registered under this Part of this Act shall enforce that order to the extent that it is for the time being registered in another court in England under Part I of the Maintenance Orders Act 1958.

(6) Except as provided by this section, no proceedings shall be taken for or with respect to the enforcement of a maintenance order which is for the time being registered in any court under this Part of this Act.

19   Functions of collecting officer etc.

(1) Where a maintenance order made in England or Northern Ireland by a court of summary jurisdiction is registered in any court under this Part of this Act, any provision of the court by virtue of which sums payable thereunder are required to be paid through or to any officer or person on behalf of the person entitled thereto shall be of no effect so long as the order is so registered.

(2) Where a maintenance order is registered under this Part of this Act in a court of summary jurisdiction in England or Northern Ireland, the court shall order that all payments to be made under the maintenance order (including any arrears accrued before the date of the registration) shall be made through the collecting officer of the court or the collecting officer of some other court of summary jurisdiction in England or Northern Ireland, as the case may be.

(3) An order made under subsection (2) of this section—

(a) by a court of summary jurisdiction in England may be varied or revoked by an exercise of the powers conferred by virtue of section 18(2ZA) or section 22(1A) or (1E) of this Act;

(b) by a court of summary jurisdiction in Northern Ireland may be varied or revoked by an exercise of the powers conferred by virtue of section 18(3ZA) or section 22(1F) or (1J) of this Act.

(4) Where by virtue of the provisions of this section or any order made thereunder payments under a maintenance order cease to be or become payable through or to any officer or person, the person liable to make the payments shall, until he is given the prescribed notice to that effect, be deemed to comply with the maintenance order if he makes payments in accordance with the maintenance order and any order under this section of which he has received such notice.

20   Arrears under registered maintenance orders

(1) Where application is made for the registration of a maintenance order under this Part of this Act, the applicant may lodge with the appropriate authority—

(a) if the payments under the order are required to be made to or through an officer of any court, a certificate in the prescribed form, signed by that officer, as to the amount of any arrears due under the order;

(b) in any other case, a statutory declaration or affidavit as to the amount of those arrears;

and if a certified copy of the maintenance order is sent to the prescribed officer of any court in pursuance of the application, the certificate, declaration or affidavit shall also be sent to that officer.

...

21 Discharge and variation of maintenance orders registered in superior courts

(1) The registration of a maintenance order in a superior court under this Part of this Act shall not confer on that court any power to vary or discharge the order, or affect any jurisdiction of the court in which the order was made to vary or discharge the order.

22 Discharge and variation of maintenance orders registered in summary or sheriff courts

(1) Where a maintenance order is for the time being registered under this Part of this Act in a court of summary jurisdiction or sheriff court, that court may, upon application made in the prescribed manner by or on behalf of the person liable to make periodical payments under the order or the person entitled to those payments, by order make such variation as the court thinks fit in the rate of the payments under the maintenance order; but no such variation shall impose on the person liable to make payments under the maintenance order a liability to make payments in excess of the maximum rate (if any) authorised by the law for the time being in force in the part of the United Kingdom in which the maintenance order was made.

(1A) The power of a magistrates' court in England and Wales to vary a maintenance order under subsection (1) of this section shall include power, if the court is satisfied that payment has not been made in accordance with the order, to vary the order by exercising one of its powers under subsection (1B) of this section.

(1B) The powers of the court are—

(a) the power to order that payments under the order be made directly to the designated officer for the court or for any other magistrates' court in England and Wales;

(b) the power to order that payments under the order be made to the designated officer for the court or for any other magistrates' court in England and Wales, by such method of payment falling within section 59(6) of the Magistrates' Courts Act 1980 (standing order, etc.) as may be specified;

(c) the power to make an attachment of earnings order under the Attachment of Earnings Act 1971 to secure payments under the order.

(1C) In deciding which of the powers under subsection (1B) of this section it is to exercise, the court shall have regard to any representations made by the person liable to make payments under the order.

(1D) Subsection (4) of section 59 of the Magistrates' Courts Act 1980 (power of court to require debtor to open account) shall apply for the purposes of subsection (1B) of this section as it applies for the purposes of that section but as if for paragraph (a)there were substituted—

'(a) the court proposes to exercise its power under paragraph (b) of section 22(1B) of the Maintenance Orders Act 1950, and'.

(1E) Subsections (4) to (11) of section 60 of the Magistrates' Courts Act 1980 (power of clerk and court to vary maintenance order) shall apply in relation to a maintenance order for the time being registered under this Part of this Act in a magistrates' court in England and Wales as they apply in relation to a maintenance order made by a magistrates' court in England and Wales but—

(a) as if in subsection (4) for paragraph (b) there were substituted—

'(b) payments under the order are required to be made to the designated officer for the court or any other magistrates' court, by any method of payment falling within section 59(6) above (standing order, etc.)';

(b) as if in subsection (5) for the words 'to the designated officer for the court there were substituted 'in accordance with paragraph (a) of section 22(1B) of the Maintenance Orders Act 1950';

(c) as if in subsection (7), paragraph (c) and the word 'and' immediately preceding it were omitted;

(d) as if in subsection (8) for the words 'paragraphs (a) to (d) of section 59(3) above' there were substituted 'section 22(1B) of the Maintenance Orders Act 1950';

(e) as if for subsections (9) and (10) there were substituted the following subsections—

'(9) In deciding which of the powers under section 22(1B) of the Maintenance Orders Act 1950 it is to exercise, the court shall have regard to any representations made by the debtor.

(10) Subsection (4) of section 59 above (power of court to require debtor to open account) shall apply for the purposes of subsection (8) above as it applies for the purposes of that section but as if for paragraph (a) there were substituted—

"(a) the court proposes to exercise its power under paragraph (b) of section 22(1B) of the Maintenance Orders Act 1950, and".'

(1F) The power of a court of summary jurisdiction in Northern Ireland to vary a maintenance order under subsection (1) of this section shall include power, if the court is satisfied that payment has not been made in accordance with the order, to vary the order by exercising one of its powers under subsection (1G) of this section.

(1G) The powers of the court are—

(a) the power to order that payments under the order be made directly to the collecting officer;

(b) the power to order that payments under the order be made to the collecting officer by such method of payment falling within Article 85(7) of the Magistrates' Courts (Northern Ireland) Order 1981 (standing order, etc.) as may be specified;

(c) the power to make an attachment of earnings order under Part IX of the Order of 1981 to secure payments under the order;

and in this subsection 'collecting officer' means the officer mentioned in Article 85(4) of the Order of 1981.

(1H) In deciding which of the powers under subsection (1G) of this section it is to exercise, the court shall have regard to any representations made by the person liable to make payments under the order.

(1I) Paragraph (5) of Article 85 of the Magistrates' Courts (Northern Ireland) Order 1981 (power of court to require debtor to open account) shall apply for the purposes of subsection (1G) of this section as it applies for the purposes of that Article but as if for subparagraph (a) there were substituted—

'(a) the court proposes to exercise its power under paragraph (b) of section 22(1G) of the Maintenance Orders Act 1950, and'.

(1J) Paragraphs (4) to (11) of Article 86 of the Magistrates' Courts (Northern Ireland) Order 1981 (power of clerk and court to vary maintenance order) shall apply in relation to a maintenance order for the time being registered under this Part of this Act in a court of summary jurisdiction in Northern Ireland as they apply in relation to a maintenance order made by a court of summary jurisdiction in Northern Ireland but—

(a) as if in paragraph (4) for sub-paragraph (b) there were substituted—

'(b) payments under the order are required to be made to the collecting officer by any method of payment falling within Article 85(7) (standing order, etc.)'; and as if after the words 'petty sessions' there were inserted 'for the petty sessions district for which the court which made the order acts';

(b) as if in paragraph (5) for the words 'to the collecting officer' there were substituted 'in accordance with paragraph (a) of section 22(1G) of the Maintenance Orders Act 1950';

(c) as if in paragraph (7), sub-paragraph (c) and the word 'and' immediately preceding it were omitted;

(d) as if in paragraph (8) for the words 'sub-paragraphs (a) to (d) of Article 85(3)' there were substituted 'section 22(1G) of the Maintenance Orders Act 1950';

(e) as if for paragraphs (9) and (10) there were substituted the following paragraphs—

'(9) In deciding which of the powers under section 22(1G) of the Maintenance Orders Act 1950 it is to exercise, the court shall have regard to any representations made by the debtor.

(10) Paragraph (5) of Article 85 (power of court to require debtor to open account) shall apply for the purposes of paragraph (8) as it applies for the purposes of that Article but as if for sub-paragraph (a) there were substituted—

"(a) the court proposes to exercise its power under paragraph (b) of section 22(1G) of the Maintenance Orders Act 1950, and".'

24   Cancellation of registration

(1) At any time while a maintenance order is registered under this Part of this Act in any court, an application for the cancellation of the registration may be made in the prescribed manner to the prescribed officer of that court by or on behalf of the person entitled to payments under the order; and upon any such application that officer shall (unless proceedings for the variation of the order are pending in that court), cancel the registration, and thereupon the order shall cease to be registered in that court.

. . .

(4) Except as provided by subsection (5) of this section, the cancellation of the registration of a maintenance order shall not affect anything done in relation to the maintenance order while it was registered.

(5) On the cancellation of the registration of a maintenance order, any order made in relation thereto under subsection (2) of section nineteen of this Act shall cease to have effect; but until the person liable to make payments under the maintenance order receives the prescribed notice of the cancellation, he shall be deemed to comply with the maintenance order if he makes payments in accordance with any order under the said subsection (2) which was in force immediately before the cancellation.

(5A) On the cancellation of the registration of a maintenance order registered in a magistrates' court in England and Wales, any order—

(a) made in relation thereto by virtue of the powers conferred by section 18(2ZA) or section 22(1A) or (1E) of this Act, and

(b) requiring payment to the designated officer for a magistrates' court in England and Wales (whether or not by any method of payment falling within section 59(6) of the Magistrates' Courts Act 1980),

shall cease to have effect; but until the person liable to make payments under the maintenance order receives the prescribed notice of the cancellation, he shall be deemed to comply with the maintenance order if he makes payments in accordance with any such order which was in force immediately before the cancellation.

(5B) On the cancellation of the registration of a maintenance order registered in a court of summary jurisdiction in Northern Ireland, any order—

(a) made in relation thereto by virtue of the powers conferred by section 18(3ZA) or section 22(1F) or (1J) of this Act, and

(b) requiring payment to the collecting officer in Northern Ireland (whether or not by any method of payment falling within Article 85(7) of the Magistrates' Courts (Northern Ireland) Order 1981),

shall cease to have effect; but until the person liable to make payments under the maintenance order receives the prescribed notice of the cancellation, he shall be deemed to comply with the maintenance order if he makes payments in accordance with any such order which was in force immediately before the cancellation.

(6) Where, by virtue of an order made under subsection (2) of section nineteen of this Act, sums payable under a maintenance order registered in a court of summary jurisdiction in England or Northern Ireland are payable through the collecting officer of any court, that

officer shall, if the person entitled to the payments so requests, make an application on behalf of that person for the cancellation of the registration.

...

Intestates' Estates Act 1952
(15 & 16 Geo. 6 & 1 Eliz. 2, c. 64)

PART I   AMENDMENTS OF LAW OF INTESTATE SUCCESSION

5   Rights of surviving spouse or civil partner as respects the matrimonial or civil partnership home

The Second Schedule to this Act shall have effect for enabling the surviving spouse or civil partner of a person dying intestate after the commencement of this Act to acquire the matrimonial or civil partnership home.

SCHEDULES

Section 5   SECOND SCHEDULE

Rights of surviving spouse or civil partner as respects the matrimonial or civil partnership home

1.—(1) Subject to the provisions of this Schedule, where the residuary estate of the intestate comprises an interest in a dwelling-house in which the surviving spouse or civil partner was resident at the time of the intestate's death, the surviving spouse or civil partner may require the personal representative, in exercise of the power conferred by section forty-one of the principal Act (and with due regard to the requirements of that section as to valuation) to appropriate the said interest in the dwelling-house in or towards satisfaction of any absolute interest of the surviving spouse or civil partner in the real and personal estate of the intestate.

(2) The right conferred by this paragraph shall not be exercisable where the interest is—

(a) a tenancy which at the date of the death of the intestate was a tenancy which would determine within the period of two years from that date; or

(b) a tenancy which the landlord by notice given after that date could determine within the remainder of that period.

(3) Nothing in subsection (5) of section forty-one of the principal Act (which requires the personal representative, in making an appropriation to any person under that section, to have regard to the rights of others) shall prevent the personal representative from giving effect to the right conferred by this paragraph.

(4) The reference in this paragraph to an absolute interest in the real and personal estate of the intestate includes a reference to the capital value of a life interest which the surviving spouse or civil partner has under this Act elected to have redeemed.

(5) Where part of a building was, at the date of the death of the intestate, occupied as a separate dwelling, that dwelling shall for the purposes of this Schedule be treated as a dwelling-house.

2. Where—

(a) the dwelling-house forms part of a building and an interest in the whole of the building is comprised in the residuary estate; or

(b) the dwelling-house is held with agricultural land and an interest in the agricultural land is comprised in the residuary estate; or

(c) the whole or part of the dwelling-house was at the time of the intestate's death used as a hotel or lodging house; or

(d) a part of the dwelling-house was at the time of the intestate's death used for purposes other than domestic purposes,

the right conferred by paragraph 1 of this Schedule shall not be exercisable unless the court, on being satisfied that the exercise of that right is not likely to diminish the value of assets in the residuary estate (other than the said interest in the dwelling-house) or make them more difficult to dispose of, so orders.

3.—(1) The right conferred by paragraph 1 of this Schedule—

    (a) shall not be exercisable after the expiration of twelve months from the first taking out of representation with respect to the intestate's estate;

    (b) shall not be exercisable after the death of the surviving spouse or civil partner;

    (c) shall be exercisable, except where the surviving spouse or civil partner is the sole personal representative, by notifying the personal representative (or, where there are two or more personal representatives of whom one is the surviving spouse or civil partner, all of them except the surviving husband or wife) in writing.

(2) A notification in writing under paragraph (c) of the foregoing sub-paragraph shall not be revocable except with the consent of the personal representative; but the surviving spouse or civil partner may require the personal representative to have the said interest in the dwelling-house valued in accordance with section forty-one of the principal Act and to inform him or her of the result of that valuation before he or she decides whether to exercise the right.

(3) Subsection (9) of the section forty-seven A added to the principal Act by section two of this Act shall apply for the purposes of the construction of the reference in this paragraph to the first taking out of representation, and the proviso to subsection (5) of that section shall apply for the purpose of enabling the surviving spouse or civil partner to apply for an extension of the period of twelve months mentioned in this paragraph.

4.—(1) During the period of twelve months mentioned in paragraph 3 of this Schedule the personal representative shall not without the written consent of the surviving spouse or civil partner sell or otherwise dispose of the said interest in the dwelling-house except in the course of administration owing to want of other assets.

(2) An application to the court under paragraph 2 of this Schedule may be made by the personal representative as well as by the surviving spouse or civil partner, and if, on an application under that paragraph, the court does not order that the right conferred by paragraph 1 of this Schedule shall be exercisable by the surviving spouse or civil partner, the court may authorise the personal representative to dispose of the said interest in the dwelling-house within the said period of twelve months.

(3) Where the court under sub-paragraph (3) of paragraph 3 of this Schedule extends the said period of twelve months, the court may direct that this paragraph shall apply in relation to the extended period as it applied in relation to the original period of twelve months.

(4) This paragraph shall not apply where the surviving spouse or civil partner is the sole personal representative or one of two or more personal representatives.

(5) Nothing in this paragraph shall confer any right on the surviving spouse or civil partner as against a purchaser from the personal representative.

5.—(1) Where the surviving spouse or civil partner is one of two or more personal representatives, the rule that a trustee may not be a purchaser of trust property shall not prevent the surviving spouse or civil partner from purchasing out of the estate of the intestate an interest in a dwelling-house in which the surviving spouse or civil partner was resident at the time of the intestate's death.

(2) The power of appropriation under section forty-one of the principal Act shall include power to appropriate an interest in a dwelling-house in which the surviving spouse or civil partner was resident at the time of the intestate's death partly in satisfaction of an interest of the surviving spouse or civil partner in the real and personal estate of the intestate and partly in return for a payment of money by the surviving spouse or civil partner to the personal representative.

6.—(1) Where the surviving spouse or civil partner lacks capacity (within the meaning of the Mental Capacity Act 2005) to make a requirement or give a consent under this Schedule, the requirement or consent may be made or given by a deputy appointed by the Court of Protection with power in that respect or, if no deputy has that power, by that court.

(2) A requirement or consent made or given under this Schedule by a surviving spouse or civil partner who is an infant shall be as valid and binding as it would be if he or she were of age; and, as respects an appropriation in pursuance of paragraph 1 of this Schedule, the provisions of section forty-one of the principal Act as to obtaining the consent of the infant's parent or guardian, or of the court on behalf of the infant, shall not apply.

7.—(1) Except where the context otherwise requires, references in this Schedule to a dwelling-house include references to any garden or portion of ground attached to and usually occupied with the dwelling-house or otherwise required for the amenity or convenience of the dwelling-house.

(2) This Schedule shall be construed as one with Part IV of the principal Act.

Matrimonial Causes (Property and Maintenance) Act 1958
(6 & 7 Eliz. 2, c. 35)

7 Extension of s. 17 of Married Women's Property Act 1882

(1) Any right of a wife, under section seventeen of the Married Women's Property Act 1882 to apply to a judge of the High Court or of a county court in any question between husband and wife as to the title to or possession of property, shall include the right to make such an application where it is claimed by the wife that her husband has had in his possession or under his control—

(a) money to which, or to a share of which, she was beneficially entitled (whether by reason that it represented the proceeds of property to which, or to an interest in which, she was beneficially entitled, or for any other reason), or

(b) property (other than money) to which, or to an interest in which, she was beneficially entitled,

and that either that money or other property has ceased to be in his possession or under his control or that she does not know whether it is still in his possession or under his control.

(2) Where, on an application made to a judge of the High Court or of a county court under the said section seventeen, as extended by the preceding subsection, the judge is satisfied—

(a) that the husband has had in his possession or under his control money or other property as mentioned in paragraph (a) or paragraph (b) of the preceding subsection, and

(b) that he has not made to the wife, in respect of that money or other property, such payment or disposition as would have been appropriate in the circumstances, the power to make orders under that section shall be extended in accordance with the next following subsection.

(3) Where the last preceding subsection applies, the power to make orders under the said section seventeen shall include power for the judge to order the husband to pay to the wife—

(a) in a case falling within paragraph (a) of subsection (1) of this section, such sum in respect of the money to which the application relates, or the wife's share thereof, as the case may be, or

(b) in a case falling within paragraph (b) of the said subsection (1), such sum in respect of the value of the property to which the application relates, or the wife's interest therein, as the case may be,

as the judge may consider appropriate.

(4) Where on an application under the said section seventeen as extended by this section it appears to the judge that there is any property which—

    (a) represents the whole or part of the money or property in question, and

    (b) is property in respect of which an order could have been made under that section if an application had been made by the wife thereunder in a question as to the title to or possession of that property,

the judge (either in substitution for or in addition to the making of an order in accordance with the last preceding subsection) may make any order under that section in respect of that property which he could have made on such an application as is mentioned in paragraph (b) of this subsection.

(5) The preceding provisions of this section shall have effect in relation to a husband as they have effect in relation to a wife, as if any reference to the husband were a reference to the wife and any reference to the wife were a reference to the husband.

(6) Any power of a judge which is exercisable on an application under the said section seventeen shall be exercisable in relation to an application made under that section as extended by this section.

(7) For the avoidance of doubt it is hereby declared that any power conferred by the said section seventeen to make orders with respect to any property includes power to order a sale of the property.

Maintenance Orders Act 1958
(6 & 7 Eliz. 2, c. 39)

PART I   REGISTRATION, ENFORCEMENT AND VARIATION OF CERTAIN MAINTENANCE ORDERS

1 Application of Part I

(1) The provisions of this Part of this Act shall have effect for the purpose of enabling maintenance orders to which this Part of this Act applies to be registered—

    (a) in the case of an order made by the High Court or a county court, in a magistrates' court; and

    (b) in the case of an order made by a magistrates' court, in the High Court, and, subject to those provisions, while so registered—

        (i)   to be enforced in like manner as an order made by the court of registration;

        (ii) in the case of an order registered in a magistrates' court, to be varied by a magistrates' court.

(1A) In the following provisions of the Act 'maintenance order' means any order specified in Schedule 8 to the Administration of Justice Act 1970.

(2) For the purposes of subsection (1) above, a maintenance order made by a court in Scotland or Northern Ireland and registered in England under Part II of the Maintenance Orders Act 1950 shall be deemed to have been made by the court in England in which it is so registered.

(2A) This Part of this Act applies—

    (a) to maintenance orders made by the High Court or a county court, or a magistrates' court, other than orders registered in Scotland or Northern Ireland under Part II of the Maintenance Orders Act 1950, and

    (b) to maintenance orders made by a court in Scotland or Northern Ireland and registered in England under Part II of the Maintenance Orders Act 1950.

...

2 Registration of orders

(1) A person entitled to receive payments under a High Court or county court order may apply for the registration of the order to the original court, and the court may, if it thinks fit, grant the application.

(2) Where an application for the registration of such an order is granted—

    (a) no proceedings shall be begun, and no writ, warrant or other process shall be issued, for the enforcement of the order before the registration of the order or the expiration of the prescribed period from the grant of the application, whichever first occurs; and

    (b) the original court shall, on being satisfied within the period aforesaid by the person who made the application that no such proceedings or process begun or issued before the grant of the application remain pending or in force, cause a certified copy of the order to be sent to the designated officer for the magistrates' court acting in the local justice area in which the defendant appears to be;

but if at the expiration of the period aforesaid the original court has not been so satisfied, the grant of the application shall become void.

(3) A person entitled to receive payments under a magistrates' court order who considers that the order could be more effectively enforced if it were registered may apply for the registration of the order to the original court, and the court may, if it thinks fit, grant the application.

(3A) Without prejudice to subsection (3) of this section, where a magistrates' court order provides both for the payment of a lump sum and for the making of periodical payments, a person entitled to receive a lump sum under the order who considers that, so far as it relates to that sum, the order could be more effectively enforced if it were registered may apply to the original court for the registration of the order so far as it so relates, and the court may, if it thinks fit, grant the application.

(3B) Where an application under subsection (3A) of this section is granted in the case of a magistrates' court order, the provisions of this Part of this Act shall have effect in relation to that order as if so far as it relates to the payment of a lump sum it were a separate order.

(4) Where an application for the registration of a magistrates' court order is granted—

    (a) no proceedings for the enforcement of the order shall be begun before the registration takes place and no warrant or other process for the enforcement thereof shall be issued in consequence of any such proceedings begun before the grant of the application; and

    (c) the original court shall, on being satisfied in the prescribed manner that no process for the enforcement of the order issued before the grant of the application remains in force, cause a certified copy of the order to be sent to the prescribed officer of the High Court.

(5) The officer of, or for, a court who receives a certified copy of an order sent to him under this section shall cause the order to be registered in that court.

(6) Where a magistrates' court order is registered under this Part of this Act in the High Court, then—

    (a) if payments under the magistrates' court order are required to be made (otherwise than to the designated officer for a magistrates' court) by any method of payment falling within section 59(6) of the Magistrates' Courts Act 1980 (standing order, etc.), any order requiring payment by that method shall continue to have effect after registration;

    (b) any order by virtue of which sums payable under the magistrates' court order are required to be paid to the designated officer for a magistrates' court (whether or not by any method of payment falling within section 59(6) of that Act) on behalf of the person entitled thereto shall cease to have effect.

(6ZA) Where a High Court or county court order is registered under this Part of this Act in a magistrates' court, then—

    (a) if a means of payment order (within the meaning of section 1(7) of the Maintenance Enforcement Act 1991) has effect in relation to the order in question, it shall continue to have effect after registration; and

    (b) in any other case, the magistrates' court shall order that all payments to be made under the order in question (including any arrears accrued before registration) shall be made to the designated officer for the court or for any other magistrates' court.

(6ZB) Any such order as to payment—

    (a) as is referred to in paragraph (a) of subsection (6) of this section may be revoked, suspended, revived or varied by an exercise of the powers conferred by section 4A of this Act; and

    (b) as is referred to in paragraph (a) or (b) of subsection (6ZA) of this section may be varied or revoked by an exercise of the powers conferred by section 3(2A) or (2B) or section 4(2A), (5A) or (5B) of this Act.

(6ZC) Where by virtue of the provisions of this section or any order under subsection (6ZA)(b) of this section payments under an order cease to be or become payable to the designated officer for a magistrates' court, the person liable to make the payments shall, until he is given the prescribed notice to that effect, be deemed to comply with the order if he makes payments in accordance with the order and any order under subsection (6ZA)(b) of this section of which he has received such notice.

(6A) In this section—

'High Court order' includes a maintenance order deemed to be made by the High Court by virtue of section 1(2) above, and

'magistrates' court order' includes a maintenance order deemed to be made by a magistrates' court by virtue of that subsection.

. . .

3 Enforcement of registered orders

(1) Subject to the provisions of section 2A of this Act and this section, a registered order shall be enforceable in all respects as if it had been made by the court of registration and as if that court had jurisdiction to make it; and proceedings for or with respect to the enforcement of a registered order may be taken accordingly.

(2) Subject to the provisions of subsections (2A) to (3) of this section, an order registered in a magistrates' court shall be enforceable as a magistrates' court maintenance order within the meaning of section 150(1) of the Magistrates' Courts Act 1980.

(2A) Where an order registered in a magistrates' court is an order other than one deemed to be made by the High Court by virtue of section 1(2) of this Act, section 76 of the Magistrates' Courts Act 1980 (enforcement of sums adjudged to be paid) shall have effect as if for subsections (4) to (6) there were substituted the following subsections—

'(4) Where proceedings are brought for the enforcement of a magistrates' court maintenance order under this section, the court may vary the order by exercising one of its powers under paragraphs (a) to (d) of section 59(3) above.

(5) In deciding which of the powers under paragraphs (a) to (d) of section 59(3) above it is to exercise, the court shall have regard to any representations made by the debtor and the creditor (which expressions have the same meaning as they have in section 59 above).

(6) Subsection (4) of section 59 above shall apply for the purposes of subsection (4) above as it applies for the purposes of that section.'

(2B) Where an order registered in a magistrates' court is an order deemed to be made by the High Court by virtue of section 1(2) of this Act, sections 76 and 93 of the Magistrates' Courts Act 1980 (enforcement of sums adjudged to be paid and complaint for arrears) shall have effect subject to the modifications specified in subsections (2ZA) and (2ZB) of section 18 of the Maintenance Orders Act 1950 (enforcement of registered orders).

(3) Where an order remains or becomes registered after the discharge of the order, no proceedings shall be taken by virtue of that registration except in respect of arrears which were due under that order at the time of the discharge and have not been remitted.

(3A) Any person under an obligation to make payments under an order registered in a magistrates' court shall give notice of any change of address to the designated officer for the court; and any person who without reasonable excuse fails to give such a notice shall be liable on summary conviction to a fine not exceeding level 2 on the standard scale.

(4) Except as provided by this section, no proceedings shall be taken for or with respect to the enforcement of a registered order.

4   Variation of orders registered in magistrates' courts

(1) The provisions of this section shall have effect with respect to the variation of orders registered in magistrates' courts, and references in this section to registered orders shall be construed accordingly.

(2) Subject to the following provisions of this section—

(a) the court of registration may exercise the same jurisdiction to vary any rate of payments specified by a registered order (other than jurisdiction in a case where a party to the order is not present in England when the application for variation is made) as is exercisable, apart from this subsection, by the original court; and

(b) a rate of payments specified by a registered order shall not be varied except by the court of registration or any other magistrates' court to which the jurisdiction conferred by the foregoing paragraph is extended by rules of court.

(2A) The power of a magistrates' court to vary a registered order under subsection (2) of this section shall include power, if the court is satisfied that payment has not been made in accordance with the order, to vary the order by exercising one of its powers under paragraphs (a) to (d) of section 59(3) of the Magistrates' Courts Act 1980.

(2B) Subsection (4) of section 59 of that Act shall apply for the purposes of subsection (2A) of this section as it applies for the purposes of that section.

(2C) In deciding which of the powers under paragraphs (a) to (d) of section 59(3) of that Act it is to exercise, the court shall have regard to any representations made by the debtor and the creditor (which expressions have the same meaning as they have in section 59 of that Act).

(4) If it appears to the court to which an application is made by virtue of subsection (2) of this section for the variation of a rate of payments specified by a registered order that it is for any reason appropriate to remit the application to the original court, the first-mentioned court shall so remit the application and the original court shall thereupon deal with the application as if the order were not registered.

(5) Nothing in subsection (2) of this section shall affect the jurisdiction of the original court to vary a rate of payments specified by a registered order if an application for the variation of that rate is made to that court—

(a) in proceedings for a variation of provisions of the order which do not specify a rate of payments; or

(b) at a time when a party to the order is not present in England.

(5A) Subject to the following provisions of this section, subsections (4) to (11) of section 60 of the Magistrates' Courts Act 1980 (power of clerk and court to vary maintenance orders) shall apply in relation to a registered order (other than one deemed to be made by the High Court by virtue of section 1(2) of this Act) as they apply in relation to a maintenance order made by a magistrates' court (disregarding section 23(2) of the Domestic Proceedings and Magistrates' Courts Act 1978, section 15(2) of the Children Act 1989) and paragraph 42 of Schedule 6 to the Civil Partnership Act 2004 but

(a) as if in subsection (8) after the words 'the court which may' there were inserted 'subject to subsection (10) below'; and

(b) as if for subsections (9) and (10) there were substituted the following subsections—

'(9) Subsection (4) of section 59 above shall apply for the purposes of subsection (8) above as it applies for the purposes of that section.

(10) In deciding which of the powers under paragraphs (a) to (d) of section 59(3) above it is to exercise, the court shall have regard to any representations made by the debtor and the creditor.'

(5B) Subject to the following provisions of this section, subsections (4) to (11) of section 60 of the Magistrates' Courts Act 1980 (power of clerk and court to vary maintenance orders) shall apply in relation to a registered order deemed to be made by the High Court by virtue of section 1(2) of this Act as they apply in relation to a maintenance order made by a magistrates' court (disregarding section 23(2) of the Domestic Proceedings and Magistrates' Courts Act 1978, section 15(2) of the Children Act 1989) and paragraph 42 of Schedule 6 to the Civil Partnership Act 2004 but—

    (a) as if in subsection (4) for paragraph (b) there were substituted—

        '(b) payments under the order are required to be made to the designated officer for the court or for any other magistrates' court by any method of payment falling within section 59(6) above (standing order, etc.)';

    (b) as if in subsection (5) for the words 'to the designated officer for the court' there were substituted 'in accordance with paragraph (a) of subsection (9) below';

    (c) as if in subsection (7), paragraph (c) and the word 'and' immediately preceding it were omitted;

    (d) as if in subsection (8) for the words 'paragraphs (a) to (d) of section 59(3) above' there were substituted 'subsection (9) below';

    (e) as if for subsections (9) and (10) there were substituted the following subsections—

    '(9) The powers of the court are—

    (a) the power to order that payments under the order be made directly to the designated officer for the court or for any other magistrates' court;

    (b) the power to order that payments under the order be made to the designated officer for the court or for any other magistrates' court by such method of payment falling within section 59(6) above (standing order, etc.) as may be specified;

    (c) the power to make an attachment of earnings order under the Attachment of Earnings Act 1971 to secure payments under the order.

(10) In deciding which of the powers under subsection (9) above it is to exercise, the court shall have regard to any representations made by the debtor.

(10A) Subsection (4) of section 59 above (power of court to require debtor to open account) shall apply for the purposes of subsection (9) above as it applies for the purposes of that section but as if for paragraph (a) there were substituted—

    "(a) the court proposes to exercise its power under paragraph (b) of section 60(9) below".'

(6) No application for any variation of a registered order shall be made to any court while proceedings for any variation of the order are pending in any other court.

(6B) No application for any variation of a registered order shall be made to any court in respect of an order for periodical or other payments made under Part III of the Matrimonial and Family Proceedings Act 1984 or under Schedule 7 to the Civil Partnership Act 2004.

(7) Where a magistrates' court, in exercise of the jurisdiction conferred by subsection (2) of this section, varies or refuses to vary a registered order, an appeal from the variation or refusal shall lie to the High Court.

4A Variation etc. of orders registered in the High Court

(1) The provisions of this section shall have effect with respect to orders registered in the High Court other than maintenance orders deemed to be made by a magistrates' court by virtue of section 1(4) of this Act, and the reference in subsection (2) of this section to a registered order shall be construed accordingly.

(2) The High Court may exercise the same powers in relation to a registered order as are exercisable by the High Court under section 1 of the Maintenance Enforcement Act 1991 in relation to a qualifying periodical maintenance order (within the meaning of that section) which has been made by the High Court, including the power under subsection (7) of that section to revoke, suspend, revive or vary—

    (a) any such order as is referred to in paragraph (a) of section 2(6) of this Act which continues to have effect by virtue of that paragraph; and

(b) any means of payment order (within the meaning of section 1(7) of that Act of 1991) made by virtue of the provisions of this section.

5 Cancellation of registration

(1) If a person entitled to receive payments under a registered order desires the registration to be cancelled, he may give notice under this section.

(2) Where the original court varies or discharges an order registered in a magistrates' court, the original court may, if it thinks fit, give notice under this section.

(3) Where the original court discharges an order registered in the High Court and it appears to the original court, whether by reason of the remission of arrears by that court or otherwise, that no arrears under the order remain to be recovered, the original court shall give notice under this section.

(4) Notice under this section shall be given to the court of registration; and where such notice is given—

(a) no proceedings for the enforcement of the registered order shall be begun before the cancellation of the registration and no writ, warrant or other process for the enforcement thereof shall be issued in consequence of any such proceedings begun before the giving of the notice; and

(c) the court of registration shall cancel the registration on being satisfied in the prescribed manner—

(i)   that no process for the enforcement of the registered order issued before the giving of the notice remains in force; and

(ii) in the case of an order registered in a magistrates' court, that no proceedings for the variation of the order are pending in a magistrates' court.

(4A) For the purposes of a notice under subsection (2) or (3) above—

'court of registration' includes any court in which an order is registered under Part II of the Maintenance Orders Act 1950, and

'registration' includes registration under that Act.

(5) On the cancellation of the registration of a High Court or county court order—

(a) any order which requires payments under the order in question to be made (otherwise than to the designated officer for a magistrates' court) by any method of payment falling within section 59(6) of the Magistrates' Courts Act 1980 or section 1(5) of the Maintenance Enforcement Act 1991 (standing order, etc.) shall continue to have effect; and

(b) any order made under section 2(6ZA)(b) of this Act or by virtue of the powers conferred by section 3(2A) or (2B) or section 4(2A), (5A) or (5B) of this Act and which requires payments under the order in question to be made to the designated officer for a magistrates' court (whether or not by any method of payment falling within section 59(6) of the Magistrates' Courts Act 1980) shall cease to have effect;

but, in a case falling within paragraph (b) of this subsection, until the defendant receives the prescribed notice of the cancellation he shall be deemed to comply with the High Court or county court order if he makes payment in accordance with any such order as is referred to in paragraph (b) of this subsection which was in force immediately before the cancellation and of which he has notice.

(6) On the cancellation of the registration of a magistrates' court order—

(a) any order which requires payments under the magistrates' court order to be made by any method of payment falling within section 59(6) of the Magistrates' Courts Act 1980 or section 1(5) of the Maintenance Enforcement Act 1991 (standing order, etc.) shall continue to have effect; and

(b) in any other case, payments shall become payable to the designated officer for the original court;

but, in a case falling within paragraph (b) of this subsection, until the defendant receives the prescribed notice of the cancellation he shall be deemed to comply with the magistrates' court order if he makes payments in accordance with any order which was in force immediately before the cancellation and of which he has notice.

(7) In subsections (5) and (6) of this section 'High Court order' and 'magistrates' court order' shall be construed in accordance with section 2(6A) of this Act.

...

Marriage (Enabling) Act 1960
(8 & 9 Eliz., c. 29)

1   Certain marriages not to be void

(1) No marriage hereafter contracted (whether in or out of Great Britain) between a man and a woman who is the sister, aunt or niece of a former wife of his (whether living or not), or was formerly the wife of his brother, uncle or nephew (whether living or not), shall by reason of that relationship be void or voidable under any enactment or rule of law applying in Great Britain as a marriage between persons within the prohibited degrees of affinity.

(2) In the foregoing subsection words of kinship apply equally to kin of the whole and of the half blood.

(3) This section does not validate a marriage, if either party to it is at the time of the marriage domiciled in a country outside Great Britain, and under the law of that country there cannot be a valid marriage between the parties.

Law Reform (Husband and Wife) Act 1962
(10 & 11 Eliz. 2, c. 48)

1   Actions in tort between husband and wife

(1) Subject to the provisions of this section, each of the parties to a marriage shall have the like right of action in tort against the other as if they were not married.

(2) Where an action in tort is brought by one of the parties to a marriage against the other during the subsistence of the marriage, the court may stay the action if it appears—

    (a) that no substantial benefit would accrue to either party from the continuation of the proceedings; or

    (b) that the question or questions in issue could more conveniently be disposed of on an application made under section seventeen of the Married Women's Property Act 1882 (determination of questions between husband and wife as to the title to or possession of property);

and without prejudice to paragraph (b) of this section the court may, in such an action, either exercise any power which could be exercised on an application under the said section seventeen, or give such directions as it thinks fit for the disposal under that section of any question arising in the proceedings.

...

3   Short title, interpretation, saving and extent

(3) The reference in subsection (1) of section one of this Act to the parties to a marriage include references to the persons who were parties to a marriage which has been dissolved.

Married Women's Property Act 1964
(1964 c. 19)

1 Money and property derived from housekeeping allowance

If any question arises as to the right of a husband or wife to money derived from any allowance made by the husband for the expenses of the matrimonial home or for similar purposes, or to any property acquired out of such money, the money or property shall, in the absence of any agreement between them to the contrary, be treated as belonging to the husband and the wife in equal shares.

Matrimonial Causes Act 1965
(1965 c. 72)

PART I DIVORCE, NULLITY AND OTHER MATRIMONIAL SUITS

Divorce

8 Remarriage of divorced persons

(2) No clergyman of the Church of England or the Church in Wales shall be compelled—

(a) to solemnize the marriage of any person whose former marriage has been dissolved and whose former spouse is still living; or

(b) to permit the marriage of such a person to be solemnized in the church or chapel of which he is the minister.

Theft Act 1968
(1968 c. 60)

General and consequential provisions

30 Spouses and civil partners

(1) This Act shall apply in relation to the parties to a marriage, and to property belonging to the wife or husband whether or not by reason of an interest derived from the marriage, as it would apply if they were not married and any such interest subsisted independently of the marriage.

(2) Subject to subsection (4) below, a person shall have the same right to bring proceedings against that person's wife or husband for any offence (whether under this Act or otherwise) as if they were not married.

(4) Proceedings shall not be instituted against a person for any offence of stealing or doing unlawful damage to property which at the time of the offence belongs to that person's wife or husband or civil partner, or for any attempt, incitement or conspiracy to commit such an offence, unless the proceedings are instituted by or with the consent of the Director of Public Prosecutions:

Provided that—

(a) this subsection shall not apply to proceedings against a person for an offence—

(i) if that person is charged with committing the offence jointly with the wife or husband or civil partner;

(ii) if by virtue of any judicial decree or order (wherever made) that person and the wife or husband are at the time of the offence under no obligation to cohabit or

(iii) an order (wherever made) is in force providing for the separation of that person and his or her civil partner.

(5) Notwithstanding section 25 of the Prosecution of Offences Act 1985 subsection (4) of this section shall apply—

    (a) to an arrest (if without warrant) made by the wife or husband, and

    (b) to a warrant of arrest issued on an information laid by the wife or husband.

31   Effect on civil proceedings and rights

(1) A person shall not be excused, by reason that to do so may incriminate that person or the spouse or civil partner of that person of an offence under this Act—

    (a) from answering any question put to that person in proceedings for the recovery or administration of any property, for the execution of any trust or for an account of any property or dealings with property; or

    (b) from complying with any order made in any such proceedings; but no statement or admission made by a person in answering a question put or complying with an order made as aforesaid shall, in proceedings for an offence under this Act, be admissible in evidence against that person or (unless they married or became civil partners after the making of the statement or admission) against the spouse or civil partner of that person.

(2) Notwithstanding any enactment to the contrary, where property has been stolen or obtained by fraud or other wrongful means, the title to that or any other property shall not be affected by reason only of the conviction of the offender.

Civil Evidence Act 1968
(1968 c. 64)

PART II   MISCELLANEOUS AND GENERAL

12   Findings of adultery and paternity as evidence in civil proceedings

(1) In any civil proceedings—

    (a) the fact that a person has been found guilty of adultery in any matrimonial proceedings; and

    (b) the fact that a person has been found to be the father of a child in relevant proceedings before any court in England or Wales or Northern Ireland or has been adjudged to be the father of a child in affiliation proceedings before any court in the United Kingdom;

shall (subject to subsection (3) below) be admissible in evidence for the purpose of proving, where to do so is relevant to any issue in those civil proceedings, that he committed the adultery to which the finding relates, or, as the case may be, is (or was) the father of that child, whether or not he offered any defence to the allegation of adultery or paternity and whether or not he is a party to the civil proceedings; but no finding or adjudication other than a subsisting one shall be admissible in evidence by virtue of this section.

(2) In any civil proceedings in which by virtue of this section a person is proved to have been found guilty of adultery as mentioned in subsection (1)(a) above or to have been found or adjudged to be the father of a child as mentioned in subsection (1)(b) above—

    (a) he shall he taken to have committed the adultery to which the finding relates, or, as the case may be, to be (or have been) the father of that child, unless the contrary is proved; and

    (b) without prejudice to the reception of any other admissible evidence for the purpose of identifying the facts on which the finding or adjudication was based, the contents of any document which was before the court, or which contains any pronouncement of the court in the other proceedings in question shall be admissible in evidence for that purpose.

(3) Nothing in this section shall prejudice the operation of any enactment whereby a finding of fact in any matrimonial or affiliation proceedings is for the purposes of any other proceedings made conclusive evidence of any fact.

...

(5) In this section—

'matrimonial proceedings' means any matrimonial cause in the High Court or a county court in England and Wales or any appeal arising out of any such cause or action;

'relevant proceedings' means—

(a) proceedings on a complaint under section 42 of the National Assistance Act 1948 or section 26 of the Social Security Act 1986;

(b) proceedings under the Children Act 1989;

...

Privilege

14   Privilege against incrimination of self or spouse or civil partner

(1) The right of a person in any legal proceedings other than criminal proceedings to refuse to answer any question or produce any document or thing if to do so would tend to expose that person to proceedings for an offence or for the recovery of a penalty—

(a) shall apply only as regards criminal offences under the law of any part of the United Kingdom and penalties provided for by such law; and

(b) shall include a like right to refuse to answer any question or produce any document or thing if to do so would tend to expose the spouse or civil partner of the person to proceedings for any such criminal offence or for the recovery of any such penalty.

...

Family Law Reform Act 1969
(1969 c. 46)

PART I   REDUCTION OF AGE OF MAJORITY AND RELATED PROVISIONS

1   Reduction of age of majority from 21 to 18

(1) As from the date on which this section comes into force a person shall attain full age on attaining the age of eighteen instead of on attaining the age of twenty-one; and a person shall attain full age on that date if he has then already attained the age of eighteen but not the age of twenty-one.

(2) The foregoing subsection applies for the purposes of any rule of law, and, in the absence of a definition or of any indication of a contrary intention, for the construction of 'full age,' 'infant,' 'infancy,' 'minor,' 'minority' and similar expressions in—

(a) any statutory provision, whether passed or made before, on or after the date on which this section comes into force; and

(b) any deed, will or other instrument of whatever nature (not being a statutory provision) made on or after that date.

...

(7) Notwithstanding any rule of law, a will or codicil executed before the date on which this section comes into force shall not be treated for the purposes of this section as made on or after that date by reason only that the will or codicil is confirmed by a codicil executed on or after that date.

8 Consent by persons over 16 to surgical, medical and dental treatment

(1) The consent of a minor who has attained the age of sixteen years to any surgical, medical or dental treatment which, in the absence of consent, would constitute a tresspass to his person, shall be as effective as it would be if he were of full age; and where a minor has by virtue of this section given an effective consent to any treatment it shall not be necessary to obtain any consent for it from his parent or guardian.

(2) In this section 'surgical, medical or dental treatment' includes any procedure undertaken for the purposes of diagnosis, and this section applies to any procedure (including, in particular, the administration of an anaesthetic) which is ancillary to any treatment as it applies to that treatment.

(3) Nothing in this section shall be construed as making ineffective any consent which would have been effective if this section had not been enacted.

9 Time at which a person attains a particular age

(1) The time at which a person attains a particular age expressed in years shall be the commencement of the relevant anniversary of the date of his birth.

(2) This section applies only where the relevant anniversary falls on a date after that on which this section comes into force, and, in relation to any enactment, deed, will or other instrument, has effect subject to any provision therein.

12 Persons under full age may be described as minors instead of infants

A person who is not of full age may be described as a minor instead of as an infant, and accordingly in this Act 'minor' means such a person as aforesaid.

19 Policies of assurance and property in industrial and provident societies

(1) In section 11 of the Married Women's Property Act 1882 (policies of assurance effected for the benefit of children) the expression 'children' shall include illegitimate children.

(3) Subsection (1) of this section does not affect the operation of the said Acts of 1882 in relation to a policy effected before the coming into force of that subsection.

. . .

PART III   PROVISIONS FOR USE OF SCIENTIFIC TESTS IN DETERMINING PARENTAGE

20 Power of court to require use of scientific tests

(1) In any civil proceedings in which the parentage of any person falls to be determined, the court may, either of its own motion or on an application by any party to the proceedings, give a direction—

    (a) for the use of scientific tests to ascertain whether such tests show that a party to the proceedings is or is not the father or mother of that person; and

    (b) for the taking, within a period specified in the direction, of bodily samples from all or any of the following, namely, that person, any party who is alleged to be the father or mother of that person and any other party to the proceedings;

and the court may at any time revoke or vary a direction previously given by it under this subsection.

(1A) Tests required by a direction under this section may only be carried out by a body which has been accredited for the purposes of this section by—

    (a) the Lord Chancellor, or

    (b) a body appointed by him for the purpose.

(2) The individual carrying out scientific tests in pursuance of a direction under subsection (1) above shall make to the court a report in which he shall state—

    (a) the results of the tests;

   (b) whether any party to whom the report relates is or is not excluded by the results from being the father or mother of the person whose parentage is to be determined; and

   (c) in relation to any party who is not so excluded, the value, if any, of the results in determining whether that party is the father or mother of that person;

and the report shall be received by the court as evidence in the proceedings of the matters stated in it.

   (2A) Where the proceedings in which the parentage of any person falls to be determined are proceedings on an application under section 55A or 56 of the Family Law Act 1986, any reference in subsection (1) or (2) of this section to any party to the proceedings shall include a reference to any person named in the application.

   (3) A report under subsection (2) of this section shall be in the form prescribed by regulations made under section 22 of this Act.

   (4) Where a report has been made to a court under subsection (2) of this section, any party may, with the leave of the court, or shall, if the court so directs, obtain from the tester a written statement explaining or amplifying any statement made in the report, and that statement shall be deemed for the purposes of this section (except subsection (3) thereof) to form part of the report made to the court.

. . .

21   Consents, etc., required for taking of bodily samples

   (1) Subject to the provisions of subsections (3) and (4) of this section, a bodily sample which is required to be taken from any person for the purpose of giving effect to a direction under section 20 of this Act shall not be taken from that person except with his consent.

   (2) The consent of a minor who has attained the age of sixteen years to the taking from himself of a bodily sample shall be as effective as it would be if he were of full age; and where a minor has by virtue of this subsection given an effective consent to the taking of a bodily sample it shall not be necessary to obtain any consent for it from any other person.

   (3) A bodily sample may be taken from a person under the age of sixteen years, not being a person as is referred to in subsection (4) of this section,

   (a) if the person who has the care and control of him consents; or

   (b) where that person does not consent, if the court considers that it would be in his best interests for the sample to be taken.

   (4) A bodily sample may be taken from a person who is suffering from mental disorder within the meaning of the Mental Health Act 1983 and is incapable of understanding the nature and purpose of scientific tests if the person who has the care and control of him consents and the medical practitioner in whose care he is has certified that the taking of a bodily sample from him will not be prejudicial to his proper care and treatment.

   (5) The foregoing provisions of this section are without prejudice to the provisions of section 23 of this Act.

. . .

23   Failure to comply with direction for taking bodily samples

   (1) Where a court gives a direction under section 20 of this Act and any person fails to take any step required of him for the purpose of giving effect to the direction, the court may draw such inferences, if any, from that fact as appear proper in the circumstances.

   (2) Where in any proceedings in which the parentage of any person falls to be determined by the court hearing the proceedings there is a presumption of law that that person is legitimate, then if—

   (a) a direction is given under section 20 of this Act in those proceedings, and

   (b) any party who is claiming any relief in the proceedings and who for the purpose of obtaining that relief is entitled to rely on the presumption fails to take any step required of him for the purpose of giving effect to the direction, the court may adjourn the hearing for such period as it thinks fit to enable that party to take that step, and if at the end of that period he has failed without reasonable cause to take it the court may, without prejudice to subsection (1) of this section, dismiss his claim for relief notwithstanding the absence of evidence to rebut the presumption.

(3) Where any person named in a direction under section 20 of this Act fails to consent to the taking of a bodily sample from himself or from any person named in the direction of whom he has the care and control, he shall be deemed for the purposes of this section to have failed to take a step required of him for the purpose of giving effect to the direction.

24 Penalty for personating another, etc., for purposes of providing bodily sample
If for the purpose of providing a bodily sample for a test required to give effect to a direction under section 20 of this Act any person personates another, or proffers a child knowing that it is not the child named in the direction, he shall be liable—

(a) on conviction on indictment, to imprisonment for a term not exceeding two years, or

(b) on summary conviction, to a fine not exceeding the prescribed sum.

25 Interpretation of Part III
In this Part of this Act the following expressions have the meanings hereby respectively assigned to them, that is to say—

'bodily sample' means a sample of bodily fluid or bodily tissue taken for the purpose of scientific tests;

'excluded' means excluded subject to the occurrence of mutation, to section 27 of the Family Law Reform Act 1987 and to sections 27 to 29 of the Human Fertilisation and Embryology Act 1990;

'scientific tests' means scientific tests carried out under this Part of this Act and made with the object of ascertaining the inheritable characteristics of bodily fluids or bodily tissue.

PART IV   MISCELLANEOUS AND GENERAL

26 Rebuttal of presumption as to legitimacy and illegitimacy
Any presumption of law as to the legitimacy or illegitimacy of any person may in any civil proceedings be rebutted by evidence which shows that it is more probable than not that that person is illegitimate or legitimate, as the case may be, and it shall not be necessary to prove that fact beyond reasonable doubt in order to rebut the presumption.
. . .

Law Reform (Miscellaneous Provisions) Act 1970
(1970 c. 33)

Legal consequences of termination of contract to marry

1 Engagements to marry not enforceable at law
(1) An agreement between two persons to marry one another shall not under the law of England and Wales have effect as a contract giving rise to legal rights and no action shall lie in England and Wales for breach of such an agreement, whatever the law applicable to the agreement.

(2) This section shall have effect in relation to agreements entered into before it comes into force, except that it shall not affect any action commenced before it comes into force.

2 Property of engaged couples
(1) Where an agreement to marry is terminated, any rule of law relating to the rights of husbands and wives in relation to property in which either or both has or have a beneficial

interest, including any such rule as explained by section 37 of the Matrimonial Proceedings and Property Act 1970, shall apply, in relation to any property in which either or both of the parties to the agreement had a beneficial interest while the agreement was in force, as it applies in relation to property in which a husband or wife has a beneficial interest.

(2) Where an agreement to marry is terminated, section 17 of the Married Women's Property Act 1882 and section 7 of the Matrimonial Causes (Property and Maintenance) Act 1958 (which sections confer power on a judge of the High Court or a county court to settle disputes between husband and wife about property) shall apply, as if the parties were married, to any dispute between, or claim by, one of them in relation to property in which either or both had a beneficial interest while the agreement was in force; but an application made by virtue of this section to the judge under the said section 17, as originally enacted or as extended by the said section 7, shall be made within three years of the termination of the agreement.

3   Gifts between engaged couples

(1) A party to an agreement to marry who makes a gift of property to the other party to the agreement on the condition (express or implied) that it shall be returned if the agreement is terminated shall not be prevented from recovering the property by reason only of his having terminated the agreement.

(2) The gift of an engagement ring shall be presumed to be an absolute gift; this presumption may be rebutted by proving that the ring was given on the condition, express or implied, that it should be returned if the marriage did not take place for any reason.

Enticement of spouse, etc.

5   Abolition of actions for enticement, seduction and harbouring of spouse or child

No person shall be liable in tort under the law of England and Wales—

    (a) to any other person on the ground only of his having induced the wife or husband of that other person to leave or remain apart from the other spouse;

    (b) to a parent (or person standing in the place of a parent) on the ground only of his having deprived the parent (or other person) of the services of his or her child by raping, seducing or enticing that child; or

    (c) to any other person for harbouring the wife or child of that other person, except in the case of action accruing before this Act comes into force if an action in respect thereof has been begun before this Act comes into force.

Marriage (Registrar General's Licence) Act 1970
(1970 c. 34)

1   Marriages which may be solemnised by Registrar General's licence

(1) Subject to the provisions of subsection (2) below, any marriage which may be solemnised on the authority of certificates of a superintendent registrar may be solemnised on the authority of the Registrar General's licence elsewhere than at a registered building, the office of a superintendent registrar, or approved premises.

Provided that any such marriage shall not be solemnised according to the rites of the Church of England or the Church in Wales.

(2) The Registrar General shall not issue any licence for the solemnisation of a marriage as is mentioned in subsection (1) above unless he is satisfied that one of the persons to be married is seriously ill and is not expected to recover and cannot be moved to a place at which under the provisions of the Marriage Act 1949 (hereinafter called the 'principal Act') the marriage could be solemnised (disregarding for this purpose the provisions of that Act relating to marriages in pursuance of section 26(1)(dd) of that Act).

2   Notice of marriage

(1) Where a marriage is intended to be solemnised on the authority of the Registrar General's licence, notice shall be given in the prescribed form by either of the persons to be married to the superintendent registrar of the registration district in which it is intended that the marriage shall be solemnised, and the notice shall state by or before whom it is intended that the marriage shall be solemnised.

(2) The provisions of section 27(4) of the principal Act (which relate to entries in the marriage notice book) shall apply to notices of marriage on the authority of the Registrar General's licence.

(3) The provisions of section 28 of the principal Act (declaration to accompany notice of marriage) shall apply to the giving of notice under this Act with the exception of paragraph (b) of subsection (1) of that section and with the modification that in section 28(2) references to the registrar of births and deaths or of marriages and deputy registrar shall be omitted.

3   Evidence of capacity, consent etc., to be produced

The person giving notice to the superintendent registrar under the provisions of the foregoing section shall produce to the superintendent registrar such evidence as the Registrar General may require to satisfy him—

  (a) that there is no lawful impediment to the marriage;
  (b) that the consent of any person whose consent to the marriage is required under section 3 of the principal Act has been duly given; and
  (c) that there is sufficient reason why a licence should be granted;
  (d) that the conditions contained in section 1(2) of this Act are satisfied and that the person in respect of whom such conditions are satisfied is able to and does understand the nature and purport of the marriage ceremony;

Provided that the certificate of a registered medical practitioner shall be sufficient evidence of any or all of the matters in subsection (1)(d) of this section referred to.

4   Application to be reported to Registrar General

Upon receipt of any notice and evidence as mentioned in sections 2 and 3 above respectively the superintendent registrar shall inform the Registrar General and shall comply with any directions he may give for verifying the evidence given.

5   Caveat against issue of Registrar General's licence

The provisions of section 29 of the principal Act (caveat against issue of certificate) shall apply to the issue of a licence by the Registrar General with the modification that aveat may be entered with either the superintendent registrar or the Registrar General and in either case it shall be for the Registrar General to examine into the matter of the caveat and to decide whether or not the licence should be granted and his decision shall be final, and with a further modification that the references to the superintendent registrar in that section shall refer to the superintendent registrar of the registration district in which the marriage is intended to be solemnised.

6   Marriage of persons under eighteen

The provisions of section 3 of the principal Act (marriage of persons under 18) shall apply for the purposes of this Act to a marriage intended to be solemnised by Registrar General's licence as they apply to a marriage intended to be solemnised on the authority of certificates of a superintendent registrar under Part III of the principal Act with the modification that if the consent of any person whose consent is required under that Act cannot be obtained by reason of absence or inaccessibility or by reason of his being under any disability, the superintendent registrar shall not be required to dispense with the necessity for the consent of that person and the Registrar General may dispense with the necessity of obtaining the consent of that person, whether or not there is any other person whose consent is also required.

7   Issue of licence by Registrar General

Where the marriage is intended to be solemnised on the authority of the Registrar General and he is satisfied that sufficient grounds exist why a licence should be granted he shall issue in the prescribed form unless—

(a) any lawful impediment to the issue of the licence has been shown to his satisfaction to exist; or

(b) the issue of the licence has been forbidden under section 30 of the principal Act.

8   Period of validity of licence

(1) A marriage may be solemnised on the authority of the Registrar General's licence at any time within one month from the day on which the notice of marriage was entered in the marriage notice book.

(2) If the marriage is not solemnised within the said period of one month, the notice of marriage and the licence shall be void, and no person shall solemnise the marriage on the authority thereof.

9   Place of solemnisation

A marriage on the authority of the Registrar General's licence shall be solemnised in the place stated in the notice of marriage.

10   Manner of solemnisation

(1) Any marriage to be solemnised on the authority of the Registrar General's licence shall be solemnised at the wish of the persons to be married either—

(a) according to such form or ceremony, not being the rites or ceremonies of the Church of England or the Church in Wales, as the persons to be married shall see fit to adopt, or

(b) by civil ceremony.

(2) Except where the marriage is solemnised according to the usages of the Society of Friends or is a marriage between two persons professing the Jewish religion according to the usages of the Jews, it shall be solemnised in the presence of a registrar:

Provided that where the marriage is to be by civil ceremony it shall be solemnised in the presence of the superintendent registrar as well as the registrar.

(3) Except where the marriage is solemnised according to the usages of the Society of Friends or is a marriage between two persons professing the Jewish religion according to the usages of the Jews, the persons to be married shall in some part of the ceremony in the presence of two or more witnesses and the registrar and, where appropriate, the superintendent registrar, make the declaration and say to one another the words prescribed by section 44(3) or (3A) of the principal Act.

(4) No person who is a clergyman within the meaning of section 78 of the principal Act shall solemnise any marriage which is solemnised on the authority of the Registrar General.

11   Civil marriage followed by religious ceremony

(1) If the parties to a marriage solemnised on the authority of the Registrar General's licence before a superintendent registrar desire to add the religious ceremony ordained or used by the church or persuasion of which they are members and have given notice of their desire so to do a clergyman or minister of that church or persuasion upon the production of a certificate of their marriage before the superintendent registrar and upon the payment of the customary fees (if any), may, if he sees fit, read or celebrate in the presence of the parties to the marriage the marriage service of the church or persuasion to which he belongs or nominate some other minister to do so.

(2) The provisions of section 46(2) and (3) of the principal Act shall apply to such a reading or celebration as they apply to the reading or celebration of a marriage service following a marriage solemnised in the office of a superintendent registrar.

12   Proof of certain matters not necessary to validity of marriages

The provisions of section 48 of the principal Act (proof of certain matters not necessary to validity of marriages) shall apply with the appropriate modifications to a marriage solemnised under the authority of the Registrar General's licence as they apply to a marriage solemnised under the authority of a certificate of a superintendent registrar.

13   Void marriages

The provisions of section 49 of the principal Act (void marriages) shall apply to a marriage under the authority of the Registrar General's licence:—

(a) with the substitution in paragraph (b) for the words from 'certificates for marriage' onwards of the words 'a Registrar General's licence';

(c) with the substitution for paragraph (d) of the words 'on the authority of a licence which is void by virtue of section 8(2) of the Marriage (Registrar General's Licence) Act 1970';

(d) with the substitution for paragraph (e) of the words 'in any place other than the place specified in the notice of marriage and the Registrar General's licence';

(e) with the substitution for paragraphs (f) and (g) of the words 'in the absence of a registrar or, where the marriage is by civil ceremony, of a superintendent registrar, except where the marriage is solemnised according to the usages of the Society of Friends or is a marriage between two persons professing the Jewish religion according to the usages of the Jews.'

14   Documentary authority for marriage

Where a marriage is to be solemnised on the authority of the Registrar General's licence a document issued by the superintendent registrar stating that the Registrar General's licence has been granted and that authority for the marriage to be solemnised has been given shall be delivered before the marriage to the following person, that is to say—

(a) if the marriage is to be solemnised according to the usages of the Society of Friends, the registering officer of that Society for the place where the marriage is to be solemnised;

(b) if the marriage is to be solemnised according to the usages of persons professing the Jewish religion, the officer of the synagogue by whom the marriage is required to be registered under Part IV of the principal Act;

(c) in any other case, the registrar in whose presence the marriage is to be solemnised.

15   Registration of marriages

A marriage solemnised on the authority of the Registrar General's licence shall be registered in accordance with the provisions of the principal Act which apply to the registration of marriages solemnised in the presence of a registrar or according to the usages of the Society of Friends or of persons professing the Jewish religion.

16   Offences

(1) It shall be an offence knowingly and wilfully—

(a) to solemnise a marriage by Registrar General's licence in any place other than the place specified in the licence;

(b) to solemnise a marriage by Registrar General's licence without the presence of a registrar except in the case of a marriage according to the usages of the Society of Friends or a marriage between two persons professing the Jewish religion according to the usages of the Jews;

(c) to solemnise a marriage by Registrar General's licence after the expiration of one month from the date of entry of the notice of marriage in the marriage notice book;

(d) to give false information by way of evidence as required by section 3 of this

(e) to give a false certificate as provided for in section 3(1)(d) of this Act; and any person found guilty of any of the above-mentioned offences shall be liable on summary conviction to a fine not exceeding the prescribed sum or on indictment to a fine or to imprisonment not exceeding three years or to both such fine and such imprisonment.

(2) A superintendent registrar who knowingly and wilfully solemnises or permits to be solemnised in his presence, or a registrar who knowingly and wilfully registers a marriage by Registrar General's licence which is void by virtue of Part III of the principal Act as amended by this Act shall be guilty of an offence and shall be liable on summary conviction to a fine not exceeding the prescribed sum or on indictment to a fine or to imprisonment not exceeding three years or to both such fine and such imprisonment.

(3) No prosecution under this section shall be commenced after the expiration of three years from the commission of the offence.

(4) The provisions of sections 75(1)(a) and 75(2)(a) of the principal Act shall not apply to a marriage solemnised on the authority of the Registrar General's licence.

Matrimonial Proceedings and Property Act 1970
(1970 c. 45)

Provisions relating to property of married persons

37 Contributions by spouse in money or money's worth to the improvement of property

It is hereby declared that where a husband or wife contributes in money or money's worth to the improvement of real or personal property in which or in the proceeds of sale of which either or both of them has or have a beneficial interest, the husband or wife so contributing shall, if the contribution is of a substantial nature and subject to any agreement between them to the contrary express or implied, be treated as having then acquired by virtue of his or her contribution a share or an enlarged share, as the case may be, in that beneficial interest of such an extent as may have been then agreed or, in default of such agreement, as may seem in all the circumstances just to any court before which the question of the existence or extent of the beneficial interest of the husband or wife arises (whether in proceedings between them or in other proceedings).

39 Extension of s. 17 of Married Women's Property Act 1882

An application may be made to the High Court or a county court under section 17 of the Married Women's Property Act 1882 (powers of the court in disputes between husband and wife about property) (including that section as extended by section 7 of the Matrimonial Causes (Property and Maintenance) Act 1958) by either of the parties to a marriage notwithstanding that their marriage has been dissolved or annulled so long as the application is made within the period of three years beginning with the date on which the marriage was dissolved or annulled; and references in the said section 17 and the said section 7 to a husband or a wife shall be construed accordingly.

Attachment of Earnings Act 1971
(1971 c. 32)

Cases in which attachment is available

1 Courts with power to attach earnings

(1) The High Court may make an attachment of earnings order to secure payments under a High Court maintenance order.

(2) A county court may make an attachment of earnings order to secure—
  (a) payments under a High Court or a county court maintenance order;
  (b) the payment of a judgment debt, other than a debt of less than £5 or such other sum as may be prescribed by county court rules; or
  (c) payments under an administration order.

(3) A magistrates' court may make an attachment of earnings order to secure—
  (a) payments under a magistrates' court maintenance order;
  (b) the payment of any sum adjudged to be paid by a conviction or treated (by any enactment relating to the collection and enforcement of fines, costs, compensation or forfeited recognisances) as so adjudged to be paid; or
  (c) the payment of any sum required to be paid by an order under section 17(2) of the Access to Justice Act 1999.

(4) The following provisions of this Act apply, except where otherwise stated, to attachment of earnings orders made, or to be made, by any court.

(5) Any power conferred by this Act to make an attachment of earnings order includes a power to make such an order to secure the discharge of liabilities arising before the coming into force of this Act.

2   Principal definitions
In this Act—
  (a) 'maintenance order' means any order specified in Schedule 1 to this Act and includes such an order which has been discharged if any arrears are recoverable thereunder;
  (b) 'High Court maintenance order', 'county court maintenance order' and 'magistrates' court maintenance order' mean respectively a maintenance order enforceable by the High Court, a county court and a magistrates' court;
  (c) 'judgment debt' means a sum payable under—
     (i) a judgment or order enforceable by a court in England and Wales (not being a magistrates' court);
     (ii) an order of a magistrates' court for the payment of money recoverable summarily as a civil debt; or
     (iii) an order of any court which is enforceable as if it were for the payment of money so recoverable,
     but does not include any sum payable under a maintenance order or an administration order;
  (d) 'the relevant adjudication', in relation to any payment secured or to be secured by an attachment of earnings order, means the conviction, judgment, order or other adjudication from which there arises the liability to make the payment; and
  (e) 'the debtor', in relation to an attachment of earnings order, or to proceedings in which a court has power to make an attachment of earnings order, or to proceedings arising out of such an order, means the person by whom payment is required by the relevant adjudication to be made.

3   Application for order and conditions of court's power to make it
(1) The following persons may apply for an attachment of earnings order:—
  (a) the person to whom payment under the relevant adjudication is required to be made (whether directly or through an officer of any court);
  (b) where the relevant adjudication is an administration order, any one of the creditors scheduled to the order;
  (c) without prejudice to paragraph (a) above, where the application is to a magistrates' court for an order to secure maintenance payments, and there is in force an order under section 59 of the Magistrates' Courts Act 1980, or section 19(2) of the Maintenance Orders Act 1950, that those payments be made to the designated officer for a magistrates' court, that officer;

    (d) in the following cases the debtor—
        (i) where the application is to a magistrates' court; or
        (ii) where the application is to the High Court or a county court for an order to
           secure maintenance payments.

  (3) Subject to subsection (3A) below for an attachment of earnings order to be made on the application of any person other than the debtor it must appear to the court that the debtor has failed to make one or more payments required by the relevant adjudication.

  (3A) Subsection (3) above shall not apply where the relevant adjudication is a maintenance order.

  (3B) Where—
    (a) a magistrates' court imposes a fine on a person in respect of an offence, and
    (b) that person consents to an order being made under this subsection, the court may
        at the time it imposes the fine, and without the need for an application, make an
        attachment of earnings order to secure the payment of the fine.

  (3C) Where—
    (a) a magistrates' court makes in the case of a person convicted of an offence an order
        under section 130 of the Powers of Criminal Courts (Sentencing) Act 2000 (a
        compensation order) requiring him to pay compensation or to make other
        payments, and
    (b) that person consents to an order being made under this subsection, the court may
        at the time it makes the compensation order, and without the need for an
        application, make an attachment of earnings order to secure the payment of the
        compensation or other payments.

  (4) Where proceedings are brought—
    (a) in the High Court or a county court for the enforcement of a maintenance order
        by committal under section 5 of the Debtors Act 1869; or
    (b) in a magistrates' court for the enforcement of a maintenance order under section
        76 of the Magistrates' Courts Act 1980 (distress or committal),
then the court may make an attachment of earnings order to secure payments under the maintenance order, instead of dealing with the case under section 5 of the said Act of 1869 or, as the case may be, section 76 of the said Act of 1980.

Administration orders in the county court

4   Extension of power to make administration order

  (1) Where, on an application to a county court for an attachment of earnings order to secure the payment of a judgment debt, it appears to the court that the debtor also has other debts, the court—
    (a) shall consider whether the case may be one in which all the debtor's liabilities
        should be dealt with together and that for that purpose an administration order
        should be made; and
    (b) if of opinion that it may be such a case, shall have power (whether or not it makes
        the attachment of earnings order applied for), with a view to making an admin-
        istration order, to order the debtor to furnish to the court a list of all his creditors
        and the amounts which he owes to them respectively.

  (2) If, on receipt of the list referred to in subsection (1)(b) above, it appears to the court that the debtor's whole indebtedness amounts to not more than the amount which for the time being is the county court limit for the purposes of section 112 of the County Courts Act 1984 (limit of total indebtedness governing county court's power to make administration order on application of debtor), the court may make such an order in respect of the debtor's estate.

  (2A) Subsection (2) above is subject to section 112(3) and (4) of the County Courts Act 1984 (which require that, before an administration order is made, notice is to be given to all the creditors and thereafter restricts the right of any creditor to institute bankruptcy proceedings).

(4) Nothing in this section is to be taken as prejudicing any right of a debtor to apply, under section 112 of the County Courts Act 1984, for an administration order.

Consequences of attachment order

6   Effect and contents of order

(1) An attachment of earnings order shall be an order directed to a person who appears to the court to have the debtor in his employment and shall operate as an instruction to that person—

(a) to make periodical deductions from the debtor's earnings in accordance with Part I of Schedule 3 to this Act; and

(b) at such times as the order may require, or as the court may allow, to pay the amounts deducted to the collecting officer of the court, as specified in the order.

(2) For the purposes of this Act, the relationship of employer and employee shall be treated as subsisting between two persons if one of them as a principal and not as a servant or agent, pays to the other any sums defined as earnings by section 24 of this Act.

(3) An attachment of earnings order shall contain prescribed particulars enabling the debtor to be identified by the employer.

(4) Except where it is made to secure maintenance payments, the order shall specify the whole amount payable under the relevant adjudication (or so much of that amount as remains unpaid), including any relevant costs.

(5) The order shall specify—

(a) the normal deduction rate, that is to say, the rate (expressed as a sum of money per week, month or other period) at which the court thinks it reasonable for the debtor's earnings to be applied to meeting his liability under the relevant adjudication; and

(b) the protected earnings rate, that is to say the rate (so expressed) below which, having regard to the debtor's resources and needs, the court thinks it reasonable that the earnings actually paid to him should not be reduced.

(6) In the case of an order made to secure payments under a maintenance order (not being an order for the payment of a lump sum), the normal deduction rate—

(a) shall be determined after taking account of any right or liability of the debtor to deduct income tax when making the payments; and

(b) shall not exceed the rate which appears to the court necessary for the purpose of—

(i) securing payment of the sums falling due from time to time under the maintenance order, and

(ii) securing payment within a reasonable period of any sums already due and unpaid under the maintenance order.

(7) For the purposes of an attachment of earnings order, the collecting officer of the court shall be (subject to later variation of the order under section 9 of this Act)—

(a) in the case of an order made by the High Court, either—

(i) the proper officer of the High Court, or

(ii) the appropriate officer of such county court as the order may specify;

(b) in the case of an order made by a county court, the appropriate officer of that court; and

(c) in the case of an order made by a magistrates' court, the designated officer for that court or for another magistrates' court specified in the order.

(8) In subsection (7) above 'appropriate officer' means an officer designated by the Lord Chancellor.

. . .

7   Compliance with order by employer

(1) Where an attachment of earnings order has been made, the employer shall, if he has been served with the order, comply with it; but he shall be under no liability for non-compliance before seven days have elapsed since the service.

(2) Where a person is served with an attachment of earnings order directed to him and he has not the debtor in his employment, or the debtor subsequently ceases to be in his employment, he shall (in either case), within ten days from the date of service or, as the case may be, the cesser, give notice of that fact to the court.

. . .

8 Interrelation with alternative remedies open to creditor

(1) Where an attachment of earnings order has been made to secure maintenance payments, no order or warrant of commitment shall be issued in consequence of any proceedings for the enforcement of the related maintenance order begun before the making of the attachment of earnings order.

. . .

Subsequent proceedings

9 Variation, lapse and discharge of orders

(1) The court may make an order discharging or varying an attachment of earnings order.

(2) Where an order is varied, the employer shall, if he has been served with notice of the variation, comply with the order as varied; but he shall be under no liability for non-compliance before seven days have elapsed since the service.

(3) Rules of court may make provision—

    (a) as to the circumstances in which an attachment of earnings order may be varied or discharged by the court of its own motion;

    (b) in the case of an attachment of earnings order made by a magistrates' court, for enabling a single justice, on an application made by the debtor on the ground of a material change in his resources and needs since the order was made or last varied, to vary the order for a period of not more than four weeks by an increase of the protected earnings rate.

(4) Where an attachment of earnings order has been made and the person to whom it is directed ceases to have the debtor in his employment, the order shall lapse (except as respects deduction from earnings paid after the cesser and payment to the collecting officer of amounts deducted at any time) and be of no effect unless and until the court again directs it to a person (whether the same as before or another) who appears to the court to have the debtor in his employment.

(5) The lapse of an order under subsection (4) above shall not prevent its being treated as remaining in force for other purposes.

. . .

11 Attachment order in respect of maintenance payments to cease to have effect on occurrence of certain events

(1) An attachment of earnings order made to secure maintenance payments shall cease to have effect—

    (a) upon the grant of an application for registration of the related maintenance order under section 2 of the Maintenance Orders Act 1958 (which provides for the registration in a magistrates' court of a High Court or county court maintenance order, and for registration in the High Court of a magistrates' court maintenance order);

    (b) where the related maintenance order is registered under Part 1 of the said Act of 1958, upon the giving of notice with respect thereto under section 5 of that Act (notice with view to cancellation or registration);

    (c) subject to subsection (3) below, upon the discharge of the related maintenance order while it is not registered under Part I of the said Act of 1958;

    (d) upon the related maintenance order ceasing to be registered in a court in England or Wales, or becoming registered in a court in Scotland or Northern Ireland, under Part II of the Maintenance Orders Act 1950.

(2) Subsection (1)(a) above shall have effect, in the case of an application for registration under section 2(1) of the said Act of 1958, notwithstanding that the grant of the application may subsequently become void under subsection (2) of that section.

(3) Where the related maintenance order is discharged as mentioned in subsection (1)(c) above and it appears to the court discharging the order that arrears thereunder will remain to be recovered after the discharge, that court may, if it thinks fit, direct that subsection (1) shall not apply.

...

14   Power of court to obtain statements of earnings etc.

(1) Where in any proceedings a court has power to make an attachment of earnings order, it may—

    (a) order the debtor to give to the court, within a specified period, a statement signed by him of—

        (i)   the name and address of any person by whom earnings are paid to him:

        (ii) specified particulars as to his earnings and anticipated earnings, as to his resources and needs; and

        (iii) specified particulars for the purpose of enabling the debtor to be identified by any employer of his;

    (b) order any person appearing to the court to have the debtor in his employment to give to the court, within a specified period, a statement signed by him or on his behalf of specified particulars of the debtor's earnings and anticipated earnings.

(2) Where an attachment of earnings order has been made, the court may at any time thereafter while the order is in force—

    (a) make such an order as is described in subsection (1)(a) or (b) above; and

    (b) order the debtor to attend before it on a day and at a time specified in the order to give the information described in subsection (1)(a) above.

(3) In the case of an application to a magistrates' court for an attachment of earnings order, or for the variation or discharge of such an order, the power to make an order under subsection (1) or (2) above shall be exercisable also, before the hearing of the application, by a single justice.

(4) Without prejudice to subsections (1) to (3) above, rules of court may provide that where notice of an application for an attachment of earnings order is served on the debtor, it shall include a requirement that he shall give to the court, within such period and in such manner as may be prescribed, a statement in writing of the matters specified in subsection (1)(a) above and of any other prescribed matters which are, or may be, relevant under section 6 of this Act to the determination of the normal deduction rate and the protected earnings rate to be specified in any order made on the application.

(5) In any proceedings in which a court has power to make an attachment of earnings order, and in any proceedings for the making, variation or discharge of such an order, a document purporting to be a statement given to the court in compliance with an order under subsection (1)(a) or (b) above, or with any such requirement of a notice of application for an attachment of earnings order as is mentioned in subsection (4) above, shall, in the absence of proof to the contrary, be deemed to be a statement so given and shall be evidence of the facts stated therein.

...

Miscellaneous Provisions

23   Enforcement provisions

(1) If, after being served with notice of an application to a county court for an attachment of earnings order or for the variation of such an order or with an order made under section 14 (2)(b) above, the debtor fails to attend on the day and at the time specified for any hearing of the application or specified in the order, the court may adjourn the hearing and

order him to attend at a specified time on another day; and if the debtor—
- (a) fails to attend at that time on that day; or
- (b) attends, but refuses to be sworn or give evidence, he may be ordered by the judge to be imprisoned for not more than fourteen days.

(1A) In any case where the judge has power to make an order of imprisonment under subsection (1) for failure to attend, he may, in lieu of or in addition to making that order, order the debtor to be arrested and brought before the court either forthwith or at such time as the judge may direct.

(2) Subject to this section, a person commits an offence if—
- (a) being required by section 7(1) or 9(2) of this Act to comply with an attachment of earnings order, he fails to do so; or
- (b) being required by section 7(2) of this Act to give a notice for the purposes of that subsection, he fails to give it, or fails to give it within the time required by that subsection; or
- (c) he fails to comply with an order under section 14(1) of this Act or with any such requirement of a notice of application for an attachment of earnings order as is mentioned in section 14(4), or fails (in either case) to comply within the time required by the order or notice; or
- (d) he fails to comply with section 15 of this Act; or
- (e) he gives a notice for the purposes of section 7(2) of this Act, or a notification for the purposes of section 15, which he knows to be false in a material particular, or recklessly gives such a notice or notification which is false in a material particular; or
- (f) in purported compliance with section 7(2) or 15 of this Act, or with an order under section 14(1), or with any such requirement of a notice of application for an attachment of earnings order as is mentioned in section 14(4), he makes any statement which he knows to be false in a material particular, or recklessly makes any statement which is false in a material particular.

(3) Where a person commits an offence under subsection (2) above in relation to proceedings in, or to an attachment of earnings order made by the High Court or a county court, he shall be liable on summary conviction to a fine of not more than level 2 on the standard scale or he may be ordered by a judge of the High Court or the county court judge (as the case may be) to pay a fine of not more than £250 or, in the case of an offence specified in subsection (4) below, to be imprisoned for not more than fourteen days; and where a person commits an offence under subsection (2) otherwise than as mentioned above in this subsection, he shall be liable on summary conviction to a fine of not more than level 2 on the standard scale.

(4) The offences referred to above in the case of which a judge may impose imprisonment are—
- (a) an offence under subsection (2)(c) or (d), if committed by the debtor; and
- (b) an offence under subsection (2)(e) or (f), whether committed by the debtor or any other person.

(5) It shall be a defence—
- (a) for a person charged with an offence under subsection (2)(a) above to prove that he took all reasonable steps to comply with the attachment of earnings order in question;
- (b) for a person charged with an offence under subsection (2)(b) to prove that he did not know, and could not reasonably be expected to know, that the debtor was not in his employment, or (as the case may be) had ceased to be so, and that he gave the required notice as soon as reasonably practicable after the fact came to his knowledge.

(6) Where a person is convicted or dealt with for an offence under subsection (2)(a), the court may order him to pay, to whoever is the collecting officer of the court for the purposes of the attachment of earnings order in question, any sums deducted by that person from the debtor's earnings and not already paid to the collecting officer.

(7) Where under this section a person is ordered by a judge of the High Court or a county court to be imprisoned, the judge may at any time revoke the order and, if the person is already in custody, order his discharge.

(8) Any fine imposed by a judge of the High Court under subsection (3) above and any sums ordered by the High Court to be paid under subsection (6) above shall be recoverable in the same way as a fine imposed by that court in the exercise of its jurisdiction to punish for contempt of court; section 129 of the County Courts Act 1984 (enforcement of fines) shall apply to payment of a fine imposed by a county court judge under subsection (3) and of any sums ordered by a county court judge to be paid under subsection (6); and any sum ordered by a magistrates' court to be paid under subsection (6) shall be recoverable as a sum adjudged to be paid on a conviction by that court.

(9) For the purposes of section 13 of the Administration of Justice Act 1960 (appeal in cases of contempt of court), subsection (3) above shall be treated as an enactment enabling the High Court or a county court to deal with an offence under subsection (2) above as if it were contempt of court.

(10) In this section references to proceedings in a court are to proceedings in which that court has power to make an attachment of earnings order or has made such an order.

(11) A district judge, assistant district judge or deputy district judge shall have the same powers under this section as a judge of a county court.

24   Meaning of 'earnings'

(1) For the purposes of this Act, but subject to the following subsection, 'earnings' are any sums payable to a person—

- (a) by way of wages or salary (including any fees, bonus, commission, overtime pay or other emoluments payable in addition to wages or salary or payable under a contract of service);
- (b) by way of pension (including an annuity in respect of past services, whether or not rendered to the person paying the annuity, and including periodical payments by way of compensation for the loss, abolition or relinquishment, or diminution in the emoluments, of any office or employment);
- (c) by way of statutory sick pay.

(2) The following shall not be treated as earnings:—

- (a) sums payable by any public department of the Government of Northern Ireland or of a territory outside the United Kingdom;
- (b) pay or allowances payable to the debtor as a member of Her Majesty's forces other than pay or allowances payable by his employer to him as a special member of a reserve force (within the meaning of the Reserve Forces Act 1996);
- (ba) a tax credit (within the meaning of the Tax Credits Act 2002);
- (c) pension, allowances or benefit payable under any enactment relating to social security;
- (d) pension or allowances payable in respect of disablement or disability;
- (e) except in relation to a maintenance order, wages payable to a person as a seaman, other than wages payable to him as a seaman of a fishing boat;
- (f) guaranteed minimum pension within the meaning of the Pension Schemes Act 1993.

...

Land Charges Act 1972
(1972 c. 61)

2   The register of land charges

(1) If a charge on or obligation affecting land falls into one of the classes described in this section, it may be registered in the register of land charges as a land charge of that class.

...

(7) A Class F land charge is a charge affecting any land by virtue of Part IV of the Family Law Act 1996.

Matrimonial Causes Act 1973
(1973 c. 18)

PART I   DIVORCE, NULLITY AND OTHER MATRIMONIAL SUITS

Divorce

1   Divorce on breakdown of marriage

(1) Subject to section 3 below, a petition for divorce may be presented to the court by either party to a marriage on the ground that the marriage has broken down irretrievably.

(2) The court hearing a petition for divorce shall not hold the marriage to have broken down irretrievably unless the petitioner satisfies the court of one or more of the following facts, that is to say—

(a) that the respondent has committed adultery and the petitioner finds it intolerable to live with the respondent;

(b) that the respondent has behaved in such a way that the petitioner cannot reasonably be expected to live with the respondent;

(c) that the respondent has deserted the petitioner for a continuous period of at least two years immediately preceding the presentation of the petition;

(d) that the parties to the marriage have lived apart for a continuous period of at least two years immediately preceding the presentation of the petition (hereafter in this Act referred to as 'two years' separation') and the respondent consents to a decree being granted;

(e) that the parties to the marriage have lived apart for a continuous period of at least five years immediately preceding the presentation of the petition (hereafter in this Act referred to as 'five years' separation').

(3) On a petition for divorce it shall be the duty of the court to enquire, so far as it reasonably can, into the facts alleged by the petitioner and into any facts alleged by the respondent.

(4) If the court is satisfied on the evidence of any such fact as is mentioned in subsection (2) above, then, unless it is satisfied on all the evidence that the marriage has not broken down irretrievably, it shall, subject to section 5 below, grant a decree of divorce.

(5) Every decree of divorce shall in the first instance be a decree nisi and shall not be made absolute before the expiration of six months from its grant unless the High Court by general order from time to time fixes a shorter period, or unless in any particular case the court in which the proceedings are for the time being pending from time to time by special order fixes a shorter period than the period otherwise applicable for the time being by virtue of this subsection.

2   Supplemental provision as to facts raising presumption of breakdown

(1) One party to a marriage shall not be entitled to rely for the purposes of section 1(2)(a) above on adultery committed by the other if, after it became known to him that the other had committed that adultery, the parties have lived with each other for a period exceeding, or periods together exceeding, six months.

(2) Where the parties to a marriage have lived with each other after it became known to one party that the other had committed adultery, but subsection (1) above does not apply, in any proceedings for divorce in which the petitioner relies on that adultery the fact that the parties have lived with each other after that time shall be disregarded in determining for the purposes of section 1(2)(a) above whether the petitioner finds it intolerable to live with the respondent.

(3) Where in any proceedings for divorce the petitioner alleges that the respondent has behaved in such a way that the petitioner cannot reasonably be expected to live with him, but the parties to the marriage have lived with each other for a period or periods after the date of the occurrence of the final incident relied on by the petitioner and held by the court to support his allegation, that fact shall be disregarded in determining for the purposes of section 1(2)(b) above whether the petitioner cannot reasonably be expected to live with the respondent if the length of that period or of those periods together was six months or less.

(4) For the purposes of section 1(2)(c) above the court may treat a period of desertion as having continued at a time when the deserting party was incapable of continuing the necessary intention if the evidence before the court is such that, had that party not been so incapable, the court would have inferred that his desertion continued at that time.

(5) In considering for the purposes of section 1(2) above whether the period for which the respondent has deserted the petitioner or the period for which the parties to a marriage have lived apart has been continuous, no account shall be taken of any one period (not exceeding six months) or of any two or more periods (not exceeding six months in all) during which the parties resumed living with each other, but no period during which the parties lived with each other shall count as part of the period of desertion, or of the period for which the parties to the marriage lived apart, as the case may be.

(6) For the purposes of section 1(2)(d) and (e) above and this section a husband and wife shall be treated as living apart unless they are living with each other in the same household, and references in this section to the parties to a marriage living with each other shall be construed as references to their living with each other in the same household.

(7) Provision shall be made by rules of court for the purpose of ensuring that where in pursuance of section 1(2)(d) above the petitioner alleges that the respondent consents to a decree being granted the respondent has been given such information as will enable him to understand the consequences to him of his consenting to a decree being granted and the steps which he must take to indicate that he consents to the grant of a decree.

3 Bar on petitions for divorce within one year of marriage

(1) No petition for divorce shall be presented to the court before the expiration of the period of one year from the date of the marriage.

(2) Nothing in this section shall prohibit the presentation of a petition based on matters which occurred before the expiration of that period.

4 Divorce not precluded by previous judicial separation

(1) A person shall not be prevented from presenting a petition for divorce, or the court from granting a decree of divorce, by reason only that the petitioner or respondent has at any time, on the same facts or substantially the same facts as those proved in support of the petition, been granted a decree of judicial separation or an order under, or having effect as if made under, the Matrimonial Proceedings (Magistrates' Courts) Act 1960 or Part I of the Domestic Proceedings and Magistrates' Courts Act 1978 or any corresponding enactments in force in Northern Ireland, the Isle of Man or any of the Channel Islands.

(2) On a petition for divorce in such a case as is mentioned in subsection (1) above, the court may treat the decree or order as sufficient proof of any adultery, desertion or other fact by reference to which it was granted, but shall not grant a decree of divorce without receiving evidence from the petitioner.

(3) Where a petition for divorce in such a case follows a decree of judicial separation or (subject to subsection (5) below) an order containing a provision exempting one party to the marriage from the obligation to cohabit with the other, for the purposes of that petition a period of desertion immediately preceding the institution of the proceedings for the decree or order shall, if the parties have not resumed cohabitation and the decree or order has been continuously in force since it was granted, be deemed immediately to precede the presentation of the petition.

(4) For the purposes of section 1(2)(c) above the court may treat as a period during which the respondent has deserted the petitioner any of the following periods, that is to say—

    (a) any period during which there is in force an injunction granted by the High Court or a county court which excludes the respondent from the matrimonial home;

    (b) any period during which there is in force an order made by the High Court or a county court under section 1 or 9 of the Matrimonial Homes Act 1983 which prohibits the exercise by the respondent of the right to occupy a dwelling-house in which the applicant and the respondent have or at any time have had a matrimonial home;

    (c) any period during which there is in force an order made by a magistrates' court under section 16(3) of the Domestic Proceedings and Magistrates' Courts Act 1978 which requires the respondent to leave the matrimonial home or prohibits the respondent from entering the matrimonial home.

(5) Where—

    (a) a petition for divorce is presented after the date on which Part I of the Domestic Proceedings and Magistrates' Courts Act 1978 comes into force, and

    (b) an order made under the Matrimonial Proceedings (Magistrates' Courts) Act 1960 containing a provision exempting the petitioner from the obligation to cohabit with the respondent is in force on that date,

then, for the purposes of section 1(2)(c) above, the court may treat a period during which such a provision was included in that order (whether before or after that date) as a period during which the respondent has deserted the petitioner.

5 Refusal of decree in five year separation cases on ground of grave hardship to respondent

(1) The respondent to a petition for divorce in which the petitioner alleges five years' separation may oppose the grant of a decree on the ground that the dissolution of the marriage will result in grave financial or other hardship to him and that it would in all the circumstances be wrong to dissolve the marriage.

(2) Where the grant of a decree is opposed by virtue of this section, then—

    (a) if the court finds that the petitioner is entitled to rely in support of his petition on the fact of five years' separation and makes no such finding as to any other fact mentioned in section 1(2) above, and

    (b) if apart from this section the court would grant a decree on the petition, the court shall consider all the circumstances, including the conduct of the parties to the marriage and the interests of those parties and of any children or other persons concerned, and if of opinion that the dissolution of the marriage will result in grave financial or other hardship to the respondent and that it would in all the circumstances be wrong to dissolve the marriage it shall dismiss the petition.

(3) For the purposes of this section hardship shall include the loss of the chance of acquiring any benefit which the respondent might acquire if the marriage were not dissolved.

6 Attempts at reconciliation of parties to marriage

(1) Provision shall be made by rules of court for requiring the solicitor acting for a petitioner for divorce to certify whether he has discussed with the petitioner the possibility of a reconciliation and given him the names and addresses of persons qualified to help effect a reconciliation between parties to a marriage who have become estranged.

(2) If at any stage of proceedings for divorce it appears to the court that there is a reasonable possibility of a reconciliation between the parties to the marriage, the court may adjourn the proceedings for such period as it thinks fit to enable attempts to be made to effect such a reconciliation.

The power conferred by the foregoing provision is additional to any other power of the court to adjourn proceedings.

7 Consideration by the court of certain agreements or arrangements

Provision may be made by rules of court for enabling the parties to a marriage, or either of them, in application made either before or after the presentation of a petition for divorce, to refer to the court any agreement or arrangement made or proposed to be made between them, being an agreement or arrangement which relates to, arises out of, or is connected with, the proceedings for divorce which are contemplated or, as the case may be, have begun, for enabling the court to express an opinion, should it think it desirable to do so, as to the reasonableness of the agreement or arrangement and to give such directions, if any, in the matter as it thinks fit.

8 Intervention of Queen's Proctor

(1) In the case of a petition for divorce—

    (a) the court may, if it thinks fit, direct all necessary papers in the matter to be sent to the Queen's Proctor, who shall under the directions of the Attorney-General instruct counsel to argue before the court any question in relation to the matter which the court considers it necessary or expedient to have fully argued;

    (b) any person may at any time during the progress of the proceedings or before the decree nisi is made absolute give information to the Queen's Proctor on any matter material to the due decision of the case, and the Queen's Proctor may thereupon take such steps as the Attorney General considers necessary or expedient.

(2) Where the Queen's Proctor intervenes or shows cause against a decree nisi in any proceedings for divorce, the court may make such order as may be just as to the payment by other parties to the proceedings of the costs incurred by any of those parties by reason of his so doing.

(3) The Queen's Proctor shall be entitled to charge as part of the expenses of his office—

    (a) the costs of any proceedings under subsection (1)(a) above;

    (b) where his reasonable costs of intervening or showing cause as mentioned in subsection (2) above are not fully satisfied by any order under that subsection, the amount of the difference;

    (c) if the Treasury so directs, any cost which he pays to any parties under an order made under subsection (2).

9 Proceedings after decree nisi: general powers of court

(1) Where a decree of divorce has been granted but not made absolute, then, without prejudice to section 8 above, any person (excluding a party to the proceedings other than the Queen's Proctor) may show cause why the decree should not be made absolute by reason of material facts not having been brought before the court; and in such a case the court may—

    (a) notwithstanding anything in section 1(5) above (but subject to sections 10(2) to (4) and 41 below) make the decree absolute; or

    (b) rescind the decree; or

    (c) require further inquiry; or

    (d) otherwise deal with the case as it thinks fit.

(2) Where a decree of divorce has been granted and no application for it to be made absolute has been made by the party to whom it was granted, then, at any time after the expiration of three months from the earliest date on which that party could have made such an application, the party against whom it was granted may make an application to the court, and on that application the court may exercise any of the powers mentioned in paragraphs (a) to (d) of subsection (1) above.

10 Proceedings after decree nisi: special protection for respondent in separation cases

(1) Where in any case the court has granted a decree of divorce on the basis of a finding that the petitioner was entitled to rely in support of his petition on the fact of two years'

separation coupled with the respondent's consent to a decree being granted and has made no such finding as to any other fact mentioned in section 1(2) above, the court may, on an application made by the respondent at any time before the decree is made absolute, rescind the decree if it is satisfied that the petitioner misled the respondent (whether intentionally or unintentionally) about any matter which the respondent took into account in deciding to give his consent.

(2) The following provisions of this section apply where—

    (a) the respondent to a petition for divorce in which the petitioner alleged two years' or five years' separation coupled, in the former case, with the respondent's consent to a decree being granted, has applied to the court for consideration under subsection (3) below of his financial position after the divorce; and

    (b) the court has granted a decree on the petition on the basis of a finding that the petitioner was entitled to rely in support of his petition on the fact of two years' or five years' separation (as the case may be) and has made no such finding as to any other fact mentioned in section 1(2) above.

(3) The court hearing an application by the respondent under subsection (2) above shall consider all the circumstances including the age, health, conduct, earning capacity, financial resources, and financial obligations of each of the parties, and the financial position of the respondent as, having regard to the divorce, it is likely to be after the death of the petitioner should the petitioner die first; and, subject to subsection (4) below, the court shall not make the decree absolute unless it is satisfied—

    (a) that the petitioner should not be required to make any financial provision for the respondent, or

    (b) that the financial provision made by the petitioner for the respondent is reasonable and fair or the best that can be made in the circumstances.

(4) The court may if it thinks fit make the decree absolute notwithstanding the requirements of subsection (3) above if—

    (a) it appears that there are circumstances making it desirable that the decree should be made absolute without delay, and

    (b) the court has obtained a satisfactory undertaking from the petitioner that he will make such financial provision for the respondent as the court may approve.

10A Proceedings after decree nisi: religious marriage

(1) This section applies if a decree of divorce has been granted but not made absolute and the parties to the marriage concerned—

    (a) were married in accordance with—

        (i)   the usages of the Jews, or

        (ii) any other prescribed religious usages; and

    (b) must co-operate if the marriage is to be dissolved in accordance with those usages.

(2) On the application of either party, the court may order that a decree of divorce is not to be made absolute until a declaration made by both parties that they have taken such steps as are required to dissolve the marriage in accordance with those usages is produced to the court.

(3) An order under subsection (2)—

    (a) may be made only if the court is satisfied that in all the circumstances of the case it is just and reasonable to do so; and

    (b) may be revoked at any time.

(4) A declaration of a kind mentioned in subsection (2)—

    (a) must be in a specified form;

    (b) must, in specified cases, be accompanied by such documents as may be specified; and

    (c) must, in specified cases, satisfy such other requirements as may be specified.

(5) The validity of a decree of divorce made by reference to such a declaration is not to be affected by any inaccuracy in that declaration.

(6) 'Prescribed' means prescribed in an order made by the Lord Chancellor after consulting the Lord Chief Justice and such an order—

(a) must be made by statutory instrument;

(b) shall be subject to annulment in pursuance of a resolution of either House of Parliament.

(7) 'Specified' means specified in rules of court.

(8) The Lord Chief Justice may nominate a judicial office holder (as defined in section 109(4) of the Constitutional Reform Act 2005) to exercise his functions under this section.

Nullity

11   Grounds on which a marriage is void

A marriage celebrated after 31st July 1971 shall be void on the following grounds only, that is to say—

(a) that it is not a valid marriage under the provisions of the Marriages Acts 1949 to 1986 (that is to say where—

(i)   the parties are within the prohibited degrees of relationship;

(ii) either party is under the age of sixteen; or

(iii) the parties have intermarried in disregard of certain requirements as to the formation of marriage);

(b) that at the time of the marriage either party was already lawfully married or a civil partner;

(c) that the parties are not respectively male and female;

(d) in the case of a polygamous marriage entered into outside England and Wales, that either party was at the time of the marriage domiciled in England and Wales.

For the purposes of paragraph (d) of this subsection a marriage is not polygamous if at its inception neither party has any spouse additional to the other.

12   Grounds on which a marriage is voidable

A marriage celebrated after 31st July 1971 shall be voidable on the following grounds only, that is to say—

(a) that the marriage has not been consummated owing to the incapacity of either party to consummate it;

(b) that the marriage has not been consummated owing to the wilful refusal of the respondent to consummate it;

(c) that either party to the marriage did not validly consent to it, whether in consequence of duress, mistake, unsoundness of mind or otherwise;

(d) that at the time of the marriage either party, though capable of giving a valid consent, was suffering (whether continuously or intermittently) from mental disorder within the meaning of the Mental Health Act 1983 of such a kind or to such an extent as to be unfitted for marriage;

(e) that at the time of the marriage the respondent was suffering from venereal disease in a communicable form;

(f) that at the time of the marriage the respondent was pregnant by some person other than the petitioner.

(g) that an interim gender recognition certificate under the Gender Recognition Act 2004 has, after the time of the marriage, been issued to either party to the marriage;

(h) that the respondent is a person whose gender at the time of the marriage had become the acquired gender under the Gender Recognition Act 2004.

13   Bars to relief where marriage is voidable

(1) The court shall not, in proceedings instituted after 31st July 1971, grant a decree of nullity on the ground that a marriage is voidable if the respondent satisfies the court—

(a) that the petitioner, with knowledge that it was open to him to have the marriage avoided, so conducted himself in relation to the respondent as to lead the respondent reasonably to believe that he would not seek to do so; and

(b) that it would be unjust to the respondent to grant the decree.

(2) Without prejudice to subsection (1) above, the court shall not grant a decree of nullity by virtue of section 12 above on the grounds mentioned in paragraph (c), (d), (e), (f) or (h) of that section unless—

(a) it is satisfied that proceedings were instituted within the period of three years from the date of the marriage, or

(b) leave for the institution of proceedings after the expiration of that period has been granted under subsection (4) below.

(2A) Without prejudice to subsection (1) above, the court shall not grant a decree of nullity by virtue of section 12 above on the ground mentioned in paragraph (g) of that section unless it is satisfied that proceedings were instituted within the period of six months from the date of issue of the interim gender recognition certificate.

(3) Without prejudice to subsections (1) and (2) above, the court shall not grant a decree of nullity by virtue of section 12 above on the grounds mentioned in paragraph (e), (f) or (h) of that section unless it is satisfied that the petitioner was at the time of the marriage ignorant of the facts alleged.

(4) In the case of proceedings for the grant of a decree of nullity by virtue of section 12 above on the grounds mentioned in paragraph (c), (d), (e), (f) or (h) of that section, a judge of the court may, on an application made to him, grant leave for the institution of proceedings after the expiration of the period of three years from the date of the marriage if—

(a) he is satisfied that the petitioner has at some time during that period suffered from mental disorder within the meaning of the Mental Health Act 1983, and

(b) he considers that in all the circumstances of the case it would be just to grant leave for the institution of proceedings.

(5) An application for leave under subsection (4) above may be made after the expiration of the period of three years from the date of the marriage.

14 Marriages governed by foreign law or celebrated abroad under English law

(1) Subject to subsection (3) where, apart from this Act, any matter affecting the validity of a marriage would fall to be determined (in accordance with the rules of private international law) by reference to the law of a country outside England and Wales, nothing in section 11, 12 or 13(1) above shall—

(a) preclude the determination of that matter as aforesaid; or

(b) require the application to the marriage of the grounds or bar there mentioned except so far as applicable in accordance with those rules.

(2) In the case of a marriage which purports to have been celebrated under the Foreign Marriage Acts 1892 to 1947 or has taken place outside England and Wales and purports to be a marriage under common law, section 11 above is without prejudice to any ground on which the marriage may be void under those Acts or, as the case may be, by virtue of the rules governing the celebration of marriages outside England and Wales under common law.

(3) No marriage is to be treated as valid by virtue of subsection (1) if, at the time when it purports to have been celebrated, either party was already a civil partner.

15 Application of ss. 1(5), 8 and 9 to nullity proceedings

Sections 1(5), 8 and 9 as above shall apply in relation to proceedings for nullity of marriage as if for any reference in those provisions to divorce there were substituted a reference to nullity of marriage.

16 Effect of decree of nullity in case of voidable marriage

A decree of nullity granted after 31st July 1971 in respect of a voidable marriage shall operate to annul the marriage only as respects any time after the decree has been made absolute, and the marriage shall, notwithstanding the decree, be treated as if it had existed up to that time.

Other matrimonial suits

17 Judicial separation

(1) A petition for judicial separation may be presented to the court by either party to a marriage on the ground that any such fact as is mentioned in section 1(2) above exists, and the provisions of section 2 above shall apply accordingly for the purposes of a petition for judicial separation alleging any such fact, as they apply in relation to a petition for divorce alleging that fact.

(2) On a petition for judicial separation it shall be the duty of the court to inquire, so far as it reasonably can, into the facts alleged by the petitioner and into any facts alleged by the respondent, but the court shall not be concerned to consider whether the marriage has broken down irretrievably, and if it is satisfied on the evidence of any such fact as is mentioned in section 1(2) above it shall, subject to section 41 below, grant a decree of judicial separation.

(3) Sections 6 and 7 above shall apply for the purpose of encouraging the reconciliation of parties to proceedings for judicial separation and of enabling the parties to a marriage to refer to the court for its opinion an agreement or arrangement relevant to actual or contemplated proceedings for judicial separation, as they apply in relation to proceedings for divorce.

18 Effects of judicial separation

(1) Where the court grants a decree of judicial separation it shall no longer be obligatory for the petitioner to cohabit with the respondent.

(2) If while a decree of judicial separation is in force and the separation is continuing either of the parties to the marriage dies intestate as respects all or any of his or her real or personal property, the property as respects which he or she died intestate shall devolve as if the other party to the marriage had then been dead.

(3) Notwithstanding anything in section 2(1)(a) of the Matrimonial Proceedings (Magistrates' Courts) Act 1960, a provision in force under an order made, or having effect as if made, under that section exempting one party to a marriage from the obligation to cohabit with the other shall not have effect as a decree of judicial separation for the purposes of subsection (2) above.

19 Presumption of death and dissolution of marriage

(1) Any married person who alleges that reasonable grounds exist for supposing that the other party to the marriage is dead may present a petition to the court to have it presumed that the other party is dead and to have the marriage dissolved, and the court may, if satisfied that such reasonable grounds exist, grant a decree of presumption of death and dissolution of marriage.

(3) In any proceedings under this section the fact that for a period of seven years or more the other party to the marriage has been continually absent from the petitioner and the petitioner has no reason to believe that the other party has been living within that time shall be evidence that the other party is dead until the contrary is proved.

(4) Sections 1(5), 8 and 9 shall apply to a petition and a decree under this section as they apply to a petition for divorce and a decree of divorce respectively.

(6) It is hereby declared that neither collusion nor any other conduct on the part of the petitioner which has at any time been a bar to relief in matrimonial proceedings constitutes a bar to the grant of a decree under this section.

General

20 Relief for respondent in divorce proceedings

If in any proceedings for divorce the respondent alleges and proves any such fact as is mentioned in subsection (2) of section 1 above (treating the respondent as the petitioner and the petitioner as the respondent for the purposes of that subsection) the court may give to the respondent the relief to which he would have been entitled if he had presented a petition seeking that relief.

PART II   FINANCIAL RELIEF FOR PARTIES TO MARRIAGE AND CHILDREN OF FAMILY

Financial provision and property adjustment orders

21   Financial provision and property adjustment orders

(1) The financial provision orders for the purposes of this Act are the orders for periodical or lump sum provision available (subject to the provisions of this Act) under section 23 below for the purpose of adjusting the financial position of the parties to a marriage and any children of the family in connection with proceedings for divorce, nullity of marriage or judicial separation and under section 27(6) below on proof of neglect by one party to a marriage to provide, or to make a proper contribution towards, reasonable maintenance for the other or a child of the family, that is to say—

   (a) any order for periodical payments in favour of a party to a marriage under section 23(1)(a) or 27(6)(a) or in favour of a child of the family under section 23(1)(d), (2) or (4) or 27(6)(d);

   (b) any order for secured periodical payments in favour of a party to a marriage under section 23(1)(b) or 27(6)(b) or in favour of a child of the family under section 23(1)(e), (2) or (4) or 27(6)(e); and

   (c) any order for lump sum provision in favour of a party to a marriage under section 23(1)(c) or 27(6)(c) or in favour of a child of the family under section 23(1)(f), (2) or (4) or 27(6)(f);

and references in this Act (except in paragraphs 17(1) and 23 of Schedule 1 below) to periodical payments orders, secured periodical payments orders, and orders for the payment of a lump sum are references to all or some of the financial provision orders requiring the sort of financial provision in question according as the context of each reference may require.

(2) The property adjustment orders for the purposes of this Act are the orders dealing with property rights available (subject to the provisions of this Act) under section 24 below for the purpose of adjusting the financial position of the parties to a marriage and any children of the family on or after the grant of a decree of divorce, nullity of marriage or judicial separation, that is to say—

   (a) any order under subsection (1)(a) of that section for a transfer of property;

   (b) any order under subsection (1)(b) of that section for a settlement of property; and

   (c) any order under subsection (1)(c) or (d) of that section for a variation of settlement.

21A   Pension sharing orders

(1) For the purposes of this Act, a pension sharing order is an order which—

   (a) provides that one party's—

      (i) shareable rights under a specified pension arrangement, or

      (ii) shareable state scheme rights, be subject to pension sharing for the benefit of the other party, and

   (b) specifies the percentage value to be transferred.

(2) In subsection (1) above—

   (a) the reference to shareable rights under a pension arrangement is to rights in relation to which pension sharing is available under Chapter I of Part IV of the Welfare Reform and Pensions Act 1999, or under corresponding Northern Ireland legislation,

   (b) the reference to shareable state scheme rights is to rights in relation to which pension sharing is available under Chapter II of Part IV of the Welfare Reform and Pensions Act 1999, or under corresponding Northern Ireland legislation, and

   (c) 'party' means a party to a marriage.

Ancillary relief in connection with divorce proceedings, etc.

22   Maintenance pending suit

On a petition for divorce, nullity of marriage or judicial separation, the court may make an order for maintenance pending suit, that is to say, an order requiring either party to the marriage to make to the other such periodical payments for his or her maintenance and for such term, being a term beginning not earlier than the date of the presentation of the petition and ending with the date of the determination of the suit, as the court thinks reasonable.

23   Financial provision orders in connection with divorce proceedings, etc.

(1) On granting a decree of divorce, a decree of nullity of marriage or a decree of judicial separation or at any time thereafter (whether, in the case of a decree of divorce or of nullity of marriage, before or after the decree is made absolute), the court may make any one or more of the following orders, that is to say—

(a) an order that either party to the marriage shall make to the other such periodical payments, for such term, as may be specified in the order;

(b) an order that either party to the marriage shall secure to the other to the satisfaction of the court such periodical payments, for such term, as may be so specified;

(c) an order that either party to the marriage shall pay to the other such lump sum or sums as may be so specified;

(d) an order that a party to the marriage shall make to such person as may be specified in the order for the benefit of a child of the family, or to such a child, such periodical payments, for such term, as may be so specified;

(e) an order that a party to the marriage shall secure to such person as may be so specified for the benefit of such a child, or to such a child, to the satisfaction of the court, such periodical payments, for such term, as may be so specified;

(f) an order that a party to the marriage shall pay to such person as may be so specified for the benefit of such a child, or to such a child, such lump sum as may be so specified;

subject however, in the case of an order under paragraph (d), (e) or (f) above, to the restrictions imposed by section 29(1) and (3) below on the making of financial provision orders in favour of children who have attained the age of eighteen.

(2) The court may also, subject to those restrictions, make any one or more of the orders mentioned in subsection (1)(d), (e) and (f) above—

(a) in any proceedings for divorce, nullity of marriage or judicial separation, before granting a decree; and

(b) where any such proceedings are dismissed after the beginning of the trial, either forthwith or within a reasonable period after the dismissal.

(3) Without prejudice to the generality of subsection (1)(c) or (f) above—

(a) an order under this section that a party to a marriage shall pay a lump sum to the other party may be made for the purpose of enabling that other party to meet any liabilities or expenses reasonably incurred by him or her in maintaining himself or herself or any child of the family before making an application for an order under this section in his or her favour;

(b) an order under this section for the payment of a lump sum to or for the benefit of a child of the family may be made for the purpose of enabling any liabilities or expenses reasonably incurred by or for the benefit of that child before the making of an application for an order under this section in his favour to be met; and

(c) an order under this section for the payment of a lump sum may provide for the payment of that sum by instalments of such amount as may be specified in the order and may require the payment of the instalments to be secured to the satisfaction of the court.

(4) The power of the court under subsection (1) or (2)(a) above to make an order in favour of a child of the family shall be exercisable from time to time; and where the court makes an order in favour of a child under subsection (2)(b) above, it may from time to time, subject to the restrictions mentioned in subsection (1) above, make a further order in his favour of any of the kinds mentioned in subsection (1)(d), (e) or (f) above.

(5) Without prejudice to the power to give a direction under section 30 below for the settlement of an instrument by conveyancing counsel, where an order is made under subsection (1)(a), (b) or (c) above on or after granting a decree of divorce or nullity of marriage, neither the order nor any settlement made in pursuance of the order shall take effect unless the decree has been made absolute.

(6) Where the court—

(a) makes an order under this section for the payment of a lump sum; and

(b) directs—

(i) that payment of that sum or any part of it shall be deferred; or

(ii) that that sum or any part of it shall be paid by instalments,

the court may order that the amount deferred or the instalments shall carry interest at such rate as may be specified by the order from such date, not earlier than the date of the order, as may be so specified, until the date when payment of it is due.

24 Property adjustment orders in connection with divorce proceedings, etc.

(1) On granting a decree of divorce, a decree of nullity of marriage or a decree of judicial separation or at any time thereafter (whether, in the case of a decree of divorce, or of nullity of marriage, before or after the decree is made absolute), the court may make any one or more of the following orders, that is to say—

(a) an order that a party to the marriage shall transfer to the other party, to any child of the family or to such person as may be specified in the order for the benefit of such a child such property as may be so specified, being property to which the first-mentioned party is entitled, either in possession or reversion;

(b) an order that a settlement of such property as may be so specified, being property to which a party to the marriage is so entitled, be made to the satisfaction of the court for the benefit of the other party to the marriage and of the children of the family or either or any of them;

(c) an order varying for the benefit of the parties to the marriage and of the children of the family or either or any of them any ante-nuptial or post-nuptial settlement (including such a settlement made by will or codicil) made on the parties to the marriage, other than one in the form of a pension arrangement (within the meaning of section 25D below);

(d) an order extinguishing or reducing the interest of either of the parties to the marriage under any such settlement, other than one in the form of a pension arrangement (within the meaning of section 25D below);

subject, however, in the case of an order under paragraph (a) above, to the restrictions imposed by section 29(1) and (3) below on the making of orders for a transfer of property in favour of children who have attained the age of eighteen.

(2) The court may make an order under subsection (1)(c) above notwithstanding that there are no children of the family.

(3) Without prejudice to the power to give a direction under section 30 below for the settlement of an instrument by conveyancing counsel, where an order is made under this section on or after granting a decree of divorce or nullity of marriage, neither the order nor any settlement made in pursuance of the order shall take effect unless the decree has been made absolute.

24A Orders for sale of property

(1) Where the court makes under section 23 or 24 of this Act a secured periodical payments order, an order for the payment of a lump sum or a property adjustment order, then,

on making that order or at any time thereafter, the court may make a further order for the sale of such property as may be specified in the order, being property in which or in the proceeds of sale of which either or both of the parties to the marriage has or have a beneficial interest, either in possession or reversion.

(2) Any order made under subsection (1) above may contain such consequential or supplementary provisions as the court thinks fit and, without prejudice to the generality of the foregoing provision, may include—

(a) provision requiring the making of a payment out of the proceeds of sale of the property to which the order relates, and

(b) provision requiring any such property to be offered for sale to a person, or class of persons, specified in the order.

(3) Where an order is made under subsection (1) above on or after the grant of a decree of divorce or nullity of marriage, the order shall not take effect unless the decree has been made absolute.

(4) Where an order is made under subsection (1) above, the court may direct that the order, or such provision thereof as the court may specify, shall not take effect until the occurrence of an event specified by the court or the expiration of a period so specified.

(5) Where an order under subsection (1) above contains a provision requiring the proceeds of sale of the property to which the order relates to be used to secure periodical payments to a party to the marriage, the order shall cease to have effect on the death or re-marriage of, or formation of a civil partnership by, that person.

(6) Where a party to a marriage has a beneficial interest in any property, or in the proceeds of sale thereof, and some other person who is not a party to the marriage also has a beneficial interest in that property or in the proceeds of sale thereof, then, before deciding whether to make an order under this section in relation to that property, it shall be the duty of the court to give that other person an opportunity to make representations with respect to the order; and any representations made by that other person shall be included among the circumstances to which the court is required to have regard under section 25(1) below.

24B   Pension sharing orders in connection with divorce proceedings, etc.

(1) On granting a decree of divorce or a decree of nullity of marriage or at any time thereafter (whether before or after the decree is made absolute), the court may, on an application made under this section, make one or more pension sharing orders in relation to the marriage.

(2) A pension sharing order under this section is not to take effect unless the decree on or after which it is made has been made absolute.

(3) A pension sharing order under this section may not be made in relation to a pension arrangement which—

(a) is the subject of a pension sharing order in relation to the marriage, or

(b) has been the subject of pension sharing between the parties to the marriage.

(4) A pension sharing order under this section may not be made in relation to shareable state scheme rights if—

(a) such rights are the subject of a pension sharing order in relation to the marriage, or

(b) such rights have been the subject of pension sharing between the parties to the marriage.

(5) A pension sharing order under this section may not be made in relation to the rights of a person under a pension arrangement if there is in force a requirement imposed by virtue of section 25B or 25C below which relates to benefits or future benefits to which he is entitled under the pension arrangement.

24C   Pension sharing orders: duty to stay

(1) No pension sharing order may be made so as to take effect before the end of such period after the making of the order as may be prescribed by regulations made by the Lord Chancellor.

(2) The power to make regulations under this section shall be exercisable by statutory instrument which shall be subject to annulment in pursuance of a resolution of either House of Parliament.

24D Pension sharing orders: apportionment of charges

If a pension sharing order relates to rights under a pension arrangement, the court may include in the order provision about the apportionment between the parties of any charge under section 41 of the Welfare Reform and Pensions Act 1999 (charges in respect of pension sharing costs), or under corresponding Northern Ireland legislation.

25 Matters to which court is to have regard in deciding how to exercise its powers under sections 23, 24 and 24A

(1) It shall be the duty of the court in deciding whether to exercise its powers under sections 23, 24, 24A or 24B above and, if so, in what manner, to have regard to all the circumstances of the case, first consideration being given to the welfare while a minor of any child of the family who has not attained the age of eighteen.

(2) As regards the exercise of the powers of the court under section 23(1)(a), (b) or (c), 24, 24A or 24B above in relation to a party to the marriage, the court shall in particular have regard to the following matters—

   (a) the income, earning capacity, property and other financial resources which each of the parties to the marriage has or is likely to have in the foreseeable future, including in the case of earning capacity any increase in that capacity which it would in the opinion of the court be reasonable to expect a party to the marriage to take steps to acquire;

   (b) the financial needs, obligations and responsibilities which each of the parties to the marriage has or is likely to have in the foreseeable future;

   (c) the standard of living enjoyed by the family before the breakdown of the marriage;

   (d) the age of each party to the marriage and the duration of the marriage;

   (e) any physical or mental disability of either of the parties to the marriage;

   (f) the contributions which each of the parties has made or is likely in the foreseeable future to make to the welfare of the family, including any contribution by looking after the home or caring for the family;

   (g) the conduct of each of the parties, if that conduct is such that it would in the opinion of the court be inequitable to disregard it;

   (h) in the case of proceedings for divorce or nullity of marriage, the value to each of the parties to the marriage of any benefit which, by reason of the dissolution or annulment of the marriage, that party will lose the chance of acquiring.

(3) As regards the exercise of the powers of the court under section 23(1)(d), (e) or (f), (2) or (4), 24 or 24A above in relation to a child of the family, the court shall in particular have regard to the following matters—

   (a) the financial needs of the child;

   (b) the income, earning capacity (if any), property and other financial resources of the child;

   (c) any physical or mental disability of the child;

   (d) the manner in which he was being and in which the parties to the marriage expected him to be educated or trained;

   (e) the considerations mentioned in relation to the parties to the marriage in paragraphs (a), (b), (c) and (e) of subsection (2) above.

(4) As regards the exercise of the powers of the court under section 23(1)(d), (e) or (f), (2) or (4), 24 or 24A above against a party to a marriage in favour of a child of the family who is not the child of that party, the court shall also have regard—

   (a) to whether that party assumed any responsibility for the child's maintenance, and, if so, to the extent to which, and the basis upon which, that party assumed such responsibility and to the length of time for which that party discharged such responsibility;

(b) to whether in assuming and discharging such responsibility that party did so knowing that the child was not his or her own;

(c) to the liability of any other person to maintain the child.

25A   Exercise of court's powers in favour of party to marriage on decree of divorce or nullity of marriage

(1) Where on or after the grant of a degree of divorce or nullity of marriage the court decides to exercise its powers under section 23(1)(a), (b) or (c), 24, 24A or 24B above in favour of a party to the marriage, it shall be the duty of the court to consider whether it would be appropriate so to exercise those powers that the financial obligations of each party towards the other will be terminated as soon after the grant of the decree as the court considers just and reasonable.

(2) Where the court decides in such a case to make a periodical payments or secured periodical payments order in favour of a party to the marriage, the court shall in particular consider whether it would be appropriate to require those payments to be made or secured only for such term as would in the opinion of the court be sufficient to enable the party in whose favour the order is made to adjust without undue hardship to the termination of his or her financial dependence on the other party.

(3) Where on or after the grant of a decree of divorce or nullity of marriage an application is made by a party to the marriage for a periodical payments order in his or her favour, then, if the court considers that no continuing obligation should be imposed on either party to make or secure periodical payments in favour of the other, the court may dismiss the application with a direction that the applicant shall not be entitled to make any further application in relation to that marriage for an order under section 23(1)(a) or (b) above.

25B   Pensions

(1) The matters to which the court is to have regard under section 25(2) above include—

(a) in the case of paragraph (a), any benefits under a pension arrangement which a party to the marriage has or is likely to have, and

(b) in the case of paragraph (h), any benefits under a pension arrangement which, by reason of the dissolution or annulment of the marriage, a party to the marriage will lose the chance of acquiring,

and, accordingly, in relation to benefits under a pension arrangement, section 25(2)(a) above shall have effect as if 'in the foreseeable future' were omitted.

(3) The following provisions apply where, having regard to any benefits under a pension arrangement, the court determines to make an order under section 23 above.

(4) To the extent to which the order is made having regard to any benefits under a pension arrangement, the order may require the person responsible for the pension arrangement in question, if at any time any payment in respect of any benefits under the arrangement becomes due to the party with pension rights, to make a payment for the benefit of the other party.

(5) The order must express the amount of any payment required to be made by virtue of subsection (4) above as a percentage of the payment which becomes due to the party with pension rights.

(6) Any such payment by the person responsible for the arrangement—

(a) shall discharge so much of his liability to the party with pension rights as corresponds to the amount of the payment, and

(b) shall be treated for all purposes as a payment made by the party with pension rights in or towards the discharge of his liability under the order.

(7) Where the party with pension rights has a right of commutation under the arrangement, the order may require him to exercise it to any extent; and this section applies to any payment due in consequence of commutation in pursuance of the order as it applies to other payments in respect of benefits under the arrangement.

(7A) The power conferred by subsection (7) above may not be exercised for the purpose of commuting a benefit payable to the party with pension rights to a benefit payable to the other party.

(7B) The power conferred by subsection (4) or (7) above may not be exercised in relation to a pension arrangement which—

(a) is the subject of a pension sharing order in relation to the marriage, or

(b) has been the subject of pension sharing between the parties to the marriage.

(7C) In subsection (1) above, references to benefits under a pension arrangement include any benefits by way of pension, whether under a pension arrangement or not.

25C   Pensions: lump sums

(1) The power of the court under section 23 above to order a party to a marriage to pay a lump sum to the other party includes, where the benefits which the party with pension rights has or is likely to have under a pension arrangement include any lump sum payable in respect of his death, power to make any of the following provision by the order.

(2) The court may—

(a) if the person responsible for the pension arrangement in question has power to determine the person to whom the sum, or any part of it, is to be paid, require him to pay the whole or part of that sum, when it becomes due, to the other party,

(b) if the party with pension rights has power to nominate the person to whom the sum, or any part of it, is to be paid, require the party with pension rights to nominate the other party in respect of the whole or part of that sum,

(c) in any other case, require the person responsible for the pension arrangement in question to pay the whole or part of that sum, when it becomes due, for the benefit of the other party instead of to the person to whom, apart from the order, it would be paid.

(3) Any payment by the person responsible for the arrangement under an order made under section 23 above by virtue of this section shall discharge so much of his liability in respect of the party with pension rights as corresponds to the amount of the payment.

(4) The powers conferred by this section may not be exercised in relation to a pension arrangement which—

(a) is the subject of a pension sharing order in relation to the marriage, or

(b) has been the subject of pension sharing between the parties to the marriage.

25D   Pensions: supplementary

(1) Where—

(a) an order made under section 23 above by virtue of section 25B or 25C above imposes any requirement on the person responsible for a pension arrangement ('the first arrangement') and the party with pension rights acquires rights under another pension arrangement ('the new arrangement') which are derived (directly or indirectly) from the whole of his rights under the first arrangement, and

(b) the person responsible for the new arrangement has been given notice in accordance with regulations made by the Lord Chancellor,

the order shall have effect as if it had been made instead in respect of the person responsible for the new arrangement.

(2) The Lord Chancellor may by regulations—

(a) in relation to any provision of sections 25B or 25C above which authorises the court making an order under section 23 above to require the person responsible for a pension arrangement to make a payment for the benefit of the other party, make provision as to the person to whom, and the terms on which, the payment is to be made,

(ab) make, in relation to payment under a mistaken belief as to the continuation in force of a provision included by virtue of section 25B or 25C above in an order under section 23 above, provision about the rights or liabilities of the payer, the payee or the person to whom the payment was due,

(b) require notices to be given in respect of changes of circumstances relevant to such orders which include provision made by virtue of sections 25B and 25C above,

(ba) make provision for the person responsible for a pension arrangement to be discharged in prescribed circumstances from a requirement imposed by virtue of section 25B or 25C above,

(e) make provision about calculation and verification in relation to the valuation of—

(i) benefits under a pension arrangement, or

(ii) shareable state scheme rights,

for the purposes of the court's functions in connection with the exercise of any of its powers under this Part of this Act.

(2A) Regulations under subsection (2)(e) above may include—

(a) provision for calculation or verification in accordance with guidance from time to time prepared by a prescribed person, and

(b) provision by reference to regulations under section 30 or 49(4) of the Welfare Reform and Pensions Act 1999.

(2B) Regulations under subsection (2) above may make different provision for different cases.

(2C) Power to make regulations under this section shall be exercisable by statutory instrument which shall be subject to annulment in pursuance of a resolution of either House of Parliament.

(3) In this section and sections 25B and 25C above—

'occupational pension scheme' has the same meaning as in the Pension Schemes Act 1993;

'the party with pension rights' means the party to the marriage who has or is likely to have benefits under a pension arrangement and 'the other party' means the other party to the marriage;

'pension arrangement' means—

(a) an occupational pension scheme,

(b) a personal pension scheme,

(c) a retirement annuity contract,

(d) an annuity or insurance policy purchased, or transferred, for the purpose of giving effect to rights under an occupational pension scheme or a personal pension scheme, and

(e) an annuity purchased, or entered into, for the purpose of discharging liability in respect of a pension credit under section 29(1)(b) of the Welfare Reform and Pensions Act 1999 or under corresponding Northern Ireland legislation;

'personal pension scheme' has the same meaning as in the Pension Schemes Act 1993;

'prescribed' means prescribed by regulations;

'retirement annuity contract' means a contract or scheme approved under Chapter III of Part XIV of the Income and Corporation Taxes Act 1988;

'shareable state scheme rights' has the same meaning as in section 21A(1) above; and 'trustees or managers', in relation to an occupational pension scheme or a personal pension scheme, means—

(a) in the case of a scheme established under a trust, the trustees of the scheme, and

(b) in any other case, the managers of the scheme.

(4) In this section and sections 25B and 25C above, references to the person responsible for a pension arrangement are—

(a) in the case of an occupational pension scheme or a personal pension scheme, to the trustees or managers of the scheme,

     (b) in the case of a retirement annuity contract or an annuity falling within paragraph (d) or (e) of the definition of 'pension arrangement' above, the provider of the annuity, and

     (c) in the case of an insurance policy falling within paragraph (d) of the definition of that expression, the insurer.

25E The Pension Protection Fund

    (1) The matters to which the court is to have regard under section 25(2) include—

     (a) in the case of paragraph (a), any PPF compensation to which a party to the marriage is or is likely to be entitled, and

     (b) in the case of paragraph (h), any PPF compensation which, by reason of the dissolution or annulment of the marriage, a party to the marriage will lose the chance of acquiring entitlement to,

and, accordingly, in relation to PPF compensation, section 25(2)(a) shall have effect as if 'in the foreseeable future' were omitted.

    (2) Subsection (3) applies in relation to an order under section 23 so far as it includes provision made by virtue of section 25B(4) which—

     (a) imposed requirements on the trustees or managers of an occupational pension scheme for which the Board has assumed responsibility in accordance with Chapter 3 of Part 2 of the Pensions Act 2004 (pension protection) or any provision in force in Northern Ireland corresponding to that Chapter, and

     (b) was made before the trustees or managers of the scheme received the transfer notice in relation to the scheme.

    (3) The order is to have effect from the time when the trustees or managers of the scheme receive the transfer notice—

     (a) as if, except in prescribed descriptions of case—

       (i) references in the order to the trustees or managers of the scheme were references to the Board, and

      (ii) references in the order to any pension or lump sum to which the party with pension rights is or may become entitled under the scheme were references to any PPF compensation to which that person is or may become entitled in respect of the pension or lump sum, and

     (b) subject to such other modifications as may be prescribed.

    (4) Subsection (5) applies to an order under section 23 if—

     (a) it includes provision made by virtue of section 25B(7) which requires the party with pension rights to exercise his right of commutation under an occupational pension scheme to any extent, and

     (b) before the requirement is complied with the Board has assumed responsibility for the scheme as mentioned in subsection (2)(a).

    (5) From the time the trustees or managers of the scheme receive the transfer notice, the order is to have effect with such modifications as may be prescribed.

    (6) Regulations may modify section 25C as it applies in relation to an occupational pension scheme at any time when there is an assessment period in relation to the scheme.

    (7) Where the court makes a pension sharing order in respect of a person's shareable rights under an occupational pension scheme, or an order which includes provision made by virtue of section 25B(4) or (7) in relation to such a scheme, the Board subsequently assuming responsibility for the scheme as mentioned in subsection (2)(a) does not affect—

     (a) the powers of the court under section 31 to vary or discharge the order or to suspend or revive any provision of it, or

     (b) on an appeal, the powers of the appeal court to affirm, reinstate, set aside or vary the order.

. . .

    (9) In this section—

'assessment period' means an assessment period within the meaning of Part 2 of the Pensions Act 2004 (pension protection) (see sections 132 and 159 of that Act) or an equivalent period under any provision in force in Northern Ireland corresponding to that Part;

'the Board' means the Board of the Pension Protection Fund;

'occupational pension scheme' has the same meaning as in the Pension Schemes Act 1993;

'prescribed' means prescribed by regulations;

'PPF compensation' means compensation payable under Chapter 3 of Part 2 of the Pensions Act 2004 (pension protection) or any provision in force in Northern Ireland corresponding to that Chapter;

'regulations' means regulations made by the Lord Chancellor;

'shareable rights' are rights in relation to which pension sharing is available under Chapter 1 of Part 4 of the Welfare Reform and Pensions Act 1999 or any provision in force in Northern Ireland corresponding to that Chapter;

'transfer notice' has the same meaning as in section 160 of the Pensions Act 2004 or any corresponding provision in force in Northern Ireland.

...

26 Commencement of proceedings for ancillary relief etc.

(1) Where a petition for divorce, nullity of marriage or judicial separation has been presented, then, subject to subsection (2) below, proceedings for maintenance pending suit under section 22 above, for a financial provision order under section 23 above, or for a property adjustment order may be begun, subject to and in accordance with rules of court, at any time after the presentation of the petition.

(2) Rules of court may provide, in such cases as may be prescribed by the rules—

    (a) that applications for any such relief as is mentioned in subsection (1) above shall be made in the petition or answer; and

    (b) that applications for any such relief which are not so made, or are not made until after the expiration of such period following the presentation of the petition or filing of the answer as may be so prescribed, shall be made only with the leave of the court.

Financial provision in case of neglect to maintain

27 Financial provision orders etc., in case of neglect by party to marriage to maintain other party or child of the family

(1) Either party to a marriage may apply to the court for an order under this section on the ground that the other party to the marriage (in this section referred to as the respondent)—

    (a) has failed to provide reasonable maintenance for the applicant, or

    (b) has failed to provide, or to make a proper contribution towards, reasonable maintenance for any child of the family.

(2) The court shall not entertain an application under this section unless—

    (a) the applicant or the respondent is domiciled in England and Wales on the date of the application; or

    (b) the applicant has been habitually resident there throughout the period of one year ending with that date; or

    (c) the respondent is resident there on that date.

(3) Where an application under this section is made on the ground mentioned in subsection (1)(a) above, then, in deciding—

    (a) whether the respondent has failed to provide reasonable maintenance for the applicant, and

    (b) what order, if any, to make under this section in favour of the applicant, the court shall have regard to all the circumstances of the case including the matters mentioned in section 25(2) above, and where an application is also made under this section in respect of a child of the family who has not attained the age of eighteen, first consideration shall be given to the welfare of the child while a minor.

(3A) Where an application under this section is made on the ground mentioned in subsection (1)(b) above then, in deciding—

    (a) whether the respondent has failed to provide, or to make a proper contribution towards, reasonable maintenance for the child of the family to whom the application relates, and

    (b) what order, if any, to make under this section in favour of the child,

the court shall have regard to all the circumstances of the case including the matters mentioned in section 25(3)(a) to (e) above, and where the child of the family to whom the application relates is not the child of the respondent, including also the matters mentioned in section 25(4) above.

(3B) In relation to an application under this section on the ground mentioned in subsection (1)(a) above, section 25(2)(c) above shall have effect as if for the reference therein to the breakdown of the marriage there were substituted a reference to the failure to provide reasonable maintenance for the applicant, and in relation to an application under this section on the ground mentioned in subsection (1)(b) above, section 25(2)(c) above (as it applies by virtue of section 25(3)(e) above) shall have effect as if for the reference therein to the breakdown of the marriage there were substituted a reference to the failure to provide, or to make a proper contribution towards, reasonable maintenance for the child of the family to whom the application relates.

(5) Where on an application under this section it appears to the court that the applicant or any child of the family to whom the application relates is in immediate need of financial assistance, but it is not yet possible to determine what order, if any, should be made on the application, the court may make an interim order for maintenance, that is to say, an order requiring the respondent to make to the applicant until the determination of the application such periodical payments as the court thinks reasonable.

(6) Where on an application under this section the applicant satisfies the court of any ground mentioned in subsection (1) above, the court may make any one or more of the following orders, that is to say—

    (a) an order that the respondent shall make to the applicant such periodical payments, for such term, as may be specified in the order;

    (b) an order that the respondent shall secure to the applicant, to the satisfaction of the court, such periodical payments, for such term, as may be so specified;

    (c) an order that the respondent shall pay to the applicant such lump sum as may be so specified;

    (d) an order that the respondent shall make to such person as may be specified in the order for the benefit of the child to whom the application relates, or to that child, such periodical payments, for such term, as may be so specified;

    (e) an order that the respondent shall secure to such person as may be so specified for the benefit of that child, or to that child, to the satisfaction of the court, such periodical payments, for such term, as may be so specified;

    (f) an order that the respondent shall pay to such person as may be so specified for the benefit of that child, or to that child, such lump sum as may be so specified;

subject, however, in the case of an order under paragraph (d), (e) or (f) above, to the restrictions imposed by section 29(1) and (3) below on the making of financial provision orders in favour of children who have attained the age of eighteen.

(6A) An application for the variation under section 31 of this Act of a periodical payments order or secured periodical payments order made under this section in favour of a child may, if the child has attained the age of sixteen, be made by the child himself.

(6B) Where a periodical payments order made in favour of a child under this section ceases to have effect on the date on which the child attains the age of sixteen or at any time after that date but before or on the date on which he attains the age of eighteen, then if, on an application made to the court for an order under this subsection, it appears to the court that—

>   (a) the child is, will be or (if an order were made under this subsection) would be receiving instruction at an educational establishment or undergoing training for a trade, profession or vocation, whether or not he also is, will be or would be in gainful employment; or
>   (b) there are special circumstances which justify the making of an order under this subsection,

the court shall have power by order to revive the first mentioned order from such date as the court may specify, not being earlier than the date of the making of the application, and to exercise its power under section 31 of this Act in relation to any order so revived.

(7) Without prejudice to the generality of subsection (6)(c) or (f) above, an order under this section for the payment of a lump sum—

>   (a) may be made for the purpose of enabling any liabilities or expenses reasonably incurred in maintaining the applicant or any child of the family to whom the application relates before the making of the application to be met;
>   (b) may provide for the payment of that sum by instalments of such amount as may be specified in the order and may require the payment of the instalments to be secured to the satisfaction of the court.

Additional provisions with respect to financial provision and property adjustment orders

28 Duration of continuing financial provision orders in favour of party to marriage, and effect of remarriage or formation of a civil partnership

(1) Subject in the case of an order made on or after the grant of a decree of divorce or nullity of marriage to the provisions of sections 25A(2) above and 31(7) below, the term to be specified in a periodical payments or secured periodical payments order in favour of a party to a marriage shall be such term as the court thinks fit, except that the term shall not begin before or extend beyond the following limits, that is to say—

>   (a) in the case of a periodical payments order, the term shall begin not earlier than the date of the making of an application for the order, and shall be so defined as not to extend beyond the death of either of the parties to the marriage or, where the order is made on or after the grant of a decree of divorce or nullity of marriage, the remarriage of, or formation of a civil partnership by, the party in whose favour the order is made; and
>   (b) in the case of a secured periodical payments order, the term shall begin not earlier than the date of the making of an application for the order, and shall be so defined as not to extend beyond the death or, where the order is made on or after the grant of such a decree, the remarriage of, or formation of a civil partnership by, the party in whose favour the order is made.

(1A) Where a periodical payments or secured periodical payments order in favour of a party to a marriage is made on or after the grant of a decree of divorce or nullity of marriage, the court may direct that that party shall not be entitled to apply under section 31 below for the extension of the term specified in the order.

(2) Where a periodical payments or secured periodical payments order in favour of a party to a marriage is made otherwise than on or after the grant of a decree of divorce or nullity of marriage, and the marriage in question is subsequently dissolved or annulled but the order continues in force, the order shall, notwithstanding anything in it, cease to have effect on the remarriage of, or formation of a civil partnership by, that party, except in relation to any arrears due under or on the date of the remarriage or formation of the civil partnership.

(3) If after the grant of a decree dissolving or annulling a marriage either party to that marriage remarries, whether at any time before or after the commencement of this Act or forms a civil partnership, that party shall not be entitled to apply, by reference to the grant of that decree, for a financial provision order in his or her favour, or for a property adjustment order, against the other party to that marriage.

29   Duration of continuing financial provision orders in favour of children, and age limit on making certain orders in their favour

(1) Subject to subsection (3) below, no financial provision order and no order for a transfer of property under section 24(1)(a) above shall be made in favour of a child who has attained the age of eighteen.

(2) The term to be specified in a periodical payments or secured periodical payments order in favour of a child may begin with the date of the making of an application for the order in question or any later date or a date ascertained in accordance with subsection (5) or (6) below but—

> (a) shall not in the first instance extend beyond the date of the birthday of the child next following his attaining the upper limit of the compulsory school age (construed in accordance with section 8 of the Education Act 1996) unless the court considers that in the circumstances of the case the welfare of the child requires that it should extend to a later date; and
>
> (b) shall not in any event, subject to subsection (3) below, extend beyond the date of the child's eighteenth birthday.

(3) Subsection (1) above, and paragraph (b) of subsection (2), shall not apply in the case of a child, if it appears to the court that—

> (a) the child is, or will be, or if an order were made without complying with either or both of those provisions would be, receiving instruction at an educational establishment or undergoing training for a trade, profession or vocation, whether or not he is also or will also be, in gainful employment; or
>
> (b) there are special circumstances which justify the making of an order without complying with either or both of those provisions.

(4) Any periodical payments order in favour of a child shall, notwithstanding anything in the order, cease to have effect on the death of the person liable to make payments under the order, except in relation to any arrears due under the order on the date of the death.

(5) Where—

> (a) a maintenance calculation ('the current calculation') is in force with respect to a child; and
>
> (b) an application is made under Part II of this Act for a periodical payments or secured periodical payments order in favour of that child—
>> (i)   in accordance with section 8 of the Child Support Act 1991; and
>> (ii) before the end of the period of 6 months beginning with the making of the current calculation,

the term to be specified in any such order made on that application may be expressed to begin on, or at any time after, the earliest permitted date.

(6) For the purposes of subsection (5) above, 'the earliest permitted date' is whichever is the later of—

> (a) the date 6 months before the application is made; or
>
> (b) the date on which the current calculation took effect or, where successive maintenance calculations have been continuously in force with respect to a child, on which the first of those calculations took effect.

(7) Where—

> (a) a maintenance calculation ceases to have effect by or under a provision of the Child Support Act 1991; and

(b) an application is made before the end of the period of 6 months beginning with the relevant date, for a periodical payments or secured periodical payments order in favour of a child with respect to whom that maintenance calculation was in force immediately before it ceased to have effect,

the term to be specified in any such order made on that application may begin with the date on which that maintenance calculation ceased to have effect, or any later date.

(8) In subsection (7)(b) above—

(a) where the maintenance calculation ceased to have effect, the relevant date is the date on which it so ceased;

30   Direction for settlement of instrument for securing payments or effecting property adjustment

Where the court decides to make a financial provision order requiring any payments to be secured or a property adjustment order—

(a) it may direct that the matter be referred to one of the conveyancing counsel of the court for him to settle a proper instrument to be executed by all necessary parties; and

(b) where the order is to be made in proceedings for divorce, nullity of marriage or judicial separation it may, if it thinks fit, defer the grant of the decree in question until the instrument has been duly executed.

Variation, discharge and enforcement of certain orders etc.

31   Variation, discharge etc., of certain orders for financial relief

(1) Where the court has made an order to which this section applies, then, subject to the provisions of this section and of section 28(1A) above, the court shall have power to vary or discharge the order or to suspend any provision thereof temporarily and to revive the operation of any provision so suspended.

(2) This section applies to the following orders, that is to say—

(a) any order for maintenance pending suit and any interim order for maintenance;

(b) any periodical payments order;

(c) any secured periodical payments order;

(d) any order made by virtue of section 23(3)(c) or 27(7)(b) above (provision for payment of a lump sum by instalments);

(dd) any deferred order made by virtue of section 23(1)(c) (lump sums) which includes provision made by virtue of—

(i)   section 25B(4) or

(ii) section 25C,

(provision in respect of pension rights);

(e) any order for a settlement of property under section 24(1)(b) or for a variation of settlement under section 24(1)(c) or (d) above, being an order made on or after the grant of a decree of judicial separation;

(f) any order made under section 24A(1) above for the sale of property;

(g) a pension sharing order under section 24B above which is made at a time before the decree has been made absolute;

(2A) Where the court has made an order referred to in subsection (2)(a), (b) or (c) above, then, subject to the provisions of this section, the court shall have power to remit the payment of any arrears due under the order or of any part thereof.

(2B) Where the court has made an order referred to in subsection (2)(dd)(ii) above, this section shall cease to apply to the order on the death of either of the parties to the marriage.

(3) The powers exercisable by the court under this section in relation to an order shall be exercisable also in relation to any instrument executed in pursuance of the order.

(4) The court shall not exercise the powers conferred by this section in relation to an order for a settlement under section 24(1)(b) or for a variation of settlement under section 24(1)(c) or (d) above except on an application made in proceedings—

(a) for the rescission of the decree of judicial separation by reference to which the order was made, or

(b) for the dissolution of the marriage in question.

(4A) In relation to an order which falls within paragraph (g) of subsection (2) above ('the subsection (2) order')—

(a) the powers conferred by this section may be exercised—

(i) only on an application made before the subsection (2) order has or, but for paragraph (b) below, would have taken effect; and

(ii) only if, at the time when the application is made, the decree has not been made absolute; and

(b) an application made in accordance with paragraph (a) above prevents the subsection (2) order from taking effect before the application has been dealt with.

(4B) No variation of a pension sharing order shall be made so as to take effect before the decree is made absolute.

(4C) The variation of a pension sharing order prevents the order taking effect before the end of such period after the making of the variation as may be prescribed by regulations made by the Lord Chancellor.

(5) Subject to subsections (7A) to (7G) below and without prejudice to any power exercisable by virtue of subsection (2)(d), (dd), (e) or (g) above or otherwise than by virtue of this section, no property adjustment order or pension sharing order shall be made on an application for the variation of a periodical payments or secured periodical payments order made (whether in favour of a party to a marriage or in favour of a child of the family) under section 23 above, and no order for the payment of a lump sum shall be made on an application for the variation of a periodical payments or secured periodical payments order in favour of a party to a marriage (whether made under section 23 or under section 27 above).

(6) Where the person liable to make payments under a secured periodical payments order has died, an application under this section relating to that order (and to any order made under section 24A(1) above which requires the proceeds of sale of property to be used for securing those payments) may be made by the person entitled to payments under the periodical payments order or by the personal representatives of the deceased person, but no such application shall, except with the permission of the court, be made after the end of the period of six months from the date on which representation in regard to the estate of that person is first taken out.

(7) In exercising the powers conferred by this section the court shall have regard to all the circumstances of the case, first consideration being given to the welfare while a minor of any child of the family who has not attained the age of eighteen, and the circumstances of the case shall include any change in any of the matters to which the court was required to have regard when making the order to which the application relates, and—

(a) in the case of a periodical payments or secured periodical payments order made on or after the grant of a decree of divorce or nullity of marriage, the court shall consider whether in all the circumstances and after having regard to any such change it would be appropriate to vary the order so that payments under the order are required to be made or secured only for such further period as will in the opinion of the court be sufficient (in the light of any proposed exercise by the court, where the marriage has been dissolved of its powers under subsection (7B) below) to enable the party in whose favour the order was made to adjust without undue hardship to the termination of those payments;

(b) in a case where the party against whom the order was made has died, the circumstances of the case shall also include the changed circumstances resulting from his or her death.

(7A) Subsection (7B) below applies where, after the dissolution of a marriage, the court—

(a) discharges a periodical payments order or secured periodical payments order made in favour of a party to the marriage; or

(b) varies such an order so that payments under the order are required to be made or secured only for such further period as is determined by the court.

(7B) The court has power, in addition to any power it has apart from this subsection, to make supplemental provision consisting of any of—

   (a) an order for the payment of a lump sum in favour of a party to the marriage;

   (b) one or more property adjustment orders in favour of a party to the marriage;

  (ba) one or more pension sharing orders;

   (c) a direction that the party in whose favour the original order discharged or varied was made is not entitled to make any further application for—

     (i) a periodical payments or secured periodical payments order, or

    (ii) an extension of the period to which the original order is limited by any variation made by the court.

(7C) An order for the payment of a lump sum made under subsection (7B) above may—

   (a) provide for the payment of that sum by instalments of such amount as may be specified in the order; and

   (b) require the payment of the instalments to be secured to the satisfaction of the court.

(7D) Subsections (7) and (8) of section 22A above apply where the court makes an order for the payment of a lump sum under subsection (7B) above as they apply where it makes such an order under section 22A above.

(7E) If under subsection (7B) above the court makes more than one property adjustment order in favour of the same party to the marriage, each of those orders must fall within a different paragraph of section 21(2) above.

(7F) Sections 24A and 30 above apply where the court makes a property adjustment order under subsection (7B) above as they apply where it makes such an order under section 23A above.

(7G) Subsections (3) to (5) of section 24B above apply in relation to a pension sharing order under subsection (7B) above as they apply in relation to a pension sharing order under that section.

(8) The personal representatives of a deceased person against whom a secured periodical payments order was made shall not be liable for having distributed any part of the estate of the deceased after the expiration of the period of six months referred to in subsection (6) above on the ground that they ought to have taken into account the possibility that the court might permit an application under this section to be made after that period by the person entitled to payments under the order; but this subsection shall not prejudice any power to recover any part of the estate so distributed arising by virtue of the making of an order in pursuance of this section.

(9) In considering for the purposes of subsection (6) above the question when representation was first taken out, a grant limited to settled land or to trust property shall be left out of account and a grant limited to real estate or to personal estate shall be left out of account unless a grant limited to the remainder of the estate has previously been made or is made at the same time.

(10) Where the court, in exercise of its powers under this section, decides to vary or discharge a periodical payments or secured periodical payments order, then, subject to section 28(1) and (2) above, the court shall have power to direct that the variation or discharge shall not take effect until the expiration of such period as may be specified in the order.

(11) Where—

   (a) a periodical payments or secured periodical payments order in favour of more than one child ('the order') is in force;

   (b) the order requires payments specified in it to be made to or for the benefit of more than one child without apportioning those payments between them;

   (c) a maintenance calculation ('the calculation') is made with respect to one or more, but not all, of the children with respect to whom those payments are to be made; and

   (d) an application is made, before the end of the period of 6 months beginning with the date on which the assessment was made, for the variation or discharge of the order, the court may, in exercise of its powers under this section to vary or discharge the order, direct that the variation or discharge shall take effect from the date on which the assessment took effect or any later date.

(12) Where—

 (a) an order ('the child order') of a kind prescribed for the purposes of section 10(1) of the Child Support Act 1991 is affected by a maintenance calculation;

 (b) on the date on which the child order became so affected there was in force a periodical payments or secured periodical payments order ('the spousal order') in favour of a party to a marriage having the care of the child in whose favour the child order was made; and

 (c) an application is made, before the end of the period of 6 months beginning with the date on which the maintenance calculation was made, for the spousal order to be varied or discharged,

the court may, in exercise of its powers under this section to vary or discharge the spousal order, direct that the variation or discharge shall take effect from the date on which the child order became so affected or any later date.

(13) For the purposes of subsection (12) above, an order is affected if it ceases to have effect or is modified by or under section 10 of the Child Support Act 1991.

(14) Subsections (11) and (12) above are without prejudice to any other power of the court to direct that the variation or discharge of an order under this section shall take effect from a date earlier than that on which the order for variation or discharge was made.

(15) The power to make regulations under subsection (4C) above shall be exercisable by statutory instrument which shall be subject to annulment in pursuance of a resolution of either House of Parliament.

32 Payment of certain arrears unenforceable without the leave of the court

(1) A person shall not be entitled to enforce through the High Court or any county court the payment of any arrears due under an order for maintenance pending suit, an interim order for maintenance or any financial provision order without the leave of that court if those arrears became due more than twelve months before proceedings to enforce the payment of them are begun.

(2) The court hearing an application for the grant of leave under this section may refuse leave, or may grant leave subject to such restrictions and conditions (including conditions as to the allowing of time for payment or the making of payments by instalments) as that court thinks proper, or may remit the payment of the arrears or any part thereof.

(3) An application for the grant of leave under this section shall be made in such manner as may be prescribed by rules of court.

33 Orders for repayment in certain cases of sums paid under certain orders

(1) Where on an application made under this section in relation to an order to which this section applies it appears to the court that by reason of—

 (a) a change in the circumstances of the person entitled to, or liable to make, payments under the order since the order was made, or

 (b) the changed circumstances resulting from the death of the person so liable, the amount received by the person entitled to payments under the order in respect of a period after those circumstances changed or after the death of the person liable to make payments under the order, as the case may be, exceeds the amount which the person so liable or his or her personal representatives should have been required to pay, the court may order the respondent to the application to pay to the applicant such sum, not exceeding the amount of the excess, as the court thinks just.

(2) This section applies to the following orders, that is to say—

 (a) any order for maintenance pending suit and any interim order for maintenance;

 (b) any periodical payments order; and

 (c) any secured periodical payments order.

(3) An application under this section may be made by the person liable to make payments under an order to which this section applies or his or her personal representatives and may be made against the person entitled to payments under the order or her or his personal representatives.

(4) An application under this section may be made in proceedings in the High Court or a county court for—

> (a) the variation or discharge of the order to which this section applies, or
>
> (b) leave to enforce, or the enforcement of, the payment of arrears under that order;

but when not made in such proceedings shall be made to a county court, and accordingly references in this section to the court are references to the High Court or a county court, as the circumstances require.

(5) The jurisdiction conferred on a county court by this section shall be exercisable notwithstanding that by reason of the amount claimed in the application the jurisdiction would not but for this subsection be exercisable by a county court.

(6) An order under this section for the payment of any sum may provide for the payment of that sum by instalments of such amount as may be specified in the order.

Consent orders

33A   Consent orders for financial provision or property adjustment

(1) Notwithstanding anything in the preceding provisions of this Part of this Act, on an application for a consent order for financial relief the court may, unless it has reason to think that there are other circumstances into which it ought to inquire, make an order in the terms agreed on the basis only of the prescribed information furnished with the application.

(2) Subsection (1) above applies to an application for a consent order varying or discharging an order for financial relief as it applies to an application for an order for financial relief.

(3) In this section—

'consent order,' in relation to an application for an order, means an order in the terms applied for to which the respondent agrees;

'order for financial relief' means an order under any of sections 23, 24, 24A, 24B or 27 above; and

'prescribed' means prescribed by rules of court.

Maintenance agreements

34   Validity of maintenance agreements

(1) If a maintenance agreement includes a provision purporting to restrict any right to apply to a court for an order containing financial arrangements, then—

> (a) that provision shall be void; but
>
> (b) any other financial arrangements contained in the agreement shall not thereby be rendered void or unenforceable and shall, unless they are void or unenforceable for any other reason (and subject to sections 35 and 36 below), be binding on the parties to the agreement.

(2) In this section and in section 35 below—

'maintenance agreement' means any agreement in writing made, whether before or after the commencement of this Act, between the parties to a marriage, being—

> (a) an agreement containing financial arrangements, whether made during the continuance or after the dissolution or annulment of the marriage; or
>
> (b) a separation agreement which contains no financial arrangements in a case where no other agreement in writing between the same parties contains such arrangements;

'financial arrangements' means provisions governing the rights and liabilities towards one another when living separately of the parties to a marriage (including a marriage which has been dissolved or annulled) in respect of the making or securing of payments or the disposition or use of any property, including such rights and liabilities with respect to the maintenance or education of any child, whether or not a child of the family.

35   Alteration of agreements by court during lives of parties

(1) Where a maintenance agreement is for the time being subsisting and each of the parties to the agreement is for the time being either domiciled or resident in England and Wales, then, subject to subsection (3) below, either party may apply to the court or to a magistrates' court for an order under this section.

(2) If the court to which the application is made is satisfied either—

(a) that by reason of a change in the circumstances in the light of which any financial arrangements contained in the agreement were made or, as the case may be, financial arrangements were omitted from it (including a change foreseen by the parties when making the agreement), the agreement should be altered so as to make different, or, as the case may be, so as to contain, financial arrangements, or

(b) that the agreement does not contain proper financial arrangements with respect to any child of the family,

then subject to subsections (3), (4) and (5) below, that court may by order make such alterations in the agreement—

(i) by varying or revoking any financial arrangements contained in it, or

(ii) by inserting in it financial arrangements for the benefit of one of the parties to the agreement or of a child of the family,

as may appear to that court to be just having regard to all the circumstances, including, if relevant, the matters mentioned in section 25(4) above; and the agreement shall have effect thereafter as if any alteration made by the order had been made by agreement between the parties and for valuable consideration.

(3) A magistrates' court shall not entertain an application under subsection (1) above unless both the parties to the agreement are resident in England and Wales and the court acts in, or is authorised by the Lord Chancellor to act for, a local justice area in which at least one of the parties is resident, and shall not have power to make any order on such an application except—

(a) in a case where the agreement includes no provision for periodical payments by either of the parties, an order inserting provision for the making by one of the parties of periodical payments for the maintenance of the other party or for the maintenance of any child of the family;

(b) in a case where the agreement includes provision for the making by one of the parties of periodical payments, an order increasing or reducing the rate of, or terminating, any of those payments.

(4) Where a court decides to alter, by order under this section, an agreement by inserting provision for the making or securing by one of the parties to the agreement of periodical payments for the maintenance of the other party or by increasing the rate of the periodical payments which the agreement provides shall be made by one of the parties for the maintenance of the other, the term for which the payments or, as the case may be, the additional payments attributable to the increase are to be made under the agreement as altered by the order shall be such term as the court may specify, subject to the following limits, that is to say—

(a) where the payments will not be secured, the term shall be so defined as not to extend beyond the death of either of the parties to the agreement or the remarriage of, or formation of a civil partnership by, the party to whom the payments are to be made;

(b) where the payments will be secured, the term shall be so defined as not to extend beyond the death or remarriage of, or formation of a civil partnership by, that party.

(5) Where a court decides to alter, by order under this section, an agreement by inserting provision for the making or securing by one of the parties to the agreement of periodical payments for the maintenance of a child of the family or by increasing the rate of the periodical payments which the agreement provides shall be made or secured by one of the parties for the maintenance of such a child, then, in deciding the term for which under the agreement as altered by the order the payments, or as the case may be, the additional payments attributable to the increase are to be made or secured for the benefit of the child, the court shall apply the provisions of section 29(2) and (3) above as to age limits as if the order in question were a periodical payments or secured periodical payments order in favour of the child.

(6) For the avoidance of doubt it is hereby declared that nothing in this section or in section 34 above affects any power of a court before which any proceedings between the parties to a maintenance agreement are brought under any other enactment (including a provision of this Act) to make an order containing financial arrangements or any right of either party to apply for such an order in such proceedings.

36 Alteration of agreements by court after death of one party

(1) Where a maintenance agreement within the meaning of section 34 above provides for the continuation of payment under the agreement after the death of one of the parties and that party dies domiciled in England and Wales, the surviving party or the personal representatives of the deceased party may, subject to subsections (2) and (3) below, apply to the High Court or a county court for an order under section 35 above.

(2) An application under this section shall not, except with the permission of the High Court or a county court, be made after the end of the period of six months from the date on which representation in regard to the estate of the deceased is first taken out.

(3) A county court shall not entertain an application under this section, or an application for permission to make an application under this section, unless it would have jurisdiction by virtue of section 22 of the Inheritance (Provision for Family and Dependants) Act 1975 (which confers jurisdiction on county courts in proceedings under that Act if the value of the property mentioned in that section does not exceed £5,000 or such larger sum as may be fixed by order of the Lord Chancellor) to hear and determine proceedings for an order under section 2 of that Act in relation to the deceased's estate.

(4) If a maintenance agreement is altered by a court on an application made in pursuance of subsection (1) above, the like consequences shall ensue as if the alteration had been made immediately before the death by agreement between the parties and for valuable consideration.

(5) The provisions of this section shall not render the personal representatives of the deceased liable for having distributed any part of the estate of the deceased after the expiration of the period of six months referred to in subsection (2) above on the ground that they ought to have taken into account the possibility that a court might permit an application by virtue of this section to be made by the surviving party after that period, but this subsection shall not prejudice any power to recover any part of the estate so distributed arising by virtue of the making of an order in pursuance of this section.

(6) Section 31(9) above shall apply for the purposes of subsection (2) above as it applies for the purposes of subsection (6) of section 31.

(7) Subsection (3) of section 22 of the Inheritance (Provision for Family and Dependants) Act 1975 (which enables rules of court to provide for the transfer from a county court to the High Court or from the High Court to a county court of proceedings for an order under section 2 of that Act) and paragraphs (a) and (b) of subsection (4) of that section (provisions relating to proceedings commenced in county court before coming into force of order of the Lord Chancellor under that section) shall apply in relation to proceedings consisting of any such application as is referred to in subsection (3) above as they apply in relation to proceedings for an order under section 2 of that Act.

Miscellaneous and supplemental

37 Avoidance of transactions intended to prevent or reduce financial relief

(1) For the purposes of this section 'financial relief' means relief under any of the provisions of sections 22, 23, 24, 24B, 27, 31 (except subsection (6)) and 35 above, and any reference in this section to defeating a person's claim for financial relief is a reference to preventing financial relief from being granted to that person, or to that person for the benefit of a child of the family, or reducing the amount of any financial relief which might be so granted, or frustrating or impeding the enforcement of any order which might be or has been made at his instance under any of those provisions.

(2) Where proceedings for financial relief are brought by one person against another, the court may, on the application of the first-mentioned person—

(a) if it is satisfied that the other party to the proceedings is, with the intention of defeating the claim for financial relief, about to make any disposition or to transfer out of the jurisdiction or otherwise deal with any property, make such order as it thinks fit for restraining the other party from so doing or otherwise for protecting the claim;

(b) if it is satisfied that the other party has, with that intention, made a reviewable disposition and that if the disposition were set aside financial relief or different financial relief would be granted to the applicant, make an order setting aside the disposition;

(c) if it is satisfied, in a case where an order has been obtained under any of the provisions mentioned in subsection (1) above by the applicant against the other party, that the other party has, with that intention, made a reviewable disposition, make an order setting aside the disposition;

and an application for the purposes of paragraph (b) above shall be made in the proceedings for the financial relief in question.

(3) Where the court makes an order under subsection (2)(b) or (c) above setting aside a disposition it shall give such consequential directions as it thinks fit for giving effect to the order (including directions requiring the making of any payments or the disposal of any property).

(4) Any disposition made by the other party to the proceedings for financial relief in question (whether before or after the commencement of those proceedings) is a reviewable disposition for the purposes of subsection (2)(b) and (c) above unless it was made for valuable consideration (other than marriage) to a person who, at the time of the disposition, acted in relation to it in good faith and without notice of any intention on the part of the other party to defeat the applicant's claim for financial relief.

(5) Where an application is made under this section with respect to a disposition which took place less than three years before the date of the application or with respect to a disposition or other dealing with property which is about to take place and the court is satisfied—

(a) in a case falling within subsection (2)(a) or (b) above, that the disposition or other dealing would (apart from this section) have the consequence, or

(b) in a case falling within subsection (2)(c) above, that the disposition has had the consequence,

of defeating the applicant's claim for financial relief, it shall be presumed, unless the contrary is shown, that the person who disposed of or is about to dispose of or deal with the property did so or, as the case may be, is about to do so, with the intention of defeating the applicant's claim for financial relief.

(6) In this section 'disposition' does not include any provision contained in a will or codicil but, with that exception, includes any conveyance, assurance or gift of property of any description, whether made by an instrument or otherwise.

(7) This section does not apply to a disposition made before 1st January 1968.

38 Order for repayment in certain cases of sums paid after cessation of order by reason of remarriage or formation of civil partnership

(1) Where—

    (a) a periodical payments or secured periodical payments order in favour of a party to a marriage (hereafter in this section referred to as 'a payments order') has ceased to have effect by reason of the remarriage of, or formation of a civil partnership by, that party, and

    (b) the person liable to make payments under the order or his or her personal representatives made payments in accordance with it in respect of a period after the date of the remarriage or formation of the civil partnership in the mistaken belief that the order was still subsisting,

the person so liable or his or her personal representatives shall not be entitled to bring proceedings in respect of a cause of action arising out of the circumstances mentioned in paragraphs (a) and (b) above against the person entitled to payments under the order or her or his personal representatives, but may instead make an application against that person or her or his personal representatives under this section.

(2) On an application under this section the court may order the respondent to pay to the applicant a sum equal to the amount of the payments made in respect of the period mentioned in subsection (1)(b) above or, if it appears to the court that it would be unjust to make that order, it may either order the respondent to pay to the applicant such lesser sum as it thinks fit or dismiss the application.

(3) An application under this section may be made in proceedings in the High Court or a county court for leave to enforce, or the enforcement of, payment of arrears under the order in question, but when not made in such proceedings shall be made to a county court; and accordingly references in this section to the court are references to the High Court or a county court, as the circumstances require.

(4) The jurisdiction conferred on a county court by this section shall be exercisable notwithstanding that by reason of the amount claimed in the application the jurisdiction would not but for this subsection be exercisable by a county court.

(5) An order under this section for the payment of any sum may provide for the payment of that sum by instalments of such amount as may be specified in the order.

(6) The designated officer for a magistrates' court to whom any payments under a payments order are required to be made, and the collecting officer under an attachment of earnings order made to secure payments under a payments order, shall not be liable—

    (a) in the case of the designated officer, for any act done by him in pursuance of the payments order after the date on which that order ceased to have effect by reason of the remarriage of, or formation of a civil partnership by, the person entitled to payments under it, and

    (b) in the case of the collecting officer, for any act done by him after that date in accordance with any enactment or rule of court specifying how payments made to him in compliance with the attachment of earnings order are to be dealt with,

if, but only if, the act was one which he would have been under a duty to do had the payments order not so ceased to have effect and the act was done before notice in writing of the fact that the person so entitled had remarried or formed civil partnership was given to him by or on behalf of that person, the person liable to make payments under the payments order or the personal representatives of either of those persons.

(7) In this section 'collecting officer,' in relation to an attachment of earnings order, means the officer of the High Court, the registrar of a county court or the designated officer for a magistrates' court to whom a person makes payments in compliance with the order.

39 Settlement, etc., made in compliance with a property adjustment order may be avoided on bankruptcy of settlor

The fact that a settlement or transfer of property had to be made in order to comply with a property adjustment order shall not prevent that settlement or transfer from being a transaction in respect of which an order may be made under section 339 or 340 of the Insolvency Act 1986 (transactions at an undervalue and preferences).

40 Payments etc., under order made in favour of person suffering from mental disorder

(1) Where the court makes an order under this Part of this Act requiring payments (including a lump sum payment) to be made, or property to be transferred, to a party to a marriage and the court is satisfied that the person in whose favour the order is made ("P") lacks capacity (within the meaning of the Mental Capacity Act 2005) in relation to the provisions of the order then, subject to any order, direction or authority made or given in relation to P under that Act, the court may order the payments to be made, or as the case may be, the property to be transferred, to such person ("D") as it may direct.

(2) In carrying out any functions of his in relation to an order made under subsection (1), D must act in P's best interests (within the meaning of that Act).

40A Appeals relating to pension sharing orders which have taken effect

(1) Subsections (2) and (3) below apply where an appeal against a pension sharing order is begun on or after the day on which the order takes effect.

(2) If the pension sharing order relates to a person's rights under a pension arrangement, the appeal court may not set aside or vary the order if the person responsible for the pension arrangement has acted to his detriment in reliance on the taking effect of the order.

(3) If the pension sharing order relates to a person's shareable state scheme rights, the appeal court may not set aside or vary the order if the Secretary of State has acted to his detriment in reliance on the taking effect of the order.

(4) In determining for the purposes of subsection (2) or (3) above whether a person has acted to his detriment in reliance on the taking effect of the order, the appeal court may disregard any detriment which in its opinion is insignificant.

(5) Where subsection (2) or (3) above applies, the appeal court may make such further orders (including one or more pension sharing orders) as it thinks fit for the purpose of putting the parties in the position it considers appropriate.

(6) Section 24C above only applies to a pension sharing order under this section if the decision of the appeal court can itself be the subject of an appeal.

(7) In subsection (2) above, the reference to the person responsible for the pension arrangement is to be read in accordance with section 25D(4) above.

PART III   PROTECTION, CUSTODY ETC., OF CHILDREN

41 Restrictions on decrees for dissolution, annulment or separation affecting children

(1) In any proceedings for a decree of divorce or nullity of marriage, or a decree of judicial separation, the court shall consider—

    (a) whether there are any children of the family to whom this section applies; and

    (b) where there are any such children, whether (in the light of the arrangements which have been, or are proposed to be, made for their upbringing and welfare) it should exercise any of its powers under the Children Act 1989 with respect to any of them.

(2) Where, in any case to which this section applies, it appears to the court that—

    (a) the circumstances of the case require it, or are likely to require it, to exercise any of its powers under the Act of 1989 with respect to any such child;

    (b) it is not in a position to exercise that power or (as the case may be) those powers without giving further consideration to the case; and

    (c) there are exceptional circumstances which make it desirable in the interests of the child that the court should give a direction under this section, it may direct that the decree of divorce or nullity is not to be made absolute, or that the decree of judicial separation is not to be granted, until the court orders otherwise.

(3) This section applies to—

(a) any child of the family who has not reached the age of sixteen at the date when the court considers the case in accordance with the requirements of this section; and

(b) any child of the family who has reached that age at that date and in relation to whom the court directs that this section shall apply.

PART IV   MISCELLANEOUS AND SUPPLEMENTAL

...

48   Evidence

(1) The evidence of a husband or wife shall be admissible in any proceedings to prove that marital intercourse did or did not take place between them during any period.

(2) In any proceedings for nullity of marriage, evidence on the question of sexual capacity shall be heard in camera unless in any case the judge is satisfied that in the interests of justice any such evidence ought to be heard in open court.

49   Parties to proceedings under this Act

(1) Where in a petition for divorce or judicial separation, or in any other pleading praying for either form of relief, one party to a marriage alleges that the other has committed adultery, he or she shall make the person alleged to have committed adultery with the other party to the marriage a party to the proceedings unless excused by the court on special grounds from doing so.

(2) Rules of court may, either generally or in such case as may be prescribed by the rules, exclude the application of subsection (1) above where the person alleged to have committed adultery with the other party to the marriage is not named in the petition or other pleading.

(3) Where in pursuance of subsection (1) above a person is made a party to proceedings for divorce or judicial separation, the court may, if after the close of the evidence on the part of the person making the allegation of adultery it is of opinion that there is not sufficient evidence against the person so made a party, dismiss him or her from the suit.

(4) Rules of court may make provision, in cases not failing within subsection (1) above, with respect to the joinder as parties to proceedings under this Act of persons involved in allegations of adultery or other improper conduct made in those proceedings, and with respect to the dismissal from such proceedings of any parties so joined, and rules of court made by virtue of this subsection may make different provision for different cases.

(5) In every case in which adultery with any party to a suit is alleged against any person not made a party to the suit or in which the court considers, in the interest of any person not already a party to the suit, that that person should be made a party to the suit, the court may if it thinks fit allow that person to intervene upon such terms, if any, as the court thinks just.

52   Interpretation

(1) In this Act—

'child', in relation to one or both of the parties to a marriage, includes an illegitimate child of that party or, as the case may be, of both parties;

'child of the family,' in relation to the parties to a marriage, means—

(a) a child of both of those parties; and

(b) any other child, not being a child who is placed with those parties as foster parents by a local authority or voluntary organisation, who has been treated by both of those parties as a child of their family;

'the court' (except where the context otherwise requires) means the High Court or, where a county court has jurisdiction by virtue of Part V of the Matrimonial and Family Proceedings Act 1984, a county court;

'education' includes training;

'maintenance calculation' has the same meaning as it has in the Child Support Act 1991 by virtue of section 54 of that Act as read with any regulations in force under that section;

(2) In this Act—

(a) references to financial provision orders, periodical payments and secured periodical payments orders and orders for the payment of a lump sum, and references to property adjustment orders, shall be construed in accordance with section 21 above;

(aa) references to pension sharing orders shall be construed in accordance with section 21A above; and

(b) references to orders for maintenance pending suit and to interim orders for maintenance shall be construed respectively in accordance with section 22 and section 27(5) above.

(3) For the avoidance of doubt it is hereby declared that references in this Act to remarriage include references to a marriage which is by law void or voidable.

(3A) References in this Act to the formation of a civil partnership by a person include references to a civil partnership which is by law void or voidable.

(4) Except where the contrary intention is indicated, references in this Act to any enactment include references to that enactment as amended, extended or applied by or under any subsequent enactment, including this Act.

. . .

Domicile and Matrimonial Proceedings Act 1973
(1973 c. 45)

PART I   DOMICILE

Husband and wife

1   Abolition of wife's dependent domicile

(1) Subject to subsection (2) below, the domicile of a married woman as at any time after the coming into force of this section shall, instead of being the same as her husband's by virtue only of marriage, be ascertained by reference to the same factors as in the case of any other individual capable of having an independent domicile.

(2) Where immediately before this section came into force a woman was married and then had her husband's domicile by dependence, she is to be treated as retaining that domicile (as a domicile of choice, if it is not also her domicile of origin) unless and until it is changed by acquisition or revival of another domicile either on or after the coming into force of this section.

(3) This section extends to England and Wales, Scotland and Northern Ireland.

Minors and pupils

3   Age at which independent domicile can be acquired

(1) The time at which a person first becomes capable of having an independent domicile shall be when he attains the age of sixteen or marries under that age; and in the case of a person who immediately before 1 January 1974 was incapable of having an independent domicile, but had then attained the age of sixteen or been married, it shall be that date.

(2) This section extends to England and Wales and Northern Ireland (but not to Scotland).

4   Dependent domicile of child not living with his father

(1) Subsection (2) of this section shall have effect with respect to the dependent domicile of a child as at any time after the coming into force of this section when his father and mother are alive but living apart.

(2) The child's domicile as at that time shall be that of his mother if—
    (a) he then has his home with her and has no home with his father; or
    (b) he has at any time had her domicile by virtue of paragraph (a) above and has not since had a home with his father.

(3) As at any time after the coming into force of this section, the domicile of a child whose mother is dead shall be that which she last had before she died if at her death he had her domicile by virtue of subsection (2) above and he has not since had a home with his father.

(4) Nothing in this section prejudices any existing rule of law as to cases in which a child's domicile is regarded as being, by dependence, that of his mother.

(5) In this section, 'child' means a person incapable of having an independent domicile.

(6) This section extends to England and Wales, Scotland and Northern Ireland.

PART II   JURISDICTION IN MATRIMONIAL PROCEEDINGS (ENGLAND AND WALES)

5 Jurisdiction of High Court and county courts

(1) Subsections (2) to (5) below shall have effect, subject to section 6(3) and (4) of this Act, with respect to the jurisdiction of the court to entertain—
    (a) proceedings for divorce, judicial separation or nullity of marriage; and
    (b) proceedings for death to be presumed and a marriage to be dissolved in pursuance of section 19 of the Matrimonial Causes Act 1973;

. . .

(4) The court shall have jurisdiction to entertain proceedings for death to be presumed and a marriage to be dissolved if (and only if) the petitioner—
    (a) is domiciled in England and Wales on the date when the proceedings are begun; or
    (b) was habitually resident in England and Wales throughout the period of one year ending with that date.

. . .

Inheritance (Provision for Family and Dependants) Act 1975
(1975 c. 63)

1 Application for financial provision from deceased's estate

(1) Where after the commencement of this Act a person dies domiciled in England and Wales and is survived by any of the following persons:—
    (a) the spouse or civil partner of the deceased;
    (b) a former spouse or former civil partner of the deceased, but not one who has formed a subsequent marriage or civil partnership;
    (ba) any person (not being a person included in paragraph (a) or (b) above) to whom subsection (1A) or (1B) below applies;
    (c) a child of the deceased;
    (d) any person (not being a child of the deceased) who, in the case of any marriage or civil partnership to which the deceased was at any time a party, was treated by the deceased as a child of the family in relation to that marriage;
    (e) any person (not being a person included in the foregoing paragraphs of this subsection) who immediately before the death of the deceased was being maintained, either wholly or partly, by the deceased;
that person may apply to the court for an order under section 2 of this Act on the ground that the disposition of the deceased's estate effected by his will or the law relating to intestacy, or

the combination of his will and that law, is not such as to make reasonable financial provision for the applicant.

(1A) This subsection applies to a person if the deceased died on or after 1st January 1996 and, during the whole of the period of two years ending immediately before the date when the deceased died, the person was living—

    (a) in the same household as the deceased, and

    (b) as the husband or wife of the deceased.

(1B) This subsection applies to a person if for the whole of the period of two years ending immediately before the date when the deceased died the person was living—

    (a) in the same household as the deceased, and

    (b) as the civil partner of the deceased.

(2) In this Act 'reasonable financial provision'—

    (a) in the case of an application made by virtue of subsection (1)(a) above by the husband or wife of the deceased (except where the marriage with the deceased was the subject of a decree of judicial separation and at the date of death the decree was in force and the separation was continuing), means such financial provision as it would be reasonable in all the circumstances of the case for a husband or wife to receive, whether or not that provision is required for his or her maintenance;

    (aa) in the case of an application made by virtue of subsection (1)(a) above by the civil partner of the deceased (except where, at the date of death, a separation order under Chapter 2 of Part 2 of the Civil Partnership Act 2004 was in force in relation to the civil partnership and the separation was continuing), means such financial provision as it would be reasonable in all the circumstances of the case for a civil partner to receive, whether or not that provision is required for his or her maintenance;

    (b) in the case of any other application made by virtue of subsection (1) above, means such financial provision as it would be reasonable in all the circumstances of the case for the applicant to receive for his maintenance.

(3) For the purposes of subsection (1)(e) above, a person shall be treated as being maintained by the deceased, either wholly or partly, as the case may be, if the deceased, otherwise than for full valuable consideration, was making a substantial contribution in money or money's worth towards the reasonable needs of that person.

2   Powers of court to make orders

(1) Subject to the provisions of this Act, where an application is made for an order under this section, the court may, if it is satisfied that the disposition of the deceased's estate effected by his will or the law relating to intestacy, or the combination of his will and that law, is not such as to make reasonable financial provision for the applicant, make any one or more of the following orders:—

    (a) an order for the making to the applicant out of the net estate of the deceased of such periodical payments and for such term as may be specified in the order;

    (b) an order for the payment to the applicant out of that estate of a lump sum of such amount as may be so specified;

    (c) an order for the transfer to the applicant of such property comprised in that estate as may be so specified;

    (d) an order for the settlement for the benefit of the applicant of such property comprised in that estate as may be so specified;

    (e) an order for the acquisition out of property comprised in that estate of such property as may be so specified and for the transfer of the property so acquired to the applicant or for the settlement thereof for his benefit;

    (f) an order varying any ante-nuptial or post-nuptial settlement (including such a settlement made by will) made on the parties to a marriage to which the deceased was one of the parties, the variation being for the benefit of the surviving party to that marriage, or any child of that marriage, or any person who was treated by the deceased as a child of the family in relation to that marriage.

(g) an order varying any settlement made—
  (i)   during the subsistence of a civil partnership formed by the deceased, or
  (ii) in anticipation of the formation of a civil partnership by the deceased,
  on the civil partners (including such a settlement made by will), the variation being for the benefit of the surviving civil partner, or any child of both the civil partners, or any person who was treated by the deceased as a child of the family in relation to that civil partnership.

(2) An order under subsection (1)(a) above providing for the making out of the net estate of the deceased of periodical payments may provide for—
  (a) payments of such amount as may be specified in the order,
  (b) payments equal to the whole of the income of the net estate or of such portion thereof as may be so specified,
  (c) payments equal to the whole of the income of such part of the net estate as the court may direct to be set aside or appropriated for the making out of the income thereof of payments under this section,
or may provide for the amount of the payments or any of them to be determined in any other way the court thinks fit.

(3) Where an order under subsection (1)(a) above provides for the making of payments of an amount specified in the order, the order may direct that such part of the net estate as may be so specified shall be set aside or appropriated for the making out of the income thereof of those payments; but no larger part of the net estate shall be so set aside or appropriated than is sufficient, at the date of the order, to produce by the income thereof the amount required for the making of those payments.

(4) An order under this section may contain such consequential and supplemental provisions as the court thinks necessary or expedient for the purpose of giving effect to the order or for the purpose of securing that the order operates fairly as between one beneficiary of the estate of the deceased and another and may, in particular, but without prejudice to the generality of this subsection—
  (a) order any person who holds any property which forms part of the net estate of the deceased to make such payment or transfer such property as may be specified in the order;
  (b) vary the disposition of the deceased's estate effected by the will or the law relating to intestacy, or by both the will and the law relating to intestacy, in such manner as the court thinks fair and reasonable having regard to the provisions of the order and all the circumstances of the case;
  (c) confer on the trustees of any property which is the subject of an order under this section such powers as appear to the court to be necessary or expedient.

3   Matters to which court is to have regard in exercising powers under s. 2

(1) Where an application is made for an order under section 2 of this Act, the court shall, in determining whether the disposition of the deceased's estate effected by his will or the law relating to intestacy, or the combination of his will and that law, is such as to make reasonable financial provision for the applicant and, if the court considers that reasonable financial provision has not been made, in determining whether and in what manner it shall exercise its powers under that section, have regard to the following matters, that is to say—
  (a) the financial resources and financial needs which the applicant has or is likely to have in the foreseeable future;
  (b) the financial resources and financial needs which any other applicant for an order under section 2 of this Act has or is likely to have in the foreseeable future;
  (c) the financial resources and financial needs which any beneficiary of the estate of the deceased has or is likely to have in the foreseeable future;

  (d) any obligations and responsibilities which the deceased had towards any appli-
      cant for an order under the said section 2 or towards any beneficiary of the estate
      of the deceased;
  (e) the size and nature of the net estate of the deceased;
  (f) any physical or mental disability of any applicant for an order under the said
      section 2 or any beneficiary of the estate of the deceased;
  (g) any other matter, including the conduct of the applicant or any other person,
      which in the circumstances of the case the court may consider relevant.

  (2) This subsection applies, without prejudice to the generality of paragraph (g) of
subsection (1) above, where an application for an order under section 2 of the Act is made by
virtue of section 1(1)(a) or (b) of this Act. The court shall, in addition to the matters specifically mentioned in paragraphs (a) to (f) of that subsection, have regard to—

  (a) the age of the applicant and the duration of the marriage or civil partnership;
  (b) the contribution made by the applicant to the welfare of the family of the deceased,
      including any contribution made by looking after the home or caring for the family.

In the case of an application by the wife or husband of the deceased, the court shall also, unless
at the date of death a decree of judicial separation was in force and the separation was continuing, have regard to the provision which the applicant might reasonably have expected to
receive if on the day on which the deceased died the marriage, instead of being terminated by
the death, had been terminated by a decree of divorce. In the case of an application by the civil
partner of the deceased, the court shall also, unless at the date of the death a separation order
under Chapter 2 of Part 2 of the Civil Partnership Act 2004 was in force and the separation was
continuing, have regard to the provision which the applicant might reasonably have expected
to receive if on the day on which the deceased died the civil partnership, instead of being
terminated by death, had been terminated by a dissolution order.

  (2A) Without prejudice to the generality of paragraph (g) of subsection (1) above, where an
application for an order under section 2 of this Act is made by virtue of section 1(1)(ba) of this
Act, the court shall, in addition to the matters specifically mentioned in paragraphs (a) to (f)
of that subsection, have regard to—

  (a) the age of the applicant and the length of the period during which the applicant
      lived as the husband or wife or civil partner of the deceased and in the same
      household as the deceased;
  (b) the contribution made by the applicant to the welfare of the family of the deceased,
      including any contribution made by looking after the home or caring for the family.

  (3) Without prejudice to the generality of paragraph (g) of subsection (1) above, where an
application for an order under section 2 of this Act is made by virtue of section 1(1)(c) or
1(1)(d) of this Act, the court shall, in addition to the matters specifically mentioned in
paragraphs (a) to (f) of that subsection, have regard to the manner in which the applicant was
being or in which he might be expected to be educated or trained, and where the application
is made by virtue of section 1(1)(d) the court shall also have regard—

  (a) to whether the deceased had assumed any responsibility for the applicant's
      maintenance and, if so, to the extent to which and the basis upon which the
      deceased assumed that responsibility and to the length of time for which the
      deceased discharged that responsibility;
  (b) to whether in assuming and discharging that responsibility the deceased did so
      knowing that the applicant was not his own child;
  (c) to the liability of any other person to maintain the applicant.

  (4) Without prejudice to the generality of paragraph (g) of subsection (1) above, where an
application for an order under section 2 of this Act is made by virtue of section 1(1)(e) of this
Act, the court shall, in addition to the matters specifically mentioned in paragraphs (a) to (f)
of that subsection, have regard to the extent to which and the basis upon which the deceased
assumed responsibility for the maintenance of the applicant and to the length of time for
which the deceased discharged that responsibility.

(5) In considering the matters to which the court is required to have regard under this section, the court shall take into account the facts as known to the court at the date of the hearing.

4   Time-limit for applications

An application for an order under section 2 of this Act shall not, except with the permission of the court, be made after the end of the period of six months from the date on which representation with respect to the estate of the deceased is first taken out.

5   Interim orders

(1) Where on an application for an order under section 2 of this Act it appears to the court—

(a) that the applicant is in immediate need of financial assistance, but it is not yet possible to determine what order (if any) should be made under that section; and

(b) that property forming part of the net estate of the deceased is or can be made available to meet the need of the applicant;

the court may order that, subject to such conditions or restrictions, if any, as the court may impose and to any further order of the court, there shall be paid to the applicant out of the net estate of the deceased such sum or sums and (if more than one) at such intervals as the court thinks reasonable; and the court may order that, subject to the provisions of this Act, such payments are to be made until such date as the court may specify, not being later than the date on which the court either makes an order under the said section 2 or decides not to exercise its powers under that section.

(2) Subsections (2), (3) and (4) of section 2 of this Act shall apply in relation to an order under this section as they apply in relation to an order under that section.

(3) In determining what order, if any, should be made under this section the court shall, so far as the urgency of the case admits, have regard to the same matters as those to which the court is required to have regard under section 3 of this Act.

(4) An order made under section 2 of this Act may provide that any sum paid to the applicant by virtue of this section shall be treated to such an extent and in such manner as may be provided by that order as having been paid on account of any payment provided for by that order.

(5) In considering the matters to which the court is required to have regard under this section, the court shall take into account the facts as known to the court at the date of the hearing.

(6) In considering the financial resources of any person for the purposes of this section the court shall take into account his earning capacity and in considering the financial needs of any person for the purposes of this section the court shall take into account his financial obligations and responsibilities.

6   Variation, discharge etc of orders for periodical payments

(1) Subject to the provisions of this Act, where the court has made an order under section 2(1)(a) of this Act (in this section referred to as 'the original order') for the making of periodical payments to any person (in this section referred to as 'the original recipient'), the court, on an application under this section, shall have power by order to vary or discharge the original order or to suspend any provision of it temporarily and to revive the operation of any provision so suspended.

(2) Without prejudice to the generality of subsection (1) above, an order made on an application for the variation of the original order may—

(a) provide for the making out of any relevant property of such periodical payments and for such term as may be specified in the order to any person who has applied, or would but for section 4 of this Act be entitled to apply, for an order under section 2 of this Act (whether or not, in the case of an application, an order was made in favour of the applicant);

    (b) provide for the payment out of any relevant property of a lump sum of such amount as may be so specified to the original recipient or to any such person as is mentioned in paragraph (a) above;

    (c) provide for the transfer of the relevant property, or such part thereof as may be so specified, to the original recipient or to any such person as is so mentioned.

(3) Where the original order provides that any periodical payments payable thereunder to the original recipient are to cease on the occurrence of an event specified in the order (other than the formation of a subsequent marriage or civil partnership by a former spouse or former civil partner) or on the expiration of a period so specified, then, if, before the end of the period of six months from the date of the occurrence of that event or of the expiration of that period, an application is made for an order under this section, the court shall have power to make any order which it would have had power to make if the application had been made before that date (whether in favour of the original recipient or any such person as is mentioned in subsection (2)(a) above and whether having effect from that date or from such later date as the court may specify).

(4) Any reference in this section to the original order shall include a reference to an order made under this section and any reference in this section to the original recipient shall include a reference to any person to whom periodical payments are required to be made by virtue of an order under this section.

(5) An application under this section may be made by any of the following persons, that is to say—

    (a) any person who by virtue of section 1(1) of this Act has applied, or would but for section 4 of this Act be entitled to apply, for an order under section 2 of this Act,

    (b) the personal representatives of the deceased,

    (c) the trustees of any relevant property, and

    (d) any beneficiary of the estate of the deceased.

(6) An order under this section may only affect—

    (a) property the income of which is at the date of the order applicable wholly or in part for the making of periodical payments to any person who has applied for an order under this Act, or

    (b) in the case of an application under subsection (3) above in respect of payments which have ceased to be payable on the occurrence of an event or the expiration of a period, property the income of which was so applicable immediately before the occurrence of that event or the expiration of that period, as the case may be,

and any such property as is mentioned in paragraph (a) or (b) above is in subsections (2) and (5) above referred to as 'relevant property'.

(7) In exercising the powers conferred by this section the court shall have regard to all the circumstances of the case, including any change in any of the matters to which the court was required to have regard when making the order to which the application relates.

(8) Where the court makes an order under this section, it may give such consequential directions as it thinks necessary or expedient having regard to the provisions of the order.

(9) No such order as is mentioned in sections 2(1)(d), (e) or (f), 9, 10 or 11 of this Act shall be made on an application under this section.

(10) For the avoidance of doubt it is hereby declared that, in relation to an order which provides for the making of periodical payments which are to cease on the occurrence of an event specified in the order (other than the formation of a subsequent marriage or civil partnership by a former spouse or former civil partner) or on the expiration of a period so specified, the power to vary an order includes powers to provide for the making of periodical payments after the expiration of that period or the occurrence of that event.

7 Payment of lump sums by instalments

(1) An order under section 2(1)(b) or 6(2)(b) of this Act for the payment of a lump sum may provide for the payment of that sum by instalments of such amount as may be specified in the order.

(2) Where an order is made by virtue of subsection (1) above the court shall have power, on an application made by the person to whom the lump sum is payable, by the personal representatives of the deceased or by the trustees of the property out of which the lump sum is payable, to vary that order by varying the number of instalments payable, the amount of any instalment and the date on which any instalment becomes payable.

Property available for financial provision

8   Property treated as part of 'net estate'

(1) Where a deceased person has in accordance with the provisions of any enactment nominated any person to receive any sum of money or other property on his death and that nomination is in force at the time of his death, that sum of money, after deducting therefrom any capital transfer tax payable in respect thereof, or that other property, to the extent of the value thereof at the date of the death of the deceased after deducting therefrom any capital transfer tax so payable, shall be treated for the purposes of this Act as part of the net estate of the deceased; but this subsection shall not render any person liable for having paid that sum or transferred that other property to the person named in the nomination in accordance with the directions given in the nomination.

(2) Where any sum of money or other property is received by any person as a donatio mortis causa made by a deceased person, that sum of money, after deducting therefrom any capital transfer tax payable thereon, or that other property, to the extent of the value thereof at the date of the death of the deceased after deducting therefrom any capital transfer tax so payable, shall be treated for the purposes of this Act as part of the net estate of the deceased; but this subsection shall not render any person liable for having paid that sum or transferred that other property in order to give effect to that donatio mortis causa.

(3) The amount of capital transfer tax to be deducted for the purposes of this section shall not exceed the amount of that tax which has been borne by the person nominated by the deceased or, as the case may be, the person who has received a sum of money or other property as a donatio mortis causa.

9   Property held on a joint tenancy

(1) Where a deceased person was immediately before his death beneficially entitled to a joint tenancy of any property, then, if, before the end of the period of six months from the date on which representation with respect to the estate of the deceased was first taken out, an application is made for an order under section 2 of this Act the court for the purpose of facilitating the making of financial provisions for the applicant under this Act may order that the deceased's severable share of that property, at the value thereof immediately before his death, shall, to such extent as appears to the court to be just in all the circumstances of the case, be treated for the purposes of this Act as part of the net estate of the deceased.

(2) In determining the extent to which any severable share is to be treated as part of the net estate of the deceased by virtue of an order under subsection (1) above, the court shall have regard to any capital transfer tax payable in respect of that severable share.

(3) Where an order is made under subsection (1) above, the provisions of this section shall not render any person liable for anything done by him before the order was made.

(4) For the avoidance of doubt it is hereby declared that for the purposes of this section there may be a joint tenancy of a chose in action.

Powers of court in relation to transactions intended to defeat applications for financial provision

10   Dispositions intended to defeat applications for financial provision

(1) Where an application is made to the court for an order under section 2 of this Act, the applicant may, in the proceedings on that application, apply to the court for an order under subsection (2) below.

(2) Where on an application under subsection (1) above the court is satisfied—

(a) that, less than six years before the date of the death of the deceased, the deceased with the intention of defeating an application for financial provision under this Act made a disposition, and

(b) that full valuable consideration for the disposition was not given by the person to whom or for the benefit of whom the disposition was made (in this section referred to as 'the donee') or by any other person, and

(c) that the exercise of the powers conferred by this section would facilitate the making of financial provision for the applicant under this Act,

then, subject to the provisions of this section and of sections 12 and 13 of this Act, the court may order the donee (whether or not at the date of the order he holds any interest in the property disposed of to him or for his benefit by the deceased) to provide, for the purpose of the making of that financial provision, such sum of money or other property as may be specified in the order.

(3) Where an order is made under subsection (2) above as respects any disposition made by the deceased which consisted of the payment of money to or for the benefit of the donee, the amount of any sum of money or the value of any property ordered to be provided under that subsection shall not exceed the amount of the payment made by the deceased after deducting therefrom any capital transfer tax borne by the donee in respect of that payment.

(4) Where an order is made under subsection (2) above as respects any disposition made by the deceased which consisted of the transfer of property (other than a sum of money) to or for the benefit of the donee, the amount of any sum of money or the value of any property ordered to be provided under that subsection shall not exceed the value at the date of the death of the deceased of the property disposed of by him to or for the benefit of the donee (or if that property has been disposed of by the person to whom it was transferred by the deceased, the value at the date of that disposal thereof) after deducting therefrom any capital transfer tax borne by the donee in respect of the transfer of that property by the deceased.

(5) Where an application (in this subsection referred to as 'the original application') is made for an order under subsection (2) above in relation to any disposition then, if, on an application under this subsection by the donee or by any applicant for an order under section 2 of this Act the court is satisfied—

(a) that, less than six years before the date of the death of the deceased, the deceased with the intention of defeating an application for financial provision under this Act made a disposition other than the disposition which is the subject of the original application, and

(b) that full valuable consideration for that other disposition was not given by the person to whom or for the benefit of whom that other disposition was made or by any other person,

the court may exercise in relation to the person to whom or for the benefit of whom that other disposition was made the powers which the court would have had under subsection (2) above if the original application had been made in respect of that other disposition and the court had been satisfied as to the matters set out in paragraphs (a), (b) and (c) of that subsection; and where any application is made under this subsection, any reference in this section (except in subsection (2)(b)) to the donee shall include a reference to the person to whom or for the benefit of whom that other disposition was made.

(6) In determining whether and in what manner to exercise its powers under this section, the court shall have regard to the circumstances in which any disposition was made and any valuable consideration which was given therefor, the relationship, if any, of the donee to the deceased, the conduct and financial resources of the donee and all the other circumstances of the case.

(7) In this section 'disposition' does not include—

(a) any provision in a will, any such nomination as is mentioned in section 8(1) of this Act or any donatio mortis causa, or

(b) any appointment of property made, otherwise than by will, in the exercise of a special power of appointment, but, subject to these exceptions, includes any payment of money (including the payment of a premium under a policy of assurance) and any conveyance, assurance, appointment or gift of property of any description, whether made by an instrument or otherwise.

(8) The provisions of this section do not apply to any disposition made before the commencement of this Act.

11   Contracts to leave property by will

(1) Where an application is made to a court for an order under section 2 of this Act, the applicant may, in the proceedings on that application, apply to the court for an order under this section.

(2) Where on an application under subsection (1) above the court is satisfied—

    (a) that the deceased made a contract by which he agreed to leave by his will a sum of money or other property to any person or by which he agreed that a sum of money or other property would be paid or transferred to any person out of his estate, and

    (b) that the deceased made that contract with the intention of defeating an application for financial provision under this Act, and

    (c) that when the contract was made full valuable consideration for that contract was not given or promised by the person with whom or for the benefit of whom the contract was made (in this section referred to as 'the donee') or by any other person, and

    (d) that the exercise of the powers conferred by this section would facilitate the making of financial provision for the applicant under this Act,

then, subject to the provisions of this section and of sections 12 and 13 of this Act, the court may make any one or more of the following orders, that is to say—

    (i) if any money has been paid or any other property has been transferred to or for the benefit of the donee in accordance with the contract, an order directing the donee to provide, for the purpose of the making of that financial provision, such sum of money or other property as may be specified in the order;

    (ii) if the money or all the money has not been paid or the property or all the property has not been transferred in accordance with the contract, an order directing the personal representatives not to make any payment or transfer any property, or not to make any further payment or transfer any further property, as the case may be, in accordance therewith or directing the personal representatives only to make such payment or transfer such property as may be specified in the order.

(3) Notwithstanding anything in subsection (2) above, the court may exercise its powers thereunder in relation to any contract made by the deceased only to the extent that the court considers that the amount of any sum of money paid or to be paid or the value of any property transferred or to be transferred in accordance with the contract exceeds the value of any valuable consideration given or to be given for that contract, and for this purpose the court shall have regard to the value of property at the date of the hearing.

(4) In determining whether and in what manner to exercise its powers under this section, the court shall have regard to the circumstances in which the contract was made, the relationship, if any, of the donee to the deceased, the conduct and financial resources of the donee and all the other circumstances of the case.

(5) Where an order has been made under subsection (2) above in relation to any contract, the rights of any person to enforce that contract or to recover damages or to obtain other relief for the breach thereof shall be subject to any adjustment made by the court under section 12(3) of this Act and shall survive to such extent only as is consistent with giving effect to the terms of that order.

(6) The provisions of this section do not apply to a contract made before the commencement of this Act.

12   Provisions supplementary to ss. 10 and 11

(1) Where the exercise of any of the powers conferred by section 10 or 11 of this Act is conditional on the court being satisfied that a disposition or contract was made by a deceased person with the intention of defeating an application for financial provision under this Act, that condition shall be fulfilled if the court is of the opinion that, on a balance of probabilities, the intention of the deceased (though not necessarily his sole intention) in making the disposition or contract was to prevent an order for financial provision being made under this Act or to reduce the amount of the provision which might otherwise be granted by an order thereunder.

(2) Where an application is made under section 11 of this Act with respect to any contract made by the deceased and no valuable consideration was given or promised by any person for that contract then, notwithstanding anything in subsection (1) above, it shall be presumed, unless the contrary is shown, that the deceased made that contract with the intention of defeating an application for financial provision under this Act.

(3) Where the court makes an order under section 10 or 11 of this Act it may give such consequential directions as it thinks fit (including directions requiring the making of any payment or the transfer of any property) for giving effect to the order or for securing a fair adjustment of the rights of the persons affected thereby.

(4) Any power conferred on the court by the said section 10 or 11 to order the donee, in relation to any disposition or contract, to provide any sum of money or other property shall be exercisable in like manner in relation to the personal representatives of the donee, and—

(a) any reference in section 10(4) to the disposal of property by the donee shall include a reference to the disposal by the personal representative of the donee, and

(b) any reference in section 10(5) to an application by the donee under that subsection shall include a reference to an application by the personal representative of the donee;

but the court shall not have the power under the said section 10 or 11 to make an order in respect of any property forming part of the estate of the donee which has been distributed by the personal representative; and the personal representative shall not be liable for having distributed any such property before he has notice of the making of an application under the said section 10 or 11 on the ground that he ought to have taken into account the possibility that such an application would be made.

13   Provisions as to trustees in relation to ss. 10 and 11

(1) Where an application is made for—

(a) an order under section 10 of this Act in respect of a disposition made by the deceased to any person as a trustee, or

(b) an order under section 11 of this Act in respect of any payment made or property transferred, in accordance with a contract made by the deceased, to any person as a trustee,

the powers of the court under the said section 10 or 11 to order that trustee to provide a sum of money or other property shall be subject to the following limitation (in addition, in a case of an application under section 10, to any provision regarding the deduction of captial transfer tax) namely, that the amount of any sum of money or the value of any property ordered to be provided—

(i) in the case of an application in respect of a disposition which consisted of the payment of money or an application in respect of the payment of money in accordance with a contract, shall not exceed the aggregate of so much of that money as is at the date of the order in the hands of the trustee and the value at that date of any property which represents that money or is derived therefrom and is at that date in the hands of the trustee;

(ii) in the case of an application in respect of a disposition which consisted of the transfer of property (other than a sum of money) or an application in respect of the transfer of property (other than a sum of money) in accordance with a contract, shall not exceed the aggregate of the value at the date of the order of so much of that property as is at that date in the hands of the trustee and the value at that date of any property which represents the first-mentioned property or is derived therefrom and is at that date in the hands of the trustee.

(2) Where any such application is made in respect of a disposition made to any person as a trustee or in respect of any payment made or property transferred in pursuance of a contract to any person as trustee, the trustee shall not be liable for having distributed any money or other property on the ground that he ought to have taken into account the possibility that such an application would be made.

(3) Where any such application is made in respect of a disposition made to any person as a trustee or in respect of any payment made or property transferred in accordance with a contract to any person as a trustee, any reference in the said section 10 or 11 to the donee shall be construed as including a reference to the trustee or trustees for the time being of the trust in question and any reference in subsection (1) or (2) above to a trustee shall be construed in the same way.

Special provisions relating to cases of divorce, separation etc.

14   Provision as to cases where no financial relief was granted in divorce proceedings etc.

(1) Where, within twelve months from the date on which a decree of divorce or nullity of marriage has been made absolute or a decree of judicial separation has been granted, a party to the marriage dies and—

(a) an application for a financial provision order under section 23 of the Matrimonial Causes Act 1973 or a property adjustment order under section 24 of that Act has not been made by the other party to that marriage, or

(b) such an application has been made but the proceedings thereon have not been determined at the time of the death of the deceased,

then, if an application for an order under section 2 of this Act is made by that other party, the court shall, notwithstanding anything in section 1 or section 3 of this Act, have power, if it thinks it just to do so, to treat that party for the purposes of that application as if the decree of divorce or nullity of marriage had not been made absolute or the decree of judicial separation had not been granted, as the case may be.

(2) This section shall not apply in relation to a decree of judicial separation unless at the date of the death of the deceased the decree was in force and the separation was continuing.

14A   Provision as to cases where no financial relief was granted in proceedings for the dissolution etc. of a civil partnership

(1) Subsection (2) below applies where—

(a) a dissolution order, nullity order, separation order or presumption of death order has been made under Chapter 2 of Part 2 of the Civil Partnership Act 2004 in relation to a civil partnership,

(b) one of the civil partners dies within twelve months from the date on which the order is made, and

(c) either—

(i) an application for a financial provision order under Part 1 of Schedule 5 to that Act or a property adjustment order under Part 2 of that Schedule has not been made by the other civil partner, or

(ii) such an application has been made but the proceedings on the application have not been determined at the time of the death of the deceased.

(2) If an application for an order under section 2 of this Act is made by the surviving civil partner, the court shall, notwithstanding anything in section 1 or section 3 of this Act, have

power, if it thinks it just to do so, to treat the surviving civil partner as if the order mentioned in subsection (1)(a) above had not been made.

(3) This section shall not apply in relation to a separation order unless at the date of the death of the deceased the separation order was in force and the separation was continuing.

15 Restriction imposed in divorce proceedings etc. on application under this Act

(1) On the grant of a decree of divorce, a decree of nullity of marriage or a decree of judicial separation or at any time thereafter the court, if it considers it just to do so, may, on the application of either party to the marriage, order that the other party to the marriage shall not on the death of the applicant be entitled to apply for an order under section 2 of this Act.

In this subsection 'the court' means the High Court or, where a county court has jurisdiction by virtue of Part V of the Matrimonial and Family Proceedings Act 1984, a county court.

(2) In the case of a decree of divorce or nullity of marriage an order may be made under subsection (1) above before or after the decree is made absolute, but if it is made before the decree is made absolute it shall not take effect unless the decree is made absolute.

(3) Where an order made under subsection (1) above on the grant of a decree of divorce or nullity of marriage has come into force with respect to a party to a marriage, then, on the death of the other party to that marriage, the court shall not entertain any application for an order under section 2 of this Act made by the first-mentioned party.

(4) Where an order made under subsection (1) above on the grant of a decree of judicial separation has come into force with respect to any party to a marriage, then, if, the other party to that marriage dies while the decree is in force and the separation is continuing, the court does not entertain any application for an order under section 2 of this Act made by the first-mentioned party.

15ZA Restriction imposed in proceedings for the dissolution etc. of a civil partnership on application under this Act

(1) On making a dissolution order, nullity order, separation order or presumption of death order under Chapter 2 of Part 2 of the Civil Partnership Act 2004, or at any time after making such an order, the court, if it considers it just to do so, may, on the application of either of the civil partners, order that the other civil partner shall not on the death of the applicant be entitled to apply for an order under section 2 of this Act.

(2) In subsection (1) above 'the court' means the High Court or, where a county court has jurisdiction by virtue of Part 5 of the Matrimonial and Family Proceedings Act 1984, a county court.

(3) In the case of a dissolution order, nullity order or presumption of death order ('the main order') an order may be made under subsection (1) above before (as well as after) the main order is made final, but if made before the main order is made final it shall not take effect unless the main order is made final.

(4) Where an order under subsection (1) above made in connection with a dissolution order, nullity order or presumption of death order has come into force with respect to a civil partner, then, on the death of the other civil partner, the court shall not entertain any application for an order under section 2 of this Act made by the surviving civil partner.

(5) Where an order under subsection (1) above made in connection with a separation order has come into force with respect to a civil partner, then, if the other civil partner dies while the separation order is in force and the separation is continuing, the court shall not entertain any application for an order under section 2 of this Act made by the surviving civil partner.

15A Restriction imposed in proceedings under Matrimonial and Family Proceedings Act 1984 on application under this Act

(1) On making an order under section 17 of the Matrimonial and Family Proceedings Act 1984 (orders for financial provision and property adjustment following overseas divorces, etc.) the court, if it considers it just to do so, may, on the application of either party to the

marriage, order that the other party to the marriage shall not on the death of the applicant be entitled to apply for an order under section 2 of this Act.

In this subsection 'the court' means the High Court or, where a county court has jurisdiction by virtue of Part V of the Matrimonial and Family Proceedings Act 1984, a county court.

(2) Where an order under subsection (1) above has been made with respect to a party to a marriage which has been dissolved or annulled, then, on the death of the other party to that marriage, the court shall not entertain an application under section 2 of this Act made by the first-mentioned party.

(3) Where an order under subsection (1) above has been made with respect to a party to a marriage the parties to which have been legally separated, then, if the other party to the marriage dies while the legal separation is in force, the court shall not entertain an application under section 2 of this Act made by the first-mentioned party.

15B   Restriction imposed in proceedings under Schedule 7 to the Civil Partnership Act 2004 on application under this Act

(1) On making an order under paragraph 9 of Schedule 7 to the Civil Partnership Act 2004 (orders for financial provision, property adjustment and pension-sharing following overseas dissolution etc. of civil partnership) the court, if it considers it just to do so, may, on the application of either of the civil partners, order that the other civil partner shall not on the death of the applicant be entitled to apply for an order under section 2 of this Act.

(2) In subsection (1) above 'the court' means the High Court or, where a county court has jurisdiction by virtue of Part 5 of the Matrimonial and Family Proceedings Act 1984, a county court.

(3) Where an order under subsection (1) above has been made with respect to one of the civil partners in a case where a civil partnership has been dissolved or annulled, then, on the death of the other civil partner, the court shall not entertain an application under section 2 of this Act made by the surviving civil partner.

(4) Where an order under subsection (1) above has been made with respect to one of the civil partners in a case where civil partners have been legally separated, then, if the other civil partner dies while the legal separation is in force, the court shall not entertain an application under section 2 of this Act made by the surviving civil partner.

16   Variation and discharge of secured periodical payments orders made under Matrimonial Causes Act 1973

(1) Where an application for an order under section 2 of this Act is made to the court by any person who was at the time of the death of the deceased entitled to payments from the deceased under a secured periodical payments order made under the Matrimonial Causes Act 1973 or Schedule 5 to the Civil Partnership Act 2004, then, in the proceedings on that application, the court shall have power, if an application is made under this section by that person or by the personal representative of the deceased, to vary or discharge that periodical payments order or to revive the operation of any provision thereof which has been suspended under section 31 of that Act of 1973 or Part II of that Schedule.

(2) In exercising the powers conferred by this section the court shall have regard to all the circumstances of the case, including any order which the court proposes to make under section 2 or section 5 of this Act and any change (whether resulting from the death of the deceased or otherwise) in any of the matters to which the court was required to have regard when making the secured periodical payments order.

(3) The powers exercisable by the court under this section in relation to an order shall be exercisable also in relation to any instrument executed in pursuance of the order.

17   Variation and revocation of maintenance agreements

(1) Where an application for an order under section 2 of this Act is made to the court by any person who was at the time of the death of the deceased entitled to payments from the deceased under a maintenance agreement which provided for the continuation of payments

under the agreement after the death of the deceased, then, in the proceedings on that application, the court shall have power, if an application is made under this section by that person or by the personal representative of the deceased, to vary or revoke that agreement.

(2) In exercising the powers conferred by this section the court shall have regard to all the circumstances of the case, including any order which the court proposes to make under section 2 or section 5 of this Act and any change (whether resulting from the death of the deceased or otherwise) in any of the circumstances in the light of which the agreement was made.

(3) If a maintenance agreement is varied by the court under this section the like consequences shall ensue as if the variation had been made immediately before the death of the deceased by agreement between the parties and for valuable consideration.

(4) In this section 'maintenance agreement', in relation to a deceased person, means any agreement made, whether in writing or not and whether before or after the commencement of this Act, by the deceased with any person with whom he formed a marriage or civil partnership, being an agreement which contained provisions governing the rights and liabilities towards one another when living separately of the parties to that marriage or of the civil partners (whether or not the marriage or civil partnership has been dissolved or annulled) in respect of the making or securing of payments or the disposition or use of any property, including such rights and liabilities with respect to the maintenance or education of any child, whether or not a child of the deceased or a person who was treated by the deceased as a child of the family in relation to that marriage or civil partnership.

18 Availability of court's powers under this Act in applications under ss. 31 and 36 of the Matrimonial Causes Act 1973

(1) Where—
    (a) a person against whom a secured periodical payments order was made under the Matrimonial Causes Act 1973 has died and an application is made under section 31(6) of that Act for the variation or discharge of that order or for the revival of the operation of any provision thereof which has been suspended, or
    (b) a party to a maintenance agreement within the meaning of section 34 of that Act has died, the agreement being one which provides for the continuation of payments thereunder after the death of one of the parties, and an application is made under section 36(1) of that Act, for the alteration of the agreement under section 35 thereof,

the court shall have power to direct that the application made under the said section 31(6) or 36(1) shall be deemed to have been accompanied by an application for an order under section 2 of this Act.

(2) Where the court gives a direction under subsection (1) above it shall have power, in the proceedings on the application under the said section 31(6) or 36(1), to make any order which the court would have had power to make under the provisions of this Act if the application under the said section 31(6) or 36(1), as the case may be, had been made jointly with an application for an order under the said section 2; and the court shall have power to give such consequential directions as may be necessary for enabling the court to exercise any of the powers available to the court under this Act in the case of an application for an order under section 2.

(3) Where an order made under section 15(1) of this Act is in force with respect to a party to a marriage, the court shall not give a direction under subsection (1) above with respect to any application made under the said section 31(6) or 36(1) by that party on the death of the other party.

18A Availability of court's powers under this Act in applications under paragraphs 60 and 73 of Schedule 5 to the Civil Partnership Act 2004

(1) Where—
    (a) a person against whom a secured periodical payments order was made under Schedule 5 to the Civil Partnership Act 2004 has died and an application is made

under paragraph 60 of that Schedule for the variation or discharge of that order or for the revival of the operation of any suspended provision of the order, or

(b) a party to a maintenance agreement within the meaning of Part 13 of that Schedule has died, the agreement being one which provides for the continuation of payments under the agreement after the death of one of the parties, and an application is made under paragraph 73 of that Schedule for the alteration of the agreement under paragraph 69 of that Schedule,

the court shall have power to direct that the application made under paragraph 60 or 73 of that Schedule shall be deemed to have been accompanied by an application for an order under section 2 of this Act.

(2) Where the court gives a direction under subsection (1) above it shall have power, in the proceedings on the application under paragraph 60 or 73 of that Schedule, to make any order which the court would have had power to make under the provisions of this Act if the application under that paragraph had been made jointly with an application for an order under section 2 of this Act; and the court shall have power to give such consequential directions as may be necessary for enabling the court to exercise any of the powers available to the court under this Act in the case of an application for an order under section 2.

(3) Where an order made under section 15ZA(1) of this Act is in force with respect to a civil partner, the court shall not give a direction under subsection (1) above with respect to any application made under paragraph 60 or 73 of that Schedule by that civil partner on the death of the other civil partner.

Miscellaneous and supplementary provisions

19 Effect, duration and form of orders

(1) Where an order is made under section 2 of this Act then for all purposes, including the purposes of the enactments relating to capital transfer tax, the will or the law relating to intestacy, or both the will and the law relating to intestacy, as the case may be, shall have effect and be deemed to have had effect as from the deceased's death subject to the provisions of the order.

(2) Any order made under section 2 or 5 of this Act in favour of—

(a) an applicant who was the former spouse or former civil partner of the deceased; or

(b) an applicant who was the husband or wife of the deceased in a case where the marriage with the deceased was the subject of a decree of judicial separation and at the date of death the decree was in force and the separation was continuing, or

(c) an applicant who was the civil partner of the deceased in a case where, at the date of death, a separation order under Chapter 2 of Part 2 of the Civil Partnership Act 2004 was in force in relation to their civil partnership and the separation was continuing,

shall, in so far as it provides for the making of periodical payments, cease to have effect on the formation by the applicant of a subsequent marriage or civil partnership, except in relation to any arrears due under the order on the date of the formation of the subsequent marriage or civil partnership.

(3) A copy of every order made under this Act other than an order made under section 15(1) or 15ZA(1) of this Act shall be sent to the principal registry of the Family Division for entry and filing, and a memorandum of the order shall be endorsed on, or permanently annexed to, the probate or letters of administration under which the estate is being administered.

20 Provisions as to personal representatives

(1) The provisions of this Act shall not render the personal representative of a deceased person liable for having distributed any part of the estate of the deceased, after the end of the period of six months from the date on which the representation with respect to the estate of the deceased is first taken out, on the ground that he ought to have taken into account the possibility—

(a) that the court might permit the making of an application for an order under section 2 of this Act after the end of that period, or

(b) that, where an order has been made under the said section 2, the court might exercise in relation thereto the powers conferred on it by section 6 of this Act, but this subsection shall not prejudice any power to recover, by reason of the making of an order under this Act, any part of the estate so distributed.

(2) Where the personal representative of a deceased person pays any sum directed by an order under section 5 of this Act to be paid out of the deceased's net estate, he shall not be under any liability by reason of that estate not being sufficient to make the payment, unless at the time of making the payment he has reasonable cause to believe that the estate is not sufficient.

(3) Where a deceased person entered into a contract by which he agreed to leave by his will any sum of money or other property to any person or by which he agreed that a sum of money or other property would be paid or transferred to any person out of his estate, then, if the personal representative of the deceased has reason to believe that the deceased entered into the contract with the intention of defeating an application for financial provision under this Act, he may, notwithstanding anything in that contract, postpone the payment of that sum of money or the transfer of that property until the expiration of the period of six months from the date on which representation with respect to the estate of the deceased is first taken out or, if during that period an application is made for an order under section 2 of this Act, until the determination of the proceedings on that application.

23   Determination of date on which representation was first taken out

In considering for the purposes of this Act when representation with respect to the estate of a deceased person was first taken out, a grant limited to settled land or to trust property shall be left out of account, and a grant limited to real estate or to personal estate shall be left out of account unless a grant limited to the remainder of the estate has previously been made or is made at the same time.

24   Effect of this Act on s. 46(1)(vi) of Administration of Estates Act 1925

Section 46(1)(vi) of the Administration of Estates Act 1925, in so far as it provides for the devolution of property on the Crown, the Duchy of Lancaster or the Duke of Cornwall as bona vacantia, shall have effect subject to the provisions of this Act.

25   Interpretation

(1) In this Act—

'beneficiary' in relation to the estate of a deceased person, means—

(a) a person who under the will of the deceased or under the law relating to intestacy is beneficially interested in the estate or would be so interested if an order had not been made under this Act, and

(b) a person who has received any sum of money or other property which by virtue of section 8(1) or 8(2) of this Act is treated as part of the net estate of the deceased or would have received that sum or other property if an order had not been made under this Act;

'child' includes an illegitimate child and a child en ventre sa mere at the death of the deceased;

'the court' means, unless the context otherwise requires, the High Court, or where a county court has jurisdiction by virtue of section 22 of this Act, a county court;

'former civil partner' means a person whose civil partnership with the deceased was during the lifetime of the deceased either—

(a) dissolved or annulled by an order made under the law of any part of the British Islands, or

...

'former spouse' means a person whose marriage with the deceased was during the lifetime of the deceased either—

(a) dissolved or annulled by a decree of divorce or a decree of nullity of marriage granted under the law of any part of the British Islands, or

(b) dissolved or annulled in any country or territory outside the British Islands by a divorce or annulment which is entitled to be recognised as valid by the law of England and Wales;

'net estate' in relation to a deceased person, means:—

(a) all property of which the deceased had power to dispose by his will (otherwise than by virtue of a special power of appointment) less the amount of his funeral, testamentary and administration expenses, debts and liabilities, including any capital transfer tax payable out of his estate on his death;

(b) any property in respect of which the deceased held a general power of appointment (not being a power exercisable by will) which has not been exercised;

(c) any sum of money or other property which is treated for the purposes of this Act as part of the net estate of the deceased by virtue of section 8(1) or (2) of this Act;

(d) any property which is treated for the purposes of this Act as part of the net estate of the deceased by virtue of an order made under section 9 of the Act;

(e) any sum of money or other property which is, by reason of a disposition or contract made by the deceased, ordered under section 10 or 11 of this Act to be provided for the purpose of the making of financial provision under this Act;

'property' includes any chose in action;

'reasonable financial provision' has the meaning assigned to it by section 1 of this Act;

'valuable consideration' does not include marriage or a promise of marriage;

'will' includes codicil.

(2) For the purposes of paragraph (a) of the definition of 'net estate' in subsection (1) above a person who is not of full age and capacity shall be treated as having power to dispose by will of all property of which he would have had power to dispose by will if he had been of full age and capacity.

(3) Any reference in this Act to provision out of the net estate of a deceased person includes a reference to provision extending to the whole of that estate.

(4) For the purpose of this Act any reference to a spouse, wife or husband shall be treated as including a reference to a person who in good faith entered into a void marriage with the deceased person unless either—

(a) the marriage of the deceased and that person was dissolved or annulled during the lifetime of the deceased and the dissolution or annulment is recognised by the law of England and Wales, or

(b) that person has during the lifetime of the deceased formed a subsequent marriage or civil partnership.

(4A) For the purposes of this Act any reference to a civil partner shall be treated as including a reference to a person who in good faith formed a void civil partnership with the deceased unless either—

(a) the civil partnership between the deceased and that person was dissolved or annulled during the lifetime of the deceased and the dissolution or annulment is recognised by the law of England and Wales, or

(b) that person has during the lifetime of the deceased formed a subsequent civil partnership or marriage.

(5) Any reference in this Act to the formation of, or to a person who has formed, a subsequent marriage or civil partnership includes (as the case may be) a reference to the formation of, or to a person who has formed, a marriage or civil partnership which is by law void or voidable.

(5A) The formation of a marriage or civil partnership shall be treated for the purposes of this Act as the formation of a subsequent marriage or civil partnership, in relation to either of the spouses or civil partners, notwithstanding that the previous marriage or civil partnership of that spouse or civil partner was void or voidable.

(6) Any reference in this Act to an order or decree made under the Matrimonial Causes Act 1973 or under any section of that Act shall be construed as including a reference to an

order or decree which is deemed to have been made under that Act or under that section thereof, as the case may be.

(6A) Any reference in this Act to an order made under, or under any provision of, the Civil Partnership Act 2004 shall be construed as including a reference to anything which is deemed to be an order made (as the case may be) under that Act or provision.

(7) Any reference in this Act to any enactment is a reference to that enactment as amended by or under any subsequent enactment.

Legitimacy Act 1976
(1976 c. 31)

1   Legitimacy of children of certain void marriages

(1) The child of a void marriage, whenever born, shall, subject to subsection (2) below and Schedule 1 to this Act, be treated as the legitimate child of his parents if at the time of the insemination resulting in the birth, or where there was no such insemination, the child's conception (or at the time of the celebration of the marriage if later) both or either of the parties reasonably believed that the marriage was valid.

(2) This section applies where the father of the child was domiciled in England and Wales at the time of the birth or, if he died before the birth, was so domiciled immediately before his death.

(3) It is hereby declared for the avoidance of doubt that subsection (1) above applies notwithstanding that the belief that the marriage was valid was due to a mistake as to law.

(4) In relation to a child born after the coming into force of section 28 of the Family Law Reform Act 1987, it shall be presumed for the purposes of subsection (1) above, unless the contrary is shown, that one of the parties to the void marriage reasonably believed at the time of the insemination resulting in the birth or, where there was no such insemination, the child's conception (or at the time of the celebration of the marriage if later) that the marriage was valid.

2   Legitimation by subsequent marriage of parents

Subject to the following provisions of this Act, where the parents of an illegitimate person marry one another, the marriage shall, if the father of the illegitimate person is at the date of marriage domiciled in England and Wales, render that person, if living, legitimate from the date of the marriage.

3   Legitimation by extraneous law

Subject to the following provisions of this Act, where the parents of an illegitimate person marry one another and the father of the illegitimate person is not at the time of the marriage domiciled in England and Wales but is domiciled in a country by the law of which the illegitimate person became legitimated by virtue of such subsequent marriage, that person, if living, shall in England and Wales be recognised as having been so legitimated from the date of the marriage notwithstanding that, at the time of his birth, his father was domiciled in a country the law of which did not permit legitimation by subsequent marriage.

4   Legitimation of adopted child

(1) Section 39 of the Adoption Act 1976 or section 67 of the Adoption and Children Act 2002 does not prevent an adopted child being legitimated under section 2 or 3 above if either natural parent is the sole adoptive parent.

(2) Where an adopted child (with a sole adoptive parent) is legitimated—

    (a) Subsection (2) of the said section 39 or subsection (3)(b) of the said section 67 shall not apply after the legitimation to the natural relationship with the other natural parent, and

(b) revocation of the adoption order in consequence of the legitimation shall not affect section 39, 41 or 42 of the Adoption Act 1976 or section 67, 68 or 69 of the Adoption and Children Act 2002 as it applies to any instrument made before the date of legitimation.

5 Rights of legitimated persons and others to take interests in property

(1) Subject to any contrary indication, the rules of construction contained in this section apply to any instrument other than an existing instrument, so far as the instrument contains a disposition of property.

(2) For the purposes of this section, provisions of the law of intestate succession applicable to the estate of a deceased person shall be treated as if contained in an instrument executed by him (while of full capacity) immediately before his death.

(3) A legitimated person, and any other person, shall be entitled to take any interest as if the legitimated person had been born legitimate.

(4) A disposition which depends on the date of birth of a child or children of the parent or parents shall be construed as if—

(a) a legitimated child had been born on the date of legitimation,

(b) two or more legitimated children legitimated on the same date had been born on that date in the order of their actual births,

but this does not affect any reference to the age of a child.

(5) Examples of phrases in wills on which subsection (4) above can operate are—

1. Children of A 'living at my death or born afterwards.'

2. Children of A 'living at my death or born afterwards before any one of such children for the time being in existence attains a vested interest, and who attain the age of 21 years.'

3. As in example 1 or 2, but referring to grandchildren of A, instead of children of A.

4. A for life 'until he has a child' and then to his child or children.

Note. Subsection (4) above will not affect the reference to the age of 21 years in example 2.

(6) If an illegitimate person or a person adopted by one of his natural parents dies, or has died before the commencement of this Act, and—

(a) after his death his parents marry or have married; and

(b) the deceased would, if living at the time of the marriage, have become a legitimated person,

this section shall apply for the construction of the instrument so far as it relates to the taking of interests by, or in succession to, his spouse, children and remoter issue as if he had been legitimated by virtue of the marriage.

(7) In this section 'instrument' includes a private Act settling property, but not any other enactment.

6 Dispositions depending on date of birth

(1) Where a disposition depends on the date of birth of a child who was born illegitimate and who is legitimated (or, if deceased, is treated as legitimated), section 5(4) above does not affect entitlement under Part II of the Family Law Reform Act 1969 (illegitimate children).

(2) Where a disposition depends on the date of birth of an adopted child who is legitimated (or, if deceased, is treated as legitimated) section 5(4) above does not affect entitlement by virtue of section 42(2) of the Adoption Act 1976 or section 69(2) of the Adoption and Children Act 2002.

(3) This section applies for example where—

(a) a testator dies in 1976 bequeathing a legacy to his eldest grandchild living at a specified time,

(b) his daughter has an illegitimate child in 1977 who is the first grandchild,

(c) his married son has a child in 1978,

(d) subsequently the illegitimate child is legitimated,

and in all those cases the daughter's child remains the eldest grandchild of the testator throughout.

7   Protection of trustees and personal representatives

(1) A trustee or personal representative is not under a duty, by virtue of the law relating to trusts or the administration of estates, to enquire, before conveying or distributing any property, whether any person is illegitimate or has been adopted by one of his natural parents, and could be legitimated (or if deceased be treated as legitimated), if the fact could affect entitlement to the property.

(2) A trustee or personal representative shall not be liable to any person by reason of a conveyance or distribution of the property made without regard to any such fact if he has not received notice of the fact before the conveyance or distribution.

(3) This section does not prejudice the right of a person to follow the property, or any property representing it, into the hands of another person, other than a purchaser, who has received it.

8   Personal rights and obligations

A legitimated person shall have the same rights, and shall be under the same obligations in respect of the maintenance and support of himself or of any other person as if he had been born legitimate, and, subject to the provisions of this Act, the provisions of any Act relating to claims for damages, compensation, allowance, benefit or otherwise by or in respect of a legitimate child shall apply in like manner in the case of a legitimated person.

9   Re-registration of birth of legitimated person

(1) It shall be the duty of the parents of a legitimated person or, in cases where re-registration can be effected on information furnished by one parent and one of the parents is dead, of the surviving parent to furnish to the Registrar General information with a view to obtaining the re-registration of the birth of that person within three months after the date of the marriage by virtue of which he was legitimated.

(2) The failure of the parents or either of them to furnish information as required by subsection (1) above in respect of any legitimated person shall not affect the legitimation of that person.

(3) This section does not apply in relation to a person who was legitimated otherwise than by virtue of the subsequent marriage of his parents.

(4) Any parent who fails to give information as required by this section shall be liable on summary conviction to a fine not exceeding level 1 on the standard scale.

10   Interpretation

(1) In this Act, except where the context otherwise requires—

'disposition' includes the conferring of a power of appointment and any other disposition of an interest in or right over property;

'existing', in relation to an instrument, means one made before 1st January 1976;

'legitimated person' means a person legitimated or recognised as legitimated—

(a) under section 2 or 3 above; or

(b) under section 1 or 8 of the Legitimacy Act 1926; or

(c) except in section 8, by a legitimation (whether or not by virtue of the subsequent marriage of his parents) recognised by the law of England and Wales and effected under the law of any other country;

and cognate expressions shall be construed accordingly;

'power of appointment' includes any discretionary power to transfer a beneficial interest in property without the furnishing of valuable consideration;

'void marriage' means a marriage not being voidable only, in respect of which the High Court has or had jurisdiction to grant a decree of nullity, or would have or would have had such jurisdiction if the parties were domiciled in England and Wales.

(2) For the purposes of this Act 'legitimated person' includes, where the context admits, a person legitimated, or recognised as legitimated, before the passing of the Children Act 1975.

(3) For the purposes of this Act, except where the context otherwise requires—

    (a) the death of the testator is the date at which a will or codicil is to be regarded as made;

    (b) an oral disposition of property shall be deemed to be contained in an instrument made when the disposition was made.

Adoption Act 1976
(1976 c. 36)

PART IV   STATUS OF ADOPTED CHILDREN

38   Meaning of 'adoption' in Part IV

(1) In this Part 'adoption' means adoption—

    (a) by an adoption order;

    (b) by an order made under the Children Act 1975, the Adoption Act 1958, the Adoption Act 1950 or any enactment repealed by the Adoption Act 1950;

    (c) by an order made in Scotland, Northern Ireland, the Isle of Man or in any of the Channel Islands;

    (cc) which is a Convention adoption;

    (d) which is an overseas adoption; or

    (e) which is an adoption recognised by the law of England and Wales and effected under the law of any other country,

and cognate expressions shall be construed accordingly.

(2) The definition of adoption includes, where the context admits, an adoption effected before the passing of the Children Act 1975 but does not include an adoption of a kind mentioned in paragraphs (c) to (e) of subsection (1) effected on or after the day which is the appointed day for the purposes of Chapter 4 of Part 1 of the Adoption and Children Act 2002, and the date of an adoption effected by an order is the date of the making of the order.

39   Status conferred by adoption

(1) An adopted child shall be treated in law—

    (a) where the adopters are a married couple, as if he had been born as a child of the marriage (whether or not he was in fact born after the marriage was solemnized);

    (b) in any other case, as if he had been born to the adopter in wedlock (but not as a child of any actual marriage of the adopter).

(2) An adopted child shall, subject to subsections (3) and (3A), be treated in law as if he were not the child of any person other than the adopters or adopter.

(3) In the case of a child adopted by one of its natural parents as sole adoptive parent, subsection (2) has no effect as respects entitlement to property depending on relationship to that parent, or as respects anything else depending on that relationship.

. . .

(4) It is hereby declared that this section prevents an adopted child from being illegitimate.

(5) This section has effect—

    (a) in the case of an adoption before 1st January 1976, from that date, and

    (b) in the case of any other adoption, from the date of the adoption.

(6) Subject to the provisions of this Part, this section—

    (a) applies to the construction of enactments or instruments passed or made before the adoption or later, and so applies subject to any contrary indication; and

    (b) has effect as respects things done, or events occurring, after the adoption, or after 31st December 1975, whichever is the later.

41   Adoptive relatives

A relationship existing by virtue of section 39 may be referred to as an adoptive relationship, and—

(a) a male adopter may be referred to as the adoptive father;

(b) a female adopter may be referred to as the adoptive mother;

(c) any other relative of any degree under an adoptive relationship may be referred to as an adoptive relative of that degree,

but this section does not prevent the term 'parent,' or any other term not qualified by the word 'adoptive' being treated as including an adoptive relative.

42 Rules of construction for instruments concerning property

(1) Subject to any contrary indication, the rules of construction contained in this section apply to any instrument, other than an existing instrument, so far as it contains a disposition of property.

(2) In applying section 39(1) to a disposition which depends on the date of birth of a child or children of the adoptive parent or parents, the disposition shall be construed as if—

(a) the adopted child had been born on the date of adoption,

(b) two or more children adopted on the same date had been born on that date in the order of their actual births,

but this does not affect any reference to the age of a child.

(3) Examples of phrases in wills on which subsection (2) can operate are—

1. Children of A 'living at my death or born afterwards.'

2. Children of A 'living at my death or born afterwards before any one of such children for the time being in existence attains a vested interest and who attain the age of 21 years.'

3. As in example 1 or 2, but referring to grandchildren of A instead of children of A.

4. A for life 'until he has a child,' and then to his child or children.

Note. Subsection (2) will not affect the reference to the age of 21 years in example 2.

(4) Section 39(2) does not prejudice any interest vested in possession in the adopted child before the adoption, or any interest expectant (whether immediately or not) upon an interest so vested.

(5) Where it is necessary to determine for the purposes of a disposition of property effected by an instrument whether a woman can have a child, it shall be presumed that once a woman has attained the age of 55 years she will not adopt a child after execution of the instrument, and, notwithstanding section 39, if she does so that child shall not be treated as her child or as the child of her spouse (if any) for the purposes of the instrument.

(6) In this section, 'instrument' includes a private Act settling property, but not any other enactment.

43 Dispositions depending on date of birth

(1) Where a disposition depends on the date of birth of a child who was born illegitimate and who is adopted by one of the natural parents as sole adoptive parent, section 42(2) does not affect entitlement under Part II of the Family Law Reform Act 1969 (illegitimate children).

(2) Subsection (1) applies for example where—

(a) a testator dies in 1976 bequeathing a legacy to his eldest grandchild living at a specified time,

(b) his daughter has an illegitimate child in 1977 who is the first grandchild,

(c) his married son has a child in 1978,

(d) subsequently the illegitimate child is adopted by the mother as sole adoptive parent,

and in all those cases the daughter's child remains the eldest grandchild of the testator throughout.

44 Property devolving with peerages etc.

(1) An adoption does not affect the descent of any peerage or dignity or title of honour.

(2) An adoption shall not affect the devolution of any property limited (expressly or not) to devolve (as nearly as the law permits) along with any peerage or dignity or title of honour.

(3) Subsection (2) applies only if and so far as a contrary intention is not expressed in the instrument, and shall have effect subject to the terms of the instrument.

45   Protection of trustees and personal representatives

(1) A trustee or personal representative is not under a duty, by virtue of the law relating to trusts or the administration of estates, to enquire, before conveying or distributing any property, whether any adoption has been effected or revoked if that fact could affect entitlement to the property.

(2) A trustee or personal representative shall not be liable to any person by reason of a conveyance or distribution of the property made without regard to any such fact if he has not received notice of the fact before the conveyance or distribution.

(3) This section does not prejudice the right of a person to follow the property, or any property representing it, into the hands of another person, other than a purchaser, who has received it.

46   Meaning of 'disposition'

(1) In this Part, unless the context otherwise requires,—

'disposition' includes the conferring of a power of appointment and any other disposition of an interest in or right over property;

'power of appointment' includes any discretionary power to transfer a beneficial interest in property without the furnishing of valuable consideration.

(2) This Part applies to an oral disposition as if contained in an instrument made when the disposition was made.

(3) For the purposes of this Part, the death of the testator is the date at which a will or codicil is to be regarded as made.

(4) For the purposes of this Part, provisions of the law of intestate succession applicable to the estate of a deceased person shall be treated as if contained in an instrument executed by him (while of full capacity) immediately before his death.

47   Miscellaneous enactments

(1) Section 39 does not apply for the purposes of section 1 of and Schedule 1 to the Marriage Act 1949 or Schedule 1 to the Civil Partnership Act 2004 (prohibited degrees of kindred and affinity), sections 10 and 11 (incest) of the Sexual Offences Act 1956.

(2) Section 39 does not apply for the purposes of any provision of—
(a) the British Nationality Act 1981,
(b) the Immigration Act 1971,
(c) any instrument having effect under an enactment within paragraph (a) or (b), or
(d) any other provision of the law for the time being in force which determines British citizenship, British Dependent Territories citizenship, the status of a British National (Overseas) or British Overseas citizenship.

. . .

Rent Act 1977

(1977 c. 42)

PART I   PRELIMINARY

Protected and statutory tenancies

1   Protected tenants and tenancies

Subject to this Part of this Act, a tenancy under which a dwelling-house (which may be a house or part of a house) is let as a separate dwelling is a protected tenancy for the purposes of this Act.

Any reference in this Act to a protected tenant shall be construed accordingly.

2 Statutory tenants and tenancies

(1) Subject to this Part of this Act—

(a) after the termination of a protected tenancy of a dwelling-house the person who, immediately before that termination, was the protected tenant of the dwelling-house shall, if and so long as he occupies the dwelling-house as his residence, be the statutory tenant of it; and

(b) Part I of Schedule 1 to this Act shall have effect for determining what person (if any) is the statutory tenant of a dwelling-house or, as the case may be, is entitled to an assured tenancy of a dwelling-house by succession at any time after the death of a person who, immediately before his death, was either a protected tenant of the dwelling-house or the statutory tenant of it by virtue of paragraph (a) above.

3 Terms and conditions of statutory tenancies

(1) So long as he retains possession, a statutory tenant shall observe and be entitled to the benefit of all the terms and conditions of the original contract of tenancy, so far as they are consistent with the provisions of this Act.

(2) It shall be a condition of a statutory tenancy of a dwelling-house that the statutory tenant shall afford to the landlord access to the dwelling-house and all reasonable facilities for executing therein any repairs which the landlord is entitled to execute.

SCHEDULE 1   STATUTORY TENANCIES

PART I   STATUTORY TENANTS BY SUCCESSION

1. Paragraph 2 below shall have effect, subject to section 2(3) of this Act, for the purpose of determining who is the statutory tenant of a dwelling-house by succession after the death of the person (in this Part of this Schedule referred to as 'the original tenant') who, immediately before his death, was a protected tenant of the dwelling-house or the statutory tenant of it by virtue of his previous protected tenancy.

2. The surviving spouse (if any) of the original tenant, if residing in the dwellinghouse immediately before the death of the original tenant, shall after the death be the statutory tenant if and so long as he or she occupies the dwelling-house as his or her residence.

(2) For the purposes of this paragraph—

(a) a person who was living with the original tenant as his or her wife or husband shall be treated as the spouse of the original tenant, and

(b) a person who was living with the original tenant as if they were civil partners shall be treated as the civil partner of the original tenant.

(3) If, immediately after the death of the original tenant, there is, by virtue of sub-paragraph (2) above, more than one person who fulfils the conditions in sub-paragraph (1) above, such one of them as may be decided by agreement or, in default of agreement, by the county court shall be treated as the surviving spouse for the purposes of this paragraph.

3. Where paragraph 2 above does not apply, but a person who was a member of the original tenant's family was residing with him in the dwelling-house at the time of and for the period of 2 years immediately before his death, then, after his death, that person or if there is more than one such person such one of them as may be decided by agreement, or in default of agreement by the county court, shall for the purposes of this paragraph be treated (according to whether that one of them is of the opposite sex to, or of the same sex as, the original tenant) as the surviving spouse or the surviving civil partner.

(2) If the original tenant died within the period of 18 months beginning on the operative date, then, for the purposes of this paragraph, a person who was residing in the dwelling-house with the original tenant at the time of his death and for the period which began 6 months before the operative date and ended at the time of his death shall be taken to have been residing with the original tenant for the period of 2 years immediately before his death.

4. A person who becomes the statutory tenant of a dwelling-house by virtue of paragraph 2 above is in this Part of this Schedule referred to as 'the first successor.'

5. If, immediately before his death, the first successor was still a statutory tenant, paragraph 6 below shall have effect for the purpose of determining who is entitled to an assured tenancy of the dwelling-house by succession.

6.—(1) Where a person who—

(a) was a member of the original tenant's family immediately before that tenant's death, and

(b) was a member of the first successor's family immediately before the first successor's death,

was residing in the dwelling-house with the first successor at the time of, and for the period of 2 years immediately before, the first successor's death, that person or, if there is more than one such person, such one of them as may be decided by agreement or, in default of agreement, by the county court shall be entitled to an assured tenancy of the dwelling-house by succession.

(2) If the first successor died within the period of 18 months beginning on the operative date, then, for the purposes of this paragraph, a person who was residing in the dwelling-house with the first successor at the time of his death and for the period which began 6 months before the operative date and ended at the time of his death shall be taken to have been residing with the first successor for the period of 2 years immediately before his death.

. . .

10.—(1) Where after a succession the successor becomes the tenant of the dwelling-house by the grant to him of another tenancy, 'the original tenant' and 'the first successor' in this Part of this Schedule shall, in relation to that other tenancy, mean the persons who were respectively the original tenant and the first successor at the time of the succession, and accordingly—

(a) if the successor was the first successor, and, immediately before his death he was still the tenant (whether protected or statutory), paragraph 6 above shall apply on his death,

(b) if the successor was not the first successor, no person shall become a statutory tenant on his death by virtue of this Schedule.

(2) Sub-paragraph (1) above applies—

(a) even if a successor enters into more than one other tenancy of the dwelling-house, and

(b) even if both the first successor and the successor on his death enter into other tenancies of the dwelling-house.

(3) In this paragraph 'succession' means the occasion on which a person becomes the statutory tenant of a dwelling-house by virtue of this Part of this Schedule and 'successor' shall be construed accordingly.

(4) This paragraph shall apply as respects a succession which took place before 27th August 1972 if, and only if, the tenancy granted after the succession, or the first of those tenancies, was granted on or after that date, and where it does not apply as respects a succession, no account should be taken of that succession in applying this paragraph as respects any later succession.

Domestic Proceedings and Magistrates' Courts Act 1978
(1978 c. 22)

PART I   MATRIMONIAL PROCEEDINGS IN MAGISTRATES' COURTS

Powers of court to make orders for financial provision for parties to a marriage and children of the family

1   Grounds of application for financial provision
Either party to a marriage may apply to a magistrates' court for an order under section 2 of this Act on the ground that the other party to the marriage—

    (a) has failed to provide reasonable maintenance for the applicant; or

    (b) has failed to provide, or to make a proper contribution towards, reasonable maintenance for any child of the family; or

    (c) has behaved in such a way that the applicant cannot reasonably be expected to live with the respondent; or

    (d) has deserted the applicant.[1]

2 Powers of court to make orders for financial provision

(1) Where on an application for an order under this section the applicant satisfies the court of any ground mentioned in section 1 of this Act, the court may, subject to the provisions of this Part of this Act, make any one or more of the following orders, that is to say—

    (a) an order that the respondent shall make to the applicant such periodical payments, and for such term, as may be specified in the order;

    (b) an order that the respondent shall pay to the applicant such lump sum as may be so specified;

    (c) an order that the respondent shall make to the applicant for the benefit of a child of the family to whom the application relates, or to such a child, such periodical payments, and for such term, as may be so specified;

    (d) an order that the respondent shall pay to the applicant for the benefit of a child of the family to whom the application relates, or to such a child, such lump sum as may be so specified.

(2) Without prejudice to the generality of subsection (1)(b) or (d) above, an order under this section for the payment of a lump sum may be made for the purpose of enabling any liability or expenses reasonably incurred in maintaining the applicant, or any child of the family to whom the application relates, before the making of the order to be met.

(3) The amount of any lump sum required to be paid by such an order under this section shall not exceed [£1,000] or such larger amount as the Lord Chancellor may from time to time by order fix for the purposes of this subsection.

(4) An order made by the Lord Chancellor under this section-

    (a) shall be made only after consultation with the Lord Chief Justice;

    (b) shall be made by statutory instrument and be subject to annulment in pursuance of a resolution of either House of Parliament.

(5) The Lord Chief Justice may nominate a judicial office holder (as defined in section 109(4) of the Constitutional Reform Act 2005) to exercise his functions under this section.

3 Matters to which court is to have regard in exercising its powers under s. 2

(1) Where an application is made for an order under section 2 of this Act, it shall be the duty of the court, in deciding whether to exercise its powers under that section and, if so, in what manner, to have regard to all the circumstances of the case, first consideration being given to the welfare while a minor of any child of the family who has not attained the age of eighteen.

(2) As regards the exercise of its powers under subsection (1)(a) or (b) of section 2, the court shall in particular have regard to the following matters—

    (a) the income, earning capacity, property and other financial resources which each of the parties to the marriage has or is likely to have in the foreseeable future, including in the case of earning capacity any increase in that capacity which it would in the opinion of the court be reasonable to expect a party to the marriage to take steps to acquire;

    (b) the financial needs, obligations and responsibilities which each of the parties to the marriage has or is likely to have in the foreseeable future;

    (c) the standard of living enjoyed by the parties to the marriage before the occurrence of the conduct which is alleged as the ground of the application;

    (d) the age of each party to the marriage and the duration of the marriage;

---

[1] Paras (c) and (d) are repealed by the Family Law Act 1996, ss. 18(1), 66(3), Sch 10, as from a day to be appointed.

(e) any physical or mental disability of either of the parties to the marriage;

(f) the contributions which each of the parties has made or is likely in the foreseeable future to make to the welfare of the family, including any contribution by looking after the home or caring for the family;

(g) the conduct of each of the parties, if that conduct is such that it would in the opinion of the court be inequitable to disregard it.

(3) As regards the exercise of its powers under subsection (1)(c) or (d) of section 2, the court shall in particular have regard to the following matters—

(a) the financial needs of the child;

(b) the income, earning capacity (if any), property and other financial resources of the child;

(c) any physical or mental disability of the child;

(d) the standard of living enjoyed by the family before the occurrence of the conduct which is alleged as the ground of the application;

(e) the manner in which the child was being and in which the parties to the marriage expected him to be educated or trained;

(f) the matters mentioned in relation to the parties to the marriage in paragraphs (a) and (b) of subsection (2) above.

(4) As regards the exercise of its powers under section 2 in favour of a child of the family who is not the child of the respondent, the court shall also have regard—

(a) to whether the respondent has assumed any responsibility for the child's maintenance and, if he did, to the extent to which, and the basis on which, he assumed that responsibility and to the length of time during which he discharged that responsibility;

(b) to whether in assuming and discharging that responsibility the respondent did so knowing that the child was not his own child;

(c) to the liability of any other person to maintain the child.

4   Duration of orders for financial provision for a party to a marriage

(1) The terms to be specified in any order made under section 2(1)(a) of this Act shall be such terms as the court thinks fit except that the term shall not begin earlier than the date of the making of the application for the order and shall not extend beyond the death of either of the parties to the marriage.

(2) Where an order is made under the said section 2(1)(a) and the marriage of the parties affected by the order is subsequently dissolved or annulled but the order continues in force, the order shall, notwithstanding anything in it, cease to have effect on the remarriage of or formation of a civil partnership by, the party in whose favour it was made, except in relation to any arrears due under the order on the date of the remarriage or formation of the civil partnership.

5   Age limit on making orders for financial provision for children and duration of such orders

(1) Subject to subsection (3) below, no order shall be made under section 2(1)(c) or (d) of this Act in favour of a child who has attained the age of eighteen.

(2) The term to be specified in an order made under section 2(1)(c) of this Act in favour of a child may begin with the date of the making of an application for the order in question or any later date or a date ascertained in accordance with subsection (5) or (6) below but—

(a) shall not in the first instance extend beyond the date of the birthday of the child next following his attaining the upper limit of the compulsory school age (construed in accordance with section 8 of the Education Act 1996) unless the court considers that in the circumstances of the case the welfare of the child requires that it should extend to a later date; and

(b) shall not in any event, subject to subsection (3) below, extend beyond the date of the child's eighteenth birthday.

   (3) The court—
     (a) may make an order under section 2(1)(c) or (d) of this Act in favour of a child who
       has attained the age of eighteen, and
     (b) may include in an order made under section 2(1)(c) of this Act in relation to a
       child who has not attained that age a provision for extending beyond the date
       when the child will attain that age the term for which by virtue of the order any
       payments are to be made to or for the benefit of that child,
if it appears to the court—
     (i)   that the child is, or will be, or if such an order or provision were made would be,
       receiving instruction at an educational establishment or undergoing training for
       a trade, profession or vocation, whether or not he is also, or will also be, in
       gainful employment; or
     (ii) that there are special circumstances which justify the making of the order or
       provison.
   (4) Any order made under section 2(1)(c) of this Act in favour of a child shall,
notwithstanding anything in the order, cease to have effect on the death of the person liable
to make payments under the order.
   (5) Where—
     (a) a maintenance calculation ('the current calculation') is in force with respect to a
       child; and
     (b) an application is made for an order under section 2(1)(c) of this Act—
       (i)   in accordance with section 8 of the Child Support Act 1991; and
       (ii) before the end of the period of 6 months beginning with the making of the
          current calculation,
the term to be specified in any such order made on that application may be expressed to
begin on, or at any time after, the earliest permitted date.
   (6) For the purposes of subsection (5) above, 'the earliest permitted date' is whichever is
the later of—
     (a) the date 6 months before the application is made; or
     (b) the date on which the current calculation took effect or, where successive
       maintenance calculations have been continuously in force with respect to a child,
       on which the first of those calculations took effect.
   (7) Where—
     (a) a maintenance calculation ceases to have effect by or under any provision of the
       Child Support Act 1991; and
     (b) an application is made, before the end of the period of 6 months beginning with
       the relevant date, for an order under section 2(1)(c) of this Act in relation to a
       child with respect to whom that maintenance calculation was in force immedi-
       ately before it ceased to have effect,
the term to be specified in any such order, or in any interim order under section 19 of this
Act, made on that application, may begin with the date on which that maintenance calculation ceased to have effect, or any later date.
   (8) In subsection (7)(b) above—
     (a) where the maintenance calculation ceased to have effect, the relevant date is the
       date on which it so ceased.

6 Orders for payments which have been agreed by the parties

   (1) Either party to a marriage may apply to a magistrates' court for an order under this
section on the ground that either the party making the application or the other party to the
marriage has agreed to make such financial provision as may be specified in the application
and, subject to subsection (3) below, the court on such an application may, if—
     (a) it is satisfied that the applicant or the respondent, as the case may be, has agreed
       to make that provision, and

(b) it has no reason to think that it would be contrary to the interests of justice to exercise its powers hereunder,

order that the applicant or the respondent, as the case may be, shall make the financial provision specified in the application.

(2) In this section 'financial provision' means the provision mentioned in any one or more of the following paragraphs, that is to say—

(a) the making of periodical payments by one party to the other,

(b) the payment of a lump sum by one party to the other,

(c) the making of periodical payments by one party to a child of the family or to the other party for the benefit of such a child,

(d) the payment by one party of a lump sum to a child of the family or to the other party for the benefit of such a child,

and any reference in this section to the financial provision specified in an application made under subsection (1) above or specified by the court under subsection (5) below is a reference to the type of provision specified in the application or by the court, as the case may be, to the amount so specified as the amount of any payment to be made thereunder and, in the case of periodical payments, to the term so specified as the term for which the payments are to be made.

(3) Where the financial provision specified in an application under subsection (1) above includes or consists of provision in respect of a child of the family, the court shall not make an order under that subsection unless it considers that the provision which the applicant or the respondent, as the case may be, has agreed to make in respect of that child provides for, or makes a proper contribution towards, the financial needs of the child.

(4) A party to a marriage who has applied for an order under section 2 of this Act shall not be precluded at any time before the determination of that application from applying for an order under this section; but if an order is made under this section on the application of either party and either of them has also made an application for an order under section 2 of this Act, the application made for the order under section 2 shall be treated as if it had been withdrawn.

(5) Where on an application under subsection (1) above the court decides—

(a) that it would be contrary to the interests of justice to make an order for the making of the financial provision specified in the application, or

(b) that any financial provision which the applicant or the respondent, as the case may be, has agreed to make in respect of a child of the family does not provide for, or make a proper contribution towards, the financial needs of that child,

but is of the opinion—

(i) that it would not be contrary to the interests of justice to make an order for the making of some other financial provision specified by the court, and

(ii) that, in so far as that other financial provision contains any provision for a child of the family, it provides for, or makes a proper contribution towards, the financial needs of that child,

then if both the parties agree, the court may order that the applicant or the respondent, as the case may be, shall make that other financial provision.

(6) Subject to subsection (8) below, the provisions of section 4 of this Act shall apply in relation to an order under this section which requires periodical payments to be made to a party to a marriage for his own benefit as they apply in relation to an order under section 2(1)(a) of this Act.

(7) Subject to subsection (8) below, the provisions of section 5 of this Act shall apply in relation to an order under this section for the making of financial provision in respect of a child of the family as they apply in relation to an order under section 2(1)(c) or (d) of this Act.

(8) Where the court makes an order under this section which contains provision for the making of periodical payments and, by virtue of subsection (4) above, an application for an order under section 2 of this Act is treated as if it had been withdrawn, then the term which

may be specified as the term for which the payments are to be made may begin with the date of the making of the application for the order under section 2 or any later date.

(9) Where the respondent is not present or respresented by counsel or solicitor at the hearing of an application for an order under subsection (1) above, the court shall not make an order under this section unless there is produced to the court such evidence as may be prescribed by rules of court of—

    (a) the consent of the respondent to the making of the order,

    (b) the financial resources of the respondent, and

    (c) in a case where the financial provision specified in the application includes or consists of provision in respect of a child of the family to be made by the applicant to the respondent for the benefit of the child or to the child, the financial resources of the child.

7 Powers of court where parties are living apart by agreement

(1) Where the parties to a marriage have been living apart for a continuous period exceeding three months, neither party having deserted the other, and one of the parties has been making periodical payments for the benefit of the other party or of a child of the family, that other party may apply to a magistrates' court for an order under this section, and any application made under this subsection shall specify the aggregate amount of the payments so made during the period of three months immediately preceding the date of the making of the application.

(2) Where on an application for an order under this section the court is satisfied that the respondent has made the payments specified in the application, the court may, subject to the provisions of this Part of this Act, make one or both of the following orders, that is to say—

    (a) an order that the respondent shall make to the applicant such periodical payments, and for such term, as may be specified in the order;

    (b) an order that the respondent shall make to the applicant for the benefit of a child of the family to whom the application relates, or to such a child, such periodical payments, and for such term, as may be so specified.

(3) The court in the exercise of its powers under this section—

    (a) shall not require the respondent to make payments which exceed in aggregate during any period of three months the aggregate amount paid by him for the benefit of the applicant or a child of the family during the period of three months immediately preceding the date of the making of the application;

    (b) shall not require the respondent to make payments to or for the benefit of any person which exceed in amount the payments which the court considers that it would have required the respondent to make to or for the benefit of that person on an application under section 1 of this Act;

    (c) shall not require payments to be made to or for the benefit of a child of the family who is not a child of the respondent unless the court considers that it would have made an order in favour of that child on an application under section 1 of this Act.

(4) Where on an application under this section the court considers that the orders which it has the power to make under this section—

    (a) would not provide reasonable maintenance for the applicant, or

    (b) if the application relates to a child of the family, would not provide, or make a proper contribution towards reasonable maintenance for that child,

the court shall refuse to make an order under this section, but the court may treat the application as if it were an application for an order under section 2 of this Act.

(5) The provisions of section 3 of this Act shall apply in relation to an application for an order under this section as they apply in relation to an application for an order under section 2 of this Act subject to the modification that for the reference in subsection 2(c) of the said section 3 to the occurrence of the conduct which is alleged as the ground of the application there shall be substituted a reference to the living apart of the parties to the marriage.

(6) The provisions of section 4 of this Act shall apply in relation to an order under this section which requires periodical payments to be made to the applicant for his own benefit as they apply in relation to an order made under section 2(1)(a) of this Act.

(7) The provisions of section 5 of this Act shall apply in relation to an order under this section for the making of periodical payments in respect of a child of the family as they apply in relation to an order under section 2(1)(c) of this Act.

Powers of court as to the custody etc. of children

8   Restrictions on making of orders under this Act: welfare of children

Where an application is made by a party to a marriage for an order under section 2, 6 or 7 of this Act, then, if there is a child of the family who is under the age of eighteen, the court shall not dismiss or make a final order on the application until it has decided whether to exercise any of its powers under the Children Act 1989 with respect to the child.

Interim orders

19   Interim orders

(1) Where an application is made for an order under section 2, 6 or 7 of this Act—

(a) the magistrates' court at any time before making a final order on, or dismissing, the application or on refusing to make an order on the application by virtue of section 27 of this Act, and

(b) the High Court on ordering the application to be reheard by a magistrates' court (either after the refusal of an order under section 27 of this Act or on an appeal under section 29 of this Act),

shall, subject to the provisions of this Part of this Act, have the

(i) power to make an order (in this Part of this Act referred to as an 'interim maintenance order') which requires the respondent to make to the applicant or to any child of the family who is under the age of eighteen, or to the applicant for the benefit of such a child, such periodical payments as the court thinks reasonable.

(3) An interim maintenance order may provide for payments to be made from such date as the court may specify, except that, subject to section 5(5) and (6) of this Act, the date shall not be earlier than the date of the making of the application for an order under section 2, 6 or 7 of this Act; and where such an order made by the High Court on an appeal under section 29 of this Act provides for payments to be made from a date earlier than the date of the making of the order, the interim order may provide that payments made by the respondent under an order made by a magistrates' court shall, to such extent and in such manner as may be provided by the interim order, be treated as having been paid on account of any payment provided for by the interim order.

(3A) Where an application is made for an order under section 6 of this Act by the party to the marriage who has agreed to make the financial provision specified in the application—

(a) subsection (1) shall apply as if the reference in paragraph (i) to the respondent were a reference to the applicant and the references to the applicant were references to the respondent; and

(b) subsection (3) shall apply accordingly.

(5) Subject to subsection (6) below, an interim order made on an application for an order under section 2, 6 or 7 of this Act shall cease to have effect on whichever of the following dates occurs first, that is to say—

(a) the date, if any, specified for the purpose of the interim order;

(b) the date of the expiration of the period of three months beginning with the date of the making of the interim order;

(c) the date on which a magistrates' court either makes a final order on or dismisses the application.

(6) Where an interim order made under subsection (1) above would, but for this subsection, cease to have effect by virtue of subsection (5)(a) or (b) above, the magistrates' court which made the order or, in the case of an interim order made by the High Court, the magistrates' court by which the application for an order under section 2, 6 or 7 of this Act is to be reheard, shall have power by order to provide that the interim order shall continue in force for a further period, and any order continued in force under this subsection shall cease to have effect on whichever of the following dates occurs first, that is to say—

(a) the date, if any, specified for the purpose in the order made under this subsection;

(b) the date of the expiration of the period of three months beginning with the date of the making of the order under this subsection or, if more than one order has been made under this subsection with respect to the application, beginning with the date of the making of the first of those orders;

(c) the date on which the court either makes a final order on, or dismisses, the application.

(7) Not more than one interim maintenance order may be made with respect to any application for an order under section 2, 6 or 7 of this Act, but without prejudice to the powers of a court under this section on any further such application.

(8) No appeal shall lie from the making of or refusal to make, the variation of or refusal to vary, or the revocation of or refusal to revoke, an interim maintenance order.

(9) An interim order made by the High Court under this section on ordering that an application be reheard by a magistrates' court shall, for the purpose of its enforcement and for the purposes of section 20 of this Act, be treated as if it were an order of that magistrates' court and not of the High Court.

Variation, revocation and cessation of orders etc.

20   Variation, revival and revocation of orders for periodical payments

(1) Where a magistrates' court has made an order under section 2(1)(a) or (c) of this Act for the making of periodical payments, the court shall have power, on an application made under this section, to vary or revoke that order and also to make an order under section 2(1)(b) or (d) of this Act.

(2) Where a magistrates' court has made an order under section 6 of this Act for the making of periodical payments by a party to a marriage the court shall have power, on an application made under this section, to vary or revoke that order and also to make an order for the payment of a lump sum by that party either—

(a) to the other party to the marriage, or

(b) to a child of the family or to that other party for the benefit of that child.

(3) Where a magistrates' court has made an order under section 7 of this Act for the making of periodical payments, the court shall have power, on an application made under this section, to vary or revoke that order.

(5) Where a magistrates' court has made an interim maintenance order under section 19 of this Act, the court, on an application made under this section, shall have power to vary or revoke that order, except that the court shall not by virtue of this subsection extend the period for which the order is in force.

(6) The power of the court under this section to vary an order for the making of periodical payments shall include power to suspend any provision thereof temporarily and to revive any provision so suspended.

(7) Where the court has power by virtue of this section to make an order for the payment of a lump sum, the amount of the lump sum shall not exceed the maximum amount that may at that time be required to be paid under section 2(3) of this Act, but the court may make an order for the payment of a lump sum not exceeding that amount notwithstanding that the person required to pay the lump sum was required to pay a lump sum by a previous order under this Part of this Act.

(8) Where the court has power by virtue of subsection (2) above to make an order for the payment of a lump sum and the respondent or the applicant as the case may be has agreed to pay a lump sum of an amount exceeding the maximum amount that may at that time be required to be paid under section 2(3) of this Act, the court may, notwithstanding anything in subsection (7) above, make an order for the payment of a lump sum of that amount.

(9) An order by virtue of this section which varies an order for the making of periodical payments may provide that the payments as so varied shall be made from such date as the court may specify, except that, subject to subsections (9A) and (9B) below, the date shall not be earlier than the date of the making of the application under this section.

(9A) Where—
   (a) there is in force an order ('the order')—
      (i)   under section 2(1)(c) of this Act,
      (ii) under section 6(1) of this Act making provision of a kind mentioned in paragraph (c) of section 6(2) of this Act (regardless of whether it makes provision of any other kind mentioned in that paragraph),
      (iii) under section 7(2)(b) of this Act, or
      (iv) which is an interim maintenance order under which the payments are to be made to a child or to the applicant for the benefit of a child;
   (b) the order requires payments specified in it to be made to or for the benefit of more than one child without apportioning those payments between them;
   (c) a maintenance calculation ('the calculation') is made with respect to one or more, but not all, of the children with respect to whom those payments are to be made; and
   (d) an application is made, before the end of the period of 6 months beginning with the date on which the calculation was made, for the variation or revocation of the order,
the court may, in exercise of its powers under this section to vary or revoke the order, direct that the variation or revocation shall take effect from the date on which the calculation took effect or any later date.

(9B) Where—
   (a) an order ('the child order') of a kind prescribed for the purposes of section 10(1) of the Child Support Act 1991 is affected by a maintenance calculation;
   (b) on the date on which the child order became so affected there was in force an order ('the spousal order')—
      (i)   under section 2(1)(a) of this Act,
      (ii) under section 6(1) of this Act making provision of a kind mentioned in section 6(2)(a) of this Act (regardless of whether it makes provision of any other kind mentioned in that paragraph),
      (iii) under section 7(2)(a) of this Act, or
      (iv) which is an interim maintenance order under which the payments are to be made to the applicant (otherwise than for the benefit of a child); and
   (c) an application is made, before the end of the period of 6 months beginning with the date on which the maintenance calculation was made, for the spousal order to be varied or revoked,
the court may, in exercise of its powers under this section to vary or revoke the spousal order, direct that the variation or revocation shall take effect from the date on which the child order became so affected or any later date.

(9C) For the purposes of subsection (9B) above, an order is affected if it ceases to have effect or is modified by or under section 10 of the Child Support Act 1991.

(11) In exercising the powers conferred by this section, the court shall, so far as it appears to the court just to do so, give effect to any agreement which has been reached between the parties in relation to the application and, if there is no such agreement or if the court decides not to give effect to the agreement, the court shall have regard to all the circumstances of the

case, first consideration being given to the welfare while a minor of any child of the family who has not attained the age of eighteen, and the circumstances of the case shall include any change in any of the matters to which the court was required to have regard when making the order to which the application relates or, in the case of an application for the variation or revocation of an order made under section 6 of this Act or on an appeal under section 29 of this Act, to which the court would have been required to have regard if that order had been made under section 2 of this Act.

(12) An application under this section may be made—

(a) where it is for the variation or revocation of an order under section 2, 6, 7 or 19 of this Act for periodical payments, by either party to the marriage in question; and

(b) where it is for the variation of an order under section 2(1)(c), 6 or 7 of this Act for periodical payments to or in respect of a child, also by the child himself, if he has attained the age of sixteen.

20ZA   Variation of orders for periodical payments: further provisions

(1) Subject to subsections (7) and (8) below, the power of the court under section 20 of this Act to vary an order for the making of periodical payments shall include power, if the court is satisfied that payment has not been made in accordance with the order, to exercise one of its powers under paragraphs (a) to (d) of section 59(3) of the Magistrates' Courts Act 1980.

(2) In any case where—

(a) a magistrates' court has made an order under this Part of this Act for the making of periodical payments, and

(b) payments under the order are required to be made by any method of payment falling within section 59(6) of the Magistrates' Courts Act 1980 (standing order, etc.),

an application may be made under this subsection to the court for the order to be varied as mentioned in subsection (3) below.

(3) Subject to subsection (5) below, where an application is made under subsection (2) above, a justices' clerk, after giving written notice (by post or otherwise) of the application to the respondent and allowing the respondent, within the period of 14 days beginning with the date of the giving of that notice, an opportunity to make written representations, may vary the order to provide that payments under the order shall be made to the designated officer for the court.

(4) The clerk may proceed with an application under subsection (2) above notwithstanding that the respondent has not received written notice of the application.

(5) Where an application has been made under subsection (2) above, the clerk may, if he considers it inappropriate to exercise his power under subsection (3) above, refer the matter to the court which, subject to subsections (7) and (8) below, may vary the order by exercising one of its powers under paragraphs (a) to (d) of section 59(3) of the Magistrates' Courts Act 1980.

(6) Subsection (4) of section 59 of the Magistrates' Courts Act 1980 (power of court to order that account be opened) shall apply for the purposes of subsections (1) and (5) above as it applies for the purposes of that section.

(7) Before varying the order by exercising one of its powers under paragraphs (a) to (d) of section 59(3) of the Magistrates' Courts Act 1980, the court shall have regard to any representations made by the parties to the application.

(8) If the court does not propose to exercise its power under paragraph (c), (cc) or (d) of subsection (3) of section 59 of the Magistrates' Courts Act 1980, the court shall, unless upon representations expressly made in that behalf by the person to whom payments under the order are required to be made it is satisfied that it is undesirable to do so, exercise its power under paragraph (b) of that subsection.

(9) Subsection (12) of section 20 of this Act shall have effect for the purposes of applications under subsection (2) above as it has effect for the purposes of applications under that section.

(10) None of the powers of the court, or of a justice's clerk, conferred by this section shall be exercisable in relation to an order under this Part of this Act for the making of periodical payments which is not a qualifying maintenance order (within the meaning of section 59 of the Magistrates' Courts Act 1980).

20A Revival of orders for periodical payments

(1) Where an order made by a magistrates' court under this Part of this Act for the making of periodical payments to or in respect of a child (other than an interim maintenance order) ceases to have effect—

    (a) on the date on which the child attains the age of sixteen, or

    (b) at any time after that date but before or on the date on which he attains the age of eighteen,

the child may apply to the court which made the order for an order for its revival.

(2) If on such an application it appears to the court that—

    (a) the child is, will be or (if an order were made under this subsection) would be receiving instruction at an educational establishment or undergoing training for a trade, profession or vocation, whether or not while in gainful employment, or

    (b) there are special circumstances which justify the making of an order under this subsection,

the court shall have power by order to revive the order from such date as the court may specify, not being earlier than the date of the making of the application.

(3) Any order revived under this section may be varied or revoked under section 20 in the same way as it could have been varied or revoked had it continued in being.

22 Variation of instalments of lump sum

Where in the exercise of its powers under section 75 of the Magistrates' Courts Act 1980 a magistrates' court orders that a lump sum required to be paid under this Part of this Act shall be paid by instalments, the court, on an application made by either the person liable to pay or the person entitled to receive that sum, shall have power to vary that order by varying the number of instalments payable, the amount of any instalment payable and the date on which any instalment becomes payable.

23 Supplementary provisions with respect to variation and revocation of orders

(2) The powers of a magistrates' court to revoke, revive or vary an order for the periodical payment of money and the power of the clerk of a magistrates' court to vary such an order under section 60 of the Magistrates' Courts Act 1980 and the power of a magistrates' court to suspend or rescind certain other orders under section 63(2) of that Act shall not apply in relation to an order made under this Part of this Act.

25 Effect on certain orders of parties living together

(1) Where—

    (a) periodical payments are required to be made to one of the parties to a marriage (whether for his own benefit or for the benefit of a child of the family) by an order made under section 2 or 6 of this Act or by an interim maintenance order made under section 19 of this Act (otherwise than on an application under section 7 of this Act),

the order shall be enforceable notwithstanding that the parties to the marriage are living with each other at the date of the making of the order or that, although they are not living with each other at that date, they subsequently resume living with each other; but the order shall cease to have effect if after that date the parties continue to live with each other, or resume living with each other, for a continuous period exceeding six months.

(2) Where any of the following orders is made under this Part of this Act, that is to say—

    (a) an order under section 2 or 6 of this Act which requires periodical payments to be made to a child of the family, or

    (b) an interim maintenance order under section 19 of this Act (otherwise than on an application under section 7 of this Act) which requires periodical payments to be made to a child of the family, then, unless the court otherwise directs, the order shall continue to have effect and be enforceable notwithstanding that the parties to the marriage in question are living with each other at the date of the making of the order or that, although they are not living with each other at that date, they subsequently resume living with each other.

(3) Any order made under section 7 of this Act, and any interim maintenance order made on an application for an order under that section, shall cease to have effect if the parties to the marriage resume living with each other.

(4) Where an order made under this Part of this Act ceases to have effect by virtue of subsection (1) or (3) above or by virtue of a direction given under subsection (2) above, a magistrates' court may, on an application made by either party to the marriage, make an order declaring that the first mentioned order ceased to have effect from such date as the court may specify.

Reconciliation

26   Reconciliation

(1) Where an application is made for an order under section 2 of this Act the court, before deciding whether to exercise its powers under that section, shall consider whether there is any possibility of reconciliation between the parties to the marriage in question: and if at any stage of the proceedings on that application it appears to the court that there is a reasonable possibility of such a reconciliation, the court may adjourn the proceedings for such period as it thinks fit to enable attempts to be made to effect a reconciliation.

(2) Where the court adjourns any proceedings under subsection (1) above, it may request an officer of the Service (within the meaning of the Criminal Justice and Court Services Act 2000), a Welsh family proceedings officer (within the meaning given by section 35 of the Children Act 2004) or any other person to attempt to effect a reconciliation between the parties to the marriage, and where any such request is made, that officer or other person shall report in writing to the court whether the attempt has been successful or not, but shall not include in that report any other information.

Provisions relating to High Court and county court

27   Refusal of order in case more suitable for High Court

Where on hearing an application for an order under section 2 of this Act a magistrates' court is of the opinion that any of the matters in question between the parties would be more conveniently dealt with by the High Court, the magistrates' court shall refuse to make any order on the application, and no appeal shall lie from that refusal; but if in any proceedings in the High Court relating to or comprising the same subject matter as that application the High Court so orders, the application shall be reheard and determined by a magistrates' court acting in the same local justice area as the first mentioned court.

28   Powers of High Court and county court in relation to certain orders under Part I

(1) Where after the making by a magistrates' court of an order under this Part of this Act proceedings between, and relating to the marriage of, the parties to the proceedings in which that order was made have been commenced in the High Court or a county court, then, except in the case of an order for the payment of a lump sum, the court in which the proceedings or any application made therein are or is pending may, if it thinks fit, direct that the order made by a magistrates' court shall cease to have effect on such date as may be specified in the direction.

29   Appeals

(1) Subject to section 27 of this Act, where a magistrates' court makes or refuses to make, varies or refuses to vary, revokes or refuses to revoke an order (other than an interim maintenance order) under this Part of this Act, an appeal shall lie to the High Court.

(2) On an appeal under this section the High Court shall have power to make such orders as may be necessary to give effect to its determination of the appeal, including such incidental or consequential orders as appear to the court to be just, and, in the case of an appeal from a decision of a magistrates' court made on an application for or in respect of an order for the making of periodical payments, the High Court shall have power to order that its determination of the appeal shall have effect from such date as the court thinks fit, not being earlier than the date of the making of the application to the magistrates' court or, in a case where there was made to the magistrates' court an application for an order under section 2 and an application under section 6 and the term of the periodical payments was or might have been ordered to begin on the date of the making of the application for an order under section 2, the date of the making of that application.

(3) Without prejudice to the generality of subsection (2) above, where, on an appeal under this section in respect of an order of a magistrates' court requiring any person to make periodical payments, the High Court reduces the amount of those payments or discharges the order, the High Court shall have power to order the person entitled to payments under the order of the magistrates' court to pay to the person liable to make payments under that order such sum in respect of payments already made in compliance with the order as the court thinks fit and, if any arrears are due under the order of the magistrates' court, the High Court shall have power to remit the payment of those arrears or any part thereof.

(5) Any order of the High Court made on an appeal under this section (other than an order directing that an application shall be reheard by a magistrates' court) shall for the purposes of the enforcement of the order and for the purposes of section 20 of this Act be treated as if it were an order of the magistrates' court from which the appeal was brought and not of the High Court.

Provisions relating to procedure, jurisdiction and enforcement

30 Provisions as to jurisdiction and procedure

(1) A magistrates' court shall, subject to section 2 of the Family Law Act 1986 and section 70 of the Magistrates' Court Act 1980 and any determination of the Lord Chancellor thereunder, have jurisdiction to hear an application for an order under this Part of this Act if it acts in, or is authorised by the Lord Chancellor to act for, a local justice area in which either the applicant or the respondent ordinarily resides at the date of the making of the application...

(5) It is hereby declared that any jurisdiction conferred on a magistrates' court by this Part of this Act is exercisable notwithstanding that any party to the proceedings is not domiciled in England.

32 Enforcement etc. of orders for payment of money

(1) An order for the payment of money made by a magistrates' court under this Part of this Act shall be enforceable as a magistrates' court maintenance order.

(2) Without prejudice to section 59 of the Magistrates' Courts Act 1980 (which relates to the power of a magistrates' court to direct periodical payments to be made through the designated officer for a magistrates' court) a magistrates' court making an order under this Part of this Act for the making of a periodical payment by one person to another may direct that it shall be made to some third party on that other person's behalf instead of directly to that other person; and, for the purposes of any order made under this Part of this Act, the said section 59 shall have effect as if, in subsection (7) thereof, for the words 'the person who applied for the maintenance order' there were substituted the words 'the person to whom the payments under the order fall to be made.'

(3) Any person for the time being under an obligation to make payments in pursuance of any order for the payment of money made under this Part of this Act shall give notice of any change of address to such person, if any, as may be specified in the order; and any person who without reasonable excuse fails to give such a notice shall be liable on summary conviction to a fine not exceeding level 2 on the standard scale.

(4) A person shall not be entitled to enforce through the High Court or any county court the payment of any arrears due under an order made by virtue of this Part of this Act without the leave of that court if those arrears became due more than twelve months before proceedings to enforce the payment of them are begun.

(5) The court hearing an application for the grant of leave under subsection (4) above may refuse to leave, or may grant leave subject to such restrictions and conditions (including conditions as to the allowing of time for payment or the making of payment by instalments) as that court thinks proper, or may remit the payment of such arrears or any part thereof.

(6) An application for the grant of leave under subsection (4) above shall be made in such manner as may be prescribed by rules of court.

35 Orders for repayment in certain cases of sums paid after cessation of order by reason of remarriage or formation of civil partnership

(1) Where—

    (a) an order made under section 2(1)(a), 6 or 7 of this Act has, by virtue of section 4(2) of this Act, ceased to have effect by reason of the remarriage of, or formation of a civil partnership by, the party in whose favour it was made, and

    (b) the person liable to make payments under the order made payments in accordance with it in respect of a period after the date of that remarriage or the formation of that civil partnership in the mistaken belief that the order was still subsisting,

no proceedings in respect of a cause of action arising out of the circumstances mentioned in paragraphs (a) and (b) above shall be maintainable by the person so liable or his personal representatives against the person so entitled or his personal representatives, but on an application made under this section the court may exercise the powers conferred on it by subsection (2) below.

(2) The court may order the respondent to an application made under this section to pay to the applicant a sum equal to the amount of the payments made in respect of the period mentioned in subsection (1)(b) above or, if it appears to the court that it would be unjust to make that order, it may either order the respondent to pay to the applicant such lesser sum as it thinks fit or dismiss the application.

. . .

PART V   SUPPLEMENTARY PROVISIONS

88 Interpretation

(1) In this Act—

'child,' in relation to one or both of the parties to a marriage, includes a child whose father and mother were not married to each other at the time of his birth;

'child of the family,' in relation to the parties to a marriage, means—

    (a) a child of both of those parties; and

    (b) any other child, not being a child who is placed with those parties as foster parents by a local authority or voluntary organisation, who has been treated by both of those parties as a child of their family;

'family proceedings' has the meaning assigned to it by section 65 of the Magistrates' Courts Act 1980;

'local authority' means the council of a county (other than a metropolitan county), of a metropolitan district or of a London borough, or the Common Council of the City of London;

'Magistrates' court maintenance order' has the same meaning as in section 150(1) of the Magistrates' Courts Act 1980;

'maintenance calculation' has the same meaning as it has in the Child Support Act 1991 by virtue of section 54 of that Act as read with any regulations in force under that section;

(2) References in this Act to the parties to a marriage living with each other shall be construed as references to their living with each other in the same household.

(3) For the avoidance of doubt it is hereby declared that references in this Act to remarriage include references to a marriage which is by law void or voidable.

...

Charging Orders Act 1979
(1979 c. 53)

Charging orders

1   Charging orders

(1) Where, under a judgment or order of the High Court or a county court, a person (the 'debtor') is required to pay a sum of money to another person (the 'creditor') then, for the purpose of enforcing that judgment or order, the appropriate court may make an order in accordance with the provisions of this Act imposing on any such property of the debtor as may be specified in the order a charge for securing the payment of any money due or to become due under the judgment or order.

(2) The appropriate court is—

(a) in a case where the property to be charged is a fund in court, the court in which that fund is lodged;

(b) in a case where paragraph (a) above does not apply and the order to be enforced is a maintenance order of the High Court, the High Court or a county court;

(c) in a case where neither paragraph (a) nor paragraph (b) above applies and the judgment or order to be enforced is a judgment or order of the High Court for a sum exceeding the county court limit, the High Court or a county court; and

(d) in any other case, a county court. In this section 'county court limit' means the county court limit for the time being specified in an Order in Council under section 145 of the County Courts Act 1984, as the county court limit for the purposes of the section and 'maintenance order' has the same meaning as in section 2(a) of the Attachment of Earnings Act 1971.

(3) An order under subsection (1) above is referred to in this Act as a 'charging order.'

(4) Where a person applies to the High Court for a charging order to enforce more than one judgment or order, that court shall be the appropriate court in relation to the application if it would be the appropriate court, apart from this subsection, on an application relating to one or more of the judgments or orders concerned.

(5) In deciding whether to make a charging order the court shall consider all the circumstances of the case and, in particular, any evidence before it as to—

(a) the personal circumstances of the debtor, and

(b) whether any other creditor of the debtor would be likely to be unduly prejudiced by the making of the order.

2   Property which may be charged

(1) Subject to subsection (3) below, a charge may be imposed by a charging order only on—

(a) any interest held by the debtor beneficially—

(i)   in any asset of a kind mentioned in subsection (2) below, or

(ii) under any trust; or

(b) any interest held by a person as trustee of a trust ('the trust'), if the interest is in such an asset or is an interest under another trust and—

(i)   the judgment or order in respect of which a charge is to be imposed was made against that person as trustee of the trust, or

(ii) the whole beneficial interest under the trust is held by the debtor unencumbered and for his own benefit, or

(iii) in a case where there are two or more debtors all of whom are liable to the creditor for the same debt, they together hold the whole beneficial interest under the trust unencumbered and for their own benefit.

(2) The assets referred to in subsection (1) above are—

(a) land,

(b) securities of any of the following kinds—

(i) government stock,

(ii) stock of any body (other than a building society) incorporated within England and Wales,

(iii) stock of any body incorporated outside England and Wales or of any state or territory outside the United Kingdom, being stock registered in a register kept at any place within England and Wales,

(iv) units of any unit trust in respect of which a register of the unit holders is kept at any place within England and Wales, or

(c) funds in court.

(3) In any case where a charge is imposed by a charging order on any interest in an asset of a kind mentioned in paragraph (b) or (c) of subsection (2) above, the court making the order may provide for the charge to extend to any interest or dividend payable in respect of the asset.

Magistrates' Courts Act 1980
(1980 c. 43)

PART II   ORDERS FOR PERIODICAL PAYMENT

59   Orders for periodical payment: means of payment

(1) In any case where a magistrates' court orders money to be paid periodically by one person (in this section referred to as 'the debtor') to another (in this section referred to as 'the creditor'), then—

(a) if the order is a qualifying maintenance order, the court shall at the same time exercise one of its powers under paragraphs (a) to (d) of subsection (3) below;

(b) if the order is not a maintenance order, the court shall at the same time exercise one of its powers under paragraphs (a) and (b) of that subsection.

(2) For the purposes of this section a maintenance order is a 'qualifying maintenance order' if, at the time it is made, the debtor is ordinarily resident in England and Wales.

(3) The powers of the court are—

(a) the power to order that payments under the order be made directly by the debtor to the creditor;

(b) the power to order that payments under the order be made to the designated officer for the court or for any other magistrates' court;

(c) the power to order that payments under the order be made by the debtor to the creditor by such method of payment falling within subsection (6) below as may be specified;

(cc) the power to order that payments under the order be made in accordance with arrangements made by the Secretary of State for their collection;

(d) the power to make an attachment of earnings order under the Attachment of Earnings Act 1971 to secure payments under the order.

(3A) No order made by a magistrates' court under paragraphs (a) to (d) of subsection (3) above (other than one made under paragraph (cc)) shall have effect at any time when the

Secretary of State is arranging for the collection of payments under the qualifying maintenance order concerned.

(4) In any case where—

(a) the court proposes to exercise its power under paragraph (c) of subsection (3) above, and

(b) having given the debtor an opportunity of opening an account from which payments under the order may be made in accordance with the method of payment proposed to be ordered under that paragraph, the court is satisfied that the debtor has failed, without reasonable excuse, to open such an account,

the court in exercising its power under that paragraph may order that the debtor open such an account.

(5) In deciding, in the case of a maintenance order, which of the powers under paragraphs (a) to (d) of subsection (3) above (other than paragraph (cc)) it is to exercise, the court having (if practicable) given them an opportunity to make representations shall have regard to any representations made—

(a) by the debtor,

(b) by the creditor, and

(c) if the person who applied for the maintenance order is a person other than the creditor, by that other person.

(6) The methods of payment referred to in subsection (3)(c) above are the following, that is to say—

(a) payment by standing order; or

(b) payment by any other method which requires one person to give his authority for payments of a specific amount to be made from an account of his to an account of another's on specific dates during the period for which the authority is in force and without the need for any further authority from him.

(7) Where the maintenance order is an order—

(a) under the Guardianship of Minors Acts 1971 and 1973,

(b) under Part I of the Domestic Proceedings and Magistrates' Courts Act 1978 or Schedule 6 to the Civil Partnership Act 2004, or

(c) under, or having effect as if made under, Schedule 1 to the Children Act 1989,

and the court does not propose to exercise its power under paragraph (c), (cc) or (d) of subsection (3) above, the court shall, unless upon representations expressly made in that behalf by the person who applied for the maintenance order it is satisfied that it is undesirable to do so, exercise its power under paragraph (b) of that subsection.

(8) The Lord Chancellor may by regulations confer on magistrates' courts, in addition to their powers under paragraphs (a) to (d) of subsection (3) above, the power (the 'additional power') to order that payments under a qualifying maintenance order be made by the debtor to the creditor or the designated officer for a magistrates' court (as the regulations may provide) by such method of payment as may be specified in the regulations.

(9) Any reference in any enactment to paragraphs (a) to (d) of subsection (3) above (but not a reference to any specific paragraph of that subsection) shall be taken to include a reference to the additional power, and the reference in subsection (10) below to the additional power shall be construed accordingly.

(10) Regulations under subsection (8) above may make provision for any enactment concerning, or connected with, payments under maintenance orders to apply, with or without modifications, in relation to the additional power.

. . .

(12) For the purposes of this section—

(a) the reference in subsection (1) above to money paid periodically by one person to another includes, in the case of a maintenance order, a reference to a lump sum paid by instalments by one person to another; and

(b) references to arrangements made by the Secretary of State for the collection of payments are to arrangements made by him under section 30 of the Child Support Act 1991 and regulations made under that section.

59A   Orders for periodical payment: proceedings by designated officer

(1) Where payments under a relevant UK order are required to be made periodically—

(a) to or through the designated officer for a magistrates' court, or

(b) by any method of payment falling within section 59(6) above,

and any sums payable under the order are in arrear, the relevant designated officer shall, if the person for whose benefit the payments are required to be made so requests in writing, and unless it appears to that designated officer that it is unreasonable in the circumstances to do so, proceed in his own name for the recovery of those sums.

(2) Where payments under a relevant UK order are required to be made periodically to or through the designated officer for a magistrates' court, the person for whose benefit the payments are required to be made may, at any time during the period in which the payments are required to be so made, give authority in writing to the relevant designated officer for him to proceed as mentioned in subsection (3) below.

(3) Where authority under subsection (2) above is given to the relevant designated officer, he shall, unless it appears to him that it is unreasonable in the circumstances to do so, proceed in his own name for the recovery of any sums payable to or through him under the orders in question which, on or after the date of the giving of the authority, fall into arrear.

(4) In any case where—

(a) authority under subsection (2) above has been given to the relevant designated officer, and

(b) the person for whose benefit the payments are required to be made gives notice in writing to the relevant delegated officer cancelling the authority,

the authority shall cease to have effect and, accordingly, the relevant designated officer shall not continue any proceedings already commenced by virtue of the authority.

(5) The person for whose benefit the payments are required to be made shall have the same liability for all the costs properly incurred in or about proceedings taken under subsection (1) above at his request or under subsection (3) above by virtue of his authority (including any costs incurred as a result of any proceedings commenced not being continued) as if the proceedings had been taken by him.

(6) Nothing in subsection (1) or (3) above shall affect any right of a person to proceed in his own name for the recovery of sums payable on his behalf under an order of any court.

(7) In this section—

'the relevant designated officer', in relation to an order, means—

(a) in a case where payments under the order are required to be made to or through the designated officer for a magistrates' court, the designated officer for that magistrates' court;

(b) in a case where such payments are required to be made by any method of payment falling within section 59(6) and the order was made by a magistrates' court, the designated officer for that magistrates' court; and

(c) in a case where such payments are required to be made by any method of payment falling within section 59(6) and the order was not made by a magistrates' court, the designated officer for the magistrates' court in which the order is registered;

'relevant UK order' means—

(a) an order made by a magistrates' court, other than an order made by virtue of Part II of the Maintenance Orders (Reciprocal Enforcement) Act 1972;

(b) an order made by the High Court or a county court (including an order deemed to be made by the High Court by virtue of section 1(2) of the Maintenance Orders Act 1958) and registered under Part I of that Act of 1958 in a magistrates' court;

. . .

and any reference to payments required to be made periodically includes, in the case of a maintenance order, a reference to instalments required to be paid in respect of a lump sum payable by instalments.

59B   Maintenance orders: penalty for breach

(1) In any case where—

(a) payments under a relevant English maintenance order are required to be made periodically in the manner mentioned in paragraph (a) or (b) of section 59A(1) above, and

(b) the debtor fails, on or after the date of commencement of this section, to comply with the order in so far as the order relates to the manner of payment concerned,

the person for whose benefit the payments are required to be made may make a complaint to a relevant justice giving details of the failure to comply.

(2) If the relevant justice is satisfied that the nature of the alleged failure to comply may be such as to justify the relevant court in exercising its power under subsection (3) below, he shall issue a summons directed to the debtor requiring him to appear before the relevant court to answer the complaint.

(3) On the hearing of the complaint, the relevant court may order the debtor to pay a sum not exceeding £1000.

(4) Any sum ordered to be paid under subsection (3) above shall for the purposes of this Act be treated as adjudged to be paid by a conviction of a magistrates court.

(5) In this section—

'debtor' has the same meaning as it has in section 59 above;

'the relevant court', in relation to an order, means—

(a) in a case where payments under the order are required to be made to or through the designated officer for a magistrates' court, that magistrates' court;

(b) in a case where such payments are required to be made by any method of payment falling within section 59(6) and the order was made by a magistrates' court, that magistrates' court; and

(c) in a case where such payments are required to be made by any method of payment falling within section 59(6) and the order was not made by a magistrates' court, the magistrates' court in which the order is registered;

'relevant English maintenance order' means—

(a) a maintenance order made by a magistrates' court, other than an order made by virtue of Part II of the Maintenance Orders (Reciprocal Enforcement) Act 1972; or

(b) an order made by the High Court or a county court (other than an order deemed to be made by the High Court by virtue of section 1(2) of the Maintenance Orders Act 1958) and registered under Part I of that Act of 1958 in a magistrates' court;

'relevant justice', in relation to a relevant court, means a justice of the peace acting in the local justice area in which the relevant court is acting;

and any reference to payments required to be made periodically includes a reference to instalments required to be paid in respect of a lump sum payable by instalments.

60   Revocation, variation etc., of orders for periodical payment

(1) Where a magistrates' court has made an order for money to be paid periodically by one person to another, the court may, by order on complaint, revoke, revive or vary the order.

(2) The power under subsection (1) above to vary an order shall include power to suspend the operation of any provision of the order temporarily and to revive the operation of any provision so suspended.

(3) Where the order mentioned in subsection (1) above is a maintenance order, the power under that subsection to vary the order shall include power, if the court is satisfied that payment has not been made in accordance with the order, to exercise one of its powers under paragraphs (a) to (d) of section 59(3) above.

(4) In any case where—

(a) a magistrates' court has made a maintenance order, and

(b) payments under the order are required to be made by any method of payment falling within section 59(6) above,

an interested party may apply in writing to the court for the order to be varied as mentioned in subsection (5) below.

(5) Subject to subsection (8) below, where an application has been made under subsection (4) above, a justice's clerk, after giving written notice (by post or otherwise) of the application to any other interested party and allowing that party, within the period of 14 days beginning with the date of the giving of that notice, an opportunity to make written representations, may vary the order to provide that payments under the order shall be made to the designated officer for the court.

(6) The clerk may proceed with an application under subsection (4) above notwithstanding that any such interested party as is referred to in subsection (5) above has not received written notice of the application.

(7) In subsections (4) to (6) above 'interested party', in relation to a maintenance order, means—

(a) the debtor;

(b) the creditor; and

(c) if the person who applied for the maintenance order is a person other than the creditor, that other person.

(8) Where an application has been made under subsection (4) above, the clerk may, if he considers it inappropriate to exercise his power under subsection (5) above, refer the matter to the court which may vary the order by exercising one of its powers under paragraphs (a) to (d) of section 59(3) above.

(9) Subsections (4), (5) and (7) of section 59 above shall apply for the purposes of subsections (3) and (8) above as they apply for the purposes of that section.

(10) None of the powers of the court, or of a justice's clerk, conferred by subsections (3) to (9) above shall be exercisable in relation to a maintenance order which is not a qualifying maintenance order (within the meaning of section 59 above).

(11) For the purposes of this section—

(a) 'creditor' and 'debtor' have the same meaning as they have in section 59 above; and

(b) the reference in subsection (1) above to money paid periodically by one person to another includes, in the case of a maintenance order, a reference to a lump sum paid by instalments by one person to another.

. . .

Payments to children

62   Provisions as to payments required to be made to a child etc.

(1) Where—

(a) periodical payments are required to be made, or a lump sum is required to be paid, to a child under an order made by a magistrates' court, or

(b) periodical payments are required to be made to a child under an order which is registered in a magistrates' court,

any sum required under the order to be paid to the child may be paid to the person with whom the child has his home, and that person—

(i)   may proceed in his own name for the variation, revival or revocation of the order, and

(ii) may either proceed in his own name for the recovery of any sum required to be paid under the order or request or authorise the designated officer for the magistrates' court under subsection (1) or subsection (2) respectively of section 59A above, to proceed for the recovery of that sum.

(2) Where a child has a right under any enactment to apply for the revival of an order made by a magistrates' court which provided for the making of periodical payments to or for the benefit of the child, the person with whom the child has his home may proceed in his own name for the revival of that order.

(3) Where any person by whom periodical payments are required to be paid to a child under an order made by or registered in a magistrates' court makes a complaint for the variation or revocation of that order, the person with whom the child has his home may answer the complaint in his own name.

(4) Nothing in subsections (1) and (2) above shall affect any right of a child to proceed in his own name for the variation, revival or revocation of an order or for the recovery of any sum payable thereunder.

(5) In this section references to the person with whom a child has his home—

    (a) in the case of any child who is being looked after by a local authority (within the meaning of section 22 of the Children Act 1989), are references to that local authority; and

    (b) in any other case, are references to the person who, disregarding any absence of the child at a hospital or boarding school and any other temporary absence, has care of the child.

(6) In this section any reference to an order registered in a magistrates' court is a reference to an order registered in a magistrates' court under Part II of the Maintenance Orders Act 1950 or Part I of the Maintenance Orders Act 1958.

(7) In this section 'child' means a person who has not attained the age of 18.

Orders other than for payment of money

63   Orders other than for payment of money

(1) Where under any Act passed after 31 December 1879 a magistrates' court has power to require the doing of anything other than payment of money, or to prohibit the doing of anything, any order of the court for the purpose of exercising that power may contain such provisions for the manner in which anything is to be done, for the time within which anything is to be done, or during which anything is not to be done, and generally for giving effect to the order, as the court thinks fit.

(2) The court may by order made on complaint suspend or rescind any such order as aforesaid.

(3) Where any person disobeys an order of a magistrates' court made under an Act passed after 31 December 1879 to do anything other than the payment of money or to abstain from doing anything the court may—

    (a) order him to pay a sum not exceeding £50 for every day during which he is in default or a sum not exceeding £5,000; or

    (b) commit him to custody until he has remedied his default or for a period not exceeding 2 months;

but a person who is ordered to pay a sum for every day during which he is in default or who is committed to custody until he has remedied his default shall not by virtue of this section be ordered to pay more than £1,000 or be committed for more than 2 months in all for doing or abstaining from doing the same thing contrary to the order (without prejudice to the operation of this section in relation to any subsequent default).

(4) Any sum ordered to be paid under subsection (3) above shall for the purposes of this Act be treated as adjudged to be paid by a conviction of a magistrates' court.

(5) The preceding provisions of this section shall not apply to any order for the enforcement of which provision is made by any other enactment.

. . .

Family proceedings

65 Meaning of family proceedings

(1) In this Act 'family proceedings' means proceedings under any of the following enactments, that is to say—

(a)	the Maintenance Orders (Facilities for Enforcement) Act 1920;
(b)	section 43 of the National Assistance Act 1948;
(c)	section 3 of the Marriage Act 1949;
(ca)	Schedule 2 to the Civil Partnership Act 2004;
(ee)	section 35 of the Matrimonial Causes Act 1973;
(ef)	paragraphs 69 to 72 of Schedule 5 to the Civil Partnership Act 2004;
(f)	Part I of the Maintenance Orders (Reciprocal Enforcement) Act 1972;
(h)	the Adoption and Children Act 2002;
(i)	section 18 of the Supplementary Benefits Act 1976;
(j)	Part I of the Domestic Proceedings and Magistrates' Courts Act 1978;
(ja)	Schedule 6 to the Civil Partnership Act 2004;
(l)	section 60 of this Act;

(m)   Part I of the Civil Jurisdiction and Judgments Act 1982, so far as that Part relates to the recognition or enforcement of maintenance orders;

(mm) section 55A of the Family Law Act 1986;

(n)   the Children Act 1989;

(na)   section 30 of the Human Fertilisation and Embryology Act 1990;

(nb)   section 106 of the Social Security Administration Act 1992;

(o)   section 20 (so far as it provides, by virtue of an order under section 45, for appeals to be made to a court) of the Child Support Act 1991), except that, subject to subsection (2) below, it does not include—

    (i) proceedings for the enforcement of any order made, confirmed or registered under any of those enactments;

    (ii) proceedings for the variation of any provision for the periodical payment of money contained in an order made, confirmed or registered under any of those enactments; or

    (iii) proceedings on an information in respect of the commission of an offence under any of those enactments;

(p)   Part IV of the Family Law Act 1996;

(q)   sections 11 and 12 of the Crime and Disorder Act 1998;

(r)   Council Regulation (EC) No. 44/2001 of 22nd December 2000 on jurisdiction and the recognition and enforcement of judgments in civil and commercial matters, so far as that Regulation relates to the recognition or enforcement of maintenance orders.

. . .

(2) The court before which there fall to be heard any of the following proceedings, that is to say—

    (a) proceedings (whether under this Act or any other enactment) for the enforcement of any order made, confirmed or registered under any of the enactments specified in paragraphs (a) to (k), (m), (n), (p) and (r) of subsection (1) above;

    (b) proceedings (whether under this Act or any other enactment) for the variation of any provision for the making of periodical payments contained in an order made, confirmed or registered under any of those enactments;

    (c) proceedings for an attachment of earnings order to secure maintenance payments within the meaning of the Attachment of Earnings Act 1971 or for the discharge or variation of such an order; or

    (d) proceedings for the enforcement of a maintenance order which is registered in a magistrates' court under Part II of the Maintenance Orders Act 1950 or Part I of the Maintenance Orders Act 1958 or for the variation of the rate of payments specified by such an order,

(e) proceedings under section 20 (so far as it provides, by virtue of an order under section 45, for appeals to be made to a court) of the Child Support Act 1991;

may if it thinks fit order that those proceedings and any other proceedings being heard therewith shall, notwithstanding anything in subsection (1) above, be treated as family proceedings for the purposes of this Act.

(3) Where the same parties are parties—

(a) to proceedings which are family proceedings by virtue of subsection (1) above, and

(b) to proceedings which the court has power to treat as family proceedings by virtue of subsection (2) above,

and the proceedings are heard together by a magistrates' court, the whole of those proceedings shall be treated as family proceedings for the purposes of this Act.

(4) No appeal shall lie from the making of, or refusal to make, an order under subsection (2) above.

66   Composition of magistrates' courts for family proceedings: general

(1) A magistrates' court when hearing family proceedings shall be composed of—

(a) two or three lay justices; or

(b) a District Judge (Magistrates' Courts) as chairman and one or two lay justices;

or, if it is not practicable for such a court to be so composed, a District Judge (Magistrates' Courts) sitting alone.

(2) Except where such a court is composed of a District Judge (Magistrates' Courts) sitting alone, it shall, so far as practicable, include both a man and a woman.

(3) In this section 'lay justice' has the same meaning as in the Courts Act 2003.

67   Family proceedings courts

(1) Magistrates' courts—

(a) constituted in accordance with this section or section 66 of the Courts Act 2003 (judges having powers of District Judges (Magistrates' Courts)), and

(b) sitting for the purpose of hearing family proceedings,

are to be known as family proceedings courts.

(2) A justice of the peace is not qualified to sit as a member of a family proceedings court to hear family proceedings of any description unless he has an authorisation extending to the proceedings.

(3) He has an authorisation extending to the proceedings only if he has been authorised by the Lord Chancellor or a person acting on his behalf to sit as a member of a family proceedings court to hear—

(a) proceedings of that description, or

(b) all family proceedings.

(4) The Lord Chancellor may by rules make provision about—

(a) the grant and revocation of authorisations,

(b) the appointment of chairmen of family proceedings courts, and

(c) the composition of family proceedings courts.

(5) Rules under subsection (4) may confer powers on the Lord Chancellor with respect to any of the matters specified in the rules.

(6) Rules under subsection (4) may be made only after consultation with the Family Procedure Rule Committee.

(7) Rules under subsection (4) are to be made by statutory instrument.

(8) A statutory instrument containing rules under subsection (4) is subject to annulment in pursuance of a resolution of either House of Parliament.

...

69 Sittings of magistrates' courts for family proceedings

(1) The business of magistrates' courts shall, so far as is consistent with the due dispatch of business, be arranged in such manner as may be requisite for separating the hearing and determination of family proceedings from other business.

(2) In the case of family proceedings in a magistrates' court other than proceedings under the Adoption and Children Act 2002, no person shall be present during the hearing and determination by the court of the proceedings except—

(a) officers of the court;

(b) parties to the case before the court, their legal representatives, witnesses and other persons directly concerned in the case;

(c) representatives of newspapers or news agencies;

(d) any other person whom the court may in its discretion permit to be present, so, however, that permission shall not be withheld from a person who appears to the court to have adequate grounds for attendance.

(3) In relation to any family proceedings under the Adoption and Children Act 2002, subsection (2) above shall apply with the omission of paragraphs (c) and (d).

(4) When hearing family proceedings, a magistrates' court may, if it thinks it necessary in the interest of the administration of justice or of public decency, direct that any persons, not being officers of the court or parties to the case, the parties' legal representatives, or other persons directly concerned in the case, be excluded during the taking of any indecent evidence.

(5) The powers conferred on a magistrates' court by this section shall be in addition and without prejudice to any other powers of the court to hear proceedings in camera.

(6) Nothing in this section shall affect the exercise by a magistrates' court of the power to direct that witnesses shall be excluded until they are called for examination.

. . .

PART III SATISFACTION AND ENFORCEMENT

General provisions

75 Power to dispense with immediate payment

(1) A magistrates' court by whose conviction or order a sum is adjudged to be paid may, instead of requiring immediate payment, allow time for payment, or order payment by instalments.

(2) Where a magistrates' court has allowed time for payment, the court may, on application by or on behalf of the person liable to make the payment, allow further time or order payment by instalments.

(2A) An order under this section that a lump sum required to be paid under a maintenance order shall be paid by instalments (a 'maintenance instalments order') shall be treated for the purposes of sections 59, 59B and 60 above as a maintenance order.

(2B) Subsections (5) and (7) of section 59 above (including those subsections as they apply for the purposes of section 60 above) shall have effect in relation to a maintenance instalments order—

(a) as if in subsection (5), paragraph (c) and the word 'and' immediately preceding it were omitted; and

(b) as if in subsection (7)—

(i) the reference to the maintenance order were a reference to the maintenance order in respect of which the maintenance instalments order in question is made;

(ii) for the words 'the person who applied for the maintenance order' there were substituted 'the debtor'.

(2C) Section 60 above shall have effect in relation to a maintenance instalments order as if in subsection (7), paragraph (c) and the word 'and' immediately preceding it were omitted.

(3) Where a court has ordered payment by instalments and default is made in the payment of any one instalment, proceedings may be taken as if the default has been made in the payment of all the instalments then unpaid.

76 Enforcement of sums adjudged to be paid

(1) Subject to the following provisions of this Part of this Act, and to section 132 below, where default is made in paying a sum adjudged to be paid by a conviction or order of a magistrates' court, the court may issue a warrant of distress for the purpose of levying the sum or issue a warrant committing the defaulter to prison.

(2) A warrant of commitment may be issued as aforesaid either—

(a) where it appears on the return to a warrant of distress that the money and goods of the defaulter are insufficient to satisfy the sum with the costs and charges of levying the sum; or

(b) instead of a warrant of distress.

(3) The period for which a person may be committed to prison under such a warrant as aforesaid shall not, subject to the provisions of any enactment passed after 31 December 1879, exceed the period applicable to the case under Schedule 4 to this Act.

(4) Where proceedings are brought for the enforcement of a magistrates' court maintenance order under this section, the court may vary the order by exercising one of its powers under paragraphs (a) to (d) of section 59(3) above.

(5) Subsections (4), (5) and (7) of section 59 above shall apply for the purposes of subsection (4) above as they apply for the purposes of that section.

(6) Subsections (4) and (5) above shall not have effect in relation to a maintenance order which is not a qualifying maintenance order (within the meaning of section 59 above).

. . .

95 Remission of arrears and manner in which arrears to be paid

(1) On the hearing of a complaint for the enforcement, revocation, revival, variation or discharge of a magistrates' court maintenance order, a magistrates' court may remit the whole or any part of the sum due under the order.

(2) If, on the hearing of a complaint for the enforcement, revocation, revival, variation or discharge of a magistrates' court maintenance order, a magistrates' court orders that the whole or any part of the sum due under the order be paid by instalments (an 'instalments order'), then—

(a) if the maintenance order is an English maintenance order, the court shall at the same time exercise one of its powers under paragraphs (a) to (d) of section 59(3) above in relation to the instalments order;

. . .

(4) The court may in the course of any proceedings concerning an instalments order or the magistrates' court maintenance order to which it relates vary the instalments order by exercising—

(a) in respect of an English maintenance order, one of the powers referred to in subsection (2)(a) above;

. . .

(5) In respect of an English maintenance order, subsections (4), (5) and (7) of section 59 above shall apply for the purposes of subsections (2)(a) and (4)(a) above as they apply for the purposes of that section.

. . .

Supreme Court Act 1981
(1981 c. 54)

PART II   JURISDICTION: THE HIGH COURT

Powers

41 Wards of court

(1) Subject to the provisions of this section, no minor shall be made a ward of court except by virtue of an order to that effect made by the High Court.

(2) Where an application is made for such an order in respect of a minor, the minor shall become a ward of court on the making of the application, but shall cease to be a ward of court at the end of such period as may be prescribed unless within that period an order has been made in accordance with the application.

(2A) Subsection (2) does not apply with respect to a child who is the subject of a care order (as defined by section 105 of the Children Act 1989).

(3) The High Court may, either upon an application in that behalf or without such an application, order that any minor who is for the time being a ward of court shall cease to be a ward of court.

PART III   PRACTICE AND PROCEDURE: THE HIGH COURT

Distribution of business

61   Distribution of business among Divisions

(1) Subject to any provision made by or under this or any other Act (and in particular to any rules of court made in pursuance of subsection (2) and any order under subsection (3)), business in the High Court of any description mentioned in Schedule 1, as for the time being in force, shall be distributed among the Divisions in accordance with that Schedule.

. . .

SCHEDULES

SCHEDULE 1   DISTRIBUTION OF BUSINESS IN HIGH COURT

Family Division

Section 61(1), (3)

3. To the Family Division are assigned—
- (a)   all matrimonial causes and matters (whether at first instance or on appeal);
- (b)   all causes and matters (whether at first instance or on appeal) relating to—
  - (i)   legitimacy;
  - (ii)   the exercise of the inherent jurisdiction of the High Court with respect to minors, the maintenance of minors and any proceedings under the Children Act 1989, except proceedings solely for the appointment of a guardian of a minor's estate;
  - (iii)   adoption;
  - (iv)   non-contentious or common form probate business;
- (c)   applications for consent to the marriage of a minor or for a declaration under section 27B(5) of the Marriage Act 1949;
- (d)   proceedings on appeal under section 13 of the Administration of Justice Act 1960 from an order or decision made under section 63(3) of the Magistrates' Courts Act 1980 to enforce an order of a magistrates' court made in matrimonial proceedings or proceedings under Part IV of the Family Law Act 1996 or with respect to the guardianship of a minor;
- (e)   applications under Part III of the Family Law Act 1986;
- (e)   proceedings under the Children Act 1989;
- (ea)   proceedings under section 79 of the Children Act 2006
- (f)   all proceedings under—
  - (i)   Part I of the Family Law Act 1996;
  - (ii)   the Child Abduction and Custody Act 1985;
  - (iii)   the Family Law Act 1986;
  - (iv)   section 30 of the Human Fertilisation and Embryology Act 1990;

. . .

(fa) all proceedings relating to a debit or credit under section 29(1) or 49(1) of the Welfare Reform and Pensions Act 1999;

(g) all proceedings for the purpose of enforcing an order made in any proceedings of a type described in this paragraph;

(h) all proceedings under the Child Support Act 1991;

(i) all proceedings under sections 6 and 8 of the Gender Recognition Act 2004;

(i) all civil partnership causes and matters (whether at first instance or on appeal);

(j) applications for consent to the formation of a civil partnership by a minor or for a declaration under paragraph 7 of Schedule 1 to the Civil Partnership Act 2004;

(k) applications under section 58 of that Act (declarations relating to civil partnerships).

. . . .

Administration of Justice Act 1982
(1982 c. 53)

2   Abolition of actions for loss of services etc

No person shall be liable in tort under the law of England and Wales or the law of Northern Ireland—

(a) to a husband on the ground only of his having deprived him of the services or society of his wife;

(b) to a parent (or person standing in the place of a parent) on the ground only of his having deprived him of the services of a child; or

(c) on the ground only—

(i)   of having deprived another of his menial servant;

(ii) of having deprived another of the services of his female servant by raping or seducing her; or

(iii) of enticement of a servant or harbouring a servant.

Marriage Act 1983
(1983 c. 32)

Marriages in England and Wales

1   Marriages of house-bound and detained persons in England and Wales

(1) Subject to the provisions of this Act and the Marriage Act 1949, the marriage of a person who is house-bound or is a detained person may be solemnized in England and Wales, on the authority of certificates of a superintendent registrar issued under Part III of the Marriage Act 1949, at the place where that person usually resides.

(2) For the purposes of this section a person is house-bound if—

(a) each notice of his or her marriage given in accordance with section 27 of the Marriage Act 1949 is accompanied by a statement, made in a form prescribed under that Act by a registered medical practitioner not more than 14 days before that notice is given, that, in his opinion—

(i) by reason of illness or disability, he or she ought not to move or be moved from his or her home or the other place where he or she is at that time, and

(ii) it is likely that it will be the case for at least the three months following the date on which the statement is made that by reason of the illness or disability he or she ought not to move or be moved from that place; and

(b) he or she is not a detained person.

(3) For the purposes of this section, a person is a detained person if he or she is for the time being detained—

      (a) otherwise than by virtue of section 2, 4, 5, 35, 36 or 136 of the Mental Health Act 1983 (short term detentions), as a patient in a hospital; or

      (b) in a prison or other place to which the Prison Act 1952 applies.

Child Abduction Act 1984
(1984 c. 37)

PART I   OFFENCES UNDER LAW OF ENGLAND AND WALES

1   Offence of abduction of child by parent etc.

(1) Subject to subsections (5) and (8) below, a person connected with a child under the age of sixteen commits an offence if he takes or sends the child out of the United Kingdom without the appropriate consent.

(2) A person is connected with a child for the purposes of this section if—

      (a) he is a parent of the child; or

      (b) in the case of a child whose parents were not married to each other at the time of his birth, there are reasonable grounds for believing that he is the father of the child; or

      (c) he is a guardian of the child; or

      (ca) he is a special guardian of the child; or

      (d) he is a person in whose favour a residence order is in force with respect to the child; or

      (e) he has custody of the child.

(3) In this section 'the appropriate consent', in relation to a child, means—

      (a) the consent of each of the following—

          (i) the child's mother;

          (ii) the child's father, if he has parental responsibility for him;

          (iii) any guardian of the child;

          (iiia) any special guardian of the child;

          (iv) any person in whose favour a residence order is in force with respect to the child;

          (v) any person who has custody of the child; or

      (b) the leave of the court granted under or by virtue of any provision of Part II of the Children Act 1989; or

      (c) if any person has custody of the child, the leave of the court which awarded custody to him.

(4) A person does not commit an offence under this section by taking or sending a child out of the United Kingdom without obtaining the appropriate consent if—

      (a) he is a person in whose favour there is a residence order in force with respect to the child, and he takes or sends the child out of the United Kingdom for a period of less than one month; or

      (b) he is a special guardian of the child and he takes or sends the child out of the United Kingdom for a period of less than three months.

(4A) Subsection (4) above does not apply if the person taking or sending the child out of the United Kingdom does so in breach of an order under Part II of the Children Act 1989.

(5) A person does not commit an offence under this section by doing anything without the consent of another person whose consent is required under the foregoing provisions if—

      (a) he does it in the belief that the other person—

          (i) has consented; or

          (ii) would consent if he was aware of all the relevant circumstances; or

(b) he has taken all reasonable steps to communicate with the other person but has been unable to communicate with him; or

(c) the other person has unreasonably refused to consent.

(5A) Subsection (5)(c) above does not apply if—

(a) the person who refused to consent is a person—

(i)   in whose favour there is a residence order in force with respect to the child;

(ia) who is a special guardian of the child; or

(ii) who has custody of the child; or

(b) the person taking or sending the child out of the United Kingdom is, by so acting, in breach of an order made by a court in the United Kingdom.

(6) Where, in proceedings for an offence under this section, there is sufficient evidence to raise an issue as to the application of subsection (5) above, it shall be for the prosecution to prove that that subsection does not apply.

(7) For the purposes of this section—

(a) 'guardian of a child', 'special guardian', 'residence order' and 'parental responsibility' have the same meaning as in the Children Act 1989; and

(b) a person shall be treated as having custody of a child if there is in force an order of a court in the United Kingdom awarding him (whether solely or jointly with another person) custody, legal custody or care and control of the child.

(8) This section shall have effect subject to the provisions of the Schedule to this Act in relation to a child who is in the care of a local authority, detained in a place of safety, remanded to a local authority accommodation or the subject of proceedings or an order relating to adoption.

2   Offence of abduction of child by other persons

(1) Subject to subsection (3) below, a person, other than one mentioned in subsection (2) below commits an offence if, without lawful authority or reasonable excuse, he takes or detains a child under the age of sixteen—

(a) so as to remove him from the lawful control of any person having lawful control of the child; or

(b) so as to keep him out of the lawful control of any person entitled to lawful control of the child.

(2) The persons are—

(a) where the father and mother of the child in question were married to each other at the time of his birth, the child's father and mother;

(b) where the father and mother of the child in question were not married to each other at the time of his birth, the child's mother; and

(c) any other person mentioned in section 1(2)(c) to (e) above.

(3) In proceedings against any person for an offence under this section, it shall be a defence for that person to prove—

(a) where the father and mother of the child in question were not married to each other at the time of his birth—

(i)   that he is the child's father; or

(ii) that, at the time of the alleged offence, he believed, on reasonable grounds, that he was the child's father; or

(b) that, at the time of the alleged offence, he believed that the child had attained the age of sixteen.

3   Construction of references to taking, sending and detaining

For the purposes of this Part of this Act—

(a) a person shall be regarded as taking a child if he causes or induces the child to accompany him or any other person or causes the child to be taken;

(b) a person shall be regarded as sending a child if he causes the child to be sent;

(c) a person shall be regarded as detaining a child if he causes the child to be detained or induces the child to remain with him or any other person; and

(d) references to a child's parents and to a child whose parents were (or were not) married to each other at the time of his birth shall be construed in accordance with section 1 of the Family Law Reform Act 1987 (which extends their meaning).

SCHEDULE

MODIFICATIONS OF SECTION 1 FOR CHILDREN IN CERTAIN CASES

Children in care of local authorities and voluntary organisations

1.—(1) This paragraph applies in the case of a child who is in the care of a local authority within the meaning of the Children Act 1989 in England or Wales.

(2) Where this paragraph applies, section 1 of this Act shall have effect as if—

(a) the reference in subsection (1) to the appropriate consent were a reference to the consent of the local authority in whose care the child is; and

(b) subsections (3) to (6) were omitted.

Children in places of safety

2.—(1) This paragraph applies in the case of a child who is—

(a) detained in a place of safety under paragraph 7(4) of Schedule 7 to the Powers of Criminal Courts (Sentencing) Act 2000; or

(b) remanded to local authority accommodation under section 23 of the Children and Young Persons Act 1969.

(2) Where this paragraph applies, section 1 of this Act shall have effect as if—

(a) the reference in subsection (1) to the appropriate consent were a reference to the leave of any magistrates' court acting for the area in which the place of safety is; and

(b) subsections (3) to (6) were omitted.

Adoption and custodianship

3.—(1) This paragraph applies where—

(a) a child is placed for adoption by an adoption agency under section 19 of the Adoption and Children Act 2002, or an adoption agency is authorised to place the child for adoption under that section; or

(b) a placement order is in force in respect of the child; or

(c) an application for such an order has been made in respect of the child and has not been disposed of; or

(d) an application for an adoption order has been made in respect of the child and has not been disposed of; or

(e) an order under section 84 of the Adoption and Children Act 2002 (giving parental responsibility prior to adoption abroad) has been made in respect of the child, or an application for such an order in respect of him has been made and has not been disposed of.

(2) Where this paragraph applies, section 1 of this Act shall have effect as if—

(a) the reference in subsection (1) to the appropriate consent were—

(i) in a case within sub-paragraph (1)(a) above, a reference to the consent of each person who has parental responsibility for the child or to the leave of the High Court;

       (ii) in a case within sub-paragraph (1)(b) above, a reference to the leave of the court which made the placement order;

       (iii) in a case within sub-paragraph (1)(c) or (d) above, a reference to the leave of the court to which the application was made;

       (iv) in a case within sub-paragraph (1)(e) above, a reference to the leave of the court which made the order or, as the case may be, to which the application was made;

    (b) subsection (3) were omitted;

    (c) in subsection (4), in paragraph (a), for the words from 'in whose favour' to the first mention of 'child' there were substituted 'who provides the child's home in a case falling within sub-paragraph (1)(a) or (b) of paragraph 3 of the Schedule to this Act'; and

    (d) subsection (4A), (5), (5A) and (6) were omitted.

   (3) Sub-paragraph (2) above shall be construed as if the references to the court included, in any case where the court is a magistrates' court, a reference to any magistrates' court acting for the same area as that court.

Cases within paragraphs 1 and 3

   4. In the case of a child falling within both paragraph 1 and paragraph 3 above, the provisions of paragraph 3 shall apply to the exclusion of those in paragraph 1.

Interpretation

   5. In this Schedule—

    (a) 'adoption agency', 'adoption order', 'placed for adoption by an adoption agency' and 'placement order' have the same meaning as in the Adoption and Children Act 2002; and

    (b) 'area', in relation to a magistrates' court, means the petty sessions area for which the court is appointed.

Matrimonial and Family Proceedings Act 1984
(1984 c. 42)

PART V   FAMILY BUSINESS: DISTRIBUTION AND TRANSFER

Preliminary

32   What is family business
In this Part of this Act—

   'family business' means business of any description which in the High Court is for the time being assigned to the Family Division and to no other Division by or under section 61 of (and Schedule 1 to) the Supreme Court Act 1981;

   'family proceedings' means proceedings which are family business;

   'civil partnership cause' means an action for the dissolution or annulment of a civil partnership or for the legal separation of civil partners;

   'matrimonial cause' means an action for divorce, nullity of marriage, or judicial separation; and 'the 1973 Act' means the Matrimonial Causes Act 1973.

Jurisdiction of county courts in matrimonial causes and matters

33   Jurisdiction of county courts in matrimonial causes
   (1) The Lord Chancellor may, with the concurrence of the Lord Chief Justice, by order designate any county court as a divorce county court and any court so designated shall have

jurisdiction to hear and determine any matrimonial cause, except that it shall have jurisdiction to try such a cause only if it is also designated in the order as a court of trial.

In this Part of this Act 'divorce county court' means a county court so designated.

(2) The jurisdiction conferred by this section on a divorce county court shall be exercisable throughout England and Wales, but rules of court may provide for a matrimonial cause pending in one such court to be heard and determined in another or partly in that and partly in another.

(3) Every matrimonial cause shall be commenced in a divorce county court and shall be heard and determined in that or another such court unless or except to the extent it is transferred to the High Court under section 39 below or section 41 of the County Courts Act 1984 (transfer to High Court by order of High Court).

(4) The Lord Chancellor may, with the concurrence of the Lord Chief Justice, by order designate a divorce county court as a court for the exercise of jurisdiction in matrimonial matters arising under Part III of this Act.

(5) The power to make an order under subsection (1) or (4) above shall be exercisable by statutory instrument.

(6) The Lord Chief Justice may nominate a judicial office holder (as defined in section 109(4) of the Constitutional Reform Act 2005) to exercise his functions under this section.

34 Jurisdiction of divorce county courts as respects financial relief and protection of children

(1) Subject to subsections (2) and (3) below, a divorce county court shall have the following jurisdiction, namely—

    (a) jurisdiction to exercise any power exercisable under Part II or Part III of the 1973 Act in connection with any petition, decree or order pending in or made by such a court and to exercise any power under section 27 or 35 of that Act;

    (b) if designated by an order under section 33(4) above, jurisdiction to exercise any power under Part III of this Act.

(2) Any proceedings for the exercise of a power which a divorce county court has jurisdiction to exercise by virtue of subsection (1)(a) or (b) above shall be commenced in such divorce county court as may be prescribed by rules of court.

(3) A divorce county court shall not by virtue of subsection (1)(a) above have jurisdiction to exercise any power under section 32, 33, 36 or 38 of the 1973 Act; but nothing in this section shall prejudice the exercise by a county court of any jurisdiction conferred on county courts by any of those sections.

(4) Nothing in this section shall affect the jurisdiction of a magistrates' court under section 35 of the 1973 Act.

35 Consideration of agreements or arrangements

Any provision to be made by rules of court for the purposes of section 7 of the 1973 Act with respect to any power exercisable by the court on an application made before the presentation of a petition shall confer jurisdiction to exercise the power on divorce county courts.

36 Assignment of Circuit judges to matrimonial proceedings

(1) The jurisdiction conferred by the preceding provisions of this Part of this Act on divorce county courts, so far as it is exercisable by judges of such courts, shall be exercised by such Circuit judges as the Lord Chief Justice may, after consulting the Lord Chancellor, direct.

(2) The Lord Chief Justice may nominate a judicial office holder (as defined in section 109(4) of the Constitutional Reform Act 2005) to exercise his functions under this section.

36A Jurisdiction of county courts in civil partnership causes and matters

(1) The Lord Chancellor may by order—

    (a) designate any county court as a civil partnership proceedings county court, and

    (b) designate, as a court of trial, any county court designated as a civil partnership proceedings county court.

(2) In this Part of this Act 'civil partnership proceedings county court' means a county court designated under subsection (1)(a) above.

(3) A civil partnership proceedings county court shall have jurisdiction to hear and determine any civil partnership cause, subject to subsection (4) below.

(4) A civil partnership proceedings county court shall have jurisdiction to try a civil partnership cause only if it is designated under subsection (1)(b) above as a court of trial.

(5) The jurisdiction conferred by this section on a civil partnership proceedings county court shall be exercisable throughout England and Wales, but rules of court may provide for a civil partnership cause pending in one such court to be heard and determined—

    (a) partly in that court and partly in another such court, or

    (b) in another such court.

(6) Every civil partnership cause shall be commenced in a civil partnership proceedings county court.

(7) Every civil partnership cause shall be heard and determined in a civil partnership proceedings county court unless, or except to the extent, it is transferred to the High Court under—

    (a) section 39 below, or

    (b) section 41 of the County Court Act 1984 (transfer to High Court by order of High Court).

(8) The Lord Chancellor may by order designate a civil partnership proceedings county court as a court for the exercise of jurisdiction in civil partnership matters under Schedule 7 to the Civil Partnership Act 2004.

(9) The power to make an order under subsection (1) or (8) above shall be exercisable by statutory instrument.

36B Jurisdiction of civil partnership proceedings county courts as respects financial relief and protection of children

(1) Subject to subsection (2) below, a civil partnership proceedings county court shall have the following jurisdiction—

    (a) a jurisdiction to exercise any power exercisable under—

        (i) section 63 of the Civil Partnership Act 2004 (restrictions on making of orders affecting children), or

        (ii) Schedule 5 to that Act (financial relief in the courts), other than Part 12 (arrears and repayments) and paragraph 73 (alteration of maintenance agreements by court after death of one party),

    in connection with any application or order pending in, or made by, a civil partnership proceedings county court;

    (b) a jurisdiction to exercise any power exercisable under—

        (i) Part 9 of that Schedule (failure to maintain: financial provision (and interim orders)), or

        (ii) paragraphs 69 to 71 of that Schedule (alteration of maintenance agreements by court during lives of parties);

    (c) if designated under section 36A(8) above, jurisdiction to exercise any power under Schedule 7 to that Act.

(2) Any proceedings for the exercise of a power which a civil partnership proceedings county court has jurisdiction to exercise by virtue of subsection (1) above shall be commenced in such civil partnership proceedings county court as may be prescribed by rules of court.

(3) Nothing in this section shall affect the jurisdiction of a magistrates' court under paragraphs 69 to 71 of Schedule 5 to the Civil Partnership Act 2004.

36C Consideration of agreements or arrangements

Where rules of court make provision for the purposes of section 43 of the Civil Partnership Act 2004 with respect to any power exercisable by the court on an application made under that section before an application is made for a dissolution or separation order, the rules shall confer jurisdiction to exercise the power on civil partnership proceedings county courts.

36D   Assignment of circuit judges to civil partnership proceedings
The jurisdiction conferred by the preceding provisions of this Part of this Act on civil partnership proceedings county courts, so far as it is exercisable by judges of such courts, shall be exercised by such Circuit judges as the Lord Chancellor may direct.

Distribution and transfer of family business and proceedings

37   Directions as to distribution and transfer of family business and proceedings
The President of the Family Division may, with the concurrence of the Lord Chancellor, give directions with respect to the distribution and transfer between the High Court and county courts of family business and family proceedings.

38   Transfer of family proceedings from High Court to county court
(1) At any stage in any family proceedings in the High Court the High Court may, if the proceedings are transferable under this section, either of its own motion or on the application of any party to the proceedings, order the transfer of the whole or any part of the proceedings to a county court.

(2) The following family proceedings are transferable to a county court under this section, namely—
   (a) all family proceedings commenced in the High Court which are within the jurisdiction of a county court, divorce county court or civil partnership county court;
   (b) wardship proceedings, except applications for an order that a minor be made, or cease to be, a ward of court, or any other proceedings which relate to the exercise of the inherent jurisdiction of the High Court with respect to minors; and
   (c) all family proceedings transferred from a county court to the High Court under section 39 below or section 41 of the County Courts Act 1984 (transfer to High Court by order of High Court); and
   (d) all matrimonial causes and matters transferred from a county court otherwise than as mentioned in paragraph (c) above.

(3) Proceedings transferred under this section shall be transferred to such county court as the High Court directs, subject to subsections (3A) and (3B) below.

(3A) Where a matrimonial cause or matter within the jurisdiction of a divorce county court only is transferred under this section, it shall be transferred to such divorce county court as the High Court directs.

(3B) Where a civil partnership cause or matter within the jurisdiction of a civil partnership proceedings county court only is transferred under this section, it shall be transferred to such civil partnership proceedings county court as the High Court directs.

(4) The transfer shall not affect any right of appeal from the order directing the transfer, or the right to enforce in the High Court any judgment signed, or order made, in that Court before the transfer.

(5) Where proceedings are transferred to a county court under this section, the county court—
   (a) if it has no jurisdiction apart from this paragraph, shall have jurisdiction to hear and determine those proceedings;
   (b) shall have jurisdiction to award any relief which could have been awarded by the High Court.

39   Transfer of family proceedings to High Court from county court
(1) At any stage in any family proceedings in a county court, the county court may, if the proceedings are transferable under this section, either of its own motion or on the application of any party to the proceedings, order the transfer of the whole or any part of the proceedings to the High Court.

(2) The following family proceedings are transferable to the High Court under this section, namely—

    (a) all family proceedings commenced in a county court, divorce county court or civil partnership proceedings county court; and

    (b) all family proceedings transferred from the High Court to a county court, divorce county court or civil partnership proceedings county court under section 38 above.

. . .

Police and Criminal Evidence Act 1984
(1984 c. 60)

80 Compellability of accused's spouse

(2) In any proceedings the spouse or civil partner of a person charged in the proceedings shall, subject to subsection (4) below, be compellable to give evidence on behalf of that person.

(2A) In any proceedings the spouse or civil partner of a person charged in the proceedings shall, subject to subsection (4) below, be compellable—

    (a) to give evidence on behalf of any other person charged in the proceedings but only in respect of any specified offence with which that other person is charged; or

    (b) to give evidence for the prosecution but only in respect of any specified offence with which any person is charged in the proceedings.

(3) In relation to the spouse or civil partner of a person charged in any proceedings, an offence is a specified offence for the purposes of subsection (2A) above if—

    (a) it involves an assault on, or injury or a threat of injury to, the spouse or civil partner or a person who was at the material time under the age of 16;

    (b) it is a sexual offence alleged to have been committed in respect of a person who was at the material time under that age; or

    (c) it consists of attempting or conspiring to commit, or of aiding, abetting, counselling, procuring or inciting the commission of, an offence falling within paragraph (a) or (b) above.

(4) No person who is charged in any proceedings shall be compellable by virtue of subsection (2) or (2A) above to give evidence in the proceedings.

(4A) References in this section to a person charged in any proceedings do not include a person who is not, or is no longer, liable to be convicted of any offence in the proceedings (whether as a result of pleading guilty or for any other reason).

(5) In any proceedings a person who has been but is no longer married to the accused shall be compellable to give evidence as if that person and the accused had never been married.

(5A) In any proceedings a person who has been but is no longer the civil partner of the accused shall be compellable to give evidence as if that person and the accused had never been civil partners.

(6) Where in any proceedings the age of any person at any time is material for the purposes of subsection (3) above, his age at the material time shall for the purposes of that provision be deemed to be or to have been that which appears to the court to be or to have been his age at that time.

(7) In subsection (3)(b) above 'sexual offence' means an offence under the Protection of Children Act 1978 or Part I of the Sexual Offences Act 2003.

80A Rule where accused's spouse or civil partner not compellable

The failure of the spouse or civil partner of a person charged in any proceedings to give evidence in the proceedings shall not be made the subject of any comment by the prosecution.

. . .

SCHEDULE 1A   SPECIFIC OFFENCES WHICH ARE ARRESTABLE OFFENCES

. . .

14A Common assault

. . .

23 An offence under section 2 of the Protection from Harassment Act 1997 (c. 40) (harassment)

. . .

Surrogacy Arrangements Act 1985
(1985 c. 49)

1   Meaning of 'surrogate mother,' 'surrogacy arrangement' and other terms

(1) The following provisions shall have effect for the interpretation of this Act.

(2) 'Surrogate mother' means a woman who carries a child in pursuance of an arrangement—

    (a) made before she began to carry the child, and

    (b) made with a view to any child carried in pursuance of it being handed over to, and parental responsibility being met (so far as practicable) by, another person or other persons.

(3) An arrangement is a surrogacy arrangement if, were a woman to whom the arrangement relates to carry a child in pursuance of it, she would be a surrogate mother.

(4) In determining whether an arrangement is made with such a view as is mentioned in subsection (2) above regard may be had to the circumstances as a whole (and, in particular, where there is a promise or understanding that any payment will or may be made to the woman or for her benefit in respect of the carrying of any child in pursuance of the arrangement, to that promise or understanding).

(5) An arrangement may be regarded as made with such a view though subject to conditions relating to the handing over of any child.

(6) A woman who carries a child is to be treated for the purposes of subsection (2)(a) above as beginning to carry it at the time of the insemination or of the placing in her of an embryo, of an egg in the process of fertilisation or of sperm and eggs, as the case may be, that results in her carrying the child.

(7) 'Body of persons' means a body of persons corporate or unincorporate.

(8) 'Payment' means payment in money or money's worth.

(9) This Act applies to arrangements whether or not they are lawful.

1A   Surrogacy arrangements unenforceable

No surrogacy arrangement is enforceable by or against any of the persons making it.

2   Negotiating surrogacy arrangements on a commercial basis, etc.

(1) No person shall on a commercial basis do any of the following acts in the United Kingdom, that is—

    (a) initiate or take part in any negotiations with a view to the making of a surrogacy arrangement,

    (b) offer or agree to negotiate the making of a surrogacy arrangement, or

    (c) compile any information with a view to its use in making, or negotiating the making of, surrogacy arrangements;

and no person shall in the United Kingdom knowingly cause another to do any of those acts on a commercial basis.

(2) A person who contravenes subsection (1) above is guilty of an offence; but it is not a contravention of that subsection—

    (a) for a woman, with a view to becoming a surrogate mother herself, to do any act mentioned in that subsection or to cause such an act to be done, or

    (b) for any person, with a view to a surrogate mother carrying a child for him, to do such an act or to cause such an act to be done.

(3) For the purposes of this section, a person does an act on a commercial basis (subject to subsection (4) below) if—

    (a) any payment is at any time received by himself or another in respect of it, or

    (b) he does it with a view to any payment being received by himself or another in respect of making, or negotiating or facilitating the making of, any surrogacy arrangement.

In this subsection 'payment' does not include payment to or for the benefit of a surrogate mother or prospective surrogate mother.

(4) In proceedings against a person for an offence under subsection (1) above, he is not to be treated as doing an act on a commercial basis by reason of any payment received by another in respect of that act if it is proved that—

    (a) in a case where the payment was received before he did the act, he did not do the act knowing or having reasonable cause to suspect that any payment had been received in respect of the act; and

    (b) in any other case, he did not do the act with a view to any payment being received in respect of it.

(5) Where—

    (a) a person acting on behalf of a body of persons takes any part in negotiating or facilitating the making of a surrogacy arrangement in the United Kingdom, and

    (b) negotiating or facilitating the making of surrogacy arrangements is an activity of the body,

then, if the body at any time receives any payment made by or on behalf of—

    (i)   a woman who carries a child in pursuance of the arrangement,

    (ii) the person or persons for whom she carries it, or

    (iii) any person connected with the woman or with that person or those persons,

the body is guilty of an offence.

For the purposes of this subsection, a payment received by a person connected with a body is to be treated as received by the body.

(6) In proceedings against a body for an offence under subsection (5) above, it is a defence to prove that the payment concerned was not made in respect of the arrangement mentioned in paragraph (a) of that subsection.

(7) A person who in the United Kingdom takes part in the management or control—

    (a) of any body of persons, or

    (b) of any of the activities of any body of persons,

is guilty of an offence if the activity described in subsection (8) below is an activity of the body concerned.

(8) The activity referred to in subsection (7) above is negotiating or facilitating the making of surrogacy arrangements in the United Kingdom, being—

    (a) arrangements the making of which is negotiated or facilitated on a commercial basis, or

    (b) arrangements in the case of which payments are received (or treated for the purposes of subsection (5) above as received) by the body concerned in contravention of subsection (5) above.

(9) In proceedings against a person for an offence under subsection (7) above, it is a defence to prove that he neither knew nor had reasonable cause to suspect that the activity described in subsection (8) above was an activity of the body concerned; and for the purposes of such proceedings any arrangement falling within subsection (8)(b) above shall be

disregarded if it is proved that the payment concerned was not made in respect of the arrangement.

3 Advertisements about surrogacy

(1) This section applies to any advertisement containing an indication (however expressed)—

(a) that any person is or may be willing to enter into a surrogacy arrangement or to negotiate or facilitate the making of a surrogacy arrangement, or

(b) that any person is looking for a woman willing to become a surrogate mother or for persons wanting a woman to carry a child as a surrogate mother.

(2) Where a newspaper or periodical containing an advertisement to which this section applies is published in the United Kingdom, any proprietor, editor or publisher of the newspaper or periodical is guilty of an offence.

(3) Where an advertisement to which this section applies is conveyed by means of an electronic telecommunications network so as to be seen or heard (or both) in the United Kingdom, any person who in the United Kingdom causes it to be so conveyed knowing it to contain such an indication as is mentioned in subsection (1) above is guilty of an offence.

(4) A person who publishes or causes to be published in the United Kingdom an advertisement to which this section applies (not being an advertisement contained in a newspaper or periodical or conveyed by means of an electronic telecommunications network) is guilty of an offence.

(5) A person who distributes or causes to be distributed in the United Kingdom an advertisement to which this section applies (not being an advertisement contained in a newspaper or periodical published outside the United Kingdom or an advertisement conveyed by means of an electronic telecommunications network) knowing it to contain such an indication as is mentioned in subsection (1) above is guilty of an offence.

4 Offences

(1) A person guilty of an offence under this Act shall be liable on summary conviction—

(b) to a fine not exceeding level 5 on the standard scale.

(2) No proceedings for an offence under this Act shall be instituted—

(a) in England and Wales, except by or with the consent of the Director of Public Prosecutions; and

(b) in Northern Ireland, except by or with the consent of the Director of Public Prosecutions for Northern Ireland.

(3) Where an offence under this Act committed by a body corporate is proved to have been committed with the consent or connivance of, or to be attributable to any neglect on the part of, any director, manager, secretary or other similar officer of the body corporate or any person who was purporting to act in any such capacity, he as well as the body corporate is guilty of the offence and is liable to be proceeded against and punished accordingly.

(4) Where the affairs of a body corporate are managed by its members, subsection (3) above shall apply in relation to the acts and defaults of a member in connection with his functions of management as if he were a director of the body corporate.

(5) In any proceedings for an offence under section 2 of this Act, proof of things done or of words written, spoken or published (whether or not in the presence of any party to the proceedings) by any person taking part in the management or control of a body of persons or of any of the activities of the body, or by any person doing any of the acts mentioned in subsection (1)(a) to (c) of that section on behalf of the body, shall be admissible as evidence of the activities of the body.

(6) In relation to an offence under this Act, section 127(1) of the Magistrates' Courts Act 1980 (information must be laid within six months of commission of offence),... shall have effect as if for the reference to six months there were substituted a reference to two years.

Housing Act 1985
(1985 c. 68)

PART IV   SECURE TENANCIES AND RIGHTS OF SECURE TENANTS

Succession on death of tenant

87   Persons qualified to succeed tenant

A person is qualified to succeed the tenant under a secure tenancy if he occupies the dwelling-house as his only or principal home at the time of the tenant's death and either—

(a) he is the tenant's spouse or civil partner, or

(b) he is another member of the tenant's family and has resided with the tenant throughout the period of twelve months ending with the tenant's death;

unless, in either case, the tenant was himself a successor, as defined in section 88.
. . .

113   Members of a person's family

(1) A person is a member of another's family within the meaning of this Part if—

(a) he is the spouse or civil partner of that person, or he and that person live together as husband and wife or as if they were civil partners, or

(b) he is that person's parent, grandparent, child, grandchild, brother, sister, uncle, aunt, nephew or niece.

(2) For the purpose of subsection (1)(b)—

(a) a relationship by marriage or civil partnership shall be treated as a relationship by blood,

(b) a relationship of the half-blood shall be treated as a relationship of the whole blood,

(c) the stepchild of a person shall be treated as his child, and

(d) an illegitimate child shall be treated as the legitimate child of his mother and reputed father.

Marriage (Prohibited Degrees of Relationship) Act 1986
(1986 c. 16)

1   Marriage between certain persons related by affinity not to be void

(1) A marriage solemnized after the commencement of this Act between a man and a woman who is the daughter or granddaughter of a former spouse of his (whether the former spouse is living or not) or who is the former spouse of his father or grandfather (whether his father or grandfather is living or not) shall not be void by reason only of that relationship if both the parties have attained the age of twenty-one at the time of the marriage and the younger party has not at any time before attaining the age of eighteen been a child of the family in relation to the other party.

(2) A marriage solemnized after the commencement of this Act between a man and a woman who is the grandmother of a former spouse of his (whether the former spouse is living or not) or is a former spouse of his grandson (whether his grandson is living or not) shall not be void by reason only of that relationship.

(3) A marriage solemnized after the commencement of this Act between a man and a woman who is the mother of a former spouse of his shall not be void by reason only of that relationship if the marriage is solemnized after the death of both that spouse and the father of that spouse and after both the parties to the marriage have attained the age of twenty-one.

(4) A marriage solemnized after the commencement of this Act between a man and a woman who is a former spouse of his son shall not be void by reason only of that relationship

if the marriage is solemnized after the death of both his son and the mother of his son and after both the parties to the marriage have attained the age of twenty-one.

(5) In this section 'child of the family' in relation to any person, means a child who has lived in the same household as that person and been treated by that person as a child of his family.

(6) The Marriage Act 1949 shall have effect subject to the amendments specified in the Schedule to this Act, being amendments consequential on the preceding provisions of this section.

(7) Where, apart from this Act, any matter affecting the validity of a marriage would fall to be determined (in accordance with the rules of private international law) by reference to the law of a country outside England and Wales nothing in this Act shall preclude the determination of that matter in accordance with that law.

(8) Nothing in this section shall affect any marriage solemnized before the commencement of this Act.

Insolvency Act 1986
(1986 c. 45)

CHAPTER IV   ADMINISTRATION BY TRUSTEE

Preliminary

305   General functions of trustee

(1) This Chapter applies in relation to any bankruptcy where either—
(a) the appointment of a person as trustee of a bankrupt's estate takes effect, or
(b) the official receiver becomes trustee of a bankrupt's estate.

(2) The function of the trustee is to get in, realise and distribute the bankrupt's estate in accordance with the following provisions of this Chapter; and in the carrying out of that function and in the management of the bankrupt's estate the trustee is entitled, subject to those provisions, to use his own discretion.

Acquisition, control and realisation of bankrupt's estate

306   Vesting of bankrupt's estate in trustee

(1) The bankrupt's estate shall vest in the trustee immediately on his appointment taking effect or, in the case of the official receiver, on his becoming trustee.

(2) Where any property which is, or is to be, comprised in the bankrupt's estate vests in the trustee (whether under this section or under any other provision of this Part), it shall so vest without any conveyance, assignment or transfer.

. . .

CHAPTER V   EFFECT OF BANKRUPTCY ON CERTAIN RIGHTS, TRANSACTIONS, ETC.

Rights under trusts of land

335A   Rights under trusts of land

(1) Any application by a trustee of a bankrupt's estate under section 14 of the Trusts of Land and Appointment of Trustees Act 1996 (powers of court in relation to trusts of land) for an order under that section for the sale of land shall be made to the court having jurisdiction in relation to the bankruptcy.

(2) On such an application the court shall make such order as it thinks just and reasonable having regard to—

(a) the interests of the bankrupt's creditors;

(b) where the application is made in respect of land which includes a dwelling house which is or has been the home of the bankrupt or the bankrupt's spouse or civil partner or former spouse or former civil partner—

(i) the conduct of the spouse, civil partner, former spouse or former civil partner, so far as contributing to the bankruptcy,

(ii) the needs and financial resources of the spouse, civil partner, former spouse or former civil partner, and

(iii) the needs of any children; and

(c) all the circumstances of the case other than the needs of the bankrupt.

(3) Where such an application is made after the end of the period of one year beginning with the first vesting under Chapter IV of this Part of the bankrupt's estate in a trustee, the court shall assume, unless the circumstances of the case are exceptional, that the interests of the bankrupt's creditors outweigh all other considerations.

(4) The powers conferred on the court by this section are exercisable on an application whether it is made before or after the commencement of this section.

Rights of occupation

336 Rights of occupation etc. of bankrupt's spouse or civil partner

(1) Nothing occurring in the initial period of the bankruptcy (that is to say, the period beginning with the day of the presentation of the petition for the bankruptcy order and ending with the vesting of the bankrupt's estate in a trustee) is to be taken as having given rise to any home rights under Part IV of the Family Law Act 1996 in relation to a dwelling house comprised in the bankrupt's estate.

(2) Where a spouse's or civil partner's home rights under the Act of 1996 are a charge on the estate or interest of the other spouse or civil partner, or of trustees for the other spouse or civil partner, and the other spouse or civil partner is adjudged bankrupt—

(a) the charge continues to subsist notwithstanding the bankruptcy and, subject to the provisions of that Act, binds the trustee of the bankrupt's estate and persons deriving title under that trustee, and

(b) any application for an order under section 33 of that Act shall be made to the court having jurisdiction in relation to the bankruptcy.

(4) On such an application as is mentioned in subsection (2) the court shall make such order under section 33 of the Act of 1996 as it thinks just and reasonable having regard to—

(a) the interests of the bankrupt's creditors,

(b) the conduct of the spouse or former spouse or civil partner or former civil partner, so far as contributing to the bankruptcy,

(c) the needs and financial resources of the spouse or former spouse or civil partner or former civil partner,

(d) the needs of any children, and

(e) all the circumstances of the case other than the needs of the bankrupt.

(5) Where such an application is made after the end of the period of one year beginning with the first vesting under Chapter IV of this Part of the bankrupt's estate in a trustee, the court shall assume, unless the circumstances of the case are exceptional, that the interests of the bankrupt's creditors outweigh all other considerations.

337 Rights of occupation of bankrupt

(1) This section applies where—

(a) a person who is entitled to occupy a dwelling house by virtue of a beneficial estate or interest is adjudged bankrupt, and

(b) any persons under the age of 18 with whom that person had at some time occupied that dwelling house had their home with that person at the time when the bankruptcy petition was presented and at the commencement of the bankpruptcy.

(2) Whether or not the bankrupt's spouse or civil partner (if any) has home rights under Part IV of the Family Law Act 1996—

   (a) the bankrupt has the following rights as against the trustee of his estate—

       (i) if in occupation, a right not to be evicted or excluded from the dwelling house or any part of it, except with the leave of the court,

       (ii) if not in occupation, a right with the leave of the court to enter into and occupy the dwelling house, and

   (b) the bankrupt's rights are a charge, having the like priority as an equitable interest created immediately before the commencement of the bankruptcy, on so much of his estate or interest in the dwelling house as vests in the trustee.

(3) The Act of 1996 has effect, with the necessary modifications, as if—

   (a) the rights conferred by paragraph (a) of subsection (2) were home rights under that Act,

   (b) any application for such leave as is mentioned in that paragraph were an application for an order under section 33 of that Act, and

   (c) any charge under paragraph (b) of that subsection on the estate or interest of the trustee were a charge under that Act on the estate or interest of a spouse or civil partner.

(4) Any application for leave such as is mentioned in subsection (2)(a) or otherwise by virtue of this section for an order under section 33 of the Act of 1996 shall be made to the court having jurisdiction in relation to the bankruptcy.

(5) On such an application the court shall make such order under section 33 of the Act of 1996 as it thinks just and reasonable having regard to the interests of the creditors, to the bankrupt's financial resources, to the needs of the children and to all the circumstances of the case other than the needs of the bankrupt.

(6) Where such an application is made after the end of the period of one year beginning with the first vesting (under Chapter IV of this Part) of the bankrupt's estate in a trustee, the court shall assume, unless the circumstances of the case are exceptional, that the interests of the bankrupt's creditors outweigh all other considerations.

Adjustment of prior transactions, etc.

339 Transactions at an undervalue

(1) Subject as follows in this section and sections 341 and 342, where an individual is adjudged bankrupt and he has at a relevant time (defined in section 341) entered into a transaction with any person at an undervalue, the trustee of the bankrupt's estate may apply to the court for an order under this section.

(2) The court shall, on such an application, make such order as it thinks fit for restoring the position to what it would have been if that individual had not entered into that transaction.

(3) For the purposes of this section and sections 341 and 342, an individual enters into a transaction with a person at an undervalue if—

   (a) he makes a gift to that person or he otherwise enters into a transaction with that person on terms that provide for him to receive no consideration,

   (b) he enters into a transaction with that person in consideration of marriage or the formation of a civil partnership, or

   (c) he enters into a transaction with that person for a consideration the value of which, in money or money's worth, is significantly less than the value, in money or money's worth, of the consideration provided by the individual.

Family Law Act 1986
(1986 c. 55)

PART III   DECLARATIONS OF STATUS

55 Declarations as to marital status

(1) Subject to the following provisions of this section, any person may apply to the High Court or a county court for one or more of the following declarations in relation to a marriage specified in the application, that is to say—

   (a) a declaration that the marriage was at its inception a valid marriage;
   (b) a declaration that the marriage subsisted on a date specified in the application;
   (c) a declaration that the marriage did not subsist on a date so specified;
   (d) a declaration that the validity of a divorce, annulment or legal separation obtained in any country outside England and Wales in respect of the marriage is entitled to recognition in England and Wales;
   (e) a declaration that the validity of a divorce, annulment or legal separation so obtained in respect of the marriage is not entitled to recognition in England and Wales.

(2) A court shall have jurisdiction to entertain an application under subsection (1) above if, and only if, either of the parties to the marriage to which the application relates—

   (a) is domiciled in England and Wales on the date of the application, or
   (b) has been habitually resident in England and Wales throughout the period of one year ending with that date, or
   (c) died before that date and either—
      (i)   was at death domiciled in England and Wales, or
      (ii) had been habitually resident in England and Wales throughout the period of one year ending with the date of death.

(3) Where an application under subsection (1) above is made to a court by any person other than a party to the marriage to which the application relates, the court shall refuse to hear the application if it considers that the applicant does not have a sufficient interest in the determination of that application.

55A Declarations of parentage

(1) Subject to the following provisions of this section, any person may apply to the High Court, a county court or a Magistrates' court for a declaration as to whether or not a person named in the application is or was the parent of another person so named.

(2) A court shall have jurisdiction to entertain an application under subsection (1) above if, and only if, either of the persons named in it for the purposes of that subsection—

   (a) is domiciled in England and Wales on the date of the application, or
   (b) has been habitually resident in England and Wales throughout the period of one year ending with that date, or
   (c) died before that date and either—
      (i)   was at death domiciled in England and Wales, or
      (ii) had been habitually resident in England and Wales throughout the period of one year ending with the date of death.

(3) Except in a case falling within subsection (4) below, the court shall refuse to hear an application under subsection (1) above unless it considers that the applicant has a sufficient personal interest in the determination of the application (but this is subject to section 27 of the Child Support Act 1991).

(4) The excepted cases are where the declaration sought is as to whether or not—

   (a) the applicant is the parent of a named person;
   (b) a named person is the parent of the applicant; or
   (c) a named person is the other parent of a named child of the applicant.

(5) Where an application under subsection (1) above is made and one of the persons named in it for the purposes of that subsection is a child, the court may refuse to hear the application if it considers that the determination of the application would not be in the best interests of the child.

(6) Where a court refuses to hear an application under subsection (1) above it may order that the applicant may not apply again for the same declaration without leave of the court.

(7) Where a declaration is made by a court on an application under subsection (1) above, the prescribed officer of the court shall notify the Registrar General, in such a manner and within such period as may be prescribed, of the making of that declaration.

56 Declarations of parentage, legitimacy or legitimation

(1) Any person may apply to the High Court or a county court for a declaration—

    (a) that he is the legitimate child of his parents.

(2) Any person may apply to the High Court or a county court for one (or for one or, in the alternative, the other) of the following declarations, that is to say—

    (a) a declaration that he has become a legitimated person;

    (b) a declaration that he has not become a legitimated person.

(3) A court shall have jurisdiction to entertain an application under this section if, and only if, the applicant—

    (a) is domiciled in England and Wales on the date of the application; or

    (b) has been habitually resident in England and Wales throughout the period of one year ending with that date.

(4) Where a declaration is made by a court on an application under subsection (1) above, the prescribed officer of the court shall notify the Registrar General, in such manner and within such period as may be prescribed, of the making of that declaration.

(5) In this section 'legitimated person' means a person legitimated or recognised as legitimated—

    (a) under section 2 or 3 of the Legitimacy Act 1976;

    (b) under section 1 or 8 of the Legitimacy Act 1926; or

    (c) by a legitimation (whether or not by virtue of the subsequent marriage of his parents) recognised by the law of England and Wales and effected under the law of another country.

. . .

58 General provisions as to the making and effect of declarations

(1) Where on an application to a court for a declaration under this Part the truth of the proposition to be declared is proved to the satisfaction of the court, the court shall make that declaration unless to do so would manifestly be contrary to public policy.

(2) Any declaration made under this Part shall be binding on Her Majesty and all other persons.

(3) A court, on the dismissal of an application for a declaration under this Part, shall not have power to make any declaration for which the application has not been made.

(4) No declaration which may be applied for under this Part may be made otherwise than under this Part by any court.

(5) No declaration may be made by any court, whether under this Part or otherwise—

    (a) that a marriage was at its inception void.

(6) Nothing in this section shall affect the powers of any court to grant a decree of nullity of marriage.

. . .

60 Supplementary provisions as to declarations

. . .

(5) An appeal shall lie to the High Court against—

    (a) the making by a Magistrates' court of a declaration under section 55A above,

    (b) any refusal by a Magistrates' court to make such a declaration, or

    (c) any order under subsection (6) of that section made on such a refusal.

61 Abolition of right to petition for jactitation of marriage

No person shall after the commencement of this Part be entitled to petition the High Court or a county court for jactitation of marriage.

. . .

Family Law Reform Act 1987
(1987 c. 42)

PART I   GENERAL PRINCIPLE

1 General principle

    (1) In this Act and enactments passed and instruments made after the coming into force of this section, references (however expressed) to any relationship between two persons shall, unless the contrary intention appears, be construed without regard to whether or not the father and mother of either of them, or the father and mother of any person through whom the relationship is deduced, have or had been married to each other at any time.

    (2) In this Act and enactments passed after the coming into force of this section, unless the contrary intention appears—

        (a) references to a person whose father and mother were married to each other at the time of his birth include; and

        (b) references to a person whose father and mother were not married to each other at the time of his birth do not include,

references to any person to whom subsection (3) below applies, and cognate references shall be construed accordingly.

    (3) This subsection applies to any person who—

        (a) is treated as legitimate by virtue of section 1 of the Legitimacy Act 1976;

        (b) is a legitimated person within the meaning of section 10 of that Act;

        (c) is an adopted person within the meaning of Chapter 4 of Part I of the Adoption and Children Act 2002; or

        (d) is otherwise treated in law as legitimate.

    (4) For the purpose of construing references falling within subsection (2) above, the time of a person's birth shall be taken to include any time during the period beginning with—

        (a) the insemination resulting in his birth; or

        (b) where there was no such insemination, his conception,

and (in either case) ending with his birth.

PART II   RIGHTS AND DUTIES OF PARENTS ETC.

Parental rights and duties: general

2 Construction of enactments relating to parental rights and duties

    (1) In the following enactments, namely—

        (a) section 42(1) of the National Assistance Act 1948;

        (b) section 6 of the Family Law Reform Act 1969;

        (c) the Guardianship of Minors Act 1971 (in this Act referred to as 'the 1971 Act');

        (d) Part I of the Guardianship Act 1973 (in this Act referred to as 'the 1973 Act');

        (e) Part II of the Children Act 1975;

        (f) the Child Care Act 1980 except Part I and sections 13, 24, 64 and 65;

references (however expressed) to any relationship between two persons shall be construed in accordance with section 1 above.

PART III   PROPERTY RIGHTS

18   Succession on intestacy

(1) In Part IV of the Administration of Estates Act 1925 (which deals with the distribution of the estate of an intestate), references (however expressed) to any relationship between two persons shall be construed in accordance with section 1 above.

(2) For the purposes of subsection (1) above and that Part of that Act, a person whose father and mother were not married to each other at the time of his birth shall be presumed not to have been survived by his father, or by any person related to him only through his father, unless the contrary is shown.

(3) In section 50(1) of that Act (which relates to the construction of documents), the reference to Part IV of that Act, or to the foregoing provisions of that Part, shall in relation to an instrument inter vivos made, or a will or codicil coming into operation, after the coming into force of this section (but not in relation to instruments inter vivos made or wills or codicils coming into operation earlier) be construed as including references to this section.

(4) This section does not affect any rights under the intestacy of a person dying before the coming into force of this section.

19   Dispositions of property

(1) In the following dispositions, namely—

    (a) dispositions inter vivos made on or after the date on which this section comes into force; and

    (b) dispositions by will or codicil where the will or codicil is made on or after that date;

references (whether express or implied) to any relationship between two persons shall be construed in accordance with section 1 above.

(2) It is hereby declared that the use, without more, of the word 'heir' or 'heirs' or any expression purporting to create an entailed interest in real or personal property does not show a contrary intention for the purposes of section 1 as applied by subsection (1) above.

(3) In relation to the dispositions mentioned in subsection (1) above, section 33 of the Trustee Act 1925 (which specifies the trust implied by a direction that income is to be held on protective trusts for the benefit of any person) shall have effect as if any reference (however expressed) to any relationship between two persons were construed in accordance with section 1 above.

(4) Where under any disposition of real or personal property, any interest in such property is limited (whether subject to any preceding limitation or charge or not) in such a way that it would, apart from this section, devolve (as nearly as the law permits) along with a dignity or title of honour, then—

    (a) whether or not the disposition contains an express reference to the dignity or title of honour; and

    (b) whether or not the property or some interest in the property may in some event become severed from it,

nothing in this section shall operate to sever the property or any interest in it from the dignity or title, but the property or interest shall devolve in all respects as if this section had not been enacted.

(5) This section is without prejudice to section 42 of the Adoption Act 1976 or section 69 of the Adoption and Children Act 2002 (construction of dispositions in cases of adoption).

(6) In this section 'disposition' means a disposition, including an oral disposition, of real or personal property whether inter vivos or by will or codicil.

(7) Notwithstanding any rule of law, a disposition made by will or codicil executed before the date on which this section comes into force shall not be treated for the purposes of this section as made on or after that date by reason only that the will or codicil is confirmed by a codicil executed on or after that date.

. . .

21   Entitlement to grant of probate etc.

(1) For the purpose of determining the person or persons who would in accordance with probate rules be entitled to a grant of probate or administration in respect of the estate of a deceased person, the deceased shall be presumed, unless the contrary is shown, not to have been survived—

    (a) by any person related to him whose father and mother were not married to each other at the time of his birth; or

    (b) by any person whose relationship with him is deduced through such a person as is mentioned in paragraph (a) above.

(2) In this section 'probate rules' means rules of court made under section 127 of the Supreme Court Act 1981.

(3) This section does not apply in relation to the estate of a person dying before the coming into force of this section.

. . .

PART VI   MISCELLANEOUS AND SUPPLEMENTAL

Miscellaneous

27   Artificial insemination

(1) Where after the coming into force of this section a child is born in England and Wales as the result of the artificial insemination of a woman who—

    (a) was at the time of the insemination a party to a marriage (being a marriage which had not at that time been dissolved or annulled); and

    (b) was artificially inseminated with the semen of some person other than the other party to that marriage,

then, unless it is proved to the satisfaction of any court by which the matter has to be determined that the other party to that marriage did not consent to the insemination, the child shall be treated in law as the child of the parties to that marriage and shall not be treated as the child of any person other than the parties to that marriage.

(2) Any reference in this section to a marriage includes a reference to a void marriage if at the time of the insemination resulting in the birth of the child both or either of the parties reasonably believed that the marriage was valid; and for the purposes of this section it shall be presumed, unless the contrary is shown, that one of the parties so believed at that time that the marriage was valid.

(3) Nothing in this section shall affect the succession to any dignity or title of honour or render any person capable of succeeding to or transmitting a right to succeed to any such dignity or title.

. . .

Supplemental

30   Orders applying section 1 to other enactments

(1) The Lord Chancellor may by order make provision for the construction in accordance with section 1 above of such enactments passed before the coming into force of that section as may be specified in the order.

. . .

Housing Act 1988
(1988 c. 50)

PART I   RENTED ACCOMMODATION

CHAPTER I   ASSURED TENANCIES

Miscellaneous

17   Succession to assured periodic tenancy by spouse or civil partner

(1) In any case where—

  (a) the sole tenant under an assured periodic tenancy dies, and

  (b) immediately before the death, the tenant's spouse or civil partner was occupying the dwelling-house as his or her only or principal home, and

  (c) the tenant was not himself a successor, as defined in subsection (2) or subsection (3) below,

then, on the death, the tenancy vests by virtue of this section in the spouse or civil partner (and, accordingly, does not devolve under the tenant's will or intestacy).

(2) For the purposes of this section, a tenant is a successor in relation to a tenancy if—

  (a) the tenancy became vested in him either by virtue of this section or under the will or intestacy of a previous tenant; or

  (b) at some time before the tenant's death the tenancy was a joint tenancy held by himself and one or more other persons and, prior to his death, he became the sole tenant by survivorship; or

  (c) he became entitled to the tenancy as mentioned in section 39(5) below.

(3) For the purposes of this section, a tenant is also a successor in relation to a tenancy (in this subsection referred to as 'the new tenancy') which was granted to him (alone or jointly with others) if—

  (a) at some time before the grant of the new tenancy, he was, by virtue of subsection (2) above, a successor in relation to an earlier tenancy of the same or substantially the same dwelling-house as is let under the new tenancy; and

  (b) at all times since he became such a successor he has been a tenant (alone or jointly with others) of the dwelling-house which is let under the new tenancy or of a dwelling-house which is substantially the same as that dwelling-house.

(4) For the purposes of this section—

  (a) a person who was living with the tenant as his or her wife or husband shall be treated as the tenant's spouse, and

  (b) a person who was living with the tenant as if they were civil partners shall be treated as the tenant's civil partner.

(5) If, on the death of the tenant, there is, by virtue of subsection (4) above, more than one person who fulfils the condition in subsection (1)(b) above, such one of them as may be decided by agreement or, in default of agreement, by the county court shall for the purposes of this section be treated (according to whether that one of them is of the opposite sex to, or of the same sex as, the tenant) as the tenant's spouse or the tenant's civil partner.

Children Act 1989
(1989 c. 41)

PART I   INTRODUCTORY

1   Welfare of the child

(1) When a court determines any question with respect to—

  (a) the upbringing of a child; or

      (b) the administration of a child's property or the application of any income arising from it,

the child's welfare shall be the court's paramount consideration.

    (2) In any proceedings in which any question with respect to the upbringing of a child arises, the court shall have regard to the general principle that any delay in determining the question is likely to prejudice the welfare of the child.

    (3) In the circumstances mentioned in subsection (4), a court shall have regard in particular to—

      (a) the ascertainable wishes and feelings of the child concerned (considered in the light of his age and understanding);

      (b) his physical, emotional and educational needs;

      (c) the likely effect on him of any change in his circumstances;

      (d) his age, sex, background and any characteristics of his which the court considers relevant;

      (e) any harm which he has suffered or is at risk of suffering;

      (f) how capable each of his parents, and any other person in relation to whom the court considers the question to be relevant, is of meeting his needs;

      (g) the range of powers available to the court under this Act in the proceedings in question.

    (4) The circumstances are that—

      (a) the court is considering whether to make, vary or discharge a section 8 order, and the making, variation or discharge of the order is opposed by any party to the proceedings; or

      (b) the court is considering whether to make, vary or discharge a special guardianship order or an order under Part IV.

    (5) Where a court is considering whether or not to make one or more orders under this Act with respect to a child, it shall not make the order or any of the orders unless it considers that doing so would be better for the child than making no order at all.

2 Parental responsibility for children

    (1) Where a child's father and mother were married to each other at the time of his birth, they shall each have parental responsibility for the child.

    (2) Where a child's father and mother were not married to each other at the time of his birth—

      (a) the mother shall have parental responsibility for the child;

      (b) the father shall have parental responsibility for the child if he has acquired it (and has not ceased to have it) in accordance with the provisions of this Act.

    (3) References in this Act to a child whose father and mother were, or (as the case may be) were not, married to each other at the time of his birth must be read with section 1 of the Family Law Reform Act 1987 (which extends their meaning).

    (4) The rule of law that a father is the natural guardian of his legitimate child is abolished.

    (5) More than one person may have parental responsibility for the same child at the same time.

    (6) A person who has parental responsibility for a child at any time shall not cease to have that responsibility solely because some other person subsequently acquires parental responsibility for the child.

    (7) Where more than one person has parental responsibility for a child, each of them may act alone and without the other (or others) in meeting that responsibility; but nothing in this Part shall be taken to affect the operation of any enactment which requires the consent of more than one person in a matter affecting the child.

    (8) The fact that a person has parental responsibility for a child shall not entitle him to act in any way which would be incompatible with any order made with respect to the child under this Act.

(9) A person who has parental responsibility for a child may not surrender or transfer any part of that responsibility to another but may arrange for some or all of it to be met by one or more persons acting on his behalf.

(10) The person with whom any such arrangement is made may himself be a person who already has parental responsibility for the child concerned.

(11) The making of any such arrangement shall not affect any liability of the person making it which may arise from any failure to meet any part of his parental responsibility for the child concerned.

3   Meaning of 'parental responsibility'

(1) In this Act 'parental responsibility' means all the rights, duties, powers, responsibilities and authority which by law a parent of a child has in relation to the child and his property.

(2) It also includes the rights, powers and duties which a guardian of the child's estate (appointed, before the commencement of section 5, to act generally) would have had in relation to the child and his property.

(3) The rights referred to in subsection (2) include, in particular, the right of the guardian to receive or recover in his own name, for the benefit of the child, property of whatever description and wherever situated which the child is entitled to receive or recover.

(4) The fact that a person has, or does not have, parental responsibility for a child shall not affect—
> (a) any obligation which he may have in relation to the child (such as a statutory duty to maintain the child); or
> (b) any rights which, in the event of the child's death, he (or any other person) may have in relation to the child's property.

(5) A person who—
> (a) does not have parental responsibility for a particular child; but
> (b) has care of the child,

may (subject to the provisions of this Act) do what is reasonable in all the circumstances of the case for the purpose of safeguarding or promoting the child's welfare.

4   Acquisition of parental responsibility by father

(1) Where a child's father and mother were not married to each other at the time of his birth, the father shall acquire parental responsibility for the child if—
> (a) he becomes registered as the child's father under any of the enactments specified in subsection (1A);
> (b) he and the child's mother make an agreement (a 'parental responsibility agreement') providing for him to have parental responsibility for the child; or
> (c) the court, on his application, orders that he shall have parental responsibility for the child.

(1A) The enactments referred to in subsection (1)(a) are—
> (a) paragraphs (a), (b) and (c) of section 10(1) and of section 10A(1) of the Births and Deaths Registration Act 1953;

. . .

(1B) The Secretary of State may by order amend subsection (1A) so as to add further enactments to the list in that subsection.

(2) No parental responsibility agreement shall have effect for the purposes of this Act unless—
> (a) it is made in the form prescribed by regulations made by the Lord Chancellor; and
> (b) where regulations are made by the Lord Chancellor prescribing the manner in which such agreements must be recorded, it is recorded in the prescribed manner.

(2A) A person who has acquired parental responsibility under subsection (1) shall cease to have that responsibility only if the court so orders.

(3) The court may make an order under subsection (2A) on the application—

    (a) of any person who has parental responsibility for the child; or

    (b) with the leave of the court, of the child himself,

subject, in the case of parental responsibility acquired under subsection (1)(c), to section 12(4).

(4) The court may only grant leave under subsection (3)(b) if it is satisfied that the child has sufficient understanding to make the proposed application.

4A Acquisition of parental responsibility by step-parent

(1) Where a child's parent ('parent A') who has parental responsibility for the child is married to, or a civil partner of, a person who is not the child's parent ('the step-parent')—

    (a) parent A or, if the other parent of the child also has parental responsibility for the child, both parents may by agreement with the step-parent provide for the step-parent to have parental responsibility for the child; or

    (b) the court may, on the application of the step-parent, order that the step-parent shall have parental responsibility for the child.

(2) An agreement under subsection (1)(a) is also a 'parental responsibility agreement', and section 4(2) applies in relation to such agreements as it applies in relation to parental responsibility agreements under section 4.

(3) A parental responsibility agreement under subsection (1)(a), or an order under subsection (1)(b), may only be brought to an end by an order of the court made on the application—

    (a) of any person who has parental responsibility for the child; or

    (b) with the leave of the court, of the child himself.

(4) The court may only grant leave under subsection (3)(b) if it is satisfied that the child has sufficient understanding to make the proposed application.

5 Appointment of guardians

(1) Where an application with respect to a child is made to the court by any individual, the court may by order appoint that individual to be the child's guardian if—

    (a) the child has no parent with parental responsibility for him; or

    (b) a residence order has been made with respect to the child in favour of a parent, guardian or special guardian of his who has died while the order was in force; or

    (c) paragraph (b) does not apply, and the child's only or last surviving special guardian dies.

(2) The power conferred by subsection (1) may also be exercised in any family proceedings if the court considers that the order should be made even though no application has been made for it.

(3) A parent who has parental responsibility for his child may appoint another individual to be the child's guardian in the event of his death.

(4) A guardian of a child may appoint another individual to take his place as the child's guardian in the event of his death; and a special guardian of a child may appoint another individual to be the child's guardian in the event of his death.

(5) An appointment under subsection (3) or (4) shall not have effect unless it is made in writing, is dated and is signed by the person making the appointment or—

    (a) in the case of an appointment made by a will which is not signed by the testator, is signed at the direction of the testator in accordance with the requirements of section 9 of the Wills Act 1837; or

    (b) in any other case, is signed at the direction of the person making the appointment, in his presence and in the presence of two witnesses who each attest the signature.

(6) A person appointed as a child's guardian under this section shall have parental responsibility for the child concerned.

(7) Where—

    (a) on the death of any person making an appointment under subsection (3) or (4), the child concerned has no parent with parental responsibility for him; or

(b) immediately before the death of any person making such an appointment, a residence order in his favour was in force with respect to the child or he was the child's only (or last surviving) special guardian,

the appointment shall take effect on the death of that person.

(8) Where, on the death of any person making an appointment under subsection (3) or (4)—

(a) the child concerned has a parent with parental responsibility for him; and

(b) subsection (7)(b) does not apply,

the appointment shall take effect when the child no longer has a parent who has parental responsibility for him.

(9) Subsections (1) and (7) do not apply if the residence order referred to in paragraph (b) of those subsections was also made in favour of a surviving parent of the child.

(10) Nothing in this section shall be taken to prevent an appointment under subsection (3) or (4) being made by two or more persons acting jointly.

(11) Subject to any provision made by rules of court, no court shall exercise the High Court's inherent jurisdiction to appoint a guardian of the estate of any child.

(12) Where rules of court are made under subsection (11) they may prescribe the circumstances in which, and conditions subject to which, an appointment of such a guardian may be made.

(13) A guardian of a child may only be appointed in accordance with the provisions of this section.

6   Guardians: revocation and disclaimer

(1) An appointment under section 5(3) or (4) revokes an earlier such appointment (including one made in an unrevoked will or codicil) made by the same person in respect of the same child, unless it is clear (whether as the result of an express provision in the later appointment or by any necessary implication) that the purpose of the later appointment is to appoint an additional guardian.

(2) An appointment under section 5(3) or (4) (including one made in an unrevoked will or codicil) is revoked if the person who made the appointment revokes it by a written and dated instrument which is signed—

(a) by him; or

(b) at his direction, in his presence and in the presence of two witnesses who each attest the signature.

(3) An appointment under section 5(3) or (4) (other than one made in a will or codicil) is revoked if, with the intention of revoking the appointment, the person who made it—

(a) destroys the instrument by which it was made; or

(b) has some other person destroy that instrument in his presence.

(3A) An appointment under section 5(3) or (4) (including one made in an unrevoked will or codicil) is revoked if the person appointed is the spouse of the person who made the appointment and either—

(a) a decree of a court of civil jurisdiction in England and Wales dissolves or annuls the marriage, or

(b) the marriage is dissolved or annulled and the divorce or annulment is entitled to recognition in England and Wales by virtue of Part II of the Family Law Act 1986,

unless a contrary intention appears by the appointment.

(3B) An appointment under section 5(3) or (4) (including one made in an unrevoked will or codicil) is revoked if the person appointed is the civil partner of the person who made the appointment and either—

(a) an order of a court of civil jurisdiction in England and Wales dissolves or annuls the civil partnership, or

(b) the civil partnership is dissolved or annulled and the dissolution or annulment is entitled to recognition in England and Wales by virtue of Chapter 3 of Part 5 of the Civil Partnership Act 2004,

unless a contrary intention appears by the appointment.

(4) For the avoidance of doubt, an appointment under section 5(3) or (4) made in a will or codicil is revoked if the will or codicil is revoked.

(5) A person who is appointed as a guardian under section 5(3) or (4) may disclaim his appointment by an instrument in writing signed by him and made within a reasonable time of his first knowing that the appointment has taken effect.

(6) Where regulations are made by the Lord Chancellor prescribing the manner in which such disclaimers must be recorded, no such disclaimer shall have effect unless it is recorded in the prescribed manner.

(7) Any appointment of a guardian under section 5 may be brought to an end at any time by order of the court—

(a) on the application of any person who has parental responsibility for the child;

(b) on the application of the child concerned, with leave of the court; or

(c) in any family proceedings, if the court considers that it should be brought to an end even though no application has been made.

7 Welfare reports

(1) A court considering any question with respect to a child under this Act may—

(a) ask an officer of the Service or a Welsh family proceedings officer; or

(b) ask a local authority to arrange for—

(i)   an officer of the authority; or

(ii) such other person (other than an officer of the Service or a Welsh family proceedings officer) as the authority considers appropriate,

to report to the court on such matters relating to the welfare of that child as are required to be dealt with in the report.

(2) The Lord Chancellor, after consulting the Lord Chief Justice, may make regulations specifying matters which, unless the court orders otherwise, must be dealt with in any report under this section.

(3) The report may be made in writing, or orally, as the court requires.

(4) Regardless of any enactment or rule of law which would otherwise prevent it from doing so, the court may take account of—

(a) any statement contained in the report; and

(b) any evidence given in respect of the matters referred to in the report,

in so far as the statement or evidence is, in the opinion of the court, relevant to the question which it is considering.

(5) It shall be the duty of the authority or officer of the Service or a Welsh family proceedings officer to comply with any request for a report under this section.

(6) The Lord Chief Justice may nominate a judicial office holder (as defined in section 109(4) of the Constitutional Reform Act 2005) to exercise his functions under subsection (2).

PART II   ORDERS WITH RESPECT TO CHILDREN IN FAMILY PROCEEDINGS

General

8 Residence, contact and other orders with respect to children

(1) In this Act—

'a contact order' means an order requiring the person with whom a child lives, or is to live, to allow the child to visit or stay with the person named in the order, or for that person and the child otherwise to have contact with each other;

'a prohibited steps order' means an order that no step which could be taken by a parent in meeting his parental responsibility for a child, and which is of a kind specified in the order, shall be taken by any person without the consent of the court;

'a residence order' means an order settling the arrangements to be made as to the person with whom a child is to live; and 'a specific issue order' means an order giving directions for the purpose of determining a specific question which has arisen, or which may arise, in connection with any aspect of parental responsibility for a child.

(2) In this Act 'a section 8 order' means any of the orders mentioned in subsection (1) and any order varying or discharging such an order.

(3) For the purposes of this Act 'family proceedings' means any proceedings—

    (a) under the inherent jurisdiction of the High Court in relation to children; and

    (b) under the enactments mentioned in subsection (4), but does not include proceedings on an application for leave under section 100(3).

(4) The enactments are—

    (a) Parts I, II and IV of this Act;

    (b) the Matrimonial Causes Act 1973;

    (ba) Schedule 5 to the Civil Partnership Act 2004;

    (d) the Adoption and Children Act 2002;

    (e) the Domestic Proceedings and Magistrates' Courts Act 1978;

    (ea) Schedule 6 to the Civil Partnership Act 2004;

    (g) Part III of the Matrimonial and Family Proceedings Act 1984;

    (h) the Family Law Act 1996;

    (i) sections 11 and 12 of the Crime and Disorder Act 1998.

9 Restrictions on making section 8 orders

(1) No court shall make any section 8 order, other than a residence order, with respect to a child who is in the care of a local authority.

(2) No application may be made by a local authority for a residence order or contact order and no court shall make such an order in favour of a local authority.

(3) A person who is, or was at any time within the last six months, a local authority foster parent of a child may not apply for leave to apply for a section 8 order with respect to the child unless—

    (a) he has the consent of the authority;

    (b) he is a relative of the child; or

    (c) the child has lived with him for at least one year preceding the application.

(5) No court shall exercise its powers to make a specific issue order or prohibited steps order—

    (a) with a view to achieving a result which could be achieved by making a residence or contact order; or

    (b) in any way which is denied to the High Court (by section 100(2)) in the exercise of its inherent jurisdiction with respect to children.

(6) Subject to section 12(5) no court shall make any section 8 order which is to have effect for a period which will end after the child has reached the age of sixteen unless it is satisfied that the circumstances of the case are exceptional.

(7) No court shall make any section 8 order, other than one varying or discharging such an order, with respect to a child who has reached the age of sixteen unless it is satisfied that the circumstances of the case are exceptional.

10 Power of court to make section 8 orders

(1) In any family proceedings in which a question arises with respect to the welfare of any child, the court may make a section 8 order with respect to the child if—

    (a) an application for the order has been made by a person who—

        (i) is entitled to apply for a section 8 order with respect to the child; or

        (ii) has obtained the leave of the court to make the application; or

    (b) the court considers that the order should be made even though no such application has been made.

(2) The court may also make a section 8 order with respect to any child on the application of a person who—

(a) is entitled to apply for a section 8 order with respect to the child; or

(b) has obtained the leave of the court to make the application.

(3) This section is subject to the restrictions imposed by section 9.

(4) The following persons are entitled to apply to the court for any section 8 order with respect to a child—

(a) any parent, guardian or special guardian of the child;

(aa) any person who by virtue of section 4A has parental responsibility for the child;

(b) any person in whose favour a residence order is in force with respect to the child.

(5) The following persons are entitled to apply for a residence or contact order with respect to a child—

(a) any party to a marriage (whether or not subsisting) in relation to whom the child is a child of the family;

(aa) any civil partner in a civil partnership (whether or not subsisting) in relation to whom the child is a child of the family;

(b) any person with whom the child has lived for a period of at least three years;

(c) any person who—

   (i) in any case where a residence order is in force with respect to the child, has the consent of each of the persons in whose favour the order was made;

   (ii) in any case where the child is in the care of a local authority, has the consent of that authority; or

   (iii) in any other case, has the consent of each of those (if any) who have parental responsibility for the child.

(5A) A local authority foster parent is entitled to apply for a residence order with respect to a child if the child has lived with him for a period of at least one year immediately preceding the application.

(6) A person who would not otherwise be entitled (under the previous provisions of this section) to apply for the variation or discharge of a section 8 order shall be entitled to do so if—

(a) the order was made on his application; or

(b) in the case of a contact order, he is named in the order.

(7) Any person who falls within a category of person prescribed by rules of court is entitled to apply for any such section 8 order as may be prescribed in relation to that category of person.

(7A) If a special guardianship order is in force with respect to a child, an application for a residence order may only be made with respect to him, if apart from this subsection the leave of the court is not required, with such leave.

(8) Where the person applying for leave to make an application for a section 8 order is the child concerned, the court may only grant leave if it is satisfied that he has sufficient understanding to make the proposed application for the section 8 order.

(9) Where the person applying for leave to make an application for a section 8 order is not the child concerned, the court shall, in deciding whether or not to grant leave, have particular regard to—

(a) the nature of the proposed application for the section 8 order;

(b) the applicant's connection with the child;

(c) any risk there might be of that proposed application disrupting the child's life to such an extent that he would be harmed by it; and

(d) where the child is being looked after by a local authority—

   (i) the authority's plans for the child's future; and

   (ii) the wishes and feelings of the child's parents.

(10) The period of three years mentioned in subsection (5)(b) need not be continuous but must not have begun more than five years before, or ended more than three months before, the making of the application.

11 General principles and supplementary provisions

(1) In proceedings in which any question of making a section 8 order, or any other question with respect to such an order arises, the court shall (in the light of any rules made by virtue of subsection (2))—

(a) draw up a timetable with a view to determining the question without delay; and

(b) give such directions as it considers appropriate for the purpose of ensuring, so far as is reasonably practicable, that that timetable is adhered to.

(2) Rules of court may—

(a) specify periods within which specified steps must be taken in relation to proceedings in which such questions arise; and

(b) make other provision with respect to such proceedings for the purpose of ensuring, so far as is reasonably practicable, that such questions are determined without delay.

(3) Where a court has power to make a section 8 order, it may do so at any time during the course of the proceedings in question even though it is not in a position to dispose finally of those proceedings.

(4) Where a residence order is made in favour of two or more persons who do not themselves all live together, the order may specify the periods during which the child is to live in the different households concerned.

(5) Where—

(a) a residence order has been made with respect to a child; and

(b) as a result of the order the child lives, or is to live, with one of two parents who each have parental responsibility for him,

the residence order shall cease to have effect if the parents live together for a continuous period of more than six months.

(6) A contact order which requires the parent with whom a child lives to allow the child to visit, or otherwise have contact with, his other parent shall cease to have effect if the parents live together for a continuous period of more than six months.

(7) A section 8 order may—

(a) contain directions about how it is to be carried into effect;

(b) impose conditions which must be complied with by any person—

(i)   in whose favour the order is made;

(ii) who is a parent of the child concerned;

(iii) who is not a parent of his but who has parental responsibility for him; or

(iv) with whom the child is living,

and to whom the conditions are expressed to apply;

(c) be made to have effect for a specified period, or contain provisions which are to have effect for a specified period;

(d) make such incidental, supplemental or consequential provision as the court thinks fit.

11A Contact activity directions

(1) This section applies in proceedings in which the court is considering whether to make provision about contact with a child by making—

(a) a contact order with respect to the child, or

(b) an order varying or discharging a contact order with respect to the child.

(2) The court may make a contact activity direction in connection with that provision about contact.

(3) A contact activity direction is a direction requiring an individual who is a party to the proceedings to take part in an activity that promotes contact with the child concerned.

(4) The direction is to specify the activity and the person providing the activity.

(5) The activities that may be so required include, in particular—

(a) programmes, classes and counselling or guidance sessions of a kind that—

      (i)   may assist a person as regards establishing, maintaining or improving contact with a child;

     (ii) may, by addressing a person's violent behaviour, enable or facilitate contact with a child;

  (b) sessions in which information or advice is given as regards making or operating arrangements for contact with a child, including making arrangements by means of mediation.

(6) No individual may be required by a contact activity direction—

  (a) to undergo medical or psychiatric examination, assessment or treatment;

  (b) to take part in mediation.

(7) A court may not on the same occasion—

  (a) make a contact activity direction, and

  (b) dispose finally of the proceedings as they relate to contact with the child concerned.

(8) Subsection (2) has effect subject to the restrictions in sections 11B and 11E.

(9) In considering whether to make a contact activity direction, the welfare of the child concerned is to be the court's paramount consideration.

11B Contact activity directions: further provision

(1) A court may not make a contact activity direction in any proceedings unless there is a dispute as regards the provision about contact that the court is considering whether to make in the proceedings.

(2) A court may not make a contact activity direction requiring an individual who is a child to take part in an activity unless the individual is a parent of the child in relation to whom the court is considering provision about contact.

(3) A court may not make a contact activity direction in connection with the making, variation or discharge of a contact order, if the contact order is, or would if made be, an excepted order.

(4) A contact order with respect to a child is an excepted order if—

  (a) it is made in proceedings that include proceedings on an application for a relevant adoption order in respect of the child; or

  (b) it makes provision as regards contact between the child and a person who would be a parent or relative of the child but for the child's adoption by an order falling within subsection (5).

(5) An order falls within this subsection if it is—

  (a) a relevant adoption order;

  (b) an adoption order, within the meaning of section 72(1) of the Adoption Act 1976, other than an order made by virtue of section 14 of that Act on the application of a married couple one of whom is the mother or the father of the child;

  (c) ....

(6) A relevant adoption order is an adoption order, within the meaning of section 46(1) of the Adoption and Children Act 2002, other than an order made—

  (a) on an application under section 50 of that Act by a couple (within the meaning of that Act) one of whom is the mother or the father of the person to be adopted, or

  (b) on an application under section 51(2) of that Act.

(7) A court may not make a contact activity direction in relation to an individual unless the individual is habitually resident in England and Wales; and a direction ceases to have effect if the individual subject to the direction ceases to be habitually resident in England and Wales.

11C Contact activity conditions

(1) This section applies if in any family proceedings the court makes—

  (a) a contact order with respect to a child, or

  (b) an order varying a contact order with respect to a child.

(2) The contact order may impose, or the contact order may be varied so as to impose, a condition (a 'contact activity condition') requiring an individual falling within subsection (3) to take part in an activity that promotes contact with the child concerned.

(3) An individual falls within this subsection if he is—

(a) for the purposes of the contact order so made or varied, the person with whom the child concerned lives or is to live;

(b) the person whose contact with the child concerned is provided for in that order; or

(c) a person upon whom that order imposes a condition under section 11(7)(b).

(4) The condition is to specify the activity and the person providing the activity.

(5) Subsections (5) and (6) of section 11A have effect as regards the activities that may be required by a contact activity condition as they have effect as regards the activities that may be required by a contact activity direction.

(6) Subsection (2) has effect subject to the restrictions in sections 11D and 11E.

11D   Contact activity conditions: further provision

(1) A contact order may not impose a contact activity condition on an individual who is a child unless the individual is a parent of the child concerned.

(2) If a contact order is an excepted order (within the meaning given by section 11B(4)), it may not impose (and it may not be varied so as to impose) a contact activity condition.

(3) A contact order may not impose a contact activity condition on an individual unless the individual is habitually resident in England and Wales; and a condition ceases to have effect if the individual subject to the condition ceases to be habitually resident in England and Wales.

11E   Contact activity directions and conditions: making

(1) Before making a contact activity direction (or imposing a contact activity condition by means of a contact order), the court must satisfy itself as to the matters falling within subsections (2) to (4).

(2) The first matter is that the activity proposed to be specified is appropriate in the circumstances of the case.

(3) The second matter is that the person proposed to be specified as the provider of the activity is suitable to provide the activity.

(4) The third matter is that the activity proposed to be specified is provided in a place to which the individual who would be subject to the direction (or the condition) can reasonably be expected to travel.

(5) Before making such a direction (or such an order), the court must obtain and consider information about the individual who would be subject to the direction (or the condition) and the likely effect of the direction (or the condition) on him.

(6) Information about the likely effect of the direction (or the condition) may, in particular, include information as to—

(a) any conflict with the individual's religious beliefs;

(b) any interference with the times (if any) at which he normally works or attends an educational establishment.

(7) The court may ask an officer of the Service or a Welsh family proceedings officer to provide the court with information as to the matters in subsections (2) to (5); and it shall be the duty of the officer of the Service or Welsh family proceedings officer to comply with any such request.

(8) In this section 'specified' means specified in a contact activity direction (or in a contact activity condition).

11F   Contact activity directions and conditions: financial assistance

(1) The Secretary of State may by regulations make provision authorising him to make payments to assist individuals falling within subsection (2) in paying relevant charges or fees.

(2) An individual falls within this subsection if he is required by a contact activity direction or condition to take part in an activity that promotes contact with a child, not being a child ordinarily resident in Wales.

(3) The National Assembly for Wales may by regulations make provision authorising it to make payments to assist individuals falling within subsection (4) in paying relevant charges or fees.

(4) An individual falls within this subsection if he is required by a contact activity direction or condition to take part in an activity that promotes contact with a child who is ordinarily resident in Wales.

(5) A relevant charge or fee, in relation to an activity required by a contact activity direction or condition, is a charge or fee in respect of the activity payable to the person providing the activity.

(6) Regulations under this section may provide that no assistance is available to an individual unless—

   (a) the individual satisfies such conditions as regards his financial resources as may be set out in the regulations;
   (b) the activity in which the individual is required by a contact activity direction or condition to take part is provided to him in England or Wales;
   (c) where the activity in which the individual is required to take Part is provided to him in England, it is provided by a person who is for the time being approved by the Secretary of State as a provider of activities required by a contact activity direction or condition;
   (d) where the activity in which the individual is required to take Part is provided to him in Wales, it is provided by a person who is for the time being approved by the National Assembly for Wales as a provider of activities required by a contact activity direction or condition.

(7) Regulations under this section may make provision—

   (a) as to the maximum amount of assistance that may be paid to or in respect of an individual as regards an activity in which he is required by a contact activity direction or condition to take part;
   (b) where the amount may vary according to an individual's financial resources, as to the method by which the amount is to be determined;
   (c) authorising payments by way of assistance to be made directly to persons pro- viding activities required by a contact activity direction or condition.

11G   Contact activity directions and conditions: monitoring

(1) This section applies if in any family proceedings the court—

   (a) makes a contact activity direction in relation to an individual, or
   (b) makes a contact order that imposes, or varies a contact order so as to impose, a contact activity condition on an individual.

(2) The court may on making the direction (or imposing the condition by means of a contact order) ask an officer of the Service or a Welsh family proceedings officer—

   (a) to monitor, or arrange for the monitoring of, the individual's compliance with the direction (or the condition);
   (b) to report to the court on any failure by the individual to comply with the direction (or the condition).

(3) It shall be the duty of the officer of the Service or Welsh family proceedings officer to comply with any request under subsection (2).

11H   Monitoring contact

(1) This section applies if in any family proceedings the court makes—

   (a) a contact order with respect to a child in favour of a person, or
   (b) an order varying such a contact order.

(2) The court may ask an officer of the Service or a Welsh family proceedings officer—

    (a) to monitor whether an individual falling within subsection (3) complies with the contact order (or the contact order as varied);

    (b) to report to the court on such matters relating to the individual's compliance as the court may specify in the request.

(3) An individual falls within this subsection if the contact order so made (or the contact order as so varied)—

    (a) requires the individual to allow contact with the child concerned;

    (b) names the individual as having contact with the child concerned; or

    (c) imposes a condition under section 11(7)(b) on the individual.

(4) If the contact order (or the contact order as varied) includes a contact activity condition, a request under subsection (2) is to be treated as relating to the provisions of the order other than the contact activity condition.

(5) The court may make a request under subsection (2)—

    (a) on making the contact order (or the order varying the contact order), or

    (b) at any time during the subsequent course of the proceedings as they relate to contact with the child concerned.

(6) In making a request under subsection (2), the court is to specify the period for which the officer of the Service or Welsh family proceedings officer is to monitor compliance with the order; and the period specified may not exceed twelve months.

(7) It shall be the duty of the officer of the Service or Welsh family proceedings officer to comply with any request under subsection (2).

(8) The court may order any individual falling within subsection (3) to take such steps as may be specified in the order with a view to enabling the officer of the Service or Welsh family proceedings officer to comply with the court's request under subsection (2).

(9) But the court may not make an order under subsection (8) with respect to an individual who is a child unless he is a parent of the child with respect to whom the order falling within subsection (1) was made.

(10) A court may not make a request under subsection (2) in relation to a contact order that is an excepted order (within the meaning given by section 11B(4)).

11I Contact orders: warning notices

Where the court makes (or varies) a contact order, it is to attach to the contact order (or the order varying the contact order) a notice warning of the consequences of failing to comply with the contact order.

11J Enforcement orders

(1) This section applies if a contact order with respect to a child has been made.

(2) If the court is satisfied beyond reasonable doubt that a person has failed to comply with the contact order, it may make an order (an 'enforcement order') imposing on the person an unpaid work requirement.

(3) But the court may not make an enforcement order if it is satisfied that the person had a reasonable excuse for failing to comply with the contact order.

(4) The burden of proof as to the matter mentioned in subsection (3) lies on the person claiming to have had a reasonable excuse, and the standard of proof is the balance of probabilities.

(5) The court may make an enforcement order in relation to the contact order only on the application of—

    (a) the person who is, for the purposes of the contact order, the person with whom the child concerned lives or is to live;

    (b) the person whose contact with the child concerned is provided for in the contact order;

(c) any individual subject to a condition under section 11(7)(b) or a contact activity condition imposed by the contact order; or

(d) the child concerned.

(6) Where the person proposing to apply for an enforcement order in relation to a contact order is the child concerned, the child must obtain the leave of the court before making such an application.

(7) The court may grant leave to the child concerned only if it is satisfied that he has sufficient understanding to make the proposed application.

(8) Subsection (2) has effect subject to the restrictions in sections 11K and 11L.

(9) The court may suspend an enforcement order for such period as it thinks fit.

(10) Nothing in this section prevents a court from making more than one enforcement order in relation to the same person on the same occasion.

(11) Proceedings in which any question of making an enforcement order, or any other question with respect to such an order, arises are to be regarded for the purposes of section 11(1) and (2) as proceedings in which a question arises with respect to a section 8 order.

(12) In Schedule A1—

(a) Part 1 makes provision as regards an unpaid work requirement;

(b) Part 2 makes provision in relation to the revocation and amendment of enforcement orders and failure to comply with such orders.

(13) This section is without prejudice to section 63(3) of the Magistrates' Courts Act 1980 as it applies in relation to contact orders.

11K Enforcement orders: further provision

(1) A court may not make an enforcement order against a person in respect of a failure to comply with a contact order unless it is satisfied that before the failure occurred the person had been given (in accordance with rules of court) a copy of, or otherwise informed of the terms of—

(a) in the case of a failure to comply with a contact order that was varied before the failure occurred, a notice under section 11I relating to the order varying the contact order or, where more than one such order has been made, the last order preceding the failure in question;

(b) in any other case, a notice under section 11I relating to the contact order.

(2) A court may not make an enforcement order against a person in respectof any failure to comply with a contact order occurring before the person attained the age of 18.

(3) A court may not make an enforcement order against a person in respectof a failure to comply with a contact order that is an excepted order (within the meaning given by section 11B(4)).

(4) A court may not make an enforcement order against a person unless the person is habitually resident in England and Wales; and an enforcement order ceases to have effect if the person subject to the order ceases to be habitually resident in England and Wales.

11L Enforcement orders: making

(1) Before making an enforcement order as regards a person in breach of a contact order, the court must be satisfied that—

(a) making the enforcement order proposed is necessary to secure the person's compliance with the contact order or any contact order that has effect in its place;

(b) the likely effect on the person of the enforcement order proposed to be made is proportionate to the seriousness of the breach of the contact order.

(2) Before making an enforcement order, the court must satisfy itself that provision for the person to work under an unpaid work requirement imposed by an enforcement order can be made in the local justice area in which the person in breach resides or will reside.

(3) Before making an enforcement order as regards a person in breach of a contact order, the court must obtain and consider information about the person and the likely effect of the enforcement order on him.

(4) Information about the likely effect of the enforcement order may, in particular, include information as to—

>(a) any conflict with the person's religious beliefs;
>
>(b) any interference with the times (if any) at which he normally works or attends an educational establishment.

(5) A court that proposes to make an enforcement order may ask an officer of the Service or a Welsh family proceedings officer to provide the court with information as to the matters in subsections (2) and (3).

(6) It shall be the duty of the officer of the Service or Welsh family proceedings officer to comply with any request under this section.

(7) In making an enforcement order in relation to a contact order, a court must take into account the welfare of the child who is the subject of the contact order.

11M Enforcement orders: monitoring

(1) On making an enforcement order in relation to a person, the court is to ask an officer of the Service or a Welsh family proceedings officer—

>(a) to monitor, or arrange for the monitoring of, the person's compliance with the unpaid work requirement imposed by the order;
>
>(b) to report to the court if a report under paragraph 8 of Schedule A1 is made in relation to the person;
>
>(c) to report to the court on such other matters relating to the person's compliance as may be specified in the request;
>
>(d) to report to the court if the person is, or becomes, unsuitable to perform work under the requirement.

(2) It shall be the duty of the officer of the Service or Welsh family proceedings officer to comply with any request under this section.

11N Enforcement orders: warning notices

Where the court makes an enforcement order, it is to attach to the order a notice warning of the consequences of failing to comply with the order.

11O Compensation for financial loss

(1) This section applies if a contact order with respect to a child has been made.

(2) If the court is satisfied that—

>(a) an individual has failed to comply with the contact order, and
>
>(b) a person falling within subsection (6) has suffered financial loss by reason of the breach,

it may make an order requiring the individual in breach to pay the person compensation in respect of his financial loss.

(3) But the court may not make an order under subsection (2) if it is satisfied that the individual in breach had a reasonable excuse for failing to comply with the contact order.

(4) The burden of proof as to the matter mentioned in subsection (3) lies on the individual claiming to have had a reasonable excuse.

(5) An order under subsection (2) may be made only on an application by the person who claims to have suffered financial loss.

(6) A person falls within this subsection if he is—

>(a) the person who is, for the purposes of the contact order, the person with whom the child concerned lives or is to live;
>
>(b) the person whose contact with the child concerned is provided for in the contact order;
>
>(c) an individual subject to a condition under section 11(7)(b) or a contact activity condition imposed by the contact order; or
>
>(d) the child concerned.

(7) Where the person proposing to apply for an order under subsection (2) is the child concerned, the child must obtain the leave of the court before making such an application.

(8) The court may grant leave to the child concerned only if it is satisfied that he has sufficient understanding to make the proposed application.

(9) The amount of compensation is to be determined by the court, but may not exceed the amount of the applicant's financial loss.

(10) In determining the amount of compensation payable by the individual in breach, the court must take into account the individual's financial circumstances.

(11) An amount ordered to be paid as compensation may be recovered by the applicant as a civil debt due to him.

(12) Subsection (2) has effect subject to the restrictions in section 11P.

(13) Proceedings in which any question of making an order under subsection (2) arises are to be regarded for the purposes of section 11(1) and (2) as proceedings in which a question arises with respect to a section 8 order.

(14) In exercising its powers under this section, a court is to take into account the welfare of the child concerned.

11P   Orders under section 11O(2): further provision

(1) A court may not make an order under section 11O(2) requiring an individual to pay compensation in respect of a failure by him to comply with a contact order unless it is satisfied that before the failure occurred the individual had been given (in accordance with rules of court) a copy of, or otherwise informed of the terms of—

(a) in the case of a failure to comply with a contact order that was varied before the failure occurred, a notice under section 11I relating to the order varying the contact order or, where more than one such order has been made, the last order preceding the failure in question;

(b) in any other case, a notice under section 11I relating to the contact order.

(2) A court may not make an order under section 11O(2) requiring an individual to pay compensation in respect of a failure by him to comply with a contact order where the failure occurred before the individual attained the age of 18.

(3) A court may not make an order under section 11O(2) requiring an individual to pay compensation in respect of a failure by him to comply with a contact order that is an excepted order (within the meaning given by section 11B(4)).

12   Residence orders and parental responsibility

(1) Where the court makes a residence order in favour of the father of a child it shall, if the father would not otherwise have parental responsibility for the child, also make an order under section 4 giving him that responsibility.

(2) Where the court makes a residence order in favour of any person who is not the parent or guardian of the child concerned that person shall have parental responsibility for the child, while the residence order remains in force.

(3) Where a person has parental responsibility for a child as a result of subsection (2), he shall not have the right—

(b) to agree, or refuse to agree, to the making of an adoption order, or an order under section 84 of the Adoption and Children Act 2002 with respect to the child; or

(c) to appoint a guardian for the child.

(4) Where subsection (1) requires the court to make an order under section 4 in respect of the father of a child, the court shall not bring that order to an end at any time while the residence order concerned remains in force.

(5) The power of a court to make a residence order in favour of any person who is not the parent or guardian of the child concerned includes power to direct, at the request of that person, that the order continue in force until the child reaches the age of eighteen (unless the order is brought to an end earlier); and any power to vary a residence order is exercisable accordingly.

(6) Where a residence order includes such a direction, an application to vary or discharge the order may only be made, if apart from this subsection the leave of the court is not required, with such leave.

13   Change of child's name or removal from jurisdiction

(1) Where a residence order is in force with respect to a child, no person may—

(a) cause the child to be known by a new surname; or

(b) remove him from the United Kingdom;

without either the written consent of every person who has parental responsibility for the child or the leave of the court.

(2) Subsection (1)(b) does not prevent the removal of a child, for a period of less than one month, by the person in whose favour the residence order is made.

(3) In making a residence order with respect to a child the court may grant the leave required by subsection (1)(b), either generally or for specified purposes.

14   Enforcement of residence orders

(1) Where—

(a) a residence order is in force with respect to a child in favour of any person; and

(b) any other person (including one in whose favour the order is also in force) is in breach of the arrangements settled by that order,

the person mentioned in paragraph (a) may, as soon as the requirement in subsection (2) is complied with, enforce the order under section 63(3) of the Magistrates' Court Act 1980 as if it were an order requiring the other person to produce the child to him.

(2) The requirement is that a copy of the residence order has been served on the other person.

(3) Subsection (1) is without prejudice to any other remedy open to the person in whose favour the residence order is in force.

Special guardianship

14A   Special guardianship orders

(1) A 'special guardianship order' is an order appointing one or more individuals to be a child's 'special guardian' (or special guardians).

(2) A special guardian—

(a) must be aged eighteen or over; and

(b) must not be a parent of the child in question,

and subsections (3) to (6) are to be read in that light.

(3) The court may make a special guardianship order with respect to any child on the application of an individual who—

(a) is entitled to make such an application with respect to the child; or

(b) has obtained the leave of the court to make the application,

or on the joint application of more than one such individual.

(4) Section 9(3) applies in relation to an application for leave to apply for a special guardianship order as it applies in relation to an application for leave to apply for a section 8 order.

(5) The individuals who are entitled to apply for a special guardianship order with respect to a child are—

(a) any guardian of the child;

(b) any individual in whose favour a residence order is in force with respect to the child;

(c) any individual listed in subsection (5)(b) or (c) of section 10 (as read with subsection (10) of that section);

(d) a local authority foster parent with whom the child has lived for a period of at least one year immediately preceding the application.

(6) The court may also make a special guardianship order with respect to a child in any family proceedings in which a question arises with respect to the welfare of the child if—

(a) an application for the order has been made by an individual who falls within subsection (3)(a) or (b) (or more than one such individual jointly); or

(b) the court considers that a special guardianship order should be made even though no such application has been made.

(7) No individual may make an application under subsection (3) or (6)(a) unless, before the beginning of the period of three months ending with the date of the application, he has given written notice of his intention to make the application—

(a) if the child in question is being looked after by a local authority, to that local authority, or

(b) otherwise, to the local authority in whose area the individual is ordinarily resident.

(8) On receipt of such a notice, the local authority must investigate the matter and prepare a report for the court dealing with—

(a) the suitability of the applicant to be a special guardian;

(b) such matters (if any) as may be prescribed by the Secretary of State; and

(c) any other matter which the local authority consider to be relevant.

(9) The court may itself ask a local authority to conduct such an investigation and prepare such a report, and the local authority must do so.

(10) The local authority may make such arrangements as they see fit for any person to act on their behalf in connection with conducting an investigation or preparing a report referred to in subsection (8) or (9).

(11) The court may not make a special guardianship order unless it has received a report dealing with the matters referred to in subsection (8).

(12) Subsections (8) and (9) of section 10 apply in relation to special guardianship orders as they apply in relation to section 8 orders.

(13) This section is subject to section 29(5) and (6) of the Adoption and Children Act 2002.

14B   Special guardianship orders: making

(1) Before making a special guardianship order, the court must consider whether, if the order were made—

(a) a contact order should also be made with respect to the child,

(b) any section 8 order in force with respect to the child should be varied or discharged,

(c) where a contact order made with respect to the child is not discharged, any enforcement order relating to that contact order should be revoked, and

(d) where a contact activity direction has been made as regards contact with the child and is in force, that contact activity direction should be discharged.

(2) On making a special guardianship order, the court may also—

(a) give leave for the child to be known by a new surname;

(b) grant the leave required by section 14C(3)(b), either generally or for specified purposes.

14C   Special guardianship orders: effect

(1) The effect of a special guardianship order is that while the order remains in force—

(a) a special guardian appointed by the order has parental responsibility for the child in respect of whom it is made; and

(b) subject to any other order in force with respect to the child under this Act, a special guardian is entitled to exercise parental responsibility to the exclusion of any other person with parental responsibility for the child (apart from another special guardian).

(2) Subsection (1) does not affect—

(a) the operation of any enactment or rule of law which requires the consent of more than one person with parental responsibility in a matter affecting the child; or

(b) any rights which a parent of the child has in relation to the child's adoption or placement for adoption.

(3) While a special guardianship order is in force with respect to a child, no person may—
  (a) cause the child to be known by a new surname; or
  (b) remove him from the United Kingdom,
without either the written consent of every person who has parental responsibility for the child or the leave of the court.

(4) Subsection (3)(b) does not prevent the removal of a child, for a period of less than three months, by a special guardian of his.

(5) If the child with respect to whom a special guardianship order is in force dies, his special guardian must take reasonable steps to give notice of that fact to—
  (a) each parent of the child with parental responsibility; and
  (b) each guardian of the child,
but if the child has more than one special guardian, and one of them has taken such steps in relation to a particular parent or guardian, any other special guardian need not do so as respects that parent or guardian.

(6) This section is subject to section 29(7) of the Adoption and Children Act 2002.

14D   Special guardianship orders: variation and discharge
  (1) The court may vary or discharge a special guardianship order on the application of—
    (a) the special guardian (or any of them, if there are more than one);
    (b) any parent or guardian of the child concerned;
    (c) any individual in whose favour a residence order is in force with respect to the child;
    (d) any individual not falling within any of paragraphs (a) to (c) who has, or immediately before the making of the special guardianship order had, parental responsibility for the child;
    (e) the child himself; or
    (f) a local authority designated in a care order with respect to the child.

  (2) In any family proceedings in which a question arises with respect to the welfare of a child with respect to whom a special guardianship order is in force, the court may also vary or discharge the special guardianship order if it considers that the order should be varied or discharged, even though no application has been made under subsection (1).

  (3) The following must obtain the leave of the court before making an application under subsection (1)—
    (a) the child;
    (b) any parent or guardian of his;
    (c) any step-parent of his who has acquired, and has not lost, parental responsibility for him by virtue of section 4A;
    (d) any individual falling within subsection (1)(d) who immediately before the making of the special guardianship order had, but no longer has, parental responsibility for him.

  (4) Where the person applying for leave to make an application under subsection (1) is the child, the court may only grant leave if it is satisfied that he has sufficient understanding to make the proposed application under subsection (1).

  (5) The court may not grant leave to a person falling within subsection (3)(b)(c) or (d) unless it is satisfied that there has been a significant change in circumstances since the making of the special guardianship order.

14E   Special guardianship orders: supplementary
  (1) In proceedings in which any question of making, varying or discharging a special guardianship order arises, the court shall (in the light of any rules made by virtue of sub-section (3))—
    (a) draw up a timetable with a view to determining the question without delay; and
    (b) give such directions as it considers appropriate for the purpose of ensuring, so far as is reasonably practicable, that the timetable is adhered to.

(2) Subsection (1) applies also in relation to proceedings in which any other question with respect to a special guardianship order arises.

(3) The power to make rules in subsection (2) of section 11 applies for the purposes of this section as it applies for the purposes of that.

(4) A special guardianship order, or an order varying one, may contain provisions which are to have effect for a specified period.

(5) Section 11(7) (apart from paragraph (c)) applies in relation to special guardianship orders and orders varying them as it applies in relation to section 8 orders.

14F   Special guardianship support services

(1) Each local authority must make arrangements for the provision within their area of special guardianship support services, which means—

    (a) counselling, advice and information; and

    (b) such other services as are prescribed,

in relation to special guardianship.

(2) The power to make regulations under subsection (1)(b) is to be exercised so as to secure that local authorities provide financial support.

(3) At the request of any of the following persons—

    (a) a child with respect to whom a special guardianship order is in force;

    (b) a special guardian;

    (c) a parent;

    (d) any other person who falls within a prescribed description,

a local authority may carry out an assessment of that person's needs for special guardianship support services (but, if the Secretary of State so provides in regulations, they must do so if he is a person of a prescribed description, or if his case falls within a prescribed description, or if both he and his case fall within prescribed descriptions).

(4) A local authority may, at the request of any other person, carry out an assessment of that person's needs for special guardianship support services.

(5) Where, as a result of an assessment, a local authority decide that a person has needs for special guardianship support services, they must then decide whether to provide any such services to that person.

(6) If—

    (a) a local authority decide to provide any special guardianship support services to a person, and

    (b) the circumstances fall within a prescribed description,

the local authority must prepare a plan in accordance with which special guardianship support services are to be provided to him, and keep the plan under review.

(7) The Secretary of State may by regulations make provision about assessments, preparing and reviewing plans, the provision of special guardianship support services in accordance with plans and reviewing the provision of special guardianship support services.

(8) The regulations may in particular make provision—

    (a) about the type of assessment which is to be carried out, or the way in which an assessment is to be carried out;

    (b) about the way in which a plan is to be prepared;

    (c) about the way in which, and the time at which, a plan or the provision of special guardianship support services is to be reviewed;

    (d) about the considerations to which a local authority are to have regard in carrying out an assessment or review or preparing a plan;

    (e) as to the circumstances in which a local authority may provide special guardianship support services subject to conditions (including conditions as to payment for the support or the repayment of financial support);

    (f) as to the consequences of conditions imposed by virtue of paragraph (e) not being met (including the recovery of any financial support provided);

(g) as to the circumstances in which this section may apply to a local authority in respect of persons who are outside that local authority's area;

(h) as to the circumstances in which a local authority may recover from another local authority the expenses of providing special guardianship support services to any person.

(9) A local authority may provide special guardianship support services (or any part of them) by securing their provision by—

(a) another local authority; or

(b) a person within a description prescribed in regulations of persons who may provide special guardianship support services,

and may also arrange with any such authority or person for that other authority or that person to carry out the local authority's functions in relation to assessments under this section.

(10) A local authority may carry out an assessment of the needs of any person for the purposes of this section at the same time as an assessment of his needs is made under any other provision of this Act or under any other enactment.

(11) Section 27 (co-operation between authorities) applies in relation to the exercise of functions of a local authority under this section as it applies in relation to the exercise of functions of a local authority under Part 3.

Financial relief

15   Orders for financial relief with respect to children

(1) Schedule 1 (which consists primarily of the re-enactment, with consequential amendments and minor modifications, of provisions of section 6 of the Family Law Reform Act 1969, the Guardianship of Minors Acts 1971 and 1973, the Children Act 1975 and of sections 15 and 16 of the Family Law Reform Act 1987) makes provision in relation to financial relief for children.

(2) The powers of a magistrates' court under section 60 of the Magistrates' Courts Act 1980 to revoke, revive or vary an order for the periodical payment of money and the power of the clerk of a magistrates' court to vary such an order shall not apply in relation to an order made under Schedule 1.

Family assistance orders

16   Family assistance orders

(1) Where, in any family proceedings, the court has power to make an order under this Part with respect to any child, it may (whether or not it makes such an order) make an order requiring—

(a) an officer of the Service or a Welsh family proceedings officer to be made available; or

(b) a local authority to make an officer of the authority available, to advise, assist and (where appropriate) befriend any person named in the order.

(2) The persons who may be named in an order under this section ('a family assistance order') are—

(a) any parent, guardian or special guardian of the child;

(b) any person with whom the child is living or in whose favour a contact order is in force with respect to the child;

(c) the child himself.

(3) No court may make a family assistance order unless—

(b) it has obtained the consent of every person to be named in the order other than the child.

(4) A family assistance order may direct—

(a) the person named in the order; or

(b) such of the persons named in the order as may be specified in the order, to take such steps as may be so specified with a view to enabling the officer concerned to be kept informed of the address of any person named in the order and to be allowed to visit any such person.

(4A) If the court makes a family assistance order with respect to a child and the order is to be in force at the same time as a contact order made with respect to the child, the family assistance order may direct the officer concerned to give advice and assistance as regards establishing, improving and maintaining contact to such of the persons named in the order as may be specified in the order.

(5) Unless it specifies a shorter period, a family assistance order shall have effect for a period of twelve months beginning with the day on which it is made.

(6) If the court makes a family assistance order with respect to a child and the order is to be in force at the same time as a section 8 order made with respect to the child, the family assistance order may direct the officer concerned to report to the court on such matters relating to the section 8 order as the court may require (including the question whether the section 8 order ought to be varied or discharged).

(7) A family assistance order shall not be made so as to require a local authority to make an officer of theirs available unless—

(a) the authority agree; or

(b) the child concerned lives or will live within their area.

16A   Risk assessments

(1) This section applies to the following functions of officers of the Service or Welsh family proceedings officers—

(a) any function in connection with family proceedings in which the court has power to make an order under this Part with respect to a child or in which a question with respect to such an order arises;

(b) any function in connection with an order made by the court in such proceedings.

(2) If, in carrying out any function to which this section applies, an officer of the Service or a Welsh family proceedings officer is given cause to suspect that the child concerned is at risk of harm, he must—

(a) make a risk assessment in relation to the child, and

(b) provide the risk assessment to the court.

(3) A risk assessment, in relation to a child who is at risk of suffering harm of a particular sort, is an assessment of the risk of that harm being suffered by the child.

PART III   LOCAL AUTHORITY SUPPORT FOR CHILDREN AND FAMILIES

Provision of services for children and their families

17   Provision of services for children in need, their families and others

(1) It shall be the general duty of every local authority (in addition to the other duties imposed on them by this Part)—

(a) to safeguard and promote the welfare of children within their area who are in need; and

(b) so far as is consistent with that duty, to promote the upbringing of such children by their families,

by providing a range and level of services appropriate to those children's needs.

(2) For the purpose principally of facilitating the discharge of their general duty under this section, every local authority shall have the specific duties and powers set out in Part 1 of Schedule 2.

(3) Any service provided by an authority in the exercise of functions conferred on them by this section may be provided for the family of a particular child in need or for any member of his family, if it is provided with a view to safeguarding or promoting the child's welfare.

(4) The Secretary of State may by order amend any provision of Part I of Schedule 2 or add any further duty or power to those for the time being mentioned there.

(4A) Before determining what (if any) services to provide for a particular child in need in the exercise of functions conferred on them by this section, a local authority shall, so far as is reasonably practicable and consistent with the child's welfare—

    (a) ascertain the child's wishes and feelings regarding the provision of those services; and

    (b) give due consideration (having regard to his age and understanding) to such wishes and feelings of the child as they have been able to ascertain.

(5) Every local authority—

    (a) shall facilitate the provision by others (including in particular voluntary organisations) of services which the authority have power to provide by virtue of this section, or section 18, 20, 23, 23B to 23D, 24A or 24B; and

    (b) may make such arrangements as they see fit for any person to act on their behalf in the provision of any such service.

(6) The services provided by a local authority in the exercise of functions conferred on them by this section may include providing accommodation and giving assistance in kind or, in exceptional circumstances, in cash.

(7) Assistance may be unconditional or subject to conditions as to the repayment of the assistance or of its value (in whole or in part).

(8) Before giving any assistance or imposing any conditions, a local authority shall have regard to the means of the child concerned and of each of his parents.

(9) No person shall be liable to make any repayment of assistance or of its value at any time when he is in receipt of income support under the Social Security Contributions and Benefits Act 1992, of any element of child tax credit other than the family element, of working tax credit or of an income-based jobseeker's allowance.

(10) For the purposes of this Part a child shall be taken to be in need if—

    (a) he is unlikely to achieve or maintain, or to have the opportunity of achieving or maintaining, a reasonable standard of health or development without the provision for him of services by a local authority under this Part;

    (b) his health or development is likely to be significantly impaired, or further impaired, without the provision for him of such services; or

    (c) he is disabled,

and 'family', in relation to such a child, includes any person who has parental responsibility for the child and any other person with whom he has been living.

(11) For the purposes of this Part, a child is disabled if he is blind, deaf or dumb or suffers from mental disorder of any kind or is substantially and permanently handicapped by illness, injury or congenital deformity or such other disability as may be prescribed; and in this Part—

'development' means physical, intellectual, emotional, social or behavioural development; and

'health' means physical or mental health.

...

17A Direct payments

(1) The Secretary of State may by regulations make provision for and in connection with requiring or authorising the responsible authority in the case of a person of a prescribed description who falls within subsection (2) to make, with that person's consent, such payments to him as they may determine in accordance with the regulations in respect of his securing the provision of the service mentioned in that subsection.

(2) A person falls within this subsection if he is—

    (a) a person with parental responsibility for a disabled child,

    (b) a disabled person with parental responsibility for a child, or

    (c) a disabled child aged 16 or 17,

and a local authority ('the responsible authority') have decided for the purposes of section 17 that the child's needs (or, if he is such a disabled child, his needs) call for the provision by them of a service in exercise of functions conferred on them under that section.

(3) Subsections (3) to (5) and (7) of section 57 of the 2001 Act shall apply, with any necessary modifications, in relation to regulations under this section as they apply in relation to regulations under that section.

(4) Regulations under this section shall provide that, where payments are made under the regulations to a person falling within subsection (5)—

(a) the payments shall be made at the rate mentioned in subsection (4)(a) of section 57 of the 2001 Act (as applied by subsection (3)); and

(b) subsection (4)(b) of that section shall not apply.

(5) A person falls within this subsection if he is—

(a) a person falling within subsection (2)(a) or (b) and the child in question is aged 16 or 17, or

(b) a person who is in receipt of income support under Part 7 of the Social Security Contributions and Benefits Act 1992 (c. 4), of any element of child tax credit other than the family element, of working tax credit or of an income-based job-seeker's allowance.

(6) In this section—

'the 2001 Act' means the Health and Social Care Act 2001;

'disabled' in relation to an adult has the same meaning as that given by section 17(11) in relation to a child;

'prescribed' means specified in or determined in accordance with regulations under this section (and has the same meaning in the provisions of the 2001 Act mentioned in subsection (3) as they apply by virtue of that subsection).

17B   Vouchers for persons with parental responsibility for disabled children

(1) The Secretary of State may by regulations make provision for the issue by a local authority of vouchers to a person with parental responsibility for a disabled child.

(2) 'Voucher' means a document whereby, if the local authority agrees with the person with parental responsibility that it would help him care for the child if the person with parental responsibility had a break from caring, that person may secure the temporary provision of services for the child under section 17.

(3) The regulations may, in particular, provide—

(a) for the value of a voucher to be expressed in terms of money, or of the delivery of a service for a period of time, or both;

(b) for the person who supplies a service against a voucher, or for the arrangement under which it is supplied, to be approved by the local authority;

(c) for a maximum period during which a service (or a service of a prescribed description) can be provided against a voucher.

18   Day care for pre-school and other children

(1) Every local authority shall provide such day care for children in need within their area who are—

(a) aged five or under; and

(b) not yet attending schools, as is appropriate.

(2) A local authority may provide day care for children within their area who satisfy the conditions mentioned in subsection (1)(a) and (b) even though they are not in need.

(3) A local authority may provide facilities (including training, advice, guidance and counselling) for those—

(a) caring for children in day care; or

(b) who at any time accompany such children while they are in day care.

(4) In this section 'day care' means any form of care or supervised activity provided for children during the day (whether or not it is provided on a regular basis).

(5) Every local authority shall provide for children in need within their area who are attending any school such care or supervised activities as is appropriate—

(a) outside school hours; or

(b) during school holidays.

(6) A local authority may provide such care or supervised activities for children within their area who are attending any school even though those children are not in need.

(7) In this section 'supervised activity' means an activity supervised by a responsible person.

19   Review of provision for day care, child minding etc.

(4) In conducting any such review the authority shall have regard to the provision made with respect to children under the age of eight in relevant establishments within their area.

(5) In this section—

'relevant establishment' means—

. . .

(b) in relation to England and Wales, any establishment which is mentioned in paragraphs 1 and 2 of Schedule 9A (establishments exempt from the registration requirements which apply in relation to the provision of day care in England and Wales);

'review period' means the period of one year beginning with the commencement of this section and each subsequent period of three years beginning with an anniversary of that commencement.

(6) Where a local authority have conducted a review under this section they shall publish the result of the review—

(a) as soon as is reasonably practicable;

(b) in such form as they consider appropriate; and

(c) together with any proposals they may have with respect to the matters reviewed.

(7) The authorities conducting any review under this section shall have regard to—

(a) any representations made to any one of them by any relevant Health Authority, Special Health Authority, Primary Care Trust, or health board; and

(b) any other representations which they consider to be relevant.

Provision of accommodation for children

20   Provision of accommodation for children: general

(1) Every local authority shall provide accommodation for any child in need within their area who appears to them to require accommodation as a result of—

(a) there being no person who has parental responsibility for him;

(b) his being lost or having been abandoned; or

(c) the person who has been caring for him being prevented (whether or not permanently, and for whatever reason) from providing him with suitable accommodation or care.

(2) Where a local authority provide accommodation under subsection (1) for a child who is ordinarily resident in the area of another local authority, that other local authority may take over the provision of accommodation for the child within—

(a) three months of being notified in writing that the child is being provided with accommodation; or

(b) such other longer period as may be prescribed.

(3) Every local authority shall provide accommodation for any child in need within their area who has reached the age of sixteen and whose welfare the authority consider is likely to be seriously prejudiced if they do not provide him with accommodation.

(4) A local authority may provide accommodation for any child within their area (even though a person who has parental responsibility for him is able to provide him with accommodation) if they consider that to do so would safeguard or promote the child's welfare.

(5) A local authority may provide accommodation for any person who has reached the age of sixteen but is under twenty-one in any community home which takes children who have reached the age of sixteen if they consider that to do so would safeguard or promote his welfare.

(6) Before providing accommodation under this section, a local authority shall, so far as is reasonably practicable and consistent with the child's welfare—

    (a) ascertain the child's wishes and feelings regarding the provision of accommodation; and

    (b) give due consideration (having regard to his age and understanding) to such wishes and feelings of the child as they have been able to ascertain.

(7) A local authority may not provide accommodation under this section for any child if any person who—

    (a) has parental responsibility for him;

    (b) is willing and able to—

        (i) provide accommodation for him; or

        (ii) arrange for accommodation to be provided for him, objects.

(8) Any person who has parental responsibility for a child may at any time remove the child from accommodation provided by or on behalf of the local authority under this section.

(9) Subsections (7) and (8) do not apply while any person—

    (a) in whose favour a residence order is in force with respect to the child;

    (aa) who is a special guardian of the child; or

    (b) who has care of the child by virtue of an order made in the exercise of the High Court's inherent jurisdiction with respect to children,

agrees to the child being looked after in accommodation provided by or on behalf of the local authority.

(10) Where there is more than one such person as is mentioned in subsection (9), all of them must agree.

(11) Subsections (7) and (8) do not apply where a child who has reached the age of sixteen agrees to being provided with accommodation under this section.

21 Provision of accommodation for children in police protection or detention or on remand, etc.

(1) Every local authority shall make provision for the reception and accommodation of children who are removed or kept away from home under Part V.

(2) Every local authority shall receive, and provide accommodation for, children—

    (a) in police protection whom they are requested to receive under section 46(3)(f);

    (b) whom they are requested to receive under section 38(6) of the Police and Criminal Evidence Act 1984;

    (c) who are—

        (i) on remand (within the meaning of the section) under paragraph 7(5) of Schedule 7 to the Powers of Criminal Courts (Sentencing) Act 2000 or section 23(1) of the Children and Young Persons Act 1969; or

        (ii) the subject of a supervision order imposing a local authority residence requirement under paragraph 5 of Schedule 6 to that Act of 2000 or a foster parent residence requirement under paragraph 5A of that Schedule,

and with respect to whom they are the designated authority.

(3) Where a child has been—

    (a) removed under Part V; or

    (b) detained under section 38 of the Police and Criminal Evidence Act 1984,

and he is not being provided with accommodation by a local authority or in a hospital vested in the Secretary of State or a Primary Care Trust or otherwise made available pursuant to arrangements made by a Health Authority or a Primary Care Trust, any reasonable expenses of accommodating him shall be recoverable from the local authority in whose area he is ordinarily resident.

Duties of local authorities in relation to children looked after by them

22   General duty of local authority in relation to children looked after by them

(1) In this Act, any reference to a child who is looked after by a local authority is a reference to a child who is—

(a) in their care; or

(b) provided with accommodation by the authority in the exercise of any functions (in particular those under this Act) which are social services functions within the meaning of the Local Authority Social Services Act 1970, apart from functions under sections 17, 23B and 24B.

(2) In subsection (1) 'accommodation' means accommodation which is provided for a continuous period of more than 24 hours.

(3) It shall be the duty of a local authority looking after any child—

(a) to safeguard and promote his welfare; and

(b) to make such use of services available for children cared for by their own parents as appears to the authority reasonable in his case.

(3A) The duty of a local authority under subsection (3)(a) to safeguard and promote the welfare of a child looked after by them includes in particular a duty to promote the child's educational achievement.

(4) Before making any decision with respect to a child whom they are looking after, or proposing to look after, a local authority shall, so far as is reasonably practicable, ascertain the wishes and feelings of—

(a) the child;

(b) his parents;

(c) any person who is not a parent of his but who has parental responsibility for him; and

(d) any other person whose wishes and feelings the authority consider to be relevant,

regarding the matter to be decided.

(5) In making any such decision a local authority shall give due consideration—

(a) having regard to his age and understanding, to such wishes and feelings of the child as they have been able to ascertain;

(b) to such wishes and feelings of any person mentioned in subsection (4)(b) to (d) as they have been able to ascertain; and

(c) to the child's religious persuasion, racial origin and cultural and linguistic background.

(6) If it appears to a local authority that it is necessary, for the purpose of protecting members of the public from serious injury, to exercise their powers with respect to a child whom they are looking after in a manner which may not be consistent with their duties under this section, they may do so.

(7) If the Secretary of State considers it necessary, for the purpose of protecting members of the public from serious injury, to give directions to a local authority with respect to the exercise of their powers with respect to a child whom they are looking after, he may give such directions to the authority.

(8) Where any such directions are given to an authority they shall comply with them even though doing so is inconsistent with their duties under this section.

23   Provision of accommodation and maintenance by local authority for children whom they are looking after

(1) It shall be the duty of any local authority looking after a child—

(a) when he is in their care, to provide accommodation for him; and

(b) to maintain him in other respects apart from providing accommodation for him.

(2) A local authority shall provide accommodation and maintenance for any child whom they are looking after by—

    (a) placing him (subject to subsection (5) and any regulations made by the Secretary of State) with—

        (i) a family;

        (ii) a relative of his; or

        (iii) any other suitable person, on such terms as to payment by the authority and otherwise as the authority may determine (subject to section 49 of the Children Act 2004);

    (aa) maintaining him in an appropriate children's home; or

    (f)   making such other arrangements as—

        (i) seem appropriate to them; and

        (ii) comply with any regulations made by the Secretary of State.

(2A) Where under subsection (2)(aa) a local authority maintains a child in a home provided, equipped and maintained by the Secretary of State under section 82(5), it shall do so on such terms as the Secretary of State may from time to time determine.

(3) Any person with whom a child has been placed under subsection (2)(a) is referred to in this Act as a local authority foster parent unless he falls within subsection (4).

(4) A person falls within this subsection if he is—

    (a) a parent of the child;

    (b) a person who is not a parent of the child but who has parental responsibility for him; or

    (c) where the child is in care and there was a residence order in force with respect to him immediately before the care order was made, a person in whose favour the residence order was made.

(5) Where a child is in the care of a local authority, the authority may only allow him to live with a person who falls within subsection (4) in accordance with regulations made by the Secretary of State.

(5A) For the purposes of subsection (5) a child shall be regarded as living with a person if he stays with that person for a continuous period of more than 24 hours.

(6) Subject to any regulations made by the Secretary of State for the purposes of this subsection, any local authority looking after a child shall make arrangements to enable him to live with—

    (a) a person falling within subsection (4); or

    (b) a relative, friend or other person connected with him,

unless that would not be reasonably practicable or consistent with his welfare.

(7) Where a local authority provide accommodation for a child whom they are looking after, they shall, subject to the provisions of this Part and so far as is reasonably practicable and consistent with his welfare, secure that—

    (a) the accommodation is near his home; and

    (b) where the authority are also providing accommodation for a sibling of his, they are accommodated together.

(8) Where a local authority provide accommodation for a child whom they are looking after and who is disabled, they shall, so far as is reasonably practicable, secure that the accommodation is not unsuitable to his particular needs.

(9) Part II of Schedule 2 shall have effect for the purposes of making further provision as to children looked after by local authorities and in particular as to the regulations that may be made under subsections (2)(a) and (f) and (5).

(10) In this Act—

'appropriate children's home' means a children's home in respect of which a person is registered under Part II of the Care Standards Act 2000; and

'children's home' has the same meaning as in that Act.

Advice and assistance for certain children and young persons

23A The responsible authority and relevant children

(1) The responsible local authority shall have the functions set out in section 23B in respect of a relevant child.

(2) In subsection (1) 'relevant child' means (subject to subsection (3)) a child who—

(a) is not being looked after by any local authority;

(b) was, before last ceasing to be looked after, an eligible child for the purposes of paragraph 19B of Schedule 2; and

(c) is aged sixteen or seventeen.

(3) The Secretary of State may prescribe—

(a) additional categories of relevant children; and

(b) categories of children who are not to be relevant children despite falling within subsection (2).

(4) In subsection (1) the 'responsible local authority' is the one which last looked after the child.

(5) If under subsection (3)(a) the Secretary of State prescribes a category of relevant children which includes children who do not fall within subsection (2)(b) (for example, because they were being looked after by a local authority in Scotland), he may in the regulations also provide for which local authority is to be the responsible local authority for those children.

23B Additional functions of the responsible authority in respect of relevant children

(1) It is the duty of each local authority to take reasonable steps to keep in touch with a relevant child for whom they are the responsible authority, whether he is within their area or not.

(2) It is the duty of each local authority to appoint a personal adviser for each relevant child (if they have not already done so under paragraph 19C of Schedule 2).

(3) It is the duty of each local authority, in relation to any relevant child who does not already have a pathway plan prepared for the purposes of paragraph 19B of Schedule 2—

(a) to carry out an assessment of his needs with a view to determining what advice, assistance and support it would be appropriate for them to provide him under this Part; and

(b) to prepare a pathway plan for him.

(4) The local authority may carry out such an assessment at the same time as any assessment of his needs is made under any enactment referred to in sub-paragraphs (a) to (c) of paragraph 3 of Schedule 2, or under any other enactment.

(5) The Secretary of State may by regulations make provision as to assessments for the purposes of subsection (3).

(6) The regulations may in particular make provision about—

(a) who is to be consulted in relation to an assessment;

(b) the way in which an assessment is to be carried out, by whom and when;

(c) the recording of the results of an assessment;

(d) the considerations to which the local authority are to have regard in carrying out an assessment.

(7) The authority shall keep the pathway plan under regular review.

(8) The responsible local authority shall safeguard and promote the child's welfare and, unless they are satisfied that his welfare does not require it, support him by—

(a) maintaining him;

(b) providing him with or maintaining him in suitable accommodation; and

(c) providing support of such other descriptions as may be prescribed.

(9) Support under subsection (8) may be in cash.

(10) The Secretary of State may by regulations make provision about the meaning of 'suitable accommodation' and in particular about the suitability of landlords or other providers of accommodation.

(11) If the local authority have lost touch with a relevant child, despite taking reasonable steps to keep in touch, they must without delay—

(a) consider how to re-establish contact; and

(b) take reasonable steps to do so,

and while the child is still a relevant child must continue to take such steps until they succeed.

(12) Subsections (7) to (9) of section 17 apply in relation to support given under this section as they apply in relation to assistance given under that section.

(13) Subsections (4) and (5) of section 22 apply in relation to any decision by a local authority for the purposes of this section as they apply in relation to the decisions referred to in that section.

23C Continuing functions in respect of former relevant children

(1) Each local authority shall have the duties provided for in this section towards—

(a) a person who has been a relevant child for the purposes of section 23A (and would be one if he were under eighteen), and in relation to whom they were the last responsible authority; and

(b) a person who was being looked after by them when he attained the age of eighteen, and immediately before ceasing to be looked after was an eligible child, and in this section such a person is referred to as a 'former relevant child'.

(2) It is the duty of the local authority to take reasonable steps—

(a) to keep in touch with a former relevant child whether he is within their area or not; and

(b) if they lose touch with him, to re-establish contact.

(3) It is the duty of the local authority—

(a) to continue the appointment of a personal adviser for a former relevant child; and

(b) to continue to keep his pathway plan under regular review.

(4) It is the duty of the local authority to give a former relevant child—

(a) assistance of the kind referred to in section 24B(1), to the extent that his welfare requires it;

(b) assistance of the kind referred to in section 24B(2), to the extent that his welfare and his educational or training needs require it;

(c) other assistance, to the extent that his welfare requires it.

(5) The assistance given under subsection (4)(c) may be in kind or, in exceptional circumstances, in cash.

(6) Subject to subsection (7), the duties set out in subsections (2), (3) and (4) subsist until the former relevant child reaches the age of twenty-one.

(7) If the former relevant child's pathway plan sets out a programme of education or training which extends beyond his twenty-first birthday—

(a) the duty set out in subsection (4)(b) continues to subsist for so long as the former relevant child continues to pursue that programme; and

(b) the duties set out in subsections (2) and (3) continue to subsist concurrently with that duty.

(8) For the purposes of subsection (7)(a) there shall be disregarded any interruption in a former relevant child's pursuance of a programme of education or training if the local authority are satisfied that he will resume it as soon as is reasonably practicable.

(9) Section 24B(5) applies in relation to a person being given assistance under subsection (4)(b) as it applies in relation to a person to whom section 24B(3) applies.

(10) Subsections (7) to (9) of section 17 apply in relation to assistance given under this section as they apply in relation to assistance given under that section.

Personal advisers and pathway plans

23D Personal advisers

(1) The Secretary of State may by regulations require local authorities to appoint a personal adviser for children or young persons of a prescribed description who have reached the age of sixteen but not the age of twenty-one who are not—

(a) children who are relevant children for the purposes of section 23A;

(b) the young persons referred to in section 23C; or

(c) the children referred to in paragraph 19C of Schedule 2.

(2) Personal advisers appointed under or by virtue of this Part shall (in addition to any other functions) have such functions as the Secretary of State prescribes.

23E Pathway plans

(1) In this Part, a reference to a 'pathway plan' is to a plan setting out—

(a) in the case of a plan prepared under paragraph 19B of Schedule 2—

(i) the advice, assistance and support which the local authority intend to provide a child under this Part, both while they are looking after him and later; and

(ii) when they might cease to look after him; and

(b) in the case of a plan prepared under section 23B, the advice, assistance and support which the local authority intend to provide under this Part,

and dealing with such other matters (if any) as may be prescribed.

(2) The Secretary of State may by regulations make provision about pathway plans and their review.

24 Persons qualifying for advice and assistance

(1) In this Part 'a person qualifying for advice and assistance' means a person to whom subsection (1A) or (1B) applies.

(1A) This subsection applies to a person—

(a) who has reached the age of sixteen but not the age of twenty-one;

(b) with respect to whom a special guardianship order is in force (or, if he has reached the age of eighteen, was in force when he reached that age); and

(c) who was, immediately before the making of that order, looked after by a local authority.

(1B) This subsection applies to a person to whom subsection (1A) does not apply, and who—

(a) is under twenty-one; and

(b) at any time after reaching the age of sixteen but while still a child was, but is no longer, looked after, accommodated or fostered.

(2) In subsection (1B)(b), 'looked after, accommodated or fostered' means—

(a) looked after by a local authority;

(b) accommodated by or on behalf of a voluntary organisation;

(c) accommodated in a private children's home;

(d) accommodated for a consecutive period of at least three months—

(i) by any Health Authority, Special Health Authority, Primary Care Trust or local education authority, or

(ii) in any care home or independent hospital or in any accommodation provided by a National Health Service trust or an NHS foundation trust; or

(e) privately fostered.

(3) Subsection (2)(d) applies even if the period of three months mentioned there began before the child reached the age of sixteen.

(4) In the case of a person qualifying for advice and assistance by virtue of subsection (2)(a), it is the duty of the local authority which last looked after him to take such steps as they think appropriate to contact him at such times as they think appropriate with a view to discharging their functions under sections 24A and 24B.

(5) In each of sections 24A and 24B, the local authority under the duty or having the power mentioned there ('the relevant authority') is—

    (za) in the case of a person to whom subsection (1A) applies, a local authority determined in accordance with regulations made by the Secretary of State;

    (a) in the case of a person qualifying for advice and assistance by virtue of subsection (2)(a), the local authority which last looked after him; or

    (b) in the case of any other person qualifying for advice and assistance, the local authority within whose area the person is (if he has asked for help of a kind which can be given under section 24A or 24B).

24A   Advice and assistance

(1) The relevant authority shall consider whether the conditions in subsection (2) are satisfied in relation to a person qualifying for advice and assistance.

    (2) The conditions are that—

    (a) he needs help of a kind which they can give under this section or section 24B; and

    (b) in the case of a person to whom section 24(1A) applies, or to whom section 24(1B) applies and who was not being looked after by any local authority, they are satisfied that the person by whom he was being looked after does not have the necessary facilities for advising or befriending him.

    (3) If the conditions are satisfied—

    (a) they shall advise and befriend him if he is a person to whom section 24(1A) applies, or he is a person to whom section 24(1B) applies and he was being looked after by a local authority or was accommodated by or on behalf of a voluntary organisation; and

    (b) in any other case they may do so.

(4) Where as a result of this section a local authority are under a duty, or are empowered, to advise and befriend a person, they may also give him assistance.

(5) The assistance may be in kind and, in exceptional circumstances, assistance may be given—

    (a) by providing accommodation, if in the circumstances assistance may not be given in respect of the accommodation under section 24B, or

    (b) in cash.

(6) Subsections (7) to (9) of section 17 apply in relation to assistance given under this section or section 24B as they apply in relation to assistance given under that section.

24B   Employment, education and training

(1) The relevant local authority may give assistance to any person who qualifies for advice and assistance by virtue of section 24(1A) or section 24(2)(a) by contributing to expenses incurred by him in living near the place where he is, or will be, employed or seeking employment.

(2) The relevant local authority may give assistance to a person to whom subsection (3) applies by—

    (a) contributing to expenses incurred by the person in question in living near the place where he is, or will be, receiving education or training; or

    (b) making a grant to enable him to meet expenses connected with his education or training.

    (3) This subsection applies to any person who—

    (a) is under twenty-four; and

    (b) qualifies for advice and assistance by virtue of section 24(1A) or section 24(2)(a), or would have done so if he were under twenty-one.

(4) Where a local authority are assisting a person under subsection (2) they may disregard any interruption in his attendance on the course if he resumes it as soon as is reasonably practicable.

(5) Where the local authority are satisfied that a person to whom subsection (3) applies who is in full-time further or higher education needs accommodation during a vacation because his term-time accommodation is not available to him then, they shall give him assistance by—

  (a) providing him with suitable accommodation during the vacation; or

  (b) paying him enough to enable him to secure such accommodation himself.

(6) The Secretary of State may prescribe the meaning of 'full-time', 'further education', 'higher education' and 'vacation' for the purposes of subsection (5).

24C Information

(1) Where it appears to a local authority that a person—

  (a) with whom they are under a duty to keep in touch under section 23B, 23C or 24; or

  (b) whom they have been advising and befriending under section 24A; or

  (c) to whom they have been giving assistance under section 24B,

proposes to live, or is living, in the area of another local authority, they must inform that other authority.

(2) Where a child who is accommodated—

  (a) by a voluntary organisation or in a private children's home;

  (b) by any Health Authority, Special Health Authority, Primary Care Trust or local education authority; or

  (c) in any care home or independent hospital or any accommodation provided by a National Health Service trust or an NHS foundation trust,

ceases to be so accommodated, after reaching the age of sixteen, the organisation, authority or (as the case may be) person carrying on the home shall inform the local authority within whose area the child proposes to live.

(3) Subsection (2) only applies, by virtue of paragraph (b) or (c), if the accommodation has been provided for a consecutive period of at least three months.

24D Representations: sections 23A to 24B

(1) Every local authority shall establish a procedure for considering representations (including complaints) made to them by—

  (a) a relevant child for the purposes of section 23A or a young person falling within section 23C;

  (b) a person qualifying for advice and assistance; or

  (c) a person falling within section 24B(2),

about the discharge of their functions under this Part in relation to him.

(1A) Regulations may be made by the Secretary of State imposing time limits on the making of representations under subsection (1).

(2) In considering representations under subsection (1), a local authority shall comply with regulations (if any) made by the Secretary of State for the purposes of this subsection.

Secure accommodation

25 Use of accommodation for restricting liberty

(1) Subject to the following provisions of this section, a child who is being looked after by a local authority may not be placed, and, if placed, may not be kept, in accommodation provided for the purpose of restricting liberty ('secure accommodation') unless it appears—

  (a) that—

   (i) he has a history of absconding and is likely to abscond from any other description of accommodation; and

   (ii) if he absconds, he is likely to suffer significant harm; or

  (b) that if he is kept in any other description of accommodation he is likely to injure himself or other persons.

(2) The Secretary of State may by regulations—

(a) specify a maximum period—
    (i) beyond which a child may not be kept in secure accommodation without the authority of the court; and
    (ii) for which the court may authorise a child to be kept in secure accommodation;
(b) empower the court from time to time to authorise a child to be kept in secure accommodation for such further period as the regulations may specify; and
(c) provide that applications to the court under this section shall be made only by local authorities.

(3) It shall be the duty of a court hearing an application under this section to determine whether any relevant criteria for keeping a child in secure accommodation are satisfied in his case.

(4) If a court determines that any such criteria are satisfied, it shall make an order authorising the child to be kept in secure accommodation and specifying the maximum period for which he may be so kept.

(5) On any adjournment of the hearing of an application under this section, a court may make an interim order permitting the child to be kept during the period of the adjournment in secure accommodation.

(6) No court shall exercise the powers conferred by this section in respect of a child who is not legally represented in that court unless, having been informed of his right to apply for representation funded by the Legal Services Commission as part of the Community Legal Service or Criminal Defence Service and having had the opportunity to do so, he refused or failed to apply.

(7) The Secretary of State may by regulations provide that—
(a) this section shall or shall not apply to any description of children specified in the regulations;
(b) this section shall have effect in relation to children of a description specified in the regulations subject to such modifications as may be so specified;
(c) such other provisions as may be so specified shall have effect for the purpose of determining whether a child of a description specified in the regulations may be placed or kept in secure accommodation.

(8) The giving of an authorisation under this section shall not prejudice any power of any court in England and Wales or Scotland to give directions relating to the child to whom the authorisation relates.

(9) This section is subject to section 20(8).

Supplemental

26   Review of cases and inquiries into representations

(1) The Secretary of State may make regulations requiring the case of each child who is being looked after by a local authority to be reviewed in accordance with the provisions of the regulations.

(2) The regulations may, in particular, make provision—
(a) as to the manner in which each case is to be reviewed;
(b) as to the considerations to which the local authority are to have regard in reviewing each case;
(c) as to the time when each case is first to be reviewed and the frequency of subsequent reviews;
(d) requiring the authority, before conducting any review, to seek the views of—
    (i) the child;
    (ii) his parents;
    (iii) any person who is not a parent of his but who has parental responsibility for him; and

(iv) any other person whose views the authority consider to be relevant, including, in particular, the views of those persons in relation to any particular matter which is to be considered in the course of the review;

(e) requiring the authority, in the case of a child who is in their care

    (i) to keep the section 31A plan for the child under review and, if they are of the opinion that some change is required, to revise the plan, or make a new plan, accordingly,

    (ii) to consider whether an application should be made to discharge the care order;

(f) requiring the authority, in the case of a child in accommodation provided by the authority,

    (i) if there is no plan for the future care of the child, to prepare one,

    (ii) if there is such a plan for the child, to keep it under review and, if they are of the opinion that some change is required, to revise the plan or make a new plan, accordingly,

    (iii) to consider whether the accommodation accords with the requirements of this Part;

(g) requiring the authority to inform the child so far as is reasonably practicable of any steps he may take under this Act;

(h) requiring the authority to make arrangements, including arrangements with such other bodies providing services as it considers appropriate, to implement any decision which they propose to make in the course, or as a result, of the review;

(i) requiring the authority to notify details of the result of the review and of any decision taken by them in consequence of the review to—

    (i) the child;

    (ii) his parents;

    (iii) any person who is not a parent of his but who has parental responsibility for him; and

    (iv) any other person whom they consider ought to be notified;

(j) requiring the authority to monitor the arrangements which they have made with a view to ensuring that they comply with the regulations;

(k) for the authority to appoint a person in respect of each case to carry out in the prescribed manner the functions mentioned in subsection (2A) and any prescribed function.

(2A) The functions referred to in subsection (2)(k) are—

(a) participating in the review of the case in question,

(b) monitoring the performance of the authority's functions in respect of the review,

(c) referring the case to an officer of the Children and Family Court Advisory and Support Service or a Welsh family proceedings officer, if the person appointed under subsection (2)(k) considers it appropriate to do so.

(2B) A person appointed under subsection (2)(k) must be a person of a prescribed description.

(2C) In relation to children whose cases are referred to officers under subsection (2A)(c), the Lord Chancellor may by regulations—

(a) extend any functions of the officers in respect of family proceedings (within the meaning of section 12 of the Criminal Justice and Court Services Act 2000) to other proceedings,

(b) require any functions of the officers to be performed in the manner prescribed by the regulations.

(2D) The power to make regulations in subsection (2C) is exercisable in relation to functions of Welsh family proceedings officers only with the consent of the National Assembly for Wales.

(3) Every local authority shall establish a procedure for considering any representations (including any complaint) made to them by—

(a) any child who is being looked after by them or who is not being looked after by them but is in need;

(b) a parent of his;

(c) any person who is not a parent of his but who has parental responsibility for him;

(d) any local authority foster parent;

(e) such other person as the authority consider has a sufficient interest in the child's welfare to warrant his representations being considered by them,

about the discharge by the authority of any of their qualifying functions in relation to the child.

(3A) The following are qualifying functions for the purposes of subsection (3)—

(a) functions under this Part,

(b) such functions under Part 4 or 5 as are specified by the Secretary of State in regulations.

(3B) The duty under subsection (3) extends to representations (including complaints) made to the authority by—

(a) any person mentioned in section 3(1) of the Adoption and Children Act 2002 (persons for whose needs provision is made by the Adoption Service) and any other person to whom arrangements for the provision of adoption support services (within the meaning of that Act) extend,

(b) such other person as the authority consider has sufficient interest in a child who is or may be adopted to warrant his representations being considered by them,

about the discharge by the authority of such functions under the Adoption and Children Act 2002 as are specified by the Secretary of State in regulations.

(3C) The duty under subsection (3) extends to any representations (including complaints) which are made to the authority by—

(a) a child with respect to whom a special guardianship order is in force,

(b) a special guardian or a parent of such a child,

(c) any other person the authority consider has a sufficient interest in the welfare of such a child to warrant his representations being considered by them, or

(d) any person who has applied for an assessment under section 14F(3) or (4),

about the discharge by the authority of such functions under section 14F as may be specified by the Secretary of State in regulations.

(4) The procedure shall ensure that at least one person who is not a member or officer of the authority takes part in—

(a) the consideration; and

(b) any discussions which are held by the authority about the action (if any) to be taken in relation to the child in the light of the consideration,

but this subsection is subject to subsection (5A).

(4A) Regulations may be made by the Secretary of State imposing time limits on the making of representations under this section.

(5) In carrying out any consideration of representations under this section a local authority shall comply with any regulations made by the Secretary of State for the purpose of regulating the procedure to be followed.

(5A) Regulations under subsection (5) may provide that subsection (4) does not apply in relation to any consideration or discussion which takes place as part of a procedure for which provision is made by the regulations for the purpose of resolving informally the matters raised in the representations.

(6) The Secretary of State may make regulations requiring local authorities to monitor the arrangements that they have made with a view to ensuring that they comply with any regulations made for the purposes of subsection (5).

(7) Where any representation has been considered under the procedure established by a local authority under this section, the authority shall—

(a) have due regard to the findings of those considering the representation; and

(b) take such steps as are reasonably practicable to notify (in writing)—

(i)   the person making the representation;

(ii) the child (if the authority consider that he has sufficient understanding); and

(iii) such other persons (if any) as appear to the authority to be likely to be affected,

of the authority's decision in the matter and their reasons for taking that decision and of any action which they have taken, or propose to take.

(8) Every local authority shall give such publicity to their procedure for considering representations under this section as they consider appropriate.

26ZA   Representations: further consideration

(1) The Secretary of State may by regulations make provision for the further consideration of representations which have been considered by a local authority in England under section 24D or section 26.

(2) The regulations may in particular make provision—

(a) for the further consideration of a representation by the Commission for Social Care Inspection ('the CSCI');

(b) for a representation to be referred by the CSCI for further consideration by an independent panel established under the regulations;

(c) about the procedure to be followed on the further consideration of a representation;

(d) for the making of recommendations about the action to be taken as the result of a representation;

(e) about the making of reports about a representation;

(f) about the action to be taken by the local authority concerned as a result of the further consideration of a representation;

(g) for a representation to be referred by the CSCI back to the local authority concerned for reconsideration by the authority;

(h) for a representation or any matter raised by the representation to be referred by the CSCI—

(i)   to a Local Commissioner in England for him to consider whether to investigate the representation or matter under Part 3 of the Local Government Act 1974 as if it were a complaint duly made under section 26 of that Act; or

(ii) to any other person or body for him or it to consider whether to take any action otherwise than under the regulations.

(3) The regulations may require—

(a) the making of a payment, in relation to the further consideration of a representation under this section, by any local authority in respect of whose functions the representation is made;

(b) any such payment to be—

(i)   made to such person or body as may be specified in the regulations;

(ii) of such amount as may be specified in, or calculated or determined under, the regulations;

(c) an independent panel to review the amount chargeable under paragraph (a) in any particular case and, if the panel thinks fit, to substitute a lesser amount.

(4) The regulations may also—

(a) provide for different parts or aspects of a representation to be treated differently;

(b) require the production of information or documents in order to enable a representation to be properly considered;

(c) authorise the disclosure of information or documents relevant to a representation—

(i)   to a person or body who is further considering a representation under the regulations; or

(ii) to a Local Commissioner in England (when a representation is referred to him under the regulations);
and any such disclosure may be authorised notwithstanding any rule of common law that would otherwise prohibit or restrict the disclosure.

. . .

26ZB   Representations: further consideration (Wales)

(1) The Secretary of State may by regulations make provision for the further consideration of representations which have been considered by a local authority in Wales under section 24D or section 26.

(2) The regulations may in particular make provision—
  (a) for the further consideration of a representation by an independent panel established under the regulations;
  (b) about the procedure to be followed on the further consideration of a representation;
  (c) for the making of recommendations about the action to be taken as the result of a representation;
  (d) about the making of reports about a representation;
  (e) about the action to be taken by the local authority concerned as a result of the further consideration of a representation;
  (f) for a representation to be referred back to the local authority concerned for reconsideration by the authority.

(3) The regulations may require—
  (a) the making of a payment, in relation to the further consideration of a representation under this section, by any local authority in respect of whose functions the representation is made;
  (b) any such payment to be—
    (i) made to such person or body as may be specified in the regulations;
    (ii) of such amount as may be specified in, or calculated or determined under, the regulations; and
  (c) for an independent panel to review the amount chargeable under paragraph (a) in any particular case and, if the panel thinks fit, to substitute a lesser amount.

(4) The regulations may also—
  (a) provide for different parts or aspects of a representation to be treated differently;
  (b) require the production of information or documents in order to enable a representation to be properly considered;
  (c) authorise the disclosure of information or documents relevant to a representation to a person or body who is further considering a representation under the regulations;
and any such disclosure may be authorised notwithstanding any rule of common law that would otherwise prohibit or restrict the disclosure.

26A   Advocacy services

(1) Every local authority shall make arrangements for the provision of assistance to—
  (a) persons who make or intend to make representations under section 24D; and
  (b) children who make or intend to make representations under section 26.

(2) The assistance provided under the arrangements shall include assistance by way of representation.

(2A) The duty under subsection (1) includes a duty to make arrangements for the provision of assistance where representations under section 24D or 26 are further considered under section 26ZA or 26ZB.

(3) The arrangements—
  (a) shall secure that a person may not provide assistance if he is a person who is prevented from doing so by regulations made by the Secretary of State; and
  (b) shall comply with any other provision made by the regulations in relation to the arrangements.

(4) The Secretary of State may make regulations requiring local authorities to monitor the steps that they have taken with a view to ensuring that they comply with regulations made for the purposes of subsection (3).

(5) Every local authority shall give such publicity to their arrangements for the provision of assistance under this section as they consider appropriate.

27 Co-operation between authorities

(1) Where it appears to a local authority that any authority mentioned in subsection (3) could, by taking any specified action, help in the exercise of any of their functions under this Part, they may request the help of that other authority, specifying the action in question.

(2) An authority whose help is so requested shall comply with the request if it is compatible with their own statutory or other duties and obligations and does not unduly prejudice the discharge of any of their functions.

(3) The authorities are—

    (a) any local authority;

    (b) any local education authority;

    (c) any local housing authority;

    (d) any Health Authority, Special Health Authority, Primary Care Trust, National Health Service trust or NHS foundation trust, and

    (e) any person authorised by the Secretary of State for the purposes of this section.

28 Consultation with local education authorities

(1) Where—

    (a) a child is being looked after by a local authority; and

    (b) the authority propose to provide accommodation for him in an establishment at which education is provided for children who are accommodated there,

they shall, so far as is reasonably practicable, consult the appropriate local education authority before doing so.

(2) Where any such proposal is carried out, the local authority shall, as soon as is reasonably practicable, inform the appropriate local education authority of the arrangements that have been made for the child's accommodation.

(3) Where the child ceases to be accommodated as mentioned in subsection (1)(b), the local authority shall inform the appropriate local education authority.

(4) In this section 'the appropriate local education authority' means—

    (a) the local education authority within whose area the local authority's area falls; or

    (b) where the child has special educational needs and a statement of his needs is maintained under Part IV of the Education Act 1996, the local education authority who maintain the statement.

29 Recoupment of cost of providing services etc.

(1) Where a local authority provide any service under section 17 or 18, other than advice, guidance or counselling, they may recover from a person specified in subsection (4) such charge for the service as they consider reasonable.

(2) Where the authority are satisfied that that person's means are insufficient for it to be reasonably practicable for him to pay the charge, they shall not require him to pay more than he can reasonably be expected to pay.

(3) No person shall be liable to pay any charge under subsection (1) for a service provided under section 17 or section 18(1) or (5) at any time when he is in receipt of income support under the Social Security Contributions and Benefits Act 1992, of any element of child tax credit other than the family element, of working tax credit or of an income-based jobseeker's allowance.

(3A) No person shall be liable to pay any charge under subsection (1) for a service provided under section 18(2) or (6) at any time when he is in receipt of income support under Part VII of the Social Security Contributions and Benefits Act 1992 or of an income-based jobseeker's allowance.

(3B) No person shall be liable to pay any charge under subsection (1) for a service provided under section 18(2) or (6) at any time when—

(a) he is in receipt of guarantee state pension credit under section 1(3)(a) of the State Pension Credit Act 2002, or

(b) he is a member of a couple (within the meaning of that Act) the other member of which is in receipt of guarantee state pension credit.

(4) The persons are—

(a) where the service is provided for a child under sixteen, each of his parents;

(b) where it is provided for a child who has reached the age of sixteen, the child himself; and

(c) where it is provided for a member of the child's family, that member.

(5) Any charge under subsection (1) may, without prejudice to any other method of recovery, be recovered summarily as a civil debt.

(6) Part III of Schedule 2 makes provision in connection with contributions towards the maintenance of children who are being looked after by local authorities and consists of the re-enactment with modifications of provisions in Part V of the Child Care Act 1980.

(7) Where a local authority provide any accommodation under section 20(1) for a child who was (immediately before they began to look after him) ordinarily resident within the area of another local authority, they may recover from that other authority any reasonable expenses incurred by them in providing the accommodation and maintaining him.

(8) Where a local authority provide accommodation under section 21(1) or (2)(a) or (b) for a child who is ordinarily resident within the area of another local authority and they are not maintaining him in—

(a) a community home provided by them;

(b) a controlled community home; or

(c) a hospital vested in the Secretary of State or a Primary Care Trust, or any other hospital made available pursuant to arrangements made by a Strategic Health Authority, a Health Authority or a Primary Care Trust;

they may recover from that other authority any reasonable expenses incurred by them in providing the accommodation and maintaining him.

(9) Except where subsection (10) applies, where a local authority comply with any request under section 27(2) in relation to a child or other person who is not ordinarily resident within their area, they may recover from the local authority in whose area the child or person is ordinarily resident any reasonable expenses incurred by them in respect of that person.

(10) Where a local authority ('authority A') comply with any request under section 27(2) from another local authority ('authority B') in relation to a child or other person—

(a) whose responsible authority is authority B for the purposes of section 23B or 23C; or

(b) whom authority B are advising or befriending or to whom they are giving assistance by virtue of section 24(5)(a),

authority A may recover from authority B any reasonable expenses incurred by them in respect of that person.

30 Miscellaneous

(1) Nothing in this Part shall affect any duty imposed on a local authority by or under any other enactment.

(2) Any question arising under section 20(2), 21(3) or 29(7) to (9) as to the ordinary residence of a child shall be determined by agreement between the local authorities concerned or, in default of agreement, by the Secretary of State.

(3) Where the functions conferred on a local authority by this Part and the functions of a local education authority are concurrent, the Secretary of State may by regulations provide by which authority the functions are to be exercised.

(4) The Secretary of State may make regulations for determining, as respects any local education authority functions specified in the regulations, whether a child who is being

looked after by a local authority is to be treated, for purposes so specified, as a child of parents of sufficient resources or as a child of parents without resources.

PART IV   CARE AND SUPERVISION

General

31   Care and supervision orders

(1) On the application of any local authority or authorised person, the court may make an order—

    (a) placing the child with respect to whom the application is made in the care of a designated local authority; or

    (b) putting him under the supervision of a designated local authority.

(2) A court may only make a care order or supervision order if it is satisfied—

    (a) that the child concerned is suffering, or is likely to suffer, significant harm; and

    (b) that the harm, or likelihood of harm, is attributable to—

        (i)   the care given to the child, or likely to be given to him if the order were not made, not being what it would be reasonable to expect a parent to give to him; or

        (ii) the child's being beyond parental control.

(3) No care order or supervision order may be made with respect to a child who has reached the age of seventeen (or sixteen, in the case of a child who is married).

(3A) No care order may be made with respect to a child until the court has considered a section 31A plan.

(4) An application under this section may be made on its own or in any other family proceedings.

(5) The court may—

    (a) on an application for a care order, make a supervision order;

    (b) on an application for a supervision order, make a care order.

(6) Where an authorised person proposes to make an application under this section he shall—

    (a) if it is reasonably practicable to do so; and

    (b) before making the application,

consult the local authority appearing to him to be the authority in whose area the child concerned is ordinarily resident.

(7) An application made by an authorised person shall not be entertained by the court if, at the time when it is made, the child concerned is—

    (a) the subject of an earlier application for a care order, or supervision order, which has not been disposed of; or

    (b) subject to—

        (i)   a care order or supervision order;

        (ii) an order under section 63(1) of the Powers of Criminal Courts (Sentencing) Act 2000; ...

(8) The local authority designated in a care order must be—

    (a) the authority within whose area the child is ordinarily resident; or

    (b) where the child does not reside in the area of a local authority, the authority within whose area any circumstances arose in consequence of which the order is being made.

(9) In this section—

'authorised person' means—

    (a) the National Society for the Prevention of Cruelty to Children and any of its officers; and

(b) any person authorised by order of the Secretary of State to bring proceedings under this section and any officer of a body which is so authorised.

'harm' means ill-treatment or the impairment of health or development including, for example, impairment suffered from seeing or hearing the ill-treatment of another;

'development' means physical, intellectual, emotional, social or behavioural development;

'health' means physical or mental health; and

'ill-treatment' includes sexual abuse and forms of ill-treatment which are not physical.

(10) Where the question of whether harm suffered by a child is significant turns on the child's health or development, his health or development shall be compared with that which could reasonably be expected of a similar child.

(11) In this Act—

'a care order' means (subject to section 105(1)) an order under subsection (1)(a) and (except where express provision to the contrary is made) includes an interim care order made under section 38; and

'a supervision order' means an order under subsection (1)(b) and (except where express provision to the contrary is made) includes an interim supervision order made under section 38.

31A   Care orders: care plans

(1) Where an application is made on which a care order might be made with respect to a child, the appropriate local authority must, within such time as the court may direct, prepare a plan ('a care plan') for the future care of the child.

(2) While the application is pending, the authority must keep any care plan prepared by them under review and, if they are of the opinion some change is required, revise the plan, or make a new plan, accordingly.

(3) A care plan must give any prescribed information and do so in the prescribed manner.

(4) For the purposes of this section, the appropriate local authority, in relation to a child in respect of whom a care order might be made, is the local authority proposed to be designated in the order.

(5) In section 31(3A) and this section, references to a care order do not include an interim care order.

(6) A plan prepared, or treated as prepared, under this section is referred to in this Act as a 'section 31A plan'.

32   Period within which application for order under this Part must be disposed of

(1) A court hearing an application for an order under this Part shall (in the light of any rules made by virtue of subsection (2))—

(a) draw up a timetable with a view to disposing of the application without delay; and

(b) give such directions as it considers appropriate for the purpose of ensuring, so far as is reasonably practicable, that that timetable is adhered to.

(2) Rules of court may—

(a) specify periods within which specified steps must be taken in relation to such proceedings; and

(b) make other provision with respect to such proceedings for the purpose of ensuring, so far as is reasonably practicable, that they are disposed of without delay.

Care orders

33   Effect of care order

(1) Where a care order is made with respect to a child it shall be the duty of the local authority designated by the order to receive the child into their care and to keep him in their care while the order remains in force.

(2) Where—

    (a) a care order has been made with respect to a child on the application of an authorised person; but

    (b) the local authority designated by the order was not informed that that person proposed to make the application,

the child may be kept in the care of that person until received into the care of the authority.

(3) While a care order is in force with respect to a child, the local authority designated by the order shall—

    (a) have parental responsibility for the child; and

    (b) have the power (subject to the following provisions of this section) to determine the extent to which

        (i)   a parent, guardian or special guardian of the child; or

        (ii) a person who by virtue of section 4A has parental responsibility for the child,

may meet his parental responsibility for him.

(4) The authority may not exercise the power in subsection (3)(b) unless they are satisfied that it is necessary to do so in order to safeguard or promote the child's welfare.

(5) Nothing in subsection (3)(b) shall prevent a person mentioned in that provision who has care of the child from doing what is reasonable in all the circumstances of the case for the purpose of safeguarding or promoting his welfare.

(6) While a care order is in force with respect to a child, the local authority designated by the order shall not—

    (a) cause the child to be brought up in any religious persuasion other than that in which he would have been brought up if the order had not been made; or

    (b) have the right—

        (ii) to agree or refuse to agree to the making of an adoption order, or an order under section 84 of the Adoption and Children Act 2002 with respect to the child; or

        (iii) to appoint a guardian for the child.

(7) While a care order is in force with respect to a child, no person may—

    (a) cause the child to be known by a new surname; or

    (b) remove him from the United Kingdom, without either the written consent of every person who has parental responsibility for the child or the leave of the court.

(8) Subsection (7)(b) does not—

    (a) prevent the removal of such a child, for a period of less than one month, by the authority in whose care he is; or

    (b) apply to arrangements for such a child to live outside England and Wales (which are governed by paragraph 19 of Schedule 2).

(9) The power in subsection (3)(b) is subject (in addition to being subject to the provisions of this section) to any right, duty, power, responsibility or authority which a person mentioned in that provision has in relation to the child and his property by virtue of any other enactment.

34   Parental contact etc. with children in care

(1) Where a child is in the care of a local authority, the authority shall (subject to the provisions of this section) allow the child reasonable contact with—

    (a) his parents;

    (b) any guardian or special guardian of his;

    (ba) any person who by virtue of section 4A has parental responsibilty for him;

    (c) where there was a residence order in force with respect to the child immediately before the care order was made, the person in whose favour the order was made; and

    (d) where, immediately before the care order was made, a person had care of the child by virtue of an order made in the exercise of the High Court's inherent jurisdiction with respect to children, that person.

(2) On the application made by the authority or the child, the court may make such order as it considers appropriate with respect to the contact which is to be allowed between the child and any named person.

(3) On an application made by—

(a) any person mentioned in paragraphs (a) to (d) of subsection (1); or

(b) any person who has obtained the leave of the court to make the application,

the court may make such order as it considers appropriate with respect to the contact which is to be allowed between the child and that person.

(4) On an application made by the authority or the child, the court may make an order authorising the authority to refuse to allow contact between the child and any person who is mentioned in paragraphs (a) to (d) of subsection (1) and named in the order.

(5) When making a care order with respect to a child, or in any family proceedings in connection with a child who is in the care of a local authority, the court may make an order under this section, even though no application for such an order has been made with respect to the child, if it considers that the order should be made.

(6) An authority may refuse to allow the contact that would otherwise be required by virtue of subsection (1) or an order under this section if—

(a) they are satisfied that it is necessary to do so in order to safeguard or promote the child's welfare; and

(b) the refusal—

(i)   is decided upon as a matter of urgency; and

(ii) does not last for more than seven days.

(7) An order under this section may impose such conditions as the court considers appropriate.

(8) The Secretary of State may by regulations make provision as to—

(a) the steps to be taken by a local authority who have exercised their powers under subsection (6);

(b) the circumstances in which, and conditions subject to which, the terms of any order made under this section may be departed from by agreement between the local authority and the person in relation to whom this order is made;

(c) notification by a local authority of any variation or suspension of arrangements made (otherwise than under an order under this section) with a view to affording any person contact with a child to whom this section applies.

(9) The court may vary or discharge any order made under this section on the application of the authority, the child concerned or the person named in the order.

(10) An order under this section may be made either at the same time as the care order itself or later.

(11) Before making a care order with respect to any child the court shall—

(a) consider the arrangements which the authority have made, or propose to make, for affording any person contact with a child to whom this section applies; and

(b) invite the parties to the proceedings to comment on those arrangements.

Supervision orders

35   Supervision orders

(1) While a supervision order is in force it shall be the duty of the supervisor—

(a) to advise, assist and befriend the supervised child;

(b) to take such steps as are reasonably necessary to give effect to the order; and

(c) where—

(i)   the order is not wholly complied with; or

(ii) the supervisor considers that the order may no longer be necessary,

to consider whether or not to apply to the court for its variation or discharge.

(2) Parts I and II of Schedule 3 make further provision with respect to supervision orders.

36 Education supervision orders

(1) On the application of any local education authority, the court may make an order putting the child with respect to whom the application is made under the supervision of a designated local education authority.

(2) In this Act 'an education supervision order' means an order under subsection (1).

(3) A court may only make an education supervision order if it is satisfied that the child concerned is of compulsory school age and is not being properly educated.

(4) For the purposes of this section, a child is being properly educated only if he is receiving efficient full-time education suitable to his age, ability and aptitude and any special educational needs he may have.

(5) Where a child is—

    (a) the subject of a school attendance order which is in force under section 437 of the Education Act 1996 and which has not been complied with; or

    (b) is not attending regularly within the meaning of section 444 of that Act—

        (i) a school at which he is a registered pupil,

        (ii) any place at which education is provided for him in the circumstances mentioned in subsection (1) of section 444ZA of that Act, or

        (iii) any place which he is required to attend in the circumstances mentioned in subsection (2) of that section,

then, unless it is proved that he is being properly educated, it shall be assumed that he is not.

(6) An education supervision order may not be made with respect to a child who is in the care of a local authority.

(7) The local education authority designated in an education supervision order must be—

    (a) the authority within whose area the child concerned is living or will live; or

    (b) where—

        (i) the child is a registered pupil at a school; and

        (ii) the authority mentioned in paragraph (a) and the authority within whose area the school is situated agree,

the latter authority.

(8) Where a local education authority propose to make an application for an education supervision order they shall, before making the application, consult the appropriate local authority.

(9) The appropriate local authority is—

    (a) in the case of a child who is being provided with accommodation by, or on behalf of, a local authority, that authority; and

    (b) in any other case, the local authority within whose area the child concerned lives, or will live.

(10) Part III of Schedule 3 makes further provision with respect to education supervision orders.

Powers of court

37 Powers of court in certain family proceedings

(1) Where, in any family proceedings in which a question arises with respect to the welfare of any child, it appears to the court that it may be appropriate for a care or supervision order to be made with respect to him, the court may direct the appropriate authority to undertake an investigation of the child's circumstances.

(2) Where the court gives a direction under this section the local authority concerned shall, when undertaking the investigation, consider whether they should—

    (a) apply for a care order or for a supervision order with respect to the child;

    (b) provide services or assistance for the child or his family; or

    (c) take any other action with respect to the child.

(3) Where a local authority undertake an investigation under this section, and decide not to apply for a care order or supervision order with respect to the child concerned, they shall inform the court of—

(a) their reasons for so deciding;

(b) any service or assistance which they have provided, or intend to provide, for the child and his family; and

(c) any other action which they have taken, or propose to take, with respect to the child.

(4) The information shall be given to the court before the end of the period of eight weeks beginning with the date of the direction, unless the court otherwise directs.

(5) The local authority named in a direction under subsection (1) must be—

(a) the authority in whose area the child is ordinarily resident; or

(b) where the child is not ordinarily resident in the area of a local authority, the authority within whose area any circumstances arose in consequence of which the direction is being given.

(6) If, on the conclusion of any investigation or review under this section, the authority decide not to apply for a care order or supervision order with respect to the child—

(a) they shall consider whether it would be appropriate to review the case at a later date; and

(b) if they decide that it would be, they shall determine the date on which that review is to begin.

38   Interim orders

(1) Where—

(a) in any proceedings on an application for a care order or supervision order, the proceedings are adjourned; or

(b) the court gives a direction under section 37(1),

the court may make an interim care order or an interim supervision order with respect to the child concerned.

(2) A court shall not make an interim care order or interim supervision order under this section unless it is satisfied that there are reasonable grounds for believing that the circumstances with respect to the child are as mentioned in section 31(2).

(3) Where, in any proceedings on an application for a care order or supervision order, a court makes a residence order with respect to the child concerned, it shall also make an interim supervision order with respect to him unless satisfied that his welfare will be satisfactorily safeguarded without an interim order being made.

(4) An interim order made under or by virtue of this section shall have effect for such period as may be specified in the order, but shall in any event cease to have effect on whichever of the following events first occurs—

(a) the expiry of the period of eight weeks beginning with the date on which the order is made;

(b) if the order is the second or subsequent such order made with respect to the same child in the same proceedings, the expiry of the relevant period;

(c) in a case which falls within subsection (1)(a), the disposal of the application;

(d) in a case which falls within subsection (1)(b), the disposal of an application for a care order or supervision order made by the authority with respect to the child;

(e) in a case which falls within subsection (1)(b) and in which—

(i)   the court has given a direction under section 37(4), but

(ii) no application for a care order or supervision order has been made with respect to the child,

the expiry of the period fixed by that direction.

(5) In subsection (4)(b) 'the relevant period' means—

(a) the period of four weeks beginning with the date on which the order in question is made; or

(b) the period of eight weeks beginning with the date on which the first order was made if that period ends later than the period mentioned in paragraph (a).

(6) Where the court makes an interim care order, or interim supervision order, it may give such directions (if any) as it considers appropriate with regard to the medical or psychiatric examination or other assessment of the child; but if the child is of sufficient understanding to make an informed decision he may refuse to submit to the examination or other assessment.

(7) A direction under subsection (6) may be to the effect that there is to be—

(a) no such examination or assessment; or

(b) no such examination or assessment unless the court directs otherwise.

(8) A direction under subsection (6) may be—

(a) given when the interim order is made or at any time while it is in force; and

(b) varied at any time on the application of any person falling within any class of person prescribed by rules of court for the purposes of this subsection.

(9) Paragraphs 4 and 5 of Schedule 3 shall not apply in relation to an interim supervision order.

(10) Where a court makes an order under or by virtue of this section it shall, in determining the period for which the order is to be in force, consider whether any party who was, or might have been, opposed to the making of the order was in a position to argue his case against the order in full.

38A Power to include exclusion requirement in interim care order

(1) Where—

(a) on being satisfied that there are reasonable grounds for believing that the circumstances with respect to a child are as mentioned in section 31(2)(a) and (b)(i), the court makes an interim care order with respect to a child, and

(b) the conditions mentioned in subsection (2) are satisfied, the court may include an exclusion requirement in the interim care order.

(2) The conditions are—

(a) that there is reasonable cause to believe that, if a person ('the relevant person') is excluded from a dwelling-house in which the child lives, the child will cease to suffer, or cease to be likely to suffer, significant harm, and

(b) that another person living in the dwelling-house (whether a parent of the child or some other person)—

(i)   is able and willing to give to the child the care which it would be reasonable to expect a parent to give him, and

(ii) consents to the inclusion of the exclusion requirement.

(3) For the purposes of this section an exclusion requirement is any one or more of the following—

(a) a provision requiring the relevant person to leave a dwelling-house in which he is living with the child,

(b) a provision prohibiting the relevant person from entering a dwelling-house in which the child lives, and

(c) a provision excluding the relevant person from a defined area in which a dwelling-house in which the child lives is situated.

(4) The court may provide that the exclusion requirement is to have effect for a shorter period than the other provisions of the interim care order.

(5) Where the court makes an interim care order containing an exclusion requirement, the court may attach a power of arrest to the exclusion requirement.

(6) Where the court attaches a power of arrest to an exclusion requirement of an interim care order, it may provide that the power of arrest is to have effect for a shorter period than the exclusion requirement.

(7) Any period specified for the purposes of subsection (4) or (6) may be extended by the court (on one or more occasions) on an application to vary or discharge the interim care order.

(8) Where a power of arrest is attached to an exclusion requirement of an interim care order by virtue of subsection (5), a constable may arrest without warrant any person whom he has reasonable cause to believe to be in breach of the requirement.

(9) Sections 47(7), (11) and (12) and 48 of, and Schedule 5 to, the Family Law Act 1996 shall have effect in relation to a person arrested under subsection (8) of this section as they have effect in relation to a person arrested under section 47(6) of that Act.

(10) If, while an interim care order containing an exclusion requirement is in force, the local authority have removed the child from the dwelling-house from which the relevant person is excluded to other accommodation for a continuous period of more than 24 hours, the interim care order shall cease to have effect in so far as it imposes the exclusion requirement.

38B　Undertakings relating to interim care orders

(1) In any case where the court has power to include an exclusion requirement in an interim care order, the court may accept an undertaking from the relevant person.

(2) No power of arrest may be attached to any undertaking given under subsection (1).

(3) An undertaking given to a court under subsection (1)—

(a) shall be enforceable as if it were an order of the court, and

(b) shall cease to have effect if, while it is in force, the local authority have removed the child from the dwelling-house from which the relevant person is excluded to other accommodation for a continuous period of more than 24 hours.

(4) This section has effect without prejudice to the powers of the High Court and county court apart from this section.

(5) In this section 'exclusion requirement' and 'relevant person' have the same meaning as in section 38A.

39　Discharge and variation etc. of care orders and supervision orders

(1) A care order may be discharged by the court on the application of—

(a) any person who has parental responsibility for the child;

(b) the child himself; or

(c) the local authority designated by the order.

(2) A supervision order may be varied or discharged by the court on the application of—

(a) any person who has parental responsibility for the child;

(b) the child himself; or

(c) the supervisor.

(3) On the application of a person who is not entitled to apply for the order to be discharged, but who is a person with whom the child is living, a supervision order may be varied by the court in so far as it imposes a requirement which affects that person.

(3A) On the application of a person who is not entitled to apply for the order to be discharged, but who is a person to whom an exclusion requirement contained in the order applies, an interim care order may be varied or discharged by the court in so far as it imposes the exclusion requirement.

(3B) Where a power of arrest has been attached to an exclusion requirement of an interim care order, the court may, on the application of any person entitled to apply for the discharge of the order so far as it imposes the exclusion requirement, vary or discharge the order in so far as it confers a power of arrest (whether or not any application has been made to vary or discharge any other provision of the order).

(4) Where a care order is in force with respect to a child the court may, on the application of any person entitled to apply for the order to be discharged, substitute a supervision order for the care order.

(5) When a court is considering whether to substitute one order for another under subsection (4) any provision of this Act which would otherwise require section 31(2) to be satisfied at the time when the proposed order is substituted or made shall be disregarded.

40 **Orders pending appeals in cases about care or supervision orders**

(1) Where—

(a) a court dismisses an application for a care order; and

(b) at the time when the court dismisses the application, the child concerned is the subject of an interim care order,

the court may make a care order with respect to the child to have effect subject to such directions (if any) as the court may see fit to include in the order.

(2) Where—

(a) a court dismisses an application for a care order, or an application for a supervision order; and

(b) at the time when the court dismisses the application, the child concerned is the subject of an interim supervision order,

the court may make a supervision order with respect to the child to have effect subject to such directions (if any) as the court may see fit to include in the order.

(3) Where a court grants an application to discharge a care order or supervision order, it may order that—

(a) its decision is not to have effect; or

(b) the care order, or supervision order, is to continue to have effect but subject to such directions as the court sees fit to include in the order.

(4) An order made under this section shall only have effect for such period, not exceeding the appeal period, as may be specified in the order.

(5) Where—

(a) an appeal is made against any decision of a court under this section; or

(b) any application is made to the appellate court in connection with a proposed appeal against that decision,

the appellate court may extend the period for which the order in question is to have effect, but not so as to extend it beyond the end of the appeal period.

(6) In this section 'the appeal period' means—

(a) where an appeal is made against the decision in question, the period between the making of that decision and the determination of the appeal; and

(b) otherwise, the period during which an appeal may be made against the decision.

Representation of child

41 **Representation of child and of his interests in certain proceedings**

(1) For the purpose of any specified proceedings, the court shall appoint an officer of the Service or a Welsh family proceedings officer for the child concerned unless satisfied that it is not necessary to do so in order to safeguard his interests.

(2) The officer of the Service or Welsh family proceedings officer shall—

(a) be appointed in accordance with rules of court; and

(b) be under a duty to safeguard the interests of the child in the manner prescribed by such rules.

(3) Where—

(a) the child concerned is not represented by a solicitor; and

(b) any of the conditions mentioned in subsection (4) is satisfied,

the court may appoint a solicitor to represent him.

(4) The conditions are that—

(a) no officer of the Service or Welsh family proceedings officer has been appointed for the child;

(b) the child has sufficient understanding to instruct a solicitor and wishes to do so;

(c) it appears to the court that it would be in the child's best interests for him to be represented by a solicitor.

(5) Any solicitor appointed under or by virtue of this section shall be appointed, and shall represent the child, in accordance with rules of court.

(6) In this section 'specified proceedings' means any proceedings—

    (a)   on an application for a care order or supervision order;

    (b)   in which the court has given a direction under section 37(1) and has made, or is considering whether to make, an interim care order;

    (c)   on an application for the discharge of a care order or the variation or discharge of a supervision order;

    (d)   on an application under section 39(4);

    (e)   in which the court is considering whether to make a residence order with respect to a child who is the subject of a care order;

    (f)   with respect to contact between a child who is the subject of a care order and any other person;

    (g)   under Part V;

    (h)   on an appeal against—

        (i)   the making of, or refusal to make, a care order, supervision order or any order under section 34;

        (ii) the making of, or refusal to make, a residence order with respect to a child who is the subject of a care order; or

        (iii) the variation or discharge, or refusal of an application to vary or discharge, an order of a kind mentioned in subparagraph (i) or (ii);

        (iv) the refusal of an application under section 39(4); or

        (v) the making of, or refusal to make, an order under Part V; or

    (hh) on an application for the making or revocation of a placement order (within the meaning of section 21 of the Adoption and Children Act 2002);

    (i)   which are specified for the time being, for the purposes of this section, by rules of court.

(6A) The proceedings which may be specified under subsection (6)(i) include (for example) proceedings for the making, varying or discharging of a section 8 order.

. . .

(11) Regardless of any enactment or rule of law which would otherwise prevent it from doing so, the court may take account of—

    (a) any statement contained in a report made by an officer of the Service or a Welsh family proceedings officer who is appointed under this section for the purpose of the proceedings in question; and

    (b) any evidence given in respect of the matters referred to in the report, in so far as the statement or evidence is, in the opinion of the court, relevant to the question which the court is considering.

. . .

42   Right of officer of the Service to have access to local authority records

(1) Where an officer of the Service or Welsh family proceedings officer has been appointed under section 41 he shall have the right at all reasonable times to examine and take copies of—

    (a) any records of, or held by, a local authority or an authorised person which were compiled in connection with the making, or proposed making, by any person of any application under this Act with respect to the child concerned;

    (b) any records of, or held by, a local authority which were compiled in connection with any functions which are social services functions within the meaning of the Local Authority Social Services Act 1970, so far as those records relate to that child; or

    (c) any records of, or held by, an authorised person which were compiled in connection with the activities of that person, so far as those records relate to that child.

(2) Where an officer of the Service or Welsh family proceedings officer takes a copy of any record which he is entitled to examine under this section, that copy or any part of it shall be admissible as evidence of any matter referred to in any—

(a) report which he makes to the court in the proceedings in question; or

(b) evidence which he gives in those proceedings.

(3) Subsection (2) has effect regardless of any enactment or rule of law which would otherwise prevent the record in question being admissible in evidence.

(4) In this section 'authorised person' has the same meaning as in section 31.

PART V   PROTECTION OF CHILDREN

43   Child assessment orders

(1) On the application of a local authority or authorised person for an order to be made under this section with respect to a child, the court may make the order if, but only if, it is satisfied that—

(a) the applicant has reasonable cause to suspect that the child is suffering, or is likely to suffer, significant harm;

(b) an assessment of the state of the child's health or development, or of the way in which he has been treated, is required to enable the applicant to determine whether or not the child is suffering, or is likely to suffer, significant harm; and

(c) it is unlikely that such an assessment will be made, or be satisfactory, in the absence of an order under this section.

(2) In this Act 'a child assessment order' means an order under this section.

(3) A court may treat an application under this section as an application for an emergency protection order.

(4) No court shall make a child assessment order if it is satisfied—

(a) that there are grounds for making an emergency protection order with respect to the child; and

(b) that it ought to make such an order rather than a child assessment order.

(5) A child assessment order shall—

(a) specify the date by which the assessment is to begin; and

(b) have effect for such period, not exceeding 7 days beginning with that date, as may be specified in the order.

(6) Where a child assessment order is in force with respect to a child it shall be the duty of any person who is in a position to produce the child—

(a) to produce him to such person as may be named in the order; and

(b) to comply with such directions relating to the assessment of the child as the court thinks fit to specify in the order.

(7) A child assessment order authorises any person carrying out the assessment, or any part of the assessment, to do so in accordance with the terms of the order.

(8) Regardless of subsection (7), if the child is of sufficient understanding to make an informed decision he may refuse to submit to a medical or psychiatric examination or other assessment.

(9) The child may only be kept away from home—

(a) in accordance with directions specified in the order;

(b) if it is necessary for the purposes of the assessment; and

(c) for such period or periods as may be specified in the order.

(10) Where the child is to be kept away from home, the order shall contain such directions as the court thinks fit with regard to the contact that he must be allowed to have with other persons while away from home.

(11) Any person making an application for a child assessment order shall take such steps as are reasonably practicable to ensure that notice of the application is given to—

(a) the child's parents;

(b) any person who is not a parent of his but who has parental responsibility for him;

(c) any other person caring for the child;

(d) any person in whose favour a contact order is in force with respect to the child;

(e) any person who is allowed to have contact with the child by virtue of an order under section 34; and

(f) the child,

before the hearing of the application.

(12) Rules of court may make provision as to the circumstances in which—

(a) any of the persons mentioned in subsection (11); or

(b) such other person as may be specified in the rules, may apply to the court for a child assessment order to be varied or discharged.

(13) In this section 'authorised person' means a person who is an authorised person for the purposes of section 31.

44   Orders for emergency protection of children

(1) Where any person ('the applicant') applies to the court for an order to be made under this section with respect to a child, the court may make the order if, but only if, it is satisfied that—

(a) there is reasonable cause to believe that the child is likely to suffer significant harm if—

(i) he is not removed to accommodation provided by or on behalf of the applicant; or

(ii) he does not remain in the place in which he is then being accommodated;

(b) in the case of an application made by a local authority—

(i) enquiries are being made with respect to the child under section 47(1)(b); and

(ii) those enquiries are being frustrated by access to the child being unreasonably refused to a person authorised to seek access and that the applicant has reasonable cause to believe that access to the child is required as a matter of urgency; or

(c) in the case of an application made by an authorised person—

(i) the applicant has reasonable cause to suspect that a child is suffering, or is likely to suffer, significant harm;

(ii) the applicant is making enquiries with respect to the child's welfare; and

(iii) those enquiries are being frustrated by access to the child being unreasonably refused to a person authorised to seek access and the applicant has reasonable cause to believe that access to the child is required as a matter of urgency.

(2) In this section—

(a) 'authorised person' means a person who is an authorised person for the purposes of section 31; and

(b) 'a person authorised to seek access' means—

(i) in the case of an application by a local authority, an officer of the local authority or a person authorised by the authority to act on their behalf in connection with the enquiries; or

(ii) in the case of an application by an authorised person, that person.

(3) Any person—

(a) seeking access to a child in connection with enquiries of a kind mentioned in subsection (1); and

(b) purporting to be a person authorised to do so,

shall, on being asked to do so, produce some duly authenticated document as evidence that he is such a person.

(4) While an order under this section ('an emergency protection order') is in force it—

(a) operates as a direction to any person who is in a position to do so to comply with any request to produce the child to the applicant;

(b) authorises—

    (i) the removal of the child at any time to accommodation provided by or on behalf of the applicant and his being kept there; or

    (ii) the prevention of the child's removal from any hospital, or other place, in which he was being accommodated immediately before the making of the order; and

(c) gives the applicant parental responsibility for the child.

(5) Where an emergency protection order is in force with respect to a child, the applicant—

    (a) shall only exercise the power given by virtue of subsection (4)(b) in order to safeguard the welfare of the child;

    (b) shall take, and shall only take, such action in meeting his parental responsibility for the child as is reasonably required to safeguard or promote the welfare of the child (having regard in particular to the duration of the order); and

    (c) shall comply with the requirements of any regulations made by the Secretary of State for the purposes of this subsection.

(6) Where the court makes an emergency protection order, it may give such directions (if any) as it considers appropriate with respect to—

    (a) the contact which is, or is not, to be allowed between the child and any named person;

    (b) the medical or psychiatric examination or other assessment of the child.

(7) Where any direction is given under subsection (6)(b), the child may, if he is of sufficient understanding to make an informed decision, refuse to submit to the examination or other assessment.

(8) A direction under subsection (6)(a) may impose conditions and one under subsection (6)(b) may be to the effect that there is to be—

    (a) no such examination or other assessment; or

    (b) no such examination or assessment unless the court directs otherwise.

(9) A direction under subsection (6) may be—

    (a) given when the emergency protection order is made or at any time while it is in force; and

    (b) varied at any time on the application of any person falling within any class of person prescribed by rules of court for the puposes of this subsection.

(10) Where an emergency protection order is in force with respect to a child and—

    (a) the applicant has exercised the power given by subsection (4)(b)(i) but it appears to him that it is safe for the child to be returned; or

    (b) the applicant has exercised the power given by subsection (4)(b)(ii) but it appears to him that it is safe for the child to be allowed to be removed from the place in question,

he shall return the child or (as the case may be) allow him to be removed.

(11) Where he is required by subsection (10) to return the child the applicant shall—

    (a) return him to the care of the person from whose care he was removed; or

    (b) if that is not reasonably practicable, return him to the care of—

        (i) a parent of his;

        (ii) any person who is not a parent of his but who has parental responsibility for him; or

        (iii) such other person as the applicant (with the agreement of the court) considers appropriate.

(12) Where the applicant has been required by subsection (10) to return the child, or to allow him to be removed, he may again exercise his powers with respect to the child (at any time while the emergency protection order remains in force) if it appears to him that a change in the circumstances of the case makes it necessary for him to do so.

(13) Where an emergency protection order has been made with respect to a child, the applicant shall, subject to any direction given under subsection (6), allow the child reasonable contact with—

    (a) his parents;

    (b) any person who is not a parent of his but who has parental responsibility for

    (c) any person with whom he was living immediately before the making of the order;

    (d) any person in whose favour a contact order is in force with respect to him;

    (e) any person who is allowed to have contact with the child by virtue of an order under section 34; and

    (f) any person acting on behalf of any of those persons.

(14) Wherever it is reasonably practicable to do so, an emergency protection order shall name the child; and where it does not name him it shall describe him as clearly as possible.

(15) A person shall be guilty of an offence if he intentionally obstructs any person exercising the power under subsection (4)(b) to remove, or prevent the removal of, a child.

(16) A person guilty of an offence under subsection (15) shall be liable on summary conviction to a fine not exceeding level 3 on the standard scale.

44A   Power to include exclusion requirement in emergency protection order

    (1) Where—

        (a) on being satisfied as mentioned in section 44(1)(a), (b) or (c), the court makes an emergency protection order with respect to a child, and

        (b) the conditions mentioned in subsection (2) are satisfied, the court may include an exclusion requirement in the emergency protection order.

    (2) The conditions are—

        (a) that there is reasonable cause to believe that, if a person ('the relevant person') is excluded from a dwelling-house in which the child lives, then—

            (i) in the case of an order made on the ground mentioned in section 44(1)(a), the child will not be likely to suffer significant harm, even though the child is not removed as mentioned in section 44(1)(a)(i) or does not remain as mentioned in section 44(1)(a)(ii), or

            (ii) in the case of an order made on the ground mentioned in paragraph (b) or (c) of section 44(1), the enquiries referred to in that paragraph will cease to be frustrated, and

        (b) that another person living in the dwelling-house (whether a parent of the child or some other person)—

            (i) is able and willing to give to the child the care which it would be reasonable to expect a parent to give him, and

            (ii) consents to the inclusion of the exclusion requirement.

    (3) For the purposes of this section an exclusion requirement is any one or more of the following—

        (a) a provision requiring the relevant person to leave a dwelling-house in which he is living with the child,

        (b) a provision prohibiting the relevant person from entering a dwelling-house in which the child lives, and

        (c) a provision excluding the relevant person from a defined area in which a dwelling-house in which the child lives is situated.

    (4) The court may provide that the exclusion requirement is to have effect for a shorter period than the other provisions of the order.

    (5) Where the court makes an emergency protection order containing an exclusion requirement, the court may attach a power of arrest to the exclusion requirement.

    (6) Where the court attaches a power of arrest to an exclusion requirement of an emergency protection order, it may provide that the power of arrest is to have effect for a shorter period than the exclusion requirement.

(7) Any period specified for the purposes of subsection (4) or (6) may be extended by the court (on one or more occasions) on an application to vary or discharge the emergency protection order.

(8) Where a power of arrest is attached to an exclusion requirement of an emergency protection order by virtue of subsection (5), a constable may arrest without warrant any person whom he has reasonable cause to believe to be in breach of the requirement.

(9) Sections 47(7), (11) and (12) and 48 of, and Schedule 5 to, the Family Law Act 1996 shall have effect in relation to a person arrested under subsection (8) of this section as they have effect in relation to a person arrested under section 47(6) of that Act.

(10) If, while an emergency protection order containing an exclusion requirement is in force, the applicant has removed the child from the dwelling-house from which the relevant person is excluded to other accommodation for a continuous period of more than 24 hours, the order shall cease to have effect in so far as it imposes the exclusion requirement.

44B Undertakings relating to emergency protection orders

(1) In any case where the court has power to include an exclusion requirement in an emergency protection order, the court may accept an undertaking from the relevant person.

(2) No power of arrest may be attached to any undertaking given under subsection (1).

(3) An undertaking given to a court under subsection (1)—

    (a) shall be enforceable as if it were an order of the court, and

    (b) shall cease to have effect if, while it is in force, the applicant has removed the child from the dwelling-house from which the relevant person is excluded to other accommodation for a continuous period of more than 24 hours.

(4) This section has effect without prejudice to the powers of the High Court and county court apart from this section.

(5) In this section 'exclusion requirement' and 'relevant person' have the same meaning as in section 44A.

45 Duration of emergency protection orders and other supplemental provisions

(1) An emergency protection order shall have effect for such period, not exceeding eight days, as may be specified in the order.

(2) Where—

    (a) the court making an emergency protection order would, but for this subsection, specify a period of eight days as the period for which the order is to have effect; but

    (b) the last of those eight days is a public holiday (that is to say, Christmas Day, Good Friday, a bank holiday or a Sunday),

the court may specify a period which ends at noon on the first later day which is not such a holiday.

(3) Where an emergency protection order is made on an application under section 46(7), the period of eight days mentioned in subsection (1) shall begin with the first day on which the child was taken into police protection under section 46.

(4) Any person who—

    (a) has parental responsibility for a child as the result of an emergency protection order; and

    (b) is entitled to apply for a care order with respect to the child,

may apply to the court for the period during which the emergency protection order is to have effect to be extended.

(5) On an application under subsection (4) the court may extend the period during which the order is to have effect by such period, not exceeding seven days, as it thinks fit, but may do so only if it has reasonable cause to believe that the child concerned is likely to suffer significant harm if the order is not extended.

(6) An emergency protection order may only be extended once.

(7) Regardless of any enactment or rule of law which would otherwise prevent it from doing so, a court hearing an application for, or with respect to, an emergency protection order may take account of—

(a) any statement contained in any report made to the court in the course of, or in connection with, the hearing; or

(b) any evidence given during the hearing, which is, in the opinion of the court, relevant to the application.

(8) Any of the following may apply to the court for an emergency protection order to be discharged—

(a) the child;

(b) a parent of his;

(c) any person who is not a parent of his but who has parental responsibility for him; or

(d) any person with whom he was living immediately before the making of the order.

(8A) On the application of a person who is not entitled to apply for the order to be discharged, but who is a person to whom an exclusion requirement contained in the order applies, an emergency protection order may be varied or discharged by the court in so far as it imposes the exclusion requirement.

(8B) Where a power of arrest has been attached to an exclusion requirement of an emergency protection order, the court may, on the application of any person entitled to apply for the discharge of the order so far as it imposes the exclusion requirement, vary or discharge the order in so far as it confers a power of arrest (whether or not any application has been made to vary or discharge any other provision of the order).

(9) No application for the discharge of an emergency protection order shall be heard by the court before the expiry of the period of 72 hours beginning with the making of the order.

(10) No appeal may be made against—

(a) the making of, or refusal to make, an emergency protection order;

(b) the extension of, or refusal to extend, the period during which such an order is to have effect;

(c) the discharge of, or refusal to discharge, such an order; or

(d) the giving of, or refusal to give, any direction in connection with such an order.

(11) Subsection (8) does not apply—

(a) where the person who would otherwise be entitled to apply for the emergency protection order to be discharged—

(i) was given notice (in accordance with rules of court) of the hearing at which the order was made; and

(ii) was present at that hearing; or

(b) to any emergency protection order the effective period of which has been extended under subsection (5).

(12) A court making an emergency protection order may direct that the applicant may, in exercising any powers which he has by virtue of the order, be accompanied by a registered medical practitioner, registered nurse or registered midwife, if he so chooses.
...

46 Removal and accommodation of children by police in cases of emergency

(1) Where a constable has reasonable cause to believe that a child would otherwise be likely to suffer significant harm, he may—

(a) remove the child to suitable accommodation and keep him there; or

(b) take such steps as are reasonable to ensure that the child's removal from any hospital, or other place, in which he is then being accommodated is prevented.

(2) For the purposes of this Act, a child with respect to whom a constable has exercised his powers under this section is referred to as having been taken into police protection.

(3) As soon as is reasonably practicable after taking a child into police protection, the constable concerned shall—

    (a) inform the local authority within whose area the child was found of the steps that have been, and are proposed to be, taken with respect to the child under this section and the reasons for taking them;

    (b) give details to the authority within whose area the child is ordinarily resident ('the appropriate authority') of the place at which the child is being accommodated;

    (c) inform the child (if he appears capable of understanding)—

        (i) of the steps that have been taken with respect to him under this section and of the reasons for taking them; and

        (ii) of the further steps that may be taken with respect to him under this section;

    (d) take such steps as are reasonably practicable to discover the wishes and feelings of the child;

    (e) secure that the case is inquired into by an officer designated for the purposes of this section by the chief officer of the police area concerned; and

    (f) where the child was taken into police protection by being removed to accommodation which is not provided—

        (i) by or on behalf of a local authority; or

        (ii) as a refuge, in compliance with the requirements of section 51, secure that he is moved to accommodation which is so provided.

(4) As soon as is reasonably practicable after taking a child into police protection, the constable concerned shall take such steps as are reasonably practicable to inform—

    (a) the child's parents;

    (b) every person who is not a parent of his but who has parental responsibility for him; and

    (c) any other person with whom the child was living immediately before being taken into police protection,

of the steps that he has taken under this section with respect to the child, the reasons for taking them and the further steps that may be taken with respect to him under this section.

(5) On completing any inquiry under subsection (3)(e), the officer conducting it shall release the child from police protection unless he considers that there is still reasonable cause for believing that the child would be likely to suffer significant harm if released.

(6) No child may be kept in police protection for more than 72 hours.

(7) While a child is being kept in police protection, the designated officer may apply on behalf of the appropriate authority for an emergency protection order to be made under section 44 with respect to the child.

(8) An application may be made under subsection (7) whether or not the authority know of it or agree to its being made.

(9) While a child is being kept in police protection—

    (a) neither the constable concerned nor the designated officer shall have parental responsibility for him; but

    (b) the designated officer shall do what is reasonable in all the circumstances of the case for the purpose of safeguarding or promoting the child's welfare (having regard in particular to the length of the period during which the child will be so protected).

(10) Where a child has been taken into police protection, the designated officer shall allow—

    (a) the child's parents;

    (b) any person who is not a parent of the child but who has parental responsibility for him;

    (c) any person with whom the child was living immediately before he was taken into police protection;

    (d) any person in whose favour a contact order is in force with respect to the child;

    (e) any person who is allowed to have contact with the child by virtue of an order under section 34; and

    (f) any person acting on behalf of any of those persons,

to have such contact (if any) with the child as, in the opinion of the designated officer, is both reasonable and in the child's best interests.

(11) Where a child who has been taken into police protection is in accommodation provided by, or on behalf of, the appropriate authority, subsection (10) shall have effect as if it referred to the authority rather than to the designated officer.

47   Local authority's duty to investigate

(1) Where a local authority—

    (a) are informed that a child who lives, or is found, in their area—

        (i)   is the subject of an emergency protection order; or

        (ii) is in police protection; or

        (iii) has contravened a ban imposed by a curfew notice within the meaning of Chapter I of Part I of the Crime and Disorder Act 1998; or

    (b) have reasonable cause to suspect that a child who lives, or is found, in their area is suffering, or is likely to suffer, significant harm,

the authority shall make, or cause to be made, such enquiries as they consider necessary to enable them to decide whether they should take any action to safeguard or promote the child's welfare.

(2) Where a local authority have obtained an emergency protection order with respect to a child, they shall make, or cause to be made, such enquiries as they consider necessary to enable them to decide what action they should take to safeguard or promote the child's welfare.

(3) The enquiries shall, in particular, be directed towards establishing—

    (a) whether the authority should make any application to the court, or exercise any of their other powers under this Act or section 11 of the Crime and Disorder Act 1998 (child safety orders), with respect to the child;

    (b) whether, in the case of a child—

        (i)   with respect to whom an emergency protection order has been made; and

        (ii) who is not in accommodation provided by or on behalf of the authority, it would be in the child's best interests (while an emergency protection order remains in force) for him to be in such accommodation; and

    (c) whether, in the case of a child who has been taken into police protection, it would be in the child's best interests for the authority to ask for an application to be made under section 46(7).

(4) Where enquiries are being made under subsection (1) with respect to a child, the local authority concerned shall (with a view to enabling them to determine what action, if any, to take with respect to him) take such steps as are reasonably practicable—

    (a) to obtain access to him; or

    (b) to ensure that access to him is obtained, on their behalf, by a person authorised by them for the purpose,

unless they are satisfied that they already have sufficient information with respect to him.

(5) Where, as a result of any such enquiries, it appears to the authority that there are matters connected with the child's education which should be investigated, they shall consult the relevant local education authority.

(5A) For the purposes of making a determination under this section as to the action to be taken with respect to a child, a local authority shall, so far as is reasonably practicable and consistent with the child's welfare—

    (a) ascertain the child's wishes and feelings regarding the action to be taken with respect to him; and

(b) give due consideration (having regard to his age and understanding) to such wishes and feelings of the child as they have been able to ascertain.

(6) Where, in the course of enquiries made under this section—

(a) any officer of the local authority concerned; or

(b) any person authorised by the authority to act on their behalf in connection with those enquiries—

    (i) is refused access to the child concerned; or

    (ii) is denied information as to his whereabouts, the authority shall apply for an emergency protection order, a child assessment order, a care order or a supervision order with respect to the child unless they are satisfied that his welfare can be satisfactorily safeguarded without their doing so.

(7) If, on the conclusion of any enquiries or review made under this section, the authority decide not to apply for an emergency protection order, a child assessment order, a care order or a supervision order they shall—

(a) consider whether it would be appropriate to review the case at a later date; and

(b) if they decide that it would be, determine the date on which that review is to begin.

(8) Where, as a result of complying with this section, a local authority conclude that they should take action to safeguard or promote the child's welfare they shall take that action (so far as it is both within their power and reasonably practicable for them to do so).

(9) Where a local authority are conducting enquiries under this section, it shall be the duty of any person mentioned in subsection (11) to assist them with those enquiries (in particular by providing relevant information and advice) if called upon by the authority to do so.

(10) Subsection (9) does not oblige any person to assist a local authority where doing so would be unreasonable in all the circumstances of the case.

(11) The persons are—

(a) any local authority;

(b) any local education authority;

(c) any local housing authority;

(d) any Health Authority, Special Health Authority, Primary Care Trust, National Health Service trust or NHS foundation trust; and

(e) any person authorised by the Secretary of State for the purposes of this section.

(12) Where a local authority are making enquiries under this section with respect to a child who appears to them to be ordinarily resident within the area of another authority, they shall consult that other authority, who may undertake the necessary enquiries in their place.

48 Powers to assist in discovery of children who may be in need of emergency protection

(1) Where it appears to a court making an emergency protection order that adequate information as to the child's whereabouts—

(a) is not available to the applicant for the order; but

(b) is available to another person,

it may include in the order a provision requiring that other person to disclose, if asked to do so by the applicant, any information that he may have as to the child's whereabouts.

(2) No person shall be excused from complying with such a requirement on the ground that complying might incriminate him or his spouse or civil partner of an offence; but a statement or admission made in complying shall not be admissible in evidence against either of them in proceedings for any offence other than perjury.

(3) An emergency protection order may authorise the appliant to enter premises specified by the order and search for the child with respect to whom the order is made.

(4) Where the court is satisfied that there is reasonable cause to believe that there may be another child on those premises with respect to whom an emergency protection order ought

to be made, it may make an order authorising the applicant to search for that other child on those premises.

(5) Where—

    (a) an order has been made under subsection (4);

    (b) the child concerned has been found on the premises; and

    (c) the applicant is satisfied that the grounds for making an emergency protection order exist with respect to him,

the order shall have effect as if it were an emergency protection order.

(6) Where an order has been made under subsection (4), the applicant shall notify the court of its effect.

(7) A person shall be guilty of an offence if he intentionally obstructs any person exercising the power of entry and search under subsection (3) or (4).

(8) A person guilty of an offence under subsection (7) shall be liable on summary conviction to a fine not exceeding level 3 on the standard scale.

(9) Where, on an application made by any person for a warrant under this section, it appears to the court—

    (a) that a person attempting to exercise powers under an emergency protection order has been prevented from doing so by being refused entry to the premises concerned or access to the child concerned; or

    (b) that any such person is likely to be so prevented from exercising any such powers,

it may issue a warrant authorising any constable to assist the person mentioned in paragraph (a) or (b) in the exercise of those powers using reasonable force if necessary.

(10) Every warrant issued under this section shall be addressed to, and executed by, a constable who shall be accompanied by the person applying for the warrant if—

    (a) that person so desires; and

    (b) the court by whom the warrant is issued does not direct otherwise.

(11) A court granting an application for a warrant under this section may direct that the constable concerned may, in executing the warrant, be accompanied by a registered medical practitioner, registered nurse or registered midwife if he so chooses.

. . .

(12) An application for a warrant under this section shall be made in the manner and form prescribed by rules of court.

(13) Wherever it is reasonably practicable to do so, an order under subsection (4), an application for a warrant under this section and any such warrant shall name the child; and where it does not name him it shall describe him as clearly as possible.

49 Abduction of children in care etc.

(1) A person shall be guilty of an offence if, knowingly and without lawful authority or reasonable excuse, he—

    (a) takes a child to whom this section applies away from the responsible person;

    (b) keeps such a child away from the responsible person; or

    (c) induces, assists or incites such a child to run away or stay away from the responsible person.

(2) This section applies in relation to a child who is—

    (a) in care;

    (b) the subject of an emergency protection order; or

    (c) in police protection,

and in this section 'the responsible person' means any person who for the time being has care of him by virtue of the care order, the emergency protection order, or section 46, as the case may be.

(3) A person guilty of an offence under this section shall be liable on summary conviction to imprisonment for a term not exceeding six months, or to a fine not exceeding level 5 on the standard scale, or to both.

50   Recovery of abducted children etc.

(1) Where it appears to the court that there is reason to believe that a child to whom this section applies—

(a) has been unlawfully taken away or is being unlawfully kept away from the responsible person;

(b) has run away or is staying away from the responsible person; or

(c) is missing,

the court may make an order under this section ('a recovery order').

(2) This section applies to the same children to whom section 49 applies and in this section 'the responsible person' has the same meaning as in section 49.

(3) A recovery order—

(a) operates as a direction to any person who is in a position to do so to produce the child on request to any authorised person;

(b) authorises the removal of the child by any authorised person;

(c) requires any person who has information as to the child's whereabouts to disclose that information, if asked to do so, to a constable or an officer of the court;

(d) authorises a constable to enter any premises specified in the order and search for the child, using reasonable force if necessary.

(4) The court may make a recovery order only on the application of—

(a) any person who has parental responsibility for the child by virtue of a care order or emergency protection order; or

(b) where the child is in police protection, the designated officer.

(5) A recovery order shall name the child and—

(a) any person who has parental responsibility for the child by virtue of a care order or emergency protection order; or

(b) where the child is in police protection, the designated officer.

(6) Premises may only be specified under subsection (3)(d) if it appears to the court that there are reasonable grounds for believing the child to be on them.

(7) In this section—

'an authorised person' means—

(a) any person specified by the court;

(b) any constable;

(c) any person who is authorised—

(i)   after the recovery order is made; and

(ii) by a person who has parental responsibility for the child by virtue of a care order or an emergency protection order,

to exercise any power under a recovery order; and

'the designated officer' means the officer designated for the purposes of section 46.

(8) Where a person is authorised as mentioned in subsection (7)(c)—

(a) the authorisation shall identify the recovery order; and

(b) any person claiming to be so authorised shall, if asked to do so, produce some duly authenticated document showing that he is so authorised.

(9) A person shall be guilty of an offence if he intentionally obstructs an authorised person exercising the power under subsection (3)(b) to remove a child.

(10) A person guilty of an offence under this section shall be liable on summary conviction to a fine not exceeding level 3 on the standard scale.

(11) No person shall be excused from complying with any request made under subsection (3)(c) on the ground that complying with it might incriminate him or his spouse or civil partner of an offence; but a statement or admission made in complying shall not be admissible in evidence against either of them in proceedings for an offence other than perjury.

(12) Where a child is made the subject of a recovery order whilst being looked after by a local authority, any reasonable expenses incurred by an authorised person in giving effect to the order shall be recoverable from the authority.

51 Refuges for children at risk

(1) Where it is proposed to use a voluntary home or private children's home to provide a refuge for children who appear to be at risk of harm, the Secretary of State may issue a certificate under this section with respect to that home.

(2) Where a local authority or voluntary organisation arrange for a foster parent to provide such a refuge, the Secretary of State may issue a certificate under this section with respect to that foster parent.

(3) In subsection (2) 'foster parent' means a person who is, or who from time to time is, a local authority foster parent or a foster parent with whom children are placed by a voluntary organisation.

(4) The Secretary of State may by regulations—

(a) make provision as to the manner in which certificates may be issued;

(b) impose requirements which must be complied with while any certificate is in force; and

(c) provide for the withdrawal of certificates in prescribed circumstances.

(5) Where a certificate is in force with respect to a home, none of the provisions mentioned in subsection (7) shall apply in relation to any person providing a refuge for any child in that home.

(6) Where a certificate is in force with respect to a foster parent, none of those provisions shall apply in relation to the provision by him of a refuge for any child in accordance with arrangements made by the local authority or voluntary organisation.

(7) The provisions are—

(a) section 49;

(b) sections 82 (recovery of certain fugitive children) and 83 (harbouring) of the Children (Scotland) Act 1995, so far as they apply in relation to anything done in England and Wales;

(c) section 32(3) of the Children and Young Persons Act 1969 (compelling, persuading, inciting or assisting any person to be absent from detention, etc.), so far as it applies in relation to anything done in England and Wales;

(d) section 2 of the Child Abduction Act 1984.

52 Rules and regulations

(1) Without prejudice to section 93 or any other power to make such rules, rules of court may be made with respect to the procedure to be followed in connection with proceedings under this Part.

(2) The rules may, in particular make provision—

(a) as to the form in which any application is to be made or direction is to be given;

(b) prescribing the persons who are to be notified of—

(i) the making, or extension, of an emergency protection order; or

(ii) the making of an application under section 45(4) or (8) or 46(7); and

(c) as to the content of any such notification and the manner in which, and person by whom, it is to be given.

(3) The Secretary of State may by regulations provide that, where—

(a) an emergency protection order has been made with respect to a child;

(b) the applicant for the order was not the local authority within whose area the child is ordinarily resident; and

(c) that local authority are of the opinion that it would be in the child's best interests for the applicant's responsibilities under the order to be transferred to them,

that authority shall (subject to their having complied with any requirements imposed by the regulations) be treated, for the purposes of this Act, as though they and not the original applicant had applied for, and been granted, the order.

(4) Regulations made under subsection (3) may, in particular, make provision as to—

(a) the considerations to which the local authority shall have regard in forming an opinion as mentioned in subsection (3)(c); and

(b) the time at which responsibility under any emergency protection order is to be treated as having been transferred to a local authority.

PART VI   COMMUNITY HOMES

53 Provision of community homes by local authorities

(1) Every local authority shall make such arrangements as they consider appropriate for securing that homes ('community homes') are available—

(a) for the care and accommodation of children looked after by them; and

(b) for purposes connected with the welfare of children (whether or not looked after by them),

and may do so jointly with one or more other local authorities.

(2) In making such arrangements, a local authority shall have regard to the need for ensuring the availability of accommodation—

(a) of different descriptions; and

(b) which is suitable for different purposes and the requirements of different descriptions of children.

(3) A community home may be a home—

(a) provided, equipped, maintained and (subject to subsection (3A)) managed by a local authority; or

(b) provided by a voluntary organisation but in respect of which a local authority and the organisation—

(i) propose that, in accordance with an instrument of management, the equipment, maintenance and (subject to subsection (3B)) management of the home shall be the responsibility of the local authority; or

(ii) so propose that the management, equipment and maintenance of the home shall be the responsibility of the voluntary organisation.

(3A) A local authority may make arrangements for the management by another person of accommodation provided by the local authority for the purpose of restricting the liberty of children.

(3B) Where a local authority are to be responsible for the management of a community home provided by a voluntary organisation, the local authority may, with the consent of the body of managers constituted by the instrument of management for the home, make arrangements for the management by another person of accommodation provided for the purpose of restricting the liberty of children.

(4) Where a local authority are to be responsible for the management of a community home provided by a voluntary organisation, the authority shall designate the home as a controlled community home.

(5) Where a voluntary organisation are to be responsible for the management of a community home provided by the organisation, the local authority shall designate the home as an assisted community home.

(6) Schedule 4 shall have effect for the purpose of supplementing the provisions of this Part.

. . .

PART VII   VOLUNTARY HOMES AND VOLUNTARY ORGANISATIONS

59 Provision of accommodation by voluntary organisations

(1) Where a voluntary organisation provide accommodation for a child, they shall do so by—

(a) placing him (subject to subsection (2)) with—

(i) a family;

(ii) a relative of his; or

(iii) any other suitable person, on such terms as to payment by the organisation and otherwise as the organisation may determine (subject to section 49 of the Children Act 2004);

(aa) maintaining him in an appropriate children's home; or

(f) making such other arrangements (subject to subsection (3)) as seem appropriate to them.

(1A) Where under subsection (1)(aa) a local authority maintains a child in a home provided, equipped and maintained by the Secretary of State under section 82(5), it shall do so on such terms as the Secretary of State may from time to time determine.

(2) The Secretary of State may make regulations as to the placing of children with foster parents by voluntary organisations and the regulations may, in particular, make provision which (with any necessary modifications) is similar to the provision that may be made under section 23(2)(a).

(3) The Secretary of State may make regulations as to the arrangements which may be made under subsection (1)(f) and the regulations may in particular make provision which (with any necessary modifications) is similar to the provision that may be made under section 23(2)(f).

(4) The Secretary of State may make regulations requiring any voluntary organisation who are providing accommodation for a child—

(a) to review his case; and

(b) to consider any representations (including any complaint) made to them by any person falling within a prescribed class of person,

in accordance with the provisions of the regulations.

(5) Regulations under subsection (4) may in particular make provision which (with any necessary modifications) is similar to the provision that may be made under section 26.

(6) Regulations under subsections (2) to (4) may provide that any person who, without reasonable excuse, contravenes or fails to comply with a regulation shall be guilty of an offence and liable on summary conviction to a fine not exceeding level 4 on the standard scale.

60   Voluntary homes

(3) In this Act 'voluntary home' means a children's home which is carried on by a voluntary organisation but does not include a community home.

(4) Schedule 5 shall have effect for the purpose of supplementing the provisions of this Part.

61   Duties of voluntary organisations

(1) Where a child is accommodated by or on behalf of a voluntary organisation, it shall be the duty of the organisation—

(a) to safeguard and promote his welfare;

(b) to make such use of the services and facilities available for children cared for by their own parents as appears to the organisation reasonable in his case; and

(c) to advise, assist and befriend him with a view to promoting his welfare when he ceases to be so accommodated.

(2) Before making any decision with respect to any such child the organisation shall, so far as is reasonably practicable, ascertain the wishes and feelings of—

(a) the child;

(b) his parents;

(c) any person who is not a parent of his but who has parental responsibility for him; and

(d) any other person whose wishes and feelings the organisation consider to be relevant,

regarding the matter to be decided.

(3) In making any such decision the organisation shall give due consideration—

(a) having regard to the child's age and understanding, to such wishes and feelings of his as they have been able to ascertain;

(b) to such other wishes and feelings mentioned in subsection (2) as they have been able to ascertain; and

(c) to the child's religious persuasion, racial origin and cultural and linguistic background.

62   Duties of local authorities

(1) Every local authority shall satisfy themselves that any voluntary organisation providing accommodation—

(a) within the authority's area for any child; or

(b) outside that area for any child on behalf of the authority,

are satisfactorily safeguarding and promoting the welfare of the children so provided with accommodation.

(2) Every local authority shall arrange for children who are accommodated within their area by or on behalf of voluntary organisations to be visited, from time to time, in the interests of their welfare.

(3) The Secretary of State may make regulations—

(a) requiring every child who is accommodated within a local authority's area, by or on behalf of a voluntary organisation, to be visited by an officer of the authority—

(i)   in prescribed circumstances; and

(ii) on specified occasions or within specified periods; and

(b) imposing requirements which must be met by any local authority, or officer of a local authority, carrying out functions under this section.

(4) Subsection (2) does not apply in relation to community homes.

(5) Where a local authority are not satisfied that the welfare of any child who is accommodated by or on behalf of a voluntary organisation is being satisfactorily safeguarded or promoted they shall—

(a) unless they consider that it would not be in the best interests of the child, take such steps as are reasonably practicable to secure that the care and accommodation of the child is undertaken by—

(i)   a parent of his;

(ii) any person who is not a parent of his but who has parental responsibility for him; or

(iii) a relative of his; and

(b) consider the extent to which (if at all) they should exercise any of their functions with respect to the child.

. . .

PART VIII   REGISTERED CHILDREN'S HOMES

63   Private children's homes etc.

(11) Schedule 6 shall have effect with respect to private children's homes.

(12) Schedule 7 shall have effect for the purpose of setting out the circumstances in which a person may foster more than three children without being treated, for the purposes of this Act and the Care Standards Act 2000, as carrying on a children's home.

64   Welfare of children in children's homes

(1) Where a child is accommodated in a private children's home, it shall be the duty of the person carrying on the home to—

(a) safeguard and promote the child's welfare;

(b) make such use of the services and facilities available for children cared for by their own parents as appears to that person reasonable in the case of the child; and

(c) advise, assist and befriend him with a view to promoting his welfare when he ceases to be so accommodated.

(2) Before making any decision with respect to any such child the person carrying on the home shall, so far as is reasonably practicable, ascertain the wishes and feelings of—

(a) the child;

(b) his parents;

(c) any other person who is not a parent of his but who has parental responsibility for him; and

(d) any person whose wishes and feelings the person carrying on the home considers to be relevant,

regarding the matter to be decided.

(3) In making any such decision the person concerned shall give due consideration—

(a) having regard to the child's age and understanding, to such wishes and feelings of his as he has been able to ascertain;

(b) to such other wishes and feelings mentioned in subsection (2) as he has been able to ascertain; and

(c) to the child's religious persuasion, racial origin and cultural and linguistic background.

(4) Section 62, except subsection (4), shall apply in relation to any person who is carrying on a private children's home as it applies in relation to any voluntary organisation.

. . .

PART IX   PRIVATE ARRANGEMENTS FOR FOSTERING CHILDREN

66   Privately fostered children

(1) In this Part—

(a) 'a privately fostered child' means a child who is under the age of sixteen and who is cared for, and provided with accommodation in their own home by, someone other than—

(i) a parent of his;

(ii) a person who is not a parent of his but who has parental responsibility for him; or

(iii) a relative of his; and

(b) 'to foster privately' means to look after the child in circumstances in which he is a privately fostered child as defined by this section.

(2) A child is not a privately fostered child if the person caring for and accommodating him—

(a) has done so for a period of less than 28 days; and

(b) does not intend to do so for any longer period.

(3) Subsection (1) is subject to—

(a) the provisions of section 63; and

(b) the exceptions made by paragraphs 1 to 5 of Schedule 8.

(4) In the case of a child who is disabled, subsection (1)(a) shall have effect as if for 'sixteen' there were substituted 'eighteen'.

(4A) The Secretary of State may by regulations make provision as to the circumstances in which a person who provides accommodation to a child is, or is not, to be treated as providing him with accommodation in the person's own home.

(5) Schedule 8 shall have effect for the purposes of supplementing the provision made by this Part.

67   Welfare of privately fostered children

(1) It shall be the duty of every local authority to satisfy themselves that the welfare of children who are or are proposed to be privately fostered within their area is being or will be

satisfactorily safeguarded and promoted and to secure that such advice is given to those concerned with them as appears to the authority to be needed.

(2) The Secretary of State may make regulations—

(a) requiring every child who is privately fostered within a local authority's area to be visited by an officer of the authority—
 (i) in prescribed circumstances; and
 (ii) on specified occasions or within specified periods; and

(b) imposing requirements which are to be met by any local authority, or officer of a local authority, in carrying out functions under this section.

(2A) Regulations under subsection (2)(b) may impose requirements as to the action to be taken by a local authority for the purposes of discharging their duty under subsection (1) where they have received notification of a proposal that a child be privately fostered.

(3) Where any person who is authorised by a local authority for the purpose has reasonable cause to believe that—

(a) any privately fostered child is being accommodated in premises within the authority's area; or

(b) it is proposed to accommodate any such child in any such premises, he may at any reasonable time inspect those premises and any children there.

(4) Any person exercising the power under subsection (3) shall, if so required, produce some duly authenticated document showing his authority to do so.

(5) Where a local authority are not satisfied that the welfare of any child who is or is proposed to be privately fostered within their area is being or will be satisfactorily safeguarded or promoted they shall—

(a) unless they consider that it would not be in the best interests of the child, take such steps as are reasonably praticable to secure that the care and accommodation of the child is undertaken by—
 (i) a parent of his;
 (ii) any person who is not a parent of his but who has parental responsibility for him; or
 (iii) a relative of his; and

(b) consider the extent to which (if at all) they should exercise any of their functions under this Act with respect to the child.

(6) The Secretary of State may make regulations requiring a local authority to monitor the way in which the authority discharge their functions under this Part (and the regulations may in particular require the authority to appoint an officer for that purpose).

68 Persons disqualified from being private foster parents

(1) Unless he has disclosed the fact to the appropriate local authority and obtained their written consent, a person shall not foster a child privately if he is disqualified from doing so by regulations made by the Secretary of State for the purposes of this section.

(2) The regulations may, in particular, provide for a person to be so disqualified where—

(a) an order of a kind specified in the regulations has been made at any time with respect to him;

(b) an order of a kind so specified has been made at any time with respect to any child who has been in his care;

(c) a requirement of a kind so specified has been imposed at any time with respect to any such child, under or by virtue of any enactment;

(d) he has been convicted of any offence of a kind so specified, or discharged absolutely or conditionally for any such offence;

(e) a prohibition has been imposed on him at any time under section 69 or under any other specified enactment;

(f) his rights and powers with respect to a child have at any time been vested in a specified authority under a specified enactment.

(2A) A conviction in respect of which a probation order was made before 1st October 1992 (which would not otherwise be treated as a conviction) is to be treated as a conviction for the purposes of subsection (2)(d).

(3) Unless he has disclosed the fact to the appropriate local authority and obtained their written consent, a person shall not foster a child privately if—

    (a) he lives in the same household as a person who is himself prevented from fostering a child by subsection (1); or

    (b) he lives in a household at which any such person is employed.

(4) Where an authority refuse to give their consent under this section, they shall inform the applicant by a written notice which states—

    (a) the reason for the refusal;

    (b) the applicant's right under paragraph 8 of Schedule 8 to appeal against the refusal; and

    (c) the time within which he may do so.

(5) In this section—

'the appropriate authority' means the local authority within whose area it is proposed to foster the child in question; and

'enactment' means any enactment having effect, at any time, in any part of the United Kingdom.

69   Power to prohibit private fostering

(1) This section applies where a person—

    (a) proposes to foster a child privately; or

    (b) is fostering a child privately.

(2) Where the local authority for the area within which the child is proposed to be, or is being, fostered are of the opinion that—

    (a) he is not a suitable person to foster a child;

    (b) the premises in which the child will be, or is being, accommodated are not suitable; or

    (c) it would be prejudicial to the welfare of the child for him to be, or continue to be, accommodated by that person in those premises,

the authority may impose a prohibition on him under subsection (3).

(3) A prohibition imposed on any person under this subsection may prohibit him from fostering privately—

    (a) any child in any premises within the area of the local authority; or

    (b) any child in premises specified in the prohibition;

    (c) a child identified in the prohibition, in premises specified in the prohibition.

(4) A local authority who have imposed a prohibition on any person under subsection (3) may, if they think fit, cancel the prohibition—

    (a) of their own motion; or

    (b) on an application made by that person, if they are satisfied that the prohibition is no longer justified.

(5) Where a local authority impose a requirement on any person under paragraph 6 of Schedule 8, they may also impose a prohibition on him under subsection (3).

(6) Any prohibition imposed by virtue of subsection (5) shall not have effect unless—

    (a) the time specified for compliance with the requirement has expired; and

    (b) the requirement has not been complied with.

(7) A prohibition imposed under this section shall be imposed by notice in writing addressed to the person on whom it is imposed and informing him of—

    (a) the reason for imposing the prohibition;

    (b) his right under paragraph 8 of Schedule 8 to appeal against the prohibition; and

    (c) the time within which he may do so.

70 Offences

(1) A person shall be guilty of an offence if—
- (a) being required, under any provision made by or under this Part, to give any notice or information—
    - (i)   he fails without reasonable excuse to give the notice within the time specified in that provision; or
    - (ii) he fails without reasonable excuse to give the information within a reasonable time; or
    - (iii) he makes, or causes or procures another person to make, any statement in the notice or information which he knows to be false or misleading in a material particular;
- (b) he refuses to allow a privately fostered child to be visited by a duly authorised officer of a local authority;
- (c) he intentionally obstructs another in the exercise of the power conferred by section 67(3);
- (d) he contravenes section 68;
- (e) he fails without reasonable excuse to comply with any requirement imposed by a local authority under this Part;
- (f) he accommodates a privately fostered child in any premises in contravention of a prohibition imposed by a local authority under this Part;
- (g) he knowingly causes to be published, or publishes, an advertisement which he knows contravenes paragraph 10 of Schedule 8.

(2) Where a person contravenes section 68(3), he shall not be guilty of an offence under this section if he proves that he did not know, and had no reasonable ground for believing, that any person to whom section 68(1) applied was living or employed in the premises in question.

(3) A person guilty of an offence under subsection (1)(a) shall be liable on summary conviction to a fine not exceeding level 5 on the standard scale.

(4) A person guilty of an offence under subsection (1)(b), (c) or (g) shall be liable on summary conviction to a fine not exceeding level 3 on the standard scale.

(5) A person guilty of a offence under subsection 1(d) or (f) shall be liable on summary conviction to imprisonment for a term not exceeding six months, or to a fine not exceeding level 5 on the standard scale, or to both.

(6) A person guilty of an offence under subsection (1)(e) shall be liable on summary conviction to a fine not exceeding level 4 on the standard scale.

(7) If any person who is required, under any provision of this Part, to give a notice fails to give the notice within the time specified in that provision, proceedings for the offence may be brought at any time within six months from the date when evidence of the offence came to the knowledge of the local authority.

(8) Subsection (7) is not affected by anything in section 127(1) of the Magistrates' Courts Act 1980 (time limit for proceedings).

. . .

PART XII   MISCELLANEOUS AND GENERAL

Notification of children accommodated in certain establishments

85 Children accommodated by health authorities and local education authorities

(1) Where a child is provided with accommodation by any Health Authority, Special Health Authority, Primary Care Trust, National Health Service trust, NHS foundation trust or local education authority ('the accommodating authority')—
- (a) for a consecutive period of at least three months; or
- (b) with the intention, on the part of that authority, of accommodating him for such a period,

the accommodating authority shall notify the responsible authority.

(2) Where subsection (1) applies with respect to a child, the accommodating authority shall also notify the responsible authority when they cease to accommodate the child.

(3) In this section 'the responsible authority' means—

    (a) the local authority appearing to the accommodating authority to be the authority within whose area the child was ordinarily resident immediately before being accommodated; or

    (b) where it appears to the accommodating authority that a child was not ordinarily resident within the area of any local authority, the local authority within whose area the accommodation is situated.

(4) Where a local authority have been notified under this section, they shall—

    (a) take such steps as are reasonably practicable to enable them to determine whether the child's welfare is adequately safeguarded and promoted while he is accommodated by the accommodating authority; and

    (b) consider the extent to which (if at all) they should exercise any of their functions under this Act with respect to the child.

. . .

Effect and duration of orders etc.

91 Effect and duration of orders etc.

(1) The making of a residence order with respect to a child who is the subject of a care order discharges the care order.

(2) The making of a care order with respect to a child who is the subject of any section 8 order discharges that order.

(2A) Where a contact activity direction has been made as regards contact with a child, the making of a care order with respect to the child discharges the direction.

(3) The making of a care order with respect to a child who is the subject of a supervision order discharges that other order.

(4) The making of a care order with respect to a child who is a ward of court brings that wardship to an end.

(5) The making of a care order with respect to a child who is the subject of a school attendance order made under section 437 of the Education Act 1996 discharges the school attendance order.

(5A) The making of a special guardianship order with respect to a child who is the subject of—

    (a) a care order; or

    (b) an order under section 34,

discharges that order.

(6) Where an emergency protection order is made with respect to a child who is in care, the care order shall have effect subject to the emergency protection order.

(7) Any order made under section 4(1), 4A(1) or 5(1) shall continue in force until the child reaches the age of eighteen, unless it is brought to an end earlier.

(8) Any—

    (a) agreement under section 4 or 4A; or

    (b) appointment under section 5(3) or (4),

shall continue in force until the child reaches the age of eighteen, unless it is brought to an end earlier.

(9) An order under Schedule 1 has effect as specified in that Schedule.

(10) A section 8 order shall, if it would otherwise still be in force, cease to have effect when the child reaches the age of sixteen, unless it is to have effect beyond that age by virtue of section 9(6) or 12(5).

(11) Where a section 8 order has effect with respect to a child who has reached the age of sixteen, it shall, if it would otherwise still be in force, cease to have effect when he reaches the age of eighteen.

(12) Any care order, other than an interim care order, shall continue in force until the child reaches the age of eighteen, unless it is brought to an end earlier.

(13) Any order made under any other provision of this Act in relation to a child shall, if it would otherwise still be in force, cease to have effect when he reaches the age of eighteen.

(14) On disposing of any application for an order under this Act, the court may (whether or not it makes any other order in response to the application) order that no application for an order under this Act of any specified kind may be made with respect to the child concerned by any person named in the order without leave of the court.

(15) Where an application ('the previous application') has been made for—

(a) the discharge of a care order;

(b) the discharge of a supervision order;

(c) the discharge of an education supervision order;

(d) the substitution of a supervision order for a care order; or

(e) a child assessment order,

no further application of a kind mentioned in paragraphs (a) to (e) may be made with respect to the child concerned, without leave of the court, unless the period between the disposal of the previous application and the making of the further application exceeds six months.

(16) Subsection (15) does not apply to applications made in relation to interim orders.

(17) Where—

(a) a person has made an application for an order under section 34;

(b) the application has been refused; and

(c) a period of less than six months has elapsed since the refusal,

that person may not make a further application for such an order with respect to the same child, unless he has obtained the leave of the court.

Jurisdiction and procedure etc.

92   Jurisdiction of courts

(1) The name 'domestic proceedings', given to certain proceedings in magistrates' courts, is hereby changed to 'family proceedings' and the names 'domestic court' and 'domestic court panel' are hereby changed to 'family proceedings court' and 'family panel', respectively.

(2) Proceedings under this Act shall be treated as family proceedings in relation to magistrates' courts.

(3) Subsection (2) is subject to the provisions of section 65(1) and (2) of the Magistrates' Courts Act 1980 (proceedings which may be treated as not being family proceedings), as amended by this Act.

(4) A magistrates' court shall not be competent to entertain any application, or make any order, involving the administration or application of—

(a) any property belonging to or held in trust for a child; or

(b) the income of any such property.

(5) The powers of a magistrates' court under section 63(2) of the Act of 1980 to suspend or rescind orders shall not apply in relation to any order made under this Act.

(6) Part I of Schedule 11 makes provision, including provision for the Lord Chancellor to make orders, with respect to the jurisdiction of courts and justices of the peace in relation to—

(a) proceedings under this Act; and

(b) proceedings under certain other enactments.

(7) For the purposes of this Act 'the court' means the High Court, a county court or a magistrates' court.

(8) Subsection (7) is subject to the provision made by or under Part I of Schedule 11 and to any express provision as to the jurisdiction of any court made by any other provision of this Act.

(9) The Lord Chancellor may, after consulting the Lord Chief Justice, by order make provision for the principal registry of the Family Division of the High Court to be treated as if it were a county court for such purposes of this Act, or of any provision made under this Act, as may be specified in the order.

(10) Any order under subsection (9) may make such provision as the Lord Chancellor thinks expedient, after consulting the Lord Chief Justice, for the purpose of applying (with or without modifications) provisions which apply in relation to the procedure in county courts to the principal registry when it acts as if it were a county court.

(10A) The Lord Chief Justice may nominate a judicial office holder (as defined in section 109(4) of the Constitutional Reform Act 2005) to exercise his functions under subsection (9) or (10).

(11) Part II of Schedule 11 makes amendments consequential on this section.

. . .

94   Appeals

(1) Subject to any express provisions to the contrary made by or under this Act, an appeal shall lie to the High Court against—

    (a) the making by a magistrates' court of any order under this Act or the Adoption and Children Act 2002; or

    (b) any refusal by a magistrates' court to make such an order.

(2) Where a magistrates' court has power, in relation to any proceedings under this Act or the Adoption and Children Act 2002, to decline jurisdiction because it considers that the case can more conveniently be dealt with by another court, no appeal shall lie against any exercise by that magistrates' court of that power.

(3) Subsection (1) does not apply in relation to an interim order for periodical payments made under Schedule 1.

(4) On an appeal under this section, the High Court may make such orders as may be necessary to give effect to its determination of the appeal.

(5) Where an order is made under subsection (4) the High Court may also make such incidental or consequential orders as appear to it to be just.

(6) Where an appeal from a magistrates' court relates to an order for the making of periodical payments, the High Court may order that its determination of the appeal shall have effect from such date as it thinks fit to specify in the order.

(7) The date so specified must not be earlier than the earliest date allowed in accordance with rules of court made for the purposes of this section.

(8) Where, on an appeal under this section in respect of an order requiring a person to make periodical payments, the High Court reduces the amount of those payments or discharges the order—

    (a) it may order the person entitled to the payments to pay to the person making them such sum in respect of payments already made as the High Court thinks fit; and

    (b) if any arrears are due under the order for periodical payments, it may remit payment of the whole, or part, of those arrears.

(9) Any order of the High Court made on an appeal under this section (other than one directing that an application be re-heard by a magistrates' court) shall, for the purposes—

    (a) of the enforcement of the order; and

    (b) of any power to vary, revive or discharge orders,

be treated as if it were an order of the magistrates' court from which the appeal was brought and not an order of the High Court.

(10) The Lord Chancellor may, after consulting the Lord Chief Justice, by order make provision as to the circumstances in which appeals may be made against decisions taken by courts on questions arising in connection with the transfer, or proposed transfer, of proceedings by virtue of any order under paragraph 2 of Schedule 11.

(11) Except to the extent provided for in any order made under subsection (10), no appeal may be made against any decision of a kind mentioned in that subsection.

(12) The Lord Chief Justice may nominate a judicial office holder (as defined in section 109(4) of the Constitutional Reform Act 2005) to exercise his functions under subsection (10).

95   Attendance of child at hearing under Part IV or V

(1) In any proceedings in which a court is hearing an application for an order under Part IV or V, or is considering whether to make any such order, the court may order the child concerned to attend such stage or stages of the proceedings as may be specified in the order.

(2) The power conferred by subsection (1) shall be exercised in accordance with rules of court.

(3) Subsections (4) to (6) apply where—

    (a) an order under subsection (1) has not been complied with; or

    (b) the court has reasonable cause to believe that it will not be complied with.

(4) The court may make an order authorising a constable, or such person as may be specified in the order—

    (a) to take charge of the child and to bring him to the court; and

    (b) to enter and search any premises specified in the order if he has reasonable cause to believe that the child may be found on the premises.

(5) The court may order any person who is in a position to do so to bring the child to the court.

(6) Where the court has reason to believe that a person has information about the whereabouts of the child it may order him to disclose it to the court.

96   Evidence given by, or with respect to, children

(1) Subsection (2) applies where a child who is called as a witness in any civil proceedings does not, in the opinion of the court, understand the nature of an oath.

(2) The child's evidence may be heard by the court if, in its opinion—

    (a) he understands that it is his duty to speak the truth; and

    (b) he has sufficient understanding to justify his evidence being heard.

(3) The Lord Chancellor may, with the concurrence of the Lord Chief Justice, by order make provision for the admissibility of evidence which would otherwise be inadmissible under any rule of law relating to hearsay.

(4) An order under subsection (3) may only be made with respect to—

    (a) civil proceedings in general or such civil proceedings, or class of civil proceedings, as may be prescribed; and

    (b) evidence in connection with the upbringing, maintenance or welfare of a child.

(5) An order under subsection (3)—

    (a) may, in particular, provide for the admissibility of statements which are made orally or in a prescribed form or which are recorded by any prescribed method of recording;

    (b) may make different provision for different purposes and in relation to different descriptions of court; and

    (c) may make such amendments and repeals in any enactment relating to evidence (other than in this Act) as the Lord Chancellor considers necessary or expedient in consequence of the provision made by the order.

(6) Subsection (5)(b) is without prejudice to section 104(4):

(7) In this section—

'civil proceedings' means civil proceedings, before any tribunal, in relation to which the strict rules of evidence apply, whether as a matter of law or by agreement of the parties, and references to 'the court' shall be construed accordingly; and

'prescribed' means prescribed by an order under subsection (3).

97 Privacy for children involved in certain proceedings

(1) Family Procedure Rules may make provision for a magistrates' court to sit in private in proceedings in which any powers under this Act or the Adoption and Children Act 2002 may be exercised by the court with respect to any child.

(2) No person shall publish to the public at large or any section of the public any material which is intended, or likely, to identify—

(a) any child as being involved in any proceedings before the High Court, a county court or a magistrates' court in which any power under this Act or the Adoption and Children Act 2002 may be exercised by the court with respect to that or any other child; or

(b) an address or school as being that of a child involved in any such proceedings.

(3) In any proceedings for an offence under this section it shall be a defence for the accused to prove that he did not know, and had no reason to suspect, that the published material was intended, or likely, to identify the child.

(4) The court or the Lord Chancellor may, if satisfied that the welfare of the child requires it and, in the case of the Lord Chancellor, if the Lord Chief Justice agrees, by order dispense with the requirements of subsection (2) to such extent as may be specified in the order.

(5) For the purposes of this section—

'publish' includes—

(a) include in a programme service (within the meaning of the Broadcasting Act 1990);

(b) cause to be published; and

'material' includes any picture or representation.

(6) Any person who contravenes this section shall be guilty of an offence and liable, on summary conviction, to a fine not exceeding level 4 on the standard scale.

(7) Subsection (1) is without prejudice to—

(a) any other power of a magistrates' court to sit in private.

(8) Sections 69 (sittings of magistrates' courts for family proceedings) and 71 (newspaper reports of certain proceedings) of the Act of 1980 shall apply in relation to any proceedings before a magistrates' court to which this section applies subject to the provisions of this section.

(9) The Lord Chief Justice may nominate a judicial office holder (as defined in section 109(4) of the Constitutional Reform Act 2005) to exercise his functions under subsection (4).

98 Self-incrimination

(1) In any proceedings in which a court is hearing an application for an order under Part IV or V, no person shall be excused from—

(a) giving evidence on any matter; or

(b) answering any question put to him in the course of his giving evidence, on the ground that doing so might incriminate him or his spouse or civil partner of an offence.

(2) A statement or admission made in such proceedings shall not be admissible in evidence against the person making it or his spouse or civil partner in proceedings for an offence other than perjury.

100 Restrictions on use of wardship jurisdiction

(1) Section 7 of the Family Law Reform Act 1969 (which gives the High Court power to place a ward of court in the care, or under the supervision, of a local authority) shall cease to have effect.

(2) No court shall exercise the High Court's inherent jurisdiction with respect to children—

(a) so as to require a child to be placed in the care, or put under the supervision, of a local authority;

(b) so as to require a child to be accommodated by or on behalf of a local authority; or

(c) so as to make a child who is the subject of a care order a ward of court; or

(d) for the purpose of conferring on any local authority power to determine any question which has arisen, or which may arise, in connection with any aspect of parental responsibility for a child.

(3) No application for any exercise of the court's inherent jurisdiction with respect to children may be made by a local authority unless the authority have obtained the leave of the court.

(4) The court may only grant leave if it is satisfied that—

(a) the result which the authority wish to achieve could not be achieved through the making of any order of a kind to which subsection (5) applies; and

(b) there is reasonable cause to believe that if the court's inherent jurisdiction is not exercised with respect to the child he is likely to suffer significant harm.

(5) This subsection applies to any order—

(a) made otherwise than in the exercise of the court's inherent jurisdiction; and

(b) which the local authority is entitled to apply for (assuming, in the case of any application which may only be made with leave, that leave is granted).

Search warrants

102 Power of constable to assist in exercise of certain powers to search for children or inspect premises

(1) Where, on an application made by any person for a warrant under this section, it appears to the court—

(a) that a person attempting to exercise powers under any enactment mentioned in subsection (6) has been prevented from doing so by being refused entry to the premises concerned or refused access to the child concerned; or

(b) that any such person is likely to be so prevented from exercising any such powers,

it may issue a warrant authorising any constable to assist that person in the exercise of those powers, using reasonable force if necessary.

(2) Every warrant issued under this section shall be addressed to, and executed by, a constable who shall be accompanied by the person applying for the warrant if—

(a) that person so desires; and

(b) the court by whom the warrant is issued does not direct otherwise.

(3) A court granting an application for a warrant under this section may direct that the constable concerned may, in executing the warrant, be accompanied by a registered medical practitioner, registered nurse or registered midwife if he so chooses.

. . .

(4) An application for a warrant under this section shall be made in the manner and form prescribed by rules of court.

(5) Where—

(a) an application for a warrant under this section relates to a particular child; and

(b) it is reasonably practicable to do so,

the application and any warrant granted on the application shall name the child; and where it does not name him it shall describe him as clearly as possible.

(6) The enactments are—

(a) sections 62, 64, 67, 76, 79U, 80, 86 and 87;

(b) paragraph 8(1)(b) and (2)(b) of Schedule 3;

. . .

General

105 Interpretation

(1) In this Act—

'adoption agency' means a body which may be referred to as an adoption agency by virtue of section 2 of the Adoption and Children Act 2002;

'appropriate children's home' has the meaning given by section 23;

'bank holiday' means a day which is a bank holiday under the Banking and Financial Dealings Act 1971;

'care home' has the same meaning as in the Care Standards Act 2000;

'care order' has the meaning given by section 31(11) and also includes any order which by or under any enactment has the effect of, or is deemed to be, a care order for the purposes of this Act; and any reference to a child who is in the care of an authority is a reference to a child who is in their care by virtue of a care order;

'child' means, subject to paragraph 16 of Schedule 1, a person under the age of eighteen;

'child assessment order' has the meaning given by section 43(2);

'child of the family', in relation to parties to a marriage, or to two people who are civil partners of each other, means—

(a) a child of both of them, and

(b) any other child, other than a child placed with them as foster parents by a local authority or voluntary organisation, who has been treated by both of them as a child of their family.

'children's home' has the meaning given by section 23;

'community home' has the meaning given by section 53;

'contact activity condition' has the meaning given by section 11C;

'contact activity direction' has the meaning given by section 11A;

'contact order' has the meaning given by section 8(1);

'day care' (except in Part XA) has the same meaning given by section 18;

'disabled', in relation to a child, has the same meaning as in section 17(11);

'domestic premises' has the meaning given by section 71(12);

'dwelling-house' includes—

(a) any building or part of a building which is occupied as a dwelling;

(b) any caravan, house-boat or structure which is occupied as a dwelling; and any yard, garden, garage or outhouse belonging to it and occupied with it;

'education supervision order' has the meaning given in section 36;

'emergency protection order' means an order under section 44;

'enforcement order' has the meaning given by section 11J;

'family assistance order' has the meaning given in section 16(2);

'family proceedings' has the meaning given by section 8(3);

'functions' includes powers and duties;

'guardian of a child' means a guardian (other than a guardian of the estate of a child) appointed in accordance with the provisions of section 5;

'harm' has the same meaning as in section 31(9) and the question of whether harm is significant shall be determined in accordance with section 31(10);

'Health Authority' means a Health Authority established under section 8 of the National Health Service Act 1977;

'health service hospital' has the same meaning as in the National Health Service Act 1977;

'hospital' (except in Schedule 9A) has the same meaning as in the Mental Health Act 1983, except that it does not include a hospital at which high security psychiatric services within the meaning of that Act are provided;

'ill-treatment' has the same meaning as in section 31(9);

'income-based jobseeker's allowance' has the same meaning as in the Jobseekers Act 1995;

'independent hospital' has the same meaning as in the Care Standards Act 2000;

'independent school' has the same meaning as in the Education Act 1996;

'local authority' means, in relation to England, the council of a county, a metropolitan district, a London Borough or the Common Council of the City of London, in relation to Wales, the council of a county or a county borough and, in relation to Scotland, a local authority within the meaning of section 1(2) of the Social Work (Scotland) Act 1968;

'local authority foster parent' has the same meaning as in section 23(3);

'local education authority' has the same meaning as in the Education Act 1996;

'local housing authority' has the same meaning as in the Housing Act 1985;

'officer of the Service' has the same meaning as in the Criminal Justice and Court Services Act 2000;

'parental responsibility' has the meaning given in section 3;

'parental responsibility agreement' has the meaning given in sections 4(1) and 4A(2);

'prescribed' means prescribed by regulations made under this Act;

'Primary Care Trust' means a Primary Care Trust established under section 16A of the National Health Service Act 1977;

'private children's home' means a children's home in respect of which a person is registered under Part II of the Care Standards Act 2000 which is not a community home or a voluntary home;

'privately fostered child' and 'to foster a child privately' have the same meaning as in section 66;

'prohibited steps order' has the meaning given by section 8(1);

'registered pupil' has the same meaning as in the Education Act 1996;

'relative', in relation to a child, means a grandparent, brother, sister, uncle or aunt (whether of the full blood or half blood or by marriage or civil partnership) or step-parent;

'residence order' has the meaning given by section 8(1);

'responsible person', in relation to a child who is the subject of a supervision order, has the meaning given in paragraph 1 of Schedule 3;

'school' has the same meaning as in the Education Act 1996 or, in relation to Scotland, in the Education (Scotland) Act 1980;

'section 31A plan' has the meaning given by section 31A(6);

'service', in relation to any provision, made under Part III, includes any facility; 'signed', in relation to any person, includes the making by that person of his mark;

'special educational needs' has the same meaning as in the Education Act 1996;

'special guardian' and 'special guardianship order' have the meaning given by section 14A;

'Special Health Authority' means a Special Health Authority established under section 11 of the National Health Service Act 1977;

'specific issue order' has the meaning given by section 8(1);

'Strategic Health Authority' means a Strategic Health Authority established under section 8 of the National Health Service Act 1977;

'supervision order' has the meaning given by section 31(11);

'supervised child' and 'supervisor', in relation to a supervision order or an education supervision order, mean respectively the child who is (or is to be) under supervision and the person under whose supervision he is (or is to be) by virtue of the order;

'upbringing', in relation to any child, includes the care of the child but not his maintenance;

'voluntary home' has the meaning given by section 60;

'voluntary organisation' means a body (other than a public or local authority) whose activities are not carried on for profit.

'Welsh family proceedings officer' has the meaning given by section 35 of the Children Act 2004.

(2) References in this Act to a child whose father and mother were, or (as the case may be) were not, married to each other at the time of his birth must be read with section 1 of the Family Law Reform Act 1987 (which extends the meaning of such references).

(3) References in this Act to—

(a) a person with whom a child lives, or is to live, as the result of a residence order; or

(b) a person in whose favour a residence order is in force,

shall be construed as references to the person named in the order as the person with whom the child is to live.

(4) References in this Act to a child who is looked after by a local authority have the same meaning as they have (by virtue of section 22) in Part III.

(5) References in this Act to accommodation provided by or on behalf of a local authority are references to accommodation so provided in the exercise of functions of that or any other local authority which are social services functions within the meaning of the Local Authority Social Services Act 1970.

(5A) References in this Act to a child minder shall be construed—

...

(b) in relation to England and Wales, in accordance with section 79A.

(6) In determining the 'ordinary residence' of a child for any purpose of this Act, there shall be disregarded any period in which he lives in any place—

(a) which is a school or other institution;

(b) in accordance with the requirements of a supervision order under this Act or an order under section 63(1) of the Powers of Criminal Courts (Sentencing) Act 2000; or

(c) while he is being provided with accommodation by or on behalf of a local authority.

...

(7) References in this Act to children who are in need shall be construed in accordance with section 17.

(8) Any notice or other document required under this Act to be served on any person may be served on him by being delivered personally to him, or being sent by post to him in a registered letter or by the recorded delivery service at his proper address.

(9) Any such notice or other document required to be served on a body corporate or a firm shall be duly served if it is served on the secretary or clerk of that body or a partner of that firm.

(10) For the purposes of this section, and of section 7 of the Interpretation Act 1978 in its application to this section, the proper address of a person—

(a) in the case of a secretary or clerk of a body corporate, shall be that of the registered or principal office of that body;

(b) in the case of a partner of a firm, shall be that of the principal office of the firm; and

(c) in any other case, shall be last known address of the person to be served.

SCHEDULES

SCHEDULE A1   ENFORCEMENT ORDERS

PART 1   UNPAID WORK REQUIREMENT

General

1. Subject to the modifications in paragraphs 2 and 3[1], Chapter 4 of Part 12 of the Criminal Justice Act 2003 has effect in relation to an enforcement order as it has effect in relation to a community order (within the meaning of Part 12 of that Act).

References to an offender

2. Subject to paragraph 3, references in Chapter 4 of Part 12 of the Criminal Justice Act 2003 to an offender are to be treated as including references to a person subject to an enforcement order.

---

[1] The modifications referred to here are incorporated into the Criminal Justice Act 2003 as reproduced in this volume.

Specific modifications

3.—(1) The power of the Secretary of State by order under section 197(3) to amend the definition of 'responsible officer' and to make consequential amendments includes power to make any amendments of this Part (including further modifications of Chapter 4 of Part 12 of the Criminal Justice Act 2003) that appear to the Secretary of State to be necessary or expedient in consequence of any amendment made by virtue of section 197(3)(a) or (b).

. . .

PART 2   REVOCATION, AMENDMENT OR BREACH OF ENFORCEMENT ORDER

Power to revoke

4. (1) This paragraph applies where a court has made an enforcement order in respect of a person's failure to comply with a contact order and the enforcement order is in force.

(2) The court may revoke the enforcement order if it appears to the court that—

    (a) in all the circumstances no enforcement order should have been made,

    (b) having regard to circumstances which have arisen since the enforcement order was made, it would be appropriate for the enforcement order to be revoked, or

    (c) having regard to the person's satisfactory compliance with the contact order or any contact order that has effect in its place, it would be appropriate for the enforcement order to be revoked.

(3) The enforcement order may be revoked by the court under subparagraph (2) of its own motion or on an application by the person subject to the enforcement order.

(4) In deciding whether to revoke the enforcement order under subparagraph (2)(b), the court is to take into account—

    (a) the extent to which the person subject to the enforcement order has complied with it, and

    (b) the likelihood that the person will comply with the contact order or any contact order that has effect in its place in the absence of an enforcement order.

(5) In deciding whether to revoke the enforcement order under subparagraph (2)(c), the court is to take into account the likelihood that the person will comply with the contact order or any contact order that has effect in its place in the absence of an enforcement order.

Amendment by reason of change of residence

5.—(1) This paragraph applies where a court has made an enforcement order in respect of a person's failure to comply with a contact order and the enforcement order is in force.

(2) If the court is satisfied that the person has changed, or proposes to change, his residence from the local justice area specified in the order to another local justice area, the court may amend the order by substituting the other area for the area specified.

(3) The enforcement order may be amended by the court under subparagraph (2) of its own motion or on an application by the person subject to the enforcement order.

Amendment of hours specified under unpaid work requirement

6.—(1) This paragraph applies where a court has made an enforcement order in respect of a person's failure to comply with a contact order and the enforcement order is in force.

(2) If it appears to the court that, having regard to circumstances that have arisen since the enforcement order was made, it would be appropriate to do so, the court may reduce the number of hours specified in the order (but not below the minimum specified in section 199(2)(a) of the Criminal Justice Act 2003).

(3) In amending the enforcement order under sub-paragraph (2), the court must be satisfied that the effect on the person of the enforcement order as proposed to be amended is

no more than is required to secure his compliance with the contact order or any contact order that has effect in its place.

(4) The enforcement order may be amended by the court under subparagraph (2) of its own motion or on an application by the person subject to the enforcement order.

Amendment to extend unpaid work requirement

7.—(1) This paragraph applies where a court has made an enforcement order in respect of a person's failure to comply with a contact order and the enforcement order is in force.

(2) If it appears to the court that, having regard to circumstances that have arisen since the enforcement order was made, it would be appropriate to do so, the court may, in relation to the order, extend the period of twelve months specified in section 200(2) of the Criminal Justice Act 2003 (as substituted by paragraph 3).

(3) The period may be extended by the court under sub-paragraph (2) of its own motion or on an application by the person subject to the enforcement order.

Warning and report following breach

8.—(1) This paragraph applies where a court has made an enforcement order in respect of a person's failure to comply with a contact order.

(2) If the responsible officer is of the opinion that the person has failed without reasonable excuse to comply with the unpaid work requirement imposed by the enforcement order, the officer must give the person a warning under this paragraph unless—
>   (a) the person has within the previous twelve months been given a warning under this paragraph in relation to a failure to comply with the unpaid work requirement, or
>   (b) the responsible officer reports the failure to the appropriate person.

(3) A warning under this paragraph must—
>   (a) describe the circumstances of the failure,
>   (b) state that the failure is unacceptable, and
>   (c) inform the person that, if within the next twelve months he again fails to comply with the unpaid work requirement, the warning and the subsequent failure will be reported to the appropriate person.

(4) The responsible officer must, as soon as practicable after the warning has been given, record that fact.

(5) If—
>   (a) the responsible officer has given a warning under this paragraph to a person subject to an enforcement order, and
>   (b) at any time within the twelve months beginning with the date on which the warning was given, the responsible officer is of the opinion that the person has since that date failed without reasonable excuse to comply with the unpaid work requirement imposed by the enforcement order,

the officer must report the failure to the appropriate person.

(6) A report under sub-paragraph (5) must include a report of the warning given to the person subject to the enforcement order.

(7) The appropriate person, in relation to an enforcement order, is the officer of the Service or the Welsh family proceedings officer who is required under section 11M to report on matters relating to the enforcement order.

(8) 'Responsible officer', in relation to a person subject to an enforcement order, has the same meaning as in section 197 of the Criminal Justice Act 2003 (as modified by paragraph 2).

Breach of an enforcement order

9.—(1) This paragraph applies where a court has made an enforcement order ('the first order') in respect of a person's failure to comply with a contact order.

(2) If the court is satisfied beyond reasonable doubt that the person has failed to comply with the unpaid work requirement imposed by the first order, the court may—

 (a) amend the first order so as to make the requirement more onerous, or

 (b) make an enforcement order ('the second order') in relation to the person and (if the first order is still in force) provide for the second order to have effect either in addition to or in substitution for the first order.

(3) But the court may not exercise its powers under sub-paragraph (2) if it is satisfied that the person had a reasonable excuse for failing to comply with the unpaid work requirement imposed by the first order.

(4) The burden of proof as to the matter mentioned in sub-paragraph (3) lies on the person claiming to have had a reasonable excuse, and the standard of proof is the balance of probabilities.

(5) The court may exercise its powers under sub-paragraph (2) in relation to the first order only on the application of a person who would be able to apply under section 11J for an enforcement order if the failure to comply with the first order were a failure to comply with the contact order to which the first order relates.

(6) Where the person proposing to apply to the court is the child with respect to whom the contact order was made, subsections (6) and (7) of section 11J have effect in relation to the application as they have effect in relation to an application for an enforcement order.

(7) An application to the court to exercise its powers under subparagraph (2) may only be made while the first order is in force.

(8) The court may not exercise its powers under sub-paragraph (2) in respect of a failure by the person to comply with the unpaid work requirement imposed by the first order unless it is satisfied that before the failure occurred the person had been given (in accordance with rules of court) a copy of, or otherwise informed of the terms of, a notice under section 11N relating to the first order.

(9) In dealing with the person under sub-paragraph (2)(a), the court may—

 (a) increase the number of hours specified in the first order (but not above the maximum specified in section 199(2)(b) of the Criminal Justice Act 2003, as substituted by paragraph 3);

 (b) in relation to the order, extend the period of twelve months specified in section 200(2) of the Criminal Justice Act 2003 (as substituted by paragraph 3).

(10) In exercising its powers under sub-paragraph (2), the court must be satisfied that, taking into account the extent to which the person has complied with the unpaid work requirement imposed by the first order, the effect on the person of the proposed exercise of those powers—

 (a) is no more than is required to secure his compliance with the contact order or any contact order that has effect in its place, and

 (b) is no more than is proportionate to the seriousness of his failures to comply with the contact order and the first order.

(11) Where the court exercises its powers under sub-paragraph (2) by making an enforcement order in relation to a person who has failed to comply with another enforcement order—

 (a) sections 11K(4), 11L(2) to (7), 11M and 11N have effect as regards the making of the order in relation to the person as they have effect as regards the making of an enforcement order in relation to a person who has failed to comply with a contact order;

 (b) this Part of this Schedule has effect in relation to the order so made as if it were an enforcement order made in respect of the failure for which the other order was made.

(12) Sub-paragraph (2) is without prejudice to section 63(3) of the Magistrates' Courts Act 1980 as it applies in relation to enforcement orders.

Provision relating to amendment of enforcement orders

10. Sections 11L(2) to (7) and 11M have effect in relation to the making of an order under paragraph 6(2), 7(2) or 9(2)(a) amending an enforcement order as they have effect in relation to the making of an enforcement order; and references in sections 11L(2) to (7) and 11M to an enforcement order are to be read accordingly.

Section 15(1)   SCHEDULE 1

FINANCIAL PROVISION FOR CHILDREN

Orders for financial relief against parents

1.—(1) On an application made by a parent, guardian or special guardian of a child, or by any person in whose favour a residence order is in force with respect to a child, the court may—

  (a) in the case of an application to the High Court or a county court, make one or more of the orders mentioned in sub-paragraph (2);
  (b) in the case of an application to a magistrates' court, make one or both of the orders mentioned in paragraphs (a) and (c) of that sub-paragraph.

(2) The orders referred to in sub-paragraph (1) are—

  (a) an order requiring either or both parents of a child—
    (i) to make to the applicant for the benefit of the child; or
    (ii) to make to the child himself, such periodical payments, for such term, as may be specified in the order;
  (b) an order requiring either or both parents of a child—
    (i) to secure to the applicant for the benefit of the child; or
    (ii) to secure to the child himself, such periodical payments, for such term, as may be so specified;
  (c) an order requiring either or both parents of a child—
    (i) to pay to the applicant for the benefit of the child; or
    (ii) to pay to the child himself, such lump sum as may be so specified;
  (d) an order requiring a settlement to be made for the benefit of the child, and to the satisfaction of the court, of property—
    (i) to which either parent is entitled (either in possession or in reversion); and
    (ii) which is specified in the order;
  (e) an order requiring either or both parents of a child—
    (i) to transfer to the applicant, for the benefit of the child; or
    (ii) to transfer to the child himself, such property to which the parent is, or the parents are, entitled (either in possession or in reversion) as may be specified in the order.

(3) The powers conferred by this paragraph may be exercised at any time.

(4) An order under sub-paragraph (2)(a) or (b) may be varied or discharged by a subsequent order made on the application of any person by or to whom payments were required to be made under the previous order.

(5) Where a court makes an order under this paragraph—

  (a) it may at any time make a further such order under sub-paragraph (2)(a), (b) or (c) with respect to the child concerned if he has not reached the age of eighteen;
  (b) it may not make more than one order under sub-paragraph (2)(d) or (e) against the same person in respect of the same child.

(6) On making, varying or discharging a residence order or a special guardianship order the court may exercise any of its powers under this Schedule even though no application has been made to it under this Schedule.

(7) Where a child is a ward of court, the court may exercise any of its powers under this Schedule even though no application has been made to it.

Orders for financial relief for persons over eighteen

2.—(1) If, on an application by a person who has reached the age of eighteen, it appears to the court—

- (a) that the applicant is, will be or (if an order were made under this paragraph) would be receiving instruction at an educational establishment or undergoing training for a trade, profession or vocation, whether or not while in gainful employment; or
- (b) that there are special circumstances which justify the making of an order under this paragraph,

the court may make one or both of the orders mentioned in sub-paragraph (2).

(2) The orders are—

- (a) an order requiring either or both of the applicant's parents to pay to the applicant such periodical payments, for such term, as may be specified in the order;
- (b) an order requiring either or both of the applicant's parents to pay to the applicant such lump sum as may be so specified.

(3) An application may not be made under this paragraph by any person if, immediately before he reached the age of sixteen, a periodical payments order was in force with respect to him.

(4) No order shall be made under this paragraph at a time when the parents of the applicant are living with each other in the same household.

(5) An order under sub-paragraph (2)(a) may be varied or discharged by a subsequent order made on the application of any person by or to whom payments were required to be made under the previous order.

(6) In sub-paragraph (3) 'periodical payments order' means an order made under—

- (a) this Schedule;
- (c) section 23 or 27 of the Matrimonial Causes Act 1973;
- (d) Part I of the Domestic Proceedings and Magistrates' Courts Act 1978,
- (e) Part 1 or 9 of Schedule 5 to the Civil Partnership Act 2004 (financial relief in the High Court or a county court etc.)
- (f) Schedule 6 to the 2004 Act (financial relief in the magistrates' courts etc.),

for the making or securing of periodical payments.

(7) The powers conferred by this paragraph shall be exercisable at any time.

(8) Where the court makes an order under this paragraph it may from time to time while that order remains in force make a further such order.

Duration of orders for financial relief

3.—(1) The term to be specified in an order for periodical payments made under paragraph 1(2)(a) or (b) in favour of a child may begin with the date of the making of an application for the order in question or any later date or a date ascertained in accordance with sub-paragraph (5) or (6) but—

- (a) shall not in the first instance extend beyond the child's seventeenth birthday unless the court thinks it right in the circumstances of the case to specify a later date; and
- (b) shall not in any event extend beyond the child's eighteenth birthday.

(2) Paragraph (b) of sub-paragraph (1) shall not apply in the case of a child if it appears to the court that—

- (a) the child is, or will be or (if an order were made without complying with that paragraph) would be receiving instruction at an educational establishment or undergoing training for a trade, profession or vocation, whether or not while in gainful employment; or

(b) there are special circumstances which justify the making of an order without complying with that paragraph.

(3) An order for periodical payments made under paragraph 1(2)(a) or 2(2)(a) shall, notwithstanding anything in the order, cease to have effect on the death of the person liable to make payments under the order.

(4) Where an order is made under paragraph 1(2)(a) or (b) requiring periodical payments to be made or secured to the parent of a child, the order shall cease to have effect if—

(a) any parent making or securing the payments; and

(b) any parent to whom the payments are made or secured,

live together for a period of more than six months.

(5) Where—

(a) a maintenance calculation ('the current calculation') is in force with respect to a child; and

(b) an application is made for an order under paragraph 1(2)(a) or (b) of this Schedule for periodical payments in favour of that child—

(i) in accordance with section 8 of the Child support Act 1991; and

(ii) before the end of the period of 6 months beginning with the making of the current calculation,

the term to be specified in any such order made on that application may be expressed to begin on, or at any time after, the earliest permitted date.

(6) For the purposes of subsection (5) above, 'the earliest permitted date' is which-ever is the later of—

(a) the date 6 months before the application is made; or

(b) the date on which the current calculation took effect or, where successive maintenance calculations have been continuously in force with respect to a child, on which the first of those calculations took effect.

(7) Where—

(a) a maintenance calculation ceases to have effect by or under any provision of the Child Support Act 1991, and

(b) an application is made, before the end of the period of 6 months beginning with the relevant date, for an order for periodical payments under paragraph 1(2)(a) or (b) in favour of a child with respect to whom that maintenance calculation was in force immediately before it ceased to have effect,

the term to be specified in any such order, or in any interim order under paragraph 9, made on that application may begin with the date on which that maintenance calculation ceased to have effect, or any later date.

(8) In subsection (7)(b)—

(a) where the maintenance calculation ceased to have effect, the relevant date is the date on which it so ceased.

Matters to which court is to have regard in making orders for financial relief

4.—(1) In deciding whether to exercise its powers under paragraph 1 or 2, and if so in what manner, the court shall have regard to all the circumstances including—

(a) the income, earning capacity, property and other financial resources which each person mentioned in sub-paragraph (3) has or is likely to have in the foreseeable future;

(b) the financial needs, obligations and responsibilities which each person mentioned in sub-paragraph (3) has or is likely to have in the foreseeable future;

(c) the financial needs of the child;

(d) the income, earning capacity (if any), property and other financial resources of the child;

(e) any physical or mental disability of the child;

    (f) the manner in which the child was being, or was expected to be, educated or trained.

  (2) In deciding whether to exercise its powers under paragraph 1 against a person who is not the mother or father of the child, and if so in what manner, the court shall in addition have regard to—

    (a) whether that person had assumed responsibility for the maintenance of the child and, if so, the extent to which and basis on which he assumed that responsibility and the length of the period during which he met that responsibility;

    (b) whether he did so knowing that the child was not his child;

    (c) the liability of any other person to maintain the child.

  (3) Where the court makes an order under paragraph 1 against a person who is not the father of the child, it shall record in the order that the order is made on the basis that the person against whom the order is made is not the child's father.

  (4) The persons mentioned in sub-paragraph (1) are—

    (a) in relation to a decision whether to exercise its powers under paragraph 1, any parent of the child;

    (b) in relation to a decision whether to exercise its powers under paragraph 2, the mother and father of the child;

    (c) the applicant for the order;

    (d) any other person in whose favour the court proposes to make the order.

Provisions relating to lump sums

  5.—(1) Without prejudice to the generality of paragraph 1, an order under that paragraph for the payment of a lump sum may be made for the purpose of enabling any liabilities or expenses—

    (a) incurred in connection with the birth of the child or in maintaining the child; and

    (b) reasonably incurred before the making of the order,

to be met.

  (2) The amount of any lump sum required to be paid by an order made by a magistrates' court under paragraph 1 or 2 shall not exceed £1000 or such larger amount as the Lord Chancellor may, after consulting the Lord Chief Justice, from time to time by order fix for the purposes of this sub-paragraph.

  (3) The power of the court under paragraph 1 or 2 to vary or discharge an order for the making or securing of periodical payments by a parent shall include power to make an order under that provision for the payment of a lump sum by that parent.

  (4) The amount of any lump sum which a parent may be required to pay by virtue of sub-paragraph (3) shall not, in the case of an order made by a magistrates' court, exceed the maximum amount that may at the time of the making of the order be required to be paid under sub-paragraph (2), but a magistrates' court may make an order for the payment of a lump sum not exceeding that amount even though the parent was required to pay a lump sum by a previous order under this Act.

  (5) An order made under paragraph 1 or 2 for the payment of a lump sum may provide for the payment of that sum by instalments.

  (6) Where the court provides for the payment of a lump sum by instalments the court, on an application made either by the person liable to pay or the person entitled to receive that sum, shall have power to vary that order by varying—

    (a) the number of instalments payable;

    (b) the amount of any instalment payable;

    (c) the date on which any instalment becomes payable.

  (7) The Lord Chief Justice may nominate a judicial office holder (as defined in section 109(4) of the Constitutional Reform Act 2005) to exercise his functions under this paragraph.

Variation etc. of orders for periodical payments

6.—(1) In exercising its powers under paragraph 1 or 2 to vary or discharge an order for the making or securing of periodical payments the court shall have regard to all the circumstances of the case, including any change in any of the matters to which the court was required to have regard when making the order.

(2) The power of the court under paragraph 1 or 2 to vary an order for the making or securing of periodical payments shall include power to suspend any provision of the order temporarily and to revive any provision so suspended.

(3) Where on an application under paragraph 1 or 2 for the variation or discharge of an order for the making or securing of periodical payments the court varies the payments required to be made under that order, the court may provide that the payments as so varied shall be made from such date as the court may specify, except that, subject to sub-paragraph (9), the date shall not be earlier than the date of the making of the application.

(4) An application for the variation of an order made under paragraph 1 for the making or securing of periodical payments to or for the benefit of a child may, if the child has reached the age of sixteen, be made by the child himself.

(5) Where an order for the making or securing of periodical payments made under paragraph 1 ceases to have effect on the date on which the child reaches the age of sixteen, or at any time after that date but before or on the date on which he reaches the age of eighteen, the child may apply to the court which made the order for an order for its revival.

(6) If on such an application it appears to the court that—

    (a) the child is, will be or (if an order were made under this sub-paragraph) would be receiving instruction at an educational establishment or undergoing training for a trade, profession or vocation, whether or not while in gainful employment; or

    (b) there are special circumstances which justify the making of an order under this paragraph,

the court shall have power by order to revive the order from such date as the court may specify, not being earlier than the date of the making of the application.

(7) Any order which is revived by an order under sub-paragraph (5) may be varied or discharged under that provision, on the application of any person by whom or to whom payments are required to be made under the revived order.

(8) An order for the making or securing of periodical payments made under paragraph 1 or 2 may be varied or discharged, after the death of either parent, on the application of a guardian or special guardian of the child concerned.

(9) Where—

    (a) an order under paragraph 1(2)(a) or (b) for the making or securing of periodical payments in favour of more than one child ('the order') is in force;

    (b) the order requires payments specified in it to be made to or for the benefit of more than one child without apportioning those payments between them;

    (c) a maintenance calculation ('the calculation') is made with respect to one or more, but not all, of the children with respect to whom those payments are to be made; and

    (d) an application is made, before the end of the period of 6 months beginning with the date on which the calculation was made, for the variation or discharge of the order,

the court may, in exercise of its powers under paragraph 1 to vary or discharge the order, direct that the variation or discharge shall take effect from the date on which the calculation took effect or any later date.

Variation of orders for periodical payments etc. made by magistrates' courts

6A.—(1) Subject to sub-paragraphs (7) and (8), the power of a magistrates' court—

    (a) under paragraph 1 or 2 to vary an order for the making of periodical payments, or

    (b) under paragraph 5(6) to vary an order for the payment of a lump sum by instalments, shall include power, if the court is satisfied that payment has not been made in accordance with the order, to exercise one of its powers under paragraphs (a) to (d) of section 59(3) of the Magistrates' Courts Act 1980.

(2) In any case where—

> (a) a magistrates' court has made an order under this Schedule for the making of periodical payments or for the payment of a lump sum by instalments, and
>
> (b) payments under the order are required to be made by any method of payment falling within section 59(6) of the Magistrates' Courts Act 1980 (standing order, etc.),

any person entitled to make an application under this Schedule for the variation of the order (in this paragraph referred to as 'the applicant') may apply to a magistrates' court acting in the same local justice area as the court which made the order for the order to be varied as mentioned in sub-paragraph (3).

(3) Subject to sub-paragraph (5), where an application is made under subparagraph (2), a justices' clerk, after giving written notice (by post or otherwise) of the application to any interested party and allowing that party, within the period of 14 days beginning with the date of the giving of that notice, an opportunity to make written representations, may vary the order to provide that payments under the order shall be made to the designated officer for the court.

(4) The clerk may proceed with an application under sub-paragraph (2) notwithstanding that any such interested party as is referred to in sub-paragraph (3) has not received written notice of the application.

(5) Where an application has been made under sub-paragraph (2), the clerk may, if he considers it inappropriate to exercise his power under sub-paragraph (3), refer the matter to the court which, subject to sub-paragraphs (7) and (8), may vary the order by exercising one of its powers under paragraphs (a) to (d) of section 59(3) of the Magistrates' Courts Act 1980.

(6) Subsection (4) of section 59 of the Magistrates' Courts Act 1980 (power of court to order that account be opened) shall apply for the purposes of sub-paragraphs (1) and (5) as it applies for the purposes of that section.

(7) Before varying the order by exercising one of its powers under paragraphs (a) to (d) of section 59(3) of the Magistrates' Courts Act 1980, the court shall have regard to any representations made by the parties to the application.

(8) If the court does not propose to exercise its power under paragraph (c), (cc) or (d) of subsection (3) of section 59 of the Magistrates' Courts Act 1980, the court shall, unless upon representations expressly made in that behalf by the applicant for the order it is satisfied that it is undesirable to do so, exercise its power under paragraph (b) of that subsection.

(9) None of the powers of the court, or of a justices' clerk, conferred by this paragraph shall be exercisable in relation to an order under this Schedule for the making of periodical payments, or for the payment of a lump sum by instalments, which is not a qualifying maintenance order (within the meaning of section 59 of the Magistrates' Courts Act 1980).

(10) In sub-paragraphs (3) and (4) 'interested party', in relation to an application made by the applicant under sub-paragraph (2), means a person who would be entitled to be a party to an application for the variation of the order made by the applicant under any other provision of this Schedule if such an application were made.

Variation of orders for secured periodical payments after death of parent

7.—(1) Where the parent liable to make payments under a secured periodical payments order has died, the persons who may apply for the variation or discharge of the order shall include the personal representatives of the deceased parent.

(2) No application for the variation of the order shall, except with the permission of the court, be made after the end of the period of six months from the date on which representation in regard to the estate of that parent is first taken out.

(3) The personal representatives of a deceased person against whom a secured periodical payments order was made shall not be liable for having distributed any part of the estate of the deceased after the end of the period of six months referred to in sub-paragraph (2) on the ground that they ought to have taken into account the possibility that the court might permit an application for variation to be made after that period by the person entitled to payments under the order.

(4) Sub-paragraph (3) shall not prejudice any power to recover any part of the estate so distributed arising by virtue of the variation of an order in accordance with this paragraph.

(5) Where an application to vary a secured periodical payments order is made after the death of the parent liable to make payments under the order, the circumstances to which the court is required to have regard under paragraph 6(1) shall include the changed circumstances resulting from the death of the parent.

(6) In considering for the purposes of sub-paragraph (2) the question when representation was first taken out, a grant limited to settled land or to trust property shall be left out of account and a grant limited to real estate or to personal estate shall be left out of account unless a grant limited to the remainder of the estate has previously been made or is made at the same time.

(7) In this paragraph 'secured periodical payments order' means an order for secured periodical payments under paragraph 1(2)(b).

Financial relief under other enactments

8.—(1) This paragraph applies where a residence order or a special guardianship order is made with respect to a child at a time when there is in force an order ('the financial relief order') made under any enactment other than this Act and requiring a person to contribute to the child's maintenance.

(2) Where this paragraph applies, the court may, on the application of—

(a) any person required by the financial relief order to contribute to the child's maintenance; or

(b) any person in whose favour a residence order with respect to the child is in force,

make an order revoking the financial relief order, or varying it by altering the amount of any sum payable under that order or by substituting the applicant for the person to whom any such sum is otherwise payable under that order.

Interim orders

9.—(1) Where an application is made under paragraph 1 or 2 the court may, at any time before it disposes of the application, make an interim order—

(a) requiring either or both parents to make such periodical payments, at such times and for such term as the court thinks fit; and

(b) giving any direction which the court thinks fit.

(2) An interim order made under this paragraph may provide for payments to be made from such date as the court may specify, except that, subject to paragraph 3(5) and (6), the date shall not be earlier than the date of the making of the application under paragraph 1 or 2.

(3) An interim order made under this paragraph shall cease to have effect when the application is disposed of or, if earlier, on the date specified for the purposes of this paragraph in the interim order.

(4) An interim order in which a date has been specified for the purposes of sub-paragraph (3) may be varied by substituting a later date.

Alteration of maintenance agreements

10.—(1) In this paragraph and in paragraph 11 'maintenance agreement' means any agreement in writing made with respect to a child, whether before or after the commencement of this paragraph, which—

(a) is or was made between the father and mother of the child; and

(b) contains provision with respect to the making or securing of payments, or the disposition or use of any property, for the maintenance or education of the child, and any such provisions are in this paragraph, and paragraph 11, referred to as 'financial arrangements'.

(2) Where a maintenance agreement is for the time being subsisting and each of the parties to the agreement is for the time being either domiciled or resident in England and Wales, then, either party may apply to the court for an order under this paragraph.

(3) If the court to which the application is made is satisfied either—

(a) that, by reason of a change in the circumstances in the light of which any financial arrangements contained in the agreement were made (including a change foreseen by the parties when making the agreement), the agreement should be altered so as to make different financial arrangements; or

(b) that the agreement does not contain proper financial arrangements with respect to the child,

then that court may by order make such alterations in the agreement by varying or revoking any financial arrangements contained in it as may appear to it to be just having regard to all the circumstances.

(4) If the maintenance agreement is altered by an order under this paragraph, the agreement shall have effect thereafter as if the alteration had been made by agreement between the parties and for valuable consideration.

(5) Where a court decides to make an order under this paragraph altering the maintenance agreement—

(a) by inserting provision for the making or securing by one of the parties to the agreement of periodical payments for the maintenance of the child; or

(b) by increasing the rate of periodical payments required to be made or secured by one of the parties for the maintenance of the child,

then, in deciding the term for which under the agreement as altered by the order the payments or (as the case may be) the additional payments attributable to the increase are to be made or secured for the benefit of the child, the court shall apply the provisions of sub-paragraphs (1) and (2) of paragraph 3 as if the order were an order under paragraph 1(2)(a) or (b).

(6) A magistrates' court shall not entertain an application under subparagraph (2) unless both the parties to the agreement are resident in England and Wales and the court acts in, or is authorised by the Lord Chancellor to act for, a local justice area in which at least one of the parties is resident, and shall not have power to make any order on such an application except—

(a) in a case where the agreement contains no provision for periodical payments by either of the parties, an order inserting provision for the making by one of the parties of periodical payments for the maintenance of the child;

(b) in a case where the agreement includes provision for the making by one of the parties of periodical payments, an order increasing or reducing the rate of, or terminating, any of those payments.

(7) For the avoidance of doubt it is hereby declared that nothing in this paragraph affects any power of a court before which any proceedings between the parties to a maintenance agreement are brought under any other enactment to make an order containing financial arrangements or any right of either party to apply for such an order in such proceedings.

11.—(1) Where a maintenance agreement provides for the continuation, after the death of one of the parties, of payments for the maintenance of a child and that party dies domiciled in England and Wales, the surviving party or the personal representatives of the deceased party may apply to the High Court or a county court for an order under paragraph 10.

(2) If a maintenance agreement is altered by a court on an application under this paragraph, the agreement shall have effect thereafter as if the alteration had been made, immediately before the death, by agreement between the parties and for valuable consideration.

(3) An application under this paragraph shall not, except with leave of the High Court or a county court, be made after the end of the period of six months beginning with the day on which representation in regard to the estate of the deceased is first taken out.

(4) In considering for the purposes of sub-paragraph (3) the question when representation was first taken out, a grant limited to settled land or to trust property shall be left out of account and a grant limited to real estate or to personal estate shall be left out of account unless a grant limited to the remainder of the estate has previously been made or is made at the same time.

(5) A county court shall not entertain an application under this paragraph, or an application for leave to make an application under this paragraph, unless it would have jurisdiction to hear and determine proceedings for an order under section 2 of the Inheritance (Provision for Family and Dependants) Act 1975 in relation to the deceased's estate by virtue of section 25 of the County Courts Act 1984 (jurisdiction under the Act of 1975).

(6) The provisions of this paragraph shall not render the personal representatives of the deceased liable for having distributed any part of the estate of the deceased after the expiry of the period of six months referred to in sub-paragraph (3) on the ground that they ought to have taken into account the possibility that a court might grant leave for an application by virtue of this paragraph to be made by the surviving party after that period.

(7) Sub-paragraph (6) shall not prejudice any power to recover any part of the estate so distributed arising by virtue of the making of an order in pursuance of this paragraph.

Enforcement of orders for maintenance

12.—(1) Any person for the time being under an obligation to make payments in pursuance of any order for the payment of money made by a magistrates' court under this Act shall give notice of any change of address to such person (if any) as may be specified in the order.

(2) Any person failing without reasonable excuse to give such a notice shall be guilty of an offence and liable on summary conviction to a fine not exceeding level 2 on the standard scale.

(3) An order for the payment of money made by a magistrates' court under this Act shall be enforceable as a magistrates' court maintenance order within the meaning of section 150(1) of the Magistrates' Courts Act 1980.

Direction for settlement of instrument by conveyancing counsel

13. Where the High Court or a county court decides to make an order under this Act for the securing of periodical payments or for the transfer or settlement of property, it may direct that the matter be referred to one of the conveyancing counsel of the court to settle a proper instrument to be executed by all necessary parties.

Financial provision for child resident in country outside England and Wales

14.—(1) Where one parent of a child lives in England and Wales and the child lives outside England and Wales with—

(a) another parent of his;

(b) a guardian or a special guardian of his; or

(c) a person in whose favour a residence order is in force with respect to the child,

the court shall have power, on an application made by any of the persons mentioned in paragraphs (a) to (c), to make one or both of the orders mentioned in paragraph 1(2)(a) and (b) against the parent living in England and Wales.

(2) Any reference in this Act to the powers of the court under paragraph 1(2) or to an order made under paragraph 1(2) shall include a reference to the powers which the court has by virtue of sub-paragraph (1) or (as the case may be) to an order made by virtue of sub-paragraph (1).

Local authority contribution to child's maintenance

15.—(1) Where a child lives, or is to live, with a person as the result of a residence order, a local authority may make contributions to that person towards the cost of the accommodation and maintenance of the child.

(2) Sub-paragraph (1) does not apply where the person with whom the child lives, or is to live, is a parent of the child or the husband or wife or civil partner of a parent of the child.

Interpretation

16.—(1) In this Schedule 'child' includes, in any case where an application is made under paragraph 2 or 6 in relation to a person who has reached the age of eighteen, that person.

(2) In this Schedule, except paragraphs 2 and 15, 'parent' includes—

(a) any party to a marriage (whether or not subsisting) in relation to whom the child concerned is a child of the family, and

(b) any civil partner in a civil partnership (whether or not subsisting) in relation to whom the child concerned is a child of the family;

and for this purpose any reference to either parent or both parents shall be read as a reference to any parent of his and to all of his parents.

(3) In this Schedule, 'maintenance calculation' has the same meaning as it has in the Child Support Act 1991 by virtue of section 54 of that Act as read with any regulations in force under that section.

SCHEDULE 2

LOCAL AUTHORITY SUPPORT FOR CHILDREN AND FAMILIES

PART I   PROVISION OF SERVICES FOR FAMILIES

Identification of children in need and provision of information

1.—(1) Every local authority shall take reasonable steps to identify the extent to which there are children in need within their area.

(2) Every local authority shall—

(a) publish information—

(i) about services provided by them under sections 17, 18, 20, 23B to 23D, 24A and 24B; and

(ii) where they consider it appropriate, about the provision by others (including, in particular, voluntary organisations) of services which the authority have power to provide under those sections; and

(b) take such steps as are reasonably practicable to ensure that those who might benefit from the services receive the information relevant to them.

Maintenance of a register of disabled children

2.—(1) Every local authority shall open and maintain a register of disabled children within their area.

(2) The register may be kept by means of a computer.

Assessment of children's needs

3. Where it appears to a local authority that a child within their area is in need, the authority may assess his needs for the purposes of this Act at the same time as any assessment of his needs is made under—

(a) the Chronically Sick and Disabled Persons Act 1970;

(b) Part IV of the Education Act 1996;
(c) the Disabled Persons (Services, Consultation and Representation) Act 1986; or
(d) any other enactment.

Prevention of neglect and abuse

4.—(1) Every local authority shall take reasonable steps, through the provision of services under Part III of this Act, to prevent children within their area suffering ill-treatment or neglect.
(2) Where a local authority believe that a child who is at any time within their area—
(a) is likely to suffer harm; but
(b) lives or proposes to live in the area of another local authority
they shall inform that other local authority.
(3) When informing that other local authority they shall specify—
(a) the harm that they believe he is likely to suffer; and
(b) (if they can) where the child lives or proposes to live.

Provision of accommodation in order to protect child

5.—(1) Where—
(a) it appears to a local authority that a child who is living on particular premises is suffering, or is likely to suffer, ill treatment at the hands of another person who is living on those premises; and
(b) that other person proposes to move from the premises, the authority may assist that other person to obtain alternative accommodation.
(2) Assistance given under this paragraph may be in cash.
(3) Subsections (7) to (9) of section 17 shall apply in relation to assistance given under this paragraph as they apply in relation to assistance given under that section.

Provision for disabled children

6. Every local authority shall provide services designed—
(a) to minimise the effect on disabled children within their area of their disabilities; and
(b) to give such children the opportunity to lead lives which are as normal as possible.

Provision to reduce need for care proceedings etc.

7. Every local authority shall take reasonable steps designed—
(a) to reduce the need to bring—
(i) proceedings for care or supervision orders with respect to children within their area;
(ii) criminal proceedings against such children;
(iii) any family or other proceedings with respect to such children which might lead to them being placed in the authority's care; or
(iv) proceedings under the inherent jurisdiction of the High Court with respect to children;
(b) to encourage children within their area not to commit criminal offences; and
(c) to avoid the need for children within their area to be placed in secure accommodation.

Provision for children living with their families

8. Every local authority shall make such provision as they consider appropriate for the following services to be available with respect to children in need within their area while they are living with their families—
(a) advice, guidance and counselling;

    (b) occupational, social, cultural or recreational activities;

    (c) home help (which may include laundry facilities);

    (d) facilities for, or assistance with, travelling to and from home for the purpose of taking advantage of any other service provided under this Act or of any similar service;

    (e) assistance to enable the child concerned and his family to have a holiday.

Family centres

    9.—(1) Every local authority shall provide such family centres as they consider appropriate in relation to children within their area.

    (2) 'Family centre' means a centre at which any of the persons mentioned in sub-paragraph (3) may—

    (a) attend for occupational, social, cultural or recreational activities;

    (b) attend for advice, guidance and counselling; or

    (c) be provided with accommodation while he is receiving advice, guidance or counselling.

    (3) The persons are—

    (a) a child;

    (b) his parents;

    (c) any person who is not a parent of his but who has parental responsibility for him;

    (d) any other person who is looking after him.

Maintenance of the family home

    10. Every local authority shall take such steps as are reasonably practicable, where any child within their area who is in need and whom they are not looking after is living apart from his family—

    (a) to enable him to live with his family; or

    (b) to promote contact between him and his family, if,

in their opinion, it is necessary to do so in order to safeguard or promote his welfare.

Duty to consider racial groups to which children in need belong

    11. Every local authority shall, in making any arrangements—

    (a) for the provision of day care within their area; or

    (b) designed to encourage persons to act as local authority foster parents, have regard to the different racial groups to which children within their area who are in need belong.

PART II   CHILDREN LOOKED AFTER BY LOCAL AUTHORITIES

Regulations as to placing of children with local authority foster parents

    12. Regulations under section 23(2)(a) may, in particular, make provision—

    (a) with regard to the welfare of children placed with local authority foster parents;

    (b) as to the arrangements to be made by local authorities in connection with the health and education of such children;

    (c) as to the records to be kept by local authorities;

    (d) for securing that a child is not placed with a local authority foster parent unless that person is for the time being approved as a local authority foster parent by such local authority as may be prescribed;

(e) for securing that where possible the local authority foster parent with whom a child is to be placed is—

    (i)   of the same religious persuasion as the child; or

    (ii) gives an undertaking that the child will be brought up in that religious persuasion;

(f) for securing that children placed with local authority foster parents, and the premises in which they are accommodated, will be supervised and inspected by a local authority and that the children will be removed from those premises if their welfare appears to require it;

(g) as to the circumstances in which local authorities may make arrangements for duties imposed on them by the regulations to be discharged, on their behalf.

Regulations as to arrangements under section 23(2)(f)

13. Regulations under section 23(2)(f) may, in particular, make provision as to—

(a) the persons to be notified of any proposed arrangements;

(b) the opportunities such persons are to have to make representations in relation to the arrangements proposed;

(c) the persons to be notified of any proposed changes in arrangements;

(d) the records to be kept by local authorities;

(e) the supervision by local authorities of any arrangements made.

Regulations as to conditions under which child in care is allowed to live with parent, etc.

14. Regulations under section 23(5) may, in particular, impose requirements on a local authority as to—

(a) the making of any decision by a local authority to allow a child to live with any person falling within section 23(4) (including requirements as to those who must be consulted before the decision is made, and those who must be notified when it has been made);

(b) the supervision or medical examination of the child concerned;

(c) the removal of the child, in such circumstances as may be prescribed, from the care of the person with whom he has been allowed to live;

(d) the records to be kept by local authorities.

Promotion and maintenance of contact between child and family

15.—(1) Where a child is being looked after by a local authority, the authority shall, unless it is not reasonably practicable or consistent with his welfare, endeavour to promote contact between the child and—

(a) his parents;

(b) any person who is not a parent of his but who has parental responsibility for him; and

(c) any relative, friend or other person connected with him.

(2) Where a child is being looked after by a local authority—

(a) the authority shall take such steps as are reasonably practicable to secure that—

    (i)   his parents; and

    (ii) any person who is not a parent of his but who has parental responsibility for him, are kept informed of where he is being accommodated; and

(b) every such person shall secure that the authority are kept informed of his or her address.

(3) Where a local authority ('the receiving authority') take over the provision of accommodation for a child from another local authority ('the transferring authority') under section 20(2)—

(a) the receiving authority shall (where reasonably practicable) inform—
    (i)   the child's parents; and
    (ii) any person who is not a parent of his but who has parental responsibility for him;
(b) sub-paragraph (2)(a) shall apply to the transferring authority, as well as the receiving authority, until at least one such person has been informed of the change; and
(c) sub-paragraph (2)(b) shall not require any person to inform the receiving authority of his address until he has been so informed.

(4) Nothing in this paragraph requires a local authority to inform any person of the whereabouts of a child if—
(a) the child is in the care of the authority; and
(b) the authority has reasonable cause to believe that informing the person would prejudice the child's welfare.

(5) Any person who fails (without reasonable excuse) to comply with sub-paragraph (2)(b) shall be guilty of an offence and liable on summary conviction to a fine not exceeding level 2 on the standard scale.

(6) It shall be a defence in any proceedings under sub-paragraph (5) to prove that the defendant was residing at the same address as another person who was the child's parent or had parental responsibility for the child and had reasonable cause to believe that the other person had informed the appropriate authority that both of them were residing at that address.

Visits to or by children: expenses

16.—(1) This paragraph applies where—
(a) a child is being looked after by a local authority; and
(b) the conditions mentioned in sub-paragraph (3) are satisfied.
(2) The authority may—
(a) make payments to—
    (i)   a parent of the child;
    (ii) any person who is not a parent of his but who has parental responsibility for him; or
    (iii) any relative, friend or other person connected with him, in respect of travelling, subsistence or other expenses incurred by that person in visiting the child; or
(b) make payments to the child, or to any person on his behalf, in respect of travelling, subsistence or other expenses incurred by or on behalf of the child in his visiting—
    (i)   a parent of his;
    (ii) any person who is not a parent of his but who has parental responsibility for him; or
    (iii) any relative, friend or other person connected with him.
(3) The conditions are that—
(a) it appears to the authority that the visit in question could not otherwise be made without undue financial hardship; and
(b) the circumstances warrant the making of the payments.

Appointment of visitor for child who is not being visited

17.—(1) Where it appears to a local authority in relation to any child that they are looking after that—
(a) communication between the child and—
    (i)   a parent of his; or
    (ii) any person who is not a parent of his but who has parental responsibility for him, has been infrequent; or

(b) he has not visited or been visited by (or lived with) any such person during the preceeding twelve months,

and that it would be in the child's best interests for an independent person to be appointed to be his visitor for the purposes of this paragraph, they shall appoint such a visitor.

(2) A person so appointed shall—

(a) have the duty of visiting, advising and befriending the child; and

(b) be entitled to recover from the authority who appointed him any reasonable expenses incurred by him for the purposes of his functions under this paragraph.

(3) A person's appointment as a visitor in pursuance of this paragraph shall be determined if—

(a) he gives notice in writing to the authority who appointed him that he resigns the appointment; or

(b) the authority give him notice in writing that they have terminated it.

(4) The determination of such an appointment shall not prejudice any duty under this paragraph to make a further appointment.

(5) Where a local authority propose to appoint a visitor for a child under this paragraph, the appointment shall not be made if—

(a) the child objects to it; and

(b) the authority are satisfied that he has sufficient understanding to make an informed decision.

(6) Where a visitor has been appointed for a child under this paragraph, the local authority shall determine the appointment if—

(a) the child objects to its continuing; and

(b) the authority are satisfied that he has sufficient understanding to make an informed decision.

(7) The Secretary of State may make regulations as to the circumstances in which a person appointed as a visitor under this paragraph is to be regarded as independent of the local authority appointing him.

Arrangements to assist children to live abroad

19.—(1) A local authority may only arrange for, or assist in arranging for, any child in their care to live outside England and Wales with the approval of the court.

(2) A local authority may, with the approval of every person who has parental responsibility for the child arrange for, or assist in arranging for, any other child looked after by them to live outside England and Wales.

(3) The court shall not give its approval under sub-paragraph (1) unless it is satisfied that—

(a) living outside England and Wales would be in the child's best interests;

(b) suitable arrangements have been, or will be, made for his reception and welfare in the country in which he will live;

(c) the child has consented to living in that country; and

(d) every person who has parental responsibility for the child has consented to his living in that country.

(4) Where the court is satisfied that the child does not have sufficient understanding to give or withhold his consent, it may disregard sub-paragraph (3)(c) and give its approval if the child is to live in the country concerned with a parent, guardian, special guardian, or other suitable person.

(5) Where a person whose consent is required by sub-paragraph (3)(d) fails to give his consent, the court may disregard that provision and give its approval if it is satisfied that that person—

(a) cannot be found;

(b) is incapable of consenting; or

(c) is withholding his consent unreasonably.

(6) Section 85 of the Adoption and Children Act 2002 (which imposes restrictions on taking children out of the United Kingdom) shall not apply in the case of any child who is to live outside England and Wales with the approval of the court given under this paragraph.

(7) Where a court decides to give its approval under this paragraph it may order that its decision is not to have effect during the appeal period.

(8) In sub-paragraph (7) 'the appeal period' means—

> (a) where an appeal is made against the decision, the period between the making of the decision and the determination of the appeal; and
>
> (b) otherwise, the period during which an appeal may be made against the decision.

(9) This paragraph does not apply to a local authority placing a child for adoption with prospective adopters.

Preparation for ceasing to be looked after

19A. It is the duty of the local authority looking after a child to advise, assist and befriend him with a view to promoting his welfare when they have ceased to look after him.

19B.—(1) A local authority shall have the following additional functions in relation to an eligible child whom they are looking after.

(2) In sub-paragraph (1) 'eligible child' means, subject to sub-paragraph (3), a child who—

> (a) is aged sixteen or seventeen; and
>
> (b) has been looked after by a local authority for a prescribed period, or periods amounting in all to a prescribed period, which began after he reached a prescribed age and ended after he reached the age of sixteen.

(3) The Secretary of State may prescribe—

> (a) additional categories of eligible children; and
>
> (b) categories of children who are not to be eligible children despite falling within sub-paragraph (2).

(4) For each eligible child, the local authority shall carry out an assessment of his needs with a view to determining what advice, assistance and support it would be appropriate for them to provide him under this Act—

> (a) while they are still looking after him; and
>
> (b) after they cease to look after him,

and shall then prepare a pathway plan for him.

(5) The local authority shall keep the pathway plan under regular review.

(6) Any such review may be carried out at the same time as a review of the child's case carried out by virtue of section 26.

(7) The Secretary of State may by regulations make provision as to assessments for the purposes of sub-paragraph (4).

(8) The regulations may in particular provide for the matters set out in section 23B(6).

Personal advisers

19C. A local authority shall arrange for each child whom they are looking after who is an eligible child for the purposes of paragraph 19B to have a personal adviser.

Death of children being looked after by local authorities

20.—(1) If a child who is being looked after by a local authority dies, the authority—

> (a) shall notify the Secretary of State and the Commission for Social Care Inspection;
>
> (b) shall, so far as is reasonably practicable, notify the child's parents and every person who is not a parent of his but who has parental responsibility for him;
>
> (c) may, with the consent (so far as it is reasonably practicable to obtain it) of every person who has parental responsibility for the child, arrange for the child's body to be buried or cremated; and

(d) may, if the conditions mentioned in sub-paragraph (2) are satisfied, make payments to any person who has parental responsibility for the child, or any relative, friend or other person connected with the child, in respect of travelling, subsistence or other expenses incurred by that person in attending the child's funeral.

(2) The conditions are that—

(a) it appears to the authority that the person concerned could not otherwise attend the child's funeral without undue financial hardship; and

(b) that the circumstances warrant the making of the payments.

(3) Sub-paragraph (1) does not authorise cremation where it does not accord with the practice of the child's religious persuasion.

(4) Where a local authority have exercised their power under sub-paragraph (1)(c) with respect to a child who was under sixteen when he died, they may recover from any parent of the child any expenses incurred by them.

(5) Any sums so recoverable shall, without prejudice to any other method of recovery, be recoverable summarily as a civil debt.

(6) Nothing in this paragraph affects any enactment regulating or authorising the burial, cremation or anatomical examination of the body of a deceased person.

PART III   CONTRIBUTIONS TOWARDS MAINTENANCE OF CHILDREN LOOKED AFTER BY LOCAL AUTHORITIES

Liability to contribute

21.—(1) Where a local authority are looking after a child (other than in the cases mentioned in sub-paragraph (7)) they shall consider whether they should recover contributions towards the child's maintenance from any person liable to contribute ('a contributor').

(2) An authority may only recover contributions from a contributor if they consider it reasonable to do so.

(3) The persons liable to contribute are—

(a) where the child is under sixteen, each of his parents;

(b) where he has reached the age of sixteen, the child himself.

(4) A parent is not liable to contribute during any period when he is in receipt of income support under the Social Security Contributions and Benefits Act 1992, of any element of child tax credit other than the family element, of working tax credit or of an income-based jobseeker's allowance.

(5) A person is not liable to contribute towards the maintenance of a child in the care of a local authority in respect of any period during which the child is allowed by the authority (under section 23(5)) to live with a parent of his.

(6) A contributor is not obliged to make any contribution towards a child's maintenance except as agreed or determined in accordance with this Part of this Schedule.

(7) The cases are where the child is looked after by a local authority under—

(a) section 21;

(b) an interim care order;

(c) section 92 of the Powers of Criminal Courts (Sentencing) Act 2000.

Agreed contributions

22.—(1) Contributions towards a child's maintenance may only be recovered if the local authority have served a notice ('a contribution notice') on the contributor specifying—

(a) the weekly sum which they consider that he should contribute; and

(b) arrangements for payment.

(2) The contribution notice must be in writing and dated.

(3) Arrangements for payment shall, in particular, include—

    (a) the date on which liability to contribute begins (which must not be earlier than the date of the notice);

    (b) the date on which liability under the notice will end (if the child has not before that date ceased to be looked after by the authority); and

    (c) the date on which the first payment is to be made.

(4) The authority may specify in a contribution notice a weekly sum which is a standard contribution determined by them for all children looked after by them.

(5) The authority may not specify in a contribution notice a weekly sum greater than that which they consider—

    (a) they would normally be prepared to pay if they had placed a similar child with local authority foster parents; and

    (b) it is reasonably practicable for the contributor to pay (having regard to his means).

(6) An authority may at any time withdraw a contribution notice (without prejudice to their power to serve another).

(7) Where the authority and the contributor agree—

    (a) the sum which the contributor is to contribute; and

    (b) arrangements for payment,

(whether as specified in the contribution notice or otherwise) and the contributor notifies the authority in writing that he so agrees, the authority may recover summarily as a civil debt any contribution which is overdue and unpaid.

(8) A contributor may, by serving a notice in writing on the authority, withdraw his agreement in relation to any period of liability falling after the date of service of the notice.

(9) Sub-paragraph (7) is without prejudice to any other method of recovery.

Contribution orders

23.—(1) Where a contributor has been served with a contribution notice and has—

    (a) failed to reach any agreement with the local authority as mentioned in paragraph 22(7) within the period of one month beginning with the day on which the contribution notice was served; or

    (b) served a notice under paragraph 22(8) withdrawing his agreement, the authority may apply to the court for an order under this paragraph.

(2) On such an application the court may make an order ('a contribution order') requiring the contributor to contribute a weekly sum towards the child's maintenance in accordance with arrangements for payment specified by the court.

(3) A contribution order—

    (a) shall not specify a weekly sum greater than that specified in the contribution notice; and

    (b) shall be made with due regard to the contributor's means.

(4) A contribution order shall not—

    (a) take effect before the date specified in the contribution notice; or

    (b) have effect while the contributor is not liable to contribute (by virtue of paragraph 21); or

    (c) remain in force after the child has ceased to be looked after by the authority who obtained the order.

(5) An authority may not apply to the court under sub-paragraph (1) in relation to a contribution notice which they have withdrawn.

(6) Where—

    (a) a contribution order is in force;

    (b) the authority serve another contribution notice; and

    (c) the contributor and the authority reach an agreement under paragraph 22(7) in respect of that other contribution notice, the effect of the agreement shall be to discharge the order from the date on which it is agreed that the agreement shall take effect.

(7) Where an agreement is reached under sub-paragraph (6) the authority shall notify the court—

(a) of the agreement; and

(b) of the date on which it took effect.

(8) A contribution order may be varied or revoked on the application of the contributor or the authority.

(9) In proceedings for the variation of a contribution order, the authority shall specify—

(a) the weekly sum which, having regard to paragraph 22, they propose that the contributor should contribute under the order as varied; and

(b) the proposed arrangements for payment.

(10) Where a contribution order is varied, the order—

(a) shall not specify a weekly sum greater than that specified by the authority in the proceedings for variation; and

(b) shall be made with due regard to the contributor's means.

(11) An appeal shall lie in accordance with rules of court from any order made under this paragraph.

Enforcement of contribution orders etc.

24.—(1) A contribution order made by a magistrates' court shall be enforceable as a magistrates' court maintenance order (within the meaning of section 150(1) of the Magistrates' Courts Act 1980).

(2) Where a contributor has agreed, or has been ordered, to make contributions to a local authority, any other local authority within whose area the contributor is for the time being living may—

(a) at the request of the local authority who served the contribution notice; and

(b) subject to agreement as to any sum to be deducted in respect of services rendered, collect from the contributor any contributions due on behalf of the authority who served the notice.

. . .

(4) The power to collect sums under sub-paragraph (2) includes the power to—

(a) receive and give a discharge for any contributions due; and

(b) (if necessary) enforce payment of any contributions,

even though those contributions may have fallen due at a time when the contributor was living elsewhere.

(5) Any contribution collected under sub-paragraph (2) shall be paid (subject to any agreed deduction) to the local authority who served the contribution notice.

(6) In any proceedings under this paragraph, a document which purports to be—

(a) a copy of an order made by a court under or by virtue of paragraph 23; and

(b) certified as a true copy by designated officer for the court, shall be evidence of the order.

(7) In any proceedings under this paragraph, a certificate which—

(a) purports to be signed by the clerk or some other duly authorised officer of the local authority who obtained the contribution order; and

(b) states that any sum due to the authority under the order is overdue and unpaid,

shall be evidence that the sum is overdue and unpaid.

Regulations

25. The Secretary of State may make regulations—

(a) as to the considerations which a local authority must take into account in deciding—

      (i)   whether it is reasonable to recover contributions; and

     (ii)   what the arrangements for payment should be;

  (b) as to the procedures they must follow in reaching agreements with—

      (i)   contributors (under paragraphs 22 and 23); and

     (ii)   any other local authority (under paragraph 23).

SCHEDULE 3

SUPERVISION ORDERS

PART I   GENERAL

Meaning of 'responsible person'

   1. In this Schedule, 'the responsible person', in relation to a supervised child, means—

  (a) any person who has parental responsibility for the child; and

  (b) any other person with whom the child is living.

Power of supervisor to give directions to supervised child

   2.—(1) A supervision order may require the supervised child to comply with any directions given from time to time by the supervisor which require him to do all or any of the following things—

  (a) to live at a place or places specified in the directions for a period or periods so specified;

  (b) to present himself to a person or persons specified in the directions at a place or places and on a day or days so specified;

  (c) to participate in activities specified in the directions on a day or days so specified.

   (2) It shall be for the supervisor to decide whether, and to what extent, he exercises his power to give directions and to decide the form of any directions which he gives.

   (3) Sub-paragraph (1) does not confer on a supervisor power to give directions in respect of any medical or psychiatric examination or treatment (which are matters dealt with in paragraphs 4 and 5).

Imposition of obligations on responsible person

   3.—(1) With the consent of any responsible person, a supervision order may include a requirement—

  (a) that he take all reasonable steps to ensure that the supervised child complies with any direction given by the supervisor under paragraph 2;

  (b) that he take all reasonable steps to ensure that the supervised child complies with any requirement included in the order under paragraph 4 or 5;

  (c) that he comply with any directions given by the supervisor requiring him to attend at a place specified in the directions for the purpose of taking part in activities so specified.

   (2) A direction given under sub-paragraph (1)(c) may specify the time at which the responsible person is to attend and whether or not the supervised child is required to attend with him.

   (3) A supervision order may require any person who is a responsible person in relation to the supervised child to keep the supervisor informed of his address, if it differs from the child's.

Psychiatric and medical examinations

   4.—(1) A supervision order may require the supervised child—

  (a) to submit to a medical or psychiatric examination; or

(b) to submit to any such examination from time to time as directed by the supervisor.

(2) Any such examination shall be required to be conducted—

    (a) by, or under the direction of, such registered medical practitioner as may be specified in the order;

    (b) at a place specified in the order and at which the supervised child is to attend as a non-resident patient; or

    (c) at—

        (i) a health service hospital; or

        (ii) in the case of a psychiatric examination, a hospital, independent hospital or care home,

at which the supervised child is, or is to attend as, a resident patient.

(3) A requirement of a kind mentioned in sub-paragraph (2)(c) shall not be included unless the court is satisfied, on the evidence of a registered medical practitioner, that—

    (a) the child may be suffering from a physical or mental condition that requires, and may be susceptible to, treatment; and

    (b) a period as a resident patient is necessary if the examination is to be carried out properly.

(4) No court shall include a requirement under this paragraph in a supervision order unless it is satisfied that—

    (a) where the child has sufficient understanding to make an informed decision, he consents to its inclusion; and

    (b) satisfactory arrangements have been, or can be, made for the examination.

Psychiatric and medical treatment

5.—(1) Where a court which proposes to make or vary a supervision order is satisfied, on the evidence of a registered medical practitioner approved for the purposes of section 12 of the Mental Health Act 1983, that the mental condition of the supervised child—

    (a) is such as requires, and may be susceptible to, treatment; but

    (b) is not such as to warrant his detention in pursuance of a hospital order under Part III of that Act,

the court may include in the order a requirement that the supervised child shall, for a period specified in the order, submit to such treatment as is so specified.

(2) The treatment specified in accordance with sub-paragraph (1) must be—

    (a) by, or under the direction of, such registered medical practitioner as may be specified in the order;

    (b) as a non-resident patient at such a place as may be so specified; or

    (c) as a resident patient in a hospital, independent hospital or care home.

(3) Where a court which proposes to make or vary a supervision order is satisfied, on the evidence of a registered medical practitioner, that the physical condition of the supervised child is such as requires, and may be susceptible to, treatment, the court may include in the order a requirement that the supervised child shall, for a period specified in the order, submit to such treatment as is so specified.

(4) The treatment specified in accordance with sub-paragraph (3) must be—

    (a) by, or under the direction of, such registered medical practitioner as may be specified in the order;

    (b) as a non-resident patient at such place as may be so specified; or

    (c) as a resident patient in a health service hospital.

(5) No court shall include a requirement under this paragraph in a supervision order unless it is satisfied—

    (a) where the child has sufficient understanding to make an informed decision, that he consents to its inclusion; and

    (b) that satisfactory arrangements have been, or can be, made for the treatment.

(6) If a medical practitioner by whom or under whose direction a supervised person is being treated in pursuance of a requirement included in a supervision order by virtue of this paragraph is unwilling to continue to treat or direct the treatment of the supervised child or is of the opinion that—

    (a) the treatment should be continued beyond the period specified in the order;

    (b) the supervised child needs different treatment;

    (c) he is not susceptible to treatment; or

    (d) he does not require further treatment,

the practitioner shall make a report in writing to that effect to the supervisor.

PART II   MISCELLANEOUS

Life of supervision order

6.—(1) Subject to sub-paragraph (2) and section 91, a supervision order shall cease to have effect at the end of the period of one year beginning with the date on which it was made.

(2) A supervision order shall also cease to have effect if an event mentioned in section 25(1)(a) or (b) of the Child Abduction and Custody Act 1985 (termination of existing orders) occurs with respect to the child.

(3) Where the supervisor applies to the court to extend, or further extend, a supervision order the court may extend the order for such period as it may specify.

(4) A supervision order may not be extended so as to run beyond the end of the period of three years beginning with the date on which it was made.

Information to be given to supervisor etc.

8.—(1) A supervision order may require the supervised child—

    (a) to keep the supervisor informed of any change in his address; and

    (b) to allow the supervisor to visit him at the place where he is living.

(2) The responsible person in relation to any child with respect to whom a supervision order is made shall—

    (a) if asked by the supervisor, inform him of the child's address (if it is known to him); and

    (b) if he is living with the child, allow the supervisor reasonable contact with the child.

Selection of supervisor

9.—(1) A supervision order shall not designate a local authority as the supervisor unless—

    (a) the authority agree; or

    (b) the supervised child lives or will live within their area.

Effect of supervision order on earlier orders

10. The making of a supervision order with respect to any child brings to an end any earlier care or supervision order which—

    (a) was made with respect to that child; and

    (b) would otherwise continue in force.

Local authority functions and expenditure

11.—(1) The Secretary of State may make regulations with respect to the exercise by a local authority of their functions where a child has been placed under their supervision by a supervision order.

(2) Where a supervision order requires compliance with directions given by virtue of this section, any expenditure incurred by the supervisor for the purposes of the directions shall be defrayed by the local authority designated in the order.

PART III   EDUCATION SUPERVISION ORDERS

Effect of orders

12.—(1) Where an education supervision order is in force with respect to a child, it shall be the duty of the supervisor—

    (a) to advise, assist and befriend, and give directions to—

        (i) the supervised child; and

        (ii) his parents, in such a way as will, in the opinion of the supervisor, secure that he is properly educated;

    (b) where any such directions given to—

        (i) the supervised child; or

        (ii) a parent of his, have not been complied with, to consider what further steps to take in the exercise of the supervisor's powers under this Act.

(2) Before giving any directions under sub-paragraph (1) the supervisor shall, so far as is reasonably practicable, ascertain the wishes and feelings of—

    (a) the child; and

    (b) his parents,

including, in particular, their wishes as to the place at which the child should be educated.

(3) When settling the terms of any such directions, the supervisor shall give due consideration—

    (a) having regard to the child's age and understanding, to such wishes and feelings of his as the supervisor has been able to ascertain; and

    (b) to such wishes and feelings of the child's parents as he has been able to ascertain.

(4) Directions may be given under this paragraph at any time while the education supervision order is in force.

13.—(1) Where an education supervision order is in force with respect to a child, the duties of the child's parents under sections 7 and 444 of the Education Act 1996 (duties to secure education of children and to secure regular attendance of registered pupils) shall be superseded by their duty to comply with any directions in force under the education supervision order.

(2) Where an education supervision order is made with respect to a child—

    (a) any school attendance order—

        (i) made under section 437 of the Education Act 1996 with respect to the child; and

        (ii) in force immediately before the making of the education supervision order, shall cease to have effect; and

    (b) while the education supervision order remains in force, the following provisions shall not apply with respect to the child—

        (i) section 437 of that Act (school attendance orders);

        (ii) section 9 of that Act (pupils to be educated in accordance with wishes of their parents);

        (iii) sections 411 and 423 of that Act (parental preference and appeals against admission decisions);

    (c) a supervision order made with respect to the child in criminal proceedings, while the education supervision order is in force, may not include an education requirement of the kind which could otherwise be included under paragraph 7 of Schedule 6 to the Powers of Criminal Courts (Sentencing) Act 2000;

(d) any education requirement of a kind mentioned in paragraph (c), which was in force with respect to the child immediately before the making of the education supervision order, shall cease to have effect.

Effect where child also subject to supervision order

14.—(1) This paragraph applies where an education supervision order and a supervision order, or order under section 63(1) of the Powers of Criminal Courts (Sentencing) Act 2000, are in force at the same time with respect to the same child.

(2) Any failure to comply with a direction given by the supervisor under the education supervision order shall be disregarded if it would not have been reasonably practicable to comply with it without failing to comply with a direction given under the other order.

Duration of orders

15.—(1) An education supervision order shall have effect for a period of one year, beginning with the date on which it is made.

(2) An education supervision order shall not expire if, before it would otherwise have expired, the court has (on the application of the authority in whose favour the order was made) extended the period during which it is in force.

(3) Such an application may not be made earlier than three months before the date on which the order would otherwise expire.

(4) The period during which an education supervision order is in force may be extended under sub-paragraph (2) on more than one occasion.

(5) No one extension may be for a period of more than three years.

(6) An education supervision order shall cease to have effect on—

(a) the child's ceasing to be of compulsory school age; or

(b) the making of a care order with respect to the child;

and sub-paragraphs (1) to (4) are subject to this sub-paragraph.

Information to be given to supervisor etc.

16.—(1) An education supervision order may require the child—

(a) to keep the supervisor informed of any change in his address; and

(b) to allow the supervisor to visit him at the place where he is living.

(2) A person who is the parent of a child with respect to whom an education supervision order has been made shall—

(a) if asked by the supervisor, inform him of the child's address (if it is known to him); and

(b) if he is living with the child, allow the supervisor reasonable contact with the child.

Discharge of orders

17.—(1) The court may discharge any education supervision order on the application of—

(a) the child concerned;

(b) a parent of his; or

(c) the local education authority concerned.

(2) On discharging an education supervision order, the court may direct the local authority within whose area the child lives, or will live, to investigate the circumstances of the child.

Offences

18.—(1) If a parent of a child with respect to whom an education supervision order is in force persistently fails to comply with a direction given under the order he shall be guilty of an offence.

(2) It shall be a defence for any person charged with such an offence to prove that—

    (a) he took all reasonable steps to ensure that the direction was complied with:

    (b) the direction was unreasonable; or

    (c) he had complied with—

        (i)   a requirement included in a supervision order made with respect to the child; or

        (ii) directions given under such a requirement, and that it was not reasonably practicable to comply both with the direction and with the requirement or directions mentioned in this paragraph.

(3) A person guilty of an offence under this paragraph shall be liable on summary conviction to a fine not exceeding level 3 on the standard scale.

Persistent failure of child to comply with directions

19.—(1) Where a child with respect to whom an education supervision order is in force persistently fails to comply with any direction given under the order, the local education authority concerned shall notify the appropriate local authority.

(2) Where a local authority have been notified under sub-paragraph (1) they shall investigate the circumstances of the child.

(3) In this paragraph 'the appropriate local authority' has the same meaning as in section 36.

Miscellaneous

20. The Secretary of State may by regulations make provision modifying, or displacing, the provisions of any enactment about education in relation to any child with respect to whom an education supervision order is in force to such extent as appears to the Secretary of State to be necessary or expedient in consequence of the provision made by this Act with respect to such orders.

Interpretation

21. In this Part of this Schedule 'parent' has the same meaning as in the Education Act 1996.

. . .

SCHEDULE 7

FOSTER PARENTS: LIMITS ON NUMBER OF FOSTER CHILDREN

Interpretation

1. For the purposes of this Schedule, a person fosters a child if—

    (a) he is a local authority foster parent in relation to the child;

    (b) he is a foster parent with whom the child has been placed by a voluntary organisation; or

    (c) he fosters the child privately.

The usual fostering limit

2. Subject to what follows, a person may not foster more than three children ('the usual fostering limit').

Siblings

3. A person may exceed the usual fostering limit if the children concerned are all siblings with respect to each other.

Exemption by local authority

4.—(1) A person may exceed the usual fostering limit if he is exempted from it by the local authority within whose area he lives.

(2) In considering whether to exempt a person, a local authority shall have regard, in particular, to—

  (a) the number of children whom the person proposes to foster;
  (b) the arrangements which the person proposes for the care and accommodation of the fostered children;
  (c) the intended and likely relationship between the person and the fostered children;
  (d) the period of time for which he proposes to foster the children; and
  (e) whether the welfare of the fostered children (and of any other children who are or will be living in the accommodation) will be safeguarded and promoted.

(3) Where a local authority exempt a person, they shall inform him by notice in writing—

  (a) that he is so exempted;
  (b) of the children, described by name, whom he may foster; and
  (c) of any condition to which the exemption is subject.

(4) A local authority may at any time by notice in writing—

  (a) vary or cancel an exemption; or
  (b) impose, vary or cancel a condition to which the exemption is subject,

and, in considering whether to do so, they shall have regard in particular to the considerations mentioned in sub-paragraph (2).

(5) The Secretary of State may make regulations amplifying or modifying the provisions of this paragraph in order to provide for cases where children need to be placed with foster parents as a matter of urgency.

Effect of exceeding fostering limit

5.—(1) A person shall cease to be treated as fostering and shall be treated, for the purposes of this Act and the Care Standards Act 2000, as carrying on a children's home if—

  (a) he exceeds the usual fostering limit; or
  (b) where he is exempted under paragraph 4,—
    (i) he fosters any child not named in the exemption; and
    (ii) in so doing, he exceeds the usual fostering limit.

(2) Sub-paragraph (1) does not apply if the children concerned are all siblings in respect of each other.

Complaints etc.

6.—(1) Every local authority shall establish a procedure for considering any representations (including any complaint) made to them about the discharge of their functions under paragraph 4 by a person exempted or seeking to be exempted under that paragraph.

(2) In carrying out any consideration of representations under subparagraph (1), a local authority shall comply with any regulations made by the Secretary of State for the purposes of this paragraph.

SCHEDULE 8

PRIVATELY FOSTERED CHILDREN

Exemptions

1. A child is not a privately fostered child while he is being looked after by a local authority.

2.—(1) A child is not a privately fostered child while he is in the care of any person—
  (a) in premises in which any—
    (i)   parent of his;
    (ii) person who is not a parent of his but who has parental responsibility for him; or
    (iii) person who is a relative of his and who has assumed responsibility for his care, is for the time being living;
  (c) in accommodation provided by or on behalf of any voluntary organisation;
  (d) in any school in which he is receiving full-time education;
  (e) in any health service hospital;
  (f) in any care home or independent hospital; or
  (g) in any home or institution not specified in this paragraph but provided, equipped and maintained by the Secretary of State.

(2) Sub-paragraph (1)(c) to (g) does not apply where the person caring for the child is doing so in his personal capacity and not in the course of carrying out his duties in relation to the establishment mentioned in the paragraph in question.

3. A child is not a privately fostered child while he is in the care of any person in compliance with—
  (a) an order under section 63(1) of the Powers of Criminal Courts (Sentencing) Act 2000; or
  (b) a supervision requirement within the meaning of Part II of the Children (Scotland) Act 1995.

4. A child is not a privately fostered child while he is liable to be detained, or subject to guardianship, under the Mental Health Act 1983.

5. A child is not a privately fostered child while he is placed in the care of a person who proposes to adopt him under arrangements made by an adoption agency within the meaning of—
  (a) section 2 of the Adoption and Children Act 2002;
  (b) section 1 of the Adoption (Scotland) Act 1978; or
  (c) Article 3 of the Adoption (Northern Ireland) Order 1987.

Power of local authority to impose requirements

6.—(1) Where a person is fostering any child privately, or proposes to foster any child privately, the appropriate local authority may impose on him requirements as to—
  (a) the number, age and sex of the children who may be privately fostered by him;
  (b) the standard of the accommodation and equipment to be provided for them;
  (c) the arrangements to be made with respect to their health and safety; and
  (d) particular arrangements which must be made with respect to the provision of care for them,
and it shall be his duty to comply with any such requirement before the end of such period as the authority may specify unless, in the case of a proposal, the proposal is not carried out.

(2) A requirement may be limited to a particular child, or class of child.

(3) A requirement (other than one imposed under sub-paragraph (1)(a)) may be limited by the authority so as to apply only when the number of children fostered by the person exceeds a specified number.

(4) A requirement shall be imposed by notice in writing addressed to the person on whom it is imposed and informing him of—
  (a) the reason for imposing the requirement;
  (b) his right under paragraph 8 to appeal against it; and
  (c) the time within which he may do so.

(5) A local authority may at any time vary any requirement, impose any additional requirement or remove any requirement.

(6) In this Schedule—
    (a) 'the appropriate local authority' means—
        (i)   the local authority within whose area the child is being fostered; or
        (ii) in the case of a proposal to foster a child, the local authority within whose area it is proposed that he will be fostered; and
    (b) 'requirement', in relation to any person, means a requirement imposed on him under this paragraph.

Regulations requiring notification of fostering etc.

7.—(1) The Secretary of State may by regulations make provision as to—
    (a) the circumstances in which notification is required to be given in connection with children who are, have been or are proposed to be fostered privately; and
    (b) the manner and form in which such notification is to be given.
(2) The regulations may, in particular—
    (a) require any person who is, or proposes to be, involved (whether or not directly) in arranging for a child to be fostered privately to notify the appropriate authority;
    (b) require any person who is—
        (i)   a parent of a child; or
        (ii) a person who is not a parent of his but who has parental responsibility for a child, and who knows that it is proposed that the child should be fostered privately, to notify the appropriate authority;
    (c) require any parent of a privately fostered child, or person who is not a parent of such a child but who has parental responsibility for him, to notify the appropriate authority of any change in his address;
    (d) require any person who proposes to foster a child privately, to notify the appropriate authority of his proposal;
    (e) require any person who is fostering a child privately, or proposes to do so, to notify the appropriate authority of—
        (i)   any offence of which he has been convicted;
        (ii) any disqualification imposed on him under section 68; or
        (iii) any prohibition imposed on him under section 69;
    (f) require any person who is fostering a child privately, to notify the appropriate authority of any change in his address;
    (g) require any person who is fostering a child privately to notify the appropriate authority in writing of any person who begins, or ceases, to be part of his household;
    (h) require any person who has been fostering a child privately, but has ceased to do so, to notify the appropriate authority (indicating, where the child has died, that this is the reason).
7A. Every local authority must promote public awareness in their area of requirements as to notification for which provision is made under paragraph 7.

Appeals

8.—(1) A person aggrieved by—
    (a) a requirement imposed under paragraph 6;
    (b) a refusal of consent under section 68;
    (c) a prohibition imposed under section 69;
    (d) a refusal to cancel such a prohibition;
    (e) a refusal to make an exemption under paragraph 4 of Schedule 7;
    (f) a condition imposed in such an exemption; or
    (g) a variation or cancellation of such an exemption,
may appeal to the court.

(2) The appeal must be made within fourteen days from the date on which the person appealing is notified of the requirement, refusal, prohibition, condition, variation or cancellation.

(3) Where the appeal is against—

(a) a requirement imposed under paragraph 6;

(b) a condition of an exemption imposed under paragraph 4 of Schedule 7; or

(c) a variation or cancellation of such an exemption,

the requirement, condition, variation or cancellation shall not have effect while the appeal is pending.

(4) Where it allows an appeal against a requirement or prohibition, the court may, instead of cancelling the requirement or prohibition—

(a) vary the requirement, or allow more time for compliance with it; or

(b) if an absolute prohibition has been imposed, substitute for it a prohibition on using the premises after such time as the court may specify unless such specified requirements as the local authority had power to impose under paragraph 6 are complied with.

(5) Any requirement or prohibition specified or substituted by a court under this paragraph shall be deemed for the purposes of Part IX (other than this paragraph) to have been imposed by the local authority under paragraph 6 or (as the case may be) section 69.

(6) Where it allows an appeal against a refusal to make an exemption, a condition imposed in such an exemption or a variation or cancellation of such an exemption, the court may—

(a) make an exemption;

(b) impose a condition; or

(c) vary the exemption.

(7) Any exemption made or varied under sub-paragraph (6), or any condition imposed under that sub-paragraph, shall be deemed for the purposes of Schedule 7 (but not for the purposes of this paragraph) to have been made, varied or imposed under that Schedule.

(8) Nothing in sub-paragraph (1)(e) to (g) confers any right of appeal on—

(a) a person who is, or would be if exempted under Schedule 7, a local authority foster parent; or

(b) a person who is, or would be if so exempted, a person with whom a child is placed by a voluntary organisation.

Extension of Part IX to certain school children during holidays

9.—(1) Where a child under sixteen who is a pupil at a school lives at the school during school holidays for a period of more than two weeks, Part IX shall apply in relation to the child as if—

(a) while living at the school, he were a privately fostered child; and

(b) paragraphs 2(1)(c) and (d) and 6 were omitted.

But this sub-paragraph does not apply to a school which is an appropriate children's home.

(2) Sub-paragraph (3) applies to any person who proposes to care for and accommodate one or more children at a school in circumstances in which some or all of them will be treated as private foster children by virtue of this paragraph.

(3) That person shall, not less than two weeks before the first of those children is treated as a private foster child by virtue of this paragraph during the holiday in question, give written notice of his proposal to the local authority within whose area the child is ordinarily resident ('the appropriate authority'), stating the estimated number of the children.

(4) A local authority may exempt any person from the duty of giving notice under sub-paragraph (3).

(5) Any such exemption may be granted for a special period or indefinitely and may be revoked at any time by notice in writing given to the person exempted.

(6) Where a child who is treated as a private foster child by virtue of this paragraph dies, the person caring for him at the school shall, not later than 48 hours after his death, give written notice of it—
    (a) to the appropriate authority; and
    (b) where reasonably practicable, to each parent of the child and to every person who is not a parent of his but who has parental responsibility for him.

(7) Where a child who is treated as a foster child by virtue of this paragraph ceases for any other reason to be such a child, the person caring for him at the school shall give written notice of the fact to the appropriate local authority.

Prohibition of advertisements relating to fostering

10. No advertisement indicating that a person will undertake, or will arrange for, a child to be privately fostered shall be published, unless it states that person's name and address.

Avoidance of insurances on lives of privately fostered children

11. A person who fosters a child privately and for reward shall be deemed for the purposes of the Life Assurance Act 1774 to have no interest in the life of the child.

. . .

Human Fertilisation and Embryology Act 1990
(1990 c. 37)

Principal terms used

1 Meaning of 'embryo', 'gamete' and associated expressions
    (1) In this Act, except where otherwise stated—
        (a) embryo means a live human embryo where fertilisation is complete, and
        (b) references to an embryo include an egg in the process of fertilisation,
and, for this purpose, fertilisation is not complete until the appearance of a two cell zygote.
    (2) This Act, so far as it governs bringing about the creation of an embryo, applies only to bringing about the creation of an embryo outside the human body; and in this Act—
        (a) references to embryos the creation of which was brought about *in vitro* (in their application to those where fertilisation is complete) are to those where fertilisation began outside the human body whether or not it was completed there, and
        (b) references to embryos taken from a woman do not include embryos whose creation was brought about *in vitro*.
    (3) This Act, so far as it governs the keeping or use of an embryo, applies only to keeping or using an embryo outside the human body.
    (4) References in this Act to gametes, eggs or sperm, except where otherwise stated, are to live human gametes, eggs or sperm but references below in this Act to gametes or eggs do not include eggs in the process of fertilisation.

2 Other terms
    (1) In this Act—
    'the Authority' means the Human Fertilisation and Embryology Authority established under section 5 of this Act,
        'directions' means directions under section 23 of this Act,
        'licence' means a licence under Schedule 2 to this Act and, in relation to a licence,
        'the person responsible' has the meaning given by section 17 of this Act, and
        'treatment services' means medical, surgical or obstetric services provided to the public or a section of the public for the purpose of assisting women to carry children.
    . . .

(3) For the purposes of this Act, a woman is not to be treated as carrying a child until the embryo has become implanted.

Status

27 Meaning of 'mother'

(1) The woman who is carrying or has carried a child as a result of the placing in her of an embryo or of sperm and eggs, and no other woman, is to be treated as the mother of the child.

(2) Subsection (1) above does not apply to any child to the extent that the child is treated by virtue of adoption as not being the woman's child.

(3) Subsection (1) above applies whether the woman was in the United Kingdom or elsewhere at the time of the placing in her of the embryo or the sperm and eggs.

28 Meaning of 'father'

(1) Subject to subsections (5A) to (5I) below, this section applies in the case of a child who is being or has been carried by a woman as the result of the placing in her of an embryo or of sperm and eggs or her artificial insemination.

(2) If—

    (a) at the time of the placing in her of the embryo or the sperm and eggs or of her insemination, the woman was a party to a marriage, and

    (b) the creation of the embryo carried by her was not brought about with the sperm of the other party to the marriage,

then, subject to subsection (5) below, the other party to the marriage shall be treated as the father of the child unless it is shown that he did not consent to the placing in her of the embryo or the sperm and eggs or to her insemination (as the case may be).

(3) If no man is treated, by virtue of subsection (2) above, as the father of the child but—

    (a) the embryo or the sperm and eggs were placed in the woman, or she was artificially inseminated, in the course of treatment services provided for her and a man together by a person to whom a licence applies, and

    (b) the creation of the embryo carried by her was not brought about with the sperm of that man,

then, subject to subsection (5) below, that man shall be treated as the father of the child.

(4) Where a person is treated as the father of the child by virtue of subsection (2) or (3) above, no other person is to be treated as the father of the child.

(5) Subsections (2) and (3) above do not apply—

    (a) in relation to England and Wales and Northern Ireland, to any child who, by virtue of the rules of common law, is treated as the legitimate child of the parties to a marriage,

    (c) to any child to the extent that the child is treated by virtue of adoption as not being the man's child.

(5A) If—

    (a) a child has been carried by a woman as the result of the placing in her of an embryo or of sperm and eggs or her artificial insemination,

    (b) the creation of the embryo carried by her was brought about by using the sperm of a man after his death, or the creation of the embryo was brought about using the sperm of a man before his death but the embryo was placed in the woman after his death,

    (c) the woman was a party to a marriage with the man immediately before his death,

    (d) the man consented in writing (and did not withdraw the consent)—

        (i) to the use of his sperm after his death which brought about the creation of the embryo carried by the woman or (as the case may be) to the placing in the woman after his death of the embryo which was brought about using his sperm before his death, and

        (ii) to being treated for the purpose mentioned in subsection (5I) below as the father of any resulting child,

(e) the woman has elected in writing not later than the end of the period of 42 days from the day on which the child was born for the man to be treated for the purpose mentioned in subsection (5I) below as the father of the child, and

(f) no-one else is to be treated as the father of the child by virtue of subsection (2) or (3) above or by virtue of adoption or the child being treated as mentioned in paragraph (a) or (b) of subsection (5) above,

then the man shall be treated for the purpose mentioned in subsection (5I) below as the father of the child.

(5B) If—

(a) a child has been carried by a woman as the result of the placing in her of an embryo or of sperm and eggs or her artificial insemination,

(b) the creation of the embryo carried by her was brought about by using the sperm of a man after his death, or the creation of the embryo was brought about using the sperm of a man before his death but the embryo was placed in the woman after his death,

(c) the woman was not a party to a marriage with the man immediately before his death but treatment services were being provided for the woman and the man together before his death either by a person to whom a licence applies or outside the United Kingdom,

(d) the man consented in writing (and did not withdraw the consent)—

(i) to the use of his sperm after his death which brought about the creation of the embryo carried by the woman or (as the case may be) to the placing in the woman after his death of the embryo which was brought about using his sperm before his death, and

(ii) to being treated for the purpose mentioned in subsection (5I) below as the father of any resulting child,

(e) the woman has elected in writing not later than the end of the period of 42 days from the day on which the child was born for the man to be treated for the purpose mentioned in subsection (5I) below as the father of the child, and

(f) no-one else is to be treated as the father of the child by virtue of subsection (2) or (3) above or by virtue of adoption or the child being treated as mentioned in paragraph (a) or (b) of subsection (5) above,

then the man shall be treated for the purpose mentioned in subsection (5I) below as the father of the child.

(5C) If—

(a) a child has been carried by a woman as the result of the placing in her of an embryo,

(b) the embryo was created at a time when the woman was a party to a marriage,

(c) the creation of the embryo was not brought about with the sperm of the other party to the marriage,

(d) the other party to the marriage died before the placing of the embryo in the woman,

(e) the other party to the marriage consented in writing (and did not withdraw the consent)—

(i) to the placing of the embryo in the woman after his death, and

(ii) to being treated for the purpose mentioned in subsection (5I) below as the father of any resulting child,

(f) the woman has elected in writing not later than the end of the period of 42 days from the day on which the child was born for the other party to the marriage to be treated for the purpose mentioned in subsection (5I) below as the father of the child, and

(g) no-one else is to be treated as the father of the child by virtue of subsection (2) or (3) above or by virtue of adoption or the child being treated as mentioned in paragraph (a) or (b) of subsection (5) above,

then the other party to the marriage shall be treated for the purpose mentioned in subsection (5I) below as the father of the child.

(5D) If—

    (a) a child has been carried by a woman as the result of the placing in her of an embryo,

    (b) the embryo was not created at a time when the woman was a party to a marriage but was created in the course of treatment services provided for the woman and a man together either by a person to whom a licence applies or outside the United Kingdom,

    (c) the creation of the embryo was not brought about with the sperm of that man,

    (d) the man died before the placing of the embryo in the woman,

    (e) the man consented in writing (and did not withdraw the consent)—

        (i)   to the placing of the embryo in the woman after his death, and

        (ii) to being treated for the purpose mentioned in subsection (5I) below as the father of any resulting child,

    (f) the woman has elected in writing not later than the end of the period of 42 days from the day on which the child was born for the man to be treated for the purpose mentioned in subsection (5I) below as the father of the child, and

    (g) no-one else is to be treated as the father of the child by virtue of subsection (2) or (3) above or by virtue of adoption or the child being treated as mentioned in paragraph (a) or (b) of subsection (5) above,

then the man shall be treated for the purpose mentioned in subsection (5I) below as the father of the child.

. . .

(5F) The requirement under subsection (5A), (5B), (5C) or (5D) above as to the making of an election (which requires an election to be made either on or before the day on which the child was born or within the period of 42 . . . days from that day) shall nevertheless be treated as satisfied if the required election is made after the end of that period but with the consent of the Registrar General under subsection (5G) below.

(5G) The Registrar General may at any time consent to the making of an election after the end of the period mentioned in subsection (5F) above if, on an application made to him in accordance with such requirements as he may specify, he is satisfied that there is a compelling reason for giving his consent to the making of such an election.

(5H) In subsections (5F) and (5G) above 'the Registrar General' means the Registrar General for England and Wales, . . .

(5I) The purpose referred to in subsections (5A) to (5D) above is the purpose of enabling the man's particulars to be entered as the particulars of the child's father in (as the case may be) a register of live-births or still-births kept under the Births and Deaths Registration Act 1953 . . .

(6) Where—

    (a) the sperm of a man who had given such consent as is required by paragraph 5 of Schedule 3 to this Act was used for a purpose for which such consent was required, or

    (b) the sperm of a man, or any embryo the creation of which was brought about with his sperm, was used after his death,

he is not, subject to subsections (5A) and (5B) above, to be treated as the father of the child.

(7) The references in subsection (2) above and subsections (5A) to (5D) above to the parties to a marriage at the time there referred to—

    (a) are to the parties to a marriage subsisting at that time, unless a judicial separation was then in force, but

    (b) include the parties to a void marriage if either or both of them reasonably believed at that time that the marriage was valid; and for the purposes of this subsection it shall be presumed, unless the contrary is shown, that one of them reasonably believed at that time that the marriage was valid.

(8) This section applies whether the woman was in the United Kingdom or elsewhere at the time of the placing in her of the embryo or the sperm and eggs or her artificial insemination.

(9) In subsection (7)(a) above, 'judicial separation' includes a legal separation obtained in a country outside the British Islands and recognised in the United Kingdom.

29   Effect of ss. 27 and 28

(1) Where by virtue of section 27 or 28 of this Act a person is to be treated as the mother or father of a child, that person is to be treated in law as the mother or, as the case may be, father of the child for all purposes.

(2) Where by virtue of section 27 or 28 of this Act a person is not be be treated as the mother or father of a child, that person is to be treated in law as not being the mother or, as the case may be, father of the child for any purpose.

(3) Where subsection (1) or (2) above has effect, references to any relationship between two people in any enactment, deed or other instrument or document (whenever passed or made) are to be read accordingly.

(3A) Subsections (1) to (3) above do not apply in relation to the treatment in law of a deceased man in a case to which section 28(5A), (5B), (5C) or (5D) of this Act applies.

(3B) Where subsection (5A), (5B), (5C) or (5D) of section 28 of this Act applies, the deceased man—

   (a) is to be treated in law as the father of the child for the purpose referred to in that subsection, but

   (b) is to be treated in law as not being the father of the child for any other purpose.

(3C) Where subsection (3B) above has effect, references to any relationship between two people in any enactment, deed or other instrument or document (whenever passed or made) are to be read accordingly.

. . .

(4) In relation to England and Wales and Northern Ireland, nothing in the provisions of section 27(1) or 28(2) to (4) or (5A) to (5I), read with this section, affects—

   (a) the succession to any dignity or title of honour or renders any person capable of succeeding to or transmitting a right to succeed to any such dignity or title, or

   (b) the devolution of any property limited (expressly or not) to devolve (as nearly as the law permits) along with any dignity or title of honour.

30   Parental orders in favour of gamete donors

(1) The court may make an order providing for a child to be treated in law as the child of the parties to a marriage (referred to in this section as 'the husband' and 'the wife') if—

   (a) the child has been carried by a woman other than the wife as the result of the placing in her of an embryo or sperm and eggs or her artificial insemination,

   (b) the gametes of the husband or the wife, or both, were used to bring about the creation of the embryo, and

   (c) the conditions in subsections (2) to (7) below are satisfied.

(2) The husband and the wife must apply for the order within six months of the birth of the child or, in the case of a child born before the coming into force of this Act, within six months of such coming into force.

(3) At the time of the application and of the making of the order—

   (a) the child's home must be with the husband and the wife, and

   (b) the husband or the wife, or both of them, must be domiciled in a part of the United Kingdom or in the Channel Islands or the Isle of Man.

(4) At the time of the making of the order both the husband and the wife must have attained the age of eighteen.

(5) The court must be satisfied that both the father of the child (including a person who is the father by virtue of section 28 of this Act), where he is not the husband, and the woman

who carried the child have freely, and with full understanding of what is involved, agreed unconditionally to the making of the order.

(6) Subsection (5) above does not require the agreement of a person who cannot be found or is incapable of giving agreement and the agreement of the woman who carried the child is ineffective for the purposes of that subsection if given by her less than six weeks after the child's birth.

(7) The court must be satisfied that no money or other benefit (other than for expenses reasonably incurred) has been given or received by the husband or the wife for or in consideration of—

(a) the making of the order,

(b) any agreement required by subsection (5) above,

(c) the handing over of the child to the husband and the wife, or

(d) the making of any arrangements with a view to the making of the order,

unless authorised by the court.

(8) For the purposes of an application under this section—

(a) in relation to England and Wales, section 92(7) to (10) of, and Part I of Schedule 11 to, the Children Act 1989 (jurisdiction of courts) shall apply for the purposes of this section to determine the meaning of 'the court' as they apply for the purposes of that Act and proceedings on the application shall be 'family proceedings' for the purposes of that Act.

(9) Regulations may provide—

(a) for any provision of the enactments about adoption to have effect, with such modifications (if any) as may be specified in the regulations, in relation to orders under this section, and applications for such orders, as it has effect in relation to adoption, and applications for adoption orders, and

(b) for references in any enactment to adoption, an adopted child or an adoptive relationship to be read (respectively) as references to the effect of an order under this section, a child to whom such an order applies and a relationship arising by virtue of the enactments about adoption, as applied by the regulations, and for similar expressions in connection with adoption to be read accordingly,

and the regulations may include such incidental or supplemental provision as appears to the Secretary of State necessary or desirable in consequence of any provision made by virtue of paragraph (a) or (b) above.

(10) In this section 'the enactments about adoption' means the Adoption and Children Act 2002, the Adoption (Scotland) Act 1978 and the Adoption (Northern Ireland) Order 1987.

(11) Subsection (1)(a) above applies whether the woman was in the United Kingdom or elsewhere at the time of the placing in her of the embryo or the sperm and eggs or her artificial insemination.

Information

31   The Authority's register of information

(1) The Authority shall keep a register which shall contain any information obtained by the Authority which falls within subsection (2) below.

(2) Information falls within this subsection if it relates to—

(a) the provision of treatment services for any identifiable individual, or

(b) the keeping or use of the gametes of any identifiable individual or of an embryo taken from any identifiable woman,

or if it shows that any identifiable individual was, or may have been, born in consequence of treatment services.

(3) A person who has attained the age of eighteen ('the applicant') may by notice to the Authority require the Authority to comply with a request under subsection (4) below, and the Authority shall do so if—

(a) the information contained in the register shows that the applicant was, or may have been, born in consequence of treatment services, and

(b) the applicant has been given a suitable opportunity to receive proper counselling about the implications of compliance with the request.

(4) The applicant may request the Authority to give the applicant notice stating whether or not the information contained in the register shows that a person other than a parent of the applicant would or might, but for sections 27 to 29 of this Act, be a parent of the applicant and, if it does show that—

(a) giving the applicant so much of that information as relates to the person concerned as the Authority is required by regulations to give (but no other information), or

(b) stating whether or not that information shows that, but for sections 27 to 29 of this Act, the applicant, and a person specified in the request as a person whom the applicant proposes to marry, would or might be related.

(5) Regulations cannot require the Authority to give any information as to the identity of a person whose gametes have been used or from whom an embryo has been taken if a person to whom a licence applied was provided with the information at a time when the Authority could not have been required to give information of the kind in question.

(6) A person who has not attained the age of eighteen ('the minor') may by notice to the Authority specifying another person ('the intended spouse') as a person whom the minor proposes to marry require the Authority to comply with a request under subsection (7) below, and the Authority shall do so if—

(a) the information contained in the register shows that the minor was, or may have been, born in consequence of treatment services, and

(b) the minor has been given a suitable opportunity to receive proper counselling about the implications of compliance with the request.

(7) The minor may request the Authority to give the minor notice stating whether or not the information contained in the register shows that, but for sections 27 to 29 of this Act, the minor and the intended spouse would or might be related.

32 Information to be provided to Registrar General

(1) This section applies where a claim is made before the Registrar General that a man is or is not the father of a child and it is necessary or desirable for the purpose of any function of the Registrar General to determine whether the claim is or may be well-founded.

(2) The Authority shall comply with any request made by the Registrar General by notice to the Authority to disclose whether any information on the register kept in pursuance of section 31 of this Act tends to show that the man may be the father of the child by virtue of section 28 of this Act and, if it does, disclose that information.

(3) In this section and section 33 of this Act, 'the Registrar General' means the Registrar General for England and Wales, the Registrar General of Births, Deaths and Marriages for Scotland or the Registrar General for Northern Ireland, as the case may be.

33 Restrictions on disclosure of information

(1) No person who is or has been a member or employee of the Authority shall disclose any information mentioned in subsection (2) below which he holds or has held as such a member or employee.

(2) The information referred to in subsection (1) above is—

(a) any information contained or required to be contained in the register kept in pursuance of section 31 of this Act, and

(b) any other information obtained by any member or employee of the Authority on terms or in circumstances requiring it to be held in confidence.

(3) Subsection (1) above does not apply to any disclosure of information mentioned in subsection (2)(a) above made—

(a) to a person as a member or employee of the Authority,

(b) to a person to whom a licence applies for the purposes of his functions as such,

(c) so that no individual to whom the information relates can be identified,

(d) in pursuance of an order of a court under section 34 or 35 of this Act,

(e) to the Registrar General in pursuance of a request under section 32 of this Act, or

(f) in accordance with section 31 of this Act.

(4) Subsection (1) above does not apply to any disclosure of information mentioned in subsection (2)(b) above—

(a) made to a person as a member or employee of the Authority,

(b) made with the consent of the person or persons whose confidence would otherwise be protected, or

(c) which has been lawfully made available to the public before the disclosure is made.

(5) No person who is or has been a person to whom a licence applies and no person to whom directions have been given shall disclose any information falling within section 31(2) of this Act which he holds or has held as such a person.

(6) Subsection (5) above does not apply to any disclosure of information made—

(a) to a person as a member or employee of the Authority,

(b) to a person to whom a licence applies for the purposes of his functions as such,

(c) so far as it identifies a person who, but for sections 27 to 29 of this Act, would or might be a parent of a person who instituted proceedings under section 1A of the Congenital Disabilities (Civil Liability) Act 1976, but only for the purpose of defending such proceedings, or instituting connected proceedings for compensation against that parent,

(d) so that no individual to whom the information relates can be identified,

(e) in pursuance of directions given by virtue of section 24(5) or (6) of this Act,

(f) necessarily—

(i) for any purpose preliminary to proceedings, or

(ii) for the purposes of, or in connection with, any proceedings,

(g) for the purpose of establishing, in any proceedings relating to an application for an order under subsection (1) of section 30 of this Act, whether the condition specified in paragraph (a) or (b) of that subsection is met,

(h) under section 3 of the Access to Health Records Act 1990 (right of access to health records), or

(i) under Article 5 of the Access to Health Records (Northern Ireland) Order 1993 (right of access to health records).

(6A) Paragraph (f) of subsection (6) above, so far as relating to disclosure for the purposes of, or in connection with, any proceedings, does not apply—

(a) to disclosure of information enabling a person to be identified as a person whose gametes were used, in accordance with consent given under paragraph 5 of Schedule 3 to this Act, for the purposes of treatment services in consequence of which an identifiable individual was or may have been, born, or

(b) to disclosure, in circumstances in which subsection (1) of section 34 of this Act applies, of information relevant to the determination of the question mentioned in that subsection.

(6B) In the case of information relating to the provision of treatment services for any identifiable individual—

(a) where one individual is identifiable, subsection (5) above does not apply to disclosure with the consent of that individual;

(b) where both a woman and a man treated together with her are identifiable, subsection (5) above does not apply—

(i) to disclosure with the consent of them both, or

(ii) if disclosure is made for the purpose of disclosing information about the provision of treatment services for one of them, to disclosure with the consent of that individual.

(6C) For the purposes of subsection (6B) above, consent must be to disclosure to a specific person, except where disclosure is to a person who needs to know—

   (a) in connection with the provision of treatment services, or any other description of medical, surgical or obstetric services, for the individual giving the consent,

   (b) in connection with the carrying out of an audit of clinical practice, or

   (c) in connection with the auditing of accounts.

(6D) For the purposes of subsection (6B) above, consent to disclosure given at the request of another shall be disregarded unless, before it is given, the person requesting it takes reasonable steps to explain to the individual from whom it is requested the implications of compliance with the request.

(6E) In the case of information which relates to the provision of treatment services for any identifiable individual, subsection (5) above does not apply to disclosure in an emergency, that is to say, to disclosure made—

   (a) by a person who is satisfied that it is necessary to make the disclosure to avert an imminent danger to the health of an individual with whose consent the information could be disclosed under subsection (6B) above, and

   (b) in circumstances where it is not reasonably practicable to obtain that individual's consent.

(6F) In the case of information which shows that any identifiable individual was, or may have been, born in consequence of treatment services, subsection (5) above does not apply to any disclosure which is necessarily incidental to disclosure under subsection (6B) or (6E) above.

(6G) Regulations may provide for additional exceptions from subsection (5) above, but no exception may be made under this subsection—

   (a) for disclosure of a kind mentioned in paragraph (a) or (b) of subsection (6A) above, or

   (b) for disclosure, in circumstances in which section 32 of this Act applies, of information having the tendency mentioned in subsection (2) of that section.

(7) This section does not apply to the disclosure to any individual of information which—

   (a) falls within section 31(2) of this Act by virtue of paragraph (a) or (b) of that subsection, and

   (b) relates only to that individual or, in the case of an individual treated together with another, only to that individual and that other.

(9) In subsection (6)(f) above, references to proceedings include any formal procedure for dealing with a complaint.

34 Disclosure in interests of justice

(1) Where in any proceedings before a court the question whether a person is or is not the parent of a child by virtue of sections 27 to 29 of this Act falls to be determined, the court may on the application of any party to the proceedings make an order requiring the Authority—

   (a) to disclose whether or not any information relevant to that question is contained in the register kept in pursuance of section 31 of this Act, and

   (b) if it is, to disclose so much of it as is specified in the order, but such an order may not require the Authority to disclose any information falling within section 31(2)(b) of this Act.

(2) The court must not make an order under subsection (1) above unless it is satisfied that the interests of justice require it to do so, taking into account—

   (a) any representations made by any individual who may be affected by the disclosure, and

   (b) the welfare of the child, if under 18 years old, and of any other person under that age who may be affected by the disclosure.

(3) If the proceedings before the court are civil proceedings, it—

    (a) may direct that the whole or any part of the proceedings on the application for an order under subsection (2) above shall be heard in camera, and

    (b) if it makes such an order, may then or later direct that the whole or any part of any later stage of the proceedings shall be heard in camera.

(4) An application for a direction under subsection (3) above shall be heard in camera unless the court otherwise directs.

35   Disclosure in interests of justice: congenital disabilities etc.

(1) Where for the purpose of instituting proceedings under section 1 of the Congenital Disabilities (Civil Liability) Act 1976 (civil liability to child born disabled) it is necessary to identify a person who would or might be the parent of a child but for sections 27 to 29 of this Act, the court may, on the application of the child, make an order requiring the Authority to disclose any information contained in the register kept in pursuance of section 31 of this Act identifying that person.

(3) Subsections (2) to (4) of section 34 of this Act apply for the purposes of this section as they apply for the purposes of that.

Offences

41   Offences

. . .

(5) A person who discloses any information in contravention of section 33 of this Act is guilty of an offence and liable—

    (a) on conviction on indictment, to imprisonment for a term not exceeding two years or a fine or both, and

    (b) on summary conviction, to imprisonment for a term not exceeding six months or a fine not exceeding the statutory maximum or both.

. . .

(11) It is a defence for a person charged with an offence under this Act to prove—

    (a) that at the material time he was a person to whom a licence applied or to whom directions had been given, and

    (b) that he took all such steps as were reasonable and exercised all due diligence to avoid committing the offence.

42   Consent to prosecution

No proceedings for an offence under this Act shall be instituted—

    (a) in England and Wales, except by or with the consent of the Director of Public Prosecutions, and

    (b) in Northern Ireland, except by or with the consent of the Director of Public Prosecutions for Northern Ireland.

. . .

49   Short title, commencement etc.

(4) Section 27 of the Family Law Reform Act 1987 (artificial insemination) does not have effect in relation to children carried by women as the result of their artificial insemination after the commencement of sections 27 to 29 of this Act.

SCHEDULE 3

CONSENTS TO USE OF GAMETES OR EMBRYOS

Consent

1. A consent under this Schedule must be given in writing and, in this Schedule, 'effective consent' means a consent under this Schedule which has not been withdrawn.

2.—(1) A consent to the use of any embryo must specify one or more of the following purposes—

    (a) use in providing treatment services to the person giving consent, or that person and another specified person together,

    (b) use in providing treatment services to persons not including the person giving consent, or

    (c) use for the purposes of any project of research,

and may specify conditions subject to which the embryo may be so used.

    (2) A consent to the storage of any gametes or any embryo must—

    (a) specify the maximum period of storage (if less than the statutory storage period), and

    (b) state what is to be done with the gametes or embryo if the person who gave the consent dies or is unable because of incapacity to vary the terms of the consent or to revoke it,

and may specify conditions subject to which the gametes or embryo may remain in storage.

    (3) A consent under this Schedule must provide for such other matters as the Authority may specify in directions.

    (4) A consent under this Schedule may apply—

    (a) to the use or storage of a particular embryo, or

    (b) in the case of a person providing gametes, to the use or storage of any embryo whose creation may be brought about using those gametes,

and in the paragraph (b) case the terms of the consent may be varied, or the consent may be withdrawn, in accordance with this Schedule either generally or in relation to a particular embryo or particular embryos.

Procedure for giving consent

3.—(1) Before a person gives consent under this Schedule—

    (a) he must be given a suitable opportunity to receive proper counselling about the implications of taking the proposed steps, and

    (b) he must be provided with such relevant information as is proper.

    (2) Before a person gives consent under this Schedule he must be informed of the effect of paragraph 4 below.

Variation and withdrawal of consent

4.—(1) The terms of any consent under this Schedule may from time to time be varied, and the consent may be withdrawn, by notice given by the person who gave the consent to the person keeping the gametes or embryo to which the consent is relevant.

    (2) The terms of any consent to the use of any embryo cannot be varied, and such consent cannot be withdrawn, once the embryo has been used—

    (a) in providing treatment services, or

    (b) for the purposes of any project of research.

Use of gametes for treatment of others

5.—(1) A person's gametes must not be used for the purposes of treatment services unless there is an effective consent by that person to their being so used and they are used in accordance with the terms of the consent.

    (2) A person's gametes must not be received for use for those purposes unless there is an effective consent by that person to their being so used.

    (3) This paragraph does not apply to the use of a person's gametes for the purpose of that person, or that person and another together, receiving treatment services.

In vitro fertilisation and subsequent use of embryo

6.—(1) A person's gametes must not be used to bring about the creation of any embryo *in vitro* unless there is an effective consent by that person to any embryo the creation of which may be brought about with the use of those gametes being used for one or more of the purposes mentioned in paragraph 2(1) above.

(2) An embryo the creation of which was brought about *in vitro* must not be received by any person unless there is an effective consent by each person whose gametes were used to bring about the creation of the embryo to the use for one or more of the purposes mentioned in paragraph 2(1) above of the embryo.

(3) An embryo the creation of which was brought about *in vitro* must not be used for any purpose unless there is an effective consent by each person whose gametes were used to bring about the creation of the embryo to the use for that purpose of the embryo and the embryo is used in accordance with those consents.

(4) Any consent required by this paragraph is in addition to any consent that may be required by paragraph 5 above.

Embryos obtained by lavage, etc.

7.—(1) An embryo taken from a woman must not be used for any purpose unless there is an effective consent by her to the use of the embryo for that purpose and it is used in accordance with the consent.

(2) An embryo taken from a woman must not be received by any person for use for any purpose unless there is an effective consent by her to the use of the embryo for that purpose.

(3) This paragraph does not apply to the use, for the purpose of providing a woman with treatment services, of an embryo taken from her.

Storage of gametes and embryos

8.—(1) A person's gametes must not be kept in storage unless there is an effective consent by that person to their storage and they are stored in accordance with the consent.

(2) An embryo the creation of which was brought about *in vitro* must not be kept in storage unless there is an effective consent, by each person whose gametes were used to bring about the creation of the embryo, to the storage of the embryo and the embryo is stored in accordance with those consents.

(3) An embryo taken from a woman must not be kept in storage unless there is an effective consent by her to its storage and it is stored in accordance with the consent.

Courts and Legal Services Act 1990
(1990 c. 41)

Family proceedings

9 Allocation of family proceedings which are within the jurisdiction of county courts

(1) The Lord Chancellor may, with the concurrence of the President of the Family Division, give directions that, in such circumstances as may be specified—

    (a) any family proceedings which are within the jurisdiction of county courts; or

    (b) any specified description of such proceedings,

shall be allocated to specified judges or to specified descriptions of judge.

(2) Any such direction shall have effect regardless of any rules of court.

(3) Where any directions have been given under this section allocating any proceedings to specified judges, the validity of anything done by a judge in, or in relation to, the

proceedings shall not be called into question by reason only of the fact that he was not a specified judge.

(4) For the purposes of subsection (1) 'county court' includes the principal registry of the Family Division of the High Court in so far as it is treated as a county court.

(5) In this section—

'family proceedings' has the same meaning as in the Matrimonial and Family Proceedings Act 1984 and also includes any other proceedings which are family proceedings for the purposes of the Children Act 1989;

'judge' means any person who—

(a) is capable of sitting as a judge for a county court district;

(b) is a district judge, an assistant district judge or a deputy district judge; or

(c) is a district judge of the principal registry of the Family Division of the High Court; and

'specified' means specified in the directions.

. . .

Miscellaneous

58 Conditional fee agreements

(1) A conditional fee agreement which satisfies all of the conditions applicable to it by virtue of this section shall not be unenforceable by reason only of its being a conditional fee agreement; but (subject to subsection (5)) any other conditional fee agreement shall be unenforceable.

(2) For the purposes of this section and section 58A—

(a) a conditional fee agreement is an agreement with a person providing advocacy or litigation services which provides for his fees and expenses, or any part of them, to be payable only in specified circumstances; and

(b) a conditional fee agreement provides for a success fee if it provides for the amount of any fees to which it applies to be increased, in specified circumstances, above the amount which would be payable if it were not payable only in specified circumstances.

(3) The following conditions are applicable to every conditional fee agreement—

(a) it must be in writing;

(b) it must not relate to proceedings which cannot be the subject of an enforceable conditional fee agreement; and

(c) it must comply with such requirements (if any) as may be prescribed by the Secretary of State.

(4) The following further conditions are applicable to a conditional fee agreement which provides for a success fee—

(a) it must relate to proceedings of a description specified by order made by the Secretary of State;

(b) it must state the percentage by which the amount of the fees which would be payable if it were not a conditional fee agreement is to be increased; and

(c) that percentage must not exceed the percentage specified in relation to the description of proceedings to which the agreement relates by order made by the Secretary of State.

(5) If a conditional fee agreement is an agreement to which section 57 of the Solicitors Act 1974 (non-contentious business agreements between solicitor and client) applies, subsection (1) shall not make it unenforceable.

58A Conditional fee agreements: supplementary

(1) The proceedings which cannot be the subject of an enforceable conditional fee agreement are—

(a) criminal proceedings, apart from proceedings under section 82 of the Environmental Protection Act 1990; and

(b) family proceedings.

(2) In subsection (1) 'family proceedings' means proceedings under any one or more of the following—

    (a) the Matrimonial Causes Act 1973;

    (b) the Adoption and Children Act 2002;

    (c) the Domestic Proceedings and Magistrates' Courts Act 1978;

    (d) Part III of the Matrimonial and Family Proceedings Act 1984;

    (e) Parts I, II and IV of the Children Act 1989;

    (f) Part IV of the Family Law Act 1996;

    (fa) Chapter 2 of Part 2 of the Civil Partnership Act 2004 (proceedings for dissolution etc. of civil partnership);

    (fb) Schedule 5 to the 2004 Act (financial relief in the High Court or a county court etc.);

    (fc) Schedule 6 to the 2004 Act (financial relief in magistrates' courts etc.);

    (fd) Schedule 7 to the 2004 Act (financial relief in England and Wales after overseas dissolution etc. of a civil partnership); and

    (g) the inherent jurisdiction of the High Court in relation to children.

. . .

(4) In section 58 and this section (and in the definitions of 'advocacy services' and 'litigation services' as they apply for their purposes) 'proceedings' includes any sort of proceedings for resolving disputes (and not just proceedings in a court), whether commenced or contemplated.

. . .

58B Litigation funding agreements

(1) A litigation funding agreement which satisfies all of the conditions applicable to it by virtue of this section shall not be unenforceable by reason only of its being a litigation funding agreement.

(2) For the purposes of this section a litigation funding agreement is an agreement under which—

    (a) a person ('the funder') agrees to fund (in whole or in part) the provision of advocacy or litigation services (by someone other than the funder) to another person ('the litigant'); and

    (b) the litigant agrees to pay a sum to the funder in specified circumstances.

(3) The following conditions are applicable to a litigation funding agreement—

    (a) the funder must be a person, or person of a description, prescribed by the Secretary of State;

    (b) the agreement must be in writing;

    (c) the agreement must not relate to proceedings which by virtue of section 58A(1) and (2) cannot be the subject of an enforceable conditional fee agreement or to proceedings of any such description as may be prescribed by the Secretary of State;

. . .

Maintenance Enforcement Act 1991
(1991 c. 17)

The High Court and county courts

1 Maintenance orders in the High Court and county courts: means of payment, attachment of earnings and revocation, variation, etc.

(1) Where the High Court or a county court makes a qualifying periodical maintenance order, it may at the same time exercise either of its powers under subsection (4) below in relation to the order, whether of its own motion or on an application made under this subsection by an interested party.

(2) For the purposes of this section, a periodical maintenance order is an order—

    (a) which requires money to be paid periodically by one person ('the debtor') to another ('the creditor'); and

    (b) which is a maintenance order;

and such an order is a 'qualifying periodical maintenance order' if, at the time it is made, the debtor is ordinarily resident in England and Wales.

(3) Where the High Court or a county court has made a qualifying periodical maintenance order, it may at any later time—

    (a) on an application made under this subsection by an interested party, or

    (b) of its own motion, in the course of any proceedings concerning the order,

exercise either of its powers under subsection (4) below in relation to the order.

(4) The powers mentioned in subsections (1) and (3) above are—

    (a) the power to order that payments required to be made by the debtor to the creditor under the qualifying periodical maintenance order in question shall be so made by such a method of payment falling within subsection (5) below as the court may specify in the particular case; or

    (b) the power, by virtue of this section, to make an attachment of earnings order under the Attachment of Earnings Act 1971 to secure payments under the qualifying periodical maintenance order in question.

(5) The methods of payment mentioned in subsection (4)(a) above are—

    (a) payment by standing order; or

    (b) payment by any other method which requires the debtor to give his authority for payments of a specific amount to be made from an account of his to an account of the creditor's on specific dates during the period for which the authority is in force and without the need for any further authority from the debtor.

(6) In any case where—

    (a) the court proposes to exercise its power under paragraph (a) of subsection (4) above, and

    (b) having given the debtor an opportunity of opening an account from which payments under the order may be made in accordance with the method of payment proposed to be ordered under that paragraph, the court is satisfied that the debtor has failed, without reasonable excuse, to open such an account,

the court in exercising its power under that paragraph may order that the debtor open such an account.

(7) Where in the exercise of its powers under subsection (1) or (3) above, the High Court or a county court has made in relation to a qualifying periodical maintenance order such an order as is mentioned in subsection (4)(a) above (a 'means of payment order'), it may at any later time—

    (a) on an application made under this subsection by an interested party, or

    (b) of its own motion, in the course of any proceedings concerning the qualifying periodical maintenance order,

revoke, suspend, revive or vary the means of payment order.

(8) In deciding whether to exercise any of its powers under this section the court in question having (if practicable) given every interested party an opportunity to make representations shall have regard to any representations made by any such party.

(9) Nothing in this section shall be taken to prejudice—

    (a) any power under the Attachment of Earnings Act 1971 which would, apart from this section, be exercisable by the High Court or a county court; or

    (b) any right of any person to make any application under that Act; and subsection (7) above is without prejudice to any other power of the High Court or a county court to revoke, suspend, revive or vary an order.

(10) For the purposes of this section—

'debtor' and 'creditor' shall be construed in accordance with subsection (2) above;

'interested party' means any of the following, that is to say—

(a) the debtor;

(b) the creditor; and

(c) in a case where the person who applied for the qualifying periodical maintenance order in question is a person other than the creditor, that other person;

'maintenance order' means any order specified in Schedule 8 to the Administration of Justice Act 1970 and includes any such order which has been discharged, if any arrears are recoverable under it;

'qualifying periodical maintenance order' shall be construed in accordance with subsection (2) above, and the references to such an order in subsections (3) and (7) above are references to any such order, whether made before or after the coming into force of this section;

and the reference in subsection (2) above to an order requiring money to be paid periodically by one person to another includes a reference to an order requiring a lump sum to be paid by instalments by one person to another.

Child Support Act 1991
(1991 c. 48)

The basic principles

1 The duty to maintain

(1) For the purposes of this Act, each parent of a qualifying child is responsible for maintaining him.

(2) For the purposes of this Act, a non-resident parent shall be taken to have met his responsibility to maintain any qualifying child of his by making periodical payments of maintenance with respect to the child of such amount, and at such intervals, as may be determined in accordance with the provisions of this Act.

(3) Where a maintenance calculation made under this Act requires the making of periodical payments, it shall be the duty of the non-resident parent with respect to whom the calculation was made to make those payments.

2 Welfare of children: the general principle

Where, in any case which falls to be dealt with under this Act, the Secretary of State is considering the exercise of any discretionary power conferred by this Act, he shall have regard to the welfare of any child likely to be affected by his decision.

3 Meaning of certain terms used in this Act

(1) A child is a 'qualifying child' if—

(a) one of his parents is, in relation to him, a non-resident parent; or

(b) both of his parents are, in relation to him, non-resident parents.

(2) The parent of any child is a 'non-resident parent', in relation to him, if—

(a) that parent is not living in the same household with the child; and

(b) the child has his home with a person who is, in relation to him, a person with care.

(3) A person is a 'person with care', in relation to any child, if he is a person—

(a) with whom the child has his home;

(b) who usually provides day to day care for the child (whether exclusively or in conjunction with any other person); and

(c) who does not fall within a prescribed category of person.

(4) The Secretary of State shall not, under subsection (3)(c), prescribe as a category—

(a) parents;

(b) guardians;

(c) persons in whose favour residence orders under section 8 of the Children Act 1989 are in force . . .

(5) For the purposes of this Act there may be more than one person with care in relation to the same qualifying child.

(6) Periodical payments which are required to be paid in accordance with a maintenance calculation are referred to in this Act as 'child support maintenance'.

(7) Expressions are defined in this section only for the purposes of this Act.

4   Child support maintenance

(1) A person who is, in relation to any qualifying child or any qualifying children, either the person with care or the non-resident parent may apply to the Secretary of State for a maintenance calculation to be made under this Act with respect to that child, or any of those children.

(2) Where a maintenance calculation has been made in response to an application under this section the Secretary of State may, if the person with care or non-resident parent with respect to whom the calculation was made applies to him under this subsection, arrange for—

(a) the collection of the child support maintenance payable in accordance with the calculation;

(b) the enforcement of the obligation to pay child support maintenance in accordance with the calculation.

(3) Where an application under subsection (2) for the enforcement of the obligation mentioned in subsection (2)(b) authorises the Secretary of State to take steps to enforce that obligation whenever he considers it necessary to do so, the Secretary of State may act accordingly.

(4) A person who applies to the Secretary of State under this section shall, so far as that person reasonably can, comply with such regulations as may be made by the Secretary of State with a view to the Secretary of State being provided with the information which is required to enable—

(a) the non-resident parent to be identified or traced (where that is necessary);

(b) the amount of child support maintenance payable by the non-resident parent to be calculated; and

(c) that amount to be recovered from the non-resident parent.

(5) Any person who has applied to the Secretary of State under this section may at any time request him to cease acting under this section.

(6) It shall be the duty of the Secretary of State to comply with any request made under subsection (5) (but subject to any regulations made under subsection (8)).

(7) The obligation to provide information which is imposed by subsection (4)—

(a) shall not apply in such circumstances as may be prescribed; and

(b) may, in such circumstances as may be prescribed, be waived by the Secretary of State.

(8) The Secretary of State may by regulations make such incidental, supplemental or transitional provision as he thinks appropriate with respect to cases in which he is requested to cease to act under this section.

(9) No application may be made under this section if there is in force with respect to the person with care and non-resident parent in question a maintenance calculation made in response to an application treated as made under section 6.

(10) No application may be made at any time under this section with respect to a qualifying child or any qualifying children if—

(a)   there is in force a written maintenance agreement made before 5th April 1993, or a maintenance order made before a prescribed date, in respect of that child or those children and the person who is, at that time, the non-resident parent; or

(aa) maintenance order made on or after the date prescribed for the purposes of paragraph (a) is in force in respect of them, but has been so for less than the period of one year beginning with the date on which it was made; or

(b) benefit is being paid to, or in respect of, a parent with care of that child or those children.

(11) In subsection (10) 'benefit' means any benefit which is mentioned in, or prescribed by regulations under, section 6(1).

5 Child support maintenance: supplemental provisions

(1) Where—

(a) there is more than one person with care of a qualifying child; and

(b) one or more, but not all, of them have parental responsibility for the child;

no application may be made for a maintenance calculation with respect to the child by any of those persons who do not have parental responsibility for the child.

(2) Where more than one application for a maintenance calculation is made with respect to the child concerned, only one of them may be proceeded with.

(3) The Secretary of State may by regulations make provision as to which of two or more applications for a maintenance calculation with respect to the same child is to be proceeded with.

6 Applications by those claiming or receiving benefit

(1) This section applies where income support, an income-based jobseeker's allowance or any other benefit of a prescribed kind is claimed by or in respect of, or paid to or in respect of, the parent of a qualifying child who is also a person with care of the child.

(2) In this section, that person is referred to as 'the parent'.

(3) The Secretary of State may—

(a) treat the parent as having applied for a maintenance calculation with respect to the qualifying child and all other children of the non-resident parent in relation to whom the parent is also a person with care; and

(b) take action under this Act to recover from the non-resident parent, on the parent's behalf, the child support maintenance so determined.

(4) Before doing what is mentioned in subsection (3), the Secretary of State must notify the parent in writing of the effect of subsections (3) and (5) and section 46.

(5) The Secretary of State may not act under subsection (3) if the parent asks him not to (a request which need not be in writing).

(6) Subsection (1) has effect regardless of whether any of the benefits mentioned there is payable with respect to any qualifying child.

(7) Unless she has made a request under subsection (5), the parent shall, so far as she reasonably can, comply with such regulations as may be made by the Secretary of State with a view to the Secretary of State's being provided with the information which is required to enable—

(a) the non-resident parent to be identified or traced;

(b) the amount of child support maintenance payable by him to be calculated; and

(c) that amount to be recovered from him.

(8) The obligation to provide information which is imposed by subsection (7)—

(a) does not apply in such circumstances as may be prescribed; and

(b) may, in such circumstances as may be prescribed, be waived by the Secretary of State.

(9) If the parent ceases to fall within subsection (1), she may ask the Secretary of State to cease acting under this section, but until then he may continue to do so.

(10) The Secretary of State must comply with any request under subsection (9) (but subject to any regulations made under subsection (11)).

(11) The Secretary of State may by regulations make such incidental or transitional provision as he thinks appropriate with respect to cases in which he is asked under subsection (9) to cease to act under this section.

(12) The fact that a maintenance calculation is in force with respect to a person with care does not prevent the making of a new maintenance calculation with respect to her as a result of the Secretary of State's acting under subsection (3).

8 Role of the courts with respect to maintenance for children

(1) This subsection applies in any case where the Secretary of State would have jurisdiction to make a maintenance calculation with respect to a qualifying child and a non-resident parent of his on an application duly made (or treated as made) by a person entitled to apply for such a calculation with respect to that child.

(2) Subsection (1) applies even though the circumstances of the case are such that the Secretary of State would not make a calculation if it were applied for.

(3) Except as provided in subsection (3A), in any case where subsection (1) applies, no court shall exercise any power which it would otherwise have to make, vary or revive any maintenance order in relation to the child and non-resident parent concerned.

(3A) Unless a maintenance calculation has been made with respect to the child concerned, subsection (3) does not prevent a court from varying a maintenance order in relation to that child and the non-resident parent concerned—

(a) if the maintenance order was made on or after the date prescribed for the purposes of section 4(10)(a) or 7(10)(a); or

(b) where the order was made before then, in any case in which section 4(10) or 7(10) prevents the making of an application for a maintenance calculation with respect to or by that child.

(4) Subsection (3) does not prevent a court from revoking a maintenance order.

(5) The Lord Chancellor or in relation to Scotland the Lord Advocate may by order provide that, in such circumstances as may be specified by the order, this section shall not prevent a court from exercising any power which it has to make a maintenance order in relation to a child if—

(a) a written agreement (whether or not enforceable) provides for the making, or securing, by a non-resident parent of the child of periodical payments to or for the benefit of the child; and

(b) the maintenance order which the court makes is, in all material respects, in the same terms as that agreement.

(5A) The Lord Chancellor may make an order under subsection (5) only with the concurrence of the Lord Chief Justice.

(6) This section shall not prevent a court from exercising any power which it has to make a maintenance order in relation to a child if—

(a) a maintenance calculation is in force with respect to the child;

(b) the non-resident parent's net weekly income exceeds the figure referred to in paragraph 10(3) of Schedule 1 (as it has effect from time to time pursuant to regulations made under paragraph 10A(1)(b)); and

(c) the court is satisfied that the circumstances of the case make it appropriate for the non-resident parent to make or secure the making of periodical payments under a maintenance order in addition to the child support maintenance payable by him in accordance with the maintenance calculation.

(7) This section shall not prevent a court from exercising any power which it has to make a maintenance order in relation to a child if—

(a) the child is, will be or (if the order were to be made) would be receiving instruction at an educational establishment or undergoing training for a trade, profession or vocation (whether or not while in gainful employment); and

(b) the order is made solely for the purposes of requiring the person making or securing the making of periodical payments fixed by the order to meet some or all of the expenses incurred in connection with the provision of the instruction or training.

(8) This section shall not prevent a court from exercising any power which it has to make a maintenance order in relation to a child if—

(a) a disability living allowance is paid to or in respect of him; or

(b) no such allowance is paid but he is disabled, and the order is made solely for the purpose of requiring the person making or securing the making of periodical payments fixed by the order to meet some or all of any expenses attributable to the child's disability.

(9) For the purposes of subsection (8), a child is disabled if he is blind, deaf or dumb or is substantially and permanently handicapped by illness, injury, mental disorder or congenital deformity or such other disability as may be prescribed.

(10) This section shall not prevent a court from exercising any power which it has to make a maintenance order in relation to a child if the order is made against a person with care of the child.

(11) In this Act 'maintenance order', in relation to any child, means an order which requires the making or securing of periodical payments to or for the benefit of the child and which is made under—

(a) Part II of the Matrimonial Causes Act 1973;

(b) the Domestic Proceedings and Magistrates' Courts Act 1978;

(c) Part III of the Matrimonial and Family Proceedings Act 1984;

. . .

(e) Schedule 1 to the Children Act 1989;

(ea) Schedule 5, 6 or 7 to the Civil Partnership Act 2004; or

(f) any other prescribed enactment, and includes any order varying or reviving such an order.

(12) The Lord Chief Justice may nominate a judicial office holder (as defined in section 109(4) of the Constitutional Reform Act 2005) to exercise his functions under this section.

9   Agreements about maintenance

(1) In this section 'maintenance agreement' means any agreement for the making, or for securing the making, of periodical payments by way of maintenance, or in Scotland aliment, to or for the benefit of any child.

(2) Nothing in this Act shall be taken to prevent any person from entering into a maintenance agreement.

(3) Subject to section 4(10)(a) and section 7(10), the existence of a maintenance agreement shall not prevent any party to the agreement, or any other person, from applying for a maintenance calculation with respect to any child to or for whose benefit periodical payments are to be made or secured under the agreement.

(4) Where any agreement contains a provision which purports to restrict the right of any person to apply for a maintenance calculation, that provision shall be void.

(5) Where section 8 would prevent any court from making a maintenance order in relation to a child and a non-resident parent of his, no court shall exercise any power that it has to vary any agreement so as—

(a) to insert a provision requiring that non-resident parent to make or secure the making of periodical payments by way of maintenance, or in Scotland aliment, to or for the benefit of that child; or

(b) to increase the amount payable under such a provision.

(6) In any case in which section 4(10) or 7(10) prevents the making of an application for a maintenance calculation, and—

(a) no parent has been treated under section 6(3) as having applied for a maintenance calculation with respect to the child; or

(b) a parent has been so treated but no maintenance calculation has been made, subsection (5) shall have effect with the omission of paragraph (b).

10   Relationship between maintenance calculations and certain court orders and related matters

(1) Where an order of a kind prescribed for the purposes of this subsection is in force with respect to any qualifying child with respect to whom a maintenance calculation is made, the order—

    (a) shall, so far as it relates to the making or securing of periodical payments, cease to have effect to such extent as may be determined in accordance with regulations made by the Secretary of State; or

    (b) where the regulations so provide, shall, so far as it so relates, have effect subject to such modifications as may be so determined.

(2) Where an agreement of a kind prescribed for the purposes of this subsection is in force with respect to any qualifying child with respect to whom a maintenance calculation is made, the agreement—

    (a) shall, so far as it relates to the making or securing of periodical payments, be unenforceable to such extent as may be determined in accordance with regulations made by the Secretary of State; or

    (b) where the regulations so provide, shall, so far as it so relates, have effect subject to such modifications as may be so determined.

(3) Any regulations under this section may, in particular, make such provision with respect to—

    (a) any case where any person with respect to whom an order or agreement of a kind prescribed for the purposes of subsection (1) or (2) has effect applies to the prescribed court, before the end of the prescribed period, for the order or agreement to be varied in the light of the maintenance calculation and of the provisions of this Act;

    (b) the recovery of any arrears under the order or agreement which fell due before the coming into force of the maintenance calculation,

as the Secretary of State considers appropriate and may provide that, in prescribed circumstances, an application to any court which is made with respect to an order of a prescribed kind relating to the making or securing of periodical payments to or for the benefit of a child shall be treated by the court as an application for the order to be revoked.

(4) The Secretary of State may by regulations make provision for—

    (a) notification to be given by the Secretary of State to the prescribed person in any case where he considers that the making of a maintenance calculation has affected, or is likely to affect, any order of a kind prescribed for the purposes of this subsection;

    (b) notification to be given by the prescribed person to the Secretary of State in any case where a court makes an order which it considers has affected, or is likely to affect, a maintenance calculation.

(5) Rules may be made under section 144 of the Magistrates' Courts Act 1980 (rules of procedure) requiring any person who, in prescribed circumstances, makes an application to a magistrates' court for a maintenance order to furnish the court with a statement in a prescribed form, and signed by an officer of the Secretary of State, as to whether or not, at the time when the statement is made, there is a maintenance calculation in force with respect to that person or the child concerned.

In this subsection—

'maintenance order' means an order of a prescribed kind for the making or securing of periodical payments to or for the benefit of a child; and

'prescribed' means prescribed by the rules.

Maintenance calculations

11 Maintenance calculations

(1) An application for a maintenance calculation made to the Secretary of State shall be dealt with by him in accordance with the provision made by or under this Act.

(2) The Secretary of State shall (unless he decides not to make a maintenance calculation in response to the application, or makes a decision under section 12) determine the application by making a decision under this section about whether any child support maintenance is payable and, if so, how much.

(3) Where—
  (a) a parent is treated under section 6(3) as having applied for a maintenance calculation; but
  (b) the Secretary of State becomes aware before determining the application that the parent has ceased to fall within section 6(1),
he shall, subject to subsection (4), cease to treat that parent as having applied for a maintenance calculation.

(4) If it appears to the Secretary of State that subsection (10) of section 4 would not have prevented the parent with care concerned from making an application for a maintenance calculation under that section he shall—
  (a) notify her of the effect of this subsection; and
  (b) if, before the end of the period of one month beginning with the day on which notice was sent to her, she asks him to do so, treat her as having applied not under section 6 but under section 4.

(5) Where subsection (3) applies but subsection (4) does not, the Secretary of State shall notify—
  (a) the parent with care concerned; and
  (b) the non-resident parent (or alleged non-resident parent), where it appears to him that that person is aware that the parent with care has been treated as having applied for a maintenance calculation.

(6) The amount of child support maintenance to be fixed by a maintenance calculation shall be determined in accordance with Part I of Schedule I unless an application for a variation has been made and agreed.

(7) If the Secretary of State has agreed to a variation, the amount of child support maintenance to be fixed shall be determined on the basis he determines under section 28F(4).

(8) Part II of Schedule I makes further provision with respect to maintenance calculations.

12 Default and interim maintenance decisions
(1) Where the Secretary of State—
  (a) is required to make a maintenance calculation; or
  (b) is proposing to make a decision under section 16 or 17, and it appears to him that he does not have sufficient information to enable him to do so, he may make a default maintenance decision.

(2) Where an application for a variation has been made under section 28A(1) in connection with an application for a maintenance calculation (or in connection with such an application which is treated as having been made), the Secretary of State may make an interim maintenance decision.

(3) The amount of child support maintenance fixed by an interim maintenance decision shall be determined in accordance with Part I of Schedule 1.

(4) The Secretary of State may by regulations make provision as to default and interim maintenance decisions.

(5) The regulations may, in particular, make provision as to—
  (a) the procedure to be followed in making a default or an interim maintenance decision; and
  (b) a default rate of child support maintenance to apply where a default maintenance decision is made.

Information

14 Information required by Secretary of State
(1) The Secretary of State may make regulations requiring any information or evidence needed for the determination of any application made or treated as made under this Act, or any question arising in connection with such an application (or application treated as made),

or needed for the making of any decision or in connection with the imposition of any condition or requirement under this Act, or needed in connection with the collection or enforcement of child support or other maintenance under this Act, to be furnished—

    (a) by such persons as may be determined in accordance with regulations made by the Secretary of State; and

    (b) in accordance with the regulations.

(1A) Regulations under subsection (1) may make provision for notifying any person who is required to furnish any information or evidence under the regulations of the possible consequences of failing to do so.

(3) The Secretary of State may by regulations make provision authorising the disclosure by him, in such circumstances as may be prescribed, of such information held by him for purposes of this Act as may be prescribed.

(4) The provisions of Schedule 2 (which relate to information which is held for purposes other than those of this Act but which is required by the Secretary of State) shall have effect.

14A Information—offences

(1) This section applies to—

    (a) persons who are required to comply with regulations under section 4(4) or 7(5); and

    (b) persons specified in regulations under section 14(1)(a).

(2) Such a person is guilty of an offence if, pursuant to a request for information under or by virtue of those regulations—

    (a) he makes a statement or representation which he knows to be false; or

    (b) he provides, or knowingly causes or knowingly allows to be provided, a document or other information which he knows to be false in a material particular.

(3) Such a person is guilty of an offence if, following such a request, he fails to comply with it.

(4) It is a defence for a person charged with an offence under subsection (3) to prove that he had a reasonable excuse for failing to comply.

(5) A person guilty of an offence under this section is liable on summary conviction to a fine not exceeding level 3 on the standard scale.

15 Powers of inspectors

(1) The Secretary of State may appoint, on such terms as he thinks fit, persons to act as inspectors under this section.

(2) The function of inspectors is to acquire information which the Secretary of State needs for any of the purposes of this Act.

(3) Every inspector is to be given a certificate of his appointment.

(4) An inspector has power, at any reasonable time and either alone or accompanied by such other persons as he thinks fit, to enter any premises which—

    (a) are liable to inspection under this section; and

    (b) are premises to which it is reasonable for him to require entry in order that he may exercise his functions under this section,

and may there make such examination and inquiry as he considers appropriate.

(4A) Premises liable to inspection under this section are those which are not used wholly as a dwelling house and which the inspector has reasonable grounds for suspecting are—

    (a) premises at which a non-resident parent is or has been employed;

    (b) premises at which a non-resident parent carries out, or has carried out, a trade, profession, vocation or business;

    (c) premises at which there is information held by a person ('A') whom the inspector has reasonable grounds for suspecting has information about a non-resident parent acquired in the course of A's own trade, profession, vocation or business.

(5) An inspector exercising his powers may question any person aged 18 or over whom he finds on the premises.

(6) If required to do so by an inspector exercising his powers, any such person shall furnish to the inspector all such information and documents as the inspector may reasonably require.

(7) No person shall be required under this section to answer any question or to give any evidence tending to incriminate himself or, in the case of a person who is married or is a civil partner, his or her spouse or civil partner.

(8) On applying for admission to any premises in the exercise of his powers, an inspector shall, if so required, produce his certificate.

(9) If any person—

(a) intentionally delays or obstructs any inspector exercising his powers; or

(b) without reasonable excuse, refuses or neglects to answer any question or furnish any information or to produce any document when required to do so under this section,

he shall be guilty of an offence and liable on summary conviction to a fine not exceeding level 3 on the standard scale.

(10) In this section—

'certificate' means a certificate of appointment issued under this section;

'inspector' means an inspector appointed under this section;

'powers' means powers conferred by this section.

(11) In this section, 'premises' includes—

(a) moveable structures and vehicles, vessels, aircraft and hovercraft;

(b) installations that are offshore installations for the purposes of the Mineral Workings (Offshore Installations) Act 1971; and

(c) places of all other descriptions whether or not occupied as land or otherwise,

and references in this section to the occupier of premises are to be construed, in relation to premises that are not occupied as land, as references to any person for the time being present at the place in question.

Reviews and appeals

16 Revision of decisions

(1) Any decision to which subsection (1A) applies may be revised by the Secretary of State—

(a) either within the prescribed period or in prescribed cases or circumstances;

and

(b) either on an application made for the purpose or on his own initiative; and regulations may prescribe the procedure by which a decision of the Secretary of State may be so revised.

(1A) This subsection applies to—

(a) a decision of the Secretary of State under section 11, 12 or 17;

(b) a reduced benefit decision under section 46;

(c) a decision of an appeal tribunal on a referral under section 28D(1)(b).

(1B) Where the Secretary of State revises a decision under section 12(1)—

(a) he may (if appropriate) do so as if he were revising a decision under section 11; and

(b) if he does that, his decision as revised is to be treated as one under section 11 instead of section 12(1) (and, in particular, is to be so treated for the purposes of an appeal against it under section 20).

(2) In making a decision under subsection (1), the Secretary of State need not consider any issue that is not raised by the application or, as the case may be, did not cause him to act on his own initiative.

(3) Subject to subsections (4) and (5) and section 28ZC, a revision under this section shall take effect as from the date on which the original decision took (or was to take) effect.

(4) Regulations may provide that, in prescribed cases or circumstances, a revision under this section shall take effect as from such other date as may be prescribed.

(5) Where a decision is revised under this section, for the purpose of any rule as to the time allowed for bringing an appeal, the decision shall be regarded as made on the date on which it is so revised.

(6) Except in prescribed circumstances, an appeal against a decision of the Secretary of State shall lapse if the decision is revised under this section before the appeal is determined.

17 Decisions superseding earlier decisions

(1) Subject to subsection (2), the following, namely—

   (a) any decision of the Secretary of State under section 11 or 12 or this section, whether as originally made or as revised under section 16;

   (b) any decision of an appeal tribunal under section 20;

   (c) any reduced benefit decision under section 46;

   (d) any decision of an appeal tribunal on a referral under section 28D(1)(b);

   (e) any decision of a Child Support Commissioner on an appeal from such a decision as is mentioned in paragraph (b) or (d);

may be superseded by a decision made by the Secretary of State, either on an application made for the purpose or on his own initiative.

(2) In making a decision under subsection (1), the Secretary of State need not consider any issue that is not raised by the application or, as the case may be, did not cause him to act on his own initiative.

(3) Regulations may prescribe the cases and circumstances in which, and the procedure by which, a decision may be made under this section.

(4) Subject to subsection (5) and section 28ZC, a decision under this section shall take effect as from the beginning of the maintenance period in which it is made or, where applicable, the beginning of the maintenance period in which the application was made.

(4A) In subsection (4), a 'maintenance period' is (except where a different meaning is prescribed for prescribed cases) a period of seven days, the first one beginning on the effective date of the first decision made by the Secretary of State under section 11 or (if earlier) his first default or interim maintenance decision (under section 12) in relation to the non-resident parent in question, and each subsequent one beginning on the day after the last day of the previous one.

(5) Regulations may provide that, in prescribed cases or circumstances, a decision under this section shall take effect as from such other date as may be prescribed.

20 Appeals to appeal tribunals

(1) A qualifying person has a right of appeal to an appeal tribunal against—

   (a) a decision of the Secretary of State under section 11, 12 or 17 (whether as originally made or as revised under section 16);

   (b) a decision of the Secretary of State not to make a maintenance calculation under section 11 or not to supersede a decision under section 17;

   (c) a reduced benefit decision under section 46;

   (d) the imposition (by virtue of section 41A) of a requirement to make penalty payments, or their amount;

   (e) the imposition (by virtue of section 47) of a requirement to pay fees.

(2) In subsection (1), 'qualifying person' means—

   (a) in relation to paragraphs (a) and (b)—

      (i) the person with care, or non-resident parent, with respect to whom the Secretary of State made the decision, or

      (ii) in a case relating to a maintenance calculation which was applied for under section 7, either of those persons or the child concerned;

   (b) in relation to paragraph (c), the person in respect of whom the benefits are payable;

(c) in relation to paragraph (d), the parent who has been required to make penalty payments; and

(d) in relation to paragraph (e), the person required to pay fees.

(3) A person with a right of appeal under this section shall be given such notice as may be prescribed of—

(a) that right; and

(b) the relevant decision, or the imposition of the requirement.

(4) Regulations may make—

(a) provision as to the manner in which, and the time within which, appeals are to be brought; and

(b) such provision with respect to proceedings before appeal tribunals as the Secretary of State considers appropriate.

(5) The regulations may in particular make any provision of a kind mentioned in Schedule 5 to the Social Security Act 1998.

(6) No appeal lies by virtue of subsection (1)(c) unless the amount of the person's benefit is reduced in accordance with the reduced benefit decision; and the time within which such an appeal may be brought runs from the date of notification of the reduction.

(7) In deciding an appeal under this section, an appeal tribunal—

(a) need not consider any issue that is not raised by the appeal; and

(b) shall not take into account any circumstances not obtaining at the time when the Secretary of State made the decision or imposed the requirement.

(8) If an appeal under this section is allowed, the appeal tribunal may—

(a) itself make such decision as it considers appropriate; or

(b) remit the case to the Secretary of State, together with such directions (if any) as it considers appropriate.

. . .

22   Child Support Commissioners

(1) Her Majesty may from time to time appoint a Chief Child Support Commissioner and such number of other Child Support Commissioners as she may think fit.

(2) The Chief Child Support Commissioner and the other Child Support Commissioners shall be appointed from among persons who—

(a) have a 10 year general qualification; or

(b) are advocates or solicitors in Scotland of 10 years' standing.

(3) The Lord Chancellor, after consulting the Secretary of State, may make such regulations with respect to proceedings before Child Support Commissioners as he considers appropriate.

(4) The regulations—

(a) may, in particular, make any provision of a kind mentioned in schedule 5 to the Social Security Act 1998; and

(b) shall provide that any hearing before a Child Support Commissioner shall be in public except in so far as the Commissioner for special reasons directs otherwise.

(5) Schedule 4 shall have effect with respect to Child Support Commissioners.

. . .

23A   Redetermination of appeals

(1) This section applies where an application is made to a person under section 24(6)(a) for leave to appeal from a decision of an appeal tribunal.

(2) If the person who constituted, or was the chairman of, the appeal tribunal considers that the decision was erroneous in law, he may set aside the decision and refer the case either for redetermination by the tribunal or for determination by a differently constituted tribunal.

(3) If each of the principal parties to the case expresses the view that the decision was erroneous in point of law, the person shall set aside the decision and refer the case for determination by a differently constituted tribunal.

(4) The 'principal parties' are—

    (a) the Secretary of State; and

    (b) those who are qualifying persons for the purposes of section 20(2) in relation to the decision in question.

24 Appeal to Child Support Commissioner

(1) Any person who is aggrieved by a decision of an appeal tribunal, and the Secretary of State, may appeal to a Child Support Commissioner on a question of law.

(2) Where, on an appeal under this section, a Child Support Commissioner holds that the decision appealed against was wrong in law he shall set it aside.

(3) Where a decision is set aside under subsection (2), the Child Support Commissioner may—

    (a) if he can do so without making fresh or further findings of fact, give the decision which he considers should have been given by the appeal tribunal;

    (b) if he considers it expedient, make such findings and give such decision as he considers appropriate in the light of those findings; or

    (c) on an appeal by the Secretary of State, refer the case to an appeal tribunal with directions for its determination; or

    (d) on any other appeal, refer the case to the Secretary of State or, if he considers it appropriate, to an appeal tribunal with directions for its determination.

(4) The reference under subsection (3) to the Secretary of State shall, subject to any direction of the Child Support Commissioner, be to an officer of his, or a person providing him with services, who has taken no part in the decision originally appealed against.

(5) On a reference under subsection (3) to an appeal tribunal, the tribunal shall, subject to any direction of the Child Support Commissioner, consist of persons who were not members of the tribunal which gave the decision which has been appealed against.

(6) No appeal lies under this section without the leave—

    (a) of the person who constituted, or was the chairman of, the appeal tribunal when the decision appealed against was given or of such other person as may be determined in accordance with regulations made by the Lord Chancellor; or

    (b) subject to and in accordance with regulations so made, of a Child Support Commissioner.

(7) The Lord Chancellor may by regulations make provision as to the manner in which, and the time within which, appeals under this section are to be brought and applications for leave under this section are to be made.

(8) Where a question which would otherwise fall to be determined by the Secretary of State first arises in the course of an appeal to a Child Support Commissioner, he may, if he thinks fit, determine it even though it has not been considered by the Secretary of State.

(9) Before making any regulations under subsection (6) or (7), the Lord Chancellor shall consult the Secretary of State.

25 Appeal from Child Support Commissioner on question of law

(1) An appeal on a question of law shall lie to the appropriate court from any decision of a Child Support Commissioner.

(2) No such appeal may be brought except—

    (a) with leave of the Child Support Commissioner who gave the decision or, where regulations made by the Lord Chancellor so provide, of a Child Support Commissioner selected in accordance with the regulations; or

    (b) if the Child Support Commissioner refuses leave, with the leave of the appropriate court.

(3) An application for leave to appeal under this section against a decision of a Child Support Commissioner ('the appeal decision') may only be made by—

    (a) a person who was a party to the proceedings in which the original decision, or appeal decision, was given;

(b) the Secretary of State; or

(c) any other person who is authorised to do so by regulations made by the Lord Chancellor.

(3A) The Child Support Commissioner to whom an application for leave to appeal under this section is made shall specify as the appropriate court either the Court of Appeal or the Court of Session.

(3B) In determining the appropriate court, the Child Support Commissioner shall have regard to the circumstances of the case, and in particular the convenience of the persons who may be parties to the appeal.

(4) In this section—

'appropriate court' except in subsections (3A) and (3B), means the court specified in accordance with those subsections; and

'original decision' meanps the decision to which the appeal decision in question relates.

(5) The Lord Chancellor may by regulations make provision with respect to—

(a) the manner in which and the time within which applications must be made to a Child Support Commissioner for leave under this section; and

(b) the procedure for dealing with such applications.

(6) Before making any regulations under subsection (2), (3) or (5), the Lord Chancellor shall consult the Secretary of State.

26 Disputes about parentage

(1) Where a person who is alleged to be a parent of the child with respect to whom an application for a maintenance calculation has been made or treated as made ('the alleged parent') denies that he is one of the child's parents, the Secretary of State shall not make a maintenance calculation on the assumption that the alleged parent is one of the child's parents unless the case falls within one of those set out in subsection (2).

(2) The Cases are—

CASE A1

Where—

(a) the child is habitually resident in England and Wales;

(b) the Secretary of State is satisfied that the alleged parent was married to the child's mother at some time in the period beginning with the conception and ending with the birth of the child; and

(c) the child has not been adopted.

CASE A2

Where—

(a) the child is habitually resident in England and Wales;

(b) the alleged parent has been registered as father of the child under section 10 or 10A of the Births and Deaths Registration Act 1953, or in any register kept under section 13 (register of births and still-births) or section 44 (Register of Corrections Etc) of the Registration of Births, Deaths and Marriages (Scotland) Act 1965, or under Article 14 or 18(1)(b)(ii) of the Births and Deaths Registration (Northern Ireland) Order 1976; and

(c) the child has not subsequently been adopted.

CASE A3

Where the result of a scientific test (within the meaning of section 27A) taken by the alleged parent would be relevant to determining the child's parentage, and the alleged parent—

(a) refuses to take such a test; or

(b) has submitted to such a test, and it shows that there is no reasonable doubt that the alleged parent is a parent of the child.

CASE A

Where the alleged parent is a parent of the child in question by virtue of having adopted him.

CASE B

Where the alleged parent is a parent of the child in question by virtue of an order under section 30 of the Human Fertilisation and Embryology Act 1990 (parental orders in favour of gamete donors).

CASE B1

Where the Secretary of State is satisfied that the alleged parent is a parent of the child in question by virtue of section 27 or 28 of that Act (meaning of 'mother' and of 'father' respectively).

CASE C

Where—
> (a) either—
> > (i)   a declaration that the alleged parent is a parent of the child in question (or a declaration which has that effect) is in force under section 55A or 56 of the Family Law Act 1986 or Article 32 of the Matrimonial and Family Proceedings (Northern Ireland) Order 1989 (declarations of parentage); or

...and
> (a) the child has not subsequently been adopted.

. . .

CASE F

Where—
> (a) the alleged parent has been found, or adjudged, to be the father of the child in question—
> > (i)   in proceedings before any court in England and Wales which are relevant proceedings for the purposes of section 12 of the Civil Evidence Act 1968 or in proceedings before any court in Northern Ireland which are relevant proceedings for the purposes of section 8 of the Civil Evidence Act (Northern Ireland) 1971; or
> > (ii) in affiliation proceedings before any court in the United Kingdom, (whether or not he offered any defence to the allegation of paternity) and that finding or adjudication still subsists; and
> (b) the child has not subsequently been adopted.

(3) In this section—
'adopted' means adopted within the meaning of Part IV of the Adoption Act 1976 or Chapter 4 of Part I of the Adoption and Children Act 2002;

. . .

27 Applications for declaration of parentage under Family Law Act 1986
(1) This section applies where—

(a) an application for a maintenance calculation has been made (or is treated as having been made), or a maintenance calculation is in force, with respect to a person ('the alleged parent') who denies that he is a parent of a child with respect to whom the application or calculation was made or treated as made;

(b) the Secretary of State is not satisfied that the case falls within one of those set out in section 26(2); and

(c) the Secretary of State or the person with care makes an application for a declaration under section 55A of the Family Law Act 1986 as to whether or not the alleged parent is one of the child's parents.

(2) Where this section applies—

(a) if it is the person with care who makes the application, she shall be treated as having a sufficient personal interest for the purposes of subsection (3) of that section; and

(b) if it is the Secretary of State who makes the application, that subsection shall not apply.

27A   Recovery of fees for scientific tests

(1) This section applies in any case where—

(a) an application for a maintenance calculation has been made or treated as made or a maintenance calculation is in force;

(b) scientific tests have been carried out (otherwise than under a direction or in response to a request) in relation to bodily samples obtained from a person who is alleged to be a parent of a child with respect to whom the application or calculation is made or, as the case may be, treated as made;

(c) the results of the tests do not exclude the alleged parent from being one of the child's parents; and

(d) one of the conditions set out in subsection (2) is satisfied.

(2) The conditions are that—

(a) the alleged parent does not deny that he is one of the child's parents;

(b) in proceedings under section 55A of the Family Law Act 1986, a court has made a declaration that the alleged parent is a parent of the child in question; or

. . .

(3) In any case to which this section applies, any fee paid by the Secretary of State in connection with scientific tests may be recovered by him from the alleged parent as a debt due to the Crown.

(4) In this section—

'bodily sample' means a sample of bodily fluid or bodily tissue taken for the purpose of scientific tests;

'direction' means a direction given by a court under section 20 of the Family Law Reform Act 1969 (tests to determine paternity);

'request' means a request made by a court under section 70 of the Law Reform (Miscellaneous Provisions) (Scotland) Act 1990 (blood and other samples in civil proceedings); and

'scientific tests' means scientific tests made with the object of ascertaining the inheritable characteristics of bodily fluids or bodily tissue.

(5) Any sum recovered by the Secretary of State under this section shall be paid by him into the Consolidated Fund.

Decisions and appeals dependent on other cases

28ZA   Decisions involving issues that arise on appeal in other cases

(1) This section applies where—

(a) a decision by the Secretary of State falls to be made under section 11, 12, 16 or 17 or with respect to a reduced benefit decision under section 46; and

(b) an appeal is pending against a decision given in relation to a different matter by a Child Support Commissioner or a court.

(2) If the Secretary of State considers it possible that the result of the appeal will be such that, if it were already determined, it would affect the decision in some way—

    (a) he need not, except in such cases or circumstances as may be prescribed, make the decision while the appeal is pending;

    (b) he may, in such cases or circumstances as may be prescribed, make the decision on such basis as may be prescribed.

(3) Where the Secretary of State acts in accordance with subsection (2)(b), following the determination of the appeal he shall if appropriate revise his decision (under section 16) in accordance with that determination.

(4) For the purposes of this section, an appeal against a decision is pending if—

    (a) an appeal against the decision has been brought but not determined;

    (b) an application for leave to appeal against the decision has been made but not determined; or

    (c) in such circumstances as may be prescribed, an appeal against the decision has not been brought (or, as the case may be, an application for leave to appeal against the decision has not been made) but the time for doing so has not yet expired.

(5) In paragraphs (a), (b) and (c) of subsection (4), any reference to an appeal, or an application for leave to appeal, against a decision includes a reference to—

    (a) an application for, or for leave to apply for, judicial review of the decision under section 31 of the Supreme Court Act 1981;

. . .

28ZB Appeals involving issues that arise on appeal in other cases

(1) This section applies where—

    (a) an appeal ('appeal A') in relation to a decision or the imposition of a requirement falling within section 20(1) is made to an appeal tribunal, or from an appeal tribunal to a Child Support Commissioner;

    (b) an appeal ('appeal B') is pending against a decision given in a different case by a Child Support Commissioner or a court.

(2) If the Secretary of State considers it possible that the result of appeal B will be such that, if it were already determined, it would affect the determination of appeal A, he may serve notice requiring the tribunal or Child Support Commissioner—

    (a) not to determine appeal A but to refer it to him; or

    (b) to deal with the appeal in accordance with subsection (4).

(3) Where appeal A is referred to the Secretary of State under subsection (2)(a), following the determination of appeal B and in accordance with that determination, he shall if appropriate—

    (a) in a case where appeal A has not been determined by the tribunal, revise (under section 16) his decision which gave rise to that appeal; or

    (b) in a case where appeal A has been determined by the tribunal, make a decision (under section 17) superseding the tribunal's decision.

(4) Where appeal A is to be dealt with in accordance with this subsection, the appeal tribunal or Child Support Commissioner shall either—

    (a) stay appeal A until appeal B is determined; or

    (b) if the tribunal or Child Support Commissioner considers it to be in the interests of the appellant to do so, determine appeal A as if—

        (i) appeal B had already been determined; and

        (ii) the issues arising on appeal B had been decided in the way that was most unfavourable to the appellant.

In this subsection 'the appellant' means the person who appealed or, as the case may be, first appealed against the decision or the imposition of the requirement mentioned in subsection (1)(a).

(5) Where the appeal tribunal or Child Support Commissioner acts in accordance with subsection (4)(b), following the determination of appeal B the Secretary of State shall, if appropriate, make a decision (under section 17) superseding the decision of the tribunal or Child Support Commissioner in accordance with that determination.

(6) For the purposes of this section, an appeal against a decision is pending if—

(a) an appeal against the decision has been brought but not determined;

(b) an application for leave to appeal against the decision has been made but not determined; or

(c) in such circumstances as may be prescribed, an appeal against the decision has not been brought (or, as the case may be, an application for leave to appeal against the decision has not been made) but the time for doing so has not yet expired.

(7) In this section—

(a) the reference in subsection (1)(a) to an appeal to a Child Support Commissioner includes a reference to an application for leave to appeal to a Child Support Commissioner; and

(b) any reference in paragraph (a), (b) or (c) of subsection (6) to an appeal, or to an application for leave to appeal, against a decision includes a reference to—

(i) an application for, or for leave to apply for, judicial review of the decision under section 31 of the Supreme Court Act 1981; or

(ii) an application to the supervisory jurisdiction of the Court of Session in respect of the decision.

(8) Regulations may make provision supplementing that made by this section.

Cases of error

28ZC—(1) Subject to subsection (2), this section applies where—

(a) the effect of the determination, whenever made, of an appeal to a Child Support Commissioner or the court ('the relevant determination') is that the adjudicating authority's decision out of which the appeal arose was erroneous in point of law; and

(b) after the date of the relevant determination a decision falls to be made by the Secretary of State in accordance with that determination (or would, apart from this section, fall to be so made)—

(i) with respect to an application for a maintenance calculation (made after the commencement date) or one treated as having been so made, or under section 46 as to the reduction of benefit;

(ii) as to whether to revise, under section 16, any decision (made after the commencement date) referred to in section 16(1A); or

(iii) on an application under section 17 (made after the commencement date) for any decision (made after the commencement date) referred to in section 17(1).

(2) This section does not apply where the decision of the Secretary of State mentioned in subsection (1)(b)—

(a) is one which, but for section 28ZA(2)(a), would have been made before the date of the relevant determination; or

(b) is one made in pursuance of section 28ZB(3) or (5).

(3) In so far as the decision relates to a person's liability or the reduction of a person's benefit in respect of a period before the date of the relevant determination, it shall be made as if the adjudicating authority's decision had been found by the Commissioner or court not to have been erroneous in point of law.

(4) Subsection (1)(a) shall be read as including a case where—

(a) the effect of the relevant determination is that part or all of a purported regulation or order is invalid; and

(b) the error of law made by the adjudicating authority was to act on the basis that the purported regulation or order (or the part held to be invalid) was valid.

(5) It is immaterial for the purposes of subsection (1)—

    (a) where such a decision as is mentioned in paragraph (b)(i) falls to be made; or

    (b) where such a decision as is mentioned in paragraph (b)(ii) or (iii) falls to be made on an application under section 16 or (as the case may be) section 17, whether the application was made before or after the date of the relevant determination.

(6) In this section—

'adjudicating authority' means the Secretary of State, or a child support officer;

'the commencement date' means the date of the coming into force of section 44 of the Social Security Act 1998 or, in the case of a decision made on a referral under section 28D(1)(b), an appeal tribunal; and

'the court' means the High Court, the Court of Appeal, the Court of Session, the High Court or Court of Appeal in Northern Ireland, the Supreme Court or the Court of Justice of the European Community.

(7) The date of the relevant determination shall, in prescribed cases, be determined for the purposes of this section in accordance with any regulations made for that purpose.

(8) Regulations made under subsection (7) may include provision—

    (a) for a determination of a higher court to be treated as if it had been made on the date of a determination of a lower court or a Child Support Commissioner; or

    (b) for a determination of a lower court or a Child Support Commissioner to be treated as if it had been made on the date of a determination of a higher court.

28ZD   Correction of errors and setting aside of decisions

(1) Regulations may make provision with respect to—

    (a) the correction of accidental errors in any decision or record of a decision given under this Act; and

    (b) the setting aside of any such decision in a case where it appears just to set the decision aside on the ground that—

        (i) a document relating to the proceedings in which the decision was given was not sent to, or was not received at an appropriate time by, a party to the proceedings or a party's representative or was not received at an appropriate time by the body or person who gave the decision; or

        (ii) a party to the proceedings or a party's representative was not present at a hearing related to the proceedings.

(2) Nothing in subsection (1) shall be construed as derogating from any power to correct errors or set aside decisions which is exercisable apart from regulations made by virtue of that subsection.

Variations

28A   Application for variation of usual rules for calculating maintenance[1]

(1) *Where an application for a maintenance calculation is made under section 4 or 7, or treated as made under section 6,* the person with care or the non-resident parent or *(in the case of an application under* section 7) either of them or the child concerned may apply to the Secretary of State for the rules by which the calculation is made to be varied in accordance with this Act.

(2) Such an application is referred to in this Act as an 'application for a variation'.

(3) An application for a variation may be made at any time before the Secretary of State has reached a decision (under section 11 or 12(1)) on the application for a maintenance calculation (or the application treated as having been made under section 6).

---

[1] Modification of section 28A in applications under section 28G

    Section 28A is modified as follows where an application is made under section 28G:

        (i) Subsection (1): for the first phrase in italics, substitute 'Where a maintenance calculation other than an interim maintenance decision is in force';

        (ii) Subsection (1): for the second phrase in italics, substitute '(where the maintenance calculation was made following an application under';

        (iii) Subsection (3) is omitted.

(4) A person who applies for a variation—

    (a) need not make the application in writing unless the Secretary of State directs in any case that he must; and

    (b) must say upon what grounds the application is made.

(5) In other respects an application for a variation is to be made in such manner as may be prescribed.

(6) Schedule 4A has effect in relation to applications for a variation.

28B   Preliminary consideration of applications[(2)]

(1) Where an application for a variation has been duly made to the Secretary of State, he may give it a preliminary consideration.

(2) Where he does so he may, on completing the preliminary consideration, reject the application *(and proceed to make his decision on the application for a maintenance calculation without any variation)* if it appears to him—

    (a) that there are no grounds on which he could agree to a variation;

    (b) that he has insufficient information to make a decision on the application for the maintenance calculation under section 11 (apart from any information needed in relation to the application for a variation), and therefore that his decision would be made under section 12(1); or

    (c) that other prescribed circumstances apply.

28C   Imposition of regular payments condition[(3)]

(1) Where—

    (a) an application for a variation is made by the non-resident parent; and

    (b) the Secretary of State makes an interim maintenance decision,

the Secretary of State may also, if he has completed his preliminary consideration (under section 28B) of the application for a variation and has not rejected it under that section, impose on the non-resident parent one of the conditions mentioned in subsection (2) (a 'regular payments condition').

(2) The conditions are that—

    (a) the non-resident parent must make the payments of child support maintenance specified in the *interim maintenance decision*;

    (b) the non-resident parent must make such lesser payments of child support maintenance as may be determined in accordance with regulations made by the Secretary of State.

[(2)] Modification of section 28B in cases of applications under section 28G

    Section 28B is modified as follows where an application is made under section 28G:

        (i)   Subsection (2): for the words in italics, substitute '(and proceed to revise or supersede a decision under section 16 or 17 respectively without taking the variation into account, or not to revise or supersede a decision under section 16 or 17)';

        (ii) Subsection (2)(b) is omitted.

[(3)] Modification of section 28C in cases of applications under section 28G

    Section 28C is modified as follows where an application is made under section 28G:

        (i)   Subsection (1): subsection (1)(b) and the word 'also' are omitted;

        (ii) Subsection (2): for the words in italics, substitute 'maintenance calculation in force';

        (iii) Subsection (3)(c): for the words in italics, substitute 'maintenance calculation in force was made in response to an application';

        (iv) Subsection (4)(a): for subsection (4)(a), substitute 'when in response to the application for a variation the Secretary of State has revised or superseded a decision under section 16 or 17 respectively (whether he agrees to a variation or not) or not revised or superseded a decision under section 16 or 17;';

        (v) Subsection (5): for the words in italics, substitute 'revise or supersede a decision under section 16 or 17 respectively, or not revise or supersede a decision under section 16 or 17, as if the application had failed';

        (vi) Subsection (7)(c): for the words in italics, substitute 'maintenance calculation in force was made in response to an application'.

(3) Where the Secretary of State imposes a regular payments condition, he shall give written notice of the imposition of the condition and of the effect of failure to comply with it to—

(a) the non-resident parent;

(b) all the persons with care concerned; and

(c) if the *application for the maintenance calculation was* made under section 7, the child who made the application.

(4) A regular payments condition shall cease to have effect—

(a) when the Secretary of State has made a decision on the application for a maintenance calculation under section 11 (whether he agrees to a variation or not);

(b) on the withdrawal of the application for a variation.

(5) Where a non-resident parent has failed to comply with a regular payments condition, the Secretary of State may in prescribed circumstances refuse to consider the application for a variation, and instead *reach his decision under section 11 as if no such application had been made.*

(6) The question whether a non-resident parent has failed to comply with a regular payments condition is to be determined by the Secretary of State.

(7) Where the Secretary of State determines that a non-resident parent has failed to comply with a regular payments condition he shall give written notice of his determination to—

(a) that parent;

(b) all the persons with care concerned; and

(c) if the *application for the maintenance calculation was* made under section 7, the child who made the application.

28D   Determination of applications[4]

(1) Where an application for a variation has not failed, the Secretary of State shall, in accordance with the relevant provisions of, or made under, this Act—

(a) either agree or not to a variation, and make a decision *under section 11 or 12(1)*; or

(b) refer the application to an appeal tribunal for the tribunal to determine what variation, if any, is to be made.

(2) For the purposes of subsection (1), an application for a variation has failed if—

(a) it has been withdrawn; or

(b) the Secretary of State has rejected it on completing a preliminary consideration under section 28B; or

(c) the Secretary of State has refused to consider it under section 28C(5).

(3) In dealing with an application for a variation which has been referred to it under subsection (1)(b), an appeal tribunal shall have the same powers, and be subject to the same duties, as would the Secretary of State if he were dealing with the application.

28E   Matters to be taken into account[5]

(1) In determining whether to agree to a variation, the Secretary of State shall have regard both to the general principles set out in subsection (2) and to such other considerations as may be prescribed.

(2) The general principles are that—

(a) parents should be responsible for maintaining their children whenever they can afford to do so;

(b) where a parent has more than one child, his obligation to maintain any one of them should be no less of an obligation than his obligation to maintain any other of them.

---

[4] Modification of section 28D in cases of applications under section 28G

Section 28D is modified as follows where an application is made under section 28G:

(i)   Subsection (1)(a): for the words in italics, substitute 'under section 16 or 17'.

[5] Modification of section 28E in cases of applications under section 28G

Section 28E is modified as follows where an application is made under section 28G:

(i)   Subsection (3)(b): for subsection (3)(b), substitute 'where the maintenance calculation in force was made in response to an application under section 7, by either of them or the child concerned.'

(3) In determining whether to agree to a variation, the Secretary of State shall take into account any representations made to him—

    (a) by the person with care or non-resident parent concerned; or

    (b) where the application for the current calculation was made under section 7, by either of them or the child concerned.

(4) In determining whether to agree to a variation, no account shall be taken of the fact that—

    (a) any part of the income of the person with care concerned is, or would be if the Secretary of State agreed to a variation, derived from any benefit; or

    (b) some or all of any child support maintenance might be taken into account in any manner in relation to any entitlement to benefit.

(5) In this section 'benefit' has such meaning as may be prescribed.

28F   Agreement to a variation[6]

(1) The Secretary of State may agree to a variation if—

    (a) he is satisfied that the case is one which falls within one or more of the cases set out in Part I of Schedule 4B or in regulations made under that Part; and

    (b) it is his opinion that, in all the circumstances of the case, it would be just and equitable to agree to a variation.

(2) In considering whether it would be just and equitable in any case to agree to a variation, the Secretary of State—

    (a) must have regard, in particular, to the welfare of any child likely to be affected if he did agree to a variation; and

    (b) must, or as the case may be must not, take any prescribed factors into account, or must take them into account (or not) in prescribed circumstances.

(3) The Secretary of State shall not agree to a variation (and shall proceed to make his decision on the application for a maintenance calculation without any variation) if he is satisfied that—

    (a) he has insufficient information to make a decision on the application for the maintenance calculation under section 11, and therefore that his decision would be made under section 12(1); or

    (b) other prescribed circumstances apply.

(4) Where the Secretary of State agrees to a variation, he shall—

    (a) determine the basis on which the amount of child support maintenance is to be calculated in response to the *application for a maintenance calculation (including an application treated as having been made); and*

    (b) make a decision under section 11 on that basis.

(5) If the Secretary of State has made an interim maintenance decision, it is to be treated as having been replaced by his decision under section 11, and except in prescribed circumstances any appeal connected with it (under section 20) shall lapse.

(6) In determining whether or not to agree to a variation, the Secretary of State shall comply with regulations made under Part II of Schedule 4B.

---

[6] Modification of section 28F in cases of applications under section 28G

    Section 28F is modified as follows where an application is made under section 28G:

      (i) Subsection (3): for subsection (3), substitute 'The Secretary of State shall not agree to a variation (and shall proceed to revise or supersede a decision under section 16 or 17 respectively without taking the variation into account, or not revise or supersede a decision under section 16 or 17) if he is satisfied that prescribed circumstances apply.';

     (ii) Subsection (4)(a): words in italics are omitted;

    (iii) Subsection (4)(b): for subsection (4)(b), substitute 'revise or supersede a decision under section 16 or 17 respectively on that basis.';

    (iv) Subsection (5) is omitted.

28G   Variations: revision and supersession

(1) An application for a variation may also be made when a maintenance calculation is in force.

(2) The Secretary of State may by regulations provide for—

(a) sections 16, 17 and 20; and

(b) sections 28A to 28F and Schedules 4A and 4B,

to apply with prescribed modifications in relation to such applications.

(3) The Secretary of State may by regulations provide that, in prescribed cases (or except in prescribed cases), a decision under section 17 made otherwise than pursuant to an application for a variation may be made on the basis of a variation agreed to for the purposes of an earlier decision without a new application for a variation having to be made.

Voluntary payments

28J   Voluntary payments

(1) This section applies where—

(a) a person has applied for a maintenance calculation under section 4(1) or 7 (1), or is treated as having applied for one by virtue of section 6;

(b) the Secretary of State has neither made a decision under section 11 or 12 on the application, nor decided not to make a maintenance calculation; and

(c) the non-resident parent makes a voluntary payment.

(2) A 'voluntary payment' is a payment—

(a) on account of child support maintenance which the non-resident parent expects to become liable to pay following the determination of the application (whether or not the amount of the payment is based on any estimate of his potential liability which the Secretary of State has agreed to give); and

(b) made before the maintenance calculation has been notified to the nonresident parent or (as the case may be) before the Secretary of State has notified the non-resident parent that he has decided not to make a maintenance calculation.

(3) In such circumstances and to such extent as may be prescribed—

(a) the voluntary payment may be set off against arrears of child support maintenance which accrued by virtue of the maintenance calculation taking effect on a date earlier than that on which it was notified to the non-resident parent;

(b) the amount payable under a maintenance calculation may be adjusted to take account of the voluntary payment.

(4) A voluntary payment shall be made to the Secretary of State unless he agrees, on such conditions as he may specify, that it may be made to the person with care, or to or through another person.

(5) The Secretary of State may by regulations make provision as to voluntary payments, and the regulations may in particular—

(a) prescribe what payments or descriptions of payment are, or are not, to count as 'voluntary payments';

(b) prescribe the extent to which and circumstances in which a payment, or a payment of a prescribed description, counts.

Collection and enforcement

29   Collection of child support maintenance

(1) The Secretary of State may arrange for the collection of any child support maintenance payable in accordance with a maintenance calculation where—

(a) the calculation is made by virtue of section 6; or

(b) an application has been made to the Secretary of State under section 4(2) or 7(3) for him to arrange for its collection.

(2) Where a maintenance calculation is made under this Act, payments of child support maintenance under the calculation shall be made in accordance with regulations made by the Secretary of State.

(3) The regulations may, in particular, make provision—
  (a) for payments of child support maintenance to be made—
      (i)   to the person caring for the child or children in question;
      (ii) to, or through, the Secretary of State; or
      (iii) to, or through, such other person as the Secretary of State may, from time to time, specify;
  (b) as to the method by which payments of child support maintenance are to be made;
  (c) as to the intervals at which such payments are to be made;
  (d) as to the method and timing of the transmission of payments which are made, to or through the Secretary of State or any other person, in accordance with the regulations;
  (e) empowering the Secretary of State to direct any person liable to make payments in accordance with the calculation—
      (i)   to make them by standing order or by any other method which requires one person to give his authority for payments to be made from an account of his to an account of another's on specific dates during the period for which the authority is in force and without the need for any further authority from him;
      (ii) to open an account from which payments under the calculation may be made in accordance with the method of payment which that person is obliged to adopt;
  (f) providing for the making of representations with respect to matters with which the regulations are concerned.

30   Collection and enforcement of other forms of maintenance
(1) Where the Secretary of State is arranging for the collection of any payments under section 29 or subsection (2), he may also arrange for the collection of any periodical payments, or secured periodical payments, of a prescribed kind which are payable to or for the benefit of any person who falls within a prescribed category.

(2) The Secretary of State may, except in prescribed cases, arrange for the collection of any periodical payments, or secured periodical payments, of a prescribed kind which are payable for the benefit of a child even though he is not arranging for the collection of child support maintenance with respect to that child.

(3) Where—
  (a) the Secretary of State is arranging, under this Act, for the collection of different payments ('the payments') from the same non-resident parent;
  (b) an amount is collected by the Secretary of State from the non-resident parent which is less than the total amount due in respect of the payments; and
  (c) the non-resident parent has not stipulated how that amount is to be allocated by the Secretary of State as between the payments,
the Secretary of State may allocate that amount as he sees fit.

(4) In relation to England and Wales, the Secretary of State may by regulations make provision for sections 29 and 31 to 40 to apply, with such modifications (if any) as he considers necessary or expedient, for the purpose of enabling him to enforce any obligation to pay any amount which he is authorised to collect under this section.

(5A) Regulations made under subsection (1) or (2) prescribing payments which may be collected by the Secretary of State may make provision for the payment to him by such person or persons as may be prescribed of such fees as may be prescribed.

31   Deduction from earnings orders
(1) This section applies where any person ('the liable person') is liable to make payments of child support maintenance.

(2) The Secretary of State may make an order ('a deduction from earnings order') against a liable person to secure the payment of any amount due under the maintenance calculation in question.

(3) A deduction from earnings order may be made so as to secure the payment of—

(a) arrears of child support maintenance payable under the calculation;

(b) amounts of child support maintenance which will become due under the calculation; or

(c) both such arrears and such future amounts.

(4) A deduction from earnings order—

(a) shall be expressed to be directed at a person ('the employer') who has the liable person in his employment; and

(b) shall have effect from such date as may be specified in the order.

(5) A deduction from earnings order shall operate as an instruction to the employer to—

(a) make deductions from the liable person's earnings; and

(b) pay the amounts deducted to the Secretary of State.

(6) The Secretary of State shall serve a copy of any deduction from earnings order which he makes under this section on—

(a) the person who appears to the Secretary of State to have the liable person in question in his employment; and

(b) the liable person.

(7) Where—

(a) a deduction from earnings order has been made; and

(b) a copy of the order has been served on the liable person's employer, it shall be the duty of that employer to comply with the order; but he shall not be under any liability for non-compliance before the end of the period of 7 days beginning with the date on which the copy was served on him.

(8) In this section and in section 32 'earnings' has such meaning as may be prescribed.

32   Regulations about deduction from earnings orders

(1) The Secretary of State may by regulations make provision with respect to deduction from earnings orders.

(2) The regulations may, in particular, make provision—

(a)   as to the circumstances in which one person is to be treated as employed by another;

(b)   requiring any deduction from earnings under an order to be made in the prescribed manner;

(bb) for the amount or amounts which are to be deducted from the liable person's earnings not to exceed a prescribed proportion of his earnings (as determined by the employer);

(c)   requiring an order to specify the amount or amounts to which the order relates and the amount or amounts which are to be deducted from the liable person's earnings in order to meet his liabilities under the maintenance calculation in question;

(d)   requiring the intervals between deductions to be made under an order to be specified in the order;

(e)   as to the payment of sums deducted under an order to the Secretary of State;

(f)   allowing the person who deducts and pays any amount under an order to deduct from the liable person's earnings a prescribed sum towards his administrative costs;

(g)   with respect to the notification to be given to the liable person of amounts deducted, and amounts paid, under the order;

(h)   requiring any person on whom a copy of an order is served to notify the Secretary of State in the prescribed manner and within a prescribed period if he does not have the liable person in his employment or if the liable person ceases to be in his employment;

(i)   as to the operation of an order where the liable person is in the employment of the Crown;

(j)   for the variation of orders;

(k) similar to that made by section 31(7), in relation to any variation of an order;

(l) for an order to lapse when the employer concerned ceases to have the liable person in his employment;

(m) as to the revival of an order in such circumstances as may be prescribed;

(n) allowing or requiring an order to be discharged;

(o) as to the giving of notice by the Secretary of State to the employer concerned that an order has lapsed or has ceased to have effect.

(3) The regulations may include provision that while a deduction from earnings order is in force—

(a) the liable person shall from time to time notify the Secretary of State, in the prescribed manner and within a prescribed period, of each occasion on which he leaves any employment or becomes employed, or re-employed, and shall include in such a notification a statement of his earnings and expected earnings from the employment concerned and of such other matters as may be prescribed;

(b) any person who becomes the liable person's employer and knows that the order is in force shall notify the Secretary of State, in the prescribed manner and within a prescribed period, that he is the liable person's employer, and shall include in such a notification a statement of the liable person's earnings and expected earnings from the employment concerned and of such other matters as may be prescribed.

(4) The regulations may include provision with respect to the priority as between a deduction from earnings order and—

(a) any other deduction from earnings order;

(b) any order under any other enactment relating to England and Wales which provides for deductions from the liable person's earnings;

(c) any diligence against earnings.

(5) The regulations may include a provision that a liable person may appeal to a magistrates' court if he is aggrieved by the making of a deduction from earnings order against him, or by the terms of any such order, or there is a dispute as to whether payments constitute earnings or as to any other prescribed matter relating to the order.

(6) On an appeal under subsection (5) the court or (as the case may be) the sheriff shall not question the maintenance calculation by reference to which the deduction from earnings order was made.

(7) Regulations made by virtue of subsection (5) may include provision as to the powers of a magistrates' court, in relation to an appeal (which may include provision as to the quashing of a deduction from earnings order or the variation of the terms of such an order).

(8) If any person fails to comply with the requirements of a deduction from earnings order, or with any regulation under this section which is designated for the purposes of this subsection, he shall be guilty of an offence.

(9) In subsection (8) 'designated' means designated by the regulations.

(10) It shall be a defence for a person charged with an offence under subsection (8) to prove that he took all reasonable steps to comply with the requirements in question.

(11) Any person guilty of an offence under subsection (8) shall be liable on summary conviction to a fine not exceeding level two on the standard scale.

33 Liability orders

(1) This section applies where—

(a) a person who is liable to make payments of child support maintenance ('the liable person') fails to make one or more of those payments; and

(b) it appears to the Secretary of State that—

(i) it is inappropriate to make a deduction from earnings order against him (because, for example, he is not employed); or

(ii) although such an order has been made against him, it has proved ineffective as a means of securing that payments are made in accordance with the maintenance calculation in question.

(2) The Secretary of State may apply to a magistrates' court for an order ('a liability order') against the liable person.

(3) Where the Secretary of State applies for a liability order, the magistrates' court shall make the order if satisfied that the payments in question have become payable by the liable person and have not been paid.

(4) On an application under subsection (2), the court shall not question the maintenance calculation under which the payments of child support maintenance fell to be made.

(5) If the Secretary of State designates a liability order for the purposes of this subsection it shall be treated as a judgment entered in a county court for the purposes of section 73 of the County Courts Act 1984 (register of judgments and orders).

(6) Where regulations have been made under section 29(3)(a)—

(a) the liable person fails to make a payment (for the purposes of subsection (1)(a) of this section); and

(b) a payment is not paid (for the purposes of subsection (3)),

unless the payment is made to, or through, the person specified in or by virtue of those regulations for the case of the liable person in question.

34 Regulations about liability orders

(1) The Secretary of State may make regulations in relation to England and Wales—

(a) prescribing the procedure to be followed in dealing with an application by the Secretary of State for a liability order;

(b) prescribing the form and contents of a liability order; and

(c) providing that where a magistrates' court has made a liability order, the person against whom it is made shall, during such time as the amount in respect of which the order was made remains wholly or partly unpaid, be under a duty to supply relevant information to the Secretary of State.

(2) In subsection (1) 'relevant information' means any information of a prescribed description which is in the possession of the liable person and which the Secretary of State has asked him to supply.

35 Enforcement of liability orders by distress

(1) Where a liability order has been made against a person ('the liable person'), the Secretary of State may levy the appropriate amount by distress and sale of the liable person's goods.

(2) In subsection (1), 'the appropriate amount' means the aggregate of—

(a) the amount in respect of which the order was made, to the extent that it remains unpaid; and

(b) an amount, determined in such manner as may be prescribed, in respect of the charges connected with the distress.

(3) The Secretary of State may, in exercising his powers under subsection (1) against the liable person's goods, seize—

(a) any of the liable person's goods except—

(i) such tools, books, vehicles and other items of equipment as are necessary to him for use personally by him in his employment, business or vocation;

(ii) such clothing, bedding, furniture, household equipment and provisions as are necessary for satisfying his basic domestic needs; and

(b) any money, banknotes, bills of exchange, promissory notes, bonds, specialties or securities for money belonging to the liable person.

(4) For the purposes of subsection (3), the liable person's domestic needs shall be taken to include those of any member of his family with whom he resides.

(5) No person levying a distress under this section shall be taken to be a trespasser—

(a) on that account; or

(b) from the beginning, on account of any subsequent irregularity in levying the distress.

(6) A person sustaining special damage by reason of any irregularity in levying a distress under this section may recover full satisfaction for the damage (and no more) by proceedings in trespass or otherwise.

(7) The Secretary of State may make regulations supplementing the provisions of this section.

(8) The regulations may, in particular—

(a) provide that a distress under this section may be levied anywhere in England and Wales;

(b) provide that such a distress shall not be deemed unlawful on account of any defect or want of form in the liability order;

(c) provide for an appeal to a magistrates' court by any person aggrieved by the levying of, or an attempt to levy, a distress under this section;

(d) make provision as to the powers of the court on an appeal (which may include provision as to the discharge of goods distrained or the payment of compensation in respect of goods distrained and sold).

36   Enforcement in county courts

(1) Where a liability order has been made against a person, the amount in respect of which the order was made, to the extent that it remains unpaid, shall, if a county court so orders, be recoverable by means of garnishee proceedings or a charging order, as if it were payable under a county court order.

(2) In subsection (1) 'charging order' has the same meaning as in section 1 of the Charging Orders Act 1979.

39A   Commitment to prison and disqualification from driving

(1) Where the Secretary of State has sought—

(a) in England and Wales to levy an amount by distress under this Act; or

(b) to recover an amount by virtue of section 36 or 38,

and that amount, or any portion of it, remains unpaid he may apply to the court under this section.

(2) An application under this section is for whichever the court considers appropriate in all the circumstances of—

(a) the issue of a warrant committing the liable person to prison; or

(b) an order for him to be disqualified from holding or obtaining a driving licence.

(3) On any such application the court shall (in the presence of the liable person) inquire as to—

(a) whether he needs a driving licence to earn his living;

(b) his means; and

(c) whether there has been wilful refusal or culpable neglect on his part.

(4) The Secretary of State may make representations to the court as to whether he thinks it more appropriate to commit the liable person to prison or to disqualify him from holding or obtaining a driving licence; and the liable person may reply to those representations.

(5) In this section and section 40B, 'driving licence' means a licence to drive a motor vehicle granted under Part III of the Road Traffic Act 1988.

(6) In this section 'the court' means—

(a) in England and Wales, a magistrates' court;

(b) in Scotland, the sheriff.

40   Commitment to prison

(3) If, but only if, the court is of the opinion that there has been wilful refusal or culpable neglect on the part of the liable person it may—

(a) issue a warrant of commitment against him; or

(b) fix a term of imprisonment and postpone the issue of the warrant until such time and on such conditions (if any) as it thinks just.

(4) Any such warrant—
- (a) shall be made in respect of an amount equal to the aggregate of—
  - (i) the amount mentioned in section 35(1) or so much of it as remains outstanding; and
  - (ii) an amount (determined in accordance with regulations made by the Secretary of State) in respect of the costs of commitment; and
- (b) shall state that amount.

(5) No warrant may be issued under this section against a person who is under the age of 18.

(6) A warrant issued under this section shall order the liable person—
- (a) to be imprisoned for a specified period; but
- (b) to be released (unless he is in custody for some other reason) on payment of the amount stated in the warrant.

(7) The maximum period of imprisonment which may be imposed by virtue of subsection (6) shall be calculated in accordance with Schedule 4 to the Magistrates' Courts Act 1980 (maximum periods of imprisonment in default of payment) but shall not exceed six weeks.

(8) The Secretary of State may by regulations make provision for the period of imprisonment specified in any warrant issued under this section to be reduced where there is part payment of the amount in respect of which the warrant was issued.

(9) A warrant issued under this section may be directed to such person or persons as the court issuing it thinks fit.

(10) Section 80 of the Magistrates' Courts Act 1980 (application of money found on defaulter) shall apply in relation to a warrant issued under this section against a liable person as it applies in relation to the enforcement of a sum mentioned in subsection (1) of that section.

(11) The Secretary of State may by regulations make provision—
- (a) as to the form of any warrant issued under this section;
- (b) allowing an application under this section to be renewed where no warrant is issued or term of imprisonment is fixed;
- (c) that a statement in writing to the effect that wages of any amount have been paid to the liable person during any period, purporting to be signed by or on behalf of his employer, shall be evidence of the facts stated;
- (d) that, for the purposes of enabling an inquiry to be made as to the liable person's conduct and means, a justice of the peace may issue a summons to him to appear before a magistrates' court and (if he does not obey) may issue a warrant for his arrest;
- (e) that for the purpose of enabling such an inquiry, a justice of the peace may issue a warrant for the liable person's arrest without issuing a summons;
- (f) as to the execution of a warrant for arrest.

. . .

40B Disqualification from driving: further provision

(1) If, but only if, the court is of the opinion that there has been wilful refusal or culpable neglect on the part of the liable person, it may—
- (a) order him to be disqualified, for such period specified in the order but not exceeding two years as it thinks fit, from holding or obtaining a driving licence (a 'disqualification order'); or
- (b) make a disqualification order but suspend its operation until such time and on such conditions (if any) as it thinks just.

(2) The court may not take action under both section 40 and this section.

(3) A disqualification order must state the amount in respect of which it is made, which is to be the aggregate of—
- (a) the amount mentioned in section 35(1), or so much of it as remains outstanding; and
- (b) an amount (determined in accordance with regulations made by the Secretary of State) in respect of the costs of the application under section 39A.

(4) A court which makes a disqualification order shall require the person to whom it relates to produce any driving licence held by him, and its counterpart (within the meaning of section 108(1) of the Road Traffic Act 1988).

(5) On an application by the Secretary of State or the liable person, the court—

    (a) may make an order substituting a shorter period of disqualification, or make an order revoking the disqualification order, if part of the amount referred to in sub-section (3) (the 'amount due') is paid to any person authorised to receive it; and

    (b) must make an order revoking the disqualification order if all of the amount due is so paid.

(6) The Secretary of State may make representations to the court as to the amount which should be paid before it would be appropriate to make an order revoking the disqualification order under subsection (5)(a), and the person liable may reply to those representations.

(7) The Secretary of State may make a further application under section 39A if the amount due has not been paid in full when the period of disqualification specified in the disqualification order expires.

(8) Where a court—

    (a) makes a disqualification order;

    (b) makes an order under subsection (5); or

    (c) allows an appeal against a disqualification order,

it shall send notice of that fact to the Secretary of State; and the notice shall contain such particulars and be sent in such manner and to such address as the Secretary of State may determine.

(9) Where a court makes a disqualification order, it shall also send the driving licence and its counterpart, on their being produced to the court, to the Secretary of State at such address as he may determine.

(10) Section 80 of the Magistrates' Courts Act 1980 (application of money found on defaulter) shall apply in relation to a disqualification order under this section in relation to a liable person as it applies in relation to the enforcement of a sum mentioned in subsection (1) of that section.

(11) The Secretary of State may by regulations make provision in relation to disqualification orders corresponding to the provision he may make under section 40(11).

41   Arrears of child support maintenance

(1) This section applies where—

    (a) the Secretary of State is authorised under section 4, 6 or 7 to recover child support maintenance payable by a non-resident parent in accordance with a maintenance calculation; and

    (b) the non-resident parent has failed to make one or more payments of child support maintenance due from him in accordance with that calculation.

(2) Where the Secretary of State recovers any such arrears he may, in such circumstances as may be prescribed and to such extent as may be prescribed, retain them if he is satisfied that the amount of any benefit paid to or in respect of the person with care of the child or children in question would have been less had the non-resident parent made the payment or payments of child support maintenance in question.

(2A) In determining for the purposes of subsection (2) whether the amount of any benefit paid would have been less at any time than the amount which was paid at that time, in a case where the maintenance calculation had effect from a date earlier than that on which it was made, the calculation shall be taken to have been in force at that time.

(6) Any sums retained by the Secretary of State by virtue of this section shall be paid by him into the Consolidated Fund.

41A   Penalty payments

(1) The Secretary of State may by regulations make provision for the payment to him by non-resident parents who are in arrears with payments of child support maintenance of penalty payments determined in accordance with the regulations.

(2) The amount of a penalty payment in respect of any week may not exceed 25% of the amount of child support maintenance payable for that week, but otherwise is to be determined by the Secretary of State.

(3) The liability of a non-resident parent to make a penalty payment does not affect his liability to pay the arrears of child support maintenance concerned.

(4) Regulations under subsection (1) may, in particular, make provision—

(a) as to the time at which a penalty payment is to be payable;

(b) for the Secretary of State to waive a penalty payment, or part of it.

(5) The provisions of this Act with respect to—

(a) the collection of child support maintenance;

(b) the enforcement of an obligation to pay child support maintenance, apply equally (with any necessary modifications) to penalty payments payable by virtue of regulations under this section.

(6) The Secretary of State shall pay penalty payments received by him into the Consolidated Fund.

41B   Repayment of overpaid child support maintenance

(1) This section applies where it appears to the Secretary of State that a non-resident parent has made a payment by way of child support maintenance which amounts to an overpayment by him of that maintenance and that—

(a) it would not be possible for the non-resident parent to recover the amount of the overpayment by way of an adjustment of the amount payable under a maintenance calculation; or

(b) it would be inappropriate to rely on an adjustment of the amount payable under a maintenance calculation as the means of enabling the non-resident parent to recover the amount of overpayment.

(1A) This section also applies where the non-resident parent has made a voluntary payment and it appears to the Secretary of State—

(a) that he is not liable to pay child support maintenance; or

(b) that he is liable, but some or all of the payment amounts to an overpayment, and, in a case falling within paragraph (b), it also appears to him that subsection (1)(a) or (b) applies.

(2) The Secretary of State may make such payment to the non-resident parent by way of reimbursement, or partial reimbursement, of the overpayment as the Secretary of State considers appropriate.

(3) Where the Secretary of State has made a payment under this section he may, in such circumstances as may be prescribed, require the relevant person to pay to him the whole, or a specified proportion, of the amount of that payment.

(4) Any such requirement shall be imposed by giving the relevant person a written demand for the amount which the Secretary of State wishes to recover from him.

(5) Any sum which a person is required to pay to the Secretary of State under this section shall be recoverable from him by the Secretary of State as a debt due to the Crown.

(6) The Secretary of State may by regulations make provision in relation to any case in which—

(a) one or more overpayments of child support maintenance are being reimbursed to the Secretary of State by the relevant person; and

(b) child support maintenance has continued to be payable by the non-resident parent concerned to the person with care concerned, or again becomes so payable.

(7) For the purposes of this section—

(a) a payment made by a person under a maintenance calculation which was not validly made; and

(b) a voluntary payment made in the circumstances set out in subsection (1A)(a), shall be treated as an overpayment of child support maintenance made by a non-resident parent.

(8) In this section 'relevant person', in relation to an overpayment, means the person with care to whom the overpayment was made.

(9) Any sum recovered by the Secretary of State under this section shall be paid by him into the Consolidated Fund.

Special cases

42   Special cases

(1) The Secretary of State may by regulations provide that in prescribed circumstances a case is to be treated as a special case for the purposes of this Act.

(2) Those regulations may, for example, provide for the following to be special cases—

    (a) each parent of a child is a non-resident parent in relation to the child;

    (b) there is more than one person who is a person with care in relation to the same child;

    (c) there is more than one qualifying child in relation to the same non-resident parent but the person who is the person with care in relation to one of those children is not the person who is the person with care in relation to all of them;

    (d) a person is a non-resident parent in relation to more than one child and the other parent of each of those children is not the same person;

    (e) the person with care has care of more than one qualifying child and there is more than one non-resident parent in relation to those children;

    (f) a qualifying child has his home in two or more separate households.

(3) The Secretary of State may by regulations make provision with respect to special cases.

(4) Regulations made under subsection (3) may, in particular—

    (a) modify any provision made by or under this Act, in its application to any special case or any special case falling within a prescribed category;

    (b) make new provision for any such case; or

    (c) provide for any prescribed provision made by or under this Act not to apply to any such case.

43   Recovery of child support maintenance by deduction from benefit

(1) This section applies where—

    (a) a non-resident parent is liable to pay a flat rate of child support maintenance (or would be so liable but for a variation having been agreed to), and that rate applies (or would have applied) because he falls within paragraph 4(1)(b) or (c) or 4(2) of Schedule 1; and

    (b) such conditions as may be prescribed for the purposes of this section are satisfied.

(2) The power of the Secretary of State to make regulations under section 5 of the Social Security Administration Act 1992 by virtue of subsection (1)(p) (deductions from benefits) may be exercised in relation to cases to which this section applies with a view to securing that payments in respect of child support maintenance are made or that arrears of child support maintenance are recovered.

(3) For the purposes of this section, the benefits to which section 5 of the 1992 Act applies are to be taken as including war disablement pensions and war widows' pensions (within the meaning of section 150 of the Social Security Contributions and Benefits Act 1992 (interpretation)).

Jurisdiction

44   Jurisdiction

(1) The Secretary of State shall have jurisdiction to make a maintenance calculation with respect to a person who is—

    (a) a person with care;

    (b) a non-resident parent; or

    (c) a qualifying child,

only if that person is habitually resident in the United Kingdom, except in the case of a non-resident parent who falls within subsection (2A).

(2) Where the person with care is not an individual, subsection (1) shall have effect as if paragraph (a) were omitted.

(2A) A non-resident parent falls within this subsection if he is not habitually resident in the United Kingdom, but is—

(a) employed in the civil service of the Crown, including Her Majesty's Diplomatic Service and Her Majesty's Overseas Civil Service;

(b) a member of the naval, military or air forces of the Crown, including any person employed by an association established for the purposes of Part XI of the Reserve Forces Act 1996;

(c) employed by a company of a prescribed description registered under the Companies Act 1985 in England and Wales or in Scotland, or under the Companies (Northern Ireland) Order 1986; or

(d) employed by a body of a prescribed description.

45   Jurisdiction of courts in certain proceedings under this Act

(1) The Lord Chancellor . . . . may by order make such provision as he considers necessary to secure that appeals, or such class of appeals as may be specified in the order—

(a) shall be made to a court instead of being made to an appeal tribunal; or

(b) shall be so made in such circumstances as may be so specified.

. . .

Miscellaneous and supplemental

46   Reduced benefit decisions

(1) This section applies where any person ('the parent')—

(a) has made a request under section 6(5);

(b) fails to comply with any regulation made under section 6(7); or

(c) having been treated as having applied for a maintenance calculation under section 6, refuses to take a scientific test (within the meaning of section 27A).

(2) The Secretary of State may serve written notice on the parent requiring her, before the end of a specified period—

(a) in a subsection (1)(a) case, to give him her reasons for making the request;

(b) in a subsection (1)(b) case, to give him her reasons for failing to do so; or

(c) in a subsection (1)(c) case, to give him her reasons for her refusal.

(3) When the specified period has expired, the Secretary of State shall consider whether, having regard to any reasons given by the parent, there are reasonable grounds for believing that—

(a) in a subsection (1)(a) case, if the Secretary of State were to do what is mentioned in section 6(3);

(b) in a subsection (1)(b) case, if she were to be required to comply; or

(c) in a subsection (1)(c) case, if she took the scientific test,

there would be a risk of her, or of any children living with her, suffering harm or undue distress as a result of his taking such action, or her complying or taking the test.

(4) If the Secretary of State considers that there are such reasonable grounds, he shall—

(a) take no further action under this section in relation to the request, the failure or the refusal in question; and

(b) notify the parent, in writing, accordingly.

(5) If the Secretary of State considers that there are no such reasonable grounds, he may, except in prescribed circumstances, make a reduced benefit decision with respect to the parent.

(6) In a subsection (1)(a) case, the Secretary of State may from time to time serve written notice on the parent requiring her, before the end of a specified period—

(a) to state whether her request under section 6(5) still stands; and

(b) if so, to give him her reasons for maintaining her request,

and subsections (3) to (5) have effect in relation to such a notice and any response to it as they have effect in relation to a notice under subsection (2)(a) and any response to it.

(7) Where the Secretary of State makes a reduced benefit decision he must send a copy of it to the parent.

(8) A reduced benefit decision is to take effect on such date as may be specified in the decision.

(9) Reasons given in response to a notice under subsection (2) or (6) need not be given in writing unless the Secretary of State directs in any case that they must.

(10) In this section—

(a) 'comply' means to comply with the requirement or with the regulation in question; and 'complied' and 'complying' are to be construed accordingly;

(b) 'reduced benefit decision' means a decision that the amount payable by way of any relevant benefit to, or in respect of, the parent concerned be reduced by such amount, and for such period, as may be prescribed;

(c) 'relevant benefit' means income support or an income-based jobseeker's allowance or any other benefit of a kind prescribed for the purposes of section 6; and

(d) 'specified', in relation to a notice served under this section, means specified in the notice; and the period to be specified is to be determined in accordance with regulations made by the Secretary of State.

. . .

46A   Finality of decisions

(1) Subject to the provisions of this Act, any decision of the Secretary of State or an appeal tribunal made in accordance with the foregoing provisions of this Act shall be final.

(2) If and to the extent that regulations so provide, any finding of fact or other determination embodied in or necessary to such a decision, or on which such a decision is based, shall be conclusive for the purposes of—

(a) further such decisions;

(b) decisions made in accordance with sections 8 to 16 of the Social Security Act 1998, or with regulations under section 11 of that Act; and

(c) decisions made under the Vaccine Damage Payments Act 1979.

46B   Matters arising as respects decisions

(1) Regulations may make provision as respects matters arising pending—

(a) any decision of the Secretary of State under section 11, 12 or 17;

(b) any decision of an appeal tribunal under section 20; or

(c) any decision of a Child Support Commissioner under section 24.

(2) Regulations may also make provision as respects matters arising out of the revision under section 16, or on appeal, of any such decision as is mentioned in subsection (1).

47   Fees

(1) The Secretary of State may by regulations provide for the payment, by the non-resident parent or the person with care (or by both), of such fees as may be prescribed in cases where the Secretary of State takes, or proposes to take, any action under section 4 or 6.

(2) The Secretary of State may by regulations provide for the payment, by the non-resident parent, the person with care or the child concerned (or by any or all of them), of such fees as may be prescribed in cases where the Secretary of State takes, or proposes to take, any action under section 7.

(3) Regulations made under this section—

(a) may require any information which is needed for the purpose of determining the amount of any such fee to be furnished, in accordance with the regulations, by such person as may be prescribed;

(b) shall provide that no such fees shall be payable by any person to or in respect of whom income support, an income-based jobseeker's allowance, any element of child tax credit other than the family element, working tax credit or any other benefit of a prescribed kind is paid; and

(c) may, in particular, make provision with respect to the recovery by the Secretary of State of any fees payable under the regulations.

(4) The provisions of this Act with respect to—

(a) the collection of child support maintenance;

(b) the enforcement of any obligation to pay child support maintenance,

shall apply equally (with any necessary modifications) to fees payable by virtue of regulations made under this section.

. . .

50 Unauthorised disclosure of information

(1) Any person who is, or has been, employed in employment to which this section applies is guilty of an offence if, without lawful authority, he discloses any information which—

(a) was acquired by him in the course of that employment; and

(b) relates to a particular person.

(2) It is not an offence under this section—

(a) to disclose information in the form of a summary or collection of information so framed as not to enable information relating to any particular person to be ascertained from it; or

(b) to disclose information which has previously been disclosed to the public with lawful authority.

(3) It is a defence for a person charged with an offence under this section to prove that at the time of the alleged offence—

(a) he believed that he was making the disclosure in question with lawful authority and had no reasonable cause to believe otherwise; or

(b) he believed that the information in question had previously been disclosed to the public with lawful authority and had no reasonable cause to believe otherwise.

. . .

54 Interpretation

In this Act—

'non-resident parent' has the meaning given in section 3(2);

'appeal tribunal' means an appeal tribunal constituted under Chapter I of Part I of the Social Security Act 1998;

'application for a variation' means an application under section 28A or 28G;

'benefit Acts' means the Social Security Contributions and Benefits Act 1992 and the Social Security Administration Act 1992;

'child benefit' has the same meaning as in the Child Benefit Act 1975;

'child support maintenance' has the meaning given in section 3(6);

'deduction from earnings order' has the meaning given in section 31(2);

'default maintenance decision' has the meaning given in section 12;

'disabled person's tax credit' has the same meaning as in the benefit Acts;

'general qualification' shall be construed in accordance with section 71 of the Courts and Legal Services Act 1990 (qualification for judicial appointments);

'income-based jobseeker's allowance' has the same meaning as in the Jobseekers Act 1995;

'income support' has the same meaning as in the benefit Acts;

'interim maintenance decision' has the meaning given in section 12;

'liability order' has the meaning given in section 33(2);

'maintenance agreement' has the meaning given in section 9(1);

'maintenance calculation' means a calculation of maintenance made under this Act and, except in prescribed circumstances, includes a default maintenance decision and an interim maintenance decision.

'maintenance order' has the meaning given in section 8(11);

'parent', in relation to any child, means any person who is in law the mother or father of the child;

'parent with care' means a person who is, in relation to a child, both a parent and a person with care.

'parental responsibility', in the application of this Act—

(a) to England and Wales, has the same meaning as in the Children Act 1989;

. . .

'person with care' has the meaning given in section 3(3);

'prescribed' means prescribed by regulations made by the Secretary of State;

'qualifying child' has the meaning given in section 3(1).

'voluntary payment' has the meaning given in section 28J.

55   Meaning of 'child'

(1) For the purposes of this Act a person is a child if—

    (a) he is under the age of 16;

    (b) he is under the age of 19 and receiving full-time education (which is not advanced education)—

        (i) by attendance at a recognised educational establishment; or

        (ii) elsewhere, if the education is recognised by the Secretary of State; or

    (c) he does not fall within paragraph (a) or (b) but—

        (i) he is under the age of 18, and

        (ii) prescribed conditions are satisfied with respect to him.

(2) A person is not a child for the purposes of this Act if he—

    (a) is or has been married or a civil partner;

    (b) has celebrated a marriage, or been a party to a civil partnership, which is void; or

    (c) has celebrated a marriage in respect of which a decree of nullity has been granted or has been a party to a civil partnership in respect of which a nullity order has been made.

(3) In this section—

'advanced education' means education of a prescribed description; and

'recognised educational establishment' means an establishment recognised by the Secretary of State for the purposes of this section as being, or as comparable to, a university, college or school.

(4) Where a person has reached the age of 16, the Secretary of State may recognise education provided for him otherwise than at a recognised educational establishment only if the Secretary of State is satisfied that education was being so provided for him immediately before he reached the age of 16.

(5) The Secretary of State may provide that in prescribed circumstances education is or is not to be treated for the purposes of this section as being full-time.

(6) In determining whether a person falls within subsection (1)(b), no account shall be taken of such interruptions in his education as may be prescribed.

(7) The Secretary of State may by regulations provide that a person who ceases to fall within subsection (1) shall be treated as continuing to fall within that subsection for a prescribed period.

(8) No person shall be treated as continuing to fall within subsection (1) by virtue of regulations made under subsection (7) after the end of the week in which he reaches the age of 19.

. . .

SCHEDULES

Section 11   ## SCHEDULE 1

MAINTENANCE CALCULATIONS

PART I   CALCULATION OF WEEKLY AMOUNT OF CHILD
SUPPORT MAINTENANCE

General rule

1.—(1) The weekly rate of child support maintenance is the basic rate unless a reduced rate, a flat rate or the nil rate applies.

(2) Unless the nil rate applies, the amount payable weekly to a person with care is—

(a) the applicable rate, if paragraph 6 does not apply; or

(b) if paragraph 6 does apply, that rate as apportioned between the persons with care in accordance with paragraph 6,

as adjusted, in either case, by applying the rules about shared care in paragraph 7 or 8.

Basic rate

2.—(1) The basic rate is the following percentage of the non-resident parent's net weekly income—

15% where he has one qualifying child;

20% where he has two qualifying children;

25% where he has three or more qualifying children.

(2) If the non-resident parent also has one or more relevant other children, the appropriate percentage referred to in sub-paragraph (1) is to be applied instead to his net weekly income less—

15% where he has one relevant other child;

20% where he has two relevant other children;

25% where he has three or more relevant other children.

Reduced rate

3.—(1) A reduced rate is payable if—

(a) neither a flat rate nor the nil rate applies; and

(b) the non-resident parent's net weekly income is less than £200 but more than £100.

(2) The reduced rate payable shall be prescribed in, or determined in accordance with, regulations.

(3) The regulations may not prescribe, or result in, a rate of less than £5.

Flat rate

4.—(1) Except in a case falling within sub-paragraph (2), a flat rate of £5 is payable if the nil rate does not apply and—

(a) the non-resident parent's net weekly income is £100 or less; or

(b) he receives any benefit, pension or allowance prescribed for the purposes of this paragraph of this sub-paragraph; or

(c) he or his partner (if any) receives any benefit prescribed for the purposes of this paragraph of this sub-paragraph.

(2) A flat rate of a prescribed amount is payable if the nil rate does not apply and—

(a) the non-resident parent has a partner who is also a non-resident parent;

(b) the partner is a person with respect to whom a maintenance calculation is in force; and

(c) the non-resident parent or his partner receives any benefit prescribed under sub-paragraph (1)(c).

(3) The benefits, pensions and allowances which may be prescribed for the purposes of sub-paragraph (1)(b) include ones paid to the non-resident parent under the law of a place outside the United Kingdom.

Nil rate

5. The rate payable is nil if the non-resident parent—
    (a) is of a prescribed description; or
    (b) has a net weekly income of below £5.

Apportionment

6.—(1) If the non-resident parent has more than one qualifying child and in relation to them there is more than one person with care, the amount of child support maintenance payable is (subject to paragraph 7 or 8) to be determined by apportioning the rate between the persons with care.

(2) The rate of maintenance liability is to be divided by the number of qualifying children, and shared among the persons with care according to the number of qualifying children in relation to whom each is a person with care.

Shared care—basic and reduced rate

7.—(1) This paragraph applies only if the rate of child support maintenance payable is the basic rate or a reduced rate.

(2) If the care of a qualifying child is shared between the non-resident parent and the person with care, so that the non-resident parent from time to time has care of the child overnight, the amount of child support maintenance which he would otherwise have been liable to pay the person with care, as calculated in accordance with the preceding paragraphs of this Part of this Schedule, is to be decreased in accordance with this paragraph.

(3) First, there is to be a decrease according to the number of such nights which the Secretary of State determines there to have been, or expects there to be, or both during a prescribed twelve-month period.

(4) The amount of that decrease for one child is set out in the following Table—

Number of nights	Fraction to subtract
52 to 103	One-seventh
104 to 155	Two-sevenths
156 to 174	Three-sevenths
175 or more	One-half

(5) If the person with care is caring for more than one qualifying child of the non-resident parent, the applicable decrease is the sum of the appropriate fractions in the Table divided by the number of such qualifying children.

(6) If the applicable fraction is one-half in relation to any qualifying child in the care of the person with care, the total amount payable to the person with care is then to be further decreased by £7 for each such child.

(7) If the application of the preceding provisions of this paragraph would decrease the weekly amount of child support maintenance (or the aggregate of all such amounts) payable by the non-resident parent to the person with care (or all of them) to less than £5, he is instead liable to pay child support maintenance at the rate of £5 a week, apportioned (if appropriate) in accordance with paragraph 6.

Shared care—flat rate

8.—(1) This paragraph applies only if—
  (a) the rate of child support maintenance payable is a flat rate; and
  (b) that rate applies because the non-resident parent falls within paragraph 4(1)(b) or (c) or 4(2).

(2) If the care of a qualifying child is shared as mentioned in paragraph 7(2) for at least 52 nights during a prescribed 12-month period, the amount of child support maintenance payable by the non-resident parent to the person with care of that child is nil.

Regulations about shared care

9. The Secretary of State may by regulations provide—
  (a) for which nights are to count for the purposes of shared care under paragraphs 7 and 8, or for how it is to be determined whether a night counts;
  (b) for what counts, or does not count, as 'care' for those purposes; and
  (c) for paragraph 7(3) or 8(2) to have effect, in prescribed circumstances, as if the period mentioned there were other than 12 months, and in such circumstances for the Table in paragraph 7(4) (or that Table as modified pursuant to regulations made under paragraph 10A(2)(a)), or the period mentioned in paragraph 8(2), to have effect with prescribed adjustments.

Net weekly income

10.—(1) For the purposes of this Schedule, net weekly income is to be determined in such manner as is provided for in regulations.

(2) The regulations may, in particular, provide for the Secretary of State to estimate any income or make an assumption as to any fact where, in his view, the information at his disposal is unreliable, insufficient, or relates to an atypical period in the life of the non-resident parent.

(3) Any amount of net weekly income (calculated as above) over £2,000 is to be ignored for the purposes of this Schedule.

Regulations about rates, figures, etc.

10A.—(1) The Secretary of State may by regulations provide that—
  (a) paragraph 2 is to have effect as if different percentages were substituted for those set out there;
  (b) paragraph 3(1) or (3), 4(1), 5, 7(7) or 10(3) is to have effect as if different amounts were substituted for those set out there.

(2) The Secretary of State may by regulations provide that—
  (a) the Table in paragraph 7(4) is to have effect as if different numbers of nights were set out in the first column and different fractions were substituted for those set out in the second column;
  (b) paragraph 7(6) is to have effect as if a different amount were substituted for that mentioned there, or as if the amount were an aggregate amount and not an amount for each qualifying child, or both.

Regulations about income

10B. The Secretary of State may by regulations provide that, in such circumstances and to such extent as may be prescribed—
  (a) where the Secretary of State is satisfied that a person has intentionally deprived himself of a source of income with a view to reducing the amount of his net weekly income, his net weekly income shall be taken to include income from that source of an amount estimated by the Secretary of State;

(b) a person is to be treated as possessing income which he does not possess;

(c) income which a person does possess is to be disregarded.

References to various terms

10C.—(1) References in this Part of this Schedule to 'qualifying children' are to those qualifying children with respect to whom the maintenance calculation falls to be made.

(2) References in this Part of this Schedule to 'relevant other children' are to—

(a) children other than qualifying children in respect of whom the non-resident parent or his partner receives child benefit under Part IX of the Social Security Contributions and Benefits Act 1992; and

(b) such other description of children as may be prescribed.

(3) In this Part of this Schedule, a person 'receives' a benefit, pension, or allowance for any week if it is paid or due to be paid to him in respect of that week.

(4) In this Part of this Schedule, a person's 'partner' is—

(a) if they are a couple, the other member of that couple;

(b) if the person is a husband or wife by virtue of a marriage entered into under a law which permits polygamy, another party to the marriage who is of the opposite sex and is a member of the same household.

(5) In sub-paragraph (4)(a), 'couple' means—

(a) a man and a woman who are married to each other and are members of the same household,

(b) a man and a woman who are not married to each other but are living together as husband and wife,

(c) two people of the same sex who are civil partners of each other and are members of the same household, or

(d) two people of the same sex who are not civil partners of each other but are living together as if they were civil partners.

(6) For the purposes of this paragraph, two people of the same sex are to be regarded as living together as if they were civil partners if, but only if, they would be regarded as living together as husband and wife were they instead two people of the opposite sex.

PART II   GENERAL PROVISIONS ABOUT MAINTENANCE CALCULATIONS

Effective date of calculation

11.—(1) A maintenance calculation shall take effect on such date as may be determined in accordance with regulations made by the Secretary of State.

(2) That date may be earlier than the date on which the calculation is made.

Form of calculation

12. Every maintenance calculation shall be made in such form and contain such information as the Secretary of State may direct.

Consolidated applications and calculations

14.—(1) The Secretary of State may by regulations provide—

(a) for two or more applications for maintenance calculations to be treated, in prescribed circumstances, as a single application; and

(b) for the replacement, in prescribed circumstances, of a maintenance calculation made on the application of one person by a later maintenance calculation made on the application of that or any other person.

(2) In sub-paragraph (1), the references (however expressed) to applications for maintenance calculations include references to applications treated as made.

Separate calculations for different periods

15. Where the Secretary of State is satisfied that the circumstances of a case require different amounts of child support maintenance to be calculated in respect of different periods, he may make separate maintenance calculations each expressed to have effect in relation to a different specified period.

Termination of calculations

16.—(1) A maintenance calculation shall cease to have effect—
  (a) on the death of the non-resident parent, or of the person with care, with respect to whom it was made;
  (b) on there no longer being any qualifying child with respect to whom it would have effect;
  (c) on the non-resident parent with respect to whom it was made ceasing to be a parent of—
    (i) the qualifying child with respect to whom it was made; or
    (ii) where it was made with respect to more than one qualifying child, all of the qualifying children with respect to whom it was made;

. . .

(10) A person with care with respect to whom a maintenance calculation is in force shall provide the Secretary of State with such information, in such circumstances, as may be prescribed, with a view to assisting the Secretary of State in determining whether the calculation has ceased to have effect.

(11) The Secretary of State may by regulations make such supplemental, incidental or transitional provision as he thinks necessary or expedient in consequence of the provisions of this paragraph.

SCHEDULE 2

PROVISION OF INFORMATION TO SECRETARY OF STATE

Inland Revenue records

1.—(1) This paragraph applies where the Secretary of State or the Department of Health and Social Services for Northern Ireland requires information for the purpose of tracing—
  (a) the current address of a non-resident parent; or
  (b) the current employer of a non-resident parent.

1A.—(1) This paragraph applies to any information which—
  (a) relates to any earnings or other income of a non-resident parent in respect of a tax year in which he is or was a self-employed earner, and
  (b) is required by the Secretary of State or the Department of Health and Social Services for Northern Ireland for any purposes of this Act or any corresponding Northern Ireland legislation.

(2) No obligation as to secrecy imposed by statute or otherwise on a Revenue and Customs official shall prevent any such information obtained or held in connection with the calculation or collection of income tax from being disclosed to—
  (a) the Secretary of State;
  (b) the Department of Health and Social Services for Northern Ireland; or
  (c) an officer of either of them authorised to receive such information in connection with the operation of this Act or any corresponding Northern Ireland legislation.

(3) This paragraph extends only to disclosure by or under the authority of the Commissioners of Inland Revenue.

(4) Information which is the subject of disclosure to any person by virtue of this paragraph shall not be further disclosed to any person except where the further disclosure is made—

      (a) to a person to whom disclosure could be made by virtue of sub-paragraph (2); or

      (b) for the purposes of any proceedings (civil or criminal) in connection with the operation of this Act or any corresponding Northern Ireland legislation.

(5) For the purposes of this paragraph 'self-employed earner' and 'tax year' have the same meaning as in Parts I to VI of the Social Security Contributions and Benefits Act 1992 or, in relation to Northern Ireland, the Social Security Contributions and Benefits (Northern Ireland) Act 1992.

...

SCHEDULE 4

CHILD SUPPORT COMMISSIONERS

...

Expenses of other persons

2A.—(1) The Lord Chancellor or, in Scotland, the Secretary of State may pay to any person who attends any proceedings before a Child Support Commissioner such travelling and other allowances as he may determine.

(2) In sub-paragraph (1), references to travelling and other allowances include references to compensation for loss of remunerative time.

(3) No compensation for loss of remunerative time shall be paid to any person under this paragraph in respect of any time during which he is in receipt of other remuneration so paid.

...

Determination of questions by other officers

4A.—(1) The Lord Chancellor may by regulations provide—

      (a) for officers authorised—

          (i) by the Lord Chancellor; or

          (ii) in Scotland, by the Secretary of State, to determine any question which is determinable by a Child Support Commissioner and which does not involve the determination of any appeal, application for leave to appeal or reference;

      (b) for the procedure to be followed by any such officer in determining any such question;

      (c) for the manner in which determinations of such questions by such officers may be called in question.

(2) A determination which would have the effect of preventing an appeal, application for leave to appeal or reference being determined by a Child Support Commissioner is not a determination of the appeal, application or reference for the purposes of sub-paragraph (1).

Tribunals of Commissioners

5.—(1) If it appears to the Chief Child Support Commissioner (or, in the case of his inability to act, to such other of the Child Support Commissioners as he may have nominated to act for the purpose) that—

      (a) an application for leave under section 24(6)(b); or

      (b) an appeal,

falling to be heard by one of the Child Support Commissioners involves a question of law of special difficulty, he may direct that the application or appeal be dealt with by a tribunal consisting of any three or more of the Child Support Commissioners.

(2) If the decision of such a tribunal is not unanimous, the decision of the majority shall be the decision of the tribunal, and the presiding Child Support Commissioner shall have a casting vote if the votes are equally divided.

(3) Where a direction is given under sub-paragraph (1)(a), section 24(6)(b) shall have effect as if the reference to a Child Support Commissioner were a reference to such a tribunal as is mentioned in subparagraph (1).

Finality of decisions

6.—(1) Subject to section 25, the decision of any Child Support Commissioner shall be final.

(2) If and to the extent that regulations so provide, any finding of fact or other determination which is embodied in or necessary to a decision, or on which a decision is based, shall be conclusive for the purposes of any further decision.

. . .

SCHEDULE 4A[1] APPLICATIONS FOR A VARIATION

Interpretation

1. In this Schedule, 'regulations' means regulations made by the Secretary of State.

Applications for a variation

2. Regulations may make provision—
    (a) as to the procedure to be followed in considering an application for a variation;
    (b) as to the procedure to be followed when an application for a variation is referred to an appeal tribunal under section 28D(1)(b).

Completion of preliminary consideration

3. Regulations may provide for determining when the preliminary consideration of an application for a variation is to be taken to have been completed.

Information

4. If any information which is required (by regulations under this Act) to be furnished to the Secretary of State in connection with an application for a variation has not been furnished within such period as may be prescribed, the Secretary of State may nevertheless proceed to consider the application.

Joint consideration of applications for a variation and appeals

5.—(1) Regulations may provide for two or more applications for a variation with respect to the same *application for a* maintenance calculation to be considered together.

(2) In sub-paragraph (1), the reference to an application for a maintenance calculation includes an application treated as having been made under section 6.

---

[1] Modification of Schedule 4A in cases of applications under section 28G
Schedule 4A is modified as follows where an application is made under section 28G:
    (i)   Paragraph 5 (1): words in italics are omitted.

(3) An appeal tribunal considering an application for a variation under section 28D(1)(b) may consider it at the same time as an appeal under section 20 in connection with an interim maintenance decision, if it considers that to be appropriate.

SCHEDULE 4B[(2)]   APPLICATIONS FOR A VARIATION: THE CASES AND CONTROLS

PART I   THE CASES

General

1.—(1) The cases in which a variation may be agreed are those set out in this Part of this Schedule or in regulations made under this Part.

(2) In this Schedule 'applicant' means the person whose application for a variation is being considered.

Special expenses

2.—(1) A variation applied for by a non-resident parent may be agreed with respect to his special expenses.

(2) In this paragraph 'special expenses' means the whole, or any amount above a prescribed amount, or any prescribed part, of expenses which fall within a prescribed description of expenses.

(3) In prescribing descriptions of expenses for the purposes of this paragraph, the Secretary of State may, in particular, make provision with respect to—

   (a) costs incurred by a non-resident parent in maintaining contact with the child, or with any of the children, with respect to whom *the application for a maintenance calculation has been made (or treated as made)*;
   (b) costs attributable to a long-term illness or disability of a relevant other child (within the meaning of paragraph 10C(2) of Schedule 1);
   (c) debts of a prescribed description incurred, before the non-resident parent became a non-resident parent in relation to a child with respect to whom the maintenance calculation *has been applied for (or treated as having been applied for)*—
      (i)   for the joint benefit of both parents;
      (ii) for the benefit of any such child; or
      (iii) for the benefit of any other child falling within a prescribed category;
   (d) boarding school fees for a child in relation to whom *the application for a maintenance calculation has been made (or treated as made)*;
   (e) the cost to the non-resident parent of making payments in relation to a mortgage on the home he and the person with care shared, if he no longer has an interest in it, and she and a child in relation to whom *the application for a maintenance calculation has been made (or treated as made)* still live there.

(4) For the purposes of sub-paragraph (3)(b)—

   (a) 'disability' and 'illness' have such meaning as may be prescribed; and
   (b) the question whether an illness or disability is long-term shall be determined in accordance with regulations made by the Secretary of State.

(5) For the purposes of sub-paragraph (3)(d), the Secretary of State may prescribe—

   (a) the meaning of 'boarding school fees'; and
   (b) components of such fees (whether or not itemised as such) which are, or are not, to be taken into account,

and may provide for estimating any such component.

[(2)] Modification of Schedule 4B in cases of applications under section 28G
   Schedule 4B is modified as follows where an application is made under section 28G:

Property or capital transfers

3.—(1) A variation may be agreed in the circumstances set out in sub-paragraph (2) if before 5th April 1993—

(a) a court order of a prescribed kind was in force with respect to the non-resident parent and either the person with care with respect to *the application for the maintenance calculation* or the child, or any of the children, with respect to whom *that application was made*; or

(b) an agreement of a prescribed kind between the non-resident parent and any of those persons was in force.

(2) The circumstances are that in consequence of one or more transfers of property of a prescribed kind and exceeding (singly or in aggregate) a prescribed minimum value—

(a) the amount payable by the non-resident parent by way of maintenance was less than would have been the case had that transfer or those transfers not been made; or

(b) no amount was payable by the non-resident parent by way of maintenance.

(3) For the purposes of sub-paragraph (2), 'maintenance' means periodical payments of maintenance made (otherwise than under this Act) with respect to the child, or any of the children, with respect to whom *the application for a maintenance calculation* has been made.

Additional cases

4.—(1) The Secretary of State may by regulations prescribe other cases in which a variation may be agreed.

(2) Regulations under this paragraph may, for example, make provision with respect to cases where—

(a) the non-resident parent has assets which exceed a prescribed value;

(b) a person's lifestyle is inconsistent with his income for the purposes of a calculation made under Part I of Schedule 1;

(c) a person has income which is not taken into account in such a calculation;

(d) a person has unreasonably reduced the income which is taken into account in such a calculation.

PART II   REGULATORY CONTROLS

5.—(1) The Secretary of State may by regulations make provision with respect to the variations from the usual rules for calculating maintenance which may be allowed when a variation is agreed.

(2) No variations may be made other than those which are permitted by the regulations.

(3) Regulations under this paragraph may, in particular, make provision for a variation to result in—

(a) a person's being treated as having more, or less, income than would be taken into account without the variation in a calculation under Part I of Schedule 1;

(b) a person's being treated as liable to pay a higher, or a lower, amount of child support maintenance than would result without the variation from a calculation under that Part.

(4) Regulations may provide for the amount of any special expenses to be taken into account in a case falling within paragraph 2, for the purposes of a variation, not to exceed such amount as may be prescribed or as may be determined in accordance with the regulations.

(5) Any regulations under this paragraph may in particular make different provision with respect to different levels of income.

(6) The Secretary of State may by regulations provide for the application, in connection with child support maintenance payable following a variation, of paragraph 7(2) to (7) of Schedule 1 (subject to any prescribed modifications).

Social Security Administration Act 1992
(1992 c. 5)

PART III   OVERPAYMENTS AND ADJUSTMENTS OF BENEFIT

74A   Payment of benefit where maintenance payments collected by Secretary of State

(1) This section applies where—
  (a) a person ('the claimant') is entitled to a benefit to which this section applies;
  (b) the Secretary of State is collecting periodical payments of child or spousal maintenance made in respect of the claimant or a member of the claimant's family; and
  (c) the inclusion of any such periodical payment in the claimant's relevant income would, apart from this section, have the effect of reducing the amount of the benefit to which the claimant is entitled.

(2) The Secretary of State may, to such extent as he considers appropriate, treat any such periodical payment as not being relevant income for the purposes of calculating the amount of benefit to which the claimant is entitled.

(3) The Secretary of State may, to the extent that any periodical payment collected by him is treated as not being relevant income for those purposes, retain the whole or any part of that payment.

(4) Any sum retained by the Secretary of State under subsection (3) shall be paid by him into the Consolidated Fund.

(5) In this section—
'child' means a person under the age of 16;
'child maintenance', 'spousal maintenance' and 'relevant income' have such meaning as may be prescribed;
'couple' has the meaning given by section 137(1) of the Contributions and Benefits Act;
'family' means—
  (a) a couple;
  (b) a couple and a member of the same household for whom one of them is, or both are, responsible and who is a child or a person of a prescribed description;
  (c) except in prescribed circumstances, a person who is not a member of a couple and a member of the same household for whom that person is responsible and who is a child or a person of a prescribed description;

(6) For the purposes of this section, the Secretary of State may by regulations make provision as to the circumstances in which—
  (a) persons are to be treated as being or not being members of the same household;
  (b) one person is to be treated as responsible or not responsible for another.

(7) The benefits to which this section applies are income support, an income-based jobseeker's allowance and such other benefits (if any) as may be prescribed.

Social fund awards

78   Recovery of social fund awards

(1) A social fund award which is repayable shall be recoverable by the Secretary of State.

(2) Without prejudice to any other method of recovery, the Secretary of State may recover an award by deduction from prescribed benefits.

(3) The Secretary of State may recover an award—

(a) from the person to or for the benefit of whom it was made;

(b) where that person is a member of a couple, from the other member of the couple;

(c) from a person who is liable to maintain the person by or on behalf of whom the application for the award was made or any person in relation to whose needs the award was made.

. . .

(5) In this section 'couple' has the meaning given by section 137(1) of the Contributions and Benefits Act.

(6) For the purposes of this section—

(a) a man shall be liable to maintain his wife or civil partner and any children of whom he is the father;

(b) a woman shall be liable to maintain her husband or civil partner and any children of whom she is the mother;

(c) a person shall be liable to maintain another person throughout any period in respect of which the first-mentioned person has, on or after 23 May 1980 (the date of the passing of the Social Security Act 1980) and either alone or jointly with a further person, given an undertaking in writing in pursuance of immigration rules within the meaning of the Immigration Act 1971 to be responsible for the maintenance and accommodation of the other person; and

(d) 'child' includes a person who has attained the age of 16 but not the age of 19 and in respect of whom either parent, or some person acting in the place of either parent, is receiving income support or an income-based jobseeker's allowance.

(7) Any reference in subsection (6) above to children of whom the man or the woman is the father or the mother shall be construed in accordance with section 1 of the Family Law Reform Act 1987.

PART V   INCOME SUPPORT AND THE DUTY TO MAINTAIN

105   Failure to maintain—general

(1) If—

(a) any person persistently refuses or neglects to maintain himself or any person whom he is liable to maintain; and

(b) in consequence of his refusal or neglect income support or an income-based jobseeker's allowance is paid to or in respect of him or such a person,

he shall be guilty of an offence and liable on summary conviction to a fine of an amount not exceeding level 4 on the standard scale.

(3) Subject to subsection (4) below, subsections (6) to (9) of section 78 above shall have effect for the purposes of this Part of this Act as they have effect for the purposes of that section.

(4) For the purposes of this section, in its application to an income-based jobseeker's allowance, a person is liable to maintain another if that other person is his or her spouse or civil partner.

106   Recovery of expenditure on benefit from person liable for maintenance

(1) Subject to the following provisions of this section, if income support is claimed by or in respect of a person whom another person is liable to maintain or paid to or in respect of such a person, the Secretary of State may make a complaint against the liable person to a magistrates' court for an order under this section.

(2) On the hearing of a complaint under this section the court shall have regard to all the circumstances and, in particular, to the income of the liable person, and may order him to pay such sum, weekly or otherwise, as it may consider appropriate, except that in a case falling within section 78(6)(c) above that sum shall not include any amount which is not attributable to income support (whether paid before or after the making of the order).

(3) In determining whether to order any payments to be made in respect of income support for any period before the complaint was made, or the amount of any such payments, the court shall disregard any amount by which the liable person's income exceeds the income which was his during that period.

(4) Any payments ordered to be made under this section shall be made—

(a) to the Secretary of State in so far as they are attributable to any income support (whether paid before or after the making of the order);

(b) to the person claiming income support or (if different) the dependant; or

(c) to such other person as appears to the court expedient in the interests of the dependant.

(5) An order under this section shall be enforceable as a magistrates' court maintenance order within the meaning of section 150(1) of the Magistrates' Courts Act 1980.

107   Recovery of expenditure on income support: additional amounts and transfer of orders

(1) In any case where—

(a) the claim for income support referred to in section 106(1) above is or was made by the parent of one or more children in respect of both himself and those children; and

(b) the other parent is liable to maintain those children but, by virtue of not being the claimant's husband or wife or civil partner, is not liable to maintain the claimant,

the sum which the court may order that other parent to pay under subsection (2) of that section may include an amount, determined in accordance with regulations, in respect of any income support paid to or for the claimant by virtue of such provisions as may be prescribed.

(3) In any case where—

(a) there is in force an order under subsection (2) of section 106 above made against a person ('the liable parent') who is the parent of one or more children, in respect of the other parent or the children; and

(b) payments under the order fall to be made to the Secretary of State by virtue of subsection (4)(a) of that section; and

(c) that other parent ('the dependent parent') ceases to claim income support, the Secretary of State may, by giving notice in writing to the court which made the order and to the liable parent and the dependent parent, transfer to the dependent parent the right to receive the payments under the order, exclusive of any personal allowance element, and to exercise the relevant rights in relation to the order, except so far as relating to that element.

(4) Notice under subsection (3) above shall not be given (and if purportedly given, shall be of no effect) at a time when there is in force a maintenance order made against the liable parent—

(a) in favour of the dependent parent or one or more of the children; or

(b) in favour of some other person for the benefit of the dependent parent or one or more of the children;

and if such a maintenance order is made at any time after notice under that subsection has been given, the order under section 106(2) above shall cease to have effect.

(5) In any case where—

(a) notice is given to a magistrates' court under subsection (3) above,

(b) payments under the order are required to be made by any method of payment falling within section 59(6) of the Magistrates' Courts Act 1980 (standing order, etc), and

(c) a justices' clerk decides that payment by that method is no longer possible, the clerk shall amend the order to provide that payments under the order shall be made by the liable parent to the designated officer for the court.

(6) Except as provided by subsections (8) and (12) below, where the Secretary of State gives notice under subsection (3) above, he shall cease to be entitled—

(a) to receive any payment under the order in respect of any personal allowance element; or

(b) to exercise the relevant rights, so far as relating to any such element,

notwithstanding that the dependent parent does not become entitled to receive any payment in respect of that element or to exercise the relevant rights so far as so relating.

(7) If, in a case where the Secretary of State gives notice under subsection (3) above, a payment under the order is or has been made to him wholly or partly in respect of the whole or any part of the period beginning with the day on which the transfer takes effect and ending with the day on which the notice under subsection (3) above is given to the liable parent, the Secretary of State shall—

(a) repay to or for the liable parent so much of the payment as is referable to any personal allowance element in respect of that period or, as the case may be, the part of it in question; and

(b) pay to or for the dependent parent so much of any remaining balance of the payment as is referable to that period or part;

and a payment under paragraph (b) above shall be taken to discharge, to that extent, the liability of the liable parent to the dependent parent under the order in respect of that period or part.

(8) If, in a case where the Secretary of State has given notice under subsection (3) above, the dependent parent makes a further claim for income support, then—

(a) the Secretary of State may, by giving a further notice in writing to the court which made the order and to the liable parent and the dependent parent, transfer back from the dependent parent to himself the right to receive the payments and to exercise the relevant rights; and

(b) that transfer shall revive the Secretary of State's right to receive payment under the order in respect of any personal allowance element and to exercise the relevant rights so far as relating to any such element.

(9) Subject to subsections (10) and (11) below, in any case where—

(a) notice is given to a magistrates' court under subsection (8) above, and

(b) the method of payment under the order which subsists immediately before the day on which the transfer under subsection (8) above takes effect differs from the method of payment which subsisted immediately before the day on which the transfer under subsection (3) above (or, if there has been more than one such transfer, the last such transfer) took effect,

a justices' clerk shall amend the order by reinstating the method of payment under the order which subsisted immediately before the day on which the transfer under subsection (3) above (or, as the case may be, the last such transfer) took effect.

(10) The clerk shall not amend the order under subsection (9) above if the Secretary of State gives notice in writing to the clerk, on or before the day on which the notice under subsection (8) above is given, that the method of payment under the order which subsists immediately before the day on which the transfer under subsection (8) above takes effect is to continue.

(11) In any case where—

(a) notice is given to a magistrates' court under subsection (8) above,

(b) the method of payment under the order which subsisted immediately before the day on which the transfer under subsection (3) above (or, if there has been more than one such transfer, the last such transfer) took effect was any method of payment falling within section 59(6) of the Magistrates' Courts Act 1980 (standing order, etc), and

(c) the clerk decides that payment by that method is no longer possible,

the clerk shall amend the order to provide that payments under the order shall be made by the liable parent to the designated officer for the court.

(12) A transfer under subsection (3) or (8) above does not transfer or otherwise affect the right of any person—

      (a) to receive a payment which fell due to him at a time before the transfer took effect; or

      (b) to exercise the relevant rights in relation to any such payment;

and, where notice is given under subsection (3), subsection (6) above does not deprive the Secretary of State of his right to receive such a payment in respect of any personal allowance element or to exercise the relevant rights in relation to such a payment.

(13) For the purposes of this section—

      (a) a transfer under subsection (3) above takes effect on the day on which the dependent parent ceases to be in receipt of income support in consequence of the cessation referred to in paragraph (c) of that subsection, and

      (b) a transfer under subsection (8) above takes effect on—

          (i) the first day in respect of which the dependent parent receives income support after the transfer under subsection (3) above took effect, or

          (ii) such later day as may be specified for the purpose in the notice under subsection (8),

      irrespective of the day on which notice under the subsection in question is given.

(14) Any notice required to be given to the liable parent under subsection (3) or (8) above shall be taken to have been given if it has been sent to his last known address.

(15) In this section—

'child' means a person under the age of 16, notwithstanding section 78(6)(d) above;

'court' (where it occurs other than in the expression 'magistrates' court') means in England and Wales a magistrates' court, and in Scotland the sheriff;

'maintenance order'—

      (a) in England and Wales, means—

          (i) any order for the making of periodical payments or for the payment of a lump sum which is, or has at any time been, a maintenance order within the meaning of the Attachment of Earnings Act 1971;

          (ii) any order under Part III of the Matrimonial and Family Proceedings Act 1984 (overseas divorce) for the making of periodical payments or for the payment of a lump sum;

          (iii) any order under Schedule 7 to the Civil Partnership Act 2004 for the making of periodical payments or for the payment of a lump sum;

'the relevant rights', in relation to an order under section 106(2) above, means the right to bring any proceedings, take any steps or do any other thing under or in relation to the order which the Secretary of State could have brought, taken or done apart from any transfer under this section.

108   Reduction of expenditure on income support: certain maintenance orders to be enforceable by the Secretary of State

(1) This section applies where—

      (a) a person ('the claimant') who is the parent of one or more children is in receipt of income support either in respect of those children or in respect of both himself and those children; and

      (b) there is in force a maintenance order made against the other parent ('the liable person')—

          (i) in favour of the claimant or one or more of the children, or

          (ii) in favour of some other person for the benefit of the claimant or one or more of the children;

and in this section 'the primary recipient' means the person in whose favour that maintenance order was made.

(2) If, in a case where this section applies, the liable person fails to comply with any of the terms of the maintenance order—

(a) the Secretary of State may bring any proceedings or take any other steps to enforce the order that could have been brought or taken by or on behalf of the primary recipient; and

(b) any court before which proceedings are brought by the Secretary of State by virtue of paragraph (a) above shall have the same powers in connection with those proceedings as it would have had if they had been brought by the primary recipient.

(3) The Secretary of State's powers under this section are exercisable at his discretion and whether or not the primary recipient or any other person consents to their exercise; but any sums recovered by virtue of this section shall be payable to or for the primary recipient, as if the proceedings or steps in question had been brought or taken by him or on his behalf.

(4) The powers conferred on the Secretary of State by subsection (2)(a) above include power—

(a) to apply for the registration of the maintenance order under—
   (i) section 17 of the Maintenance Orders Act 1950;
   (ii) section 2 of the Maintenance Orders Act 1958;
   (iii) the Civil Jurisdiction and Judgments Act 1982; or
   (iv) Council Regulation (EC) No 44/2001 of 22nd December 2000 on jurisdiction and the recognition and enforcement of judgments in civil and commercial matters; and

(b) to make an application under section 2 of the Maintenance Orders (Reciprocal Enforcement) Act 1972 (application for enforcement in reciprocating country).

(5) Where this section applies, the prescribed person shall in prescribed circumstances give the Secretary of State notice of any application—

(a) to alter, vary, suspend, discharge, revoke, revive or enforce the maintenance order in question; or

(b) to remit arrears under that maintenance order;

and the Secretary of State shall be entitled to appear and be heard on the application.

(6) Where, by virtue of this section, the Secretary of State commences any proceedings to enforce a maintenance order, he shall, in relation to those proceedings, be treated for the purposes of any enactment or instrument relating to maintenance orders as if he were a person entitled to payment under the maintenance order in question (but shall not thereby become entitled to any such payment).

. . .

Pensions Act 1995
(1995 c. 26)

PART IV   MISCELLANEOUS AND GENERAL

Pensions on divorce etc.

166   Pensions on divorce etc.

(4) Nothing in the provisions mentioned in subsection (5) applies to a court exercising its powers under section 23 of the Matrimonial Causes Act 1973 (financial provision in connection with divorce proceedings, etc.) in respect of any benefits under a pension arrangement (within the meaning of section 25B(1) of the Matrimonial Causes Act 1973) which a party to the marriage has or is likely to have.

(4A) Nothing in the provisions mentioned in subsection (5) applies to a court exercising its powers under Part 6 of Schedule 5 to the Civil Partnership Act 2004 (making Part 1 orders having regard to pension benefits).

(5) The provisions referred to in subsection (4) and (4A) are—

(a) section 203(1) and (2) of the Army Act 1955, 203(1) and (2) of the Air Force Act 1955, 128G(1) and (2) of the Naval Discipline Act 1957 or 159(4) and (4A) of the Pension Schemes Act 1993 (which prevent assignment, or orders being made restraining a person from receiving anything which he is prevented from assigning),

(b) section 91 of this Act,

(c) any provision of any enactment (whether passed or made before or after this Act is passed) corresponding to any of the enactments mentioned in paragraphs (a) and (b), and

(d) any provision of the arrangement in question corresponding to any of those enactments.

(6) Subsections (3) to (7) of section 25B, and section 25C of the Matrimonial Causes Act 1973, as inserted by this section, do not affect the powers of the court under section 31 of that Act (variation, discharge, etc.) in relation to any order made before the commencement of this section.

Child Support Act 1995
(1995 c. 34)

Miscellaneous

18 Deferral of right to apply for maintenance assessment

(6) Neither section 4(10) nor section 7(10) of the 1991 Act shall apply in relation to a maintenance order made in the circumstances mentioned in subsection (7) or (8) of section 8 of the 1991 Act.

(7) The Secretary of State may by regulations make provision for section 4(10), or section 7(10), of the 1991 Act not to apply in relation to such other cases as may be prescribed.

. . .

Supplemental

26 Regulations and orders

(1) Any power under this Act to make regulations or orders shall be exercisable by statutory instrument.

(2) Any such power may be exercised to make different provision for different cases, including different provision for different areas.

(3) Any such power includes power—

(a) to make such incidental, supplemental, consequential or transitional provision as appears to the Secretary of State to be expedient; and

(b) to provide for a person to exercise a discretion in dealing with any matter.

. . .

27 Interpretation

(1) In this Act 'the 1991 Act' means the Child Support Act 1991.

(2) Expressions in this Act which are used in the 1991 Act have the same meaning in this Act as they have in that Act.

28 Financial provisions

There shall be paid out of money provided by Parliament—

(a) any expenditure incurred by the Secretary of State under or by virtue of this Act;

(b) any increase attributable to this Act in the sums payable out of money so provided under or by virtue of any other enactment.

Family Law Act 1996
(1996 c. 27)

PART I PRINCIPLES OF PARTS II AND III

1 The general principles underlying Parts II and III

The court and any person, in exercising functions under or in consequence of Parts II and III, shall have regard to the following general principles—

   (a) that the institution of marriage is to be supported;
   (b) that the parties to a marriage which may have broken down are to be encouraged to take all practicable steps, whether by marriage counselling or otherwise, to save the marriage;
   (c) that a marriage which has irretrievably broken down and is being brought to an end should be brought to an end—
      (i) with minimum distress to the parties and to the children affected;
      (ii) with questions dealt with in a manner designed to promote as good a continuing relationship between the parties and any children affected as is possible in the circumstances; and
      (iii) without costs being unreasonably incurred in connection with the procedures to be followed in bringing the marriage to an end; and
   (d) that any risk to one of the parties to a marriage, and to any children, of violence from the other party should, so far as reasonably practicable, be removed or diminished.

. . .

PART II DIVORCE AND SEPARATION

Marriage support services

22 Funding for marriage support services

   (1) The Secretary of State may, with the approval of the Treasury, make grants in connection with—
      (a) the provision of marriage support services;
      (b) research into the causes of marital breakdown;
      (c) research into ways of preventing marital breakdown.

   (2) Any grant under this section may be made subject to such conditions as the Secretary of State considers appropriate.

   (3) In exercising his power to make grants in connection with the provision of marriage support services, the Secretary of State is to have regard, in particular, to the desirability of services of that kind being available when they are first needed.

PART IV FAMILY HOMES AND DOMESTIC VIOLENCE

Rights to occupy matrimonial or civil partnership home

30 Rights concerning home where one spouse or civil partner has no estate, etc.

   (1) This section applies if—
      (a) one spouse or civil partner ('A') is entitled to occupy a dwelling-house by virtue of—
         (i) a beneficial estate or interest or contract; or
         (ii) any enactment giving A the right to remain in occupation; and
      (b) the other spouse or civil partner ('B') is not so entitled.
   (2) Subject to the provisions of this Part, B has the following rights ('home rights')—

    (a) if in occupation, a right not to be evicted or excluded from the dwelling-house or any part of it by A except with the leave of the court given by an order under section 33;

    (b) if not in occupation, a right with the leave of the court so given to enter into and occupy the dwelling-house.

  (3) If B is entitled under this section to occupy a dwelling-house or any part of a dwelling-house, any payment or tender made or other thing done by B in or towards satisfaction of any liability of A in respect of rent, mortgage payments or other outgoings affecting the dwelling-house is, whether or not it is made or done in pursuance of an order under section 40, as good as if made or done by A.

  (4) B's occupation by virtue of this section—

    (a) is to be treated, for the purposes of the Rent (Agriculture) Act 1976 and the Rent Act 1977 (other than Part V and sections 103 to 106 of that Act), as occupation by A as A's residence, and

    (b) if B occupies the dwelling-house as B's only or principal home, is to be treated, for the purposes of the Housing Act 1985, Part I of the Housing Act 1988 and Chapter I of Part V of the Housing Act 1996, as occupation by A as A's only or principal home.

  (5) If B—

    (a) is entitled under this section to occupy a dwelling-house or any part of a dwelling-house, and

    (b) makes any payment in or towards satisfaction of any liability of A in respect of mortgage payments affecting the dwelling-house,

the person to whom the payment is made may treat it as having been made by A, but the fact that that person has treated any such payment as having been so made does not affect any claim of B against A to an interest in the dwelling-house by virtue of the payment.

  (6) If B is entitled under this section to occupy a dwelling-house or part of a dwelling-house by reason of an interest of A under a trust, all the provisions of subsections (3) to (5) apply in relation to the trustees as they apply in relation to A.

  (7) This section does not apply to a dwelling-house which—

    (a) in the case of spouses, has at no time been, and was at no time intended by them to be, a matrimonial home of theirs; and

    (b) in the case of civil partners, has at no time been, and was at no time intended by them to be, a civil partnership home of theirs.

  (8) B's home rights rights continue—

    (a) only so long as the marriage or civil partnership subsists, except to the extent that an order under section 33(5) otherwise provides; and

    (b) only so long as A is entitled as mentioned in subsection (1) to occupy the dwelling-house, except where provision is made by section 31 for those rights to be a charge on an estate or interest in the dwelling-house.

  (9) It is hereby declared that a person—

    (a) who has an equitable interest in a dwelling-house or in its proceeds of sale, but

    (b) is not a person in whom there is vested (whether solely or as joint tenant) a legal estate in fee simple or a legal term of years absolute in the dwelling-house,

is to be treated, only for the purpose of determining whether he has home rights, as not being entitled to occupy the dwelling-house by virtue of that interest.

31 Effect of home rights as charge on dwelling-house

  (1) Subsections (2) and (3) apply if, at any time during a marriage or civil partnership, A is entitled to occupy a dwelling-house by virtue of a beneficial estate or interest.

  (2) B's home rights are a charge on the estate or interest.

  (3) The charge created by subsection (2) has the same priority as if it were an equitable interest created at whichever is the latest of the following dates—

    (a) the date on which A acquires the estate or interest;

(b) the date of the marriage or of the formation of the civil partnership; and

(c) 1st January 1968 (the commencement date of the Matrimonial Homes Act 1967).

(4) Subsections (5) and (6) apply if, at any time when B's home rights are a charge on an interest of A under a trust, there are, apart from A or B, no persons, living or unborn, who are or could become beneficiaries under the trust.

(5) The rights are a charge also on the estate or interest of the trustees for A.

(6) The charge created by subsection (5) has the same priority as if it were an equitable interest created (under powers overriding the trusts) on the date when it arises.

(7) In determining for the purposes of subsection (4) whether there are any persons who are not, but could become, beneficiaries under the trust, there is to be disregarded any potential exercise of a general power of appointment exercisable by either or both of A and B alone (whether or not the exercise of it requires the consent of another person).

(8) Even though B's home rights are a charge on an estate or interest in the dwelling-house, those rights are brought to an end by—

(a) the death of A, or

(b) the termination (otherwise than by death) of the marriage or civil partnership, unless the court directs otherwise by an order made under section 33(5).

(9) If—

(a) B's home rights are a charge on an estate or interest in the dwelling-house, and

(b) that estate or interest is surrendered to merge in some other estate or interest expectant on it in such circumstances that, but for the merger, the person taking the estate or interest would be bound by the charge,

the surrender has effect subject to the charge and the persons thereafter entitled to the other estate or interest are, for so long as the estate or interest surrendered would have endured if not so surrendered, to be treated for all purposes of this Part as deriving title to the other estate or interest under A or, as the case may be, under the trustees for A, by virtue of the surrender.

(10) If the title to the legal estate by virtue of which A is entitled to occupy a dwelling-house (including any legal estate held by trustees for A) is registered under the Land Registration Act 2002 or any enactment replaced by that Act—

(a) registration of a land charge affecting the dwelling-house by virtue of this Part is to be effected by registering a notice under that Act; and

(b) B's home rights are not to be capable of falling within paragraph 2 of Schedule 1 or 3 to that Act.

(12) If—

(a) B's home rights are a charge on the estate of A or of trustees of A, and

(b) that estate is the subject of a mortgage,

then if, after the date of the creation of the mortgage ('the first mortgage'), the charge is registered under section 2 of the Land Charges Act 1972, the charge is, for the purposes of section 94 of the Law of Property Act 1925 (which regulates the rights of mortgagees to make further advances ranking in priority to subsequent mortgages), to be deemed to be a mortgage subsequent in date to the first mortgage.

(13) It is hereby declared that a charge under subsection (2) or (5) is not registrable under subsection (10) or under section 2 of the Land Charges Act 1972 unless it is a charge on a legal estate.

32 Further provisions relating to home rights

Schedule 4 (provisions supplementary to sections 30 and 31) has effect.

Occupation orders

33 Occupation orders where applicant has estate or interest etc. or has home rights

(1) If—

(a) a person ('the person entitled')—

(i) is entitled to occupy a dwelling-house by virtue of a beneficial estate or interest or contract or by virtue of any enactment giving him the right to remain in occupation, or

(ii) has home rights in relation to a dwelling-house, and

(b) the dwelling-house—

(i) is or at any time has been the home of the person entitled and of another person with whom he is associated, or

(ii) was at any time intended by the person entitled and any such other person to be their home,

the person entitled may apply to the court for an order containing any of the provisions specified in subsections (3), (4) and (5).

(2) If an agreement to marry is terminated, no application under this section may be made by virtue of section 62(3)(e) by reference to that agreement after the end of the period of three years beginning with the day on which it is terminated.

(2A) If a civil partnership agreement (as defined by section 73 of the Civil Partnership Act 2004) is terminated, no application under this section may be made by virtue of section 62(3)(eza) by reference to that agreement after the end of the period of three years beginning with the day on which it is terminated.

(3) An order under this section may—

(a) enforce the applicant's entitlement to remain in occupation as against the other person ('the respondent');

(b) require the respondent to permit the applicant to enter and remain in the dwelling-house or part of the dwelling-house;

(c) regulate the occupation of the dwelling-house by either or both parties;

(d) if the respondent is entitled as mentioned in subsection (1)(a)(i), prohibit, suspend or restrict the exercise by him of his right to occupy the dwelling-house;

(e) if the respondent has home rights in relation to the dwelling-house and the applicant is the other spouse or civil partner, restrict or terminate those rights;

(f) require the respondent to leave the dwelling-house or part of the dwelling-house; or

(g) exclude the respondent from a defined area in which the dwelling-house is included.

(4) An order under this section may declare that the applicant is entitled as mentioned in subsection (1)(a)(i) or has home rights.

(5) If the applicant has home rights and the respondent is the other spouse or civil partner, an order under this section made during the marriage or civil partnership may provide that those rights are not brought to an end by—

(a) the death of the other spouse or civil partner; or

(b) the termination (otherwise than by death) of the marriage or civil partnership.

(6) In deciding whether to exercise its powers under subsection (3) and (if so) in what manner, the court shall have regard to all the circumstances including—

(a) the housing needs and housing resources of each of the parties and of any relevant child;

(b) the financial resources of each of the parties;

(c) the likely effect of any order, or of any decision by the court not to exercise its powers under subsection (3), on the health, safety or well-being of the parties and of any relevant child; and

(d) the conduct of the parties in relation to each other and otherwise.

(7) If it appears to the court that the applicant or any relevant child is likely to suffer significant harm attributable to conduct of the respondent if an order under this section containing one or more of the provisions mentioned in subsection (3) is not made, the court shall make the order unless it appears to it that—

(a) the respondent or any relevant child is likely to suffer significant harm if the order is made; and

(b) the harm likely to be suffered by the respondent or child in that event is as great as, or greater than, the harm attributable to conduct of the respondent which is likely to be suffered by the applicant or child if the order is not made.

(8) The court may exercise its powers under subsection (5) in any case where it considers that in all the circumstances it is just and reasonable to do so.

(9) An order under this section—

(a) may not be made after the death of either of the parties mentioned in subsection (1); and

(b) except in the case of an order made by virtue of subsection (5)(a), ceases to have effect on the death of either party.

(10) An order under this section may, in so far as it has continuing effect, be made for a specified period, until the occurrence of a specified event or until further order.

34   Effect of order under s. 33 where rights are charge on dwelling-house

(1) If B's home rights are a charge on the estate or interest of A or of trustees for A—

(a) an order under section 33 against the other spouse has, except so far as a contrary intention appears, the same effect against persons deriving title under the other spouse or under the trustees and affected by the charge, and

(b) sections 33(1), (3), (4) and (10) and 30(3) to (6) apply in relation to any person deriving title under the other spouse or under the trustees and affected by the charge as they apply in relation to the other spouse.

(2) The court may make an order under section 33 by virtue of subsection (1)(b) if it considers that in all the circumstances it is just and reasonable to do so.

35   One former spouse or former civil partner with no existing right to occupy

(1) This section applies if—

(a) one former spouse or former civil partner is entitled to occupy a dwelling-house by virtue of a beneficial estate or interest or contract, or by virtue of any enactment giving him the right to remain in occupation;

(b) the other former spouse or former civil partner is not so entitled; and

(c) the dwelling-house—

(i) in the case of former spouses, was at any time their matrimonial home or was at any time intended by them to be their matrimonial home, or

(ii) in the case of former civil partners, was at any time their civil partnership home or was at any time intended by them to be their civil partnership home.

(2) The former spouse or former civil partner not so entitled may apply to the court for an order under this section against the other former spouse or former civil partner ('the respondent').

(3) If the applicant is in occupation, an order under this section must contain provision—

(a) giving the applicant the right not to be evicted or excluded from the dwelling-house or any part of it by the respondent for the period specified in the order; and

(b) prohibiting the respondent from evicting or excluding the applicant during that period.

(4) If the applicant is not in occupation, an order under this section must contain provision—

(a) giving the applicant the right to enter into and occupy the dwelling-house for the period specified in the order; and

(b) requiring the respondent to permit the exercise of that right.

(5) An order under this section may also—

(a) regulate the occupation of the dwelling-house by either or both of the parties;

(b) prohibit, suspend or restrict the exercise by the respondent of his right to occupy the dwelling-house;

(c) require the respondent to leave the dwelling-house or part of the dwelling-house; or

(d) exclude the respondent from a defined area in which the dwelling-house is included.

(6) In deciding whether to make an order under this section containing provision of the kind mentioned in subsection (3) or (4) and (if so) in what manner, the court shall have regard to all the circumstances including—

(a) the housing needs and housing resources of each of the parties and of any relevant child;

(b) the financial resources of each of the parties;

(c) the likely effect of any order, or of any decision by the court not to exercise its powers under subsection (3) or (4), on the health, safety or well-being of the parties and of any relevant child;

(d) the conduct of the parties in relation to each other and otherwise;

(e) the length of time that has elapsed since the parties ceased to live together;

(f) the length of time that has elapsed since the marriage or civil partnership was dissolved or annulled; and

(g) the existence of any pending proceedings between the parties—

(i) for an order under section 23A or 24 of the Matrimonial Causes Act 1973 (property adjustment orders in connection with divorce proceedings etc.);

(ia) for a property adjustment order under Part 2 of Schedule 5 to the Civil Partnership Act 2004;

(ii) for an order under paragraph 1(2)(d) or (e) of Schedule 1 to the Children Act 1989 (orders for financial relief against parents); or

(iii) relating to the legal or beneficial ownership of the dwelling-house.

(7) In deciding whether to exercise its power to include one or more of the provisions referred to in subsection (5) ('a subsection (5) provision') and (if so) in what manner, the court shall have regard to all the circumstances including the matters mentioned in sub-section (6)(a) to (e).

(8) If the court decides to make an order under this section and it appears to it that, if the order does not include a subsection (5) provision, the applicant or any relevant child is likely to suffer significant harm attributable to conduct of the respondent, the court shall include the subsection (5) provision in the order unless it appears to the court that—

(a) the respondent or any relevant child is likely to suffer significant harm if the provision is included in the order; and

(b) the harm likely to be suffered by the respondent or child in that event is as great as or greater than the harm attributable to conduct of the respondent which is likely to be suffered by the applicant or child if the provision is not included.

(9) An order under this section—

(a) may not be made after the death of either of the former spouses or former civil partners; and

(b) ceases to have effect on the death of either of them.

(10) An order under this section must be limited so as to have effect for a specified period not exceeding six months, but may be extended on one or more occasions for a further specified period not exceeding six months.

(11) A former spouse or former civil partner who has an equitable interest in the dwelling-house or in the proceeds of sale of the dwelling-house but in whom there is not vested (whether solely or as joint tenant) a legal estate in fee simple or a legal term of years absolute in the dwelling-house is to be treated (but only for the purpose of determining whether he is eligible to apply under this section) as not being entitled to occupy the dwelling-house by virtue of that interest.

(12) Subsection (11) does not prejudice any right of such a former spouse or former civil partner to apply for an order under section 33.

(13) So long as an order under this section remains in force, subsections (3) to (6) of section 30 apply in relation to the applicant—

(a) as if he were B (the person entitled to occupy the dwelling-house by virtue of that section); and

(b) as if the respondent were A (the person entitled as mentioned in subsection (1)(a) of that section).

36   One cohabitant or former cohabitant with no existing right to occupy

(1) This section applies if—

(a) one cohabitant or former cohabitant is entitled to occupy a dwelling-house by virtue of a beneficial estate or interest or contract or by virtue of any enactment giving him the right to remain in occupation;

(b) the other cohabitant or former cohabitant is not so entitled; and

(c) that dwelling-house is the home in which they cohabit or a home in which they at any time cohabited or intended to cohabit.

(2) The cohabitant or former cohabitant not so entitled may apply to the court for an order under this section against the other cohabitant or former cohabitant ('the respondent').

(3) If the applicant is in occupation, an order under this section must contain provision—

(a) giving the applicant the right not to be evicted or excluded from the dwelling-house or any part of it by the respondent for the period specified in the order; and

(b) prohibiting the respondent from evicting or excluding the applicant during that period.

(4) If the applicant is not in occupation, an order under this section must contain provision—

(a) giving the applicant the right to enter into and occupy the dwelling-house for the period specified in the order; and

(b) requiring the respondent to permit the exercise of that right.

(5) An order under this section may also—

(a) regulate the occupation of the dwelling-house by either or both of the parties;

(b) prohibit, suspend or restrict the exercise by the respondent of his right to occupy the dwelling-house;

(c) require the respondent to leave the dwelling-house or part of the dwellinghouse; or

(d) exclude the respondent from a defined area in which the dwelling-house is included.

(6) In deciding whether to make an order under this section containing provision of the kind mentioned in subsection (3) or (4) and (if so) in what manner, the court shall have regard to all the circumstances including—

(a) the housing needs and housing resources of each of the parties and of any relevant child;

(b) the financial resources of each of the parties;

(c) the likely effect of any order, or of any decision by the court not to exercise its powers under subsection (3) or (4), on the health, safety or well-being of the parties and of any relevant child;

(d) the conduct of the parties in relation to each other and otherwise;

(e) the nature of the parties' relationship and in particular the level of commitment involved in it;

(f) the length of time during which they have cohabited;

(g) whether there are or have been any children who are children of both parties or for whom both parties have or have had parental responsibility;

(h) the length of time that has elapsed since the parties ceased to live together; and

(i) the existence of any pending proceedings between the parties—

    (i) for an order under paragraph 1(2)(d) or (e) of Schedule 1 to the Children Act 1989 (orders for financial relief against parents); or

    (ii) relating to the legal or beneficial ownership of the dwelling-house.

(7) In deciding whether to exercise its powers to include one or more of the provisions referred to in subsection (5) ('a subsection (5) provision') and (if so) in what manner, the court shall have regard to all the circumstances including—

    (a) the matters mentioned in subsection (6)(a) to (d); and

    (b) the questions mentioned in subsection (8).

(8) The questions are—

    (a) whether the applicant or any relevant child is likely to suffer significant harm attributable to conduct of the respondent if the subsection (5) provision is not included in the order; and

    (b) whether the harm likely to be suffered by the respondent or child if the provision is included is as great as or greater than the harm attributable to conduct of the respondent which is likely to be suffered by the applicant or child if the provision is not included.

(9) An order under this section—

    (a) may not be made after the death of either of the parties; and

    (b) ceases to have effect on the death of either of them.

(10) An order under this section must be limited so as to have effect for a specified period not exceeding six months, but may be extended on one occasion for a further specified period not exceeding six months.

(11) A person who has an equitable interest in the dwelling-house or in the proceeds of sale of the dwelling-house but in whom there is not vested (whether solely or as joint tenant) a legal estate in fee simple or a legal term of years absolute in the dwelling-house is to be treated (but only for the purpose of determining whether he is eligible to apply under this section) as not being entitled to occupy the dwelling-house by virtue of that interest.

(12) Subsection (11) does not prejudice any right of such a person to apply for an order under section 33.

(13) So long as the order remains in force, subsections (3) to (6) of section 30 apply in relation to the applicant—

    (a) as if he were B (the person entitled to occupy the dwelling-house by virtue of that section); and

    (b) as if the respondent were A (the person entitled as mentioned in subsection (1)(a) of that section).

37 Neither spouse or civil partner entitled to occupy

(1) This section applies if—

    (a) one spouse or former spouse and the other spouse or former spouse occupy a dwelling-house which is or was the matrimonial home; but

    (b) neither of them is entitled to remain in occupation—

        (i) by virtue of a beneficial estate or interest or contract; or

        (ii) by virtue of any enactment giving him the right to remain in occupation.

(1A) This section also applies if—

    (a) one civil partner or former civil partner and the other civil partner or former civil partner occupy a dwelling-house which is or was the civil partnership home; but

    (b) neither of them is entitled to remain in occupation—

        (i) by virtue of a beneficial estate or interest or contract; or

        (ii) by virtue of any enactment giving him the right to remain in occupation.

(2) Either of the parties may apply to the court for an order against the other under this section.

(3) An order under this section may—

(a) require the respondent to permit the applicant to enter and remain in the dwelling-house or part of the dwelling-house;

(b) regulate the occupation of the dwelling-house by either or both of the parties;

(c) require the respondent to leave the dwelling-house or part of the dwelling-house; or

(d) exclude the respondent from a defined area in which the dwelling-house is included.

(4) Subsections (6) and (7) of section 33 apply to the exercise by the court of its powers under this section as they apply to the exercise by the court of its powers under subsection (3) of that section.

(5) An order under this section must be limited so as to have effect for a specified period not exceeding six months, but may be extended on one or more occasions for a further specified period not exceeding six months.

38   Neither cohabitant or former cohabitant entitled to occupy

(1) This section applies if—

(a) one cohabitant or former cohabitant and the other cohabitant or former cohabitant occupy a dwelling-house which is the home in which they cohabit or cohabited; but

(b) neither of them is entitled to remain in occupation—

(i)   by virtue of a beneficial estate or interest or contract; or

(ii) by virtue of any enactment giving him the right to remain in occupation.

(2) Either of the parties may apply to the court for an order against the other under this section.

(3) An order under this section may—

(a) require the respondent to permit the applicant to enter and remain in the dwelling-house or part of the dwelling-house;

(b) regulate the occupation of the dwelling-house by either or both of the parties;

(c) require the respondent to leave the dwelling-house or part of the dwelling-house; or

(d) exclude the respondent from a defined area in which the dwelling-house is included.

(4) In deciding whether to exercise its powers to include one or more of the provisions referred to in subsection (3) ('a subsection (3) provision') and (if so) in what manner, the court shall have regard to all the circumstances including—

(a) the housing needs and housing resources of each of the parties and of any relevant child;

(b) the financial resources of each of the parties;

(c) the likely effect of any order, or of any decision by the court not to exercise its powers under subsection (3), on the health, safety or well-being of the parties and of any relevant child;

(d) the conduct of the parties in relation to each other and otherwise; and

(e) the questions mentioned in subsection (5).

(5) The questions are—

(a) whether the applicant or any relevant child is likely to suffer significant harm attributable to conduct of the respondent if the subsection (3) provision is not included in the order; and

(b) whether the harm likely to be suffered by the respondent or child if the provision is included is as great as or greater than the harm attributable to conduct of the respondent which is likely to be suffered by the applicant or child if the provision is not included.

(6) An order under this section shall be limited so as to have effect for a specified period not exceeding six months, but may be extended on one occasion for a further specified period not exceeding six months.

39 Supplementary provisions

(1) In this Part an 'occupation order' means an order under section 33, 35, 36, 37 or 38.

(2) An application for an occupation order may be made in other family proceedings or without any other family proceedings being instituted.

(3) If—

(a) an application for an occupation order is made under section 33, 35, 36, 37 or 38, and

(b) the court considers that it has no power to make the order under the section concerned, but that it has power to make an order under one of the other sections,

the court may make an order under that other section.

(4) The fact that a person has applied for an occupation order under sections 35 to 38, or that an occupation order has been made, does not affect the right of any person to claim a legal or equitable interest in any property in any subsequent proceedings (including subsequent proceedings under this Part).

40 Additional provisions that may be included in certain occupation orders

(1) The court may on, or at any time after, making an occupation order under section 33, 35 or 36—

(a) impose on either party obligations as to—

(i) the repair and maintenance of the dwelling-house; or

(ii) the discharge of rent, mortgage payments or other outgoings affecting the dwelling-house;

(b) order a party occupying the dwelling-house or any part of it (including a party who is entitled to do so by virtue of a beneficial estate or interest or contract or by virtue of any enactment giving him the right to remain in occupation) to make periodical payments to the other party in respect of the accommodation, if the other party would (but for the order) be entitled to occupy the dwelling-house by virtue of a beneficial estate or interest or contract or by virtue of any such enactment;

(c) grant either party possession or use of furniture or other contents of the dwelling-house;

(d) order either party to take reasonable care of any furniture or other contents of the dwelling-house;

(e) order either party to take reasonable steps to keep the dwelling-house and any furniture or other contents secure.

(2) In deciding whether and, if so, how to exercise its powers under this section, the court shall have regard to all the circumstances of the case including—

(a) the financial needs and financial resources of the parties; and

(b) the financial obligations which they have, or are likely to have in the foreseeable future, including financial obligations to each other and to any relevant child.

(3) An order under this section ceases to have effect when the occupation order to which it relates ceases to have effect.

Non-molestation orders

42 Mon-molestation orders

(1) In this Part a 'non-molestation order' means an order containing either or both of the following provisions—

(a) provision prohibiting a person ('the respondent') from molesting another person who is associated with the respondent;

(b) provision prohibiting the respondent from molesting a relevant child.

(2) The court may make a non-molestation order—

(a) if an application for the order has been made (whether in other family proceedings or without any other family proceedings being instituted) by a person who is associated with the respondent; or

(b) if in any family proceedings to which the respondent is a party the court considers that the order should be made for the benefit of any other party to the proceedings or any relevant child even though no such application has been made.

(3) In subsection (2) 'family proceedings' includes proceedings in which the court has made an emergency protection order under section 44 of the Children Act 1989 which includes an exclusion requirement (as defined in section 44A(3) of that Act).

(4) Where an agreement to marry is terminated, no application under subsection (2)(a) may be made by virtue of section 62(3)(e) by reference to that agreement after the end of the period of three years beginning with the day on which it is terminated.

(4ZA) If a civil partnership agreement (as defined by section 73 of the Civil Partnership Act 2004) is terminated, no application under this section may be made by virtue of section 62(3)(eza) by reference to that agreement after the end of the period of three years beginning with the day on which it is terminated.

(4A) A court considering whether to make an occupation order shall also consider whether to exercise the power conferred by subsection (2)(b).

(4B) In this Part 'the applicant', in relation to a non-molestation order, includes (where the context permits) the person for whose benefit such an order would be or is made in exercise of the power conferred by subsection (2)(b).

(5) In deciding whether to exercise its powers under this section and, if so, in what manner, the court shall have regard to all the circumstances including the need to secure the health, safety and well-being—

(a) of the applicant; and

(b) of any relevant child.

(6) A non-molestation order may be expressed so as to refer to molestation in general, to particular acts of molestation, or to both.

(7) A non-molestation order may be made for a specified period or until further order.

(8) A non-molestation order which is made in other family proceedings ceases to have effect if those proceedings are withdrawn or dismissed.

42A Offence of breaching non-molestation order

(1) A person who without reasonable excuse does anything that he is prohibited from doing by a non-molestation order is guilty of an offence.

(2) In the case of a non-molestation order made by virtue of section 45(1), a person can be guilty of an offence under this section only in respect of conduct engaged in at a time when he was aware of the existence of the order.

(3) Where a person is convicted of an offence under this section in respect of any conduct, that conduct is not punishable as a contempt of court.

(4) A person cannot be convicted of an offence under this section in respect of any conduct which has been punished as a contempt of court.

(5) A person guilty of an offence under this section is liable—

(a) on conviction on indictment, to imprisonment for a term not exceeding five years, or a fine, or both;

(b) on summary conviction, to imprisonment for a term not exceeding 12 months, or a fine not exceeding the statutory maximum, or both.

(6) A reference in any enactment to proceedings under this Part, or to an order under this Part, does not include a reference to proceedings for an offence under this section or to an order made in such proceedings.

'Enactment' includes an enactment contained in subordinate legislation within the meaning of the Interpretation Act 1978.

Further provisions relating to occupation and non-molestation orders

43 Leave of court required for applications by children under sixteen

(1) A child under the age of sixteen may not apply for an occupation order or a non-molestation order except with the leave of the court.

(2) The court may grant leave for the purposes of subsection (1) only if it is satisfied that the child has sufficient understanding to make the proposed application for the occupation order or non-molestation order.

44 Evidence of agreement to marry or form a civil partnership

(1) Subject to subsection (2), the court shall not make an order under section 33 or 42 by virtue of section 62(3)(e) unless there is produced to it evidence in writing of the existence of the agreement to marry.

(2) Subsection (1) does not apply if the court is satisfied that the agreement to marry was evidenced by—

    (a) the gift of an engagement ring by one party to the agreement to the other in contemplation of their marriage, or

    (b) a ceremony entered into by the parties in the presence of one or more other persons assembled for the purpose of witnessing the ceremony.

(3) Subject to subsection (4), the court shall not make an order under section 33 or 42 by virtue of section 62(3)(eza) unless there is produced to it evidence in writing of the existence of the civil partnership agreement (as defined by section 73 of the Civil Partnership Act 2004).

(4) Subsection (3) does not apply if the court is satisfied that the civil partnership agreement was evidenced by—

    (a) a gift by one party to the agreement to the other as a token of the agreement, or

    (b) a ceremony entered into by the parties in the presence of one or more other persons assembled for the purpose of witnessing the ceremony.

45 Ex parte orders

(1) The court may, in any case where it considers that it is just and convenient to do so, make an occupation order or a non-molestation order even though the respondent has not been given such notice of the proceedings as would otherwise be required by rules of court.

(2) In determining whether to exercise its powers under subsection (1), the court shall have regard to all the circumstances including—

    (a) any risk of significant harm to the applicant or a relevant child, attributable to conduct of the respondent, if the order is not made immediately;

    (b) whether it is likely that the applicant will be deterred or prevented from pursuing the application if an order is not made immediately; and

    (c) whether there is reason to believe that the respondent is aware of the proceedings but is deliberately evading service and that the applicant or a relevant child will be seriously prejudiced by the delay involved—

        (i) where the court is a magistrates' court, in effecting service of proceedings; or

        (ii) in any other case, in effecting substituted service.

(3) If the court makes an order by virtue of subsection (1) it must afford the respondent an opportunity to make representations relating to the order as soon as just and convenient at a full hearing.

(4) If, at a full hearing, the court makes an occupation order ('the full order'), then—

    (a) for the purposes of calculating the maximum period for which the full order may be made to have effect, the relevant section is to apply as if the period for which the full order will have effect began on the date on which the initial order first had effect; and

    (b) the provisions of section 36(10) or 38(6) as to the extension of orders are to apply as if the full order and the initial order were a single order.

(5) In this section—

'full hearing' means a hearing of which notice has been given to all the parties in accordance with rules of court;

'initial order' means an occupation order made by virtue of subsection (1); and
'relevant section' means section 33(10), 35(10), 36(10), 37(5) or 38(6).

46   Undertakings

(1) In any case where the court has power to make an occupation order or non-molestation order, the court may accept an undertaking from any party to the proceedings.

(2) No power of arrest may be attached to any undertaking given under subsection (1).

(3) The court shall not accept an undertaking under subsection (1) instead of making an occupation order in any case where apart from this section a power of arrest would be attached to the order.

(3A) The court shall not accept an undertaking under subsection (1) instead of making a non-molestation order in any case where it appears to the court that—

(a) the respondent has used or threatened violence against the applicant or a relevant child; and

(b) for the protection of the applicant or child it is necessary to make a non-molestation order so that any breach may be punishable under section 42A.

(4) An undertaking given to a court under subsection (1) is enforceable as if the court had made an occupation order or a non-molestation order in terms corresponding to those of the undertaking.

(5) This section has effect without prejudice to the powers of the High Court and the county court apart from this section.

47   Arrest for breach of order

(2) If—

(a) the court makes an occupation order; and

(b) it appears to the court that the respondent has used or threatened violence against the applicant or a relevant child,

it shall attach a power of arrest to one or more provisions of the order unless satisfied that in all the circumstances of the case the applicant or child will be adequately protected without such a power of arrest.

(3) Subsection (2) does not apply in any case where the occupation order is made by virtue of section 45(1), but in such a case the court may attach a power of arrest to one or more provisions of the order if it appears to it—

(a) that the respondent has used or threatened violence against the applicant or a relevant child; and

(b) that there is a risk of significant harm to the applicant or child, attributable to conduct of the respondent, if the power of arrest is not attached to those provisions immediately.

(4) If, by virtue of subsection (3), the court attaches a power of arrest to any provisions of an occupation order, it may provide that the power of arrest is to have effect for a shorter period than the other provisions of the order.

(5) Any period specified for the purposes of subsection (4) may be extended by the court (on one or more occasions) on an application to vary or discharge the occupation order.

(6) If, by virtue of subsection (2) or (3), a power of arrest is attached to certain provisions of an order, a constable may arrest without warrant a person whom he has reasonable cause for suspecting to be in breach of any such provision.

(7) If a power of arrest is attached under subsection (2) or (3) to certain provisions of the order and the respondent is arrested under subsection (6)—

(a) he must be brought before the relevant judicial authority within the period of 24 hours beginning at the time of his arrest; and

(b) if the matter is not then disposed of forthwith, the relevant judicial authority before whom he is brought may remand him.

In reckoning for the purposes of this subsection any period of 24 hours, no account is to be taken of Christmas Day, Good Friday or any Sunday.

(8) If the court—

(a) has made a non-molestation order, or

(b) has made an occupation order but has not attached a power of arrest under subsection (2) or (3) to any provision of the order, or has attached that power only to certain provisions of the order,

then, if at any time the applicant considers that the respondent has failed to comply with the order, he may apply to the relevant judicial authority for the issue of a warrant for the arrest of the respondent.

(9) The relevant judicial authority shall not issue a warrant on an application under subsection (8) unless—

(a) the application is substantiated on oath; and

(b) the relevant judicial authority has reasonable grounds for believing that the respondent has failed to comply with the order.

(10) If a person is brought before a court by virtue of a warrant issued under subsection (9) and the court does not dispose of the matter forthwith, the court may remand him.

(11) Schedule 5 (which makes provision corresponding to that applying in magistrates' courts in civil cases under sections 128 and 129 of the Magistrates' Courts Act 1980) has effect in relation to the powers of the High Court and a county court to remand a person by virtue of this section.

(12) If a person remanded under this section is granted bail (whether in the High Court or a county court under Schedule 5 or in a magistrates' court under section 128 or 129 of the Magistrates' Courts Act 1980), he may be required by the relevant judicial authority to comply, before release on bail or later, with such requirements as appear to that authority to be necessary to secure that he does not interfere with witnesses or otherwise obstruct the course of justice.

48   Remand for medical examination and report

(1) If the relevant judicial authority has reason to consider that a medical report will be required, any power to remand a person under section 47(7)(b) or (10) may be exercised for the purpose of enabling a medical examination and report to be made.

(2) If such a power is so exercised, the adjournment must not be for more than 4 weeks at a time unless the relevant judicial authority remands the accused in custody.

(3) If the relevant judicial authority so remands the accused, the adjournment must not be for more than 3 weeks at a time.

(4) If there is reason to suspect that a person who has been arrested—

(a) under section 47(6), or

(b) under a warrant issued on an application made under section 47(8),

is suffering from mental illness or severe mental impairment, the relevant judicial authority has the same power to make an order under section 35 of the Mental Health Act 1983 (remand for report on accused's mental condition) as the Crown Court has under section 35 of the Act of 1983 in the case of an accused person within the meaning of that section.

49   Variation and discharge of orders

(1) An occupation order or non-molestation order may be varied or discharged by the court on an application by—

(a) the respondent, or

(b) the person on whose application the order was made.

(2) In the case of a non-molestation order made by virtue of section 42(2)(b), the order may be varied or discharged by the court even though no such application has been made.

(3) If B's home rights are, under section 31, a charge on the estate or interest of A or of trustees for A, an order under section 33 against A may also be varied or discharged by the court on an application by any person deriving title under A or under the trustees and affected by the charge.

(4) If, by virtue of section 47(3), a power of arrest has been attached to certain provisions of an occupation order, the court may vary or discharge the order under subsection (1) in so far as it confers a power of arrest (whether or not any application has been made to vary or discharge any other provision of the order).

Enforcement powers of magistrates' courts

50   Power of magistrates' court to suspend execution of committal order
(1) If, under section 63(3) of the Magistrates' Courts Act 1980, a magistrates' court has power to commit a person to custody for breach of a relevant requirement, the court may by order direct that the execution of the order of committal is to be suspended for such period or on such terms and conditions as it may specify.
(2) In subsection (1) 'a relevant requirement' means—
   (a) an occupation order or non-molestation order;
   (b) an exclusion requirement included by virtue of section 38A of the Children Act 1989 in an interim care order made under section 38 of that Act, or
   (c) an exclusion requirement included by virtue of section 44A of the Children Act 1989 in an emergency protection order under section 44 of that Act.

51   Power of magistrates' court to order hospital admission or guardianship
(1) A magistrates' court has the same power to make a hospital order or guardianship order under section 37 of the Mental Health Act 1983 or an interim hospital order under section 38 of that Act in the case of a person suffering from mental illness or severe mental impairment who could otherwise be committed to custody for breach of a relevant requirement as a magistrates' court has under those sections in the case of a person convicted of an offence punishable on summary conviction with imprisonment.
(2) In subsection (1) 'a relevant requirement' has the meaning given by section 50(2).

Transfer of tenancies

53   Transfer of certain tenancies
Schedule 7 makes provision in relation to the transfer of certain tenancies on divorce etc. or on separation of cohabitants.

Dwelling-house subject to mortgage

54   Dwelling-house subject to mortgage
(1) In determining for the purposes of this Part whether a person is entitled to occupy a dwelling-house by virtue of an estate or interest, any right to possession of the dwelling-house conferred on a mortgagee of the dwelling-house under or by virtue of his mortgage is to be disregarded.
(2) Subsection (1) applies whether or not the mortgagee is in possession.
(3) Where a person ('A') is entitled to occupy a dwelling-house by virtue of an estate or interest, a connected person does not by virtue of—
   (a) any home rights conferred by section 30, or
   (b) any rights conferred by an order under section 35 or 36,
have any larger right against the mortgagee to occupy the dwelling-house than A has by virtue of his estate or interest and of any contract with the mortgagee.
(4) Subsection (3) does not apply, in the case of home rights, if under section 31 those rights are a charge, affecting the mortgagee, on the estate or interest mortgaged.
(5) In this section 'connected person', in relation to any person, means that person's spouse, former spouse, civil partner, former civil partner, cohabitant or former cohabitant.

55   Actions by mortgagees: joining connected persons as parties
(1) This section applies if a mortgagee of land which consists of or includes a dwelling-house brings an action in any court for the enforcement of his security.

(2) A connected person who is not already a party to the action is entitled to be made a party in the circumstances mentioned in subsection (3).

(3) The circumstances are that—

(a) the connected person is enabled by section 30(3) or (6) (or by section 30(3) or (6) as applied by section 35(13) or 36(13)), to meet the mortgagor's liabilities under the mortgage;

(b) he has applied to the court before the action is finally disposed of in that court; and

(c) the court sees no special reason against his being made a party to the action and is satisfied—

(i) that he may be expected to make such payments or do such other things in or towards satisfaction of the mortgagor's liabilities or obligations as might affect the outcome of the proceedings; or

(ii) that the expectation of it should be considered under section 36 of the Administration of Justice Act 1970.

(4) In this section 'connected person' has the same meaning as in section 54.

56 Actions by mortgagees: service of notice on certain persons

(1) This section applies if a mortgagee of land which consists, or substantially consists, of a dwelling-house brings an action for the enforcement of his security, and at the relevant time there is—

(a) in the case of unregistered land, a land charge of Class F registered against the person who is the estate owner at the relevant time or any person who, where the estate owner is a trustee, preceded him as trustee during the subsistence of the mortgage; or

(b) in the case of registered land, a subsisting registration of—

(i) a notice under section 31(10);

(ii) a notice under section 2(8) of the Matrimonial Homes Act 1983; or

(iii) a notice or caution under section 2(7) of the Matrimonial Homes Act 1967.

(2) If the person on whose behalf—

(a) the land charge is registered, or

(b) the notice or caution is entered, is not a party to the action, the mortgagee must serve notice of the action on him.

(3) If—

(a) an official search has been made on behalf of the mortgagee which would disclose any land charge of Class F, notice or caution within subsection (1)(a) or (b),

(b) a certificate of the result of the search has been issued, and

(c) the action is commenced within the priority period,

the relevant time is the date of the certificate.

(4) In any other case the relevant time is the time when the action is commenced.

(5) The priority period is, for both registered and unregistered land, the period for which, in accordance with section 11(5) and (6) of the Land Charges Act 1972, a certificate on an official search operates in favour of a purchaser.

Jurisdiction and procedure etc.

57 Jurisdiction of courts

(1) For the purposes of this Part 'the court' means the High Court, a county court or a magistrates' court.

(2) Subsection (1) is subject to the provision made by or under the following provisions of this section, to section 59 and to any express provision as to the jurisdiction of any court made by any other provision of this Part.

(3) The Lord Chancellor, after consulting the Lord Chief Justice, may by order specify proceedings under this Part which may only be commenced in—

(a) a specified level of court;

(b) a court which falls within a specified class of court; or

(c) a particular court determined in accordance with, or specified in, the order.

(4) The Lord Chancellor, after consulting the Lord Chief Justice, may by order specify circumstances in which specified proceedings under this Part may only be commenced in—

(a) a specified level of court;

(b) a court which falls within a specified class of court; or

(c) a particular court determined in accordance with, or specified in, the order.

(5) The Lord Chancellor, after consulting the Lord Chief Justice, may by order provide that in specified circumstances the whole, or any specified part of any specified proceedings under this Part is to be transferred to—

(a) a specified level of court;

(b) a court which falls within a specified class of court; or

(c) a particular court determined in accordance with, or specified in, the order.

(6) An order under subsection (5) may provide for the transfer to be made at any stage, or specified stage, of the proceedings and whether or not the proceedings, or any part of them, have already been transferred.

(7) An order under subsection (5) may make such provision as the Lord Chancellor thinks appropriate, after consulting the Lord Chief Justice, for excluding specified proceedings from the operation of section 38 or 39 of the Matrimonial and Family Proceedings Act 1984 (transfer of family proceedings) or any other enactment which would otherwise govern the transfer of those proceedings, or any part of them.

(8) For the purposes of subsections (3), (4) and (5), there are three levels of court—

(a) the High Court;

(b) any county court; and

(c) any magistrates' court.

(9) The Lord Chancellor may, after consulting the Lord Chief Justice, by order make provision for the principal registry of the Family Division of the High Court to be treated as if it were a county court for specified purposes of this Part, or of any provision made under this Part.

(10) Any order under subsection (9) may make such provision as the Lord Chancellor thinks expedient, after consulting the Lord Chief Justice, for the purpose of applying (with or without modifications) provisions which apply in relation to the procedure in county courts to the principal registry when it acts as if it were a county court.

(11) In this section 'specified' means specified by an order under this section.

(12) The Lord Chief Justice may nominate a judicial office holder (as defined in section 109(4) of the Constitutional Reform Act 2005) to exercise his functions under this section.

58 Contempt proceedings

The powers of the court in relation to contempt of court arising out of a person's failure to comply with an order under this Part may be exercised by the relevant judicial authority.

59 Magistrates' courts

(1) A magistrates' court shall not be competent to entertain any application, or make any order, involving any disputed question as to a party's entitlement to occupy any property by virtue of a beneficial estate or interest or contract or by virtue of any enactment giving him the right to remain in occupation, unless it is unnecessary to determine the question in order to deal with the application or make the order.

(2) A magistrates' court may decline jurisdiction in any proceedings under this Part if it considers that the case can more conveniently be dealt with by another court.

(3) The powers of a magistrates' court under section 63(2) of the Magistrates' Courts Act 1980 to suspend or rescind orders shall not apply in relation to any order made under this Part.

60 Provision for third parties to act on behalf of victims of domestic violence

(1) Rules of court may provide for a prescribed person, or any person in a prescribed category, ('a representative') to act on behalf of another in relation to proceedings to which this Part applies.

(2) Rules made under this section may, in particular, authorise a representative to apply for an occupation order or for a non-molestation order for which the person on whose behalf the representative is acting could have applied.

(3) Rules made under this section may prescribe—

(a) conditions to be satisfied before a representative may make an application to the court on behalf of another; and

(b) considerations to be taken into account by the court in determining whether, and if so how, to exercise any of its powers under this Part when a representative is acting on behalf of another.

(4) Any rules made under this section may be made so as to have effect for a specified period and may make consequential or transitional provision with respect to the expiry of the specified period.

(5) Any such rules may be replaced by further rules made under this section.

61 Appeals

(1) An appeal shall lie to the High Court against—

(a) the making by a magistrates' court of any order under this Part, or

(b) any refusal by a magistrates' court to make such an order,

but no appeal shall lie against any exercise by a magistrates' court of the power conferred by section 59(2).

(2) On an appeal under this section, the High Court may make such orders as may be necessary to give effect to its determination of the appeal.

(3) Where an order is made under subsection (2), the High Court may also make such incidental or consequential orders as appear to it to be just.

(4) Any order of the High Court made on an appeal under this section (other than one directing that an application be re-heard by a magistrates' court) shall, for the purposes—

(a) of the enforcement of the order, and

(b) of any power to vary, revive or discharge orders,

be treated as if it were an order of the magistrates' court from which the appeal was brought and not an order of the High Court.

(5) The Lord Chancellor may, after consulting the Lord Chief Justice, by order make provision as to the circumstances in which appeals may be made against decisions taken by courts on questions arising in connection with the transfer, or proposed transfer, of proceedings by virtue of any order under section 57(5).

(6) Except to the extent provided for in any order made under subsection (5), no appeal may be made against any decision of a kind mentioned in that subsection.

(7) The Lord Chief Justice may nominate a judicial office holder (as defined in section 109(4) of the Constitutional Reform Act 2005) to exercise his functions under this section.

General

62 Meaning of 'cohabitants', 'relevant child' and 'associated persons'

(1) For the purposes of this Part—

(a) 'cohabitants' are two persons who are neither married to each other nor civil partners of each other but are living together as husband and wife or as if they were civil partners; and

(b) 'cohabit' and 'former cohabitants' are to be read accordingly, but the latter expression does not include cohabitants who have subsequently married each other or become civil partners of each other.

(2) In this Part, 'relevant child', in relation to any proceedings under this Part, means—

(a) any child who is living with or might reasonably be expected to live with either party to the proceedings;

(b) any child in relation to whom an order under the Adoption Act 1976, the Adoption and Children Act 2002 or the Children Act 1989 is in question in the proceedings; and

(c) any other child whose interests the court considers relevant.

(3) For the purposes of this Part, a person is associated with another person if—

(a)   they are or have been married to each other;

(aa)   they are or have been civil partners of each other;

(b)   they are cohabitants or former cohabitants;

(c)   they live or have lived in the same household, otherwise than merely by reason of one of them being the other's employee, tenant, lodger or boarder;

(d)   they are relatives;

(e)   they have agreed to marry one another (whether or not that agreement has been terminated);

(eza) they have entered into a civil partnership agreement (as defined by section 73 of the Civil Partnership Act 2004) (whether or not that agreement has been terminated);

(ea)   they have or have had an intimate personal relationship with each other which is or was of significant duration;

(f)   in relation to any child, they are both persons falling within subsection (4); or

(g)   they are parties to the same family proceedings (other than proceedings under this Part).

(4) A person falls within this subsection in relation to a child if—

(a) he is a parent of the child; or

(b) he has or has had parental responsibility for the child.

(5) If a child has been adopted or falls within subsection (7), two persons are also associated with each other for the purposes of this Part if—

(a) one is a natural parent of the child or a parent of such a natural parent; and

(b) the other is the child or any person—

(i)   who has become a parent of the child by virtue of an adoption order or has applied for an adoption order, or

(ii) with whom the child has at any time been placed for adoption.

(6) A body corporate and another person are not, by virtue of subsection (3)(f) or (g), to be regarded for the purposes of this Part as associated with each other.

(7) A child falls within this subsection if—

(a) an adoption agency, within the meaning of section 2 of the Adoption and Children Act 2002, has power to place him for adoption under section 19 of that Act (placing children with parental consent) or he has become the subject of an order under section 21 of that Act (placement orders), or

(b) he is freed for adoption by virtue of an order made—

(i)   in England and Wales, under section 18 of the Adoption Act 1976,

. . .

(iii) in Northern Ireland, under Article 17(1) or 18(1) of the Adoption (Northern Ireland) Order 1987.

63   Interpretation of Part IV

(1) In this Part—

'adoption order' means an adoption order within the meaning of section 72(1) of the Adoption Act 1976 or section 46(1) of the Adoption and Children Act 2002;

'associated', in relation to a person, is to be read with section 62(3) to (6);

'child' means a person under the age of eighteen years;

'cohabit', 'cohabitant' and 'former cohabitant' have the meaning given by section 62(1);

'the court' is to be read with section 57;

'development' means physical, intellectual, emotional, social or behavioural development;

'dwelling-house' includes (subject to subsection (4))—

 (a) any building or part of a building which is occupied as a dwelling,

 (b) any caravan, house-boat or structure which is occupied as a dwelling, and any yard, garden, garage or outhouse belonging to it and occupied with it;

'family proceedings' means any proceedings—

 (a) under the inherent jurisdiction of the High Court in relation to children; or

 (b) under the enactments mentioned in subsection (2);

'harm'—

 (a) in relation to a person who has reached the age of eighteen years, means ill-treatment or the impairment of health; and

 (b) in relation to a child, means ill-treatment or the impairment of health or development;

'health' includes physical or mental health;

'home rights' has the meaning given by section 30;

'ill-treatment' includes forms of ill-treatment which are not physical and, in relation to a child, includes sexual abuse;

'mortgage', 'mortgagor' and 'mortgagee' have the same meaning as in the Law of Property Act 1925;

'mortgage payments' includes any payments which, under the terms of the mortgage, the mortgagor is required to make to any person;

'non-molestation order' has the meaning given by section 42(1);

'occupation order' has the meaning given by section 39;

'parental responsibility' has the same meaning as in the Children Act 1989;

'relative', in relation to a person, means—

 (a) the father, mother, stepfather, stepmother, son, daughter, stepson, stepdaughter, grandmother, grandfather, grandson or granddaughter of that person or of that person's spouse, former spouse, civil partner or former civil partner, or

 (b) the brother, sister, uncle, aunt, niece, nephew or first cousin (whether of the full blood or of the half blood or by marriage or civil partnership) of that person or of that person's spouse, former spouse, civil partner or former civil partner,

and includes, in relation to a person who is cohabiting or has cohabited with another person, any person who would fall within paragraph (a) or (b) if the parties were married to each other or were civil partners of each other;

'relevant child', in relation to any proceedings under this Part, has the meaning given by section 62(2);

'the relevant judicial authority', in relation to any order under this Part, means—

 (a) where the order was made by the High Court, a judge of that court;

 (b) where the order was made by a county court, a judge or district judge of that or any other county court; or

 (c) where the order was made by a magistrates' court, any magistrates' court.

(2) The enactments referred to in the definition of 'family proceedings' are—

 (a) Part II;

 (b) this Part;

 (c) the Matrimonial Causes Act 1973;

 (d) the Adoption Act 1976;

 (e) the Domestic Proceedings and Magistrates' Courts Act 1978;

 (f) Part III of the Matrimonial and Family Proceedings Act 1984;

 (g) Parts I, II and IV of the Children Act 1989;

 (h) section 30 of the Human Fertilisation and Embryology Act 1990;

 (i) the Adoption and Children Act 2002.

 (j) Schedules 5 to 7 to the Civil Partnership Act 2004.

(3) Where the question of whether harm suffered by a child is significant turns on the child's health or development, his health or development shall be compared with that which could reasonably be expected of a similar child.

(4) For the purposes of sections 31, 32, 53 and 54 and such other provisions of this Part (if any) as may be prescribed, this Part is to have effect as if paragraph (b) of the definition of 'dwelling-house' were omitted.

(5) It is hereby declared that this Part applies as between the parties to a marriage even though either of them is, or has at any time during the marriage been, married to more than one person.

PART V   SUPPLEMENTAL

64   Provision for separate representation for children

(1) The Lord Chancellor may by regulations provide for the separate representation of children in proceedings in England and Wales which relate to any matter in respect of which a question has arisen, or may arise, under—

    (a) Part II;

    (b) Part IV;

    (c) the 1973 Act;

    (d) the Domestic Proceedings and Magistrates' Courts Act 1978; or

    (e) Schedule 5 or 6 to the Civil Partnership Act 2004.

(2) The regulations may provide for such representation only in specified circumstances.

. . .

Section 32   **SCHEDULE 4**

PROVISIONS SUPPLEMENTARY TO SECTIONS 30 AND 31

Interpretation

    1.—(1) In this Schedule—

        (a) any reference to a solicitor includes a reference to a licensed conveyancer or a recognised body, and

        (b) any reference to a person's solicitor includes a reference to a licensed conveyancer or recognised body acting for that person.

    (2) In sub-paragraph (1)—

'licensed conveyancer' has the meaning given by section 11(2) of the Administration of Justice Act 1985;

'recognised body' means a body corporate for the time being recognised under section 9 (incorporated practices) or section 32 (provision of conveyancing by recognised bodies) of that Act.

Restriction on registration where spouse or civil partner entitled to more than one charge

2. Where one spouse or civil partner is entitled by virtue of section 31 to a registrable charge in respect of each of two or more dwelling-houses, only one of the charges to which that spouse or civil partner is so entitled shall be registered under section 31(10) or under section 2 of the Land Charges Act 1972 at any one time, and if any of those charges is registered under either of those provisions the Chief Land Registrar, on being satisfied that any other of them is so registered, shall cancel the registration of the charge first registered.

Contract for sale of house affected by registered charge to include term requiring cancellation of registration before completion

3.—(1) Where one spouse or civil partner is entitled by virtue of section 31 to a charge on an estate in a dwelling-house and the charge is registered under section 31(10) or section 2 of the Land Charges Act 1972, it shall be a term of any contract for the sale of that estate whereby the vendor agrees to give vacant possession of the dwelling-house on completion of the contract that the vendor will before such completion procure the cancellation of the registration of the charge at his expense.

(2) Sub-paragraph (1) shall not apply to any such contract made by a vendor who is entitled to sell the estate in the dwelling-house freed from any such charge.

(3) If, on the completion of such a contract as is referred to in sub-paragraph (1), there is delivered to the purchaser or his solicitor an application by the spouse or civil partner entitled to the charge for the cancellation of the registration of that charge, the term of the contract for which sub-paragraph (1) provides shall be deemed to have been performed.

(4) This paragraph applies only if and so far as a contrary intention is not expressed in the contract.

(5) This paragraph shall apply to a contract for exchange as it applies to a contract for sale.

(6) This paragraph shall, with the necessary modifications, apply to a contract for the grant of a lease or underlease of a dwelling-house as it applies to a contract for the sale of an estate in a dwelling-house.

Cancellation of registration after termination of marriage or civil partnership, etc.

4.—(1) Where a spouse's or civil partner's home rights are a charge on an estate in the dwelling-house and the charge is registered under section 31(10) or under section 2 of the Land Charges Act 1972, the Chief Land Registrar shall, subject to sub-paragraph (2), cancel the registration of the charge if he is satisfied—

(a) in the case of a marriage—
    (i) by the production of a certificate or other sufficient evidence, that either spouse is dead,
    (ii) by the production of an official copy of a decree or order of a court, that the marriage has been terminated otherwise than by death, or
    (iii) by the production of an order of the court, that the spouse's home rights constituting the charge have been terminated by the order, and

(b) in the case of a civil partnership—
    (i) by the production of a certificate or other sufficient evidence, that either civil partner is dead,
    (ii) by the production of an official copy of an order or decree of a court, that the civil partnership has been terminated otherwise than by death, or
    (iii) by the production of an order of the court, that the civil partner's home rights constituting the charge have been terminated by the order.

(2) Where—

(a) the marriage or civil partnership in question has been terminated by the death of the spouse or civil partner entitled to an estate in the dwelling-house or otherwise than by death, and

(b) an order affecting the charge of the spouse or civil partner not so entitled had been made under section 33(5),

then if, after the making of the order, registration of the charge was renewed or the charge registered in pursuance of sub-paragraph (3), the Chief Land Registrar shall not cancel the registration of the charge in accordance with sub-paragraph (1) unless he is also satisfied that the order has ceased to have effect.

(3) Where such an order has been made, then, for the purposes of sub-paragraph (2), the spouse or civil partner entitled to the charge affected by the order may—

(a) if before the date of the order the charge was registered under section 31(10) or under section 2 of the Land Charges Act 1972, renew the registration of the charge, and

(b) if before the said date the charge was not so registered, register the charge under section 31(10) or under section 2 of the Land Charges Act 1972.

(4) Renewal of the registration of a charge in pursuance of sub-paragraph (3) shall be effected in such manner as may be prescribed, and an application for such renewal or for registration of a charge in pursuance of that sub-paragraph shall contain such particulars of any order affecting the charge made under section 33(5) as may be prescribed.

(5) The renewal in pursuance of sub-paragraph (3) of the registration of a charge shall not affect the priority of the charge.

(6) In this paragraph 'prescribed' means prescribed by rules made under section 16 of the Land Charges Act 1972 or by land registration rules under the Land Registration Act 2002, as the circumstances of the case require.

Release of home rights

5.—(1) A spouse or civil partner entitled to home rights may by a release in writing release those rights or release them as respects part only of the dwelling-house affected by them.

(2) Where a contract is made for the sale of an estate or interest in a dwelling-house, or for the grant of a lease or underlease of a dwelling-house, being (in either case) a dwelling-house affected by a charge registered under section 31(10) or under section 2 of the Land Charges Act 1972, then, without prejudice to sub-paragraph (1), the home rights constituting the charge shall be deemed to have been released on the happening of whichever of the following events first occurs—

(a) the delivery to the purchaser or lessee, as the case may be, or his solicitor on completion of the contract of an application by the spouse or civil partner entitled to the charge for the cancellation of the registration of the charge; or
(b) the lodging of such an application at Her Majesty's Land Registry.

Postponement of priority of charge

6. A spouse or civil partner entitled by virtue of section 31 to a charge on an estate or interest may agree in writing that any other charge on, or interest in, that estate or interest shall rank in priority to the charge to which that spouse or civil partner is so entitled.

SCHEDULE 5

POWERS OF HIGH COURT AND COUNTY COURT TO REMAND

Interpretation

1. In this Schedule 'the court' means the High Court or a county court and includes—
(a) in relation to the High Court, a judge of that court, and
(b) in relation to a county court, a judge or district judge of that court.

Remand in custody or on bail

2.—(1) Where a court has power to remand a person under section 47, the court may—
(a) remand him in custody, that is to say, commit him to custody to be brought before the court at the end of the period of remand or at such earlier time as the court may require, or
(b) remand him on bail—
(i) by taking from him a recognizance (with or without sureties) conditioned as provided in sub-paragraph (3), or
(ii) by fixing the amount of the recognizances with a view to their being taken subsequently in accordance with paragraph 4 and in the meantime committing the person to custody in accordance with paragraph (a).

(2) Where a person is brought before the court after remand, the court may further remand him.

(3) Where a person is remanded on bail under sub-paragraph (1), the court may direct that his recognizance be conditioned for his appearance—

    (a) before that court at the end of the period of remand, or

    (b) at every time and place to which during the course of the proceedings the hearing may from time to time be adjourned.

(4) Where a recognizance is conditioned for a person's appearance in accordance with sub-paragraph (l)(b), the fixing of any time for him next to appear shall be deemed to be a remand; but nothing in this sub-paragraph or sub-paragraph (3) shall deprive the court of power at any subsequent hearing to remand him afresh.

(5) Subject to paragraph 3, the court shall not remand a person under this paragraph for a period exceeding 8 clear days, except that—

    (a) if the court remands him on bail, it may remand him for a longer period if he and the other party consent, and

    (b) if the court adjourns a case under section 48(1), the court may remand him for the period of the adjournment.

(6) Where the court has power under this paragraph to remand a person in custody it may, if the remand is for a period not exceeding 3 clear days, commit him to the custody of a constable.

Further remand

3.—(1) If the court is satisfied that any person who has been remanded under paragraph 2 is unable by reason of illness or accident to appear or be brought before the court at the expiration of the period for which he was remanded, the court may, in his absence, remand him for a further time; and paragraph 2(5) shall not apply.

(2) Notwithstanding anything in paragraph 2(1), the power of the court under sub-paragraph (1) to remand a person on bail for a further time may be exercised by enlarging his recognizance and those of any sureties for him to a later time.

(3) Where a person remanded on bail under paragraph 2 is bound to appear before the court at any time and the court has no power to remand him under sub-paragraph (1), the court may in his absence enlarge his recognizance and those of any sureties for him to a later time; and the enlargement of his recognizance shall be deemed to be a further remand.

Postponement of taking of recognizance

4. Where under paragraph 2(1)(b)(ii) the court fixes the amount in which the principal and his sureties, if any, are to be bound, the recognizance may thereafter be taken by such person as may be prescribed by rules of court, and the same consequences shall follow as if it had been entered into before the court.

SCHEDULE 7

TRANSFER OF CERTAIN TENANCIES ON DIVORCE ETC. OR ON SEPARATION OF COHABITANTS

PART I   GENERAL

Interpretation

1. In this Schedule—

'civil partner', except in paragraph 2, includes (where the context requires) former civil partner;

'cohabitant', except in paragraph 3, includes (where the context requires) former cohabitant;

'the court' does not include a magistrates' court;

'landlord' includes—

(a) any person from time to time deriving title under the original landlord; and

(b) in relation to any dwelling-house, any person other than the tenant who is, or (but for Part VII of the Rent Act 1977 or Part II of the Rent (Agriculture) Act 1976) would be, entitled to possession of the dwelling-house;

'Part II order' means an order under Part II of this Schedule;

'a relevant tenancy' means—

(a) a protected tenancy or statutory tenancy within the meaning of the Rent Act 1977;

(b) a statutory tenancy within the meaning of the Rent (Agriculture) Act 1976;

(c) a secure tenancy within the meaning of section 79 of the Housing Act 1985;

(d) an assured tenancy or assured agricultural occupancy within the meaning of Part I of the Housing Act 1988; or

(e) an introductory tenancy within the meaning of Chapter I of Part V of the Housing Act 1996;

'spouse', except in paragraph 2, includes (where the context requires) former spouse; and

'tenancy' includes sub-tenancy.

Cases in which the court may make an order

2.—(1) This paragraph applies if one spouse or civil partner is entitled, either in his own right or jointly with the other spouse or civil partner, to occupy a dwelling-house by virtue of a relevant tenancy.

(2) The court may make a Part II order—

(a) on granting a decree of divorce, a decree of nullity of marriage or a decree of judicial separation or at any time thereafter (whether, in the case of a decree of divorce or nullity of marriage, before or after the decree is made absolute), or

(b) at any time when it has power to make a property adjustment order under Part 2 of Schedule 5 to the Civil Partnership Act 2004 with respect to the civil partnership.

3.—(1) This paragraph applies if one cohabitant is entitled, either in his own right or jointly with the other cohabitant, to occupy a dwelling-house by virtue of a relevant tenancy.

(2) If the cohabitants cease to cohabit, the court may make a Part II order.

4. The court shall not make a Part II order unless the dwelling-house is or was—

(a) in the case of spouses, a matrimonial home;

(aa) in the case of civil partners, a civil partnership home; or

(b) in the case of cohabitants, a home in which they cohabited.

Matters to which the court must have regard

5. In determining whether to exercise its powers under Part II of this Schedule and, if so, in what manner, the court shall have regard to all the circumstances of the case including—

(a) the circumstances in which the tenancy was granted to either or both of the spouses, civil partners or cohabitants or, as the case requires, the circumstances in which either or both of them became tenant under the tenancy;

(b) the matters mentioned in section 33(6)(a), (b) and (c) and, where the parties are cohabitants and only one of them is entitled to occupy the dwelling-house by virtue of the relevant tenancy, the further matters mentioned in section 36(6)(e), (f), (g) and (h); and

(c) the suitability of the parties as tenants.

PART II   ORDERS THAT MAY BE MADE

References to entitlement to occupy

6. References in this Part of this Schedule to a spouse, a civil partner or a cohabitant being entitled to occupy a dwelling-house by virtue of a relevant tenancy apply whether that entitlement is in his own right or jointly with the other spouse, civil partner or cohabitant.

Protected, secure or assured tenancy or assured agricultural occupancy

7.—(1) If a spouse, civil partner or cohabitant is entitled to occupy the dwelling-house by virtue of a protected tenancy within the meaning of the Rent Act 1977, a secure tenancy within the meaning of the Housing Act 1985, an assured tenancy or assured agricultural occupancy within the meaning of Part I of the Housing Act 1988 or an introductory tenancy within the meaning of Chapter I of Part V of the Housing Act 1996, the court may by order direct that, as from such date as may be specified in the order, there shall, by virtue of the order and without further assurance, be transferred to, and vested in, the other spouse, civil partner or cohabitant—

    (a) the estate or interest which the spouse, civil partner or cohabitant so entitled had in the dwelling-house immediately before that date by virtue of the lease or agreement creating the tenancy and any assignment of that lease or agreement, with all rights, privileges and appurtenances attaching to that estate or interest but subject to all covenants, obligations, liabilities and incumbrances to which it is subject; and

    (b) where the spouse, civil partner or cohabitant so entitled is an assignee of such lease or agreement, the liability of that spouse, civil partner or cohabitant under any covenant of indemnity by the assignee express or implied in the assignment of the lease or agreement to that spouse, civil partner or cohabitant.

(2) If an order is made under this paragraph, any liability or obligation to which the spouse, civil partner or cohabitant so entitled is subject under any covenant having reference to the dwelling-house in the lease or agreement, being a liability or obligation falling due to be discharged or performed on or after the date so specified, shall not be enforceable against that spouse, civil partner or cohabitant.

(3) If the spouse, civil partner or cohabitant so entitled is a successor within the meaning of Part 4 of the Housing Act 1985—

    (a) his former spouse (or, in the case of judicial separation, his spouse),

    (b) his former civil partner (or, if a separation order is in force, his civil partner), or

    (c) his former cohabitant,

is to be deemed also to be a successor within the meaning of that Part.

(3A) If the spouse, civil partner or cohabitant so entitled is a successor within the meaning of section 132 of the Housing Act 1996—

    (a) his former spouse (or, in the case of judicial separation, his spouse),

    (b) his former civil partner (or, if a separation order is in force, his civil partner), or

    (c) his former cohabitant,

is to be deemed also to be a successor within the meaning of that section.

(4) If the spouse, civil partner or cohabitant so entitled is for the purposes of section 17 of the Housing Act 1988 a successor in relation to the tenancy or occupancy—

    (a) his former spouse (or, in the case of judicial separation, his spouse),

    (b) his former civil partner (or, if a separation order is in force, his civil partner), or

    (c) his former cohabitant,

is to be deemed to be a successor in relation to the tenancy or occupancy for the purposes of that section.

(5) If the transfer under sub-paragraph (1) is of an assured agricultural occupancy, then, for the purposes of Chapter III of Part I of the Housing Act 1988—

    (a) the agricultural worker condition is fulfilled with respect to the dwelling-house while the spouse, civil partner or cohabitant to whom the assured agricultural occupancy is transferred continues to be the occupier under that occupancy, and

    (b) that condition is to be treated as so fulfilled by virtue of the same paragraph of Schedule 3 to the Housing Act 1988 as was applicable before the transfer.

Statutory tenancy within the meaning of the Rent Act 1977

8.—(1) This paragraph applies if the spouse, civil partner or cohabitant is entitled to occupy the dwelling-house by virtue of a statutory tenancy within the meaning of the Rent Act 1977.

(2) The court may by order direct that, as from the date specified in the order—

    (a) that spouse, civil partner or cohabitant is to cease to be entitled to occupy the dwelling-house; and

    (b) the other spouse, civil partner or cohabitant is to be deemed to be the tenant or, as the case may be, the sole tenant under that statutory tenancy.

(3) The question whether the provisions of paragraphs 1 to 3, or (as the case may be) paragraphs 5 to 7 of Schedule 1 to the Rent Act 1977, as to the succession by the surviving spouse or surviving civil partner of a deceased tenant, or by a member of the deceased tenant's family, to the right to retain possession are capable of having effect in the event of the death of the person deemed by an order under this paragraph to be the tenant or sole tenant under the statutory tenancy is to be determined according as those provisions have or have not already had effect in relation to the statutory tenancy.

Statutory tenancy within the meaning of the Rent (Agriculture) Act 1976

9.—(1) This paragraph applies if the spouse, civil partner or cohabitant is entitled to occupy the dwelling-house by virtue of a statutory tenancy within the meaning of the Rent (Agriculture) Act 1976.

(2) The court may by order direct that, as from such date as may be specified in the order—

    (a) that spouse, civil partner or cohabitant is to cease to be entitled to occupy the dwelling-house; and

    (b) the other spouse, civil partner or cohabitant is to be deemed to be the tenant or, as the case may be, the sole tenant under that statutory tenancy.

(3) A spouse, civil partner or cohabitant who is deemed under this paragraph to be the tenant under a statutory tenancy is (within the meaning of that Act) a statutory tenant in his own right, or a statutory tenant by succession, according as the other spouse, civil partner or cohabitant was a statutory tenant in his own right or a statutory tenant by succession.

PART III   SUPPLEMENTARY PROVISIONS

Compensation

10.—(1) If the court makes a Part II order, it may by the order direct the making of a payment by the spouse, civil partner or cohabitant to whom the tenancy is transferred ('the transferee') to the other spouse, civil partner or cohabitant ('the transferor').

(2) Without prejudice to that, the court may, on making an order by virtue of sub-paragraph (1) for the payment of a sum—

    (a) direct that payment of that sum or any part of it is to be deferred until a specified date or until the occurrence of a specified event, or

    (b) direct that that sum or any part of it is to be paid by instalments.

(3) Where an order has been made by virtue of sub-paragraph (1), the court may, on the application of the transferee or the transferor—

(a) exercise its powers under sub-paragraph (2), or

(b) vary any direction previously given under that sub-paragraph, at any time before the sum whose payment is required by the order is paid in full.

(4) In deciding whether to exercise its powers under this paragraph and, if so, in what manner, the court shall have regard to all the circumstances including—

(a) the financial loss that would otherwise be suffered by the transferor as a result of the order;

(b) the financial needs and financial resources of the parties; and

(c) the financial obligations which the parties have, or are likely to have in the foreseeable future, including financial obligations to each other and to any relevant child.

(5) The court shall not give any direction under sub-paragraph (2) unless it appears to it that immediate payment of the sum required by the order would cause the transferee financial hardship which is greater than any financial hardship that would be caused to the transferor if the direction were given.

Liabilities and obligations in respect of the dwelling-house

11.—(1) If the court makes a Part II order, it may by the order direct that both spouses, civil partners or cohabitants are to be jointly and severally liable to discharge or perform any or all of the liabilities and obligations in respect of the dwelling-house (whether arising under the tenancy or otherwise) which—

(a) have at the date of the order fallen due to be discharged or performed by one only of them; or

(b) but for the direction, would before the date specified as the date on which the order is to take effect fall due to be discharged or performed by one only of them.

(2) If the court gives such a direction, it may further direct that either spouse, civil partner or cohabitant is to be liable to indemnify the other in whole or in part against any payment made or expenses incurred by the other in discharging or performing any such liability or obligation.

Date when order made between spouses or civil partners takes effect

12. The date specified in a Part II order as the date on which the order is to take effect must not be earlier than—

(a) in the case of a marriage in respect of which a decree of divorce or nullity has been granted, the date on which the decree is made absolute;

(b) in the case of a civil partnership in respect of which a dissolution or nullity order has been made, the date on which the order is made final.

Effect of remarriage or subsequent civil partnership

13.—(1) If after the grant of a decree dissolving or annulling a marriage either spouse remarries or forms a civil partnership, that spouse is not entitled to apply, by reference to the grant of that decree, for a Part II order.

(2) If after the making of a dissolution or nullity order either civil partner forms a subsequent civil partnership or marries, that civil partner is not entitled to apply, by reference to the making of that order, for a Part II order.

(3) In sub-paragraphs (1) and (2)—

(a) the references to remarrying and marrying include references to cases where the marriage is by law void or voidable, and

(b) the references to forming a civil partnership include references to cases where the civil partnership is by law void or voidable.

Rules of court

14.—(1) Rules of court shall be made requiring the court, before it makes an order under this Schedule, to give the landlord of the dwelling-house to which the order will relate an opportunity of being heard.

(2) Rules of court may provide that an application for a Part II order by reference to an order or decree may not, without the leave of the court by which that order was made or decree was granted, be made after the expiration of such period from the order or grant as may be prescribed by the rules.

Saving for other provisions of Act

15.—(1) If a spouse or civil partner is entitled to occupy a dwelling-house by virtue of a tenancy, this Schedule does not affect the operation of sections 30 and 31 in relation to the other spouse's or civil partner's home rights.

(2) If a spouse, civil partner or cohabitant is entitled to occupy a dwelling-house by virtue of a tenancy, the court's powers to make orders under this Schedule are additional to those conferred by sections 33, 35 and 36.

Trusts of Land and Appointment of Trustees Act 1996
(1996 c. 47)

PART I   TRUSTS OF LAND

Introductory

1   Meaning of 'trust of land'
(1) In this Act—
    (a) 'trust of land' means (subject to subsection (3)) any trust of property which consists of or includes land, and
    (b) 'trustees of land' means trustees of a trust of land.
(2) The reference in subsection (1)(a) to a trust—
    (a) is to any description of trust (whether express, implied, resulting or constructive), including a trust for sale and a bare trust, and
    (b) includes a trust created, or arising, before the commencement of this Act.

Settlements and trusts for sale as trusts of land

2   Trusts in place of settlements
(1) No settlement created after the commencement of this Act is a settlement for the purposes of the Settled Land Act 1925; and no settlement shall be deemed to be made under that Act after that commencement.

(2) Subsection (1) does not apply to a settlement created on the occasion of an alteration in any interest in, or of a person becoming entitled under, a settlement which—
    (a) is in existence at the commencement of this Act, or
    (b) derives from a settlement within paragraph (a) or this paragraph.

(3) But a settlement created as mentioned in subsection (2) is not a settlement for the purposes of the Settled Land Act 1925 if provision to the effect that it is not is made in the instrument, or any of the instruments by which it is created.

(4) Where at any time after the commencement of this Act there is in the case of any settlement which is a settlement for the purposes of the Settled Land Act 1925 no relevant property which is, or is deemed to be, subject to the settlement, the settlement permanently ceases at that time to be a settlement for the purposes of that Act.

In this subsection 'relevant property' means land and personal chattels to which section 67(1) of the Settled Land Act 1925 (heirlooms) applies.

(5) No land held on charitable, ecclesiastical or public trusts shall be or be deemed to be settled land after the commencement of this Act, even if it was or was deemed to be settled land before that commencement.

(6) Schedule 1 has effect to make provision consequential on this section (including provision to impose a trust in circumstances in which apart from this section, there would be a settlement for the purposes of the Settled Land Act 1925 (and there would not otherwise be a trust)).

3   Abolition of doctrine of conversion

(1) Where land is held by trustees subject to a trust for sale, the land is not to be regarded as personal property; and where personal property is subject to a trust for sale in order that the trustees may acquire land, the personal property is not to be regarded as land.

(2) Subsection (1) does not apply to a trust created by a will if the testator died before the commencement of this Act.

(3) Subject to that, subsection (1) applies to a trust whether it is created, or arises, before or after that commencement.

4   Express trusts for sale as trusts of land

(1) In the case of every trust for sale of land created by a disposition there is to be implied, despite any provision to the contrary made by the disposition, a power for the trustees to postpone sale of the land; and the trustees are not liable in any way for postponing sale of the land, in the exercise of their discretion, for an indefinite period.

(2) Subsection (1) applies to a trust whether it is created, or arises, before or after the commencement of this Act.

(3) Subsection (1) does not affect any liability incurred by trustees before that commencement.

5   Implied trusts for sale as trusts of land

(1) Schedule 2 has effect in relation to statutory provisions which impose a trust for sale of land in certain circumstances so that in those circumstances there is instead a trust of the land (without a duty to sell).

(2) Section 1 of the Settled Land Act 1925 does not apply to land held on any trust arising by virtue of that Schedule (so that any such land is subject to a trust of land).

Functions of trustees of land

6   General powers of trustees

(1) For the purpose of exercising their functions as trustees, the trustees of land have in relation to the land subject to the trust all the powers of an absolute owner.

(2) Where in the case of any land subject to a trust of land each of the beneficiaries interested in the land is a person of full age and capacity who is absolutely entitled to the land, the powers conferred on the trustees by subsection (1) include the power to convey the land to the beneficiaries even though they have not required the trustees to do so; and where land is conveyed by virtue of this subsection—

(a) the beneficiaries shall do whatever is necessary to secure that it vests in them, and

(b) if they fail to do so, the court may make an order requiring them to do so.

(3) The trustees of land have power to acquire land under the power conferred by section 8 of the Trustee Act 2000.

(5) In exercising the powers conferred by this section trustees shall have regard to the rights of the beneficiaries.

(6) The powers conferred by this section shall not be exercised in contravention of, or of any order made in pursuance of, any other enactment or any rule of law or equity.

(7) The reference in subsection (6) to an order includes an order of any court or of the Charity Commissioners.

(8) Where any enactment other than this section confers on trustees authority to act subject to any restriction, limitation or condition, trustees of land may not exercise the powers conferred by this section to do any act which they are prevented from doing under the other enactment by reason of the restriction, limitation or condition.

(9) The duty of care under section 1 of the Trustee Act 2000 applies to trustees of land when exercising the powers conferred by this section.

7   Partition by trustees

(1) The trustees of land may, where beneficiaries of full age are absolutely entitled in undivided shares to land subject to the trust, partition the land, or any part of it, and provide (by way of mortgage or otherwise) for the payment of any equality money.

(2) The trustees shall give effect to any such partition by conveying the partitioned land in severalty (whether or not subject to any legal mortgage created for raising equality money), either absolutely or in trust, in accordance with the rights of those beneficiaries.

(3) Before exercising their powers under subsection (2) the trustees shall obtain the consent of each of those beneficiaries.

(4) Where a share in the land is affected by an incumbrance, the trustees may either give effect to it or provide for its discharge from the property allotted to that share as they think fit.

(5) If a share in the land is absolutely vested in a minor, subsections (1) to (4) apply as if he were of full age, except that the trustees may act on his behalf and retain land or other property representing his share in trust for him.

(6) Subsection (1) is subject to sections 21 (part-unit: interests) and 22 (part-unit: charging) of the Commonhold and Leasehold Reform Act 2002.

8   Exclusion and restriction of powers

(1) Sections 6 and 7 do not apply in the case of a trust of land created by a disposition in so far as provision to the effect that they do not apply is made by the disposition.

(2) If the disposition creating such a trust makes provision requiring any consent to be obtained to the exercise of any power conferred by section 6 or 7, the power may not be exercised without that consent.

(3) Subsection (1) does not apply in the case of charitable, ecclesiastical or public trusts.

(4) Subsections (1) and (2) have effect subject to any enactment which prohibits or restricts the effect of provision of the description mentioned in them.

9   Delegation by trustees

(1) The trustees of land may, by power of attorney, delegate to any beneficiary or beneficiaries of full age and beneficially entitled to an interest in possession in land subject to the trust any of their functions as trustees which relate to the land.

(2) Where trustees purport to delegate to a person by a power of attorney under subsection (1) functions relating to any land and another person in good faith deals with him in relation to the land, he shall be presumed in favour of that other person to have been a person to whom the functions could be delegated unless that other person has knowledge at the time of the transaction that he was not such a person.

And it shall be conclusively presumed in favour of any purchaser whose interest depends on the validity of that transaction that that other person dealt in good faith and did not have such knowledge if that other person makes a statutory declaration to that effect before or within three months after the completion of the purchase.

(3) A power of attorney under subsection (1) shall be given by all the trustees jointly and (unless expressed to be irrevocable and to be given by way of security) may be revoked by any one or more of them; and such a power is revoked by the appointment as a trustee of a person other than those by whom it is given (though not by any of those persons dying or otherwise ceasing to be a trustee).

(4) Where a beneficiary to whom functions are delegated by a power of attorney under subsection (1) ceases to be a person beneficially entitled to an interest in possession in land subject to the trust—

    (a) if the functions are delegated to him alone, the power is revoked,

    (b) if the functions are delegated to him and to other beneficiaries to be exercised by them jointly (but not separately), the power is revoked if each of the other beneficiaries ceases to be so entitled (but otherwise functions exercisable in accordance with the power are so exercisable by the remaining beneficiary or beneficiaries), and

    (c) if the functions are delegated to him and to other beneficiaries to be exercised by them separately (or either separately or jointly), the power is revoked in so far as it relates to him.

(5) A delegation under subsection (1) may be for any period or indefinite.

(6) A power of attorney under subsection (1) cannot be an enduring power of attorney or lasting power of attorney within the meaning of the Mental Capacity Act 2005.

(7) Beneficiaries to whom functions have been delegated under subsection (1) are, in relation to the exercise of the functions, in the same position as trustees (with the same duties and liabilities); but such beneficiaries shall not be regarded as trustees for any other purposes (including, in particular, the purposes of any enactment permitting the delegation of functions by trustees or imposing requirements relating to the payment of capital money).

(9) Neither this section nor the repeal by this Act of section 29 of the Law of Property Act 1925 (which is superseded by this section) affects the operation after the commencement of this Act of any delegation effected before that commencement.

9A   Duties of trustees in connection with delegation etc.

(1) The duty of care under section 1 of the Trustee Act 2000 applies to trustees of land in deciding whether to delegate any of their functions under section 9.

(2) Subsection (3) applies if the trustees of land—

    (a) delegate any of their functions under section 9, and

    (b) the delegation is not irrevocable.

(3) While the delegation continues, the trustees—

    (a) must keep the delegation under review,

    (b) if circumstances make it appropriate to do so, must consider whether there is a need to exercise any power of intervention that they have, and

    (c) if they consider that there is a need to exercise such a power, must do so.

(4) 'Power of intervention' includes—

    (a) a power to give directions to the beneficiary;

    (b) a power to revoke the delegation.

(5) The duty of care under section 1 of the 2000 Act applies to trustees in carrying out any duty under subsection (3).

(6) A trustee of land is not liable for any act or default of the beneficiary, or beneficiaries, unless the trustee fails to comply with the duty of care in deciding to delegate any of the trustees' functions under section 9 or in carrying out any duty under subsection (3).

(7) Neither this section nor the repeal of section 9(8) by the Trustee Act 2000 affects the operation after the commencement of this section of any delegation effected before that commencement.

Consents and consultation

10 Consents

(1) If a disposition creating a trust of land requires the consent of more than two persons to the exercise by the trustees of any function relating to the land, the consent of any two of them to the exercise of the function is sufficient in favour of a purchaser.

(2) Subsection (1) does not apply to the exercise of a function by trustees of land held on charitable, ecclesiastical or public trusts.

(3) Where at any time a person whose consent is expressed by a disposition creating a trust of land to be required to the exercise by the trustees of any function relating to the land is not of full age—

    (a) his consent is not, in favour of a purchaser, required to the exercise of the function, but

    (b) the trustees shall obtain the consent of a parent who has parental responsibility for him (within the meaning of the Children Act 1989) or of a guardian of his.

11 Consultation with beneficiaries

(1) The trustees of land shall in the exercise of any function relating to land subject to the trust—

    (a) so far as practicable, consult the beneficiaries of full age and beneficially entitled to an interest in possession in the land, and

    (b) so far as consistent with the general interest of the trust, give effect to the wishes of those beneficiaries, or (in case of dispute) of the majority (according to the value of their combined interests).

(2) Subsection (1) does not apply—

    (a) in relation to a trust created by a disposition in so far as provision that it does not apply is made by the disposition,

    (b) in relation to a trust created or arising under a will made before the commencement of this Act, or

    (c) in relation to the exercise of the power mentioned in section 6(2).

(3) Subsection (1) does not apply to a trust created before the commencement of this Act by a disposition, or a trust created after that commencement by reference to such a trust, unless provision to the effect that it is to apply is made by a deed executed—

    (a) in a case in which the trust was created by one person and he is of full capacity, by that person, or

    (b) in a case in which the trust was created by more than one person, by such of the persons who created the trust as are alive and of full capacity.

(4) A deed executed for the purposes of subsection (3) is irrevocable.

Right of beneficiaries to occupy trust land

12 The right to occupy

(1) A beneficiary who is beneficially entitled to an interest in possession in land subject to a trust of land is entitled by reason of his interest to occupy the land at any time if at that time—

    (a) the purposes of the trust include making the land available for his occupation (or for the occupation of beneficiaries of a class of which he is a member or of beneficiaries in general), or

    (b) the land is held by the trustees so as to be so available.

(2) Subsection (1) does not confer on a beneficiary a right to occupy land if it is either unavailable or unsuitable for occupation by him.

(3) This section is subject to section 13.

13 Exclusion and restriction of right to occupy

(1) Where two or more beneficiaries are (or apart from this subsection would be) entitled under section 12 to occupy land, the trustees of land may exclude or restrict the entitlement of any one or more (but not all) of them.

(2) Trustees may not under subsection (1)—

(a) unreasonably exclude any beneficiary's entitlement to occupy land, or

(b) restrict any such entitlement to an unreasonable extent.

(3) The trustees of land may from time to time impose reasonable conditions on any beneficiary in relation to his occupation of land by reason of his entitlement under section 12.

(4) The matters to which trustees are to have regard in exercising the powers conferred by this section include—

(a) the intentions of the person or persons (if any) who created the trust,

(b) the purposes for which the land is held, and

(c) the circumstances and wishes of each of the beneficiaries who is (or apart from any previous exercise by the trustees of those powers would be) entitled to occupy the land under section 12.

(5) The conditions which may be imposed on a beneficiary under subsection (3) include, in particular, conditions requiring him—

(a) to pay any outgoings or expenses in respect of the land, or

(b) to assume any other obligation in relation to the land or to any activity which is or is proposed to be conducted there.

(6) Where the entitlement of any beneficiary to occupy land under section 12 has been excluded or restricted, the conditions which may be imposed on any other beneficiary under subsection (3) include, in particular, conditions requiring him to—

(a) make payments by way of compensation to the beneficiary whose entitlement has been excluded or restricted, or

(b) forgo any payment or other benefit to which he would otherwise be entitled under the trust so as to benefit that beneficiary.

(7) The powers conferred on trustees by this section may not be exercised—

(a) so as prevent any person who is in occupation of land (whether or not by reason of an entitlement under section 12) from continuing to occupy the land, or

(b) in a manner likely to result in any such person ceasing to occupy the land, unless he consents or the court has given approval.

(8) The matters to which the court is to have regard in determining whether to give approval under subsection (7) include the matters mentioned in subsection (4)(a) to (c).

Powers of court

14 Applications for order

(1) Any person who is a trustee of land or has an interest in property subject to a trust of land may make an application to the court for an order under this section.

(2) On an application for an order under this section the court may make any such order—

(a) relating to the exercise by the trustees of any of their functions (including an order relieving them of any obligation to obtain the consent of, or to consult, any person in connection with the exercise of any of their functions), or

(b) declaring the nature or extent of a person's interest in property subject to the trust, as the court thinks fit.

(3) The court may not under this section make any order as to the appointment or removal of trustees.

(4) The powers conferred on the court by this section are exercisable on an application whether it is made before or after the commencement of this Act.

15 Matters relevant in determining applications

(1) The matters to which the court is to have regard in determining an application for an order under section 14 include—

(a) the intentions of the person or persons (if any) who created the trust,

(b) the purposes for which the property subject to the trust is held,

(c) the welfare of any minor who occupies or might reasonably be expected to occupy any land subject to the trust as his home, and

(d) the interests of any secured creditor of any beneficiary.

(2) In the case of an application relating to the exercise in relation to any land of the powers conferred on the trustees by section 13, the matters to which the court is to have regard also include the circumstances and wishes of each of the beneficiaries who is (or apart from any previous exercise by the trustees of those powers would be) entitled to occupy the land under section 12.

(3) In the case of any other application, other than one relating to the exercise of the power mentioned in section 6(2), the matters to which the court is to have regard also include the circumstances and wishes of any beneficiaries of full age and entitled to an interest in possession in property subject to the trust or (in case of dispute) of the majority (according to the value of their combined interests).

(4) This section does not apply to an application if section 335A of the Insolvency Act 1986 (which is inserted by Schedule 3 and relates to applications by a trustee of a bankrupt) applies to it.

Purchaser protection

16 Protection of purchasers

(1) A purchaser of land which is or has been subject to a trust need not be concerned to see that any requirement imposed on the trustees by section 6(5), 7(3) or 11(1) has been complied with.

(2) Where—

(a) trustees of land who convey land which (immediately before it is conveyed) is subject to the trust contravene section 6(6) or (8), but

(b) the purchaser of the land from the trustees has no actual notice of the contravention,

the contravention does not invalidate the conveyance.

(3) Where the powers of trustees of land are limited by virtue of section 8—

(a) the trustees shall take all reasonable steps to bring the limitation to the notice of any purchaser of the land from them, but

(b) the limitation does not invalidate any conveyance by the trustees to a purchaser who has no actual notice of the limitation.

(4) Where trustees of land convey land which (immediately before it is conveyed) is subject to the trust to persons believed by them to be beneficiaries absolutely entitled to the land under the trust and of full age and capacity—

(a) the trustees shall execute a deed declaring that they are discharged from the trust in relation to that land, and

(b) if they fail to do so, the court may make an order requiring them to do so.

(5) A purchaser of land to which a deed under subsection (4) relates is entitled to assume that, as from the date of the deed, the land is not subject to the trust unless he has actual notice that the trustees were mistaken in their belief that the land was conveyed to beneficiaries absolutely entitled to the land under the trust and of full age and capacity.

(6) Subsections (2) and (3) do not apply to land held on charitable, ecclesiastical or public trusts.

(7) This section does not apply to registered land.

Supplementary

17 Application of provisions to trusts of proceeds of sale

(2) Section 14 applies in relation to a trust of proceeds of sale of land and trustees of such a trust as in relation to a trust of land and trustees of land.

(3) In this section 'trust of proceeds of sale of land' means (subject to subsection (5)) any trust of property (other than a trust of land) which consists of or includes—

(a) any proceeds of a disposition of land held in trust (including settled land), or

(b) any property representing any such proceeds.

(4) The references in subsection (3) to a trust—

(a) are to any description of trust (whether express, implied, resulting or constructive), including a trust for sale and a bare trust, and

(b) include a trust created, or arising, before the commencement of this Act.

(5) A trust which (despite section 2) is a settlement for the purposes of the Settled Land Act 1925 cannot be a trust of proceeds of sale of land.

(6) In subsection (3)—

(a) 'disposition' includes any disposition made, or coming into operation, before the commencement of this Act, and

(b) the reference to settled land includes personal chattels to which section 67(1) of the Settled Land Act 1925 (heirlooms) applies.

18 Application of Part to personal representatives

(1) The provisions of this Part relating to trustees, other than sections 10, 11 and 14, apply to personal representatives, but with appropriate modifications and without prejudice to the functions of personal representatives for the purposes of administration.

(2) The appropriate modifications include—

(a) the substitution of references to persons interested in the due administration of the estate for references to beneficiaries, and

(b) the substitution of references to the will for references to the disposition creating the trust.

(3) Section 3(1) does not apply to personal representatives if the death occurs before the commencement of this Act.

PART II   APPOINTMENT AND RETIREMENT OF TRUSTEES

19 Appointment and retirement of trustee at instance of beneficiaries

(1) This section applies in the case of a trust where—

(a) there is no person nominated for the purpose of appointing new trustees by the instrument, if any, creating the trust, and

(b) the beneficiaries under the trust are of full age and capacity and (taken together) are absolutely entitled to the property subject to the trust.

(2) The beneficiaries may give a direction or directions of either or both of the following descriptions—

(a) a written direction to a trustee or trustees to retire from the trust, and

(b) a written direction to the trustees or trustee for the time being (or, if there are none, to the personal representative of the last person who was a trustee) to appoint by writing to be a trustee or trustees the person or persons specified in the direction.

(3) Where—

(a) a trustee has been given a direction under subsection (2)(a),

(b) reasonable arrangements have been made for the protection of any rights of his in connection with the trust,

(c) after he has retired there will be either a trust corporation or at least two persons to act as trustees to perform the trust, and

(d) either another person is to be appointed to be a new trustee on his retirement (whether in compliance with a direction under subsection (2)(b) or otherwise) or the continuing trustees by deed consent to his retirement, he shall make a deed declaring his retirement and shall be deemed to have retired and be discharged from the trust.

(4) Where a trustee retires under subsection (3) he and the continuing trustees (together with any new trustee) shall (subject to any arrangements for the protection of his rights) do anything necessary to vest the trust property in the continuing trustees (or the continuing and new trustees).

(5) This section has effect subject to the restrictions imposed by the Trustee Act 1925 on the number of trustees.

. . .

21 Supplementary

(1) For the purposes of section 19 or 20 a direction is given by beneficiaries if—

(a) a single direction is jointly given by all of them, or

(b) (subject to subsection (2)) a direction is given by each of them (whether solely or jointly with one or more, but not all, of the others),

and none of them by writing withdraws the direction given by him before it has been complied with.

(2) Where more than one direction is given each must specify for appointment or retirement the same person or persons.

(3) Subsection (7) of section 36 of the Trustee Act 1925 (powers of trustees appointed under that section) applies to a trustee appointed under section 19 or 20 as if he were appointed under that section.

(4) A direction under section 19 or 20 must not specify a person or persons for appointment if the appointment of that person or those persons would be in contravention of section 35(1) of the Trustee Act 1925 or section 24(1) of the Law of Property Act 1925 (requirements as to identity of trustees).

(5) Sections 19 and 20 do not apply in relation to a trust created by a disposition in so far as provision that they do not apply is made by the disposition.

(6) Sections 19 and 20 do not apply in relation to a trust created before the commencement of this Act by a disposition in so far as provision to the effect that they do not apply is made by a deed executed—

(a) in a case in which the trust was created by one person and he is of full capacity, by that person, or

(b) in a case in which the trust was created by more than one person, by such of the persons who created the trust as are alive and of full capacity.

(7) A deed executed for the purposes of subsection (6) is irrevocable.

(8) Where a deed is executed for the purposes of subsection (6)—

(a) it does not affect anything done before its execution to comply with a direction under section 19 or 20, but

(b) a direction under section 19 or 20 which has been given but not complied with before its execution shall cease to have effect.

PART III   SUPPLEMENTARY

22   Meaning of 'beneficiary'

(1) In this Act 'beneficiary', in relation to a trust, means any person who under the trust has an interest in property subject to the trust (including a person who has such an interest as a trustee or a personal representative).

(2) In this Act references to a beneficiary who is beneficially entitled do not include a beneficiary who has an interest in property subject to the trust only by reason of being a trustee or personal representative.

(3) For the purposes of this Act a person who is a beneficiary only by reason of being an annuitant is not to be regarded as entitled to an interest in possession in land subject to the trust.

23   Other interpretation provisions

(1) In this Act 'purchaser' has the same meaning as in Part I of the Law of Property Act 1925.

(2) Subject to that, where an expression used in this Act is given a meaning by the Law of Property Act 1925 it has the same meaning as in that Act unless the context otherwise requires.

(3) In this Act 'the court' means—

   (a) the High Court, or

   (b) a county court.

SCHEDULES

Section 2   SCHEDULE 1

PROVISIONS CONSEQUENTIAL ON SECTION 2

Minors

1.—(1) Where after the commencement of this Act a person purports to convey a legal estate in land to a minor, or two or more minors, alone, the conveyance—

   (a) is not effective to pass the legal estate, but

   (b) operates as a declaration that the land is held in trust for the minor or minors (or if he purports to convey it to the minor or minors in trust for any persons, for those persons).

(2) Where after the commencement of this Act a person purports to convey a legal estate in land to—

   (a) a minor or two or more minors, and

   (b) another person who is, or other persons who are, of full age,

the conveyance operates to vest the land in the other person or persons in trust for the minor or minors and the other person or persons (or if he purports to convey it to them in trust for any persons, for those persons).

(3) Where immediately before the commencement of this Act a conveyance is operating (by virtue of section 27 of the Settled Land Act 1925) as an agreement to execute a settlement in favour of a minor or minors—

   (a) the agreement ceases to have effect on the commencement of this Act, and

   (b) the conveyance subsequently operates instead as a declaration that the land is held in trust for the minor or minors.

2. Where after the commencement of this Act a legal estate in land would, by reason of intestacy or in any other circumstances not dealt with in paragraph 1, vest in a person who is a minor if he were a person of full age, the land is held in trust for the minor.

Family charges

3. Where, by virtue of an instrument coming into operation after the commencement of this Act, land becomes charged voluntarily (or in consideration of marriage or the formation of a civil partnership) or by way of family arrangement, whether immediately or after an interval, with the payment of—

   (a) a rentcharge for the life of a person or a shorter period, or

   (b) capital, annual or periodical sums for the benefit of a person,

the instrument operates as a declaration that the land is held in trust for giving effect to the charge.

. . .

Housing Act 1996
(1996 c. 52)

PART V   CONDUCT OF TENANTS

CHAPTER I   INTRODUCTORY TENANCIES

Succession on death of tenant

131 Persons qualified to succeed tenant

A person is qualified to succeed the tenant under an introductory tenancy if he occupies the dwelling-house as his only or principal home at the time of the tenant's death and either—
> (a) he is the tenant's spouse or civil partner, or
> (b) he is another member of the tenant's family and has resided with the tenant throughout the period of twelve months ending with the tenant's death;

unless, in either case, the tenant was himself a successor, as defined in section 132.

132 Cases where the tenant is a successor

(1) The tenant is himself a successor if—
> (a) the tenancy vested in him by virtue of section 133 (succession to introductory tenancy),
> (b) he was a joint tenant and has become the sole tenant,
> (c) he became the tenant on the tenancy being assigned to him (but subject to subsections (2) and (3)), or
> (d) he became the tenant on the tenancy being vested in him on the death of the previous tenant.

(2) A tenant to whom the tenancy was assigned in pursuance of an order under section 24 of the Matrimonial Causes Act 1973 (property adjustment orders in connection with matrimonial proceedings) or section 17(1) of the Matrimonial and Family Proceedings Act 1984 (property adjustment orders after overseas divorce, &c.) is a successor only if the other party to the marriage was a successor.

(2A) A tenant to whom the tenancy was assigned in pursuance of an order under Part 2 of Schedule 5, or paragraph 9(2) or (3) of Schedule 7, to the Civil Partnership Act 2004 (property adjustment orders in connection with civil partnership proceedings or after overseas dissolution of civil partnership, etc.) is a successor only if the other civil partner was a successor.

(3) Where within six months of the coming to an end of an introductory tenancy ('the former tenancy') the tenant becomes a tenant under another introductory tenancy, and—
> (a) the tenant was a successor in relation to the former tenancy, and
> (b) under the other tenancy either the dwelling-house or the landlord, or both, are the same as under the former tenancy,

the tenant is also a successor in relation to the other tenancy unless the agreement creating that tenancy otherwise provides.

133 Succession to introductory tenancy

(1) This section applies where a tenant under an introductory tenancy dies.

(2) Where there is a person qualified to succeed the tenant, the tenancy vests by virtue of this section in that person, or if there is more than one such person in the one to be preferred in accordance with the following rules—
> (a) the tenant's spouse or civil partner is to be preferred to another member of the tenant's family;
> (b) of two or more other members of the tenant's family such of them is to be preferred as may be agreed between them or as may, where there is no such agreement, be selected by the landlord.

(3) Where there is no person qualified to succeed the tenant, the tenancy ceases to be an introductory tenancy—

    (a) when it is vested or otherwise disposed of in the course of the administration of the tenant's estate, unless the vesting or other disposal is in pursuance of an order made under—

        (i) section 24 of the Matrimonial Causes Act 1973 (property adjustment orders made in connection with matrimonial proceedings),

        (ii) section 17(1) of the Matrimonial and Family Proceedings Act 1984 (property adjustment orders after overseas divorce, &c.),

        (iii) paragraph 1 of Schedule 1 to the Children Act 1989 (orders for financial relief against parents); or

        (iv) Part 2 of Schedule 5, or paragraph 9(2) or (3) of Schedule 7, to the Civil Partnership Act 2004 (property adjustment orders in connection with civil partnership proceedings or after overseas dissolution of civil partnership, etc.)

    (b) when it is known that when the tenancy is so vested or disposed of it will not be in pursuance of such an order.

Assignment

134   Assignment in general prohibited

(1) An introductory tenancy is not capable of being assigned except in the cases mentioned in subsection (2).

    (2) The exceptions are—

    (a) an assignment in pursuance of an order made under—

        (i) section 24 of the Matrimonial Causes Act 1973 (property adjustment orders in connection with matrimonial proceedings),

        (ii) section 17(1) of the Matrimonial and Family Proceedings Act 1984 (property adjustment orders after overseas divorce, &c.),

        (iii) paragraph 1 of Schedule 1 to the Children Act 1989 (orders for financial relief against parents); or

        (iv) Part 2 of Schedule 5, or paragraph 9(2) or (3) of Schedule 7, to the Civil Partnership Act 2004 (property adjustment orders in connection with civil partnership proceedings or after overseas dissolution of civil partnership, etc.)

    (b) an assignment to a person who would be qualified to succeed the tenant if the tenant died immediately before the assignment.

(3) Subsection (1) also applies to a tenancy which is not an introductory tenancy but would be if the tenant, or where the tenancy is a joint tenancy, at least one of the tenants, were occupying or continuing to occupy the dwelling-house as his only or principal home.

Supplementary

140   Members of a person's family: Chapter I

(1) A person is a member of another's family within the meaning of this Chapter if—

    (a) he is the spouse or civil partner of that person, or he and that person live together as husband and wife or as if they were civil partners, or

    (b) he is that person's parent, grandparent, child, grandchild, brother, sister, uncle, aunt, nephew or niece.

    (2) For the purpose of subsection (1)(b)—

    (a) a relationship by marriage or civil partnership shall be treated as a relationship by blood,

    (b) a relationship of the half-blood shall be treated as a relationship of the whole blood, and

(c) the stepchild of a person shall be treated as his child.

. . . .

CHAPTER III   INJUNCTIONS AGAINST ANTI-SOCIAL BEHAVIOUR

153A   Anti-social behaviour injunction

(1) This section applies to conduct—
- (a) which is capable of causing nuisance or annoyance to any person, and
- (b) which directly or indirectly relates to or affects the housing management functions of a relevant landlord.

(2) The court on the application of a relevant landlord may grant an injunction (an anti-social behaviour injunction) if each of the following two conditions is satisfied.

(3) The first condition is that the person against whom the injunction is sought is engaging, has engaged or threatens to engage in conduct to which this section applies.

(4) The second condition is that the conduct is capable of causing nuisance or annoyance to any of the following—
- (a) a person with a right (of whatever description) to reside in or occupy housing accommodation owned or managed by the relevant landlord;
- (b) a person with a right (of whatever description) to reside in or occupy other housing accommodation in the neighbourhood of housing accommodation mentioned in paragraph (a);
- (c) a person engaged in lawful activity in or in the neighbourhood of housing accommodation mentioned in paragraph (a);
- (d) a person employed (whether or not by the relevant landlord) in connection with the exercise of the relevant landlord's housing management functions.

(5) It is immaterial where conduct to which this section applies occurs.

(6) An anti-social behaviour injunction prohibits the person in respect of whom it is granted from engaging in conduct to which this section applies.

. . . .

153C   Injunctions: exclusion order and power of arrest

(1) This section applies if the court grants an injunction under subsection (2) of section 153A or 153B and it thinks that either of the following paragraphs applies—
- (a) the conduct consists of or includes the use or threatened use of violence;
- (b) there is a significant risk of harm to a person mentioned in section 153A(4).

(2) The court may include in the injunction a provision prohibiting the person in respect of whom it is granted from entering or being in—
- (a) any premises specified in the injunction;
- (b) any area specified in the injunction.

(3) The court may attach a power of arrest to any provision of the injunction.

153D   Injunction against breach of tenancy agreement

(1) This section applies if a relevant landlord applies for an injunction against a tenant in respect of the breach or anticipated breach of a tenancy agreement on the grounds that the tenant—
- (a) is engaging or threatening to engage in conduct that is capable of causing nuisance or annoyance to any person, or
- (b) is allowing, inciting or encouraging any other person to engage or threaten to engage in such conduct.

(2) The court may proceed under subsection (3) or (4) if it is satisfied—
- (a) that the conduct includes the use or threatened use of violence, or
- (b) that there is a significant risk of harm to any person.

(3) The court may include in the injunction a provision prohibiting the person in respect of whom it is granted from entering or being in—

(a) any premises specified in the injunction;

(b) any area specified in the injunction.

(4) The court may attach a power of arrest to any provision of the injunction.

(5) Tenancy agreement includes any agreement for the occupation of residential accommodation owned or managed by a relevant landlord.

153E   Injunctions: supplementary

(1) This section applies for the purposes of sections 153A to 153D.

(2) An injunction may—

(a) be made for a specified period or until varied or discharged;

(b) have the effect of excluding a person from his normal place of residence.

(3) An injunction may be varied or discharged by the court on an application by—

(a) the person in respect of whom it is made;

(b) the relevant landlord.

(4) If the court thinks it just and convenient it may grant or vary an injunction without the respondent having been given such notice as is otherwise required by rules of court.

(5) If the court acts under subsection (4) it must give the person against whom the injunction is made an opportunity to make representations in relation to the injunction as soon as it is practicable for him to do so.

(6) The court is the High Court or a county court.

(7) Each of the following is a relevant landlord—

(a) a housing action trust;

(b) a local authority (within the meaning of the Housing Act 1985);

(c) a registered social landlord.

(8) A charitable housing trust which is not a registered social landlord is also a relevant landlord for the purposes of section 153D.

. . .

(12) Harm includes serious ill-treatment or abuse (whether physical or not).

154   Powers of arrest: ex-parte applications for injunctions

(1) In determining whether to exercise its power under section 153C(3) or 153D(4) to attach a power of arrest to an injunction which it intends to grant on an ex-parte application, the High Court or a county court shall have regard to all the circumstances including—

(a) whether it is likely that the applicant will be deterred or prevented from seeking the exercise of the power if the power is not exercised immediately, and

(b) whether there is reason to believe that the respondent is aware of the proceedings for the injunction but is deliberately evading service and that the applicant or any person of a description mentioned in section 153A(4) (as the case may be) will be seriously prejudiced if the decision as to whether to exercise the power were delayed until substituted service is effected.

(2) Where the court exercises its power as mentioned in subsection (1), it shall afford the respondent an opportunity to make representations relating to the exercise of the power as soon as just and convenient at a hearing of which notice has been given to all the parties in accordance with rules of court.

155   Arrest and remand

(1) If a power of arrest is attached to certain provisions of an injunction by virtue of section 153C(3) or 153D(4), a constable may arrest without warrant a person whom he has reasonable cause for suspecting to be in breach of any such provision or otherwise in contempt of court in relation to a breach of any such provision.

A constable shall after making any such arrest forthwith inform the person on whose application the injunction was granted.

(2) Where a person is arrested under subsection (1)—

    (a) he shall be brought before the relevant judge within the period of 24 hours beginning at the time of his arrest, and

    (b) if the matter is not then disposed of forthwith, the judge may remand him.

In reckoning for the purposes of this subsection any period of 24 hours no account shall be taken of Christmas Day, Good Friday or any Sunday.

(3) If the court has granted an injunction in circumstances such that a power of arrest could have been attached under section 153C(3) or 153D(4) but—

    (a) has not attached a power of arrest under the section in question to any provisions of the injunction, or

    (b) has attached that power only to certain provisions of the injunction,

then, if at any time the applicant considers that the respondent has failed to comply with the injunction, he may apply to the relevant judge for the issue of a warrant for the arrest of the respondent.

(4) The relevant judge shall not issue a warrant on an application under subsection (3) unless—

    (a) the application is substantiated on oath, and

    (b) he has reasonable grounds for believing that the respondent has failed to comply with the injunction.

(5) If a person is brought before a court by virtue of a warrant issued under subsection (4) and the court does not dispose of the matter forthwith, the court may remand him.

(6) Schedule 15 (which makes provision corresponding to that applying in magistrates' courts in civil cases under sections 128 and 129 of the Magistrates' Courts Act 1980) applies in relation to the powers of the High Court and a county court to remand a person under this section.

(7) If a person remanded under this section is granted bail by virtue of subsection (6), he may be required by the relevant judge to comply, before release on bail or later, with such requirements as appear to the judge to be necessary to secure that he does not interfere with witnesses or otherwise obstruct the course of justice.

156   Remand for medical examination and report

(1) If the relevant judge has reason to consider that a medical report will be required, any power to remand a person under section 155 may be exercised for the purpose of enabling a medical examination and report to be made.

(2) If such a power is so exercised the adjournment shall not be for more than 4 weeks at a time unless the judge remands the accused in custody.

(3) If the judge so remands the accused, the adjournment shall not be for more than 3 weeks at a time.

(4) If there is reason to suspect that a person who has been arrested—

    (a) under section 155(1), or

    (b) under a warrant issued under section 155(4),

is suffering from mental illness or severe mental impairment, the relevant judge shall have the same power to make an order under section 35 of the Mental Health Act 1983 (remand for report on accused's mental condition) as the Crown Court has under section 35 of that Act in the case of an accused person within the meaning of that section.

157   Powers of arrest: supplementary provisions

(1) If in exercise of its power under section 153C(3) or 153D(4) the High Court or a county court attaches a power of arrest to any provisions of an injunction, it may provide that the power of arrest is to have effect for a shorter period than the other provisions of the injunction.

(2) Any period specified for the purposes of subsection (1) may be extended by the court (on one or more occasions) on an application to vary or discharge the injunction.

(3) If a power of arrest has been attached to certain provisions of an injunction by virtue of section 153C(3) or 153D(4), the court may vary or discharge the injunction in so far as it confers a power of arrest (whether or not any application has been made to vary or discharge any other provision of the injunction).

(4) An injunction may be varied or discharged under subsection (3) on an application by the respondent or the person on whose application the injunction was made.

...

PART VII   HOMELESSNESS

Homelessness and threatened homelessness

175   Homelessness and threatened homelessness

(1) A person is homeless if he has no accommodation available for his occupation, in the United Kingdom or elsewhere, which he—
  (a) is entitled to occupy by virtue of an interest in it or by virtue of an order of a court,
  (b) has an express or implied licence to occupy, or
  (c) occupies as a residence by virtue of any enactment or rule of law giving him the right to remain in occupation or restricting the right of another person to recover possession.

(2) A person is also homeless if he has accommodation but—
  (a) he cannot secure entry to it, or
  (b) it consists of a moveable structure, vehicle or vessel designed or adapted for human habitation and there is no place where he is entitled or permitted both to place it and to reside in it.

(3) A person shall not be treated as having accommodation unless it is accommodation which it would be reasonable for him to continue to occupy.

(4) A person is threatened with homelessness if it is likely that he will become homeless within 28 days.

176   Meaning of accommodation available for occupation

Accommodation shall be regarded as available for a person's occupation only if it is available for occupation by him together with—
  (a) any other person who normally resides with him as a member of his family, or
  (b) any other person who might reasonably be expected to reside with him.

References in this Part to securing that accommodation is available for a person's occupation shall be construed accordingly.

177   Whether it is reasonable to continue to occupy accommodation

(1) It is not reasonable for a person to continue to occupy accommodation if it is probable that this will lead to domestic violence or other violence against him, or against—
  (a) a person who normally resides with him as a member of his family, or
  (b) any other person who might reasonably be expected to reside with him.

(1A) For this purpose 'violence' means—
  (a) violence from another person; or
  (b) threats of violence from another person which are likely to be carried out;
and violence is 'domestic violence' if it is from a person who is associated with the victim.

(2) In determining whether it would be, or would have been, reasonable for a person to continue to occupy accommodation, regard may be had to the general circumstances prevailing in relation to housing in the district of the local housing authority to whom he has applied for accommodation or for assistance in obtaining accommodation.

(3) The Secretary of State may by order specify—

(a) other circumstances in which it is to be regarded as reasonable or not reasonable for a person to continue to occupy accommodation, and

(b) other matters to be taken into account or disregarded in determining whether it would be, or would have been, reasonable for a person to continue to occupy accommodation.

178 Meaning of associated person

(1) For the purposes of this Part, a person is associated with another person if—

   (a) they are or have been married to each other;

  (aa) they are or have been civil partners of each other;

   (b) they are cohabitants or former cohabitants;

   (c) they live or have lived in the same household;

   (d) they are relatives;

   (e) they have agreed to marry one another (whether or not that agreement has been terminated);

  (ea) they have entered into a civil partnership agreement between them (whether or not that agreement has been terminated);

   (f) in relation to a child, each of them is a parent of the child or has, or has had, parental responsibility for the child.

(2) If a child has been adopted or falls within subsection (2A), two persons are also associated with each other for the purposes of this Part if—

   (a) one is a natural parent of the child or a parent of such a natural parent, and

   (b) the other is the child or a person—

     (i)   who has become a parent of the child by virtue of an adoption order or who has applied for an adoption order, or

     (ii) with whom the child has at any time been placed for adoption.

(2A) A child falls within this subsection if—

   (a) an adoption agency, within the meaning of section 2 of the Adoption and Children Act 2002, is authorised to place him for adoption under section 19 of that Act (placing children with parental consent) or he has become the subject of an order under section 21 of that Act (placement orders), or

   (b) he is freed for adoption by virtue of an order made—

     (i)   in England and Wales, under section 18 of the Adoption Act 1976,

     . . .

(3) In this section—

'adoption order' means an adoption order within the meaning of section 72(1) of the Adoption Act 1976 or section 46(1) of the Adoption and Children Act 2002;

'child' means a person under the age of 18 years;

'civil partnership agreement' has the meaning given by section 73 of the Civil Partnership Act 2004;

'cohabitants' means—

   (a) a man and a woman who, although not married to each other, are living together as husband and wife, or

   (b) two people of the same sex who, although not civil partners of each other, are living together as if they were civil partners;

and 'former cohabitants' shall be construed accordingly;

'parental responsibility' has the same meaning as in the Children Act 1989; and

'relative', in relation to a person, means—

   (a) the father, mother, stepfather, stepmother, son, daughter, stepson, stepdaughter, grandmother, grandfather, grandson or granddaughter of that person or of that person's spouse, civil partner, former spouse or former civil partner, or

(b) the brother, sister, uncle, aunt, niece or nephew (whether of the full blood or of the half blood or by marriage or civil partnership) of that person or of that person's spouse, civil partner, former spouse or former civil partner,

and includes, in relation to a person who is living or has lived with another person as husband and wife, a person who would fall within paragraph (a) or (b) if the parties were married to each other.

. . .

Interim duty to accommodate

188 Interim duty to accommodate in case of apparent priority need

(1) If the local housing authority have reason to believe that an applicant may be homeless, eligible for assistance and have a priority need, they shall secure that accommodation is available for his occupation pending a decision as to the duty (if any) owed to him under the following provisions of this Part.

(2) The duty under this section arises irrespective of any possibility of the referral of the applicant's case to another local housing authority (see sections 198 to 200).

(3) The duty ceases when the authority's decision is notified to the applicant, even if the applicant requests a review of the decision (see section 202).

The authority may secure that accommodation is available for the applicant's occupation pending a decision on a review.

189 Priority need for accommodation

(1) The following have a priority need for accommodation—
   (a) a pregnant woman or a person with whom she resides or might reasonably be expected to reside;
   (b) a person with whom dependent children reside or might reasonably be expected to reside;
   (c) a person who is vulnerable as a result of old age, mental illness or handicap or physical disability or other special reason, or with whom such a person resides or might reasonably be expected to reside;
   (d) a person who is homeless or threatened with homelessness as a result of an emergency such as flood, fire or other disaster.

Duties to persons found to be homeless or threatened with homelessness

190 Duties to persons becoming homeless intentionally

(1) This section applies where the local housing authority are satisfied that an applicant is homeless and is eligible for assistance but are also satisfied that he became homeless intentionally.

(2) If the authority are satisfied that the applicant has a priority need, they shall—
   (a) secure that accommodation is available for his occupation for such period as they consider will give him a reasonable opportunity of securing accommodation for his occupation, and
   (b) provide him with (or secure that he is provided with) advice and assistance in any attempts he may make to secure that accommodation becomes available for his occupation.

(3) If they are not satisfied that he has a priority need, they shall provide him with (or secure that he is provided with) advice and assistance in any attempts he may make to secure that accommodation becomes available for his occupation.

(4) The applicant's housing needs shall be assessed before advice and assistance is provided under subsection (2)(b) or (3).

(5) The advice and assistance provided under subsection (2)(b) or (3) must include information about the likely availability in the authority's district of types of accommodation

appropriate to the applicant's housing needs (including, in particular, the location and sources of such types of accommodation).

191   Becoming homeless intentionally

(1) A person becomes homeless intentionally if he deliberately does or fails to do anything in consequence of which he ceases to occupy accommodation which is available for his occupation and which it would have been reasonable for him to continue to occupy.

(2) For the purposes of subsection (1) an act or omission in good faith on the part of a person who was unaware of any relevant fact shall not be treated as deliberate.

(3) A person shall be treated as becoming homeless intentionally if—

   (a) he enters into an arrangement under which he is required to cease to occupy accommodation which it would have been reasonable for him to continue to occupy, and

   (b) the purpose of the arrangement is to enable him to become entitled to assistance under this Part,

and there is no other good reason why he is homeless.

192   Duty to persons not in priority need who are not homeless intentionally

(1) This section applies where the local housing authority—

   (a) are satisfied that an applicant is homeless and eligible for assistance, and

   (b) are not satisfied that he became homeless intentionally, but are not satisfied that he has a priority need.

(2) The authority shall provide the applicant with (or secure that he is provided with) advice and assistance in any attempts he may make to secure that accommodation becomes available for his occupation.

(3) The authority may secure that accommodation is available for occupation by the applicant.

(4) The applicant's housing needs shall be assessed before advice and assistance is provided under subsection (2).

(5) The advice and assistance provided under subsection (2) must include information about the likely availability in the authority's district of types of accommodation appropriate to the applicant's housing needs (including, in particular, the location and sources of such types of accommodation).

193   Duty to persons with priority need who are not homeless intentionally

(1) This section applies where the local housing authority are satisfied that an applicant is homeless, eligible for assistance and has a priority need, and are not satisfied that he became homeless intentionally.

(2) Unless the authority refer the application to another local housing authority (see section 198), they shall secure that accommodation is available for occupation by the applicant.

. . .

195   Duties in case of threatened homelessness

(1) This section applies where the local housing authority are satisfied that an applicant is threatened with homelessness and is eligible for assistance.

(2) If the authority—

   (a) are satisfied that he has a priority need, and

   (b) are not satisfied that he became threatened with homelessness intentionally,

they shall take reasonable steps to secure that accommodation does not cease to be available for his occupation.

(3) Subsection (2) does not affect any right of the authority, whether by virtue of a contract, enactment or rule of law, to secure vacant possession of any accommodation.

(3A) The authority shall, on becoming subject to the duty under this section, give the applicant a copy of the statement included in their allocation scheme by virtue of section 167(1A) (policy on offering choice to people allocated housing accommodation under Part 6).

(4) Where in pursuance of the duty under subsection (2) the authority secure that accommodation other than that occupied by the applicant when he made his application is available for occupation by him, the provisions of section 193(3) to (9) (period for which duty owed) apply, with any necessary modifications, in relation to the duty under this section as they apply in relation to the duty under section 193.

(5) If the authority—
    (a) are not satisfied that the applicant has a priority need, or
    (b) are satisfied that he has a priority need but are also satisfied that he became threatened with homelessness intentionally,
they shall provide him with (or secure that he is provided with) advice and assistance in any attempts he may make to secure that accommodation does not cease to be available for his occupation.

(6) The applicant's housing needs shall be assessed before advice and assistance is provided under subsection (5).

(7) The advice and assistance provided under subsection (5) must include information about the likely availability in the authority's district of types of accommodation appropriate to the applicant's housing needs (including, in particular, the location and sources of such types of accommodation).

(8) If the authority decide that they owe the applicant the duty under subsection (5) by virtue of paragraph (b) of that subsection, they may, pending a decision on a review of that decision—
    (a) secure that accommodation does not cease to be available for his occupation; and
    (b) if he becomes homeless, secure that accommodation is so available.

(9) If the authority—
    (a) are not satisfied that the applicant has a priority need; and
    (b) are not satisfied that he became threatened with homelessness intentionally,
the authority may take reasonable steps to secure that accommodation does not cease to be available for the applicant's occupation.

196   Becoming threatened with homelessness intentionally

(1) A person becomes threatened with homelessness intentionally if he deliberately does or fails to do anything the likely result of which is that he will be forced to leave accommodation which is available for his occupation and which it would have been reasonable for him to continue to occupy.

(2) For the purposes of subsection (1) an act or omission in good faith on the part of a person who was unaware of any relevant fact shall not be treated as deliberate.

(3) A person shall be treated as becoming threatened with homelessness intentionally if—
    (a) he enters into an arrangement under which he is required to cease to occupy accommodation which it would have been reasonable for him to continue to occupy, and
    (b) the purpose of the arrangement is to enable him to become entitled to assistance under this Part,
and there is no other good reason why he is threatened with homelessness.

. . .

Supplementary provisions

213A   Co-operation in certain cases involving children

(1) This section applies where a local housing authority have reason to believe that an applicant with whom a person under the age of 18 normally resides, or might reasonably be expected to reside—

(a) may be ineligible for assistance;

(b) may be homeless and may have become so intentionally; or

(c) may be threatened with homelessness intentionally.

(2) A local housing authority shall make arrangements for ensuring that, where this section applies—

(a) the applicant is invited to consent to the referral of the essential facts of his case to the social services authority for the district of the housing authority (where that is a different authority); and

(b) if the applicant has given that consent, the social services authority are made aware of those facts and of the subsequent decision of the housing authority in respect of his case.

(3) Where the local housing authority and the social services authority for a district are the same authority (a 'unitary authority'); that authority shall make arrangements for ensuring that, where this section applies—

(a) the applicant is invited to consent to the referral to the social services department of the essential facts of his case; and

(b) if the applicant has given that consent, the social services department is made aware of those facts and of the subsequent decision of the authority in respect of his case.

(4) Nothing in subsection (2) or (3) affects any power apart from this section to disclose information relating to the applicant's case to the social services authority or to the social services department (as the case may be) without the consent of the applicant.

(5) Where a social services authority—

(a) are aware of a decision of a local housing authority that the applicant is ineligible for assistance, became homeless intentionally or became threatened with homelessness intentionally, and

(b) request the local housing authority to provide them with advice and assistance in the exercise of their social services functions under Part 3 of the Children Act 1989,

the local housing authority shall provide them with such advice and assistance as is reasonable in the circumstances.

(6) A unitary authority shall make arrangements for ensuring that, where they make a decision of a kind mentioned in subsection (5)(a), the housing department provide the social services department with such advice and assistance as the social services department may reasonably request.

(7) In this section, in relation to a unitary authority—

'the housing department' means those persons responsible for the exercise of their housing functions; and

'the social services department' means those persons responsible for the exercise of their social services functions under Part 3 of the Children Act 1989.

Education Act 1996
(1996 c. 56)

PART I   GENERAL

CHAPTER I   THE STATUTORY SYSTEM OF EDUCATION

Compulsory education

7 Duty of parents to secure education of children of compulsory school age

The parent of every child of compulsory school age shall cause him to receive efficient full-time education suitable—

(a) to his age, ability and aptitude, and

(b) to any special educational needs he may have,

either by regular attendance at school or otherwise.

8 Compulsory school age

(1) Subsections (2) and (3) apply to determine for the purposes of any enactment whether a person is of compulsory school age.

(2) A person begins to be of compulsory school age—

(a) when he attains the age of five, if he attains that age on a prescribed day, and

(b) otherwise at the beginning of the prescribed day next following his attaining that age.

(3) A person ceases to be of compulsory school age at the end of the day which is the school leaving date for any calendar year—

(a) if he attains the age of 16 after that day but before the beginning of the school year next following,

(b) if he attains that age on that day, or

(c) (unless paragraph (a) applies) if that day is the school leaving date next following his attaining that age.

(4) The Secretary of State may by order—

(a) provide that such days in the year as are specified in the order shall be, for each calendar year, prescribed days for the purposes of subsection (2);

(b) determine the day in any calendar year which is to be the school leaving date for that year.

Education in accordance with parental wishes

9 Pupils to be educated in accordance with parents' wishes

In exercising or performing all their respective powers and duties under the Education Acts, the Secretary of State and local education authorities shall have regard to the general principle that pupils are to be educated in accordance with the wishes of their parents, so far as that is compatible with the provision of efficient instruction and training and the avoidance of unreasonable public expenditure.

. . .

PART V   THE CURRICULUM

. . .

CHAPTER III   RELIGIOUS EDUCATION AND WORSHIP

Miscellaneous

398 No requirement of attendance at Sunday school etc.

(1) It shall not be required, as a condition of—

(a) a pupil attending a maintained school, or

(b) a person attending such a school to receive further education or any training for members of the school workforce,

that he must attend or abstain from attending a Sunday school or a place of religious worship.

(2) In subsection (1)(b), the reference to training for members of the school workforce is to be read in accordance with sections 75(5) and 96(1) of the Education Act 2005.

CHAPTER IV   MISCELLANEOUS AND SUPPLEMENTARY
PROVISIONS

Sex education

403   Sex education: manner of provision

(1) The governing body and head teacher shall take such steps as are reasonably practicable to secure that where sex education is given to any registered pupils at a maintained
school, it is given in such a manner as to encourage those pupils to have due regard to moral
considerations and the value of family life.

(1A) The Secretary of State must issue guidance designed to secure that when sex education is given to registered pupils at maintained schools—

    (a) they learn the nature of marriage and its importance for family life and the
bringing up of children, and

    (b) they are protected from teaching and materials which are inappropriate having
regard to the age and the religious and cultural background of the pupils concerned.

. . .

404   Sex education: statements of policy

(1) The governing body of a maintained school shall—

    (a) make, and keep up to date, a separate written statement of their policy with regard
to the provision of sex education, and

    (b) make copies of the statement available for inspection (at all reasonable times) by
parents of registered pupils at the school and provide a copy of the statement free
of charge to any such parent who asks for one.

(1A) A statement under subsection (1) must include a statement of the effect of
section 405.

. . .

405   Exemption from sex education

If the parent of any pupil in attendance at a maintained school requests that he may be
wholly or partly excused from receiving sex education at the school, the pupil shall, except so
far as such education is comprised in the National Curriculum, be so excused accordingly
until the request is withdrawn.

Politics

406   Political indoctrination

(1) The local education authority, governing body and head teacher shall forbid—

    (a) the pursuit of partisan political activities by any of those registered pupils at a
maintained school who are junior pupils, and

    (b) the promotion of partisan political views in the teaching of any subject in the
school.

(2) In the case of activities which take place otherwise than on the school premises,
subsection (1)(a) applies only where arrangements for junior pupils to take part in the
activities are made by—

    (a) any member of the school's staff (in his capacity as such), or

    (b) anyone acting on behalf of the school or of a member of the school's staff (in his
capacity as such).

407   Duty to secure balanced treatment of political issues

(1) The local education authority, governing body and head teacher shall take such steps
as are reasonably practicable to secure that where political issues are brought to the attention
of pupils while they are—

(a) in attendance at a maintained school, or

(b) taking part in extra-curricular activities which are provided or organised for registered pupils at the school by or on behalf of the school,

they are offered a balanced presentation of opposing views.

. . .

PART VI   SCHOOL ADMISSIONS, ATTENDANCE AND CHARGES

. . .

CHAPTER II   SCHOOL ATTENDANCE

School attendance orders

437   School attendance orders

(1) If it appears to a local education authority that a child of compulsory school age in their area is not receiving suitable education, either by regular attendance at school or otherwise, they shall serve a notice in writing on the parent requiring him to satisfy them within the period specified in the notice that the child is receiving such education.

(2) That period shall not be less than 15 days beginning with the day on which the notice is served.

(3) If—

(a) a parent on whom a notice has been served under subsection (1) fails to satisfy the local education authority, within the period specified in the notice, that the child is receiving suitable education, and

(b) in the opinion of the authority it is expedient that the child should attend school,

the authority shall serve on the parent an order (referred to in this Act as a 'school attendance order'), in such form as may be prescribed, requiring him to cause the child to become a registered pupil at a school named in the order.

(4) A school attendance order shall (subject to any amendment made by the local education authority) continue in force for so long as the child is of compulsory school age, unless—

(a) it is revoked by the authority, or

(b) a direction is made in respect of it under section 443(2) or 447(5).

(5) Where a maintained school is named in a school attendance order, the local education authority shall inform the governing body and the head teacher.

(6) Where a maintained school is named in a school attendance order, the governing body (and, in the case of a maintained school, the local education authority) shall admit the child to the school.

(7) Subsection (6) does not affect any power to exclude from a school a pupil who is already a registered pupil there.

(8) In this Chapter—

'maintained school' means any community, foundation or voluntary school or any community or foundation special school not established in a hospital; and

'suitable education', in relation to a child, means efficient full-time education suitable to his age, ability and aptitude and to any special educational needs he may have.

438   Choice of school: child without statement of special educational needs

(1) This section applies where a local education authority are required by virtue of section 437(3) to serve a school attendance order in respect of a child, other than a child for whom they maintain a statement under section 324.

(2) Before serving the order, the authority shall serve on the parent a notice in writing—

(a) informing him of their intention to serve the order,

(b) specifying the school which the authority intend to name in the order and, if they think fit, one or more other schools which they regard as suitable alternatives, and

(c) stating the effect of subsections (3) to (6).

(3) If the notice specifies one or more alternative schools and the parent selects one of them within the period of 15 days beginning with the day on which the notice is served, the school selected by him shall be named in the order.

(4) If—

(a) within the period mentioned in subsection (3) the parent applies for the child to be admitted to a school maintained by a local education authority and, where that authority are not the authority by whom the notice was served, notifies the latter authority of the application, and

(b) the child is offered a place at the school as a result of the application, that school shall be named in the order.

(5) If—

(a) within the period mentioned in subsection (3), the parent applies to the local education authority by whom the notice was served for education to be provided at a school which is not a school maintained by a local education authority, and

(b) the child is offered a place at the school and the authority are required by virtue of regulations under section 18(3) to pay the fees payable in respect of the education provided for him at the school,

that school shall be named in the order.

(6) If, within the period mentioned in subsection (3)—

(a) the parent—

(i) applies for the child to be admitted to a school which is not maintained by a local education authority, and in respect of which no application is made under subsection (5), and

(ii) notifies the local education authority by whom the notice was served of the application,

(b) the child is offered a place at the school as a result of the application, and

(c) the school is suitable to his age, ability and aptitude and to any special educational needs he may have,

that school shall be named in the order.

. . .

442   Revocation of order at request of parent

(1) This section applies where a school attendance order is in force in respect of a child.

(2) If at any time the parent applies to the local education authority requesting that the order be revoked on the ground that arrangements have been made for the child to receive suitable education otherwise than at school, the authority shall comply with the request, unless they are of the opinion that no satisfactory arrangements have been made for the education of the child otherwise than at school.

(3) If a parent is aggrieved by a refusal of the local education authority to comply with a request under subsection (2), he may refer the question to the Secretary of State.

(4) Where a question is referred to the Secretary of State under subsection (3), he shall give such direction determining the question as he thinks fit.

School attendance: offences and education supervision orders

443   Offence: failure to comply with school attendance order

(1) If a parent on whom a school attendance order is served fails to comply with the requirements of the order, he is guilty of an offence, unless he proves that he is causing the child to receive suitable education otherwise than at school.

(2) If, in proceedings for an offence under this section, the parent is acquitted, the court may direct that the school attendance order shall cease to be in force.

(3) A direction under subsection (2) does not affect the duty of the local education authority to take further action under section 437 if at any time the authority are of the opinion that, having regard to any change of circumstances, it is expedient to do so.

(4) A person guilty of an offence under this section is liable on summary conviction to a fine not exceeding level 3 on the standard scale.

444   Offence: failure to secure regular attendance at school of registered pupil

(1) If a child of compulsory school age who is a registered pupil at a school fails to attend regularly at the school, his parent is guilty of an offence.

(1A) If in the circumstances mentioned in subsection (1) the parent knows that his child is failing to attend regularly at the school and fails without reasonable justification to cause him to do so, he is guilty of an offence.

(2) Subsections (3) to (6) below apply in proceedings for an offence under this section in respect of a child who is not a boarder at the school at which he is a registered pupil.

(3) The child shall not be taken to have failed to attend regularly at the school by reason of his absence from the school—
  (a) with leave,
  (b) at any time when he was prevented from attending by reason of sickness or any unavoidable cause, or
  (c) on any day exclusively set apart for religious observance by the religious body to which his parent belongs.

(4) The child shall not be taken to have failed to attend regularly at the school if the parent proves—
  (a) that the school at which the child is a registered pupil is not within walking distance of the child's home, and
  (b) that no suitable arrangements have been made by the local education authority for any of the following—
    (i)   his transport to and from the school,
    (ii) boarding accommodation for him at or near the school, or
    (iii) enabling him to become a registered pupil at a school nearer to his home.

(5) In subsection (4) 'walking distance'—
  (a) in relation to a child who is under the age of eight, means 3.218688 kilometres (two miles), and
  (b) in relation to a child who has attained the age of eight, means 4.828032 kilometres (three miles),
in each case measured by the nearest available route.

(6) If it is proved that the child has no fixed abode, subsection (4) shall not apply, but the parent shall be acquitted if he proves—
  (a) that he is engaged in a trade or business of such a nature as to require him to travel from place to place,
  (b) that the child has attended at a school as a registered pupil as regularly as the nature of that trade or business permits, and
  (c) if the child has attained the age of six, that he has made at least 200 attendances during the period of 12 months ending with the date on which the proceedings were instituted.

(7) In proceedings for an offence under this section in respect of a child who is a boarder at the school at which he is a registered pupil, the child shall be taken to have failed to attend regularly at the school if he is absent from it without leave during any part of the school term at a time when he was not prevented from being present by reason of sickness or any unavoidable cause.

(8) A person guilty of an offence under subsection (1) is liable on summary conviction to a fine not exceeding level 3 on the standard scale.

(8A) A person guilty of an offence under subsection (1A) is liable on summary conviction—

    (a) to a fine not exceeding level 4 on the standard scale, or

    (b) to imprisonment for a term not exceeding 51 weeks, or both.

(8B) If, on the trial of an offence under subsection (1A), the court finds the defendant not guilty of that offence but is satisfied that he is guilty of an offence under subsection (1), the court may find him guilty of that offence.

(9) In this section 'leave', in relation to a school, means leave granted by any person authorised to do so by the governing body or proprietor of the school.

444ZA   Application of section 444 to alternative educational provision

(1) Where, in the case of a child of compulsory school age who is not a registered pupil at any school—

    (a) a local education authority has made arrangements under section 19 for the provision of education for him otherwise than at a school or at his home, and

    (b) notice in writing of the arrangements has been given to the child's parent,

subsections (1) to (7) of section 444 have effect as if the place at which the education is provided were a school and the child were a registered pupil at that school.

(2) Where—

    (a) a child of compulsory school age has been excluded from a relevant school,

    (b) he remains for the time being a registered pupil at the school,

    (c) he is required by the appropriate authority for the school to attend at a place outside the school premises for the purpose of receiving any instruction or training, and

    (d) notice in writing of the requirement has been given to the child's parent,

subsections (1) to (7) of section 444 have effect as if the place at which the child is required to attend were a school and the child were a registered pupil at that school (and not at the school mentioned in paragraph (b)).

(3) In relation to a maintained school or a pupil referral unit—

    (a) the reference in subsection (2)(a) to exclusion is a reference to exclusion under section 52 of the Education Act 2002, and

    (b) the requirement referred to in subsection (2)(c) is a requirement imposed under section 29(3) of that Act.

(4) A child shall not be taken to have failed to attend regularly—

    (a) in a case falling within subsection (1), at the place at which education is provided for him, or

    (b) in a case falling within subsection (2), at the place at which he is required to attend,

unless he has failed to attend regularly since the giving of the notice mentioned in subsection (1)(b) or (2)(d).

(5) Section 572, which provides for the methods by which notices may be served under this Act, does not preclude the notice mentioned in subsection (1)(b) or (2)(d) from being given to a child's parent by any other effective method.

(6) In proceedings for an offence under section 444 in a case falling within subsection (1) of this section, the parent shall be acquitted if he proves that the child is receiving suitable education otherwise than by regular attendance at a school or at the place mentioned in subsection (1).

(7) In section 444 'leave'—

    (a) in relation to a place at which education is provided as mentioned in subsection (1) of this section, means leave granted by any person authorised to do so by the local education authority;

    (b) in relation to a place at which a child is required to attend as mentioned in subsection (2)(c) of this section, means leave granted by any person authorised to do so by the appropriate authority for the school.

(8) In this section—

    (a) 'relevant school' means—

        (i)   a maintained school,

        (ii) a pupil referral unit,

        (iii) an Academy,

        (iv) a city technology college, or

        (v)   a city college for the technology of the arts;

    (b) 'appropriate authority' means—

        (i)   in relation to a maintained school, the governing body,

        (ii) in relation to a pupil referral unit, the local education authority, and

        (iii) in relation to a school falling within paragraph (a)(iii), (iv) or (v), the proprietor of the school.

444A Penalty notice in respect of failure to secure regular attendance at school of registered pupil

    (1) Where an authorised officer has reason to believe—

    (a) that a person has committed an offence under section 444(1), and

    (b) that the offence relates—

        (i)   to a relevant school in England,

        (ii) in a case falling within subsection (1) of section 444ZA, to a place at which education is provided by a local education authority in England, or

        (iii) in a case falling within subsection (2) of that section, to a place at which a child is required to attend by the appropriate authority (within the meaning of that section) for a relevant school in England,

he may give the person a penalty notice in respect of the offence.

    (2) A penalty notice is a notice offering a person the opportunity of discharging any liability to conviction for the offence under section 444(1) to which the notice relates by payment of a penalty in accordance with the notice.

    (3) Where a person is given a penalty notice, proceedings for the offence to which the notice relates (or an offence under section 444(1A) arising out of the same circumstances) may not be instituted before the end of such period as may be prescribed.

    (4) Where a person is given a penalty notice, he cannot be convicted of the offence to which the notice relates (or an offence under section 444(1A) arising out of the same circumstances) if he pays a penalty in accordance with the notice.

    (5) Penalties under this section shall be payable to local education authorities in England.

    (6) Sums received by a local education authority under this section may be used by the authority for the purposes of any of its functions which may be specified in regulations.

444B Penalty notices: supplemental

    (1) Regulations may make—

    (a) provision as to the form and content of penalty notices,

    (b) provision as to the monetary amount of any penalty and the time by which it is to be paid,

    (c) provision for determining the local education authority to which a penalty is payable,

    (d) provision as to the methods by which penalties may be paid,

    (e) provision as to the records which are to be kept in relation to penalty notices,

    (f) provision as to the persons who may be authorised by a local education authority or a head teacher to give penalty notices,

    (g) provision limiting the circumstances in which authorised officers of a prescribed description may give penalty notices,

    (h) provision for or in connection with the withdrawal, in prescribed circumstances, of a penalty notice, including—

      (i) repayment of any amount paid by way of penalty under a penalty notice which is withdrawn, and

      (ii) prohibition of the institution or continuation of proceedings for the offence to which the withdrawn notice relates (and any offence under section 444(1A) arising out of the same circumstances),

    (i) provision for a certificate—

      (i) purporting to be signed by or on behalf of a prescribed person, and

      (ii) stating that payment of any amount paid by way of penalty was or, as the case may be, was not received on or before a date specified in the certificate, to be received in evidence of the matters so stated,

    (j) provision as to the action to be taken if a penalty is not paid in accordance with a penalty notice,

    (k) provision for or in connection with the preparation of codes of conduct in relation to the giving of penalty notices,

    (l) such other provision in relation to penalties or penalty notices as the Secretary of State thinks necessary or expedient.

(2) Without prejudice to the generality of subsection (1) or section 569(4), regulations under subsection (1)(b) may make provision for penalties of different amounts to be payable in different cases or circumstances (including provision for the penalty payable under a penalty notice to differ according to the time by which it is paid).

(3) Local education authorities, head teachers and authorised officers shall, in carrying out their functions in relation to penalty notices, have regard to any guidance which is published by the Secretary of State from time to time in relation to penalty notices.

(4) In this section and section 444A—

'authorised officer' means—

    (a) a constable,

    (b) an officer of a local education authority in England who is authorised by the authority to give penalty notices, or

    (c) an authorised staff member,

'authorised staff member' means—

    (a) a head teacher of a relevant school in England, or

    (b) a member of the staff of a relevant school in England who is authorised by the head teacher of the school to give penalty notices,

'penalty' means a penalty under a penalty notice,

'penalty notice' has the meaning given by section 444A(2),

'relevant school' means—

    (a) a maintained school,

    (b) a pupil referral unit,

    (c) an Academy,

    (d) a city technology college, or

    (e) a city college for the technology of the arts.

445 Presumption of age

(1) This section applies for the purposes of any proceedings for an offence under section 443 or 444.

(2) In so far as it is material, the child in question shall be presumed to have been of compulsory school age at any time unless the parent proves the contrary.

(3) Where a court is obliged by virtue of subsection (2) to presume a child to have been of compulsory school age, section 565(1) (provisions as to evidence) does not apply.

446 Institution of proceedings

Proceedings for an offence under section 443 or 444 shall not be instituted except by a local education authority.

447 Education supervision orders

(1) Before instituting proceedings for an offence under section 443 or 444, a local education authority shall consider whether it would be appropriate (instead of or as well as instituting the proceedings) to apply for an education supervision order with respect to the child.

(2) The court—

(a) by which a person is convicted of an offence under section 443, or

(b) before which a person is charged with an offence under section 444,

may direct the local education authority instituting the proceedings to apply for an education supervision order with respect to the child unless the authority, having consulted the appropriate local authority, decide that the child's welfare will be satisfactorily safeguarded even though no education supervision order is made.

(3) Where, following such a direction, a local education authority decide not to apply for an education supervision order, they shall inform the court of the reasons for their decision.

(4) Unless the court has directed otherwise, the information required under subsection (3) shall be given to the court before the end of the period of eight weeks beginning with the date on which the direction was given.

(5) Where—

(a) a local education authority apply for an education supervision order with respect to a child who is the subject of a school attendance order, and

(b) the court decides that section 36(3) of the Children Act 1989 (education supervision orders) prevents it from making the order,

the court may direct that the school attendance order shall cease to be in force.

(6) In this section—

'the appropriate local authority' has the same meaning as in section 36(9) of the Children Act 1989, and

'education supervision order' means an education supervision order under that Act.

. . .

PART X   MISCELLANEOUS AND GENERAL

CHAPTER II   PUNISHMENT AND RESTRAINT OF PUPILS

Corporal punishment

548 No right to give corporal punishment

(1) Corporal punishment given by, or on the authority of, a member of staff to a child—

(a) for whom education is provided at any school, or

(b) for whom education is provided, otherwise than at school, under any arrangements made by a local education authority, or

(c) for whom specified nursery education is provided otherwise than at school, cannot be justified in any proceedings on the ground that it was given in pursuance of a right exercisable by the member of staff by virtue of his position as such.

(2) Subsection (1) applies to corporal punishment so given to a child at any time, whether at the school or other place at which education is provided for the child, or elsewhere.

(3) The following provisions have effect for the purposes of this section.

(4) Any reference to giving corporal punishment to a child is to doing anything for the purpose of punishing that child (whether or not there are other reasons for doing it) which, apart from any justification, would constitute battery.

(5) However, corporal punishment shall not be taken to be given to a child by virtue of anything done for reasons that include averting—

(a) an immediate danger of personal injury to, or

(b) an immediate danger to the property of, any person (including the child himself).

(6) 'Member of staff', in relation to the child concerned, means—

    (a) any person who works as a teacher at the school or other place at which education is provided for the child, or

    (b) any other person who (whether in connection with the provision of education for the child or otherwise)—

        (i) works at that school or place, or

        (ii) otherwise provides his services there (whether or not for payment), and has lawful control or charge of the child.

(7) 'Child' (except in subsection (8)) means a person under the age of 18.

(8) 'Specified nursery education' means full-time or part-time education suitable for children who have not attained compulsory school age which is provided—

    (a) by a local education authority; or

    (b) by any other person—

        (i) who is (or is to be) in receipt of financial assistance given by such an authority and whose provision of nursery education is taken into account by the authority in formulating proposals for the purposes of section 120(2)(a) of the School Standards and Framework Act 1998.

Power to restrain pupils

550A Power of members of staff to restrain pupils

(1) A member of the staff of a school may use, in relation to any pupil at the school, such force as is reasonable in the circumstances for the purpose of preventing the pupil from doing (or continuing to do) any of the following, namely—

    (a) committing any offence,

    (b) causing personal injury to, or damage to the property of, any person (including the pupil himself), or

    (c) engaging in any behaviour prejudicial to the maintenance of good order and discipline at the school or among any of its pupils, whether that behaviour occurs during a teaching session or otherwise.

(2) Subsection (1) applies where a member of the staff of a school is—

    (a) on the premises of the school, or

    (b) elsewhere at a time when, as a member of its staff, he has lawful control or charge of the pupil concerned;

but it does not authorise anything to be done in relation to a pupil which constitutes the giving of corporal punishment within the meaning of section 548.

(3) Subsection (1) shall not be taken to prevent any person from relying on any defence available to him otherwise than by virtue of this section.

(4) In this section—

'member of the staff', in relation to a school, means any teacher who works at the school and any other person who, with the authority of the head teacher, has lawful control or charge of pupils at the school;

'offence' includes anything that would be an offence but for the operation of any presumption that a person under a particular age is incapable of committing an offence.

Detention

550B Detention outside school hours lawful despite absence of parental consent

(1) Where a pupil to whom this section applies is required on disciplinary grounds to spend a period of time in detention at his school after the end of any school session, his detention shall not be rendered unlawful by virtue of the absence of his parent's consent to it if the conditions set out in subsection (3) are satisfied.

(2) This section applies to any pupil who has not attained the age of 18 and is attending—

    (a) a school maintained by a local education authority; or

(c) a city technology college, city college for the technology of the arts or Academy.
(3) The conditions referred to in subsection (1) are as follows—
  (a) the head teacher of the school must have previously determined, and have—
      (i) made generally known within the school, and
      (ii) taken steps to bring to the attention of the parent of every person who is for the time being a registered pupil there,
    that the detention of pupils after the end of a school session is one of the measures that may be taken with a view to regulating the conduct of pupils;
  (b) the detention must be imposed by the head teacher or by another teacher at the school specifically or generally authorised by him for the purpose;
  (c) the detention must be reasonable in all the circumstances; and
  (d) the pupil's parent must have been given at least 24 hours' notice in writing that the detention was due to take place.
(4) In determining for the purposes of subsection (3)(c) whether a pupil's detention is reasonable, the following matters in particular shall be taken into account—
  (a) whether the detention constitutes a proportionate punishment in the circumstances of the case; and
  (b) any special circumstances relevant to its imposition on the pupil which are known to the person imposing it (or of which he ought reasonably to be aware) including in particular—
      (i)   the pupil's age,
      (ii) any special educational needs he may have,
      (iii) any religious requirements affecting him, and
      (iv) where arrangements have to be made for him to travel from the school to his home, whether suitable alternative arrangements can reasonably be made by his parent.
(5) Section 572, which provides for the methods by which notices may be served under this Act, does not preclude a notice from being given to a pupil's parent under this section by any other effective method.
. . .

Protection from Harassment Act 1997
(1997 c. 40)

England and Wales

1 Prohibition of harassment
  (1) A person must not pursue a course of conduct—
      (a) which amounts to harassment of another, and
      (b) which he knows or ought to know amounts to harassment of the other.
  (2) For the purposes of this section, the person whose course of conduct is in question ought to know that it amounts to harassment of another if a reasonable person in possession of the same information would think the course of conduct amounted to harassment of the other.
  (3) Subsection (1) does not apply to a course of conduct if the person who pursued it shows—
      (a) that it was pursued for the purpose of preventing or detecting crime,
      (b) that it was pursued under any enactment or rule of law or to comply with any condition or requirement imposed by any person under any enactment, or

(c) that in the particular circumstances the pursuit of the course of conduct was reasonable.

2 Offence of harassment

(1) A person who pursues a course of conduct in breach of section 1 is guilty of an offence.

(2) A person guilty of an offence under this section is liable on summary conviction to imprisonment for a term not exceeding six months, or a fine not exceeding level 5 on the standard scale, or both.

3 Civil remedy

(1) An actual or apprehended breach of section 1 may be the subject of a claim in civil proceedings by the person who is or may be the victim of the course of conduct in question.

(2) On such a claim, damages may be awarded for (among other things) any anxiety caused by the harassment and any financial loss resulting from the harassment.

(3) Where—
   (a) in such proceedings the High Court or a county court grants an injunction for the purpose of restraining the defendant from pursuing any conduct which amounts to harassment, and
   (b) the plaintiff considers that the defendant has done anything which he is prohibited from doing by the injunction,
the plaintiff may apply for the issue of a warrant for the arrest of the defendant.

(4) An application under subsection (3) may be made—
   (a) where the injunction was granted by the High Court, to a judge of that court, and
   (b) where the injunction was granted by a county court, to a judge or district judge of that or any other county court.

(5) The judge or district judge to whom an application under subsection (3) is made may only issue a warrant if—
   (a) the application is substantiated on oath, and
   (b) the judge or district judge has reasonable grounds for believing that the defendant has done anything which he is prohibited from doing by the injunction.

(6) Where—
   (a) the High Court or a county court grants an injunction for the purpose mentioned in subsection (3)(a), and
   (b) without reasonable excuse the defendant does anything which he is prohibited from doing by the injunction,
he is guilty of an offence.

(7) Where a person is convicted of an offence under subsection (6) in respect of any conduct, that conduct is not punishable as a contempt of court.

(8) A person cannot be convicted of an offence under subsection (6) in respect of any conduct which has been punished as a contempt of court.

(9) A person guilty of an offence under subsection (6) is liable—
   (a) on conviction on indictment, to imprisonment for a term not exceeding five years, or a fine, or both, or
   (b) on summary conviction, to imprisonment for a term not exceeding six months, or a fine not exceeding the statutory maximum, or both.

4 Putting people in fear of violence

(1) A person whose course of conduct causes another to fear, on at least two occasions, that violence will be used against him is guilty of an offence if he knows or ought to know that his course of conduct will cause the other so to fear on each of those occasions.

(2) For the purposes of this section, the person whose course of conduct is in question ought to know that it will cause another to fear that violence will be used against him on any occasion if a reasonable person in possession of the same information would think the course of conduct would cause the other so to fear on that occasion.

(3) It is a defence for a person charged with an offence under this section to show that—

(a) his course of conduct was pursued for the purpose of preventing or detecting crime,

(b) his course of conduct was pursued under any enactment or rule of law or to comply with any condition or requirement imposed by any person under any enactment, or

(c) the pursuit of his course of conduct was reasonable for the protection of himself or another or for the protection of his or another's property.

(4) A person guilty of an offence under this section is liable—

(a) on conviction on indictment, to imprisonment for a term not exceeding five years, or a fine, or both, or

(b) on summary conviction, to imprisonment for a term not exceeding six months, or a fine not exceeding the statutory maximum, or both.

(5) If on the trial on indictment of a person charged with an offence under this section the jury find him not guilty of the offence charged, they may find him guilty of an offence under section 2.

(6) The Crown Court has the same powers and duties in relation to a person who is by virtue of subsection (5) convicted before it of an offence under section 2 as a magistrates' court would have on convicting him of the offence.

5   Restraining orders on conviction

(1) A court sentencing or otherwise dealing with a person ('the defendant') convicted of an offence may (as well as sentencing him or dealing with him in any other way) make an order under this section.

(2) The order may, for the purpose of protecting the victim of the offence, or any other person mentioned in the order, from conduct which—

(a) amounts to harassment, or

(b) will cause a fear of violence, prohibit the defendant from doing anything described in the order.

(3) The order may have effect for a specified period or until further order.

(3A) In proceedings under this section both the prosecution and the defence may lead, as further evidence, any evidence that would be admissible in proceedings for an injunction under section 3.

(4) The prosecutor, the defendant or any other person mentioned in the order may apply to the court which made the order for it to be varied or discharged by a further order.

(4A) Any person mentioned in the order is entitled to be heard on the hearing of an application under subsection (4).

(5) If without reasonable excuse the defendant does anything which he is prohibited from doing by an order under this section, he is guilty of an offence.

(6) A person guilty of an offence under this section is liable—

(a) on conviction on indictment, to imprisonment for a term not exceeding five years, or a fine, or both, or

(b) on summary conviction, to imprisonment for a term not exceeding six months, or a fine not exceeding the statutory maximum, or both.

(7) A court dealing with a person for an offence under this section may vary or discharge the order in question by a further order.

5A   Restraining orders on acquittal

(1) A court before which a person ('the defendant') is acquitted of an offence may, if it considers it necessary to do so to protect a person from harassment by the defendant, make an order prohibiting the defendant from doing anything described in the order.

(2) Subsections (3) to (7) of section 5 apply to an order under this section as they apply to an order under that one.

(3) Where the Court of Appeal allow an appeal against conviction they may remit the case to the Crown Court to consider whether to proceed under this section.

(4) Where—

(a) the Crown Court allows an appeal against conviction, or

(b) a case is remitted to the Crown Court under subsection (3),

the reference in subsection (1) to a court before which a person is acquitted of an offence is to be read as referring to that court.

(5) A person made subject to an order under this section has the same right of appeal against the order as if—

(a) he had been convicted of the offence in question before the court which made the order, and

(b) the order had been made under section 5.

7   Interpretation of this group of sections

(1) This section applies for the interpretation of sections 1 to 5A.

(2) References to harassing a person include alarming the person or causing the person distress.

(3) A 'course of conduct' must involve conduct on at least two occasions.

(3A) A person's conduct on any occasion shall be taken, if aided, abetted, counselled or procured by another—

(a) to be conduct on that occasion of the other (as well as conduct of the person whose conduct it is); and

(b) to be conduct in relation to which the other's knowledge and purpose, and what he ought to have known, are the same as they were in relation to what was contemplated or reasonably foreseeable at the time of the aiding, abetting, counselling or procuring.

(4) 'Conduct' includes speech.

School Standards and Framework Act 1998
(1998 c. 31)

PART II   NEW FRAMEWORK FOR MAINTAINED SCHOOLS
CHAPTER VI   RELIGIOUS EDUCATION AND WORSHIP

Religious education

69   Duty to secure due provision of religious education

(1) Subject to section 71, in relation to any community, foundation or voluntary school—

(a) the local education authority and the governing body shall exercise their functions with a view to securing, and

(b) the head teacher shall secure,

that religious education is given in accordance with the provision for such education included in the school's basic curriculum by virtue of section 80(1)(a) or 101(1)(a) of the Education Act 2002.

. . .

Religious worship

70   Requirements relating to collective worship

(1) Subject to section 71, each pupil in attendance at a community, foundation or voluntary school shall on each school day take part in an act of collective worship.

. . .

Exceptions and special arrangements etc.

71 Exceptions and special arrangements; provision for special schools

(1) If the parent of a pupil at a community, foundation or voluntary school requests that he may be wholly or partly excused—

>   (a) from receiving religious education given in the school in accordance with the school's basic curriculum,
>   (b) from attendance at religious worship in the school, or
>   (c) both from receiving such education and from such attendance,

the pupil shall be so excused until the request is withdrawn.

. . .

(3) Where in accordance with subsection (1) a pupil has been wholly or partly excused from receiving religious education or from attendance at religious worship and the local education authority are satisfied—

>   (a) that the parent of the pupil desires him to receive religious education of a kind which is not provided in the school during the periods of time during which he is so excused,
>   (b) that the pupil cannot with reasonable convenience be sent to another community, foundation or voluntary school where religious education of the kind desired by the parent is provided, and
>   (c) that arrangements have been made for him to receive religious education of that kind during school hours elsewhere,

the pupil may be withdrawn from the school during such periods of time as are reasonably necessary for the purpose of enabling him to receive religious education in accordance with the arrangements.

(4) A pupil may not be withdrawn from school under subsection (3) unless the local education authority are satisfied that the arrangements there mentioned are such as will not interfere with the attendance of the pupil at school on any day except at the beginning or end of a school session (or, if there is only one, the school session) on that day.

. . .

PART III   SCHOOL ADMISSIONS

CHAPTER I   ADMISSION ARRANGEMENTS

Parental preferences

86 Parental preferences

(1) A local education authority shall make arrangements for enabling the parent of a child in the area of the authority—

>   (a) to express a preference as to the school at which he wishes education to be provided for his child in the exercise of the authority's functions, and
>   (b) to give reasons for his preference.

(2) Subject to subsections (3) and (3A) and section 87 (children excluded from two or more schools), a local education authority and the governing body of a maintained school shall comply with any preference expressed in accordance with arrangements made under subsection (1).

(2A) Arrangements made under subsection (1) may allow the parent of a child to express preferences for more than one school; but nothing in this section requires the admission authority for a maintained school for which a child's parent has expressed a preference to offer the child admission to the school if, in accordance with a scheme adopted or made by virtue of section 89B, the child is offered admission to a different school for which the parent has also expressed a preference.

(3) The duty imposed by subsection (2) does not apply—

(a) if compliance with the preference would prejudice the provision of efficient education or the efficient use of resources; or

(c) if the arrangements for admission to the preferred school—

(i)   are wholly based on selection by reference to ability or aptitude, and

(ii) are so based with a view to admitting only pupils with high ability or with aptitude,

and compliance with the preference would be incompatible with selection under those arrangements.

. . .

(3A) In relation to a preference expressed by a parent as to the school at which he wishes secondary education suitable to the requirements of pupils who are over compulsory school age to be provided for his child, the duty imposed by subsection (2) also does not apply if the relevant selection arrangements are wholly based on selection by reference to ability or aptitude and compliance with the preference would be incompatible with selection under those arrangements.

(3B) In subsection (3A) 'the relevant selection arrangements', in relation to a school, means—

(a) the arrangements for admission to the school for secondary education suitable to the requirements of pupils who are over compulsory school age, or

(b) those arrangements and the arrangements for entry to the sixth form of children who have been admitted to the school;

and references in this subsection to entry to the sixth form of children who have been admitted to a school shall be construed in accordance with section 94(7).

. . .

PART V   NURSERY EDUCATION

Nursery education

117   Definition of 'nursery education'

In this Part 'nursery education' means full-time or part-time education suitable for children who have not attained compulsory school age (whether provided at schools or elsewhere).

General duty of local education authority

118   Duty of LEA as respects availability of nursery education

(1) A local education authority shall secure that the provision (whether or not by them) of nursery education for children who—

(a) have not attained compulsory school age, but

(b) have attained such age as may be prescribed, is sufficient for their area.

(2) In determining for the purposes of subsection (1) whether the provision of such education is sufficient for their area a local education authority—

(a) may have regard to any facilities which they expect to be available outside their area for providing such education; and

(b) shall have regard to any guidance given from time to time by the Secretary of State.

118A   Duties of LEA in respect of childcare

(1) A local education authority shall review annually the sufficiency of childcare provision for their area.

(2) In carrying out a review for the purposes of subsection (1), a local education authority—

  (a) may have regard to any facilities which they expect to be available outside their area for providing childcare; and

  (b) shall have regard to any guidance given from time to time by the Secretary of State.

(3) A local education authority shall also establish and maintain a service providing information to the public relating to the provision of childcare and related services in their area.

(4) In relation to the function, form and content of a service established and maintained under subsection (3), a local education authority shall have regard to any guidance given from time to time by the Secretary of State.

. . .

Crime and Disorder Act 1998
(1998 c. 37)

PART I   PREVENTION OF CRIME AND DISORDER
CHAPTER I   ENGLAND AND WALES

Youth crime and disorder

8   Parenting orders

(1) This section applies where, in any court proceedings—

  (a) a child safety order is made in respect of a child or the court determines on an application under section 12(6) below that a child has failed to comply with any requirement included in such an order;

  (aa) parental compensation order is made in relation to a child's behaviour;

  (b) an anti-social behaviour order or sex offender order is made in respect of a child or young person;

  (c) a child or young person is convicted of an offence; or

  (d) a person is convicted of an offence under section 443 (failure to comply with school attendance order) or section 444 (failure to secure regular attendance at school of registered pupil) of the Education Act 1996.

(2) Subject to subsection (3) and section 9(1) below, if in the proceedings the court is satisfied that the relevant condition is fulfilled, it may make a parenting order in respect of a person who is a parent or guardian of the child or young person or, as the case may be, the person convicted of the offence under section 443 or 444 ('the parent').

(3) A court shall not make a parenting order unless it has been notified by the Secretary of State that arrangements for implementing such orders are available in the area in which it appears to the court that the parent resides or will reside and the notice has not been withdrawn.

(4) A parenting order is an order which requires the parent—

  (a) to comply, for a period not exceeding twelve months, with such requirements as are specified in the order, and

  (b) subject to subsection (5) below, to attend, for a concurrent period not exceeding three months, such counselling or guidance programme as may be specified in directions given by the responsible officer.

(5) A parenting order may, but need not, include such a requirement as is mentioned in subsection (4)(b) above in any case where a parenting order under this section or any other enactment has been made in respect of the parent on a previous occasion.

(6) The relevant condition is that the parenting order would be desirable in the interests of preventing—

    (a) in a case falling within paragraph (a), (aa), or (b) of subsection (1) above, any repetition of the kind of behaviour which led to the child safety order, parental compensation order, anti-social behaviour order or sex offender order being made;

    (b) in a case falling within paragraph (c) of that subsection, the commission of any further offence by the child or young person;

    (c) in a case falling within paragraph (d) of that subsection, the commission of any further offence under section 443 or 444 of the Education Act 1996.

(7) The requirements that may be specified under subsection (4)(a) above are those which the court considers desirable in the interests of preventing any such repetition or, as the case may be, the commission of any such further offence.

(7A) A counselling or guidance programme which a parent is required to attend by virtue of subsection (4)(b) above may be or include a residential course but only if the court is satisfied—

    (a) that the attendance of the parent at a residential course is likely to be more effective than his attendance at a non-residential course in preventing any such repetition or, as the case may be, the commission of any such further offence, and

    (b) that any interference with family life which is likely to result from the attendance of the parent at a residential course is proportionate in all the circumstances.

(8) In this section and section 9 below 'responsible officer', in relation to a parenting order, means one of the following who is specified in the order, namely—

    (a)   an officer of a local probation board;

    (b)   a social worker of a local authority; and

    (bb) a person nominated by a person appointed as director of children's services under section 18 of the Children Act 2004 or by a person appointed as chief education officer under section 532 of the Education Act 1996;

    (c)   a member of a youth offending team.

9 Parenting orders: supplemental

(1) Where a person under the age of 16 is convicted of an offence, the court by or before which he is so convicted—

    (a) if it is satisfied that the relevant condition is fulfilled, shall make a parenting order; and

    (b) if it is not so satisfied, shall state in open court that it is not and why it is not.

(1A) The requirements of subsection (1) do not apply where the court makes a referral order in respect of the offence.

(1B) If an anti-social behaviour order is made in respect of a person under the age of 16 the court which makes the order—

    (a) must make a parenting order if it is satisfied that the relevant condition is fulfilled;

    (b) if it is not so satisfied, must state in open court that it is not and why it is not.

(2) Before making a parenting order—

    (a) in a case falling within paragraph (a) of subsection (1) of section 8 above;

    (b) in a case falling within paragraph (b) or (c) of that subsection, where the person concerned is under the age of 16; or

    (c) in a case falling within paragraph (d) of that subsection, where the person to whom the offence related is under that age,

a court shall obtain and consider information about the person's family circumstances and the likely effect of the order on those circumstances.

(2A) In a case where a court proposes to make both a referral order in respect of a child or young person convicted of an offence and a parenting order, before making the parenting order the court shall obtain and consider a report by an appropriate officer—

> (a) indicating the requirements proposed by that officer to be included in the parenting order;
>
> (b) indicating the reasons why he considers those requirements would be desirable in the interests of preventing the commission of any further offence by the child or young person; and
>
> (c) if the child or young person is aged under 16, containing the information required by subsection (2) above.

(2B) In subsection (2A) above 'an appropriate officer' means—

> (a) an officer of a local probation board;
>
> (b) a social worker of a local authority; or
>
> (c) a member of a youth offending team.

(3) Before making a parenting order, a court shall explain to the parent in ordinary language—

> (a) the effect of the order and of the requirements proposed to be included in it;
>
> (b) the consequences which may follow (under subsection (7) below) if he fails to comply with any of those requirements; and
>
> (c) that the court has power (under subsection (5) below) to review the order on the application either of the parent or of the responsible officer.

(4) Requirements specified in, and directions given under, a parenting order shall, as far as practicable, be such as to avoid—

> (a) any conflict with the parent's religious beliefs; and
>
> (b) any interference with the times, if any, at which he normally works or attends an educational establishment.

(5) If while a parenting order is in force it appears to the court which made it, on the application of the responsible officer or the parent, that it is appropriate to make an order under this subsection, the court may make an order discharging the parenting order or varying it—

> (a) by cancelling any provision included in it; or
>
> (b) by inserting in it (either in addition to or in substitution for any of its provisions) any provision that could have been included in the order if the court had then had power to make it and were exercising the power.

(6) Where an application under subsection (5) above for the discharge of a parenting order is dismissed, no further application for its discharge shall be made under that subsection by any person except with the consent of the court which made the order.

(7) If while a parenting order is in force the parent without reasonable excuse fails to comply with any requirement included in the order, or specified in directions given by the responsible officer, he shall be liable on summary conviction to a fine not exceeding level 3 on the standard scale.

(7A) In this section 'referral order' means an order under section 16(2) or (3) of the Powers of Criminal Courts (Sentencing) Act 2000 (referral of offender to youth offender panel).

10   Appeals against parenting orders

(1) An appeal shall lie—

> (a) to the High Court against the making of a parenting order by virtue of paragraph (a) of subsection (1) of section 8 above; and
>
> (b) to the Crown Court against the making of a parenting order by virtue of paragraph (b) of that subsection.

(2) On an appeal under subsection (1) above the High Court or the Crown Court—

> (a) may make such orders as may be necessary to give effect to its determination of the appeal; and

  (b) may also make such incidental or consequential orders as appear to it to
    be just.

  (3) Any order of the High Court or the Crown Court made on an appeal under subsection
(1) above (other than one directing that an application be reheard by a magistrates' court)
shall, for the purposes of subsections (5) to (7) of section 9 above, be treated as if it were an
order of the court from which the appeal was brought and not an order of the High Court or
the Crown Court.

  (4) A person in respect of whom a parenting order is made by virtue of section 8(1)(c)
above shall have the same right of appeal against the making of the order as if—

  (a) the offence that led to the making of the order were an offence committed by
    him; and

  (b) the order were a sentence passed on him for the offence.

  (5) A person in respect of whom a parenting order is made by virtue of section 8(1)(d)
above shall have the same right of appeal against the making of the order as if the order were
a sentence passed on him for the offence that led to the making of the order.

  . . .

11 Child safety orders

  (1) Subject to subsection (2) below, if a magistrates' court, on the application of a local
authority, is satisfied that one or more of the conditions specified in subsection (3) below are
fulfilled with respect to a child under the age of 10, it may make an order (a 'child safety
order') which—

  (a) places the child, for a period (not exceeding the permitted maximum) specified in
    the order, under the supervision of the responsible officer; and

  (b) requires the child to comply with such requirements as are so specified.

  (2) A court shall not make a child safety order unless it has been notified by the Secretary
of State that arrangements for implementing such orders are available in the area in which it
appears that the child resides or will reside and the notice has not been withdrawn.

  (3) The conditions are—

  (a) that the child has committed an act which, if he had been aged 10 or over, would
    have constituted an offence;

  (b) that a child safety order is necessary for the purpose of preventing the commis-
    sion by the child of such an act as is mentioned in paragraph (a) above;

  (c) that the child has contravened a ban imposed by a curfew notice; and

  (d) that the child has acted in a manner that caused or was likely to cause harassment,
    alarm or distress to one or more persons not of the same household as himself.

  (4) The maximum period permitted for the purposes of subsection (1)(a) above is twelve
months.

  (5) The requirements that may be specified under subsection (1)(b) above are those
which the court considers desirable in the interests of—

  (a) securing that the child receives appropriate care, protection and support and is
    subject to proper control; or

  (b) preventing any repetition of the kind of behaviour which led to the child safety
    order being made.

  (6) Proceedings under this section or section 12 below shall be family proceedings for the
purposes of the 1989 Act or section 65 of the Magistrates' Courts Act 1980 ('the 1980 Act');
and the standard of proof applicable to such proceedings shall be that applicable to civil
proceedings.

  (7) In this section 'local authority' has the same meaning as in the 1989 Act.

  (8) In this section and section 12 below, 'responsible officer', in relation to a child safety
order, means one of the following who is specified in the order, namely—

  (a) a social worker of a local authority; and

  (b) a member of a youth offending team.

12 Child safety orders: supplemental

(1) Before making a child safety order, a magistrates' court shall obtain and consider information about the child's family circumstances and the likely effect of the order on those circumstances.

(2) Before making a child safety order, a magistrates' court shall explain to the parent or guardian of the child in ordinary language—

(a) the effect of the order and of the requirements proposed to be included in it;

(b) the consequences which may follow (under subsection (6) below) if the child fails to comply with any of those requirements; and

(c) that the court has power (under subsection (4) below) to review the order on the application either of the parent or guardian or of the responsible officer.

(3) Requirements included in a child safety order shall, as far as practicable, be such as to avoid—

(a) any conflict with the parent's religious beliefs; and

(b) any interference with the times, if any, at which the child normally attends school.

(4) If while a child safety order is in force in respect of a child it appears to the court which made it, on the application of the responsible officer or a parent or guardian of the child, that it is appropriate to make an order under this subsection, the court may make an order discharging the child safety order or varying it—

(a) by cancelling any provision included in it; or

(b) by inserting in it (either in addition to or in substitution for any of its provisions) any provision that could have been included in the order if the court had then had power to make it and were exercising the power.

(5) Where an application under subsection (4) above for the discharge of a child safety order is dismissed, no further application for its discharge shall be made under that subsection by any person except with the consent of the court which made the order.

(6) Where a child safety order is in force and it is proved to the satisfaction of the court which made it or another magistrates' court acting in the same local justice area, on the application of the responsible officer, that the child has failed to comply with any requirement included in the order, the court—

. . .

(b) may make an order varying the order—

(i) by canceling any provision included in it; or

(ii) by inserting in it (either in addition to or in substitution for any of its provisions) any provision that could have been included in the order if the court had then had power to make it and were exercising the power.

13 Appeals against child safety orders

(1) An appeal shall lie to the High Court against the making by a magistrates' court of a child safety order; and on such an appeal the High Court—

(a) may make such orders as may be necessary to give effect to its determination of the appeal; and

(b) may also make such incidental or consequential orders as appear to it to be just.

(2) Any order of the High Court made on an appeal under this section (other than one directing that an application be re-heard by a magistrates' court) shall, for the purposes of subsections (4) to (6) of section 12 above, be treated as if it were an order of the magistrates' court from which the appeal was brought and not an order of the High Court.

(3) Subsections (6) and (7) of section 10 above shall apply for the purposes of subsection (1) above as they apply for the purposes of subsection (1)(a) of that section.

13A   Parental compensation orders

(1) A magistrates' court may make an order under this section (a 'parental compensation order') if on the application of a local authority it is satisfied, on the civil standard of proof—

(a) that the condition mentioned in subsection (2) below is fulfilled with respect to a child under the age of 10; and

(b) that it would be desirable to make the order in the interests of preventing a repetition of the behaviour in question.

(2) The condition is that the child has taken, or caused loss of or damage to, property in the course of—

(a) committing an act which, if he had been aged 10 or over, would have constituted an offence; or

(b) acting in a manner that caused or was likely to cause harassment, alarm or distress to one or more persons not of the same household as himself.

(3) A parental compensation order is an order which requires any person specified in the order who is a parent or guardian of the child (other than a local authority) to pay compensation of an amount specified in the order to any person or persons specified in the order who is, or are, affected by the taking of the property or its loss or damage.

(4) The amount of compensation specified may not exceed £5,000 in all.

. . .

13B   Parental compensation orders: the compensation

(1) When specifying the amount of compensation for the purposes of section 13A(3) above, the magistrates' court shall take into account—

(a) the value of the property taken or damaged, or whose loss was caused, by the child;

(b) any further loss which flowed from the taking of or damage to the property, or from its loss;

(c) whether the child, or any parent or guardian of his, has already paid any compensation for the property (and if so, how much);

(d) whether the child, or any parent or guardian of his, has already made any reparation (and if so, what it consisted of);

(e) the means of those to be specified in the order as liable to pay the compensation, so far as the court can ascertain them;

(f) whether there was any lack of care on the part of the person affected by the taking of the property or its loss or damage which made it easier for the child to take or damage the property or to cause its loss.

. . .

13C   Parental compensation orders: supplemental

(1) Before deciding whether or not to make a parental compensation order in favour of any person, the magistrates' court shall take into account the views of that person about whether a parental compensation order should be made in his favour.

(2) Before making a parental compensation order, the magistrates' court shall obtain and consider information about the child's family circumstances and the likely effect of the order on those circumstances.

. . .

14   Local child curfew schemes

(1) A local authority or a chief officer of police may make a scheme (a 'local child curfew scheme') for enabling the authority or (as the case may be) the officer—

(a) subject to and in accordance with the provisions of the scheme; and

(b) if, after such consultation as is required by the scheme, the authority or (as the case may be) the officer considers it necessary to do so for the purpose of maintaining order,

to give a notice imposing, for a specified period (not exceeding 90 days), a ban to which subsection (2) below applies.

(2) This subsection applies to a ban on children of specified ages (under 16) being in a public place within a specified area—

(a) during specified hours (between 9 pm, and 6 am); and

(b) otherwise than under the effective control of a parent or a responsible person aged 18 or over.

(3) Before making a local child curfew scheme, a local authority shall consult—

(a) every chief officer of police any part of whose police area lies within its area; and

(b) such other persons or bodies as it considers appropriate.

(3A) Before making a local child curfew scheme, a chief officer of police shall consult—

(a) every local authority any part of whose area lies within the area to be specified; and

(b) such other persons or bodies as he considers appropriate.

(4) A local child curfew scheme shall, if made by a local authority, be made under the common seal of the authority.

(4A) A local child curfew scheme shall not have effect until it is confirmed by the Secretary of State.

(5) The Secretary of State—

(a) may confirm, or refuse to confirm, a local child curfew scheme submitted under this section for confirmation; and

(b) may fix the date on which such a scheme is to come into operation;

and if no date is so fixed, the scheme shall come into operation at the end of the period of one month beginning with the date of its confirmation.

(6) A notice given under a local child curfew scheme (a 'curfew notice') may specify different hours in relation to children of different ages.

(7) A curfew notice shall be given—

(a) by posting the notice in some conspicuous place or places within the specified area; and

(b) in such other manner, if any, as appears to the local authority or (as the case may be) the chief officer of police to be desirable for giving publicity to the notice.

(8) In this section—

'local authority' means—

(a) in relation to England, the council of a district or London borough, the Common Council of the City of London, the Council of the Isle of Wight and the Council of the Isles of Scilly;

(b) in relation to Wales, the council of a county or county borough; 'public place' has the same meaning as in Part II of the Public Order Act 1986.

15 Contravention of curfew notices

(1) Subsections (2) and (3) below apply where a constable has reasonable cause to believe that a child is in contravention of a ban imposed by a curfew notice.

(2) The constable shall, as soon as practicable, inform the local authority for the area that the child has contravened the ban.

(3) The constable may remove the child to the child's place of residence unless he has reasonable cause to believe that the child would, if removed to that place, be likely to suffer significant harm.

16 Removal of truants to designated premises etc.

(1) This section applies where a local authority—

(a) designates premises in a police area ('designated premises') as premises to which children and young persons of compulsory school age may be removed under this section; and

(b) notifies the chief officer of police for that area of the designation.

(2) A police officer of or above the rank of superintendent may direct that the powers conferred on a constable by subsection (3) below—

　　(a) shall be exercisable as respects any area falling within the police area and specified in the direction; and

　　(b) shall be so exercisable during a period so specified; and references in that subsection to a specified area and a specified period shall be construed accordingly.

(3) If a constable has reasonable cause to believe that a child or young person found by him in a public place in a specified area during a specified period—

　　(a) is of compulsory school age; and

　　(b) is absent from a school without lawful authority, the constable may remove the child or young person to designated premises, or to the school from which he is so absent.

(3A) Subsection (2) shall have effect in relation to The British Transport Police Force; and for that purpose the reference to any area falling within the police area shall be treated as a reference to any area in a place specified in section 31(1)(a) to (f) of the Railways and Transport Safety Act 2003.

(4) A child's or young person's absence from a school shall be taken to be without lawful authority unless it falls within subsection (3) (leave, sickness, unavoidable cause or day set apart for religious observance) of section 444 of the Education Act 1996.

(5) In this section—

'local authority' means—

　　(a) in relation to England, a county council, a district council whose district does not form part of an area that has a county council, a London borough council or the Common Council of the City of London;

　　(b) in relation to Wales, a county council or a county borough council;

'public place' has the same meaning as in section 14 above;

'school' has the same meaning as in the Education Act 1996.

Miscellaneous and supplemental

18　Interpretation etc. of Chapter I

(1) In this Chapter—

'anti-social behaviour order' has the meaning given by section 1(4) above;

'chief officer of police' has the meaning given by section 101(1) of the Police Act 1996;

'child safety order' has the meaning given by section 11(1) above;

'curfew notice' has the meaning given by section 14(6) above;

'individual support order' has the meaning given by section 1AA(2) above;

'local child curfew scheme' has the meaning given by section 14(1) above;

'parental compensation order' has the meaning given by section 13A(1) above;

'parenting order' has the meaning given by section 8(4) above;

'police area' has the meaning given by section 1(2) of the Police Act 1996;

'police authority' has the meaning given by section 101(1) of that Act;

'responsible officer'—

　　(za) in relation to an individual support order, has the meaning given by section 1AA(10) above;

　　(a) in relation to a parenting order, has the meaning given by section 8(8) above;

　　(b) in relation to a child safety order, has the meaning given by section 11(8) above;

'serious harm' shall be construed in accordance with section 224 of the Criminal Justice Act 2003;

'sex offender order' has the meaning given by section 2(3) above.

(3) Where directions under a parenting order are to be given by an officer of a local probation board, the officer of a local probation board shall be an officer appointed for or assigned to the local justice area area within which it appears to the court that the child or, as the case may be, the parent resides or will reside.

(4) Where the supervision under a child safety order is to be provided, or directions under an individual support order or a parenting order are to be given, by—

    (a) a social worker of a local authority; or

    (b) a member of a youth offending team,

the social worker or member shall be a social worker of, or a member of a youth offending team established by, the local authority within whose area it appears to the court that the child, defendant or parent, as the case may be, resides or will reside,

(5) For the purposes of this Chapter the Inner Temple and the Middle Temple form part of the City of London.

. . .

Access to Justice Act 1999
(1999 c. 22)

PART I   LEGAL SERVICES COMMISSION

Commission

1   Legal Services Commission

(1) There shall be a body known as the Legal Services Commission (in this Part referred to as 'the Commission').

(2) The Commission shall have the functions relating to—

    (a) the Community Legal Service, and

    (b) the Criminal Defence Service,

which are conferred or imposed on it by the provisions of this Act or any other enactment.

(3) The Commission shall consist of—

    (a) not fewer than seven members, and

    (b) not more than twelve members;

but the Secretary of State may by order substitute for either or both of the numbers for the time being specified in paragraphs (a) and (b) such other number or numbers as he thinks appropriate.

. . .

Community Legal Service

4   Community Legal Service

(1) The Commission shall establish, maintain and develop a service known as the Community Legal Service for the purpose of promoting the availability to individuals of services of the descriptions specified in subsection (2) and, in particular, for securing (within the resources made available, and priorities set, in accordance with this Part) that individuals have access to services that effectively meet their needs.

(2) The descriptions of services referred to in subsection (1) are—

    (a) the provision of general information about the law and legal system and the availability of legal services,

    (b) the provision of help by the giving of advice as to how the law applies in particular circumstances,

    (c) the provision of help in preventing, or settling or otherwise resolving, disputes about legal rights and duties,

    (d) the provision of help in enforcing decisions by which such disputes are resolved, and

    (e) the provision of help in relation to legal proceedings not relating to disputes.

. . .

6 Services which may be funded

(1) The Commission shall set priorities in its funding of services as part of the Community Legal Service and the priorities shall be set—

(a) in accordance with any directions given by the Secretary of State, and

(b) after taking into account the need for services of the descriptions specified in section 4(2).

(6) The Commission may not fund as part of the Community Legal Service any of the services specified in Schedule 2.

. . .

7 Individuals for whom services may be funded

(1) The Commission may only fund services for an individual as part of the Community Legal Service if his financial resources are such that, under regulations, he is an individual for whom they may be so funded.

(2) Regulations may provide that, in prescribed circumstances and subject to any prescribed conditions, services of a prescribed description may be so funded for individuals without reference to their financial resources.

(3) Regulations under this section may include provision requiring the furnishing of information.

8 Code about provision of funded services

(1) The Commission shall prepare a code setting out the criteria according to which it is to decide whether to fund (or continue to fund) services as part of the Community Legal Service for an individual for whom they may be so funded and, if so, what services are to be funded for him.

(2) In settling the criteria to be set out in the code the Commission shall consider the extent to which they ought to reflect the following factors—

(a) the likely cost of funding the services and the benefit which may be obtained by their being provided,

(b) the availability of sums in the Community Legal Service Fund for funding the services and (having regard to present and likely future demands on that Fund) the appropriateness of applying them to fund the services,

(c) the importance of the matters in relation to which the services would be provided for the individual,

(d) the availability to the individual of services not funded by the Commission and the likelihood of his being able to avail himself of them,

(e) if the services are sought by the individual in relation to a dispute, the prospects of his success in the dispute,

(f) the conduct of the individual in connection with services funded as part of the Community Legal Service (or an application for funding) or in, or in connection with, any proceedings,

(g) the public interest, and

(h) such other factors as the Secretary of State may by order require the Commission to consider.

(3) The criteria set out in the code shall reflect the principle that in many family disputes mediation will be more appropriate than court proceedings.

(4) The code shall seek to secure that, where more than one description of service is available, the service funded is that which (in all the circumstances) is the most appropriate having regard to the criteria set out in the code.

. . .

10 Terms of provision of funded services

(1) An individual for whom services are funded by the Commission as part of the Community Legal Service shall not be required to make any payment in respect of the services except where regulations otherwise provide.

(2) Regulations may provide that, in prescribed circumstances, an individual for whom services are so funded shall—

(a) pay a fee of such amount as is fixed by or determined under the regulations,

(b) if his financial resources are, or relevant conduct is, such as to make him liable to do so under the regulations, pay the cost of the services or make a contribution in respect of the cost of the services of such amount as is so fixed or determined, or

(c) if the services relate to a dispute and he has agreed to make a payment (which may exceed the cost of the services) only in specified circumstances, make in those circumstances a payment of the amount agreed, or determined in the manner agreed, by him;

and in paragraph (b) 'relevant conduct' means conduct in connection with the services (or any application for their funding) or in, or in connection with, any proceedings in relation to which they are provided.

(3) The regulations may include provision for any amount payable in accordance with the regulations to be payable by periodical payments or one or more capital sums, or both.

(4) The regulations may also include provision for the payment by an individual of interest (on such terms as may be prescribed) in respect of—

(a) any loan made to him by the Commission as part of the Community Legal Service,

(b) any payment in respect of the cost of services required by the regulations to be made by him later than the time when the services are provided, or

(c) so much of any payment required by the regulations to be made by him which remains unpaid after the time when it is required to be paid.

(5) The regulations shall include provision for the repayment to an individual of any payment made by him in excess of his liability under the regulations.

(6) The regulations may—

(a) include provision requiring the furnishing of information, and

(b) make provision for the determination of the cost of services for the purposes of the regulations.

(7) Except so far as regulations otherwise provide, where services have been funded by the Commission for an individual as part of the Community Legal Service—

(a) sums expended by the Commission in funding the services (except to the extent that they are recovered under section 11), and

(b) other sums payable by the individual by virtue of regulations under this section,

shall constitute a first charge on any property recovered or preserved by him (whether for himself or any other person) in any proceedings or in any compromise or settlement of any dispute in connection with which the services were provided.

(8) Regulations may make provision about the charge, including—

(a) provision as to whether it is in favour of the Commission or the body or person by whom the services were provided, and

(b) provision about its enforcement.

11 Costs in funded cases

(1) Except in prescribed circumstances, costs ordered against an individual in relation to any proceedings or part of proceedings funded for him shall not exceed the amount (if any) which is a reasonable one for him to pay having regard to all the circumstances including—

(a) the financial resources of all the parties to the proceedings, and

(b) their conduct in connection with the dispute to which the proceedings relate;

and for this purpose proceedings, or a part of proceedings, are funded for an individual if services relating to the proceedings or part are funded for him by the Commission as part of the Community Legal Service.

(2) In assessing for the purposes of subsection (1) the financial resources of an individual for whom services are funded by the Commission as part of the Community Legal Service, his clothes and household furniture and the tools and implements of his trade shall not be taken into account, except so far as may be prescribed.

(3) Subject to subsections (1) and (2), regulations may make provision about costs in relation to proceedings in which services are funded by the Commission for any of the parties as part of the Community Legal Service.

(4) The regulations may, in particular, make provision—

(a) specifying the principles to be applied in determining the amount of any costs which may be awarded against a party for whom services are funded by the Commission as part of the Community Legal Service,

(b) limiting the circumstances in which, or extent to which, an order for costs may be enforced against such a party,

(c) as to the cases in which, and extent to which, such a party may be required to give security for costs and the manner in which it is to be given,

(d) requiring the payment by the Commission of the whole or part of any costs incurred by a party for whom services are not funded by the Commission as part of the Community Legal Service,

(e) specifying the principles to be applied in determining the amount of any costs which may be awarded to a party for whom services are so funded,

(f) requiring the payment to the Commission, or the person or body by which the services were provided, of the whole or part of any sum awarded by way of costs to such a party, and

(g) as to the court, tribunal or other person or body by whom the amount of any costs is to be determined and the extent to which any determination of that amount is to be final.

. . .

Supplementary

. . .

21   Misrepresentation etc.

(1) Any person who—

(a) intentionally fails to comply with any requirement imposed by virtue of this Part as to the information to be furnished by him, or

(b) in furnishing any information required by virtue of this Part makes any statement or representation which he knows or believes to be false,

shall be guilty of an offence.

(2) A person guilty of an offence under subsection (1) is liable on summary conviction to—

(a) a fine not exceeding level 4 on the standard scale, or

(b) imprisonment for a term not exceeding 51 weeks, or to both.

(3) Proceedings in respect of an offence under subsection (1) may (despite anything in the Magistrates' Courts Act 1980) be brought at any time within the period of six months beginning with the date on which evidence sufficient in the opinion of the prosecutor to justify a prosecution comes to his knowledge.

(4) But subsection (3) does not authorise the commencement of proceedings for an offence at a time more than two years after the date on which the offence was committed.

(5) A county court shall have jurisdiction to hear and determine any action brought by the Commission to recover loss sustained by reason of—

(a) the failure of any person to comply with any requirement imposed by virtue of this Part as to the information to be furnished by him, or

(b) a false statement or false representation made by any person in furnishing any information required by virtue of this Part.

22 Position of service providers and other parties etc.

(1) Except as expressly provided by regulations, the fact that services provided for an individual are or could be funded by the Commission as part of the Community Legal Service or Criminal Defence Service shall not affect—

(a) the relationship between that individual and the person by whom they are provided or any privilege arising out of that relationship, or

(b) any right which that individual may have to be indemnified in respect of expenses incurred by him by any other person.

(2) A person who provides services funded by the Commission as part of the Community Legal Service or Criminal Defence Service shall not take any payment in respect of the services apart from—

(a) that made by way of that funding, and

(b) any authorised by the Commission to be taken.

. . .

(4) Except as expressly provided by regulations, any rights conferred by or by virtue of this Part on an individual for whom services are funded by the Commission as part of the Community Legal Service or Criminal Defence Service in relation to any proceedings shall not affect—

(a) the rights or liabilities of other parties to the proceedings, or

(b) the principles on which the discretion of any court or tribunal is normally exercised.

. . .

26 Interpretation

In this Part—

'the Commission' means the Legal Services Commission,

'the Community Legal Service Fund' has the meaning given by section 5(1),

'criminal proceedings' has the meaning given in section 12(2),

'prescribed' means prescribed by regulations and 'prescribe' shall be construed accordingly,

'regulations' means regulations made by the Secretary of State, and

'representation' means representation for the purposes of proceedings and includes the assistance which is usually given by a representative in the steps preliminary or incidental to any proceedings and, subject to any time limits which may be prescribed, advice and assistance as to any appeal.

. . .

SCHEDULE 2

COMMUNITY LEGAL SERVICE: EXCLUDED SERVICES

The services which may not be funded as part of the Community Legal Service are as follows.

1. Services consisting of the provision of help (beyond the provision of general information about the law and the legal system and the availability of legal services) in relation to—

(a) allegations of negligently caused injury, death or damage to property, apart from allegations relating to clinical negligence,

. . .

(d) the making of wills,

(e) matters of trust law,

(ea) the creation of lasting powers of attorney under the Mental Capacity Act 2005, (eb) the making of advance decisions under that Act,

. . .

2. Advocacy in any proceedings except—
(1) proceedings in—
- (a) the House of Lords in its judicial capacity,
- (b) the Judicial Committee of the Privy Council in the exercise of its jurisdiction under the Government of Wales Act 1998, the Scotland Act 1998 or the Northern Ireland Act 1998,
- (c) the Court of Appeal,
- (d) the High Court,
- (e) any county court,
- (f) the Employment Appeal Tribunal,
- (g) any Mental Health Review Tribunal,
- (h) the Immigration Appeal Tribunal or before an adjudicator,
- (ha) the Special Immigration Appeals Commission, or
- (i) the Proscribed Organisations Appeal Commission
(2) proceedings in the Crown Court—
- (a) for the variation or discharge of an order under section 5 of the Protection from Harassment Act 1997,
- (b) which relate to an order under section 10 of the Crime and Disorder Act 1998,

. . .

(3) proceedings in a magistrates' court—
- (a) under section 43 or 47 of the National Assistance Act 1948, section 22 of the Maintenance Orders Act 1950, section 4 of the Maintenance Orders Act 1958 or section 106 of the Social Security Administration Act 1992,
- (b) under Part I of the Maintenance Orders (Reciprocal Enforcement) Act 1972 relating to a maintenance order made by a court of a country outside the United Kingdom,
- (c) in relation to an application for leave of the court to remove a child from a person's custody under section 36 of the Adoption and Children Act 2002 or in which the making of a placement order or adoption order (within the meaning of the Adoption and Children Act 2002) or an order under section 41 or 84 of that Act is opposed by any party to the proceedings,
- (d) for or in relation to an order under Part I of the Domestic Proceedings and Magistrates' Courts Act 1978 or Schedule 6 to the Civil Partnership Act 2004,
- (da) under section 55A of the Family Law Act 1986 (declarations of parentage),
- (e) under the Children Act 1989,
- (f) under section 30 of the Human Fertilisation and Embryology Act 1990,
- (g) under section 20 of the Child Support Act 1991,
- (h) under Part IV of the Family Law Act 1996,
- (i) for the variation or discharge of an order under section 5 of the Protection from Harassment Act 1997,
- (j) under section 8 or 11 of the Crime and Disorder Act 1998,

. . .

(4) proceedings before any person to whom a case is referred (in whole or in part) in any proceedings within paragraphs (1) to (3).

Powers of Criminal Courts (Sentencing) Act 2000
(2000 c. 6)

...

PART IV   COMMUNITY ORDERS AND REPARATION ORDERS

CHAPTER I   COMMUNITY ORDERS: GENERAL PROVISIONS

...

Exclusion orders

40A   Exclusion orders

(1) Where a person aged under 16 is convicted of an offence, the court by or before which he is convicted may (subject to sections 148, 150 and 156 of the Criminal Justice Act 2003) make an order prohibiting him from entering a place specified in the order for a period so specified of not more than three months.

(2) An order under subsection (1) above is in this Act referred to as an 'exclusion order'.

(3) An exclusion order—

(a) may provide for the prohibition to operate only during the periods specified in the order;

(b) may specify different places for different periods or days.

(5) The requirements in an exclusion order shall, as far as practicable, be such as to avoid—

(a) any conflict with the offender's religious beliefs or with the requirements of any other youth community order to which he may be subject; and

(b) any interference with the times, if any, at which he normally works or attends school or any other educational establishment.

(6) An exclusion order shall include provision for making a person responsible for monitoring the offender's whereabouts during the periods when the prohibition operates; and a person who is made so responsible shall be of a description specified in an order made by the Secretary of State.

...

(12) In this section, 'place' includes an area.

...

PART VI   FINANCIAL PENALTIES AND ORDERS

...

Young offenders

137   Power to order parent or guardian to pay fine, costs, compensation or surcharge

(1) Where—

(a) a child or young person (that is to say, any person aged under 18) is convicted of any offence for the commission of which a fine or costs may be imposed or a compensation order may be made, and

(b) the court is of the opinion that the case would best be met by the imposition of a fine or costs or the making of such an order, whether with or without any other punishment,

the court shall order that the fine, compensation or costs awarded be paid by the parent or guardian of the child or young person instead of by the child or young person himself, unless the court is satisfied—

(i)   that the parent or guardian cannot be found; or

(ii) that it would be unreasonable to make an order for payment, having regard to the circumstances of the case.

(1A) Where but for this subsection a court would order a child or young person to pay a surcharge under section 161A of the Criminal Justice Act 2003, the court shall order that the surcharge be paid by the parent or guardian of the child or young person instead of by the child or young person himself, unless the court is satisfied—

> (a) that the parent or guardian cannot be found; or
> (b) that it would be unreasonable to make an order for payment, having regard to the circumstances of the case.

(2) Where but for this subsection a court would impose a fine on a child or young person under—

> (b) paragraph 2(1)(a) of Schedule 5 to this Act (breach of attendance centre order or attendance centre rules),
> (c) paragraph 2(2)(a) of Schedule 7 to this Act (breach of supervision order),
> (d) paragraph 2(2)(a) of Schedule 8 to this Act (breach of action plan order or reparation order),
> (e) section 104(3)(b) above (breach of requirements of supervision under a detention and training order), or
> (f) section 4(3)(b) of the Criminal Justice and Public Order Act 1994 (breach of requirements of supervision under a secure training order),

the court shall order that the fine be paid by the parent or guardian of the child or young person instead of by the child or young person himself, unless the court is satisfied—

> (i) that the parent or guardian cannot be found; or
> (ii) that it would be unreasonable to make an order for payment, having regard to the circumstances of the case.

(3) In the case of a young person aged 16 or over, subsections (1) to (2) above shall have effect as if, instead of imposing a duty, they conferred a power to make such an order as is mentioned in those subsections.

(4) Subject to subsection (5) below, no order shall be made under this section without giving the parent or guardian an opportunity of being heard.

(5) An order under this section may be made against a parent or guardian who, having been required to attend, has failed to do so.

(6) A parent or guardian may appeal to the Crown Court against an order under this section made by a magistrates' court.

(7) A parent or guardian may appeal to the Court of Appeal against an order under this section made by the Crown Court, as if he had been convicted on indictment and the order were a sentence passed on his conviction.

(8) In relation to a child or young person for whom a local authority have parental responsibility and who—

> (a) is in their care, or
> (b) is provided with accommodation by them in the exercise of any functions (in particular those under the Children Act 1989) which are social services functions within the meaning of the Local Authority Social Services Act 1970,

references in this section to his parent or guardian shall be construed as references to that authority.

(9) In subsection (8) above 'local authority' and 'parental responsibility' have the same meanings as in the Children Act 1989.

138   Fixing of fine, compensation or surcharge to be paid by parent or guardian

(1) For the purposes of any order under section 137 above made against the parent or guardian of a child or young person—

> (za) Subsection (3) of section 161A of the Criminal Justice Act 2003 (surcharges) and subsection (4A) of section 164 of that Act (fixing of fines) shall have effect as if any reference in those subsections to the offender's means were a reference to those of the parent or guardian;
> (a) section 164 of the Criminal Justice Act 2003 (fixing of fines) shall have effect as if any reference in subsections (1) to (4) to the financial circumstances of the offender were a reference to the financial circumstances of the parent or guardian, and as if subsection (5) were omitted;
> (b) section 130(11) above (determination of compensation order) shall have effect as if any reference to the means of the person against whom the compensation

order is made were a reference to the financial circumstances of the parent or guardian; and

(c) section 130(12) above (preference to be given to compensation if insufficient means to pay both compensation and a fine) shall have effect as if the reference to the offender were a reference to the parent or guardian;

but in relation to an order under section 137 made against a local authority this subsection has effect subject to subsection (2) below.

(2) For the purposes of any order under section 137 above made against a local authority, section 164(1) of the Criminal Justice Act 2003 and section 130(11) above shall not apply.

(3) For the purposes of any order under section 137 above, where the parent or guardian of an offender who is a child or young person—

(a) has failed to comply with an order under section 136 above, or

(b) has otherwise failed to co-operate with the court in its inquiry into his financial circumstances,

and the court considers that it has insufficient information to make a proper determination of the parent's or guardian's financial circumstances, it may make such determination as it thinks fit.

(4) Where a court has, in fixing the amount of a fine, determined the financial circumstances of a parent or guardian under subsection (3) above, subsections (2) to (4) of section 165 of the Criminal Justice Act 2003 (remission of fines) shall (so far as applicable) have effect as they have effect in the case mentioned in section 165(1), but as if the reference in section 165(2) to the offender's financial circumstances were a reference to the financial circumstances of the parent or guardian.

(5) In this section 'local authority' has the same meaning as in the Children Act 1989.

. . .

PART VII   FURTHER POWERS OF COURTS

Young offenders

150   Binding over of parent or guardian

(1) Where a child or young person (that is to say, any person aged under 18) is convicted of an offence, the powers conferred by this section shall be exercisable by the court by which he is sentenced for that offence, and where the offender is aged under 16 when sentenced it shall be the duty of that court—

(a) to exercise those powers if it is satisfied, having regard to the circumstances of the case, that their exercise would be desirable in the interests of preventing the commission by him of further offences; and

(b) if it does not exercise them, to state in open court that it is not satisfied as mentioned in paragraph (a) above and why it is not so satisfied;

but this subsection has effect subject to section 19(5) above and paragraph 13(5) of Schedule 1 to this Act (cases where referral orders made or extended).

(2) The powers conferred by this section are as follows—

(a) with the consent of the offender's parent or guardian, to order the parent or guardian to enter into a recognizance to take proper care of him and exercise proper control over him; and

(b) if the parent or guardian refuses consent and the court considers the refusal unreasonable, to order the parent or guardian to pay a fine not exceeding £1,000;

and where the court has passed a community sentence on the offender, it may include in the recognizance a provision that the offender's parent or guardian ensure that the offender complies with the requirements of that sentence.

(3) An order under this section shall not require the parent or guardian to enter into a recognizance for an amount exceeding £1,000.

(4) An order under this section shall not require the parent or guardian to enter into a recognizance—

> (a) for a period exceeding three years; or
>
> (b) where the offender will attain the age of 18 in a period shorter than three years, for a period exceeding that shorter period.

. . .

(8) A parent or guardian may appeal to the Crown Court against an order under this section made by a magistrates' court.

(9) A parent or guardian may appeal to the Court of Appeal against an order under this section made by the Crown Court, as if he had been convicted on indictment and the order were a sentence passed on his conviction.

(10) A court may vary or revoke an order made by it under this section if, on the application of the parent or guardian, it appears to the court, having regard to any change in the circumstances since the order was made, to be in the interests of justice to do so.

(11) For the purposes of this section, taking 'care' of a person includes giving him protection and guidance and 'control' includes discipline.

. . .

Care Standards Act 2000
(2000 c. 14)

PART I   INTRODUCTORY

Preliminary

1   Children's homes

(1) Subsections (2) to (6) have effect for the purposes of this Act.

(2) An establishment is a children's home (subject to the following provisions of this section) if it provides care and accommodation wholly or mainly for children.

(3) An establishment is not a children's home merely because a child is cared for and accommodated there by a parent or relative of his or by a foster parent.

(4) An establishment is not a children's home if it is—

> (a) a health service hospital;
>
> (b) an independent hospital or an independent clinic; or
>
> (c) a residential family centre,

or if it is of a description excepted by regulations.

(5) Subject to subsection (6), an establishment is not a children's home if it is a school.

(6) A school is a children's home at any time if at that time accommodation is provided for children at the school and either—

> (a) in each year that fell within the period of two years ending at that time, accommodation was provided for children, either at the school or under arrangements made by the proprietor of the school, for more than 295 days; or
>
> (b) it is intended to provide accommodation for children, either at the school or under arrangements made by the proprietor of the school, for more than 295 days in any year;

and in this subsection 'year' means a period of twelve months.

But accommodation shall not for the purposes of paragraph (a) be regarded as provided to children for a number of days unless there is at least one child to whom it is provided for that number of days; and paragraph (b) shall be construed accordingly.

(7) For the purposes of this section a person is a foster parent in relation to a child if—

    (a) he is a local authority foster parent in relation to the child;

    (b) he is a foster parent with whom a child has been placed by a voluntary organisation under section 59(1)(a) of the 1989 Act; or

    (c) he fosters the child privately.

. . .

4   Other basic definitions

(1) This section has effect for the purposes of this Act.

. . .

(4) 'Fostering agency' means, subject to subsection (6)—

    (a) an undertaking which consists of or includes discharging functions of local authorities in connection with the placing of children with foster parents; or

    (b) a voluntary organisation which places children with foster parents under section 59(1) of the 1989 Act.

. . .

(6) The definitions in subsections (2) to (5) do not include any description of establishment, undertaking or organisation excepted from those definitions by regulations.

(7) 'Voluntary adoption agency' means an adoption society within the meaning of the Adoption and Children Act 2002 which is a voluntary organisation within the meaning of that Act.

(7A) 'Adoption support agency' has the meaning given by section 8 of the Adoption and Children Act 2002.

(8) Below in this Act—

    (a) any reference to a description of establishment is a reference to a children's home, a children's home providing accommodation for the purpose of restricting liberty, an independent hospital, an independent hospital in which treatment or nursing (or both) are provided for persons liable to be detained under the Mental Health Act 1983, an independent clinic, a care home or a residential family centre;

    (b) a reference to any establishment is a reference to an establishment of any of those descriptions.

(9) Below in this Act—

    (a) any reference to a description of agency is a reference to an independent medical agency, a domiciliary care agency, a nurses agency, a fostering agency, a voluntary adoption agency or an adoption support agency;

    (b) a reference to any agency is a reference to an agency of any of those descriptions.

Registration authorities

5   Registration authorities

For the purposes of this Act—

    (a) the registration authority in relation to England is

        (i) the CHAI, in the case of independent hospitals, independent clinics and independent medical agencies;

        (ii) the CSCI, in the case of children's homes, care homes, residential family centres, domiciliary care agencies, nurses agencies, fostering agencies, voluntary adoption agencies and adoption support agencies;

    (b) the registration authority in relation to Wales is the National Assembly for Wales (referred to in this Act as 'the Assembly').

. . .

6   National Care Standards Commission

(1) There shall be a body corporate, to be known as the National Care Standards Commission (referred to in this Act as 'the Commission'), which shall exercise in relation to England the functions conferred on it by or under this Act or any other enactment.

. . .

PART II   ESTABLISHMENTS AND AGENCIES

Registration

11   Requirement to register

(1) Any person who carries on or manages an establishment or agency of any description without being registered under this Part in respect of it (as an establishment or, as the case may be, agency of that description) shall be guilty of an offence.

(2) Where the activities of an agency are carried on from two or more branches, each of those branches shall be treated as a separate agency for the purposes of this Part.

(3) References in subsections (1) and (2) to an agency do not include a reference to a voluntary adoption agency.

...

Regulations and standards

22   Regulation of establishments and agencies

(1) Regulations may impose in relation to establishments and agencies any requirements which the appropriate Minister thinks fit for the purposes of this Part and may in particular make any provision such as is mentioned in subsection (2), (7) or (8).

(2) Regulations may—

    (a) make provision as to the persons who are fit to carry on or manage an establishment or agency;

    (b) make provision as to the persons who are fit to work at an establishment or for the purposes of an agency;

    (c) make provision as to the fitness of premises to be used as an establishment or for the purposes of an agency;

    (d) make provision for securing the welfare of persons accommodated in an establishment or provided with services by an establishment, an independent medical agency or a domiciliary care agency;

    (e) make provision for securing the welfare of children placed, under section 23(2)(a) of the 1989 Act, by a fostering agency;

    (f) make provision as to the management and control of the operations of an establishment or agency;

    (g) make provision as to the numbers of persons, or persons of any particular type, working at an establishment or for the purposes of an agency;

    (h) make provision as to the management and training of such persons;

    (i) impose requirements as to the financial position of an establishment or agency;

    (j) make provision requiring the person carrying on an establishment or agency to appoint a manager in prescribed circumstances.

...

(5) Regulations under paragraph (d) of subsection (2) may, in particular, make provision—

    (a) as to the promotion and protection of the health of persons such as are mentioned in that paragraph;

    ...

    (c) as to the control, restraint and discipline of children accommodated in, or provided with services by, an establishment.

(6) Regulations under paragraph (e) of subsection (2) may, in particular, make provision—

    (a) as to the promotion and protection of the health of children such as are mentioned in that paragraph;

    (b) as to the control, restraint and discipline of such children.

(7) Regulations may make provision as to the conduct of establishments and agencies, and such regulations may in particular—

(a) make provision as to the facilities and services to be provided in establishments and by agencies;

...

(j) make provision requiring arrangements to be made by the person who carries on, or manages, an establishment or agency for dealing with complaints made by or on behalf of those seeking, or receiving, any of the services provided in the establishment or by the agency and requiring that person to take steps for publicising the arrangements;

...

(8) Regulations may make provision—

(b) imposing other requirements (in addition to those imposed by section 25 of the 1989 Act (use of accommodation for restricting liberty)) as to the placing of a child in accommodation provided for the purpose of restricting liberty, including a requirement to obtain the permission of any local authority who are looking after the child;

(c) as to the facilities which are to be provided for giving religious instruction to children in children's homes.

...

(10) References in this section to agencies do not include references to voluntary adoption agencies or adoption support agencies.

...

23   National minimum standards

(1) The appropriate Minister may prepare and publish statements of national minimum standards applicable to establishments or agencies.

(2) The appropriate Minister shall keep the standards set out in the statements under review and may publish amended statements whenever he considers it appropriate to do so.

(3) Before issuing a statement, or an amended statement which in the opinion of the appropriate Minister effects a substantial change in the standards, the appropriate Minister shall consult any persons he considers appropriate.

...

PART III   LOCAL AUTHORITY SERVICES

43   Introductory

(1) This section has effect for the purposes of this Part.

(2) 'Relevant functions', in relation to a local authority, means relevant adoption functions and relevant fostering functions.

(3) In relation to a local authority—

(a) 'relevant adoption functions' means functions under the Adoption and Children Act 2002 of making or participating in arrangements for the adoption of children or the provision of adoption support services (as defined in section 2(6) of the Adoption and Children Act 2002); and

(b) 'relevant fostering functions' means functions under section 23(2)(a) of the 1989 Act or regulations under any of paragraphs (a), (b) or (d) to (f) of paragraph 12 of Schedule 2 to that Act.

...

48   Regulation of the exercise of relevant fostering functions

(1) Regulations may make provision about the exercise by local authorities of relevant fostering functions, and may in particular make provision—

(a) as to the persons who are fit to work for local authorities in connection with the exercise of such functions;

(b) as to the fitness of premises to be used by local authorities in their exercise of such functions;

(c) as to the management and control of the operations of local authorities in their exercise of such functions;

(d) as to the numbers of persons, or persons of any particular type, working for local authorities in connection with the exercise of such functions;

(e) as to the management and training of such persons;

(f) as to the fees or expenses which may be paid to persons assisting local authorities in making decisions in the exercise of such functions.

(2) Regulations under subsection (1)(a) may, in particular, make provision for prohibiting persons from working for local authorities in such positions as may be prescribed unless they are registered in, or in a particular part of, one of the registers maintained under section 56(1).

49 National minimum standards

(1) Subsections (1), (2) and (3) of section 23 shall apply to local authorities in their exercise of relevant functions as they apply to establishments and agencies.

. . .

PART V   THE CHILDREN'S COMMISSIONER FOR WALES

72 Children's Commissioner for Wales

(1) There shall be an office of the Children's Commissioner for Wales or Comisiynydd Plant Cymru.

. . .

73 Review and monitoring of arrangements

(1) The Commissioner may review, and monitor the operation of, arrangements falling within subsection (2), (2A), (2B), (2C), (3) or (4) for the purpose of ascertaining whether, and to what extent, the arrangements are effective in safeguarding and promoting the rights and welfare of children—

(a) to or in respect of whom services are provided in Wales by, or on behalf of or under arrangements with, a person mentioned in Schedule 2B; or

(b) to or in respect of whom regulated children's services in Wales are provided.

(1A) The Commissioner may also assess the effect on such children of the failure of any person to make such arrangements.

(2) The arrangements falling within this subsection are the arrangements made by the providers of regulated children's services in Wales, or by the Assembly, for dealing with complaints or representations about such services made by or on behalf of children to whom such services are provided.

(2A) The arrangements falling within this subsection are the arrangements made by a person mentioned in Schedule 2B for dealing with complaints or representations made to the person by or on behalf of a child about services provided in Wales by the person to or in respect of the child.

(2B) The arrangements falling within this subsection are the arrangements made by a person providing services in Wales on behalf of, or under arrangements with, a person mentioned in Schedule 2B for dealing with complaints or representations made to the person by or on behalf of a child about a service which is so provided to or in respect of the child.

(2C) The arrangements falling within this subsection are the arrangements made by the Assembly for dealing with complaints or representations made by or on behalf of a child about a service which is provided in Wales to or in respect of the child by, or on behalf of or under arrangements with, a person mentioned in Schedule 2B (other than the Assembly).

(3) The arrangements falling within this subsection are arrangements made by the providers of regulated children's services in Wales, by the Assembly, or by another person

mentioned in Schedule 2B or subsection (2B) for ensuring that proper action is taken in response to any disclosure of information which may tend to show—

(a) that a criminal offence has been committed;

(b) that a person has failed to comply with any legal obligation to which he is subject;

(c) that the health and safety of any person has been endangered; or

(d) that information tending to show that any matter falling within one of the preceding paragraphs has been deliberately concealed,

in the course of or in connection with the provision of the services mentioned in subsection (3A).

(3A) The services are—

(a) in the case of a person mentioned in Schedule 2B, services provided in Wales by the person to or in respect of a child;

(b) in the case of a person mentioned in subsection (2B), services provided in Wales by the person to or in respect of a child on behalf of, or under arrangements with, a person mentioned in Schedule 2B;

(c) in the case of a provider of regulated children's services in Wales, those services.

(4) The arrangements falling within this subsection are arrangements made (whether by providers of regulated children's services in Wales, by the Assembly or by any other person) for making persons available—

(a) to represent the views and wishes of children—

(i) to or in respect of whom services are provided in Wales by, or on behalf of or under arrangements with, a person mentioned in Schedule 2B; or

(ii) to or in respect of whom regulated children's services in Wales are provided; or

(b) to provide such children with advice and support of any prescribed kind.

(5) Regulations may confer power on the Commissioner to require prescribed persons to provide any information which the Commissioner considers it necessary or expedient to have for the purposes of his functions under this section.

. . .

74 Examination of cases

(1) Regulations may, in connection with the Commissioner's functions under this Part, make provision for the examination by the Commissioner of the cases of particular children to whom this Part applies.

. . .

(2) The regulations may include provision about—

(a) the types of case which may be examined;

(b) the circumstances in which an examination may be made;

(c) the procedure for conducting an examination, including provision about the representation of parties;

(d) the publication of reports following an examination.

(3) The regulations may make provision for—

(a) requiring persons to provide the Commissioner with information; or

(b) requiring persons who hold or are accountable for information to provide the Commissioner with explanations or other assistance,

for the purposes of an examination or for the purposes of determining whether any recommendation made in a report following an examination has been complied with.

(4) For the purposes mentioned in subsection (3), the Commissioner shall have the same powers as the High Court in respect of—

(a) the attendance and examination of witnesses (including the administration of oaths and affirmations and the examination of witnesses abroad); and

(b) the provision of information.

(5) No person shall be compelled for the purposes mentioned in subsection (3) to give any evidence or provide any information which he could not be compelled to give or provide in civil proceedings before the High Court.

(6) The regulations may make provision for the payment by the Commissioner of sums in respect of expenses or allowances to persons who attend or provide information for the purposes mentioned in subsection (3).

75 Obstruction etc.

(1) The Commissioner may certify an offence to the High Court where—

    (a) a person, without lawful excuse, obstructs him or any member of his staff in the exercise of any of his functions under regulations made by virtue of section 73(5) or 74; or

    (b) a person is guilty of any act or omission in relation to an examination under regulations made by virtue of section 74 which, if that examination were proceedings in the High Court, would constitute contempt of court.

(2) Where an offence is so certified the High Court may inquire into the matter; and after hearing—

    (a) any witnesses who may be produced against or on behalf of the person charged with the offence; and

    (b) any statement that may be offered in defence,

the High Court may deal with the person charged with the offence in any manner in which it could deal with him if he had committed the same offence in relation to the High Court.

. . .

76 Further functions

(1) Regulations may confer power on the Commissioner to assist a child to whom this Part applies—

    (a) in making a complaint or representation to or in respect of a provider of regulated children's services in Wales;

    (aa) in making a complaint or representation to or in respect of a person mentioned in Schedule 2B or section 73(2B); or

    (b) in any prescribed proceedings,

and in this subsection 'proceedings' includes a procedure of any kind and any prospective proceedings.

. . .

(2) For the purposes of subsection (1), assistance includes—

    (a) financial assistance; and

    (b) arranging for representation, or the giving of advice or assistance, by any person,

and the regulations may provide for assistance to be given on conditions, including (in the case of financial assistance) conditions requiring repayment in circumstances specified in the regulations.

(3) The Commissioner may, in connection with his functions under this Part, give advice and information to any person.

(4) Regulations may, in connection with the Commissioner's functions under this Part, confer further functions on him.

(5) The regulations may, in particular, include provision about the making of reports on any matter connected with any of his functions.

. . .

(6) Apart from identifying any person investigated, a report by the Commissioner shall not—

    (a) mention the name of any person; or

    (b) include any particulars which, in the opinion of the Commissioner, are likely to identify any person and can be omitted without impairing the effectiveness of the report, unless, after taking account of the public interest (as well as the interests of any person who made a complaint and other persons), the Commissioner considers it necessary for the report to mention his name or include such particulars.

(7) For the purposes of the law of defamation, the publication of any matter by the Commissioner in a report is absolutely privileged.

(8) The Commissioner or a person authorised by him may for the purposes of any function of the Commissioner under section 72B or 73 or subsection (4) of this section at any reasonable time—

  (a) enter any premises, other than a private dwelling, for the purposes of interviewing any child accommodated or cared for there; and

  (b) if the child consents, interview the child in private.

77 Restrictions

(1) This Part does not authorise the Commissioner to enquire into or report on any matter so far as it is the subject of legal proceedings before, or has been determined by, a court or tribunal.

(2) This Part does not authorise the Commissioner to exercise any function which by virtue of an enactment is also exercisable by a prescribed person.

78 Interpretation

(1) This Part applies to a child—

  (a) who is ordinarily resident in Wales;

  (b) to or in respect of whom services are provided in Wales by, or on behalf of or under arrangements with, a person mentioned in Schedule 2B; or

  (c) to or in respect of whom regulated children's services in Wales are provided.

(1A) Regulations may provide that, for the purposes of this Part of this Act, 'child' includes a person aged 18 or over who falls within subsection (1B).

(1B) A person falls within this subsection if he is a person to or in respect of whom services are provided in Wales by, or on behalf of or under arrangements with, a county council or county borough council in Wales by virtue of—

  (a) section 23C, 24, 24A or 24B of the Children Act 1989 (c. 41) (which provide for the continuing duties of such councils towards young persons); or

  (b) regulations made under section 23D of that Act (which may provide for the appointment of personal advisers for certain young persons).

(2) In this Part, 'regulated children's services in Wales' means any of the following services for the time being provided in respect of children—

  (a) services of a description provided by or in Part II undertakings, so far as provided in Wales;

  (b) services provided by local authorities in Wales in the exercise of relevant adoption functions or relevant fostering functions;

  (c) services of a description provided by persons registered under Part XA of the 1989 Act, so far as provided in Wales;

  (d) accommodation provided by schools or by an institution within the further education sector (as defined in section 91 of the Further and Higher Education Act 1992), so far as provided in Wales.

(3) For the purposes of this Part—

  (a) in the case of the services mentioned in subsection (2)(a), the person who carries on the Part II undertaking is to be treated as the provider of the services;

  (b) in the case of the services mentioned in subsection (2)(d), the relevant person (as defined in section 87 of the 1989 Act) is to be treated as the provider of the services.

(4) For the purposes of this section, an establishment or agency, and an undertaking of any other description, is a Part II undertaking if the provider of the services in question is for the time being required to be registered under that Part.

(5) Where the activities of an undertaking are carried on from two or more branches, each of those branches shall be treated as a separate undertaking for the purposes of this Part.

(6) Regulations may provide for the references to a child in subsection (1) to include references to a person (including a child) who was at any time (including a time before the commencement of this Part)—

    (a) a child ordinarily resident in Wales;

    (b) a child to or in respect of whom services were provided in Wales by, or on behalf of or under arrangements with, a person mentioned in Schedule 2B; or

    (c) a child to or in respect of whom regulated children's services in Wales were provided.

(7) In this Part—

'information' includes information recorded in any form;

'regulations' means regulations made by the Assembly.

(8) In this section, 'relevant adoption functions' and 'relevant fostering functions' have the same meanings as in Part III.

. . .

Carers and Disabled Children Act 2000
(2000 c. 16)

1 Right of carers to assessment

(1) If an individual aged 16 or over ('the carer')—

    (a) provides or intends to provide a substantial amount of care on a regular basis for another individual aged 18 or over ('the person cared for'); and

    (b) asks a local authority to carry out an assessment of his ability to provide and to continue to provide care for the person cared for,

the local authority must carry out such an assessment if it is satisfied that the person cared for is someone for whom it may provide or arrange for the provision of community care services

(2) For the purposes of such an assessment, the local authority may take into account, so far as it considers it to be material, an assessment under section 1(1) of the Carers (Recognition and Services) Act 1995.

(3) Subsection (1) does not apply if the individual provides or will provide the care in question—

    (a) by virtue of a contract of employment or other contract with any person; or

    (b) as a volunteer for a voluntary organisation.

(3A) An assessment under subsection (1) must include consideration of whether the carer—

    (a) works or wishes to work,

    (b) is undertaking, or wishes to undertake, education, training or any leisure activity.

(4) The Secretary of State (or, in relation to Wales, the National Assembly for Wales) may give directions as to the manner in which an assessment under subsection (1) is to be carried out or the form it is to take.

(5) Subject to any such directions, it is to be carried out in such manner, and is to take such form, as the local authority considers appropriate.

(6) In this section, 'voluntary organisation' has the same meaning as in the National Assistance Act 1948.

2 Services for carers

(1) The local authority must consider the assessment and decide—

    (a) whether the carer has needs in relation to the care which he provides or intends to provide;

(b) if so, whether they could be satisfied (wholly or partly) by services which the local authority may provide; and

(c) if they could be so satisfied, whether or not to provide services to the carer.

(2) The services referred to are any services which—

(a) the local authority sees fit to provide; and

(b) will in the local authority's view help the carer care for the person cared for,

and may take the form of physical help or other forms of support.

(3) A service, although provided to the carer—

(a) may take the form of a service delivered to the person cared for if it is one which, if provided to him instead of to the carer, could fall within community care services and they both agree it is to be so delivered; but

(b) if a service is delivered to the person cared for it may not, except in prescribed circumstances, include anything of an intimate nature.

(4) Regulations may make provision about what is, or is not, of an intimate nature for the purposes of subsection (3).

. . .

6   Assessments: persons with parental responsibility for disabled children

(1) If a person with parental responsibility for a disabled child—

(a) provides or intends to provide a substantial amount of care on a regular basis for the child; and

(b) asks a local authority to carry out an assessment of his ability to provide and to continue to provide care for the child,

the local authority must carry out such an assessment if it is satisfied that the child and his family are persons for whom it may provide or arrange for the provision of services under section 17 of the Children Act 1989 ('the 1989 Act').

(2) For the purposes of such an assessment, the local authority may take into account, so far as it considers it to be material, an assessment under section 1(2) of the Carers (Recognition and Services) Act 1995.

(2A) An assessment under subsection (1) must include consideration of whether the person with parental responsibility for the child—

(a) works or wishes to work,

(b) is undertaking, or wishes to undertake, education, training or any leisure activity.

(3) The Secretary of State (or, in relation to Wales, the National Assembly for Wales) may give directions as to the manner in which an assessment under subsection (1) is to be carried out or the form it is to take.

(4) Subject to any such directions, it is to be carried out in such manner, and is to take such form, as the local authority considers appropriate.

(5) The local authority must take the assessment into account when deciding what, if any, services to provide under section 17 of the 1989 Act.

(6) Terms used in this section have the same meaning as in Part III of the 1989 Act.

6A   Duty to inform carers of right to assessment

(1) Subsection (2) applies if it appears to a local authority that it would be required to carry out a carer's assessment on being asked to do so by—

(a) the carer, or

(b) a person with parental responsibility for a disabled child ('the responsible person').

(2) The local authority must inform the carer or, as appropriate, the responsible person that he may be entitled to a carer's assessment (but this is subject to subsections (3) and (4)).

(3) Subsection (2) does not apply in relation to the carer if the local authority has previously—

(a) carried out a carer's assessment for him in relation to the person cared for,

(b) informed him that he may be entitled to a carer's assessment in relation to the person cared for, or

(c) carried out an assessment of him under section 4(3) of the Community Care (Delayed Discharges etc.) Act 2003 in relation to the person cared for.

(4) Subsection (2) does not apply in relation to the responsible person if the local authority has previously carried out a carer's assessment for him in relation to the disabled child or informed him that he may be entitled to a carer's assessment in relation to the disabled child.

(5) In this section 'carer's assessment' means—

(a) in the case of the carer, an assessment under section 1 of his ability to provide and to continue to provide care for the person cared for,

(b) in the case of the responsible person, an assessment under section 6 of his ability to provide and to continue to provide care for the disabled child.

. . .

Trustee Act 2000

(2000 c. 29)

PART I   THE DUTY OF CARE

1   The duty of care

(1) Whenever the duty under this subsection applies to a trustee, he must exercise such care and skill as is reasonable in the circumstances, having regard in particular—

(a) to any special knowledge or experience that he has or holds himself out as having, and

(b) if he acts as trustee in the course of a business or profession, to any special knowledge or experience that it is reasonable to expect of a person acting in the course of that kind of business or profession.

(2) In this Act the duty under subsection (1) is called 'the duty of care'.

2   Application of duty of care

Schedule 1 makes provision about when the duty of care applies to a trustee.

. . .

PART III   ACQUISITION OF LAND

8   Power to acquire freehold and leasehold land

(1) A trustee may acquire freehold or leasehold land in the United Kingdom—

(a) as an investment,

(b) for occupation by a beneficiary, or

(c) for any other reason.

(2) 'Freehold or leasehold land' means—

(a) in relation to England and Wales, a legal estate in land,

and

. . .

(c) in relation to Northern Ireland, a legal estate in land, including land held under a fee farm grant.

(3) For the purpose of exercising his functions as a trustee, a trustee who acquires land under this section has all the powers of an absolute owner in relation to the land.

9   Restriction or exclusion of this Part etc.

The powers conferred by this Part are—

(a) in addition to powers conferred on trustees otherwise than by this Part, but

(b) subject to any restriction or exclusion imposed by the trust instrument or by any enactment or any provision of subordinate legislation.

10 Existing trusts

(1) This Part does not apply in relation to—

(a) a trust of property which consists of or includes land which (despite section 2 of the Trusts of Land and Appointment of Trustees Act 1996) is settled land,

. . .

(2) Subject to subsection (1), this Part applies in relation to trusts whether created before or after its commencement.

. . .

PART VI   MISCELLANEOUS AND SUPPLEMENTARY

. . .

35 Personal representatives

(1) Subject to the following provisions of this section, this Act applies in relation to a personal representative administering an estate according to the law as it applies to a trustee carrying out a trust for beneficiaries.

(2) For this purpose this Act is to be read with the appropriate modifications and in particular—

(a) references to the trust instrument are to be read as references to the will,

(b) references to a beneficiary or to beneficiaries, apart from the reference to a beneficiary in section 8(1)(b), are to be read as references to a person or the persons interested in the due administration of the estate, and

(c) the reference to a beneficiary in section 8(1)(b) is to be read as a reference to a person who under the will of the deceased or under the law relating to intestacy is beneficially interested in the estate.

. . .

SCHEDULES

Section 2   SCHEDULE 1

APPLICATION OF DUTY OF CARE

. . .

Acquisition of land

2. The duty of care applies to a trustee—

(a) when exercising the power under section 8 to acquire land;

(b) when exercising any other power to acquire land, however conferred;

(c) when exercising any power in relation to land acquired under a power mentioned in sub-paragraph (a) or (b).

. . .

Exclusion of duty of care

7. The duty of care does not apply if or in so far as it appears from the trust instrument that the duty is not meant to apply.

Children (Leaving Care) Act 2000
(2000 c. 35)

. . .

6 Exclusion from benefits

(1) No person is entitled to income-based jobseekers allowance under the Jobseekers Act 1995, or to income support or housing benefit under the Social Security Contributions and Benefits Act 1992, while he is a person to whom this section applies.

(2) Subject to subsection (3), this section applies to—

    (a) an eligible child for the purposes of paragraph 19B of Schedule 2 to the Children Act 1989;

    (b) a relevant child for the purposes of section 23A of that Act: and

    (c) any person of a description prescribed in regulations under subsection (4).

. . .

Criminal Justice and Court Services Act 2000
(2000 c. 43)

PART I   THE NEW SERVICES

. . .

CHAPTER II   CHILDREN AND FAMILY COURT ADVISORY AND SUPPORT SERVICE

11 Establishment of the Service

(1) There shall be a body corporate to be known as the Children and Family Court Advisory and Support Service (referred to in this Part as the Service) which is to exercise the functions conferred on it by virtue of this Act and any other enactment.

(2) Schedule 2 (which makes provision about the constitution of the Service, its powers and other matters relating to it) is to have effect.

(3) References in this Act or any other enactment to an officer of the Service are references to—

    (a) any member of the staff of the Service appointed under paragraph 5(1)(a) of that Schedule, and

    (b) any other individual exercising functions of an officer of the Service by virtue of section 13(2) or (4).

12 Principal functions of the Service

(1) In respect of family proceedings in which the welfare of children other than children ordinarily resident in Wales is or may be in question, it is a function of the Service to—

    (a) safeguard and promote the welfare of the children,

    (b) give advice to any court about any application made to it in such proceedings,

    (c) make provision for the children to be represented in such proceedings,

    (d) provide information, advice and other support for the children and their families.

(2) The Service must also make provision for the performance of any functions conferred on officers of the Service by virtue of this Act or any other enactment (whether or not they are exercisable for the purposes of the functions conferred on the Service by subsection (1)).

(3) Regulations may provide for grants to be paid by the Service to any person for the purpose of furthering the performance of any of the Service's functions.

(4) The regulations may provide for the grants to be paid on conditions, including conditions—

    (a) regulating the purposes for which the grant or any part of it may be used,

    (b) requiring repayment to the Service in specified circumstances.

(5) In this section, 'family proceedings' has the same meaning as in the Matrimonial and Family Proceedings Act 1984 and also includes any other proceedings which are family proceedings for the purposes of the Children Act 1989, but—

    (a) references to family proceedings include (where the context allows) family proceedings which are proposed or have been concluded.

. . .

13   Other powers of the Service

(1) The Service may make arrangements with organisations under which the organisations perform functions of the Service on its behalf.

(2) Arrangements under subsection (1) may provide for the organisations to designate individuals who may perform functions of officers of the Service.

. . .

15   Right to conduct litigation and right of audience

(1) The Service may authorise an officer of the Service of a prescribed description—

    (a) to conduct litigation in relation to any proceedings in any court,

    (b) to exercise a right of audience in any proceedings before any court, in the exercise of his functions.

. . .

SCHEDULE 2

CHILDREN AND FAMILY COURT ADVISORY AND SUPPORT SERVICE

Constitution

1. The Service is to consist of a chairman, and not less than nine other members, appointed by the Secretary of State.

2.—(1) Regulations may provide—

    (a) for the appointment of the chairman and other members and for the co-option by the Service for particular purposes of additional members (including the number, or limits on the number, of persons who may be appointed or co-opted and any conditions to be fulfilled for appointment or co-option),

    (b) for the tenure of office of the chairman and other members and any co-opted members (including the circumstances in which they cease to hold office or may be removed or suspended from office).

(2) References below in this Schedule to members of the Service do not include co-opted members.

. . .

Delegation

7. The Service may arrange for the chairman or any other member to discharge functions of the Service on its behalf.

. . .

Supervision

9.—(1) Functions and other powers of the Service, and functions of any officer of the Service, must be performed in accordance with any directions given by the Secretary of State.

(2) In particular, the directions may make provision for the purpose of ensuring that the services provided are of appropriate quality and meet appropriate standards.

. . .

Complaints

15. The Service must make and publicise a scheme for dealing with complaints made by or on behalf of prescribed persons in relation to the performance by the Service and its officers of their functions.

. . .

Health and Social Care Act 2001
(2001 c. 15)

. . .

PART 4   SOCIAL CARE

. . .

Direct payments

57   Direct payments

(1) Regulations may make provision for and in connection with requiring or authorising the responsible authority in the case of a person of a prescribed description who falls within subsection (2) to make, with that person's consent, such payments to him as they may determine in accordance with the regulations in respect of his securing the provision of the service mentioned in paragraph (a) or (b) of that subsection.

(2) A person falls within this subsection if a local authority ('the responsible authority') have decided—

. . .

    (b) under section 2(1) of the Carers and Disabled Children Act 2000 (c. 16) (services for carers) to provide him with a particular service under that Act.

. . .

Human Reproductive Cloning Act 2001
(2001 c. 23)

1   The offence

(1) A person who places in a woman a human embryo which has been created otherwise than by fertilisation is guilty of an offence.

(2) A person who is guilty of the offence is liable on conviction on indictment to imprisonment for a term not exceeding 10 years or a fine or both.

(3) No proceedings for the offence may be instituted—

    (a) in England and Wales, except with the consent of the Director of Public Prosecutions;

    (b) in Northern Ireland, except with the consent of the Director of Public Prosecutions for Northern Ireland.

Land Registration Act 2002
(2002 c. 9)

PART 3   DISPOSITIONS OF REGISTERED LAND

. . .

26   Protection of disponees

(1) Subject to subsection (2), a person's right to exercise owner's powers in relation to a registered estate or charge is to be taken to be free from any limitation affecting the validity of a disposition.

(2) Subsection (1) does not apply to a limitation—

    (a) reflected by an entry in the register, or

    (b) imposed by, or under, this Act.

(3) This section has effect only for the purpose of preventing the title of a disponee being questioned (and so does not affect the lawfulness of a disposition).

. . .

PART 4   NOTICES AND RESTRICTIONS

Notices

. . .

33   Excluded interests

No notice may be entered in the register in respect of any of the following—

    (a) an interest under—

        (i)   a trust of land, or

        (ii)   a settlement under the Settled Land Act 1925 (c. 18),

. . .

Restrictions

40   Nature

(1) A restriction is an entry in the register regulating the circumstances in which a disposition of a registered estate or charge may be the subject of an entry in the register.

(2) A restriction may, in particular—

    (a) prohibit the making of an entry in respect of any disposition, or a disposition of a kind specified in the restriction;

    (b) prohibit the making of an entry—

        (i)   indefinitely,

        (ii)   for a period specified in the restriction, or

        (iii)   until the occurrence of an event so specified.

(3) Without prejudice to the generality of subsection (2)(b)(iii), the events which may be specified include—

    (a) the giving of notice,

    (b) the obtaining of consent, and

    (c) the making of an order by the court or registrar.

(4) The entry of a restriction is to be made in relation to the registered estate or charge to which it relates.

41   Effect

(1) Where a restriction is entered in the register, no entry in respect of a disposition to which the restriction applies may be made in the register otherwise than in accordance with the terms of the restriction, subject to any order under subsection (2).

(2) The registrar may by order—
>   (a) disapply a restriction in relation to a disposition specified in the order or dispositions of a kind so specified, or
>   (b) provide that a restriction has effect, in relation to a disposition specified in the order or dispositions of a kind so specified, with modifications so specified.

(3) The power under subsection (2) is exercisable only on the application of a person who appears to the registrar to have a sufficient interest in the restriction.

42 Power of registrar to enter

(1) The registrar may enter a restriction in the register if it appears to him that it is necessary or desirable to do so for the purpose of—
>   (a) preventing invalidity or unlawfulness in relation to dispositions of a registered estate or charge,
>   (b) securing that interests which are capable of being overreached on a disposition of a registered estate or charge are overreached, or
>   (c) protecting a right or claim in relation to a registered estate or charge.

(2) No restriction may be entered under subsection (1)(c) for the purpose of protecting the priority of an interest which is, or could be, the subject of a notice.

(3) The registrar must give notice of any entry made under this section to the proprietor of the registered estate or charge concerned, except where the entry is made in pursuance of an application under section 43.

(4) For the purposes of subsection (1)(c), a person entitled to the benefit of a charging order relating to an interest under a trust shall be treated as having a right or claim in relation to the trust property.

43 Applications

(1) A person may apply to the registrar for the entry of a restriction under section 42(1) if—
>   (a) he is the relevant registered proprietor, or a person entitled to be registered as such proprietor,
>   (b) the relevant registered proprietor, or a person entitled to be registered as such proprietor, consents to the application, or
>   (c) he otherwise has a sufficient interest in the making of the entry.

. . .

46 Power of court to order entry

(1) If it appears to the court that it is necessary or desirable to do so for the purpose of protecting a right or claim in relation to a registered estate or charge, it may make an order requiring the registrar to enter a restriction in the register.

(2) No order under this section may be made for the purpose of protecting the priority of an interest which is, or could be, the subject of a notice.

(3) The court may include in an order under this section a direction that an entry made in pursuance of the order is to have overriding priority.

(4) If an order under this section includes a direction under subsection (3), the registrar must make such entry in the register as rules may provide.

(5) The court may make the exercise of its power under subsection (3) subject to such terms and conditions as it thinks fit.

. . .

PART 6   REGISTRATION: GENERAL

. . .

Applications

71   Duty to disclose unregistered interests

Where rules so provide—

    (a) a person applying for registration under Chapter 1 of Part 2 must provide to the registrar such information as the rules may provide about any interest affecting the estate to which the application relates which—

        (i)   falls within any of the paragraphs of Schedule 1, and

        (ii) is of a description specified by the rules;

    (b) a person applying to register a registrable disposition of a registered estate must provide to the registrar such information as the rules may provide about any unregistered interest affecting the estate which—

        (i)   falls within any of the paragraphs of Schedule 3, and

        (ii) is of description specified by the rules.

. . .

Miscellaneous

77   Duty to act reasonably

    (1) A person must not exercise any of the following rights without reasonable cause—

        (a) the right to lodge a caution under section 15,

        (b) the right to apply for the entry of a notice or restriction, and

        (c) the right to object to an application to the registrar.

    (2) The duty under this section is owed to any person who suffers damage in consequence of its breach.

. . .

PART 12   MISCELLANEOUS AND GENERAL

Miscellaneous

. . .

116   Proprietary estoppel and mere equities

It is hereby declared for the avoidance of doubt that, in relation to registered land, each of the following—

    (a) an equity by estoppel, and

    (b) a mere equity,

has effect from the time the equity arises as an interest capable of binding successors in title (subject to the rules about the effect of dispositions on priority).

. . .

SCHEDULE 1

UNREGISTERED INTERESTS WHICH OVERRIDE FIRST REGISTRATION

. . .

Interests of persons in actual occupation

    2. An interest belonging to a person in actual occupation, so far as relating to land of which he is in actual occupation, except for an interest under a settlement under the Settled Land Act 1925 (c. 18).

. . .

Sections 29 and 30   SCHEDULE 3

UNREGISTERED INTERESTS WHICH OVERRIDE
REGISTERED DISPOSITIONS

. . .

Interests of persons in actual occupation

2. An interest belonging at the time of the disposition to a person in actual occupation, so far as relating to land of which he is in actual occupation, except for—
  (a) an interest under a settlement under the Settled Land Act 1925 (c. 18);
  (b) an interest of a person of whom inquiry was made before the disposition and who failed to disclose the right when he could reasonably have been expected to do so;
  (c) an interest—
    (i) which belongs to a person whose occupation would not have been obvious on a reasonably careful inspection of the land at the time of the disposition, and
    (ii) of which the person to whom the disposition is made does not have actual knowledge at that time;
  (d) a leasehold estate in land granted to take effect in possession after the end of the period of three months beginning with the date of the grant and which has not taken effect in possession at the time of the disposition.

. . .

Education Act 2002
(2002 c. 32)

PART 6   THE CURRICULUM IN ENGLAND

General duties in respect of the curriculum

78 General requirements in relation to curriculum

(1) The curriculum for a maintained school or maintained nursery school satisfies the requirements of this section if it is a balanced and broadly based curriculum which—
  (a) promotes the spiritual, moral, cultural, mental and physical development of pupils at the school and of society, and
  (b) prepares pupils at the school for the opportunities, responsibilities and experiences of later life.

. . .

80 Basic curriculum for every maintained school in England

(1) The curriculum for every maintained school in England shall comprise a basic curriculum which includes—
  (a) provision for religious education for all registered pupils at the school (in accordance with such of the provisions of Schedule 19 to the School Standards and Framework Act 1998 (c. 31) as apply in relation to the school),
  (b) a curriculum for all registered pupils at the school who have attained the age of three but are not over compulsory school age (known as 'the National Curriculum for England'),
  (c) in the case of a secondary school, provision for sex education for all registered pupils at the school, and

(d) in the case of a special school, provision for sex education for all registered pupils at the school who are provided with secondary education.

(2) Subsection (1)(a) does not apply—

(a) in relation to a nursery class in a primary school, or

(b) in the case of a maintained special school (provision as to religious education in special schools being made by regulations under section 71(7) of the School Standards and Framework Act 1998).

(3) The Secretary of State may by order—

(a) amend subsection (1) so as to add further requirements (otherwise than in relation to religious education or sex education),

(b) amend subsection (1)(b) by substituting for the reference to compulsory school age (or to any age specified there by virtue of this paragraph) a reference to such other age as may be specified in the order, and

(c) amend any provision included in subsection (1) by virtue of paragraph (a) of this subsection.

. . .

Adoption and Children Act 2002
(2002 c. 38)

PART 1   ADOPTION

CHAPTER 1   INTRODUCTORY

1   Considerations applying to the exercise of powers

(1) This section applies whenever a court or adoption agency is coming to a decision relating to the adoption of a child.

(2) The paramount consideration of the court or adoption agency must be the child's welfare, throughout his life.

(3) The court or adoption agency must at all times bear in mind that, in general, any delay in coming to the decision is likely to prejudice the child's welfare.

(4) The court or adoption agency must have regard to the following matters (among others)—

(a) the child's ascertainable wishes and feelings regarding the decision (considered in the light of the child's age and understanding),

(b) the child's particular needs,

(c) the likely effect on the child (throughout his life) of having ceased to be a member of the original family and become an adopted person,

(d) the child's age, sex, background and any of the child's characteristics which the court or agency considers relevant,

(e) any harm (within the meaning of the Children Act 1989 (c. 41)) which the child has suffered or is at risk of suffering,

(f) the relationship which the child has with relatives, and with any other person in relation to whom the court or agency considers the relationship to be relevant, including—

(i) the likelihood of any such relationship continuing and the value to the child of its doing so,

(ii) the ability and willingness of any of the child's relatives, or of any such person, to provide the child with a secure environment in which the child can develop, and otherwise to meet the child's needs,

(iii) the wishes and feelings of any of the child's relatives, or of any such person, regarding the child.

(5) In placing the child for adoption, the adoption agency must give due consideration to the child's religious persuasion, racial origin and cultural and linguistic background.

(6) The court or adoption agency must always consider the whole range of powers available to it in the child's case (whether under this Act or the Children Act 1989); and the court must not make any order under this Act unless it considers that making the order would be better for the child than not doing so.

(7) In this section, 'coming to a decision relating to the adoption of a child', in relation to a court, includes—

(a) coming to a decision in any proceedings where the orders that might be made by the court include an adoption order (or the revocation of such an order), a placement order (or the revocation of such an order) or an order under section 26 (or the revocation or variation of such an order),

(b) coming to a decision about granting leave in respect of any action (other than the initiation of proceedings in any court) which may be taken by an adoption agency or individual under this Act,

but does not include coming to a decision about granting leave in any other circumstances.

(8) For the purposes of this section—

(a) references to relationships are not confined to legal relationships,

(b) references to a relative, in relation to a child, include the child's mother and father.

CHAPTER 2   THE ADOPTION SERVICE

The Adoption Service

2 Basic definitions

(1) The services maintained by local authorities under section 3(1) may be collectively referred to as 'the Adoption Service', and a local authority or registered adoption society may be referred to as an adoption agency.

(2) In this Act, 'registered adoption society' means a voluntary organisation which is an adoption society registered under Part 2 of the Care Standards Act 2000 (c. 14); but in relation to the provision of any facility of the Adoption Service, references to a registered adoption society or to an adoption agency do not include an adoption society which is not registered in respect of that facility.

(3) A registered adoption society is to be treated as registered in respect of any facility of the Adoption Service unless it is a condition of its registration that it does not provide that facility.

(4) No application for registration under Part 2 of the Care Standards Act 2000 may be made in respect of an adoption society which is an unincorporated body.

(5) In this Act—

'the 1989 Act' means the Children Act 1989 (c. 41),

'adoption society' means a body whose functions consist of or include making arrangements for the adoption of children,

'voluntary organisation' means a body other than a public or local authority the activities of which are not carried on for profit.

(6) In this Act, 'adoption support services' means—

(a) counselling, advice and information, and

(b) any other services prescribed by regulations,

in relation to adoption.

(7) The power to make regulations under subsection (6)(b) is to be exercised so as to secure that local authorities provide financial support.

(8) In this Chapter, references to adoption are to the adoption of persons, wherever they may be habitually resident, effected under the law of any country or territory, whether within or outside the British Islands.

3 Maintenance of Adoption Service

(1) Each local authority must continue to maintain within their area a service designed to meet the needs, in relation to adoption, of—

(a) children who may be adopted, their parents and guardians,

(b) persons wishing to adopt a child, and

(c) adopted persons, their parents, natural parents and former guardians;

and for that purpose must provide the requisite facilities.

(2) Those facilities must include making, and participating in, arrangements—

(a) for the adoption of children, and

(b) for the provision of adoption support services.

(3) As part of the service, the arrangements made for the purposes of subsection (2)(b)—

(a) must extend to the provision of adoption support services to persons who are within a description prescribed by regulations,

(b) may extend to the provision of those services to other persons.

(4) A local authority may provide any of the requisite facilities by securing their provision by—

(a) registered adoption societies, or

(b) other persons who are within a description prescribed by regulations of persons who may provide the facilities in question.

(5) The facilities of the service must be provided in conjunction with the local authority's other social services and with registered adoption societies in their area, so that help may be given in a co-ordinated manner without duplication, omission or avoidable delay.

(6) The social services referred to in subsection (5) are the functions of a local authority which are social services functions within the meaning of the Local Authority Social Services Act 1970 (c. 42) (which include, in particular, those functions in so far as they relate to children).

4 Assessments etc. for adoption support services

(1) A local authority must at the request of—

(a) any of the persons mentioned in paragraphs (a) to (c) of section 3(1), or

(b) any other person who falls within a description prescribed by regulations (subject to subsection (7)(a)),

carry out an assessment of that person's needs for adoption support services.

(2) A local authority may, at the request of any person, carry out an assessment of that person's needs for adoption support services.

(3) A local authority may request the help of the persons mentioned in paragraph (a) or (b) of section 3(4) in carrying out an assessment.

(4) Where, as a result of an assessment, a local authority decide that a person has needs for adoption support services, they must then decide whether to provide any such services to that person.

(5) If—

(a) a local authority decide to provide any adoption support services to a person, and

(b) the circumstances fall within a description prescribed by regulations,

the local authority must prepare a plan in accordance with which adoption support services are to be provided to the person and keep the plan under review.

(6) Regulations may make provision about assessments, preparing and reviewing plans, the provision of adoption support services in accordance with plans and reviewing the provision of adoption support services.

(7) The regulations may in particular make provision—

(a) as to the circumstances in which a person mentioned in paragraph (b) of sub-section (1) is to have a right to request an assessment of his needs in accordance with that subsection,

(b) about the type of assessment which, or the way in which an assessment, is to be carried out,

(c) about the way in which a plan is to be prepared,

(d) about the way in which, and time at which, a plan or the provision of adoption support services is to be reviewed,

(e) about the considerations to which a local authority are to have regard in carrying out an assessment or review or preparing a plan,

(f) as to the circumstances in which a local authority may provide adoption support services subject to conditions,

(g) as to the consequences of conditions imposed by virtue of paragraph (f) not being met (including the recovery of any financial support provided by a local authority),

(h) as to the circumstances in which this section may apply to a local authority in respect of persons who are outside that local authority's area,

(i) as to the circumstances in which a local authority may recover from another local authority the expenses of providing adoption support services to any person.

(8) A local authority may carry out an assessment of the needs of any person under this section at the same time as an assessment of his needs is made under any other enactment.

(9) If at any time during the assessment of the needs of any person under this section, it appears to a local authority that—

(a) there may be a need for the provision of services to that person by a Primary Care Trust (in Wales, a Health Authority or Local Health Board), or

(b) there may be a need for the provision to him of any services which fall within the functions of a local education authority (within the meaning of the Education Act 1996 (c. 56)),

the local authority must notify that Primary Care Trust, Health Authority, Local Health Board or local education authority.

(10) Where it appears to a local authority that another local authority could, by taking any specified action, help in the exercise of any of their functions under this section, they may request the help of that other local authority, specifying the action in question.

(11) A local authority whose help is so requested must comply with the request if it is consistent with the exercise of their functions.

. . .

8   Adoption support agencies

(1) In this Act, 'adoption support agency' means an undertaking the purpose of which, or one of the purposes of which, is the provision of adoption support services; but an under-taking is not an adoption support agency—

(a) merely because it provides information in connection with adoption other than for the purpose mentioned in section 98(1), or

(b) if it is excepted by virtue of subsection (2).

'Undertaking' has the same meaning as in the Care Standards Act 2000 (c. 14).

(2) The following are excepted—

(a) a registered adoption society, whether or not the society is registered in respect of the provision of adoption support services,

(b) a local authority,

(c) a local education authority (within the meaning of the Education Act 1996 (c. 56)),

(d) a Special Health Authority, Primary Care Trust (in Wales, a Health Authority or Local Health Board), NHS trust or NHS foundation trust,

(e) the Registrar General,

(f) any person, or description of persons, excepted by regulations.

. . .

Supplemental

13 Information concerning adoption

(1) Each adoption agency must give to the appropriate Minister any statistical or other general information he requires about—

(a) its performance of all or any of its functions relating to adoption,

(b) the children and other persons in relation to whom it has exercised those functions.

(2) The following persons—

(a) the designated officer for each magistrates' court,

(b) the relevant officer of each county court,

(c) the relevant officer of the High Court,

must give to the appropriate Minister any statistical or other general information he requires about the proceedings under this Act of the court in question.

(3) In subsection (2), 'relevant officer', in relation to a county court or the High Court, means the officer of that court who is designated to act for the purposes of that subsection by a direction given by the Lord Chancellor.

(4) The information required to be given to the appropriate Minister under this section must be given at the times, and in the form, directed by him.

(5) The appropriate Minister may publish from time to time abstracts of the information given to him under this section.

. . .

15 Inspection of premises etc.

(1) The appropriate Minister may arrange for any premises in which—

(a) a child is living with a person with whom the child has been placed by an adoption agency, or

(b) a child in respect of whom a notice of intention to adopt has been given under section 44 is, or will be, living,

to be inspected from time to time.

(2) The appropriate Minister may require an adoption agency—

(a) to give him any information, or

(b) to allow him to inspect any records (in whatever form they are held),

relating to the discharge of any of its functions in relation to adoption which the appropriate Minister specifies.

(3) An inspection under this section must be conducted by a person authorised by the appropriate Minister.

(4) An officer of a local authority may only be so authorised with the consent of the authority.

(5) A person inspecting any premises under subsection (1) may—

(a) visit the child there,

(b) make any examination into the state of the premises and the treatment of the child there which he thinks fit.

(6) A person authorised to inspect any records under this section may at any reasonable time have access to, and inspect and check the operation of, any computer (and associated apparatus) which is being or has been used in connection with the records in question.

(7) A person authorised to inspect any premises or records under this section may—

(a) enter the premises for that purpose at any reasonable time,

(b) require any person to give him any reasonable assistance he may require.

(8) A person exercising a power under this section must, if required to do so, produce a duly authenticated document showing his authority.

(9) Any person who intentionally obstructs another in the exercise of a power under this section is guilty of an offence and liable on summary conviction to a fine not exceeding level 3 on the standard scale.

. . .

CHAPTER 3   PLACEMENT FOR ADOPTION AND ADOPTION ORDERS

Placement of children by adoption agency for adoption

18   Placement for adoption by agencies

(1) An adoption agency may—

(a) place a child for adoption with prospective adopters, or

(b) where it has placed a child with any persons (whether under this Part or not), leave the child with them as prospective adopters,

but, except in the case of a child who is less than six weeks old, may only do so under section 19 or a placement order.

(2) An adoption agency may only place a child for adoption with prospective adopters if the agency is satisfied that the child ought to be placed for adoption.

(3) A child who is placed or authorised to be placed for adoption with prospective adopters by a local authority is looked after by the authority.

(4) If an application for an adoption order has been made by any persons in respect of a child and has not been disposed of—

(a) an adoption agency which placed the child with those persons may leave the child with them until the application is disposed of, but

(b) apart from that, the child may not be placed for adoption with any prospective adopters.

'Adoption order' includes a Scottish or Northern Irish adoption order.

(5) References in this Act (apart from this section) to an adoption agency placing a child for adoption—

(a) are to its placing a child for adoption with prospective adopters, and

(b) include, where it has placed a child with any persons (whether under this Act or not), leaving the child with them as prospective adopters;

and references in this Act (apart from this section) to a child who is placed for adoption by an adoption agency are to be interpreted accordingly.

(6) References in this Chapter to an adoption agency being, or not being, authorised to place a child for adoption are to the agency being or (as the case may be) not being authorised to do so under section 19 or a placement order.

(7) This section is subject to sections 30 to 35 (removal of children placed by adoption agencies).

19   Placing children with parental consent

(1) Where an adoption agency is satisfied that each parent or guardian of a child has consented to the child—

(a) being placed for adoption with prospective adopters identified in the consent, or

(b) being placed for adoption with any prospective adopters who may be chosen by the agency,

and has not withdrawn the consent, the agency is authorised to place the child for adoption accordingly.

(2) Consent to a child being placed for adoption with prospective adopters identified in the consent may be combined with consent to the child subsequently being placed for adoption with any prospective adopters who may be chosen by the agency in circumstances where the child is removed from or returned by the identified prospective adopters.

(3) Subsection (1) does not apply where—

(a) an application has been made on which a care order might be made and the application has not been disposed of, or

(b) a care order or placement order has been made after the consent was given.

(4) References in this Act to a child placed for adoption under this section include a child who was placed under this section with prospective adopters and continues to be placed with them, whether or not consent to the placement has been withdrawn.

(5) This section is subject to section 52 (parental etc. consent).

20 Advance consent to adoption

(1) A parent or guardian of a child who consents to the child being placed for adoption by an adoption agency under section 19 may, at the same or any subsequent time, consent to the making of a future adoption order.

(2) Consent under this section—

(a) where the parent or guardian has consented to the child being placed for adoption with prospective adopters identified in the consent, may be consent to adoption by them, or

(b) may be consent to adoption by any prospective adopters who may be chosen by the agency.

(3) A person may withdraw any consent given under this section.

(4) A person who gives consent under this section may, at the same or any subsequent time, by notice given to the adoption agency—

(a) state that he does not wish to be informed of any application for an adoption order, or

(b) withdraw such a statement.

(5) A notice under subsection (4) has effect from the time when it is received by the adoption agency but has no effect if the person concerned has withdrawn his consent.

(6) This section is subject to section 52 (parental etc. consent).

21 Placement orders

(1) A placement order is an order made by the court authorising a local authority to place a child for adoption with any prospective adopters who may be chosen by the authority.

(2) The court may not make a placement order in respect of a child unless—

(a) the child is subject to a care order,

(b) the court is satisfied that the conditions in section 31(2) of the 1989 Act (conditions for making a care order) are met, or

(c) the child has no parent or guardian.

(3) The court may only make a placement order if, in the case of each parent or guardian of the child, the court is satisfied—

(a) that the parent or guardian has consented to the child being placed for adoption with any prospective adopters who may be chosen by the local authority and has not withdrawn the consent, or

(b) that the parent's or guardian's consent should be dispensed with.

This subsection is subject to section 52 (parental etc. consent).

(4) A placement order continues in force until—

(a) it is revoked under section 24,

(b) an adoption order is made in respect of the child, or

(c) the child marries, forms a civil partnership or attains the age of 18 years.

'Adoption order' includes a Scottish or Northern Irish adoption order.

22 Applications for placement orders

(1) A local authority must apply to the court for a placement order in respect of a child if—

(a) the child is placed for adoption by them or is being provided with accommodation by them,

(b) no adoption agency is authorised to place the child for adoption,

(c) the child has no parent or guardian or the authority consider that the conditions in section 31(2) of the 1989 Act are met, and

(d) the authority are satisfied that the child ought to be placed for adoption.

(2) If—

(a) an application has been made (and has not been disposed of) on which a care order might be made in respect of a child, or

(b) a child is subject to a care order and the appropriate local authority are not authorised to place the child for adoption,

the appropriate local authority must apply to the court for a placement order if they are satisfied that the child ought to be placed for adoption.

(3) If—

(a) a child is subject to a care order, and

(b) the appropriate local authority are authorised to place the child for adoption under section 19,

the authority may apply to the court for a placement order.

(4) If a local authority—

(a) are under a duty to apply to the court for a placement order in respect of a child, or

(b) have applied for a placement order in respect of a child and the application has not been disposed of,

the child is looked after by the authority.

(5) Subsections (1) to (3) do not apply in respect of a child—

(a) if any persons have given notice of intention to adopt, unless the period of four months beginning with the giving of the notice has expired without them applying for an adoption order or their application for such an order has been withdrawn or refused, or

(b) if an application for an adoption order has been made and has not been disposed of.

'Adoption order' includes a Scottish or Northern Irish adoption order.

(6) Where—

(a) an application for a placement order in respect of a child has been made and has not been disposed of, and

(b) no interim care order is in force,

the court may give any directions it considers appropriate for the medical or psychiatric examination or other assessment of the child; but a child who is of sufficient understanding to make an informed decision may refuse to submit to the examination or other assessment.

(7) The appropriate local authority—

(a) in relation to a care order, is the local authority in whose care the child is placed by the order, and

(b) in relation to an application on which a care order might be made, is the local authority which makes the application.

23 Varying placement orders

(1) The court may vary a placement order so as to substitute another local authority for the local authority authorised by the order to place the child for adoption.

(2) The variation may only be made on the joint application of both authorities.

24 Revoking placement orders

(1) The court may revoke a placement order on the application of any person.

(2) But an application may not be made by a person other than the child or the local authority authorised by the order to place the child for adoption unless—

    (a) the court has given leave to apply, and

    (b) the child is not placed for adoption by the authority.

(3) The court cannot give leave under subsection (2)(a) unless satisfied that there has been a change in circumstances since the order was made.

(4) If the court determines, on an application for an adoption order, not to make the order, it may revoke any placement order in respect of the child.

(5) Where—

    (a) an application for the revocation of a placement order has been made and has not been disposed of, and

    (b) the child is not placed for adoption by the authority,

the child may not without the court's leave be placed for adoption under the order.

25   Parental responsibility

(1) This section applies while—

    (a) a child is placed for adoption under section 19 or an adoption agency is authorised to place a child for adoption under that section, or

    (b) a placement order is in force in respect of a child.

(2) Parental responsibility for the child is given to the agency concerned.

(3) While the child is placed with prospective adopters, parental responsibility is given to them.

(4) The agency may determine that the parental responsibility of any parent or guardian, or of prospective adopters, is to be restricted to the extent specified in the determination.

26   Contact

(1) On an adoption agency being authorised to place a child for adoption, or placing a child for adoption who is less than six weeks old, any provision for contact under the 1989 Act ceases to have effect and any contact activity direction relating to contact with the child is discharged.

(2) While an adoption agency is so authorised or a child is placed for adoption—

    (a) no application may be made for any provision for contact under that Act, but

    (b) the court may make an order under this section requiring the person with whom the child lives, or is to live, to allow the child to visit or stay with the person named in the order, or for the person named in the order and the child otherwise to have contact with each other.

(3) An application for an order under this section may be made by—

    (a) the child or the agency,

    (b) any parent, guardian or relative,

    (c) any person in whose favour there was provision for contact under the 1989 Act which ceased to have effect by virtue of subsection (1),

    (d) if a residence order was in force immediately before the adoption agency was authorised to place the child for adoption or (as the case may be) placed the child for adoption at a time when he was less than six weeks old, the person in whose favour the order was made,

    (e) if a person had care of the child immediately before that time by virtue of an order made in the exercise of the High Court's inherent jurisdiction with respect to children, that person,

    (f) any person who has obtained the court's leave to make the application.

(4) When making a placement order, the court may on its own initiative make an order under this section.

(5) This section does not prevent an application for a contact order under section 8 of the 1989 Act being made where the application is to be heard together with an application for an adoption order in respect of the child.

(6) In this section, 'contact activity direction' has the meaning given by section 11A of the 1989 Act and 'provision for contact under the 1989 Act' means a contact order under section 8 of that Act or an order under section 34 of that Act (parental contact with children in care).

27   Contact: supplementary

(1) An order under section 26—

   (a) has effect while the adoption agency is authorised to place the child for adoption or the child is placed for adoption, but

   (b) may be varied or revoked by the court on an application by the child, the agency or a person named in the order.

(2) The agency may refuse to allow the contact that would otherwise be required by virtue of an order under that section if—

   (a) it is satisfied that it is necessary to do so in order to safeguard or promote the child's welfare, and

   (b) the refusal is decided upon as a matter of urgency and does not last for more than seven days.

(3) Regulations may make provision as to —

   (a) the steps to be taken by an agency which has exercised its power under subsection (2),

   (b) the circumstances in which, and conditions subject to which, the terms of any order under section 26 may be departed from by agreement between the agency and any person for whose contact with the child the order provides,

   (c) notification by an agency of any variation or suspension of arrangements made (otherwise than under an order under that section) with a view to allowing any person contact with the child.

(4) Before making a placement order the court must —

   (a) consider the arrangements which the adoption agency has made, or proposes to make, for allowing any person contact with the child, and

   (b) invite the parties to the proceedings to comment on those arrangements.

(5) An order under section 26 may provide for contact on any conditions the court considers appropriate.

28   Further consequences of placement

(1) Where a child is placed for adoption under section 19 or an adoption agency is authorised to place a child for adoption under that section—

   (a) a parent or guardian of the child may not apply for a residence order unless an application for an adoption order has been made and the parent or guardian has obtained the court's leave under subsection (3) or (5) of section 47,

   (b) if an application has been made for an adoption order, a guardian of the child may not apply for a special guardianship order unless he has obtained the court's leave under subsection (3) or (5) of that section.

(2) Where—

   (a) a child is placed for adoption under section 19 or an adoption agency is authorised to place a child for adoption under that section, or

   (b) a placement order is in force in respect of a child,

then (whether or not the child is in England and Wales) a person may not do either of the following things, unless the court gives leave or each parent or guardian of the child gives written consent.

(3) Those things are—

   (a) causing the child to be known by a new surname, or

   (b) removing the child from the United Kingdom.

(4) Subsection (3) does not prevent the removal of a child from the United Kingdom for a period of less than one month by a person who provides the child's home.

29 Further consequences of placement orders

(1) Where a placement order is made in respect of a child and either—

(a) the child is subject to a care order, or

(b) the court at the same time makes a care order in respect of the child,

the care order does not have effect at any time when the placement order is in force.

(2) On the making of a placement order in respect of a child, any order mentioned in section 8(1) of the 1989 Act, and any supervision order in respect of the child, ceases to have effect.

(3) Where a placement order is in force—

(a) no prohibited steps order, residence order or specific issue order, and

(b) no supervision order or child assessment order,

may be made in respect of the child.

(4) Subsection (3)(a) does not apply in respect of a residence order if—

(a) an application for an adoption order has been made in respect of the child, and

(b) the residence order is applied for by a parent or guardian who has obtained the court's leave under subsection (3) or (5) of section 47 or by any other person who has obtained the court's leave under this subsection.

(5) Where a placement order is in force, no special guardianship order may be made in respect of the child unless—

(a) an application has been made for an adoption order, and

(b) the person applying for the special guardianship order has obtained the court's leave under this subsection or, if he is a guardian of the child, has obtained the court's leave under section 47(5).

(6) Section 14A(7) of the 1989 Act applies in respect of an application for a special guardianship order for which leave has been given as mentioned in subsection (5)(b) with the omission of the words 'the beginning of the period of three months ending with'.

(7) Where a placement order is in force—

(a) section 14C(1)(b) of the 1989 Act (special guardianship: parental responsibility) has effect subject to any determination under section 25(4) of this Act,

(b) section 14C(3) and (4) of the 1989 Act (special guardianship: removal of child from UK etc.) does not apply.

Removal of children who are or may be placed by adoption agencies

30 General prohibitions on removal

(1) Where—

(a) a child is placed for adoption by an adoption agency under section 19, or

(b) a child is placed for adoption by an adoption agency and either the child is less than six weeks old or the agency has at no time been authorised to place the child for adoption,

a person (other than the agency) must not remove the child from the prospective adopters.

(2) Where—

(a) a child who is not for the time being placed for adoption is being provided with accommodation by a local authority, and

(b) the authority have applied to the court for a placement order and the application has not been disposed of,

only a person who has the court's leave (or the authority) may remove the child from the accommodation.

(3) Where subsection (2) does not apply, but—

(a) a child who is not for the time being placed for adoption is being provided with accommodation by an adoption agency, and

(b) the agency is authorised to place the child for adoption under section 19 or would be so authorised if any consent to placement under that section had not been withdrawn,

a person (other than the agency) must not remove the child from the accommodation.

(4) This section is subject to sections 31 to 33 but those sections do not apply if the child is subject to a care order.

(5) This group of sections (that is, this section and those sections) apply whether or not the child in question is in England and Wales.

(6) This group of sections does not affect the exercise by any local authority or other person of any power conferred by any enactment, other than section 20(8) of the 1989 Act (removal of children from local authority accommodation).

(7) This group of sections does not prevent the removal of a child who is arrested.

(8) A person who removes a child in contravention of this section is guilty of an offence and liable on summary conviction to imprisonment for a term not exceeding three months, or a fine not exceeding level 5 on the standard scale, or both.

31   Recovery by parent etc. where child not placed or is a baby

(1) Subsection (2) applies where—
   (a) a child who is not for the time being placed for adoption is being provided with accommodation by an adoption agency, and
   (b) the agency would be authorised to place the child for adoption under section 19 if consent to placement under that section had not been withdrawn.

(2) If any parent or guardian of the child informs the agency that he wishes the child to be returned to him, the agency must return the child to him within the period of seven days beginning with the request unless an application is, or has been, made for a placement order and the application has not been disposed of.

(3) Subsection (4) applies where—
   (a) a child is placed for adoption by an adoption agency and either the child is less than six weeks old or the agency has at no time been authorised to place the child for adoption, and
   (b) any parent or guardian of the child informs the agency that he wishes the child to be returned to him,

unless an application is, or has been, made for a placement order and the application has not been disposed of.

(4) The agency must give notice of the parent's or guardian's wish to the prospective adopters who must return the child to the agency within the period of seven days beginning with the day on which the notice is given.

(5) A prospective adopter who fails to comply with subsection (4) is guilty of an offence and liable on summary conviction to imprisonment for a term not exceeding three months, or a fine not exceeding level 5 on the standard scale, or both.

(6) As soon as a child is returned to an adoption agency under subsection (4), the agency must return the child to the parent or guardian in question.

32   Recovery by parent etc. where child placed and consent withdrawn

(1) This section applies where—
   (a) a child is placed for adoption by an adoption agency under section 19, and
   (b) consent to placement under that section has been withdrawn,

unless an application is, or has been, made for a placement order and the application has not been disposed of.

(2) If a parent or guardian of the child informs the agency that he wishes the child to be returned to him—
   (a) the agency must give notice of the parent's or guardian's wish to the prospective adopters, and

(b) the prospective adopters must return the child to the agency within the period of 14 days beginning with the day on which the notice is given.

(3) A prospective adopter who fails to comply with subsection (2)(b) is guilty of an offence and liable on summary conviction to imprisonment for a term not exceeding three months, or a fine not exceeding level 5 on the standard scale, or both.

(4) As soon as a child is returned to an adoption agency under this section, the agency must return the child to the parent or guardian in question.

(5) Where a notice under subsection (2) is given, but—

(a) before the notice was given, an application for an adoption order (including a Scottish or Northern Irish adoption order), special guardianship order or residence order, or for leave to apply for a special guardianship order or residence order, was made in respect of the child, and

(b) the application (and, in a case where leave is given on an application to apply for a special guardianship order or residence order, the application for the order) has not been disposed of,

the prospective adopters are not required by virtue of the notice to return the child to the agency unless the court so orders.

33   Recovery by parent etc. where child placed and placement order refused

(1) This section applies where—

(a) a child is placed for adoption by a local authority under section 19,

(b) the authority have applied for a placement order and the application has been refused, and

(c) any parent or guardian of the child informs the authority that he wishes the child to be returned to him.

(2) The prospective adopters must return the child to the authority on a date determined by the court.

(3) A prospective adopter who fails to comply with subsection (2) is guilty of an offence and liable on summary conviction to imprisonment for a term not exceeding three months, or a fine not exceeding level 5 on the standard scale, or both.

(4) As soon as a child is returned to the authority, they must return the child to the parent or guardian in question.

34   Placement orders: prohibition on removal

(1) Where a placement order in respect of a child—

(a) is in force, or

(b) has been revoked, but the child has not been returned by the prospective adopters or remains in any accommodation provided by the local authority,

a person (other than the local authority) may not remove the child from the prospective adopters or from accommodation provided by the authority.

(2) A person who removes a child in contravention of subsection (1) is guilty of an offence.

(3) Where a court revoking a placement order in respect of a child determines that the child is not to remain with any former prospective adopters with whom the child is placed, they must return the child to the local authority within the period determined by the court for the purpose; and a person who fails to do so is guilty of an offence.

(4) Where a court revoking a placement order in respect of a child determines that the child is to be returned to a parent or guardian, the local authority must return the child to the parent or guardian as soon as the child is returned to the authority or, where the child is in accommodation provided by the authority, at once.

(5) A person guilty of an offence under this section is liable on summary conviction to imprisonment for a term not exceeding three months, or a fine not exceeding level 5 on the standard scale, or both.

(6) This section does not affect the exercise by any local authority or other person of a power conferred by any enactment, other than section 20(8) of the 1989 Act.

(7) This section does not prevent the removal of a child who is arrested.

(8) This section applies whether or not the child in question is in England and Wales.

35 Return of child in other cases

(1) Where a child is placed for adoption by an adoption agency and the prospective adopters give notice to the agency of their wish to return the child, the agency must—

    (a) receive the child from the prospective adopters before the end of the period of seven days beginning with the giving of the notice, and

    (b) give notice to any parent or guardian of the child of the prospective adopters' wish to return the child.

(2) Where a child is placed for adoption by an adoption agency, and the agency—

    (a) is of the opinion that the child should not remain with the prospective adopters, and

    (b) gives notice to them of its opinion,

the prospective adopters must, not later than the end of the period of seven days beginning with the giving of the notice, return the child to the agency.

(3) If the agency gives notice under subsection (2)(b), it must give notice to any parent or guardian of the child of the obligation to return the child to the agency.

(4) A prospective adopter who fails to comply with subsection (2) is guilty of an offence and liable on summary conviction to imprisonment for a term not exceeding three months, or a fine not exceeding level 5 on the standard scale, or both.

(5) Where—

    (a) an adoption agency gives notice under subsection (2) in respect of a child,

    (b) before the notice was given, an application for an adoption order (including a Scottish or Northern Irish adoption order), special guardianship order or residence order, or for leave to apply for a special guardianship order or residence order, was made in respect of the child, and

    (c) the application (and, in a case where leave is given on an application to apply for a special guardianship order or residence order, the application for the order) has not been disposed of,

prospective adopters are not required by virtue of the notice to return the child to the agency unless the court so orders.

(6) This section applies whether or not the child in question is in England and Wales.

Removal of children in non-agency cases

36 Restrictions on removal

(1) At any time when a child's home is with any persons ('the people concerned') with whom the child is not placed by an adoption agency, but the people concerned—

    (a) have applied for an adoption order in respect of the child and the application has not been disposed of,

    (b) have given notice of intention to adopt, or

    (c) have applied for leave to apply for an adoption order under section 42(6) and the application has not been disposed of,

a person may remove the child only in accordance with the provisions of this group of sections (that is, this section and sections 37 to 40).

The reference to a child placed by an adoption agency includes a child placed by a Scottish or Northern Irish adoption agency.

(2) For the purposes of this group of sections, a notice of intention to adopt is to be disregarded if—

    (a) the period of four months beginning with the giving of the notice has expired without the people concerned applying for an adoption order, or

(b) the notice is a second or subsequent notice of intention to adopt and was given during the period of five months beginning with the giving of the preceding notice.

(3) For the purposes of this group of sections, if the people concerned apply for leave to apply for an adoption order under section 42(6) and the leave is granted, the application for leave is not to be treated as disposed of until the period of three days beginning with the granting of the leave has expired.

(4) This section does not prevent the removal of a child who is arrested.

(5) Where a parent or guardian may remove a child from the people concerned in accordance with the provisions of this group of sections, the people concerned must at the request of the parent or guardian return the child to the parent or guardian at once.

(6) A person who—
    (a) fails to comply with subsection (5), or
    (b) removes a child in contravention of this section,
is guilty of an offence and liable on summary conviction to imprisonment for a term not exceeding three months, or a fine not exceeding level 5 on the standard scale, or both.

(7) This group of sections applies whether or not the child in question is in England and Wales.

37 Applicants for adoption

If section 36(1)(a) applies, the following persons may remove the child—
    (a) a person who has the court's leave,
    (b) a local authority or other person in the exercise of a power conferred by any enactment, other than section 20(8) of the 1989 Act.

38 Local authority foster parents

(1) This section applies if the child's home is with local authority foster parents.

(2) If—
    (a) the child has had his home with the foster parents at all times during the period of five years ending with the removal and the foster parents have given notice of intention to adopt, or
    (b) an application has been made for leave under section 42(6) and has not been disposed of,
the following persons may remove the child.

(3) They are—
    (a) a person who has the court's leave,
    (b) a local authority or other person in the exercise of a power conferred by any enactment, other than section 20(8) of the 1989 Act.

(4) If subsection (2) does not apply but—
    (a) the child has had his home with the foster parents at all times during the period of one year ending with the removal, and
    (b) the foster parents have given notice of intention to adopt,
the following persons may remove the child.

(5) They are—
    (a) a person with parental responsibility for the child who is exercising the power in section 20(8) of the 1989 Act,
    (b) a person who has the court's leave,
    (c) a local authority or other person in the exercise of a power conferred by any enactment, other than section 20(8) of the 1989 Act.

39 Partners of parents

(1) This section applies if a child's home is with a partner of a parent and the partner has given notice of intention to adopt.

(2) If the child's home has been with the partner for not less than three years (whether continuous or not) during the period of five years ending with the removal, the following

persons may remove the child—

    (a) a person who has the court's leave,

    (b) a local authority or other person in the exercise of a power conferred by any enactment, other than section 20(8) of the 1989 Act.

  (3) If subsection (2) does not apply, the following persons may remove the child—

    (a) a parent or guardian,

    (b) a person who has the court's leave,

    (c) a local authority or other person in the exercise of a power conferred by any enactment, other than section 20(8) of the 1989 Act.

40   Other non-agency cases

  (1) In any case where sections 37 to 39 do not apply but—

    (a) the people concerned have given notice of intention to adopt, or

    (b) the people concerned have applied for leave under section 42(6) and the application has not been disposed of,

the following persons may remove the child.

  (2) They are—

    (a) a person who has the court's leave,

    (b) a local authority or other person in the exercise of a power conferred by any enactment, other than section 20(8) of the 1989 Act.

Breach of restrictions on removal

41   Recovery orders

  (1) This section applies where it appears to the court—

    (a) that a child has been removed in contravention of any of the preceding provisions of this Chapter or that there are reasonable grounds for believing that a person intends to remove a child in contravention of those provisions, or

    (b) that a person has failed to comply with section 31(4), 32(2), 33(2), 34(3) or 35(2).

  (2) The court may, on the application of any person, by an order—

    (a) direct any person who is in a position to do so to produce the child on request to any person mentioned in subsection (4),

    (b) authorise the removal of the child by any person mentioned in that subsection,

    (c) require any person who has information as to the child's whereabouts to disclose that information on request to any constable or officer of the court,

    (d) authorise a constable to enter any premises specified in the order and search for the child, using reasonable force if necessary.

  (3) Premises may only be specified under subsection (2)(d) if it appears to the court that there are reasonable grounds for believing the child to be on them.

  (4) The persons referred to in subsection (2) are—

    (a) any person named by the court,

    (b) any constable,

    (c) any person who, after the order is made under that subsection, is authorised to exercise any power under the order by an adoption agency which is authorised to place the child for adoption.

  (5) A person who intentionally obstructs a person exercising a power of removal conferred by the order is guilty of an offence and liable on summary conviction to a fine not exceeding level 3 on the standard scale.

  (6) A person must comply with a request to disclose information as required by the order even if the information sought might constitute evidence that he had committed an offence.

  (7) But in criminal proceedings in which the person is charged with an offence (other than one mentioned in subsection (8))—

    (a) no evidence relating to the information provided may be adduced, and

    (b) no question relating to the information may be asked,

by or on behalf of the prosecution, unless evidence relating to it is adduced, or a question relating to it is asked, in the proceedings by or on behalf of the person.

(8) The offences excluded from subsection (7) are—

    (a) an offence under section 2 or 5 of the Perjury Act 1911 (c. 6) (false statements made on oath otherwise than in judicial proceedings or made otherwise than on oath),

. . .

Preliminaries to adoption

42   Child to live with adopters before application

(1) An application for an adoption order may not be made unless—

    (a) if subsection (2) applies, the condition in that subsection is met,

    (b) if that subsection does not apply, the condition in whichever is applicable of subsections (3) to (5) applies.

(2) If—

    (a) the child was placed for adoption with the applicant or applicants by an adoption agency or in pursuance of an order of the High Court, or

    (b) the applicant is a parent of the child,

the condition is that the child must have had his home with the applicant or, in the case of an application by a couple, with one or both of them at all times during the period of ten weeks preceding the application.

(3) If the applicant or one of the applicants is the partner of a parent of the child, the condition is that the child must have had his home with the applicant or, as the case may be, applicants at all times during the period of six months preceding the application.

(4) If the applicants are local authority foster parents, the condition is that the child must have had his home with the applicants at all times during the period of one year preceding the application.

(5) In any other case, the condition is that the child must have had his home with the applicant or, in the case of an application by a couple, with one or both of them for not less than three years (whether continuous or not) during the period of five years preceding the application.

(6) But subsections (4) and (5) do not prevent an application being made if the court gives leave to make it.

(7) An adoption order may not be made unless the court is satisfied that sufficient opportunities to see the child with the applicant or, in the case of an application by a couple, both of them together in the home environment have been given—

    (a) where the child was placed for adoption with the applicant or applicants by an adoption agency, to that agency,

    (b) in any other case, to the local authority within whose area the home is.

. . .

43   Reports where child placed by agency

Where an application for an adoption order relates to a child placed for adoption by an adoption agency, the agency must—

    (a) submit to the court a report on the suitability of the applicants and on any other matters relevant to the operation of section 1, and

    (b) assist the court in any manner the court directs.

44   Notice of intention to adopt

(1) This section applies where persons (referred to in this section as 'proposed adopters') wish to adopt a child who is not placed for adoption with them by an adoption agency.

(2) An adoption order may not be made in respect of the child unless the proposed adopters have given notice to the appropriate local authority of their intention to apply for the adoption order (referred to in this Act as a 'notice of intention to adopt').

(3) The notice must be given not more than two years, or less than three months, before the date on which the application for the adoption order is made.

(4) Where—

(a) if a person were seeking to apply for an adoption order, subsection (4) or (5) of section 42 would apply, but

(b) the condition in the subsection in question is not met,

the person may not give notice of intention to adopt unless he has the court's leave to apply for an adoption order.

(5) On receipt of a notice of intention to adopt, the local authority must arrange for the investigation of the matter and submit to the court a report of the investigation.

(6) In particular, the investigation must, so far as practicable, include the suitability of the proposed adopters and any other matters relevant to the operation of section 1 in relation to the application.

(7) If a local authority receive a notice of intention to adopt in respect of a child whom they know was (immediately before the notice was given) looked after by another local authority, they must, not more than seven days after the receipt of the notice, inform the other local authority in writing that they have received the notice.

(8) Where—

(a) a local authority have placed a child with any persons otherwise than as prospective adopters, and

(b) the persons give notice of intention to adopt,

the authority are not to be treated as leaving the child with them as prospective adopters for the purposes of section 18(1)(b).

(9) In this section, references to the appropriate local authority, in relation to any proposed adopters, are—

(a) in prescribed cases, references to the prescribed local authority,

(b) in any other case, references to the local authority for the area in which, at the time of giving the notice of intention to adopt, they have their home,

and 'prescribed' means prescribed by regulations.

45 Suitability of adopters

(1) Regulations under section 9 may make provision as to the matters to be taken into account by an adoption agency in determining, or making any report in respect of, the suitability of any persons to adopt a child.

(2) In particular, the regulations may make provision for the purpose of securing that, in determining the suitability of a couple to adopt a child, proper regard is had to the need for stability and permanence in their relationship.

46 Adoption orders

(1) An adoption order is an order made by the court on an application under section 50 or 51 giving parental responsibility for a child to the adopters or adopter.

(2) The making of an adoption order operates to extinguish—

(a) the parental responsibility which any person other than the adopters or adopter has for the adopted child immediately before the making of the order,

(b) any order under the 1989 Act or the Children (Northern Ireland) Order 1995 (S.I. 1995/755 (N.I. 2)),

(c) any order under the Children (Scotland) Act 1995 (c. 36) other than an excepted order, and

(d) any duty arising by virtue of an agreement or an order of a court to make payments, so far as the payments are in respect of the adopted child's maintenance or upbringing for any period after the making of the adoption order.

'Excepted order' means an order under section 9, 11(1)(d) or 13 of the Children (Scotland) Act 1995 or an exclusion order within the meaning of section 76(1) of that Act.

(3) An adoption order—
- (a) does not affect parental responsibility so far as it relates to any period before the making of the order, and
- (b) in the case of an order made on an application under section 51(2) by the partner of a parent of the adopted child, does not affect the parental responsibility of that parent or any duties of that parent within subsection (2)(d).

(4) Subsection (2)(d) does not apply to a duty arising by virtue of an agreement—
- (a) which constitutes a trust, or
- (b) which expressly provides that the duty is not to be extinguished by the making of an adoption order.

(5) An adoption order may be made even if the child to be adopted is already an adopted child.

(6) Before making an adoption order, the court must consider whether there should be arrangements for allowing any person contact with the child; and for that purpose the court must consider any existing or proposed arrangements and obtain any views of the parties to the proceedings.

47   Conditions for making adoption orders

(1) An adoption order may not be made if the child has a parent or guardian unless one of the following three conditions is met; but this section is subject to section 52 (parental etc. consent).

(2) The first condition is that, in the case of each parent or guardian of the child, the court is satisfied—
- (a) that the parent or guardian consents to the making of the adoption order,
- (b) that the parent or guardian has consented under section 20 (and has not withdrawn the consent) and does not oppose the making of the adoption order, or
- (c) that the parent's or guardian's consent should be dispensed with.

(3) A parent or guardian may not oppose the making of an adoption order under subsection (2)(b) without the court's leave.

(4) The second condition is that—
- (a) the child has been placed for adoption by an adoption agency with the prospective adopters in whose favour the order is proposed to be made,
- (b) either—
  - (i) the child was placed for adoption with the consent of each parent or guardian and the consent of the mother was given when the child was at least six weeks old, or
  - (ii) the child was placed for adoption under a placement order, and
- (c) no parent or guardian oppose the making of the adoption order.

(5) A parent or guardian may not oppose the making of an adoption order under the second condition without the court's leave.

(6) The third condition is that the child is free for adoption by virtue of an order made—
- (a) in Scotland, under section 18 of the Adoption (Scotland) Act 1978 (c. 28), or
- (b) in Northern Ireland, under Article 17(1) or 18(1) of the Adoption (Northern Ireland) Order 1987 (S.I. 1987/2203 (N.I. 22)).

(7) The court cannot give leave under subsection (3) or (5) unless satisfied that there has been a change in circumstances since the consent of the parent or guardian was given or, as the case may be, the placement order was made.

(8) An adoption order may not be made in relation to a person who is or has been married.

(8A) An adoption order may not be made in relation to a person who is or has been a civil partner.

(9) An adoption order may not be made in relation to a person who has attained the age of 19 years.

48   Restrictions on making adoption orders

(1) The court may not hear an application for an adoption order in relation to a child, where a previous application to which subsection (2) applies made in relation to the child by the same persons was refused by any court, unless it appears to the court that, because of a change in circumstances or for any other reason, it is proper to hear the application.

(2) This subsection applies to any application—

(a) for an adoption order or a Scottish or Northern Irish adoption order, or

(b) for an order for adoption made in the Isle of Man or any of the Channel Islands.

49   Applications for adoption

(1) An application for an adoption order may be made by—

(a) a couple, or

(b) one person,

but only if it is made under section 50 or 51 and one of the following conditions is met.

(2) The first condition is that at least one of the couple (in the case of an application under section 50) or the applicant (in the case of an application under section 51) is domiciled in a part of the British Islands.

(3) The second condition is that both of the couple (in the case of an application under section 50) or the applicant (in the case of an application under section 51) have been habitually resident in a part of the British Islands for a period of not less than one year ending with the date of the application.

(4) An application for an adoption order may only be made if the person to be adopted has not attained the age of 18 years on the date of the application.

(5) References in this Act to a child, in connection with any proceedings (whether or not concluded) for adoption, (such as 'child to be adopted' or 'adopted child') include a person who has attained the age of 18 years before the proceedings are concluded.

50   Adoption by couple

(1) An adoption order may be made on the application of a couple where both of them have attained the age of 21 years.

(2) An adoption order may be made on the application of a couple where—

(a) one of the couple is the mother or the father of the person to be adopted and has attained the age of 18 years, and

(b) the other has attained the age of 21 years.

51   Adoption by one person

(1) An adoption order may be made on the application of one person who has attained the age of 21 years and is not married or a civil partner.

(2) An adoption order may be made on the application of one person who has attained the age of 21 years if the court is satisfied that the person is the partner of a parent of the person to be adopted.

(3) An adoption order may be made on the application of one person who has attained the age of 21 years and is married if the court is satisfied that—

(a) the person's spouse cannot be found,

(b) the spouses have separated and are living apart, and the separation is likely to be permanent, or

(c) the person's spouse is by reason of ill-health, whether physical or mental, incapable of making an application for an adoption order.

(3A) An adoption order may be made on the application of one person who has attained the age of 21 years and is a civil partner if the court is satisfied that—

(a) the person's civil partner cannot be found,

(b) the civil partners have separated and are living apart, and the separation is likely to be permanent, or

(c) the person's civil partner is by reason of ill-health, whether physical or mental, incapable of making an application for an adoption order.

(4) An adoption order may not be made on an application under this section by the mother or the father of the person to be adopted unless the court is satisfied that—

(a) the other natural parent is dead or cannot be found,

(b) by virtue of section 28 of the Human Fertilisation and Embryology Act 1990 (c. 37) (disregarding subsections (5A)—(5I) of that section), there is no other parent, or

(c) there is some other reason justifying the child's being adopted by the applicant alone,

and, where the court makes an adoption order on such an application, the court must record that it is satisfied as to the fact mentioned in paragraph (a) or (b) or, in the case of paragraph (c), record the reason.

Placement and adoption: general

52 Parental etc. consent

(1) The court cannot dispense with the consent of any parent or guardian of a child to the child being placed for adoption or to the making of an adoption order in respect of the child unless the court is satisfied that—

(a) the parent or guardian cannot be found or lacks capacity (within the meaning of the Mental Capacity Act 2005) to give consent, or

(b) the welfare of the child requires the consent to be dispensed with.

(2) The following provisions apply to references in this Chapter to any parent or guardian of a child giving or withdrawing—

(a) consent to the placement of a child for adoption, or

(b) consent to the making of an adoption order (including a future adoption order).

(3) Any consent given by the mother to the making of an adoption order is ineffective if it is given less than six weeks after the child's birth.

(4) The withdrawal of any consent to the placement of a child for adoption, or of any consent given under section 20, is ineffective if it is given after an application for an adoption order is made.

(5) 'Consent' means consent given unconditionally and with full understanding of what is involved; but a person may consent to adoption without knowing the identity of the persons in whose favour the order will be made.

(6) 'Parent' (except in subsections (9) and (10) below) means a parent having parental responsibility.

(7) Consent under section 19 or 20 must be given in the form prescribed by rules, and the rules may prescribe forms in which a person giving consent under any other provision of this Part may do so (if he wishes).

(8) Consent given under section 19 or 20 must be withdrawn—

(a) in the form prescribed by rules, or

(b) by notice given to the agency.

(9) Subsection (10) applies if—

(a) an agency has placed a child for adoption under section 19 in pursuance of consent given by a parent of the child, and

(b) at a later time, the other parent of the child acquires parental responsibility for the child.

(10) The other parent is to be treated as having at that time given consent in accordance with this section in the same terms as those in which the first parent gave consent.

53 Modification of 1989 Act in relation to adoption

(1) Where—

(a) a local authority are authorised to place a child for adoption, or

(b) a child who has been placed for adoption by a local authority is less than six weeks old,

regulations may provide for the following provisions of the 1989 Act to apply with modifications, or not to apply, in relation to the child.

(2) The provisions are—

(a) section 22(4)(b), (c) and (d) and (5)(b) (duty to ascertain wishes and feelings of certain persons),

(b) paragraphs 15 and 21 of Schedule 2 (promoting contact with parents and parents' obligation to contribute towards maintenance).

(3) Where a registered adoption society is authorised to place a child for adoption or a child who has been placed for adoption by a registered adoption society is less than six weeks old, regulations may provide—

(a) for section 61 of that Act to have effect in relation to the child whether or not he is accommodated by or on behalf of the society,

(b) for subsections (2)(b) to (d) and (3)(b) of that section (duty to ascertain wishes and feelings of certain persons) to apply with modifications, or not to apply, in relation to the child.

(4) Where a child's home is with persons who have given notice of intention to adopt, no contribution is payable (whether under a contribution order or otherwise) under Part 3 of Schedule 2 to that Act (contributions towards maintenance of children looked after by local authorities) in respect of the period referred to in subsection (5).

(5) That period begins when the notice of intention to adopt is given and ends if—

(a) the period of four months beginning with the giving of the notice expires without the prospective adopters applying for an adoption order, or

(b) an application for such an order is withdrawn or refused.

. . .

54 Disclosing information during adoption process

Regulations under section 9 may require adoption agencies in prescribed circumstances to disclose in accordance with the regulations prescribed information to prospective adopters.

55 Revocation of adoptions on legitimation

(1) Where any child adopted by one natural parent as sole adoptive parent subsequently becomes a legitimated person on the marriage of the natural parents, the court by which the adoption order was made may, on the application of any of the parties concerned, revoke the order.

(2) In relation to an adoption order made by a magistrates' court, the reference in subsection (1) to the court by which the order was made includes a court acting for the same local justice area.

Disclosure of information in relation to a person's adoption

56 Information to be kept about a person's adoption

(1) In relation to an adopted person, regulations may prescribe—

(a) the information which an adoption agency must keep in relation to his adoption,

(b) the form and manner in which it must keep that information.

(2) Below in this group of sections (that is, this section and sections 57 to 65), any information kept by an adoption agency by virtue of subsection (1)(a) is referred to as section 56 information.

(3) Regulations may provide for the transfer in prescribed circumstances of information held, or previously held, by an adoption agency to another adoption agency.

57 Restrictions on disclosure of protected etc. information

(1) Any section 56 information kept by an adoption agency which—

(a) is about an adopted person or any other person, and

(b) is or includes identifying information about the person in question,

may only be disclosed by the agency to a person (other than the person the information is about) in pursuance of this group of sections.

(2) Any information kept by an adoption agency—

    (a) which the agency has obtained from the Registrar General on an application under section 79(5) and any other information which would enable the adopted person to obtain a certified copy of the record of his birth, or

    (b) which is information about an entry relating to the adopted person in the Adoption Contact Register,

may only be disclosed to a person by the agency in pursuance of this group of sections.

(3) In this group of sections, information the disclosure of which to a person is restricted by virtue of subsection (1) or (2) is referred to (in relation to him) as protected information.

(4) Identifying information about a person means information which, whether taken on its own or together with other information disclosed by an adoption agency, identifies the person or enables the person to be identified.

(5) This section does not prevent the disclosure of protected information in pursuance of a prescribed agreement to which the adoption agency is a party.

(6) Regulations may authorise or require an adoption agency to disclose protected information to a person who is not an adopted person.

58 Disclosure of other information

(1) This section applies to any section 56 information other than protected information.

(2) An adoption agency may for the purposes of its functions disclose to any person in accordance with prescribed arrangements any information to which this section applies.

(3) An adoption agency must, in prescribed circumstances, disclose prescribed information to a prescribed person.

59 Offence

Regulations may provide that a registered adoption society which discloses any information in contravention of section 57 is to be guilty of an offence and liable on summary conviction to a fine not exceeding level 5 on the standard scale.

60 Disclosing information to adopted adult

(1) This section applies to an adopted person who has attained the age of 18 years.

(2) The adopted person has the right, at his request, to receive from the appropriate adoption agency—

    (a) any information which would enable him to obtain a certified copy of the record of his birth, unless the High Court orders otherwise,

    (b) any prescribed information disclosed to the adopters by the agency by virtue of section 54.

(3) The High Court may make an order under subsection (2)(a), on an application by the appropriate adoption agency, if satisfied that the circumstances are exceptional.

(4) The adopted person also has the right, at his request, to receive from the court which made the adoption order a copy of any prescribed document or prescribed order relating to the adoption.

(5) Subsection (4) does not apply to a document or order so far as it contains information which is protected information.

61 Disclosing protected information about adults

(1) This section applies where—

    (a) a person applies to the appropriate adoption agency for protected information to be disclosed to him, and

(b) none of the information is about a person who is a child at the time of the application.

(2) The agency is not required to proceed with the application unless it considers it appropriate to do so.

(3) If the agency does proceed with the application it must take all reasonable steps to obtain the views of any person the information is about as to the disclosure of the information about him.

(4) The agency may then disclose the information if it considers it appropriate to do so.

(5) In deciding whether it is appropriate to proceed with the application or disclose the information, the agency must consider—
    (a) the welfare of the adopted person,
    (b) any views obtained under subsection (3),
    (c) any prescribed matters,
and all the other circumstances of the case.

(6) This section does not apply to a request for information under section 60(2) or to a request for information which the agency is authorised or required to disclose in pursuance of regulations made by virtue of section 57(6).

62   Disclosing protected information about children

(1) This section applies where—
    (a) a person applies to the appropriate adoption agency for protected information to be disclosed to him, and
    (b) any of the information is about a person who is a child at the time of the application.

(2) The agency is not required to proceed with the application unless it considers it appropriate to do so.

(3) If the agency does proceed with the application, then, so far as the information is about a person who is at the time a child, the agency must take all reasonable steps to obtain—
    (a) the views of any parent or guardian of the child, and
    (b) the views of the child, if the agency considers it appropriate to do so having regard to his age and understanding and to all the other circumstances of the case,
as to the disclosure of the information.

(4) And, so far as the information is about a person who has at the time attained the age of 18 years, the agency must take all reasonable steps to obtain his views as to the disclosure of the information.

(5) The agency may then disclose the information if it considers it appropriate to do so.

(6) In deciding whether it is appropriate to proceed with the application, or disclose the information, where any of the information is about a person who is at the time a child—
    (a) if the child is an adopted child, the child's welfare must be the paramount consideration,
    (b) in the case of any other child, the agency must have particular regard to the child's welfare.

(7) And, in deciding whether it is appropriate to proceed with the application or disclose the information, the agency must consider—
    (a) the welfare of the adopted person (where subsection (6)(a) does not apply),
    (b) any views obtained under subsection (3) or (4),
    (c) any prescribed matters,
and all the other circumstances of the case.

(8) This section does not apply to a request for information under section 60(2) or to a request for information which the agency is authorised or required to disclose in pursuance of regulations made by virtue of section 57(6).

63   Counselling

(1) Regulations may require adoption agencies to give information about the availability of counselling to persons—

>   (a) seeking information from them in pursuance of this group of sections,
>   (b) considering objecting or consenting to the disclosure of information by the agency in pursuance of this group of sections, or
>   (c) considering entering with the agency into an agreement prescribed for the purposes of section 57(5).

(2) Regulations may require adoption agencies to make arrangements to secure the provision of counselling for persons seeking information from them in prescribed circumstances in pursuance of this group of sections.

(3) The regulations may authorise adoption agencies—

>   (a) to disclose information which is required for the purposes of such counselling to the persons providing the counselling,
>   (b) where the person providing the counselling is outside the United Kingdom, to require a prescribed fee to be paid.

(4) The regulations may require any of the following persons to provide counselling for the purposes of arrangements under subsection (2)—

>   (a) a local authority...
>   (b) a registered adoption society...
>   (c) an adoption support agency in respect of which a person is registered under Part 2 of the Care Standards Act 2000 (c. 14).

...

64   Other provision to be made by regulations

(1) Regulations may make provision for the purposes of this group of sections, including provision as to—

>   (a) the performance by adoption agencies of their functions,
>   (b) the manner in which information may be received, and
>   (c) the matters mentioned below in this section.

(2) Regulations may prescribe—

>   (a) the manner in which agreements made by virtue of section 57(5) are to be recorded,
>   (b) the information to be provided by any person on an application for the disclosure of information under this group of sections.

(3) Regulations may require adoption agencies—

>   (a) to give to prescribed persons prescribed information about the rights or opportunities to obtain information, or to give their views as to its disclosure, given by this group of sections,
>   (b) to seek prescribed information from, or give prescribed information to, the Registrar General in prescribed circumstances.

(4) Regulations may require the Registrar General—

>   (a) to disclose to any person (including an adopted person) at his request any information which the person requires to assist him to make contact with the adoption agency which is the appropriate adoption agency in the case of an adopted person specified in the request (or, as the case may be, in the applicant's case),
>   (b) to disclose to the appropriate adoption agency any information which the agency requires about any entry relating to the adopted person on the Adoption Contact Register.

(5) Regulations may provide for the payment of a prescribed fee in respect of the disclosure in prescribed circumstances of any information in pursuance of section 60, 61 or 62; but an adopted person may not be required to pay any fee in respect of any information

disclosed to him in relation to any person who (but for his adoption) would be related to him by blood (including half-blood), marriage or civil partnership.

(6) Regulations may provide for the payment of a prescribed fee by an adoption agency obtaining information under subsection (4)(b).

65   Sections 56 to 65: interpretation

(1) In this group of sections—

'appropriate adoption agency', in relation to an adopted person or to information relating to his adoption, means—

    (a) if the person was placed for adoption by an adoption agency, that agency or (if different) the agency which keeps the information in relation to his adoption,

    (b) in any other case, the local authority to which notice of intention to adopt was given,

'prescribed' means prescribed by subordinate legislation,

'regulations' means regulations under section 9,

'subordinate legislation' means regulations or, in relation to information to be given by a court, rules.

. . .

CHAPTER 4   STATUS OF ADOPTED CHILDREN

66   Meaning of adoption in Chapter 4

(1) In this Chapter 'adoption' means—

    (a) adoption by an adoption order or a Scottish or Northern Irish adoption order,

    (b) adoption by an order made in the Isle of Man or any of the Channel Islands,

    (c) an adoption effected under the law of a Convention country outside the British Islands, and certified in pursuance of Article 23(1) of the Convention (referred to in this Act as a 'Convention adoption'),

    (d) an overseas adoption, or

    (e) an adoption recognised by the law of England and Wales and effected under the law of any other country;

and related expressions are to be interpreted accordingly.

(2) But references in this Chapter to adoption do not include an adoption effected before the day on which this Chapter comes into force (referred to in this Chapter as 'the appointed day').

(3) Any reference in an enactment to an adopted person within the meaning of this Chapter includes a reference to an adopted child within the meaning of Part 4 of the Adoption Act 1976 (c. 36).

67   Status conferred by adoption

(1) An adopted person is to be treated in law as if born as the child of the adopters or adopter.

(2) An adopted person is the legitimate child of the adopters or adopter and, if adopted by—

    (a) a couple, or

    (b) one of a couple under section 51(2),

is to be treated as the child of the relationship of the couple in question.

(3) An adopted person—

    (a) if adopted by one of a couple under section 51(2), is to be treated in law as not being the child of any person other than the adopter and the other one of the couple, and

    (b) in any other case, is to be treated in law, subject to subsection (4), as not being the child of any person other than the adopters or adopter;

but this subsection does not affect any reference in this Act to a person's natural parent or to any other natural relationship.

(4) In the case of a person adopted by one of the person's natural parents as sole adoptive parent, subsection (3)(b) has no effect as respects entitlement to property depending on relationship to that parent, or as respects anything else depending on that relationship.

(5) This section has effect from the date of the adoption.

(6) Subject to the provisions of this Chapter and Schedule 4, this section—

    (a) applies for the interpretation of enactments or instruments passed or made before as well as after the adoption, and so applies subject to any contrary indication, and

    (b) has effect as respects things done, or events occurring, on or after the adoption.

68   Adoptive relatives

(1) A relationship existing by virtue of section 67 may be referred to as an adoptive relationship, and—

    (a) an adopter may be referred to as an adoptive parent or (as the case may be) as an adoptive father or adoptive mother,

    (b) any other relative of any degree under an adoptive relationship may be referred to as an adoptive relative of that degree.

(2) Subsection (1) does not affect the interpretation of any reference, not qualified by the word 'adoptive', to a relationship.

(3) A reference (however expressed) to the adoptive mother and father of a child adopted by—

    (a) a couple of the same sex, or

    (b) a partner of the child's parent, where the couple are of the same sex,

is to be read as a reference to the child's adoptive parents.

69   Rules of interpretation for instruments concerning property

(1) The rules of interpretation contained in this section apply (subject to any contrary indication and to Schedule 4) to any instrument so far as it contains a disposition of property.

(2) In applying section 67(1) and (2) to a disposition which depends on the date of birth of a child or children of the adoptive parent or parents, the disposition is to be interpreted as if—

    (a) the adopted person had been born on the date of adoption,

    (b) two or more people adopted on the same date had been born on that date in the order of their actual births;

but this does not affect any reference to a person's age.

(3) Examples of phrases in wills on which subsection (2) can operate are—

    1. Children of A 'living at my death or born afterwards'.

    2. Children of A 'living at my death or born afterwards before any one of such children for the time being in existence attains a vested interest and who attain the age of 21 years'.

    3. As in example 1 or 2, but referring to grandchildren of A instead of children of A.

    4. A for life 'until he has a child', and then to his child or children.

Note. Subsection (2) will not affect the reference to the age of 21 years in example 2.

(4) Section 67(3) does not prejudice—

    (a) any qualifying interest, or

    (b) any interest expectant (whether immediately or not) upon a qualifying interest.

'Qualifying interest' means an interest vested in possession in the adopted person before the adoption.

(5) Where it is necessary to determine for the purposes of a disposition of property effected by an instrument whether a woman can have a child—

    (a) it must be presumed that once a woman has attained the age of 55 years she will not adopt a person after execution of the instrument, and

(b) if she does so, then (in spite of section 67) that person is not to be treated as her child or (if she does so as one of a couple) as the child of the other one of the couple for the purposes of the instrument.

(6) In this section, 'instrument' includes a private Act settling property, but not any other enactment.

70 Dispositions depending on date of birth

(1) Where a disposition depends on the date of birth of a person who was born illegitimate and who is adopted by one of the natural parents as sole adoptive parent, section 69(2) does not affect entitlement by virtue of Part 3 of the Family Law Reform Act 1987 (c. 42) (dispositions of property).

(2) Subsection (1) applies for example where—
(a) a testator dies in 2001 bequeathing a legacy to his eldest grandchild living at a specified time,
(b) his unmarried daughter has a child in 2002 who is the first grandchild,
(c) his married son has a child in 2003,
(d) subsequently his unmarried daughter adopts her child as sole adoptive parent.

In that example the status of the daughter's child as the eldest grandchild of the testator is not affected by the events described in paragraphs (c) and (d).

71 Property devolving with peerages etc.

(1) An adoption does not affect the descent of any peerage or dignity or title of honour.

(2) An adoption does not affect the devolution of any property limited (expressly or not) to devolve (as nearly as the law permits) along with any peerage or dignity or title of honour.

(3) Subsection (2) applies only if and so far as a contrary intention is not expressed in the instrument, and has effect subject to the terms of the instrument.

72 Protection of trustees and personal representatives

(1) A trustee or personal representative is not under a duty, by virtue of the law relating to trusts or the administration of estates, to enquire, before conveying or distributing any property, whether any adoption has been effected or revoked if that fact could affect entitlement to the property.

(2) A trustee or personal representative is not liable to any person by reason of a conveyance or distribution of the property made without regard to any such fact if he has not received notice of the fact before the conveyance or distribution.

(3) This section does not prejudice the right of a person to follow the property, or any property representing it, into the hands of another person, other than a purchaser, who has received it.

73 Meaning of disposition

(1) This section applies for the purposes of this Chapter.

(2) A disposition includes the conferring of a power of appointment and any other disposition of an interest in or right over property; and in this subsection a power of appointment includes any discretionary power to transfer a beneficial interest in property without the furnishing of valuable consideration.

(3) This Chapter applies to an oral disposition as if contained in an instrument made when the disposition was made.

(4) The date of death of a testator is the date at which a will or codicil is to be regarded as made.

(5) The provisions of the law of intestate succession applicable to the estate of a deceased person are to be treated as if contained in an instrument executed by him (while of full capacity) immediately before his death.

74 Miscellaneous enactments

(1) Section 67 does not apply for the purposes of—

    (a) section 1 of and Schedule 1 to the Marriage Act 1949 or Schedule 1 to the Civil Partnership Act 2004 (prohibited degrees of kindred and affinity),

    (b) sections 64 and 65 of the Sexual Offences Act 2003 (sex with an adult relative).

(2) Section 67 does not apply for the purposes of any provision of—

    (a) the British Nationality Act 1981 (c. 61),

    (b) the Immigration Act 1971 (c. 77),

    (c) any instrument having effect under an enactment within paragraph (a) or (b), or

    (d) any other provision of the law for the time being in force which determines British citizenship, British overseas territories citizenship, the status of a British National (Overseas) or British Overseas citizenship.

75 Pensions

Section 67(3) does not affect entitlement to a pension which is payable to or for the benefit of a person and is in payment at the time of the person's adoption.

76 Insurance

(1) Where a child is adopted whose natural parent has effected an insurance with a friendly society or a collecting society or an industrial insurance company for the payment on the death of the child of money for funeral expenses, then—

    (a) the rights and liabilities under the policy are by virtue of the adoption transferred to the adoptive parents, and

    (b) for the purposes of the enactments relating to such societies and companies, the adoptive parents are to be treated as the person who took out the policy.

(2) Where the adoption is effected by an order made by virtue of section 51(2), the references in subsection (1) to the adoptive parents are to be read as references to the adopter and the other one of the couple.

CHAPTER 5   THE REGISTERS

Adopted Children Register etc.

77 Adopted Children Register

(1) The Registrar General must continue to maintain in the General Register Office a register, to be called the Adopted Children Register.

(2) The Adopted Children Register is not to be open to public inspection or search.

(3) No entries may be made in the Adopted Children Register other than entries—

    (a) directed to be made in it by adoption orders, or

    (b) required to be made under Schedule 1.

(4) A certified copy of an entry in the Adopted Children Register, if purporting to be sealed or stamped with the seal of the General Register Office, is to be received as evidence of the adoption to which it relates without further or other proof.

(5) Where an entry in the Adopted Children Register contains a record—

    (a) of the date of birth of the adopted person, or

    (b) of the country, or the district and sub-district, of the birth of the adopted person,

a certified copy of the entry is also to be received, without further or other proof, as evidence of that date, or country or district and sub-district, (as the case may be) in all respects as if the copy were a certified copy of an entry in the registers of live-births.

(6) Schedule 1 (registration of adoptions and the amendment of adoption orders) is to have effect.

78 Searches and copies

(1) The Registrar General must continue to maintain at the General Register Office an index of the Adopted Children Register.

(2) Any person may—

(a) search the index,

(b) have a certified copy of any entry in the Adopted Children Register.

(3) But a person is not entitled to have a certified copy of an entry in the Adopted Children Register relating to an adopted person who has not attained the age of 18 years unless the applicant has provided the Registrar General with the prescribed particulars.

'Prescribed' means prescribed by regulations made by the Registrar General with the approval of the Chancellor of the Exchequer.

(4) The terms, conditions and regulations as to payment of fees, and otherwise, applicable under the Births and Deaths Registration Act 1953 (c. 20), and the Registration Service Act 1953 (c. 37), in respect of—

(a) searches in the index kept in the General Register Office of certified copies of entries in the registers of live-births,

(b) the supply from that office of certified copies of entries in those certified copies, also apply in respect of searches, and supplies of certified copies, under subsection (2).

79 Connections between the register and birth records

(1) The Registrar General must make traceable the connection between any entry in the registers of live-births or other records which has been marked 'Adopted' and any corresponding entry in the Adopted Children Register.

(2) Information kept by the Registrar General for the purposes of subsection (1) is not to be open to public inspection or search.

(3) Any such information, and any other information which would enable an adopted person to obtain a certified copy of the record of his birth, may only be disclosed by the Registrar General in accordance with this section.

(4) In relation to a person adopted before the appointed day the court may, in exceptional circumstances, order the Registrar General to give any information mentioned in subsection (3) to a person.

(5) On an application made in the prescribed manner by the appropriate adoption agency in respect of an adopted person a record of whose birth is kept by the Registrar General, the Registrar General must give the agency any information relating to the adopted person which is mentioned in subsection (3).

'Appropriate adoption agency' has the same meaning as in section 65.

(6) In relation to a person adopted before the appointed day, Schedule 2 applies instead of subsection (5).

(7) On an application made in the prescribed manner by an adopted person a record of whose birth is kept by the Registrar General and who—

(a) is under the age of 18 years, and

(b) intends to be married or form a civil partnership,

the Registrar General must inform the applicant whether or not it appears from information contained in the registers of live-births or other records that the applicant and the intended spouse or civil partner may be within the prohibited degrees of relationship for the purposes of the Marriage Act 1949 (c. 76) or for the purposes of the Civil Partnership Act 2004 (c 33).

(8) Before the Registrar General gives any information by virtue of this section, any prescribed fee which he has demanded must be paid.

(9) In this section—

'appointed day' means the day appointed for the commencement of sections 56 to 65,

'prescribed' means prescribed by regulations made by the Registrar General with the approval of the Chancellor of the Exchequer.

80 Adoption Contact Register

(1) The Registrar General must continue to maintain at the General Register Office in accordance with regulations a register in two Parts to be called the Adoption Contact Register.

(2) Part 1 of the register is to contain the prescribed information about adopted persons who have given the prescribed notice expressing their wishes as to making contact with their relatives.

(3) The Registrar General may only make an entry in Part 1 of the register for an adopted person—

    (a) a record of whose birth is kept by the Registrar General,

    (b) who has attained the age of 18 years, and

    (c) who the Registrar General is satisfied has such information as is necessary to enable him to obtain a certified copy of the record of his birth.

(4) Part 2 of the register is to contain the prescribed information about persons who have given the prescribed notice expressing their wishes, as relatives of adopted persons, as to making contact with those persons.

(5) The Registrar General may only make an entry in Part 2 of the register for a person—

    (a) who has attained the age of 18 years, and

    (b) who the Registrar General is satisfied is a relative of an adopted person and has such information as is necessary to enable him to obtain a certified copy of the record of the adopted person's birth.

(6) Regulations may provide for—

    (a) the disclosure of information contained in one Part of the register to persons for whom there is an entry in the other Part,

    (b) the payment of prescribed fees in respect of the making or alteration of entries in the register and the disclosure of information contained in the register.

81 Adoption Contact Register: supplementary

(1) The Adoption Contact Register is not to be open to public inspection or search.

(2) In section 80, 'relative', in relation to an adopted person, means any person who (but for his adoption) would be related to him by blood (including half-blood), marriage or civil partnership.

(3) The Registrar General must not give any information entered in the register to any person except in accordance with subsection (6)(a) of that section or regulations made by virtue of section 64(4)(b).

(4) In section 80, 'regulations' means regulations made by the Registrar General with the approval of the Chancellor of the Exchequer, and 'prescribed' means prescribed by such regulations.

General

82 Interpretation

(1) In this Chapter—

'records' includes certified copies kept by the Registrar General of entries in any register of births,

'registers of live-births' means the registers of live-births made under the Births and Deaths Registration Act 1953 (c. 20).

(2) Any register, record or index maintained under this Chapter may be maintained in any form the Registrar General considers appropriate; and references (however expressed) to entries in such a register, or to their amendment, marking or cancellation, are to be read accordingly.

. . .

CHAPTER 7   MISCELLANEOUS

Restrictions

92   Restriction on arranging adoptions etc.

(1) A person who is neither an adoption agency nor acting in pursuance of an order of the High Court must not take any of the steps mentioned in subsection (2).

(2) The steps are—

    (a) asking a person other than an adoption agency to provide a child for adoption,

    (b) asking a person other than an adoption agency to provide prospective adopters for a child,

    (c) offering to find a child for adoption,

    (d) offering a child for adoption to a person other than an adoption agency,

    (e) handing over a child to any person other than an adoption agency with a view to the child's adoption by that or another person,

    (f) receiving a child handed over to him in contravention of paragraph (e),

    (g) entering into an agreement with any person for the adoption of a child, or for the purpose of facilitating the adoption of a child, where no adoption agency is acting on behalf of the child in the adoption,

    (h) initiating or taking part in negotiations of which the purpose is the conclusion of an agreement within paragraph (g),

    (i) causing another person to take any of the steps mentioned in paragraphs (a) to (h).

(3) Subsection (1) does not apply to a person taking any of the steps mentioned in paragraphs (d), (e), (g), (h) and (i) of subsection (2) if the following condition is met.

(4) The condition is that—

    (a) the prospective adopters are parents, relatives or guardians of the child (or one of them is), or

    (b) the prospective adopter is the partner of a parent of the child.

(5) References to an adoption agency in subsection (2) include a prescribed person outside the United Kingdom exercising functions corresponding to those of an adoption agency, if the functions are being exercised in prescribed circumstances in respect of the child in question.

(6) The Secretary of State may, after consultation with the Assembly, by order make any amendments of subsections (1) to (4), and any consequential amendments of this Act, which he considers necessary or expedient.

(7) In this section—

    (a) 'agreement' includes an arrangement (whether or not enforceable),

    (b) 'prescribed' means prescribed by regulations made by the Secretary of State after consultation with the Assembly.

93   Offence of breaching restrictions under section 92

(1) If a person contravenes section 92(1), he is guilty of an offence; and, if that person is an adoption society, the person who manages the society is also guilty of the offence.

(2) A person is not guilty of an offence under subsection (1) of taking the step mentioned in paragraph (f) of section 92(2) unless it is proved that he knew or had reason to suspect that the child was handed over to him in contravention of paragraph (e) of that subsection.

(3) A person is not guilty of an offence under subsection (1) of causing a person to take any of the steps mentioned in paragraphs (a) to (h) of section 92(2) unless it is proved that he knew or had reason to suspect that the step taken would contravene the paragraph in question.

(4) But subsections (2) and (3) only apply if sufficient evidence is adduced to raise an issue as to whether the person had the knowledge or reason mentioned.

(5) A person guilty of an offence under this section is liable on summary conviction to imprisonment for a term not exceeding six months, or a fine not exceeding £10,000, or both.

94   Restriction on reports

(1) A person who is not within a prescribed description may not, in any prescribed circumstances, prepare a report for any person about the suitability of a child for adoption or of a person to adopt a child or about the adoption, or placement for adoption, of a child.

'Prescribed' means prescribed by regulations made by the Secretary of State after consultation with the Assembly.

(2) If a person—

(a) contravenes subsection (1), or

(b) causes a person to prepare a report, or submits to any person a report which has been prepared, in contravention of that subsection,

he is guilty of an offence.

(3) If a person who works for an adoption society—

(a) contravenes subsection (1), or

(b) causes a person to prepare a report, or submits to any person a report which has been prepared, in contravention of that subsection,

the person who manages the society is also guilty of the offence.

(4) A person is not guilty of an offence under subsection (2)(b) unless it is proved that he knew or had reason to suspect that the report would be, or had been, prepared in contravention of subsection (1).

But this subsection only applies if sufficient evidence is adduced to raise an issue as to whether the person had the knowledge or reason mentioned.

(5) A person guilty of an offence under this section is liable on summary conviction to imprisonment for a term not exceeding six months, or a fine not exceeding level 5 on the standard scale, or both.

95   Prohibition of certain payments

(1) This section applies to any payment (other than an excepted payment) which is made for or in consideration of—

(a) the adoption of a child,

(b) giving any consent required in connection with the adoption of a child,

(c) removing from the United Kingdom a child who is a Commonwealth citizen, or is habitually resident in the United Kingdom, to a place outside the British Islands for the purpose of adoption,

(d) a person (who is neither an adoption agency nor acting in pursuance of an order of the High Court) taking any step mentioned in section 92(2),

(e) preparing, causing to be prepared or submitting a report the preparation of which contravenes section 94(1).

(2) In this section and section 96, removing a child from the United Kingdom has the same meaning as in section 85.

(3) Any person who—

(a) makes any payment to which this section applies,

(b) agrees or offers to make any such payment, or

(c) receives or agrees to receive or attempts to obtain any such payment,

is guilty of an offence.

(4) A person guilty of an offence under this section is liable on summary conviction to imprisonment for a term not exceeding six months, or a fine not exceeding £10,000, or both.

96   Excepted payments

(1) A payment is an excepted payment if it is made by virtue of, or in accordance with provision made by or under, this Act, the Adoption (Scotland) Act 1978 (c. 28) or the Adoption (Northern Ireland) Order 1987 (S.I. 1987/2203 (N.I.22)).

(2) A payment is an excepted payment if it is made to a registered adoption society by—

(a) a parent or guardian of a child, or

(b) a person who adopts or proposes to adopt a child,

in respect of expenses reasonably incurred by the society in connection with the adoption or proposed adoption of the child.

(3) A payment is an excepted payment if it is made in respect of any legal or medical expenses incurred or to be incurred by any person in connection with an application to a court which he has made or proposes to make for an adoption order, a placement order, or an order under section 26 or 84.

. . .

97 Sections 92 to 96: interpretation
In sections 92 to 96—
> (a) 'adoption agency' includes a Scottish or Northern Irish adoption agency,
> (b) 'payment' includes reward,
> (c) references to adoption are to the adoption of persons, wherever they may be habitually resident, effected under the law of any country or territory, whether within or outside the British Islands.

. . .

Proceedings

99 Proceedings for offences
Proceedings for an offence by virtue of section 9 or 59 may not, without the written consent of the Attorney General, be taken by any person other than the Commission for Social Care Inspection or the Assembly.

. . .

101 Privacy
(1) Proceedings under this Act in the High Court or a County Court may be heard and determined in private.

. . .

The Children and Family Court Advisory and Support Service

102 Officers of the Service
(1) For the purposes of—
> (a) any relevant application,
> (b) the signification by any person of any consent to placement or adoption,

rules must provide for the appointment in prescribed cases of an officer of the Children and Family Court Advisory and Support Service ('the Service') or a Welsh family proceedings officer.

(2) The rules may provide for the appointment of such an officer in other circumstances in which it appears to the Lord Chancellor to be necessary or expedient to do so.

(3) The rules may provide for the officer—
> (a) to act on behalf of the child upon the hearing of any relevant application, with the duty of safeguarding the interests of the child in the prescribed manner,
> (b) where the court so requests, to prepare a report on matters relating to the welfare of the child in question,
> (c) to witness documents which signify consent to placement or adoption,
> (d) to perform prescribed functions.

(4) A report prepared in pursuance of the rules on matters relating to the welfare of a child must—
> (a) deal with prescribed matters (unless the court orders otherwise), and
> (b) be made in the manner required by the court.

(5) A person who—
> (a) in the case of an application for the making, varying or revocation of a placement order, is employed by the local authority which made the application,

    (b) in the case of an application for an adoption order in respect of a child who was placed for adoption, is employed by the adoption agency which placed him, or

    (c) is within a prescribed description,

is not to be appointed under subsection (1) or (2).

    (6) In this section, 'relevant application' means an application for—

      (a) the making, varying or revocation of a placement order,

      (b) the making of an order under section 26, or the varying or revocation of such an order,

      (c) the making of an adoption order, or

      (d) the making of an order under section 84.

    (7) Rules may make provision as to the assistance which the court may require an officer of the Service or a Welsh family proceedings officer to give to it.

    (8) In this section and section 103 'Welsh family proceedings officer' has the meaning given by section 35 of the Children Act 2004.

103   Right of officers of the Service to have access to adoption agency records

    (1) Where an officer of the Service or a Welsh family proceedings officer has been appointed to act under section 102(1), he has the right at all reasonable times to examine and take copies of any records of, or held by, an adoption agency which were compiled in connection with the making, or proposed making, by any person of any application under this Part in respect of the child concerned.

    (2) Where an officer of the Service or a Welsh family proceedings officer takes a copy of any record which he is entitled to examine under this section, that copy or any part of it is admissible as evidence of any matter referred to in any—

      (a) report which he makes to the court in the proceedings in question, or

      (b) evidence which he gives in those proceedings.

    (3) Subsection (2) has effect regardless of any enactment or rule of law which would otherwise prevent the record in question being admissible in evidence.

Evidence

104   Evidence of consent

    (1) If a document signifying any consent which is required by this Part to be given is witnessed in accordance with rules, it is to be admissible in evidence without further proof of the signature of the person by whom it was executed.

    (2) A document signifying any such consent which purports to be witnessed in accordance with rules is to be presumed to be so witnessed, and to have been executed and witnessed on the date and at the place specified in the document, unless the contrary is proved.

. . .

PART 2   AMENDMENTS OF THE CHILDREN ACT 1989

111   Parental responsibility of unmarried father

. . .

    (7) Paragraph (a) of section 4(1) of the 1989 Act, as substituted by subsection (2) of this section, does not confer parental responsibility on a man who was registered under an enactment referred to in paragraph (a), (b) or (c) of section 4(1A) of that Act, as inserted by subsection (3) of this section, before the commencement of subsection (3) in relation to that paragraph.

. . .

PART 3   MISCELLANEOUS AND FINAL PROVISIONS

CHAPTER 1   MISCELLANEOUS

Advertisements in the United Kingdom

123   Restriction on advertisements etc.

(1) A person must not—

    (a) publish or distribute an advertisement or information to which this section applies, or

    (b) cause such an advertisement or information to be published or distributed.

(2) This section applies to an advertisement indicating that—

    (a) the parent or guardian of a child wants the child to be adopted,

    (b) a person wants to adopt a child,

    (c) a person other than an adoption agency is willing to take any step mentioned in paragraphs (a) to (e), (g) and (h) and (so far as relating to those paragraphs) (i) of section 92(2),

    (d) a person other than an adoption agency is willing to receive a child handed over to him with a view to the child's adoption by him or another, or

    (e) a person is willing to remove a child from the United Kingdom for the purposes of adoption.

(3) This section applies to—

    . . .

    (b) information about a particular child as a child available for adoption.

(4) For the purposes of this section and section 124—

    (a) publishing or distributing an advertisement or information means publishing it or distributing it to the public and includes doing so by electronic means (for example, by means of the internet),

    (b) the public includes selected members of the public as well as the public generally or any section of the public.

(5) Subsection (1) does not apply to publication or distribution by or on behalf of an adoption agency.

(6) The Secretary of State may by order make any amendments of this section which he considers necessary or expedient in consequence of any developments in technology relating to publishing or distributing advertisements or other information by electronic or electromagnetic means.

. . .

124   Offence of breaching restriction under section 123

(1) A person who contravenes section 123(1) is guilty of an offence.

(2) A person is not guilty of an offence under this section unless it is proved that he knew or had reason to suspect that section 123 applied to the advertisement or information.

But this subsection only applies if sufficient evidence is adduced to raise an issue as to whether the person had the knowledge or reason mentioned.

(3) A person guilty of an offence under this section is liable on summary conviction to imprisonment for a term not exceeding three months, or a fine not exceeding level 5 on the standard scale, or both.

Adoption and Children Act Register

125   Adoption and Children Act Register

(1) Her Majesty may by Order in Council make provision for the Secretary of State to establish and maintain a register, to be called the Adoption and Children Act Register, containing—

    (a) prescribed information about children who are suitable for adoption and prospective adopters who are suitable to adopt a child,

(b) prescribed information about persons included in the register in pursuance of paragraph (a) in respect of things occurring after their inclusion.

(2) For the purpose of giving assistance in finding persons with whom children may be placed for purposes other than adoption, an Order under this section may—

(a) provide for the register to contain information about such persons and the children who may be placed with them, and

(b) apply any of the other provisions of this group of sections (that is, this section and sections 126 to 131), with or without modifications.

(3) The register is not to be open to public inspection or search.

(4) An Order under this section may make provision about the retention of information in the register.

(5) Information is to be kept in the register in any form the Secretary of State considers appropriate.

126   Use of an organisation to establish the register

(1) The Secretary of State may make an arrangement with an organisation under which any function of his under an Order under section 125 of establishing and maintaining the register, and disclosing information entered in, or compiled from information entered in, the register to any person is performed wholly or partly by the organisation on his behalf.

(2) The arrangement may include provision for payments to be made to the organisation by the Secretary of State.

(3) If the Secretary of State makes an arrangement under this section with an organisation, the organisation is to perform the functions exercisable by virtue of this section in accordance with any directions given by the Secretary of State and the directions may be of general application (or general application in any part of Great Britain) or be special directions.

(4) An exercise of the Secretary of State's powers under subsection (1) or (3) requires the agreement of the Scottish Ministers (if the register applies to Scotland) and of the Assembly (if the register applies to Wales).

(5) References in this group of sections to the registration organisation are to any organisation for the time being performing functions in respect of the register by virtue of arrangements under this section.

127   Use of an organisation as agency for payments

(1) An Order under section 125 may authorise an organisation with which an arrangement is made under section 126 to act as agent for the payment or receipt of sums payable by adoption agencies to other adoption agencies and may require adoption agencies to pay or receive such sums through the organisation.

(2) The organisation is to perform the functions exercisable by virtue of this section in accordance with any directions given by the Secretary of State; and the directions may be of general application (or general application in any part of Great Britain) or be special directions.

(3) An exercise of the Secretary of State's power to give directions under subsection (2) requires the agreement of the Scottish Ministers (if any payment agency provision applies to Scotland) and of the Assembly (if any payment agency provision applies to Wales).

128   Supply of information for the register

(1) An Order under section 125 may require adoption agencies to give prescribed information to the Secretary of State or the registration organisation for entry in the register.

(2) Information is to be given to the Secretary of State or the registration organisation when required by the Order and in the prescribed form and manner.

(3) An Order under section 125 may require an agency giving information which is entered on the register to pay a prescribed fee to the Secretary of State or the registration organisation.

(4) But an adoption agency is not to disclose any information to the Secretary of State or the registration organisation—

    (a) about prospective adopters who are suitable to adopt a child, or persons who were included in the register as such prospective adopters, without their consent,

    (b) about children suitable for adoption, or persons who were included in the register as such children, without the consent of the prescribed person.

(5) Consent under subsection (4) is to be given in the prescribed form.

129   Disclosure of information

(1) Information entered in the register, or compiled from information entered in the register, may only be disclosed under subsection (2) or (3).

(2) Prescribed information entered in the register may be disclosed by the Secretary of State or the registration organisation—

    (a) where an adoption agency is acting on behalf of a child who is suitable for adoption, to the agency to assist in finding prospective adopters with whom it would be appropriate for the child to be placed,

    (b) where an adoption agency is acting on behalf of prospective adopters who are suitable to adopt a child, to the agency to assist in finding a child appropriate for adoption by them.

(3) Prescribed information entered in the register, or compiled from information entered in the register, may be disclosed by the Secretary of State or the registration organisation to any prescribed person for use for statistical or research purposes, or for other prescribed purposes.

(4) An Order under section 125 may prescribe the steps to be taken by adoption agencies in respect of information received by them by virtue of subsection (2).

(5) Subsection (1) does not apply—

    (a) to a disclosure of information with the authority of the Secretary of State, or

    (b) to a disclosure by the registration organisation of prescribed information to the Scottish Ministers (if the register applies to Scotland) or the Assembly (if the register applies to Wales).

(6) Information disclosed to any person under subsection (2) or (3) may be given on any prescribed terms or conditions.

(7) An Order under section 125 may, in prescribed circumstances, require a prescribed fee to be paid to the Secretary of State or the registration organisation—

    (a) by a prescribed adoption agency in respect of information disclosed under subsection (2), or

    (b) by a person to whom information is disclosed under subsection (3).

(8) If any information entered in the register is disclosed to a person in contravention of subsection (1), the person disclosing it is guilty of an offence.

(9) A person guilty of an offence under subsection (8) is liable on summary conviction to imprisonment for a term not exceeding three months, or a fine not exceeding level 5 on the standard scale, or both.

. . .

131   Supplementary

(1) In this group of sections—

    (a) 'organisation' includes a public body and a private or voluntary organisation,

    (b) 'prescribed' means prescribed by an Order under section 125,

    (c) 'the register' means the Adoption and Children Act Register,

    . . .

    (e) 'voluntary organisation providing a registered adoption service' has the same meaning as in section 144(3).

(2) For the purposes of this group of sections—

(a) a child is suitable for adoption if an adoption agency is satisfied that the child ought to be placed for adoption,

(b) prospective adopters are suitable to adopt a child if an adoption agency is satisfied that they are suitable to have a child placed with them for adoption.

(3) Nothing authorised or required to be done by virtue of this group of sections constitutes an offence under section 93, 94 or 95.

(4) No recommendation to make an Order under section 125 is to be made to Her Majesty in Council unless a draft has been laid before and approved by resolution of each House of Parliament.

...

138 Proceedings in Great Britain

Proceedings for an offence by virtue of section 9, 59, 93, 94, 95 or 129—

(a) may not be brought more than six years after the commission of the offence but, subject to that,

(b) may be brought within a period of six months from the date on which evidence sufficient in the opinion of the prosecutor to warrant the proceedings came to his knowledge.

...

CHAPTER 2   FINAL PROVISIONS

...

144   General interpretation etc.

(1) In this Act—

'appropriate Minister' means—

(a) in relation to England, Scotland or Northern Ireland, the Secretary of State,

(b) in relation to Wales, the Assembly,

and in relation to England and Wales means the Secretary of State and the Assembly acting jointly,

'the Assembly' means the National Assembly for Wales,

'body' includes an unincorporated body,

'by virtue of' includes 'by' and 'under',

'child', except where used to express a relationship, means a person who has not attained the age of 18 years,

'the Convention' means the Convention on Protection of Children and Co-operation in respect of Intercountry Adoption, concluded at the Hague on 29th May 1993,

'Convention adoption order' means an adoption order which, by virtue of regulations under section 1 of the Adoption (Intercountry Aspects) Act 1999 (c. 18) (regulations giving effect to the Convention), is made as a Convention adoption order,

'Convention country' means a country or territory in which the Convention is in force,

'court' means, subject to any provision made by virtue of Part 1 of Schedule 11 to the 1989 Act, the High Court, a county court or a magistrates' court,

'enactment' includes an enactment comprised in subordinate legislation,

'fee' includes expenses,

'guardian' has the same meaning as in the 1989 Act and includes a special guardian within the meaning of that Act,

'information' means information recorded in any form,

'local authority' means any unitary authority, or any county council so far as they are not a unitary authority,

...

'notice' means a notice in writing,

'registration authority' (in Part 1) has the same meaning as in the Care Standards Act 2000 (c. 14),

'regulations' means regulations made by the appropriate Minister, unless they are required to be made by the Lord Chancellor, the Secretary of State or the Registrar General,

'relative', in relation to a child, means a grandparent, brother, sister, uncle or aunt, whether of the full blood or half-blood or by marriage or civil partnership,

'rules' means Family Procedure Rules made by virtue of section 141(1),

. . .

'subordinate legislation' has the same meaning as in the Interpretation Act 1978 (c. 30),

'unitary authority' means—

(a) the council of any county so far as they are the council for an area for which there are no district councils,

(b) the council of any district comprised in an area for which there is no county council,

(c) the council of a county borough,

(d) the council of a London borough,

(e) the Common Council of the City of London.

. . .

(4) In this Act, a couple means—

(a) a married couple, or

(aa) two people who are civil partners of each other, or

(b) two people (whether of different sexes or the same sex) living as partners in an enduring family relationship.

(5) Subsection (4)(b) does not include two people one of whom is the other's parent, grandparent, sister, brother, aunt or uncle.

(6) References to relationships in subsection (5)—

(a) are to relationships of the full blood or half blood or, in the case of an adopted person, such of those relationships as would exist but for adoption, and

(b) include the relationship of a child with his adoptive, or former adoptive, parents, but do not include any other adoptive relationships.

(7) For the purposes of this Act, a person is the partner of a child's parent if the person and the parent are a couple but the person is not the child's parent.

. . .

SCHEDULES

SCHEDULE 1

REGISTRATION OF ADOPTIONS

Registration of adoption orders

1. (1) Every adoption order must contain a direction to the Registrar General to make in the Adopted Children Register an entry in the form prescribed by regulations made by the Registrar General with the approval of the Chancellor of the Exchequer.

(2) Where, on an application to a court for an adoption order in respect of a child, the identity of the child with a child to whom an entry in the registers of live-births or other records relates is proved to the satisfaction of the court, any adoption order made in pursuance of the application must contain a direction to the Registrar General to secure that the entry in the register or, as the case may be, record in question is marked with the word 'Adopted'.

(3) Where an adoption order is made in respect of a child who has previously been the subject of an adoption order made by a court in England or Wales under Part 1 of this Act or any other enactment—

>   (a) sub-paragraph (2) does not apply, and

>   (b) the order must contain a direction to the Registrar General to mark the previous entry in the Adopted Children Register with the word 'Re-adopted'.

(4) Where an adoption order is made, the prescribed officer of the court which made the order must communicate the order to the Registrar General in the prescribed manner; and the Registrar General must then comply with the directions contained in the order.

'Prescribed' means prescribed by rules.

. . .

Amendment of orders and rectification of Registers and other records

4. (1) The court by which an adoption order has been made may, on the application of the adopter or the adopted person, amend the order by the correction of any error in the particulars contained in it.

(2) The court by which an adoption order has been made may, if satisfied on the application of the adopter or the adopted person that within the period of one year beginning with the date of the order any new name—

>   (a) has been given to the adopted person (whether in baptism or otherwise), or

>   (b) has been taken by the adopted person,

either in place of or in addition to a name specified in the particulars required to be entered in the Adopted Children Register in pursuance of the order, amend the order by substituting or, as the case may be, adding that name in those particulars.

(3) The court by which an adoption order has been made may, if satisfied on the application of any person concerned that a direction for the marking of an entry in the registers of live-births, the Adopted Children Register or other records included in the order in pursuance of paragraph 1(2) or (3) was wrongly so included, revoke that direction.

(4) Where an adoption order is amended or a direction revoked under subparagraphs (1) to (3), the prescribed officer of the court must communicate the amendment in the prescribed manner to the Registrar General.

'Prescribed' means prescribed by rules.

(5) The Registrar General must then—

>   (a) amend the entry in the Adopted Children Register accordingly, or

>   (b) secure that the marking of the entry in the registers of live-births, the Adopted Children Register or other records is cancelled,

as the case may be.

(6) Where an adoption order is quashed or an appeal against an adoption order allowed by any court, the court must give directions to the Registrar General to secure that—

>   (a) any entry in the Adopted Children Register, and

>   (b) any marking of an entry in that Register, the registers of live-births or other records as the case may be, which was effected in pursuance of the order,

is cancelled.

(7) Where an adoption order has been amended, any certified copy of the relevant entry in the Adopted Children Register which may be issued pursuant to section 78(2)(b) must be a copy of the entry as amended, without the reproduction of—

>   (a) any note or marking relating to the amendment, or

>   (b) any matter cancelled in pursuance of it.

(8) A copy or extract of an entry in any register or other record, being an entry the marking of which has been cancelled, is not to be treated as an accurate copy unless both the marking and the cancellation are omitted from it.

. . .

Marking of entries on re-registration of birth on legitimation

5. (1) Without prejudice to paragraphs 2(4) and 4(5), where, after an entry in the registers of live-births or other records has been marked in accordance with paragraph 1 or 2, the birth is re-registered under section 14 of the Births and Deaths Registration Act 1953 (c. 20) (re-registration of births of legitimated persons), the entry made on the re-registration must be marked in the like manner.

(2) Without prejudice to paragraph 4(9), where an entry in the registers of live-births or other records is marked in pursuance of paragraph 3 and the birth in question is subsequently re-registered under section 14 of that Act, the entry made on re-registration must be marked in the like manner.

Cancellations in registers on legitimation

6. (1) This paragraph applies where an adoption order is revoked under section 55(1).

(2) The prescribed officer of the court must communicate the revocation in the prescribed manner to the Registrar General who must then cancel or secure the cancellation of—
- (a) the entry in the Adopted Children Register relating to the adopted person, and
- (b) the marking with the word 'Adopted' of any entry relating to the adopted person in the registers of live-births or other records.

'Prescribed' means prescribed by rules.

(3) A copy or extract of an entry in any register or other record, being an entry the marking of which is cancelled under this paragraph, is not to be treated as an accurate copy unless both the marking and the cancellation are omitted from it.

SCHEDULE 2

DISCLOSURE OF BIRTH RECORDS BY REGISTRAR GENERAL

1. On an application made in the prescribed manner by an adopted person—
- (a) a record of whose birth is kept by the Registrar General, and
- (b) who has attained the age of 18 years,

the Registrar General must give the applicant any information necessary to enable the applicant to obtain a certified copy of the record of his birth.

'Prescribed' means prescribed by regulations made by the Registrar General with the approval of the Chancellor of the Exchequer.

2. (1) Before giving any information to an applicant under paragraph 1, the Registrar General must inform the applicant that counselling services are available to the applicant—
- (a) from a registered adoption society, an organisation within section 144(3)(b) or an adoption society which is registered under Article 4 of the Adoption (Northern Ireland) Order 1987 (S.I. 1987/2203 (N.I. 22)),
- (b) if the applicant is in England and Wales, at the General Register Office or from any local authority or registered adoption support agency,

...

(2) In sub-paragraph (1)(b), 'registered adoption support agency' means an adoption support agency in respect of which a person is registered under Part 2 of the Care Standards Act 2000 (c. 14).

...

(4) If the applicant chooses to receive counselling from a person or body within sub-paragraph (1), the Registrar General must send to the person or body the information to which the applicant is entitled under paragraph 1.

...

4. (1) Where a person—

    (a) was adopted before 12th November 1975, and

    (b) applies for information under paragraph 1,

the Registrar General must not give the information to the applicant unless the applicant has attended an interview with a counsellor arranged by a person or body from whom counselling services are available as mentioned in paragraph 2.

(2) Where the Registrar General is prevented by sub-paragraph (1) from giving information to a person who is not living in the United Kingdom, the Registrar General may give the information to any body which—

    (a) the Registrar General is satisfied is suitable to provide counselling to that person, and

    (b) has notified the Registrar General that it is prepared to provide such counselling.

...

SCHEDULE 6

GLOSSARY

In this Act, the expressions listed in the left-hand column below have the meaning given by, or are to be interpreted in accordance with, the provisions of this Act or (where stated) of the 1989 Act listed in the right-hand column.

Expression	Provision
the 1989 Act	section 2(5)
Adopted Children Register	section 77
Adoption and Children Act Register	section 125
adoption (in relation to Chapter 4 of Part 1)	section 66
adoption agency	section 2(1)
adoption agency placing a child for adoption	section 18(5)
Adoption Contact Register	section 80
adoption order	section 46(1)
Adoption Service	section 2(1)
adoption society	section 2(5)
adoption support agency	section 8
adoption support services	section 2(6)
appointed day (in relation to Chapter 4 of Part 1)	section 66(2)
appropriate Minister	section 144
Assembly	section 144
body	section 144
by virtue of	section 144
care order	section 105(1) of the 1989 Act
child	sections 49(5) and 144
child assessment order	section 43(2) of the 1989 Act
child in the care of a local authority	section 105(1) of the 1989 Act
child looked after by a local authority	section 22 of the 1989 Act
child placed for adoption by an adoption agency	section 18(5)
child to be adopted, adopted child	section 49(5)
consent (in relation to making adoption orders or placing for adoption)	section 52
the Convention	section 144
Convention adoption	section 66(1)(c)
Convention adoption order	section 144
Convention country	section 144

Expression	Provision
couple	section 144(4)
court	section 144
disposition (in relation to Chapter 4 of Part 1)	section 73
enactment	section 144
fee	section 144
guardian	section 144
information	section 144
interim care order	section 38 of the 1989 Act
local authority	section 144
local authority foster parent	section 23(3) of the 1989 Act
Northern Irish adoption agency	section 144
Northern Irish adoption order	section 144
notice	section 144
notice of intention to adopt	section 44(2)
overseas adoption	section 87
parental responsibility	section 3 of the 1989 Act
partner, in relation to a parent of a child	section 144(7)
placement order	section 21
placing, or placed, for adoption	sections 18(5) and 19(4)
prohibited steps order	section 8(1) of the 1989 Act
records (in relation to Chapter 5 of Part 1)	section 82
registered adoption society	section 2(2)
registers of live-births (in relation to Chapter 5 of Part 1)	section 82
registration authority (in Part 1)	section 144
regulations	section 144
relative	section 144, read with section 1(8)
residence order	section 8(1) of the 1989 Act
rules	section 144
Scottish adoption agency	section 144(3)
Scottish adoption order	section 144
specific issue order	section 8(1) of the 1989 Act
subordinate legislation	section 144
supervision order	section 31(11) of the 1989 Act
unitary authority	section 144
voluntary organisation	section 2(5)

Human Fertilisation and Embryology
(Deceased Fathers) Act 2003
(2003 c. 24)

3   Retrospective, transitional and transitory provision

(1) This Act shall (in addition to any case where the sperm or embryo is used on or after the coming into force of section 1) apply to any case where the sperm of a man, or any embryo the creation of which was brought about with the sperm of a man, was used on or after 1st August 1991 and before the coming into force of that section.

(2) Where the child concerned was born before the coming into force of section 1 of this Act, section 28(5A) or (as the case may be) (5B) of the Human Fertilisation and Embryology

Act 1990 (c. 37) shall have effect as if for paragraph (e) there were substituted—

'(e) the woman has elected in writing not later than the end of the period of six months beginning with the coming into force of this subsection for the man to be treated for the purpose mentioned in subsection (5I) below as the father of the child,'.

(3) Where the child concerned was born before the coming into force of section 1 of this Act, section 28(5C) of the Act of 1990 shall have effect as if for paragraph (f) there were substituted—

'(f) the woman has elected in writing not later than the end of the period of six months beginning with the coming into force of this subsection for the other party to the marriage to be treated for the purpose mentioned in subsection (5I) below as the father of the child,'.

(4) Where the child concerned was born before the coming into force of section 1 of this Act, section 28(5D) of the Act of 1990 shall have effect as if for paragraph (f) there were substituted—

'(f) the woman has elected in writing not later than the end of the period of six months beginning with the coming into force of this subsection for the man to be treated for the purpose mentioned in subsection (5I) below as the father of the child,'.

(5) Where the child concerned was born before the coming into force of section 1 of this Act, section 28 of the Act of 1990 shall have effect as if—

    (a) subsection (5E) were omitted; and

    (b) in subsection (5F) for the words from '(which requires' to 'that day)' there were substituted '(which requires an election to be made not later than the end of a period of six months)'.

(6) Where the man who might be treated as the father of the child died before the passing of this Act—

    (a) subsections (5A) and (5B) of section 28 of the Act of 1990 shall have effect as if paragraph (d) of each subsection were omitted;

    (b) subsections (5C) and (5D) of that section of that Act shall have effect as if paragraph (e) of each subsection were omitted;

. . .

Anti-social Behaviour Act 2003
(2003 c. 38)

PART 3   PARENTAL RESPONSIBILITIES

Truancy and exclusion from school

19   Parenting contracts in cases of exclusion from school or truancy

(1) This section applies where a pupil has been excluded on disciplinary grounds from a relevant school for a fixed period or permanently.

(2) This section also applies where a child of compulsory school age has failed to attend regularly at

    (a) a relevant school at which he is a registered pupil,

    (b) any place at which education is provided for him in the circumstances mentioned in subsection (1) of section 444ZA of the Education Act 1996, and

    (c) any place at which he is required to attend in the circumstances mentioned in subsection (2) of that section.

(3) A local education authority or the governing body of a relevant school may enter into a parenting contract with a parent of the pupil or child.

(4) A parenting contract is a document which contains—

    (a) a statement by the parent that he agrees to comply with such requirements as may be specified in the document for such period as may be so specified, and

    (b) a statement by the local education authority or governing body that it agrees to provide support to the parent for the purpose of complying with those requirements.

(5) The requirements mentioned in subsection (4) may include (in particular) a requirement to attend a counselling or guidance programme.

(6) The purpose of the requirements mentioned in subsection (4)—

    (a) in a case falling within subsection (1), is to improve the behaviour of the pupil,

    (b) in a case falling within subsection (2), is to ensure that the child attends regularly at the relevant school at which he is a registered pupil.

(7) A parenting contract must be signed by the parent and signed on behalf of the local education authority or governing body.

(8) A parenting contract does not create any obligations in respect of whose breach any liability arises in contract or in tort.

(9) Local education authorities and governing bodies of relevant schools must, in carrying out their functions in relation to parenting contracts, have regard to any guidance which is issued by the appropriate person from time to time for that purpose.

20 Parenting orders in cases of exclusion from school

(1) This section applies where—

    (a) a pupil has been excluded on disciplinary grounds from a relevant school for a fixed period or permanently, and

    (b) such conditions as may be prescribed in regulations made by the appropriate person are satisfied.

(2) A local education authority may apply to a magistrates' court for a parenting order in respect of a parent of the pupil.

(3) If such an application is made, the court may make a parenting order in respect of a parent of the pupil if it is satisfied that making the order would be desirable in the interests of improving the behaviour of the pupil.

(4) A parenting order is an order which requires the parent—

    (a) to comply, for a period not exceeding twelve months, with such requirements as are specified in the order, and

    (b) subject to subsection (5), to attend, for a concurrent period not exceeding three months, such counselling or guidance programme as may be specified in directions given by the responsible officer.

(5) A parenting order under this section may, but need not, include a requirement mentioned in subsection (4)(b) in any case where a parenting order under this section or any other enactment has been made in respect of the parent on a previous occasion.

(6) A counselling or guidance programme which a parent is required to attend by virtue of subsection (4)(b) may be or include a residential course but only if the court is satisfied that the following two conditions are fulfilled.

(7) The first condition is that the attendance of the parent at a residential course is likely to be more effective than his attendance at a non-residential course in improving the behaviour of the pupil.

(8) The second condition is that any interference with family life which is likely to result from the attendance of the parent at a residential course is proportionate in all the circumstances.

21 Parenting orders: supplemental

(1) In deciding whether to make a parenting order under section 20, a court must take into account (amongst other things)—

    (a) any refusal by the parent to enter into a parenting contract under section 19 in respect of the pupil in a case falling within subsection (1) of that section, or

(b) if the parent has entered into such a parenting contract, any failure by the parent to comply with the requirements specified in the contract.

(2) Before making a parenting order under section 20 in the case of a pupil under the age of 16, a court must obtain and consider information about the pupil's family circumstances and the likely effect of the order on those circumstances.

(3) Subsections (3) to (7) of section 9 of the Crime and Disorder Act 1998 (c. 37) (supplemental provisions about parenting orders) are to apply in relation to a parenting order under section 20 as they apply in relation to a parenting order under section 8 of that Act.

(4) The appropriate person may by regulations make provision as to how the costs associated with the requirements of parenting orders under section 20 (including the costs of providing counselling or guidance programmes) are to be borne.

(5) Local education authorities, head teachers and responsible officers must, in carrying out their functions in relation to parenting orders, have regard to any guidance which is issued by the appropriate person from time to time for that purpose.

22   Parenting orders: appeals

(1) An appeal lies to the Crown Court against the making of a parenting order under section 20.

(2) Subsections (2) and (3) of section 10 of the Crime and Disorder Act 1998 (appeals against parenting orders) are to apply in relation to an appeal under this section as they apply in relation to an appeal under subsection (1)(b) of that section.

. . .

24   Interpretation

In this section and sections 19 to 21—

'the appropriate person' means—

(a) in relation to England, the Secretary of State, and

(b) in relation to Wales, the National Assembly for Wales,

'child of compulsory school age' has the same meaning as in the 1996 Act, and 'child' is to be construed accordingly,

'head teacher' includes acting head teacher, teacher in charge and acting teacher in charge,

'local education authority' has the same meaning as in the 1996 Act,

'parent', in relation to a pupil or child, is to be construed in accordance with section 576 of the 1996 Act, but does not include a person who is not an individual,

'pupil' is to be construed in accordance with section 3(1) and (1A) of the 1996 Act,

'registered pupil' has the meaning given by section 434(5) of the 1996 Act,

'relevant school' means—

(a) a qualifying school as defined in section 1(3) of the Education Act 2002 (c. 32), or

(b) a pupil referral unit as defined in section 19(2) of the 1996 Act,

'responsible officer', in relation to a parenting order, means one of the following who is specified in the order, namely—

(a) an officer of a local education authority, and

(b) a head teacher or a person nominated by a head teacher,

but a person falling within paragraph (b) may not be specified in the order without his consent,

'the 1996 Act' means the Education Act 1996 (c. 56).

Criminal conduct and anti-social behaviour

25   Parenting contracts in respect of criminal conduct and anti-social behaviour

(1) This section applies where a child or young person has been referred to a youth offending team.

(2) The youth offending team may enter into a parenting contract with a parent of the child or young person if a member of that team has reason to believe that the child or young person has engaged, or is likely to engage, in criminal conduct or anti-social behaviour.

(3) A parenting contract is a document which contains—

   (a) a statement by the parent that he agrees to comply with such requirements as may be specified in the document for such period as may be so specified, and

   (b) a statement by the youth offending team that it agrees to provide support to the parent for the purpose of complying with those requirements.

(4) The requirements mentioned in subsection (3)(a) may include (in particular) a requirement to attend a counselling or guidance programme.

(5) The purpose of the requirements mentioned in subsection (3)(a) is to prevent the child or young person from engaging in criminal conduct or anti-social behaviour or further criminal conduct or further anti-social behaviour.

(6) A parenting contract must be signed by the parent and signed on behalf of the youth offending team.

(7) A parenting contract does not create any obligations in respect of whose breach any liability arises in contract or in tort.

(8) Youth offending teams must, in carrying out their functions in relation to parenting contracts, have regard to any guidance which is issued by the Secretary of State from time to time for that purpose.

26 Parenting orders in respect of criminal conduct and anti-social behaviour

(1) This section applies where a child or young person has been referred to a youth offending team.

(2) A member of the youth offending team may apply to a magistrates' court for a parenting order in respect of a parent of the child or young person.

(3) If such an application is made, the court may make a parenting order in respect of a parent of the child or young person if it is satisfied—

   (a) that the child or young person has engaged in criminal conduct or anti-social behaviour, and

   (b) that making the order would be desirable in the interests of preventing the child or young person from engaging in further criminal conduct or further anti-social behaviour.

(4) A parenting order is an order which requires the parent—

   (a) to comply, for a period not exceeding twelve months, with such requirements as are specified in the order, and

   (b) subject to subsection (5), to attend, for a concurrent period not exceeding three months, such counselling or guidance programme as may be specified in directions given by the responsible officer.

(5) A parenting order under this section may, but need not, include a requirement mentioned in subsection (4)(b) in any case where a parenting order under this section or any other enactment has been made in respect of the parent on a previous occasion.

(6) A counselling or guidance programme which a parent is required to attend by virtue of subsection (4)(b) may be or include a residential course but only if the court is satisfied that the following two conditions are fulfilled.

(7) The first condition is that the attendance of the parent at a residential course is likely to be more effective than his attendance at a non-residential course in preventing the child or young person from engaging in further criminal conduct or further anti-social behaviour.

(8) The second condition is that any interference with family life which is likely to result from the attendance of the parent at a residential course is proportionate in all the circumstances.

27 Parenting orders: supplemental

(1) In deciding whether to make a parenting order under section 26, a court must take into account (amongst other things)—

    (a) any refusal by the parent to enter into a parenting contract under section 25 in respect of the child or young person, or

    (b) if the parent has entered into such a parenting contract, any failure by the parent to comply with the requirements specified in the contract.

(2) Before making a parenting order under section 26 in the case of a child or a young person under the age of 16, a court must obtain and consider information about the child or young person's family circumstances and the likely effect of the order on those circumstances.

(3) Subsections (3) to (7) of section 9 of the 1998 Act (supplemental provisions about parenting orders) are to apply in relation to a parenting order under section 26 as they apply in relation to a parenting order under section 8 of that Act.

(4) Members of youth offending teams and responsible officers must, in carrying out their functions in relation to parenting orders, have regard to any guidance which is issued by the Secretary of State from time to time for that purpose.

28 Parenting orders: appeals

(1) An appeal lies to the Crown Court against the making of a parenting order under section 26.

(2) Subsections (2) and (3) of section 10 of the 1998 Act (appeals against parenting orders) are to apply in relation to an appeal under this section as they apply in relation to an appeal under subsection (1)(b) of that section.

29 Interpretation and consequential amendment

(1) In this section and sections 25 to 28—

'anti-social behaviour' means behaviour by a person which causes or is likely to cause harassment, alarm or distress to one or more other persons not of the same household as the person,

'child' has the same meaning as in the 1998 Act,

'criminal conduct' means conduct which—

    (a) constitutes a criminal offence, or

    (b) in the case of conduct by a person under the age of 10, would constitute a criminal offence if that person were not under that age,

'guardian' has the same meaning as in the Children and Young Persons Act 1933 (c. 12),

'parent' includes guardian,

'responsible officer', in relation to a parenting order, means a member of a youth offending team who is specified in the order,

'the 1998 Act' means the Crime and Disorder Act 1998 (c. 37),

'young person' has the same meaning as in the 1998 Act,

'youth offending team' means a team established under section 39 of the 1998 Act.

. . .

PART 9 MISCELLANEOUS POWERS

. . .

91 Proceedings under section 222 of the Local Government Act 1972: power of arrest attached to injunction

(1) This section applies to proceedings in which a local authority is a party by virtue of section 222 of the Local Government Act 1972 (c. 70) (power of local authority to bring, defend or appear in proceedings for the promotion or protection of the interests of inhabitants of their area).

(2) If the court grants an injunction which prohibits conduct which is capable of causing nuisance or annoyance to a person it may, if subsection (3) below applies, attach a power of arrest to any provision of the injunction.

(3) This subsection applies if the local authority applies to the court to attach the power of arrest and the court thinks that either—

    (a) the conduct mentioned in subsection (2) consists of or includes the use or threatened use of violence, or

    (b) there is a significant risk of harm to the person mentioned in that subsection.

(4) Harm includes serious ill-treatment or abuse (whether physical or not).

. . .

Courts Act 2003
(2003 c. 39)

PART 7   PROCEDURE RULES AND PRACTICE DIRECTIONS

. . .

Family Procedure Rules and practice directions

75 Family Procedure Rules

(1) There are to be rules of court (to be called 'Family Procedure Rules') governing the practice and procedure to be followed in family proceedings in—

    (a) the High Court,

    (b) county courts, and

    (c) magistrates' courts.

(2) Family Procedure Rules are to be made by a committee known as the Family Procedure Rule Committee.

(3) 'Family proceedings', in relation to a court, means proceedings in that court which are family proceedings as defined by either—

    (a) section 65 of the 1980 Act, or

    (b) section 32 of the Matrimonial and Family Proceedings Act 1984 (c. 42).

(4) The power to make Family Procedure Rules includes power to make different provision for different areas, including different provision—

    (a) for a specified court or description of courts, or

    (b) for specified descriptions of proceedings or a specified jurisdiction.

(5) Any power to make Family Procedure Rules is to be exercised with a view to securing that—

    (a) the family justice system is accessible, fair and efficient, and

    (b) the rules are both simple and simply expressed.

76 Further provision about scope of Family Procedure Rules

(1) Family Procedure Rules may not be made in respect of matters which may be dealt with in probate rules made under section 127 of the 1981 Act.

(2) Family Procedure Rules may—

    (a) modify or exclude the application of any provision of the County Courts Act 1984 (c. 28), and

    (b) provide for the enforcement in the High Court of orders made in a divorce county court or civil partnership proceedings county court (within the meaning of Part 5 of the Matrimonial and Family Proceedings Act 1984).

(2A) Family Procedure Rules may, for the purposes of the law relating to contempt of court, authorise the publication in such circumstances as may be specified of information relating to family proceedings held in private.

(3) Family Procedure Rules may modify the rules of evidence as they apply to family proceedings in any court within the scope of the rules.

(4) Family Procedure Rules may apply any rules of court (including in particular Civil Procedure Rules) which relate to—

(a) courts which are outside the scope of Family Procedure Rules, or

(b) proceedings other than family proceedings.

(5) Any rules of court, not made by the Family Procedure Rule Committee, which apply to proceedings of a particular kind in a court within the scope of Family Procedure Rules may be applied by Family Procedure Rules to family proceedings in such a court.

(6) In subsections (4) and (5) 'rules of court' includes any provision governing the practice and procedure of a court which is made by or under an enactment.

(7) Where Family Procedure Rules may be made by applying other rules, the other rules may be applied—

(a) to any extent,

(b) with or without modification, and

(c) as amended from time to time.

(8) Family Procedure Rules may, instead of providing for any matter, refer to provision made or to be made about that matter by directions.

. . .

81 Practice directions relating to family proceedings

(1) Directions may be given in accordance with Part 1 of Schedule 2 to the Constitutional Reform Act 2005 as to the practice and procedure of—

(za) the civil division of the Court of Appeal,

(zb) the High Court

(a) county courts, and

(b) magistrates' courts,

in family proceedings.

(2) Directions as to the practice and procedure of those courts in family proceedings given otherwise than under subsection (1) may not be given without the approval of—

(a) the Lord Chancellor, and

(b) the Lord Chief Justice.

(2A) Directions as to the practice and procedure of any relevant court in family proceedings (whether given under subsection (1) or otherwise) may provide for any matter which, by virtue of paragraph 3 of Schedule 1 to the Civil Procedure Act 1997, may be provided for by Civil Procedure Rules.

(3) The power to give directions under subsection (1) includes power—

(a) to vary or revoke directions as to the practice and procedure of any relevant court in family proceedings, whether given under subsection (1) or otherwise,

(b) to give directions containing different provision for different cases (including different areas), and

(c) to give directions containing provision for a specific court, for specific proceedings or for a specific jurisdiction.

(4) Subsection (2)(a) does not apply to directions to the extent that they consist of guidance about any of the following—

(a) the application or interpretation of the law;

(b) the making of judicial decisions.

(5) Subsection (2)(a) does not apply to directions to the extent that they consist of criteria for determining which judges may be allocated to hear particular categories of case; but the directions may, to that extent, be given only—

    (a) after consulting the Lord Chancellor, and

    (b) with the approval of the Lord Chief Justice.

(5) In this section—

'Civil Procedure Rules' has the same meaning as in the Civil Procedure Act 1997;

'relevant court' means a court listed in subsection (1)

. . .

PART 9   FINAL PROVISIONS

107   Interpretation

    (1) In this Act—

'the 1933 Act' means the Children and Young Persons Act 1933 (c. 12);

'the 1968 Act' means the Criminal Appeal Act 1968 (c. 19);

. . .

    'the 1980 Act' means the Magistrates' Courts Act 1980 (c. 43);

    'the 1981 Act' means the Supreme Court Act 1981 (c. 54);

    'the 1990 Act' means the Courts and Legal Services Act 1990 (c. 41);

    'the 1997 Act' means the Civil Procedure Act 1997 (c. 12).

. . .

SCHEDULE 5

Section 97(1)   COLLECTION OF FINES

PART 1   INTRODUCTORY

Application of Schedule

    1. (1) This Schedule applies if a person aged 18 or over ('P') is liable to pay a sum which—

        (a) consists of or includes a fine or a surcharge imposed under section 161A of the Criminal Justice Act 2003, and

        (b) is or is treated for the purposes of Part 3 of the 1980 Act as a sum adjudged to be paid by conviction of a magistrates' court.

    (2) In sub-paragraph (1)(a) 'fine' does not include any pecuniary forfeiture or pecuniary compensation payable on conviction.

Meaning of 'the sum due'

    2. In this Schedule 'the sum due' means the sum adjudged to be paid as mentioned in paragraph 1(1).

Meaning of 'existing defaulter' etc.

    3. (1) For the purposes of this Schedule, P is an existing defaulter if it is shown that—

        (a) he was required to pay the sum due immediately but failed to do so,

        (b) the sum due or any other sum is registered for enforcement against him as a fine under—

           (i)   section 71 of the Road Traffic Offenders Act 1988,

           (ii) section 9 of the Criminal Justice and Police Act 2001, or

           (iii) any other enactment specified in fines collection regulations,

(c) he is in default on a collection order in respect of another sum falling within paragraph 1(1), or

(d) he is in default in payment of another sum falling within paragraph 1(1) but in respect of which no collection order has been made.

(2) For the purposes of this Schedule, P's existing default can be disregarded only if he shows that there was an adequate reason for it.

(3) Sub-paragraph (2) is subject to sub-paragraph (4).

(4) Where a sum is registered for enforcement against P as mentioned in sub-paragraph (1)(b), P's existing default is not one which can be disregarded for the purposes of the following provisions of this Schedule.

(5) In sub-paragraph (1)(a) 'immediately' means, where P is informed of his liability to pay the sum due in a notice, within the period specified in the notice.

(6) The period so specified must be a period which—

(a) is not longer than 10 working days, and

(b) begins with the date of the notice.

(7) 'Collection order' means an order made under Part 4 of this Schedule.

. . .

PART 3   ATTACHMENT OF EARNINGS ORDERS AND APPLICATIONS FOR BENEFIT DEDUCTIONS

Application of Part

7. (1) This Part applies if—

(a) the court which is imposing the liability to pay the sum due concludes that P should not be required to pay the sum due immediately, or

(b) P was required to pay the sum due immediately but failed to do so.

(2) In the following provisions of this Part, 'the relevant court' means—

(a) the court which is imposing the liability to pay the sum due, or

(b) if sub-paragraph (1)(b) applies, the magistrates' court responsible for enforcing payment of the sum due.

Attachment of earnings order or application for benefit deductions without P's consent

8. (1) This paragraph applies if the relevant court concludes that P is an existing defaulter and that his existing default (or defaults) cannot be disregarded.

(2) The court must make an attachment of earnings order if it appears to the court—

(a) that P is in employment, and

(b) that it is not impracticable or inappropriate to make the order.

(3) The court must make an application for benefit deductions if it appears to the court—

(a) that P is entitled to a relevant benefit, and

(b) that it is not impracticable or inappropriate to make the application.

(4) If it appears to the court that (apart from this sub-paragraph) both sub-paragraph (2) and sub-paragraph (3) would apply, the court must make either an attachment of earnings order or an application for benefit deductions.

Attachment of earnings order or application for benefit deductions with P's consent

9. (1) This paragraph applies if the relevant court concludes that P is not an existing defaulter or, if he is, that his existing default (or defaults) can be disregarded.

(2) The court may make—

(a) an attachment of earnings order, or

(b) an application for benefit deductions,

if P consents.

Meaning of 'relevant benefit' and 'application for benefit deductions'

10. In this Schedule—
   (a) 'relevant benefit' means a benefit from which the Secretary of State may make deductions by virtue of section 24 of the Criminal Justice Act 1991 (recovery of fines etc. by deductions from income support etc.), and
   (b) 'application for benefit deductions', in relation to a relevant benefit, means an application to the Secretary of State asking him to deduct sums from any amounts payable to P by way of the benefit.

. . .

Sexual Offences Act 2003
(2003 c. 42)

PART 2   NOTIFICATION AND ORDERS

Risk of sexual harm orders

123   Risk of sexual harm orders: applications, grounds and effect

(1) A chief officer of police may by complaint to a magistrates' court apply for an order under this section (a 'risk of sexual harm order') in respect of a person aged 18 or over ('the defendant') who resides in his police area or who the chief officer believes is in, or is intending to come to, his police area if it appears to the chief officer that—
   (a) the defendant has on at least two occasions, whether before or after the commencement of this Part, done an act within subsection (3), and
   (b) as a result of those acts, there is reasonable cause to believe that it is necessary for such an order to be made.

(2) An application under subsection (1) may be made to any magistrates' court whose commission area includes—
   (a) any part of the applicant's police area, or
   (b) any place where it is alleged that the defendant acted in a way mentioned in subsection (1)(a).

(3) The acts are—
   (a) engaging in sexual activity involving a child or in the presence of a child;
   (b) causing or inciting a child to watch a person engaging in sexual activity or to look at a moving or still image that is sexual;
   (c) giving a child anything that relates to sexual activity or contains a reference to such activity;
   (d) communicating with a child, where any part of the communication is sexual.

(4) On the application, the court may make a risk of sexual harm order if it is satisfied that—
   (a) the defendant has on at least two occasions, whether before or after the commencement of this section, done an act within subsection (3); and
   (b) it is necessary to make such an order, for the purpose of protecting children generally or any child from harm from the defendant.

(5) Such an order—
   (a) prohibits the defendant from doing anything described in the order;
   (b) has effect for a fixed period (not less than 2 years) specified in the order or until further order.

(6) The only prohibitions that may be imposed are those necessary for the purpose of protecting children generally or any child from harm from the defendant.

(7) Where a court makes a risk of sexual harm order in relation to a person already subject to such an order (whether made by that court or another), the earlier order ceases to have effect.

124 Section 123: interpretation

(1) Subsections (2) to (7) apply for the purposes of section 123.

(2) 'Protecting children generally or any child from harm from the defendant' means protecting children generally or any child from physical or psychological harm, caused by the defendant doing acts within section 123(3).

(3) 'Child' means a person under 16.

(4) 'Image' means an image produced by any means, whether of a real or imaginary subject.

(5) 'Sexual activity' means an activity that a reasonable person would, in all the circumstances but regardless of any person's purpose, consider to be sexual.

(6) A communication is sexual if—
  (a) any part of it relates to sexual activity, or
  (b) a reasonable person would, in all the circumstances but regardless of any person's purpose, consider that any part of the communication is sexual.

(7) An image is sexual if—
  (a) any part of it relates to sexual activity, or
  (b) a reasonable person would, in all the circumstances but regardless of any person's purpose, consider that any part of the image is sexual.

. . .

125 RSHOs: variations, renewals and discharges

(1) A person within subsection (2) may by complaint to the appropriate court apply for an order varying, renewing or discharging a risk of sexual harm order.

(2) The persons are—
  (a) the defendant;
  (b) the chief officer of police on whose application the risk of sexual harm order was made;
  (c) the chief officer of police for the area in which the defendant resides;
  (d) a chief officer of police who believes that the defendant is in, or is intending to come to, his police area.

(3) Subject to subsections (4) and (5), on the application the court, after hearing the person making the application and (if they wish to be heard) the other persons mentioned in subsection (2), may make any order, varying, renewing or discharging the risk of sexual harm order, that the court considers appropriate.

(4) An order may be renewed, or varied so as to impose additional prohibitions on the defendant, only if it is necessary to do so for the purpose of protecting children generally or any child from harm from the defendant (and any renewed or varied order may contain only such prohibitions as are necessary for this purpose).

(5) The court must not discharge an order before the end of 2 years beginning with the day on which the order was made, without the consent of the defendant and—
  (a) where the application is made by a chief officer of police, that chief officer, or
  (b) in any other case, the chief officer of police for the area in which the defendant resides.

(6) Section 124(2) applies for the purposes of this section.

(7) In this section 'the appropriate court' means—
  (a) the court which made the risk of sexual harm order;
  (b) a magistrates' court for the area in which the defendant resides; or

(c) where the application is made by a chief officer of police, any magistrates' court whose commission area includes any part of his police area.

126   Interim RSHOs

(1) This section applies where an application for a risk of sexual harm order ('the main application') has not been determined.

(2) An application for an order under this section ('an interim risk of sexual harm order')—

(a) may be made by the complaint by which the main application is made, or

(b) if the main application has been made, may be made by the person who has made that application, by complaint to the court to which that application has been made.

(3) The court may, if it considers it just to do so, make an interim risk of sexual harm order, prohibiting the defendant from doing anything described in the order.

(4) Such an order—

(a) has effect only for a fixed period, specified in the order;

(b) ceases to have effect, if it has not already done so, on the determination of the main application.

(5) The applicant or the defendant may by complaint apply to the court that made the interim risk of sexual harm order for the order to be varied, renewed or discharged.

127   RSHOs and interim RSHOs: appeals

(1) A defendant may appeal to the Crown Court—

(a) against the making of a risk of sexual harm order;

(b) against the making of an interim risk of sexual harm order; or

(c) against the making of an order under section 125, or the refusal to make such an order.

(2) On any such appeal, the Crown Court may make such orders as may be necessary to give effect to its determination of the appeal, and may also make such incidental or consequential orders as appear to it to be just.

(3) Any order made by the Crown Court on an appeal under subsection (1)(a) or (b) (other than an order directing that an application be re-heard by a magistrates' court) is for the purpose of section 125(7) or 126(5) (respectively) to be treated as if it were an order of the court from which the appeal was brought (and not an order of the Crown Court).

128   Offence: breach of RSHO or interim RSHO

(1) A person commits an offence if, without reasonable excuse, he does anything which he is prohibited from doing by—

(a) a risk of sexual harm order; or

(b) an interim risk of sexual harm order.

(2) A person guilty of an offence under this section is liable—

(a) on summary conviction, to imprisonment for a term not exceeding 6 months or a fine not exceeding the statutory maximum or both;

(b) on conviction on indictment, to imprisonment for a term not exceeding 5 years.

(3) Where a person is convicted of an offence under this section, it is not open to the court by or before which he is convicted to make, in respect of the offence, an order for conditional discharge.

. . .

Criminal Justice Act 2003

(2003 c. 44)

*   The provisions reproduced here are as modified for the purposes of enforcement of contact orders under the Children Act 1989, as amended by the Children and Adoption Act 2006.

. . .

PART 12   SENTENCING

...

CHAPTER 4   FURTHER PROVISIONS ABOUT ORDERS UNDER CHAPTERS 2 AND 3

Introductory

196   Meaning of 'relevant order'

(1) In this Chapter 'relevant order' means—

    (a) a community order,

    (b) a custody plus order,

    (c) a suspended sentence order, or

    (d) an intermittent custody order.

(2) In this Chapter any reference to a requirement being imposed by, or included in, a relevant order is, in relation to a custody plus order or an intermittent custody order, a reference to compliance with the requirement being required by the order to be a condition of a licence.

...

197   Meaning of 'the responsible officer'

(1) For the purposes of this Part, 'the responsible officer', in relation to an offender to whom a relevant order relates, means—

    ...

    (c) in any other case, the qualifying officer who, as respects the offender, is for the time being responsible for discharging the functions conferred by this Part on the responsible officer.

(2) The following are qualifying officers for the purposes of subsection (1)(c)—

    (a) in a case where the offender is aged under 18 at the time when the relevant order is made, an officer of a local probation board appointed for or assigned to the petty sessions area for the time being specified in the order or a member of a youth offending team established by a local authority for the time being specified in the order;

    (b) in any other case, an officer of a local probation board appointed for or assigned to the petty sessions area for the time being specified in the order.

(3) The Secretary of State may by order—

    (a) amend subsections (1) and (2), and

    (b) make any other amendments of this Part that appear to him to be necessary or expedient in consequence of any amendment made by virtue of paragraph (a).

(4) An order under subsection (3) may, in particular, provide for the court to determine which of two or more descriptions of 'responsible officer' is to apply in relation to any relevant order.

198   Duties of responsible officer

(1) Where a relevant order has effect, it is the duty of the responsible officer—

    (a) to make any arrangements that are necessary in connection with the requirements imposed by the order, and

    (b) to promote the offender's compliance with those requirements.

(1A) Subsection (1B) applies where—

    (a) an enforcement order is in force, and

    (b) an officer of the Children and Family Court Advisory and Support Service or a Welsh family proceedings officer (as defined in section 35 of the Children Act 2004) is required under section 11M of the Children Act 1989 to report on matters relating to the order.

(1B) The officer of the Service or the Welsh family proceedings officer may request the responsible officer to report to him on such matters relating to the order as he may require for the purpose of making a report under section 11M(1)(c) or (d); and it shall be the duty of the responsible officer to comply with such a request.

(2) In this section 'responsible officer' does not include a person falling within section 197(1)(a).

Requirements available in case of all offenders

199 Unpaid work requirement

(1) In this Part 'unpaid work requirement', in relation to a relevant order, means a requirement that the offender must perform unpaid work in accordance with section 200.

(2) The number of hours which a person may be required to work under an unpaid work requirement must be specified in the relevant order and must be in the aggregate—

(a) not less than 40, and

(b) not more than 200.

. . .

(5) Where on the same occasion and in relation to the same person the court makes more than one enforcement order imposing an unpaid work requirement, the court may direct that the hours of work specified in any of those requirements is to be concurrent with or additional to those specified in any other of those orders, but so that the total number of hours which are not concurrent does not exceed the maximum specified in subsection (2)(b).

200 Obligations of person subject to unpaid work requirement

(1) An offender in respect of whom an unpaid work requirement of a relevant order is in force must perform for the number of hours specified in the order such work at such times as he may be instructed by the responsible officer.

(2) Subject to paragraphs 7 and 9 of Schedule A1 to the Children Act 1989, the work required to be performed under an unpaid work requirement imposed by an enforcement order must be performed during a period of twelve months.

(2A) But the period of twelve months is not to run while the enforcement order is suspended under section 11J(9) of the Children Act 1989.

(3) Unless revoked, a community order imposing an unpaid work requirement remains in force until the offender has worked under it for the number of hours specified in it.

(4) Where an unpaid work requirement is imposed by a suspended sentence order, the supervision period as defined by section 189(1)(a) continues until the offender has worked under the order for the number of hours specified in the order, but does not continue beyond the end of the operational period as defined by section 189(1)(b)(ii).

. . .

Gender Recognition Act 2004
(2004 c. 7)

Applications for gender recognition certificate

1 Applications

(1) A person of either gender who is aged at least 18 may make an application for a gender recognition certificate on the basis of—

    (a) living in the other gender, or

    (b) having changed gender under the law of a country or territory outside the United Kingdom.

(2) In this Act 'the acquired gender', in relation to a person by whom an application under subsection (1) is or has been made, means—

    (a) in the case of an application under paragraph (a) of that subsection, the gender in which the person is living, or

    (b) in the case of an application under paragraph (b) of that subsection, the gender to which the person has changed under the law of the country or territory concerned.

(3) An application under subsection (1) is to be determined by a Gender Recognition Panel.

(4) Schedule 1 (Gender Recognition Panels) has effect.

2 Determination of applications

(1) In the case of an application under section 1(1)(a), the Panel must grant the application if satisfied that the applicant—

    (a) has or has had gender dysphoria,

    (b) has lived in the acquired gender throughout the period of two years ending with the date on which the application is made,

    (c) intends to continue to live in the acquired gender until death, and

    (d) complies with the requirements imposed by and under section 3.

(2) In the case of an application under section 1(1)(b), the Panel must grant the application if satisfied—

    (a) that the country or territory under the law of which the applicant has changed gender is an approved country or territory, and

    (b) that the applicant complies with the requirements imposed by and under section 3.

(3) The Panel must reject an application under section 1(1) if not required by subsection (1) or (2) to grant it.

(4) In this Act 'approved country or territory' means a country or territory prescribed by order made by the Secretary of State after consulting the Scottish Ministers and the Department of Finance and Personnel in Northern Ireland.

3 Evidence

(1) An application under section 1(1)(a) must include either—

    (a) a report made by a registered medical practitioner practising in the field of gender dysphoria and a report made by another registered medical practitioner (who may, but need not, practise in that field), or

    (b) a report made by a chartered psychologist practising in that field and a report made by a registered medical practitioner (who may, but need not, practise in that field).

(2) But subsection (1) is not complied with unless a report required by that subsection and made by—

    (a) a registered medical practitioner, or

    (b) a chartered psychologist,

practising in the field of gender dysphoria includes details of the diagnosis of the applicant's gender dysphoria.

(3) And subsection (1) is not complied with in a case where—

    (a) the applicant has undergone or is undergoing treatment for the purpose of modifying sexual characteristics, or

    (b) treatment for that purpose has been prescribed or planned for the applicant,

unless at least one of the reports required by that subsection includes details of it.

(4) An application under section 1(1)(a) must also include a statutory declaration by the applicant that the applicant meets the conditions in section 2(1)(b) and (c).

(5) An application under section 1(1)(b) must include evidence that the applicant has changed gender under the law of an approved country or territory.

(6) Any application under section 1(1) must include—

>   (a) a statutory declaration as to whether or not the applicant is married or a civil partner,
>
>   (b) any other information or evidence required by an order made by the Secretary of State, and
>
>   (c) any other information or evidence which the Panel which is to determine the application may require,

and may include any other information or evidence which the applicant wishes to include.

. . .

(8) If the Panel which is to determine the application requires information or evidence under subsection (6)(c) it must give reasons for doing so.

4   Successful applications

(1) If a Gender Recognition Panel grants an application under section 1(1) it must issue a gender recognition certificate to the applicant.

(2) Unless the applicant is married or a civil partner, the certificate is to be a full gender recognition certificate.

(3) If the applicant is married or a civil partner, the certificate is to be an interim gender recognition certificate.

(4) Schedule 2 (annulment or dissolution of marriage after issue of interim gender recognition certificate) has effect.

. . .

5   Issue of full certificates where applicant has been married

(1) A court which—

>   (a) makes absolute a decree of nullity granted on the ground that an interim gender recognition certificate has been issued to a party to the marriage, or
>
>   (b) . . .

must, on doing so, issue a full gender recognition certificate to that party and send a copy to the Secretary of State.

(2) If an interim gender recognition certificate has been issued to a person and either—

>   (a) the person's marriage is dissolved or annulled (otherwise than on the ground mentioned in subsection (1)) in proceedings instituted during the period of six months beginning with the day on which it was issued, or
>
>   (b) the person's spouse dies within that period,

the person may make an application for a full gender recognition certificate at any time within the period specified in subsection (3) (unless the person is again married or is a civil partner).

(3) That period is the period of six months beginning with the day on which the marriage is dissolved or annulled or the death occurs.

(4) An application under subsection (2) must include evidence of the dissolution or annulment of the marriage and the date on which proceedings for it were instituted, or of the death of the spouse and the date on which it occurred.

(5) An application under subsection (2) is to be determined by a Gender Recognition Panel.

(6) The Panel—

>   (a) must grant the application if satisfied that the applicant is neither married nor a civil partner, and
>
>   (b) otherwise must reject it.

(7) If the Panel grants the application it must issue a full gender recognition certificate to the applicant.

5A Issue of full certificates where applicant has been a civil partner

(1) A court which—

(a) makes final a nullity order made on the ground that an interim gender recognition certificate has been issued to a civil partner, or

(b) (in Scotland) grants a decree of dissolution on that ground,

must, on doing so, issue a full gender recognition certificate to that civil partner and send a copy to the Secretary of State.

(2) If an interim gender recognition certificate has been issued to a person and either—

(a) the person's civil partnership is dissolved or annulled (otherwise than on the ground mentioned in subsection (1)) in proceedings instituted during the period of six months beginning with the day on which it was issued, or

(b) the person's civil partner dies within that period,

the person may make an application for a full gender recognition certificate at any time within the period specified in subsection (3) (unless the person is again a civil partner or is married).

(3) That period is the period of six months beginning with the day on which the civil partnership is dissolved or annulled or the death occurs.

(4) An application under subsection (2) must include evidence of the dissolution or annulment of the civil partnership and the date on which proceedings for it were instituted, or of the death of the civil partner and the date on which it occurred.

(5) An application under subsection (2) is to be determined by a Gender Recognition Panel.

(6) The Panel—

(a) must grant the application if satisfied that the applicant is neither a civil partner nor married, and

(b) otherwise must reject it.

(7) If the Panel grants the application it must issue a full gender recognition certificate to the applicant.

6 Errors in certificates

(1) Where a gender recognition certificate has been issued to a person, the person or the Secretary of State may make an application for a corrected certificate on the ground that the certificate which has been issued contains an error.

(2) If the certificate was issued by a court the application is to be determined by the court but in any other case it is to be determined by a Gender Recognition Panel.

(3) The court or Panel—

(a) must grant the application if satisfied that the gender recognition certificate contains an error, and

(b) otherwise must reject it.

(4) If the court or Panel grants the application it must issue a corrected gender recognition certificate to the applicant.

. . .

8 Appeals etc.

(1) An applicant to a Gender Recognition Panel under section 1(1), 5(2), 5A(2) or 6(1) may appeal to the High Court. . . . on a point of law against a decision by the Panel to reject the application.

(2) An appeal under subsection (1) must be heard in private if the applicant so requests.

(3) On such an appeal the court must—

(a) allow the appeal and issue the certificate applied for,

(b) allow the appeal and refer the matter to the same or another Panel for re-consideration, or

(c) dismiss the appeal.

(4) If an application under section 1(1) is rejected, the applicant may not make another application before the end of the period of six months beginning with the date on which it is rejected.

(5) If an application under section 1(1), 5(2), 5A(2) or 6(1) is granted but the Secretary of State considers that its grant was secured by fraud, the Secretary of State may refer the case to the High Court...

(6) On a reference under subsection (5) the court—

(a) must either quash or confirm the decision to grant the application, and

(b) if it quashes it, must revoke the gender recognition certificate issued on the grant of the application and may make any order which it considers appropriate in consequence of, or otherwise in connection with, doing so.

Consequences of issue of gender recognition certificate etc.

9 General

(1) Where a full gender recognition certificate is issued to a person, the person's gender becomes for all purposes the acquired gender (so that, if the acquired gender is the male gender, the person's sex becomes that of a man and, if it is the female gender, the person's sex becomes that of a woman).

(2) Subsection (1) does not affect things done, or events occurring, before the certificate is issued; but it does operate for the interpretation of enactments passed, and instruments and other documents made, before the certificate is issued (as well as those passed or made afterwards).

(3) Subsection (1) is subject to provision made by this Act or any other enactment or any subordinate legislation.

10 Registration

(1) Where there is a UK birth register entry in relation to a person to whom a full gender recognition certificate is issued, the Secretary of State must send a copy of the certificate to the appropriate Registrar General.

(2) In this Act 'UK birth register entry', in relation to a person to whom a full gender recognition certificate is issued, means—

(a) an entry of which a certified copy is kept by a Registrar General, or

(b) an entry in a register so kept,

containing a record of the person's birth or adoption (or, if there would otherwise be more than one, the most recent).

. . .

12 Parenthood

The fact that a person's gender has become the acquired gender under this Act does not affect the status of the person as the father or mother of a child.

13 Social security benefits and pensions

Schedule 5 (entitlement to benefits and pensions) has effect.

. . .

15 Succession etc.

The fact that a person's gender has become the acquired gender under this Act does not affect the disposal or devolution of property under a will or other instrument made before the appointed day.

16 Peerages etc.

The fact that a person's gender has become the acquired gender under this Act—

(a) does not affect the descent of any peerage or dignity or title of honour, and

(b) does not affect the devolution of any property limited (expressly or not) by a will or other instrument to devolve (as nearly as the law permits) along with any peerage or dignity or title of honour unless an intention that it should do so is expressed in the will or other instrument.

17   Trustees and personal representatives

(1) A trustee or personal representative is not under a duty, by virtue of the law relating to trusts or the administration of estates, to enquire, before conveying or distributing any property, whether a full gender recognition certificate has been issued to any person or revoked (if that fact could affect entitlement to the property).

(2) A trustee or personal representative is not liable to any person by reason of a conveyance or distribution of the property made without regard to whether a full gender recognition certificate has been issued to any person or revoked if the trustee or personal representative has not received notice of the fact before the conveyance or distribution.

(3) This section does not prejudice the right of a person to follow the property, or any property representing it, into the hands of another person who has received it unless that person has purchased it for value in good faith and without notice.

18   Orders where expectations defeated

(1) This section applies where the disposition or devolution of any property under a will or other instrument (made on or after the appointed day) is different from what it would be but for the fact that a person's gender has become the acquired gender under this Act.

(2) A person may apply to the High Court. . . . for an order on the ground of being adversely affected by the different disposition or devolution of the property.

(3) The court may, if it is satisfied that it is just to do so, make in relation to any person benefiting from the different disposition or devolution of the property such order as it considers appropriate.

(4) An order may, in particular, make provision for—

(a) the payment of a lump sum to the applicant,

(b) the transfer of property to the applicant,

(c) the settlement of property for the benefit of the applicant,

(d) the acquisition of property and either its transfer to the applicant or its settlement for the benefit of the applicant.

(5) An order may contain consequential or supplementary provisions for giving effect to the order or for ensuring that it operates fairly as between the applicant and the other person or persons affected by it; and an order may, in particular, confer powers on trustees.

19   Sport

(1) A body responsible for regulating the participation of persons as competitors in an event or events involving a gender-affected sport may, if subsection (2) is satisfied, prohibit or restrict the participation as competitors in the event or events of persons whose gender has become the acquired gender under this Act.

(2) This subsection is satisfied if the prohibition or restriction is necessary to secure—

(a) fair competition, or

(b) the safety of competitors,

at the event or events.

(3) 'Sport' means a sport, game or other activity of a competitive nature.

(4) A sport is a gender-affected sport if the physical strength, stamina or physique of average persons of one gender would put them at a disadvantage to average persons of the other gender as competitors in events involving the sport.

. . .

20 Gender-specific offences

(1) Where (apart from this subsection) a relevant gender-specific offence could be committed or attempted only if the gender of a person to whom a full gender recognition certificate has been issued were not the acquired gender, the fact that the person's gender has become the acquired gender does not prevent the offence being committed or attempted.

(2) An offence is a 'relevant gender-specific offence' if—

(a) either or both of the conditions in subsection (3) are satisfied, and

(b) the commission of the offence involves the accused engaging in sexual activity.

(3) The conditions are—

(a) that the offence may be committed only by a person of a particular gender, and

(b) that the offence may be committed only on, or in relation to, a person of a particular gender,

and the references to a particular gender include a gender identified by reference to the gender of the other person involved.

. . .

Supplementary

22 Prohibition on disclosure of information

(1) It is an offence for a person who has acquired protected information in an official capacity to disclose the information to any other person.

(2) 'Protected information' means information which relates to a person who has made an application under section 1(1) and which—

(a) concerns that application or any application by the person under section 5(2), 5A(2) or 6(1), or

(b) if the application under section 1(1) is granted, otherwise concerns the person's gender before it becomes the acquired gender.

(3) A person acquires protected information in an official capacity if the person acquires it—

(a) in connection with the person's functions as a member of the civil service, a constable or the holder of any other public office or in connection with the functions of a local or public authority or of a voluntary organisation,

(b) as an employer, or prospective employer, of the person to whom the information relates or as a person employed by such an employer or prospective employer, or

(c) in the course of, or otherwise in connection with, the conduct of business or the supply of professional services.

(4) But it is not an offence under this section to disclose protected information relating to a person if—

(a) the information does not enable that person to be identified,

(b) that person has agreed to the disclosure of the information,

(c) the information is protected information by virtue of subsection (2)(b) and the person by whom the disclosure is made does not know or believe that a full gender recognition certificate has been issued,

(d) the disclosure is in accordance with an order of a court or tribunal,

(e) the disclosure is for the purpose of instituting, or otherwise for the purposes of, proceedings before a court or tribunal,

(f) the disclosure is for the purpose of preventing or investigating crime,

(g) the disclosure is made to the Registrar General for England and Wales. . . .

(h) the disclosure is made for the purposes of the social security system or a pension scheme,

(i) the disclosure is in accordance with provision made by an order under subsection (5), or

(j) the disclosure is in accordance with any provision of, or made by virtue of, an enactment other than this section.

. . .

(8) A person guilty of an offence under this section is liable on summary conviction to a fine not exceeding level 5 on the standard scale.

. . .

25 Interpretation

In this Act—

'the acquired gender' is to be construed in accordance with section 1(2),

'approved country or territory' has the meaning given by section 2(4),

'the appointed day' means the day appointed by order under section 26,

'chartered psychologist' means a person for the time being listed in the British Psychological Society's Register of Chartered Psychologists,

. . .

'full gender recognition certificate' and 'interim gender recognition certificate' mean the certificates issued as such under section 4, 5 or 5A and 'gender recognition certificate' means either of those sorts of certificate,

'gender dysphoria' means the disorder variously referred to as gender dysphoria, gender identity disorder and transsexualism,

'Gender Recognition Panel' (and 'Panel') is to be construed in accordance with Schedule 1,

'subordinate legislation' means an Order in Council, an order, rules, regulations, a scheme, a warrant, bye-laws or any other instrument made under an enactment, and

'UK birth register entry' has the meaning given by section 10(2).

. . .

27 Applications within two years of commencement

(1) This section applies where applications are made under section 1(1)(a) during the period of two years beginning with the appointed day ('the initial period').

(2) Section 2(1)(a) has effect as if there were inserted at the end 'or has undergone surgical treatment for the purpose of modifying sexual characteristics,'.

(3) In the case of an application which—

(a) is made during the first six months of the initial period, or

(b) is made during the rest of the initial period and is based on the applicant having undergone surgical treatment for the purpose of modifying sexual characteristics,

section 2(1)(b) has effect as if for 'two' there were substituted 'six'.

(4) Subsections (5) and (6) apply in the case of an application to which subsection (3) applies and in the case of an application—

(a) made during the rest of the initial period,

(b) based on the applicant having or having had gender dysphoria, and

(c) including a statutory declaration by the applicant that the applicant has lived in the acquired gender throughout the period of six years ending with the date on which the application is made.

(5) Section 3 has effect as if for subsections (1) to (3) there were substituted—

'(1) An application under section 1(1)(a) must include either—

(a) a report made by a registered medical practitioner, or

(b) a report made by a chartered psychologist practising in the field of gender dysphoria.

(2) Where the application is based on the applicant having or having had gender dysphoria—

(a) the reference in subsection (1) to a registered medical practitioner is to one practising in the field of gender dysphoria, and

(b) that subsection is not complied with unless the report includes details of the diagnosis of the applicant's gender dysphoria.

(3) Subsection (1) is not complied with in a case where—

(a) the applicant has undergone or is undergoing treatment for the purpose of modifying sexual characteristics, or

(b) treatment for that purpose has been prescribed or planned for the applicant,

unless the report required by that subsection includes details of it.'

(6) Paragraph 4(2) of Schedule 1 has effect with the omission of paragraph (b).

SCHEDULE 1   GENDER RECOGNITION PANELS

List of persons eligible to sit

1. (1) The Lord Chancellor must … make appointments to a list of persons eligible to sit as members of Gender Recognition Panels.

(2) The only persons who may be appointed to the list are persons who—

(a) have a relevant legal qualification ('legal members'), or

(b) are registered medical practitioners or chartered psychologists ('medical members').

(3) The following have a relevant legal qualification—

(a) a person who has a 7 year general qualification within the meaning of section 71 of the Courts and Legal Services Act 1990 (c. 41),

(b) …

President

2. (1) The Lord Chancellor must … —

(a) appoint one of the legal members to be the President of Gender Recognition Panels ('the President'), and

(b) appoint another of the legal members to be the Deputy President of Gender Recognition Panels ('the Deputy President').

…

Membership of Panels

4. (1) The President must make arrangements for determining the membership of Panels.

(2) The arrangements must ensure that a Panel determining an application under section 1(1)(a) includes—

(a) at least one legal member, and

(b) at least one medical member.

5. The arrangements must ensure that a Panel determining an application under section 1(1)(b), 5(2), 5A(2) or 6(1) includes at least one legal member.

Procedure

6. (1) Where a Panel consists of more than one member, either the President or Deputy President or another legal member nominated by the President must preside.

(2) Decisions of a Panel consisting of more than one member may be taken by majority vote (and, if its members are evenly split, the member presiding has a casting vote).

(3) Panels are to determine applications in private.

(4) A Panel must determine an application without a hearing unless the Panel considers that a hearing is necessary.

(5) The President may, after consulting the Council on Tribunals, give directions about the practice and procedure of Panels.

(6) Panels must give reasons for their decisions.

(7) Where a Panel has determined an application, the Secretary of State must communicate to the applicant the Panel's decision and its reasons for making its decision.

…

SCHEDULE 3   REGISTRATION

PART 1   ENGLAND AND WALES

Introductory

1. In this Part—

'the Registrar General' means the Registrar General for England and Wales, and 'the 1953 Act' means the Births and Deaths Registration Act 1953 (c. 20).

Gender Recognition Register

2. (1) The Registrar General must maintain, in the General Register Office, a register to be called the Gender Recognition Register.

(2) In this Part 'the Gender Recognition Register' means the register maintained under sub-paragraph (1).

(3) The form in which the Gender Recognition Register is maintained is to be determined by the Registrar General.

(4) The Gender Recognition Register is not to be open to public inspection or search.

Entries in Gender Recognition Register and marking of existing birth register entries

3. (1) If the Registrar General receives under section 10(1) a copy of a full gender recognition certificate issued to a person, the Registrar General must—

   (a) make an entry in the Gender Recognition Register containing such particulars as may be prescribed in relation to the person's birth and any other prescribed matter,

   (b) secure that the UK birth register entry is marked in such manner as may be prescribed, and

   (c) make traceable the connection between the entry in the Gender Recognition Register and the UK birth register entry.

(2) Sub-paragraph (1) does not apply if the certificate was issued after an application under section 6(1) and that sub-paragraph has already been complied with in relation to the person.

(3) No certified copy of the UK birth register entry and no short certificate of birth compiled from that entry is to include anything marked by virtue of sub-paragraph (1)(b).

(4) Information kept by the Registrar General for the purposes of sub-paragraph (1)(c) is not to be open to public inspection or search.

(5) 'Prescribed' means prescribed by regulations made by the Registrar General with the approval of the Chancellor of the Exchequer.

Indexing of entries in Gender Recognition Register

4. (1) The Registrar General must make arrangements for each entry made in the Gender Recognition Register to be included in the relevant index kept in the General Register Office.

(2) Any right to search the relevant index includes the right to search entries included in it by virtue of sub-paragraph (1).

(3) Where by virtue of sub-paragraph (1) an index includes entries in the Gender Recognition Register, the index must not disclose that fact.

(4) 'The relevant index', in relation to an entry made in the Gender Recognition Register in relation to a person, means the index of the certified copies of entries in registers, or of entries in registers, which includes the person's UK birth register entry.

Certified copies of entries in Gender Recognition Register

5. (1) Anyone who may have a certified copy of the UK birth register entry of a person issued with a full gender recognition certificate may have a certified copy of the entry made in relation to the person in the Gender Recognition Register.

(2) Any fee which would be payable for a certified copy of the person's UK birth register entry is payable for a certified copy of the entry made in relation to the person in the Gender Recognition Register.

(3) If the person's UK birth register entry is an entry in the Gender Recognition Register, sub-paragraph (1) applies as if the person's UK birth register entry were the most recent entry within section 10(2)(a) or (b) containing a record of the person's birth or adoption which is not an entry in the Gender Recognition Register.

(4) A certified copy of an entry in the Gender Recognition Register must not disclose the fact that the entry is contained in the Gender Recognition Register.

(5) A certified copy of an entry in the Gender Recognition Register must be sealed or stamped with the seal of the General Register Office.

Short certificates of birth compiled from Gender Recognition Register

6. Where a short certificate of birth under section 33 of the 1953 Act is compiled from the Gender Recognition Register, the certificate must not disclose that fact.

Gender Recognition Register: re-registration

7. (1) Section 10A of the 1953 Act (re-registration where parents not married) applies where an entry relating to a person's birth has been made in the Gender Recognition Register as where the birth of a child has been registered under that Act.

(2) In its application by virtue of sub-paragraph (1) section 10A has effect—

    (a) as if the reference to the registrar in subsection (1) were to the Registrar General, and

    (b) with the omission of subsection (2).

(3) Sections 14 and 14A of the 1953 Act (re-registration in cases of legitimation and after declaration of parentage) apply where an entry relating to a person's birth has been made in the Gender Recognition Register as if the references in those sections to the Registrar General authorising re-registration of the person's birth were to the Registrar General's re-registering it.

Correction etc. of Gender Recognition Register

8. (1) Any power or duty of the Registrar General or any other person to correct, alter, amend, mark or cancel the marking of a person's UK birth register entry is exercisable, or falls to be performed, by the Registrar General in relation to an entry in the Gender Recognition Register which—

    (a) relates to that person, and

    (b) under paragraph 4(1) is included in the index which includes the person's UK birth register entry.

(2) If the person's UK birth register entry is an entry in the Gender Recognition Register, the references in sub-paragraph (1) to the person's UK birth register entry are to the most recent entry within section 10(2)(a) or (b) containing a record of the person's birth or adoption which is not an entry in the Gender Recognition Register.

(3) The Registrar General may correct the Gender Recognition Register by entry in the margin (without any alteration of the original entry) in consequence of the issue of a full gender recognition certificate after an application under section 6(1).

Revocation of gender recognition certificate etc.

9. (1) This paragraph applies if, after an entry has been made in the Gender Recognition Register in relation to a person, the High Court...makes an order under section 8(6) quashing the decision to grant the person's application under section 1(1), 5(2) or 5A(2).
    (2) The High Court...must inform the Registrar General.
    (3) Subject to any appeal, the Registrar General must—
        (a) cancel the entry in the Gender Recognition Register, and
        (b) cancel, or secure the cancellation, of any marking of an entry relating to the person made by virtue of paragraph 3(1)(b).

Evidence

10. (1) Section 34(5) of the 1953 Act (certified copy of entry in register under that Act deemed to be true copy) applies in relation to the Gender Recognition Register as if it were a register under that Act.
    (2) A certified copy of an entry made in the Gender Recognition Register in relation to a person is to be received, without further or other proof, as evidence—
        (a) if the relevant index is the index of the Adopted Children Register, of the matters of which a certified copy of an entry in that Register is evidence,
        (b) if the relevant index is the index of the Parental Order Register, of the matters of which a certified copy of an entry in that Register is evidence, and
        (c) otherwise, of the person's birth.
. . .

SCHEDULE 5   BENEFITS AND PENSIONS

PART 1   INTRODUCTORY

1. This Schedule applies where a full gender recognition certificate is issued to a person.

PART 2   STATE BENEFITS

Introductory

2. (1) In this Part of this Schedule 'the 1992 Act' means—
        (a) in England and Wales and Scotland, the Social Security Contributions and Benefits Act 1992 (c. 4), . . .
    (2) In this Part of this Schedule 'the Administration Act' means—
        (a) in England and Wales and Scotland, the Social Security Administration Act 1992 (c. 5), . . .
    (3) Expressions used in this Part of this Schedule and in Part 2 of the 1992 Act have the same meaning in this Part of this Schedule as in Part 2 of the 1992 Act.

Widowed mother's allowance

3. (1) If (immediately before the certificate is issued) the person is, or but for section 1 of the Administration Act would be, entitled to a widowed mother's allowance under section 37 of the 1992 Act (allowance for woman whose husband died before 9th April 2001)—
        (a) the person is not entitled to that allowance afterwards, but

(b) (instead) subsections (2) to (5) of section 39A of the 1992 Act (widowed parent's allowance) apply in relation to the person.

(2) If (immediately before the certificate is issued) the person is (actually) entitled to a widowed mother's allowance, the entitlement to widowed parent's allowance conferred by sub-paragraph (1) is not subject to section 1 of the Administration Act.

Widow's pension

4. If (immediately before the certificate is issued) the person is entitled to a widow's pension under section 38 of the 1992 Act (pension for woman whose husband died before 9th April 2001), the person is not entitled to that pension afterwards.

Widowed parent's allowance

5. If (immediately before the certificate is issued) the person is, or but for section 1 of the Administration Act would be, entitled to a widowed parent's allowance by virtue of sub-section (1)(b) of section 39A of the 1992 Act (allowance for man whose wife died before 9th April 2001), subsections (2) to (5) of that section continue to apply in relation to the person afterwards.

Long-term incapacity benefit etc.

6. If (immediately before the certificate is issued) the person is entitled to incapacity benefit, or a Category A retirement pension, under—
  (a) section 40 of the 1992 Act (long-term incapacity benefit etc. for woman whose husband died before 9th April 2001), or
  (b) section 41 of the 1992 Act (long-term incapacity benefit etc. for man whose wife died before that date),
the person is not so entitled afterwards.

Category A retirement pension

7. (1) Any question—
  (a) whether the person is entitled to a Category A retirement pension (under section 44 of the 1992 Act) for any period after the certificate is issued, and
  (b) (if so) the rate at which the person is so entitled for the period,
is to be decided as if the person's gender had always been the acquired gender.

  (2) Accordingly, if (immediately before the certificate is issued) the person—
  (a) is a woman entitled to a Category A retirement pension, but
  (b) has not attained the age of 65,
the person ceases to be so entitled when it is issued.

  (3) And, conversely, if (immediately before the certificate is issued) the person—
  (a) is a man who has attained the age at which a woman of the same age attains pensionable age, but
  (b) has not attained the age of 65,
the person is to be treated for the purposes of section 44 of the 1992 Act as attaining pensionable age when it is issued.

  (4) But sub-paragraph (1) does not apply if and to the extent that the decision of any question to which it refers is affected by—
  (a) the payment or crediting of contributions, or the crediting of earnings, in respect of a period ending before the certificate is issued, or
  (b) preclusion from regular employment by responsibilities at home for such a period.
  (5) Paragraph 10 makes provision about deferment of Category A retirement pensions.

Category B retirement pension etc.

8. (1) Any question whether the person is entitled to—

    (a) a Category B retirement pension (under section 48A, 48B, 48BB or 51 of the 1992 Act), or

    (b) an increase in a Category A retirement pension under section 51A or 52 of the 1992 Act (increase in Category A retirement pension by reference to amount of Category B retirement pension),

for any period after the certificate is issued is (in accordance with section 9(1)) to be decided as if the person's gender were the acquired gender (but subject to sub-paragraph (4)).

    (2) Accordingly, if (immediately before the certificate is issued) the person is a woman entitled to—

    (a) a Category B retirement pension, or

    (b) an increase in a Category A retirement pension under section 51A or 52 of the 1992 Act,

the person may cease to be so entitled when it is issued.

    (3) And, conversely, if (immediately before the certificate is issued) the person—

    (a) is a man who has attained the age at which a woman of the same age attains pensionable age, but

    (b) has not attained the age of 65,

the person is to be treated for the purposes of sections 48A, 48B and 48BB of the 1992 Act as attaining pensionable age when it is issued.

    (4) But a person who is a man (immediately before the certificate is issued) is not entitled to a Category B retirement pension under section 48B of the 1992 Act for any period after it is issued if the person—

    (a) attains (or has attained) the age of 65 before 6th April 2010, and

    (b) would not have been entitled to a Category B retirement pension under section 51 of the 1992 Act for that period if still a man.

    (5) Paragraph 10 makes provision about deferment of Category B retirement pensions.

Shared additional pension

9. (1) Any question—

    (a) whether the person is entitled to a shared additional pension (under section 55A of the 1992 Act) for any period after the certificate is issued, and

    (b) (if so) the rate at which the person is so entitled for the period,

is to be decided on the basis of the person attaining pensionable age on the same date as someone of the acquired gender (and the same age).

    (2) Accordingly, if (immediately before the certificate is issued) the person—

    (a) is a woman entitled to a shared additional pension, but

    (b) has not attained the age of 65,

the person ceases to be so entitled when it is issued.

    (3) And, conversely, if (immediately before the certificate is issued) the person—

    (a) is a man who has attained the age at which a woman of the same age attains pensionable age, but

    (b) has not attained the age of 65,

the person is to be treated for the purposes of section 55A of the 1992 Act as attaining pensionable age when it is issued.

    (4) Paragraph 10 makes provision about deferment of shared additional pensions.

Deferment of pensions

10. (1) The person's entitlement to—

    (a) a Category A retirement pension,

(b) a Category B retirement pension, or

(c) a shared additional pension,

is not to be taken to have been deferred for any period ending before the certificate is issued unless the condition in sub-paragraph (2) is satisfied.

(2) The condition is that the entitlement both—

(a) was actually deferred during the period, and

(b) would have been capable of being so deferred had the person's gender been the acquired gender.

Category C retirement pension for widows

11. If (immediately before the certificate is issued) the person is entitled to a Category C retirement pension under section 78(2) of the 1992 Act, the person is not entitled to that pension afterwards.

Graduated retirement benefit: Great Britain

12. (1)The provision that may be made by regulations under paragraph 15 of Schedule 3 to the Social Security (Consequential Provisions) Act 1992 (c. 6) (power to retain provisions repealed by Social Security Act 1973 (c. 38), with or without modification, for transitional purposes) includes provision modifying the preserved graduated retirement benefit provisions in consequence of this Act.

(2) 'The preserved graduated retirement benefit provisions' are the provisions of the National Insurance Act 1965 (c. 51) relating to graduated retirement benefit continued in force, with or without modification, by regulations having effect as if made under that paragraph.

. . . .

PART 3   OCCUPATIONAL PENSION SCHEMES

Guaranteed minimum pensions etc.: Great Britain

14. (1) In this paragraph 'the 1993 Act' means the Pension Schemes Act 1993 (c. 48); and expressions used in this paragraph and in that Act have the same meaning in this paragraph as in that Act.

(2) The fact that the person's gender has become the acquired gender does not affect the operation of section 14 of the 1993 Act (guaranteed minimum) in relation to the person, except to the extent that its operation depends on section 16 of the 1993 Act (revaluation); and sub-paragraphs (3) and (5) have effect subject to that.

(3) If (immediately before the certificate is issued) the person is a woman who is entitled to a guaranteed minimum pension but has not attained the age of 65—

(a) the person is for the purposes of section 13 of the 1993 Act and the guaranteed minimum pension provisions to be treated after it is issued as not having attained pensionable age (so that the entitlement ceases) but as attaining pensionable age on subsequently attaining the age of 65, and

(b) in a case where the person's guaranteed minimum pension has commenced before the certificate is issued, it is to be treated for the purposes of Chapter 3 of Part 4 of the 1993 Act (anti-franking) as if it had not.

(4) But sub-paragraph (3)(a) does not—

(a) affect any pension previously paid to the person, or

(b) prevent section 15 of the 1993 Act (increase of guaranteed minimum where commencement of guaranteed minimum pension postponed) operating to increase the person's guaranteed minimum by reason of a postponement of the commencement of the person's guaranteed minimum pension for a period ending before the certificate is issued.

(5) If (immediately before the certificate is issued) the person is a man who—

(a) has attained the age of 60, but

(b) has not attained the age of 65,

the person is to be treated for the purposes of section 13 of the 1993 Act and the guaranteed minimum pension provisions as attaining pensionable age when it is issued.

(6) If at that time the person has attained the age of 65, the fact that the person's gender has become the acquired gender does not affect the person's pensionable age for those purposes.

(7) The fact that the person's gender has become the acquired gender does not affect any guaranteed minimum pension to which the person is entitled as a widow or widower immediately before the certificate is issued (except in consequence of the operation of the previous provisions of this Schedule).

(8) If a transaction to which section 19 of the 1993 Act applies which is carried out before the certificate is issued discharges a liability to provide a guaranteed minimum pension for or in respect of the person, it continues to do so afterwards.

(9) 'The guaranteed minimum pension provision' means so much of the 1993 Act (apart from section 13) and of any other enactment as relates to guaranteed minimum pensions.

. . .

Domestic Violence, Crime and Victims Act 2004
(2004 c. 28)

PART 1   DOMESTIC VIOLENCE ETC

. . .

Causing or allowing the death of a child or vulnerable adult

5   The offence

(1) A person ('D') is guilty of an offence if—

(a) a child or vulnerable adult ('V') dies as a result of the unlawful act of a person who—

    (i)   was a member of the same household as V, and

    (ii)   had frequent contact with him,

(b) D was such a person at the time of that act,

(c) at that time there was a significant risk of serious physical harm being caused to V by the unlawful act of such a person, and

(d) either D was the person whose act caused V's death or—

    (i)   D was, or ought to have been, aware of the risk mentioned in paragraph (c),

    (ii)   D failed to take such steps as he could reasonably have been expected to take to protect V from the risk, and

    (iii) the act occurred in circumstances of the kind that D foresaw or ought to have foreseen.

(2) The prosecution does not have to prove whether it is the first alternative in subsection (1)(d) or the second (sub-paragraphs (i) to (iii)) that applies.

(3) If D was not the mother or father of V—

(a) D may not be charged with an offence under this section if he was under the age of 16 at the time of the act that caused V's death;

(b) for the purposes of subsection (1)(d)(ii) D could not have been expected to take any such step as is referred to there before attaining that age.

(4) For the purposes of this section—

(a) a person is to be regarded as a 'member' of a particular household, even if he does not live in that household, if he visits it so often and for such periods of time that it is reasonable to regard him as a member of it;

(b) where V lived in different households at different times, 'the same household as V' refers to the household in which V was living at the time of the act that caused V's death.

(5) For the purposes of this section an 'unlawful' act is one that—

(a) constitutes an offence, or

(b) would constitute an offence but for being the act of—

(i) a person under the age of ten, or

(ii) a person entitled to rely on a defence of insanity.

Paragraph (b) does not apply to an act of D.

(6) In this section—

'act' includes a course of conduct and also includes omission;

'child' means a person under the age of 16;

'serious' harm means harm that amounts to grievous bodily harm for the purposes of the Offences against the Person Act 1861 (c. 100);

'vulnerable adult' means a person aged 16 or over whose ability to protect himself from violence, abuse or neglect is significantly impaired through physical or mental disability or illness, through old age or otherwise.

(7) A person guilty of an offence under this section is liable on conviction on indictment to imprisonment for a term not exceeding 14 years or to a fine, or to both.

6   Evidence and procedure: England and Wales

(1) Subsections (2) to (4) apply where a person ('the defendant') is charged in the same proceedings with an offence of murder or manslaughter and with an offence under section 5 in respect of the same death ('the section 5 offence').

(2) Where by virtue of section 35(3) of the Criminal Justice and Public Order Act 1994 (c. 33) a court or jury is permitted, in relation to the section 5 offence, to draw such inferences as appear proper from the defendant's failure to give evidence or refusal to answer a question, the court or jury may also draw such inferences in determining whether he is guilty—

(a) of murder or manslaughter, or

(b) of any other offence of which he could lawfully be convicted on the charge of murder or manslaughter,

even if there would otherwise be no case for him to answer in relation to that offence.

(3) The charge of murder or manslaughter is not to be dismissed under paragraph 2 of Schedule 3 to the Crime and Disorder Act 1998 (c. 37) (unless the section 5 offence is dismissed).

(4) At the defendant's trial the question whether there is a case for the defendant to answer on the charge of murder or manslaughter is not to be considered before the close of all the evidence (or, if at some earlier time he ceases to be charged with the section 5 offence, before that earlier time).

(5) An offence under section 5 is an offence of homicide for the purposes of the following enactments—

sections 24 and 25 of the Magistrates' Courts Act 1980 (c. 43) (mode of trial of child or young person for indictable offence);

section 51A of the Crime and Disorder Act 1998 (sending cases to the Crown Court: children and young persons);

section 8 of the Powers of Criminal Courts (Sentencing) Act 2000 (c. 6) (power and duty to remit young offenders to youth courts for sentence).

. . .

Domestic homicide reviews

9   Establishment and conduct of reviews

(1) In this section 'domestic homicide review' means a review of the circumstances in which the death of a person aged 16 or over has, or appears to have, resulted from violence, abuse or neglect by—

    (a) a person to whom he was related or with whom he was or had been in an intimate personal relationship, or

    (b) a member of the same household as himself,

held with a view to identifying the lessons to be learnt from the death.

(2) The Secretary of State may in a particular case direct a specified person or body within subsection (4) to establish, or to participate in, a domestic homicide review.

(3) It is the duty of any person or body within subsection (4) establishing or participating in a domestic homicide review (whether or not held pursuant to a direction under subsection (2)) to have regard to any guidance issued by the Secretary of State as to the establishment and conduct of such reviews.

(4) The persons and bodies within this subsection are—

    (a) in relation to England and Wales—

        chief officers of police for police areas in England and Wales;

        local authorities;

        local probation boards established under section 4 of the Criminal Justice and Court Services Act 2000 (c. 43);

        Strategic Health Authorities established under section 8 of the National Health Service Act 1977 (c. 49);

        Primary Care Trusts established under Section 16A of that Act;

        Local Health Boards established under section 16BA of that Act;

        NHS trusts established under section 5 of the National Health Service and Community Care Act 1990 (c. 19);

. . .

(5) In subsection (4)(a) 'local authority' means—

    (a) in relation to England, the council of a district, county or London borough, the Common Council of the City of London and the Council of the Isles of Scilly;

    (b) in relation to Wales, the council of a county or county borough.

(6) The Secretary of State may by order amend subsection (4) or (5).

. . .

PART 3   VICTIMS ETC

CHAPTER 1   THE VICTIMS' CODE

32   Code of practice for victims

(1) The Secretary of State must issue a code of practice as to the services to be provided to a victim of criminal conduct by persons appearing to him to have functions relating to—

    (a) victims of criminal conduct, or

    (b) any aspect of the criminal justice system.

(2) The code may restrict the application of its provisions to—

    (a) specified descriptions of victims;

    (b) victims of specified offences or descriptions of conduct;

    (c) specified persons or descriptions of persons appearing to the Secretary of State to have functions of the kind mentioned in subsection (1).

(3) The code may include provision requiring or permitting the services which are to be provided to a victim to be provided to one or more others—

    (a) instead of the victim (for example where the victim has died);

(b) as well as the victim.

(4) The code may make different provision for different purposes, including different provision for—

(a) different descriptions of victims;

(b) persons who have different functions or descriptions of functions;

(c) different areas.

(5) The code may not require anything to be done by—

(a) a person acting in a judicial capacity;

(b) a person acting in the discharge of a function of a member of the Crown Prosecution Service which involves the exercise of a discretion.

(6) In determining whether a person is a victim of criminal conduct for the purposes of this section, it is immaterial that no person has been charged with or convicted of an offence in respect of the conduct.

(7) In this section—

'criminal conduct' means conduct constituting an offence;

'specified' means specified in the code.

. . .

34   Effect of non-compliance

(1) If a person fails to perform a duty imposed on him by a code issued under section 32, the failure does not of itself make him liable to criminal or civil proceedings.

(2) But the code is admissible in evidence in criminal or civil proceedings and a court may take into account a failure to comply with the code in determining a question in the proceedings.

CHAPTER 2   REPRESENTATIONS AND INFORMATION

Imprisonment or detention

35   Victims' rights to make representations and receive information

(1) This section applies if—

(a) a court convicts a person ('the offender') of a sexual or violent offence, and

(b) a relevant sentence is imposed on him in respect of the offence.

(2) But section 39 applies (instead of this section) if a hospital direction and a limitation direction are given in relation to the offender.

(3) The local probation board for the area in which the sentence is imposed must take all reasonable steps to ascertain whether a person who appears to the board to be the victim of the offence or to act for the victim of the offence wishes—

(a) to make representations about the matters specified in subsection (4);

(b) to receive the information specified in subsection (5).

(4) The matters are—

(a) whether the offender should be subject to any licence conditions or supervision requirements in the event of his release;

(b) if so, what licence conditions or supervision requirements.

(5) The information is information about any licence conditions or supervision requirements to which the offender is to be subject in the event of his release.

(6) If a person whose wishes have been ascertained under subsection (3) makes representations to the local probation board mentioned in that subsection or the relevant local probation board about a matter specified in subsection (4), the relevant local probation board must forward those representations to the persons responsible for determining the matter.

(7) If a local probation board has ascertained under subsection (3) that a person wishes to receive the information specified in subsection (5), the relevant local probation board must take all reasonable steps—

> (a) to inform the person whether or not the offender is to be subject to any licence conditions or supervision requirements in the event of his release,
>
> (b) if he is, to provide the person with details of any licence conditions or supervision requirements which relate to contact with the victim or his family, and
>
> (c) to provide the person with such other information as the relevant local probation board considers appropriate in all the circumstances of the case.
>
> (8) The relevant local probation board is—
>
> (a) in a case where the offender is to be supervised on release by an officer of a local probation board, that local probation board;
>
> (b) in any other case, the local probation board for the area in which the prison or other place in which the offender is detained is situated.

. . .

Interpretation

45 Interpretation: sections 35 to 44

(1) In sections 35 to 44—

'court' does not include a court-martial or the Courts-Martial Appeal Court;

'hospital direction' has the meaning given in section 45A(3)(a) of the Mental Health Act 1983 (c. 20);

'hospital order' has the meaning given in section 37(4) of that Act;

'licence condition' means a condition in a licence;

'limitation direction' has the meaning given in section 45A(3)(b) of the Mental Health Act 1983;

'local probation board' means a local probation board established under section 4 of the Criminal Justice and Court Services Act 2000 (c. 43);

'relevant sentence' means any of these—

> (a) a sentence of imprisonment for a term of 12 months or more;
>
> (b) a sentence of detention during Her Majesty's pleasure;
>
> (c) a sentence of detention for a period of 12 months or more under section 91 of the Powers of Criminal Courts (Sentencing) Act 2000 (c. 6) (offenders under 18 convicted of certain serious offences);
>
> (d) a detention and training order for a term of 12 months or more;

'restriction direction' has the meaning given in section 49(2) of the Mental Health Act 1983;

'restriction order' has the meaning given in section 41(1) of that Act;

'supervision requirements' means requirements specified in a notice under section 103(6) of the Powers of Criminal Courts (Sentencing) Act 2000;

'transfer direction' has the meaning given in section 47(1) of the Mental Health Act 1983.

(2) For the purposes of sections 35 to 44, an offence is a sexual or violent offence if it is any of these—

> (a) murder or an offence specified in Schedule 15 to the Criminal Justice Act 2003 (c. 44);
>
> (b) an offence in respect of which the patient or offender is subject to the notification requirements of Part 2 of the Sexual Offences Act 2003 (c. 42));
>
> (c) an offence against a child within the meaning of Part 2 of the Criminal Justice and Court Services Act 2000.

. . .

CHAPTER 3   OTHER MATTERS RELATING TO VICTIMS ETC

. . .

Commissioner for Victims and Witnesses

48   Commissioner for Victims and Witnesses

(1) The Secretary of State must appoint a Commissioner for Victims and Witnesses (referred to in this Part as the Commissioner).

(2) Before appointing the Commissioner the Secretary of State must consult the Attorney General and the Lord Chancellor as to the person to be appointed.

(3) The Commissioner is a corporation sole.

(4) The Commissioner is not to be regarded—

(a) as the servant or agent of the Crown, or

(b) as enjoying any status, immunity or privilege of the Crown.

(5) The Commissioner's property is not to be regarded as property of, or held on behalf of, the Crown.

(6) Schedule 8 (which make further provision in connection with the Commissioner) has effect.

49   General functions of Commissioner

(1) The Commissioner must—

(a) promote the interests of victims and witnesses;

(b) take such steps as he considers appropriate with a view to encouraging good practice in the treatment of victims and witnesses;

(c) keep under review the operation of the code of practice issued under section 32.

(2) The Commissioner may, for any purpose connected with the performance of his duties under subsection (1)—

(a) make proposals to the Secretary of State for amending the code (at the request of the Secretary of State or on his own initiative);

(b) make a report to the Secretary of State;

(c) make recommendations to an authority within his remit;

(d) undertake or arrange for or support (financially or otherwise) the carrying out of research;

(e) consult any person he thinks appropriate.

(3) If the Commissioner makes a report to the Secretary of State under subsection (2)(b)—

(a) the Commissioner must send a copy of the report to the Attorney General and the Lord Chancellor;

(b) the Secretary of State must lay a copy of the report before Parliament and arrange for the report to be published.

50   Advice

(1) If he is required to do so by a Minister of the Crown, the Commissioner must give advice to the Minister of the Crown in connection with any matter which—

(a) is specified by the Minister, and

(b) relates to victims or witnesses.

(2) If he is required to do so by or on behalf of an authority within his remit, the Commissioner must give advice to the authority in connection with the information provided or to be provided by or on behalf of the authority to victims or witnesses.

(3) In this section 'Minister of the Crown' includes the Treasury.

51   Restrictions on exercise of functions

The Commissioner must not exercise any of his functions in relation to—

(a) a particular victim or witness;

(b) the bringing or conduct of particular proceedings;

(c) anything done or omitted to be done by a person acting in a judicial capacity or on the instructions of or on behalf of such a person.

52   **'Victims' and 'witnesses'**

    (1) This section applies for the purposes of sections 48 to 51.

    (2) 'Victim' means—

        (a) a victim of an offence, or

        (b) a victim of anti-social behaviour.

    (3) It is immaterial for the purposes of subsection (2)(a) that—

        (a) no complaint has been made about the offence;

        (b) no person has been charged with or convicted of the offence.

    (4) 'Witness' means a person (other than a defendant)—

        (a) who has witnessed conduct in relation to which he may be or has been called to give evidence in relevant proceedings;

        (b) who is able to provide or has provided anything which might be used or has been used as evidence in relevant proceedings; or

        (c) who is able to provide or has provided anything mentioned in subsection (5) (whether or not admissible in evidence in relevant proceedings).

    (5) The things referred to in subsection (4)(c) are—

        (a) anything which might tend to confirm, has tended to confirm or might have tended to confirm evidence which may be, has been or could have been admitted in relevant proceedings;

        (b) anything which might be, has been or might have been referred to in evidence given in relevant proceedings by another person;

        (c) anything which might be, has been or might have been used as the basis for any cross examination in the course of relevant proceedings.

    (6) For the purposes of subsection (4)—

        (a) a person is a defendant in relation to any criminal proceedings if he might be, has been or might have been charged with or convicted of an offence in the proceedings;

        (b) a person is a defendant in relation to any other relevant proceedings if he might be, has been or might have been the subject of an order made in those proceedings.

    (7) In subsections (4) to (6) 'relevant proceedings' means—

        (a) criminal proceedings;

        (b) proceedings of any other kind in respect of anti-social behaviour.

    (8) For the purposes of this section—

        (a) 'anti-social behaviour' means behaviour by a person which causes or is likely to cause harassment, alarm or distress to one or more persons not of the same household as the person;

        (b) a person is a victim of anti-social behaviour if the behaviour has caused him harassment, alarm or distress and he is not of the same household as the person who engages in the behaviour.

53   **Authorities within Commissioner's remit**

    (1) For the purposes of this Part the authorities within the Commissioner's remit are those specified in Schedule 9.

. . .

Disclosure of information

54   **Disclosure of information**

    (1) A person may disclose information to a relevant authority for a purpose specified in subsection (2).

    (2) The purposes are purposes connected with any of these—

        (a) compliance with the code issued under section 32;

        (b) compliance with sections 35 to 44;

        (c) the carrying out of the functions of the Commissioner.

(3) These are relevant authorities—
  (a) a person required to do anything under the code issued under section 32;
  (b) a local probation board established under section 4 of the Criminal Justice and Court Services Act 2000 (c. 43);
  (c) the Commissioner;
  (d) an authority within the Commissioner's remit.

(4) The Secretary of State may by order—
  (a) amend subsection (2) by adding any purpose appearing to him to be connected with the assistance of victims of offences or anti-social behaviour, witnesses of offences or anti-social behaviour or other persons affected by offences or anti-social behaviour;
  (b) amend subsection (3) by adding any authority appearing to him to exercise functions of a public nature.

(5) The reference in subsection (4)(a) to persons affected by offences does not include persons accused or convicted of offences.

(6) The Secretary of State may exercise the power in subsection (4) only after consulting the Attorney General and the Lord Chancellor.

(7) Nothing in this section authorises the making of a disclosure which contravenes the Data Protection Act 1998 (c. 29).

(8) This section does not affect a power to disclose which exists apart from this section.

Victims' Advisory Panel

55 Victims' Advisory Panel

(1) The Secretary of State must appoint persons to form a panel, to be known as the Victims' Advisory Panel.

(2) The Secretary of State must consult the Attorney General and the Lord Chancellor before—
  (a) appointing a person to the Panel, or
  (b) removing a person from the Panel.

(3) The Secretary of State must consult the Panel at such times and in such manner as he thinks appropriate on matters appearing to him to relate to victims of offences or anti-social behaviour or witnesses of offences or anti-social behaviour.

(4) The Secretary of State may reimburse the members of the Panel for such of their travelling and other expenses as he thinks appropriate.

(5) If the Secretary of State consults the Panel under subsection (3) in a particular year, he must arrange for the Panel to prepare a report for the year—
  (a) summarising what the Panel has done in response to the consultation, and
  (b) dealing with such other matters as the Panel consider appropriate.

(6) If a report is prepared under subsection (5), the Secretary of State must—
  (a) arrange for it to be published, and
  (b) lay it before Parliament.

(7) The non-statutory Victims' Advisory Panel is to be treated as having been established in accordance with this section.

(8) If the Secretary of State consults the non-statutory Victims' Advisory Panel on a matter mentioned in subsection (3) before the date on which this section comes into force, the consultation is to be treated as taking place under subsection (3).

(9) The non-statutory Victims' Advisory Panel is the unincorporated body of persons known as the Victims' Advisory Panel established by the Secretary of State before the date on which this section comes into force.

(10) In this section 'year' means a period of 12 months beginning on 1 April.

Grants

56   Grants for assisting victims, witnesses etc

(1) The Secretary of State may pay such grants to such persons as he considers appropriate in connection with measures which appear to him to be intended to assist victims, witnesses or other persons affected by offences.

(2) The Secretary of State may make a grant under this section subject to such conditions as he considers appropriate.

. . .

SCHEDULE 8

COMMISSIONER FOR VICTIMS AND WITNESSES

Deputy Commissioner

(1) The Secretary of State must appoint a Deputy Commissioner for Victims and Witnesses (referred to in this Schedule as the Deputy Commissioner).

(2) Before appointing the Deputy Commissioner the Secretary of State must consult the Attorney General and the Lord Chancellor as to the person to be appointed.

(3) The Deputy Commissioner must act as the Commissioner—

   (a) during any period when the office of Commissioner is vacant;

   (b) at any time when the Commissioner is absent or is unable to act.

(4) The Deputy Commissioner is not to be regarded—

   (a) as the servant or agent of the Crown, or

   (b) as enjoying any status, immunity or privilege of the Crown.

. . .

SCHEDULE 9

AUTHORITIES WITHIN COMMISSIONER'S REMIT

Government departments

1. The Department for Constitutional Affairs.
2. The Department for Education and Skills.
3. The Department of Health.
4. The Department of Trade and Industry.
5. The Department for Transport.
6. The Department for Work and Pensions.
7. The Foreign and Commonwealth Office.
8. The Home Office.
9. The Office of the Deputy Prime Minister.

Customs and Excise

10. The Commissioners of Customs and Excise.

Police forces etc

11. A police force for a police area in England or Wales.
12. The Serious Fraud Office.
13. The Serious Organised Crime Agency
15. The force of constables appointed under section 53 of the British Transport Commission Act 1949 (c. xxix).
16. The Ministry of Defence Police.

Children Act 2004

(2004 c. 31)

PART 1   CHILDREN'S COMMISSIONER

1   Establishment

(1) There is to be an office of Children's Commissioner.

(2) Schedule 1 has effect with respect to the Children's Commissioner.

2   General function

(1) The Children's Commissioner has the function of promoting awareness of the views and interests of children in England.

(2) The Children's Commissioner may in particular under this section—

    (a) encourage persons exercising functions or engaged in activities affecting children to take account of their views and interests;

    (b) advise the Secretary of State on the views and interests of children;

    (c) consider or research the operation of complaints procedures so far as relating to children;

    (d) consider or research any other matter relating to the interests of children;

    (e) publish a report on any matter considered or researched by him under this section.

(3) The Children's Commissioner is to be concerned in particular under this section with the views and interests of children so far as relating to the following aspects of their well-being—

    (a) physical and mental health and emotional well-being;

    (b) protection from harm and neglect;

    (c) education, training and recreation;

    (d) the contribution made by them to society;

    (e) social and economic well-being.

(4) The Children's Commissioner must take reasonable steps to involve children in the discharge of his function under this section, and in particular to—

    (a) ensure that children are made aware of his function and how they may communicate with him; and

    (b) consult children, and organisations working with children, on the matters he proposes to consider or research under subsection (2)(c) or (d).

(5) Where the Children's Commissioner publishes a report under this section he must, if and to the extent that he considers it appropriate, also publish the report in a version which is suitable for children (or, if the report relates to a particular group of children, for those children).

(6) The Children's Commissioner must for the purposes of subsection (4) have particular regard to groups of children who do not have other adequate means by which they can make their views known.

(7) The Children's Commissioner is not under this section to conduct an investigation of the case of an individual child.

(8) The Children's Commissioner or a person authorised by him may for the purposes of his function under this section at any reasonable time—

    (a) enter any premises, other than a private dwelling, for the purposes of interviewing any child accommodated or cared for there; and

    (b) if the child consents, interview the child in private.

(9) Any person exercising functions under any enactment must supply the Children's Commissioner with such information in that person's possession relating to those functions as the Children's Commissioner may reasonably request for the purposes of his function under this section (provided that the information is information which that person may, apart from this subsection, lawfully disclose to him).

(10) Where the Children's Commissioner has published a report under this section containing recommendations in respect of any person exercising functions under any enactment, he may require that person to state in writing, within such period as the Children's Commissioner may reasonably require, what action the person has taken or proposes to take in response to the recommendations.

(11) In considering for the purpose of his function under this section what constitutes the interests of children (generally or so far as relating to a particular matter) the Children's Commissioner must have regard to the United Nations Convention on the Rights of the Child.

(12) In subsection (11) the reference to the United Nations Convention on the Rights of the Child is to the Convention on the Rights of the Child adopted by the General Assembly of the United Nations on 20th November 1989, subject to any reservations, objections or interpretative declarations by the United Kingdom for the time being in force.

3 Inquiries initiated by Commissioner

(1) Where the Children's Commissioner considers that the case of an individual child in England raises issues of public policy of relevance to other children, he may hold an inquiry into that case for the purpose of investigating and making recommendations about those issues.

(2) The Children's Commissioner may only conduct an inquiry under this section if he is satisfied that the inquiry would not duplicate work that is the function of another person (having consulted such persons as he considers appropriate).

(3) Before holding an inquiry under this section the Children's Commissioner must consult the Secretary of State.

(4) The Children's Commissioner may, if he thinks fit, hold an inquiry under this section, or any part of it, in private.

(5) As soon as possible after completing an inquiry under this section the Children's Commissioner must—

    (a) publish a report containing his recommendations; and

    (b) send a copy to the Secretary of State.

(6) The report need not identify any individual child if the Children's Commissioner considers that it would be undesirable for the identity of the child to be made public.

(7) Where the Children's Commissioner has published a report under this section containing recommendations in respect of any person exercising functions under any enactment, he may require that person to state in writing, within such period as the Children's Commissioner may reasonably require, what action the person has taken or proposes to take in response to the recommendations.

(8) Subsections (2) and (3) of section 250 of the Local Government Act 1972 (c. 70) apply for the purposes of an inquiry held under this section with the substitution for references to the person appointed to hold the inquiry of references to the Children's Commissioner.

4   Other inquiries held by Commissioner

(1) Where the Secretary of State considers that the case of an individual child in England raises issues of relevance to other children, he may direct the Children's Commissioner to hold an inquiry into that case.

(2) The Children's Commissioner may, if he thinks fit, hold an inquiry under this section, or any part of it, in private.

(3) The Children's Commissioner must, as soon as possible after the completion of an inquiry under this section, make a report in relation to the inquiry and send a copy to the Secretary of State.

(4) The Secretary of State must, subject to subsection (5), publish each report received by him under this section as soon as possible.

(5) Where a report made under this section identifies an individual child and the Secretary of State considers that it would be undesirable for the identity of the child to be made public—

    (a) the Secretary of State may make such amendments to the report as are necessary to protect the identity of the child and publish the amended report only; or

    (b) if he considers that it is not possible to publish the report without identifying the child, he need not publish the report.

(6) The Secretary of State must lay a copy of each report published by him under this section before each House of Parliament.

(7) Subsections (2) to (5) of section 250 of the Local Government Act 1972 (c. 70) apply for the purposes of an inquiry held under this section.

5   Functions of Commissioner in Wales

(1) The Children's Commissioner has the function of promoting awareness of the views and interests of children in Wales, except in so far as relating to any matter falling within the remit of the Children's Commissioner for Wales under section 72B, 73 or 74 of the Care Standards Act 2000 (c. 14).

(2) Subsections (2) to (12) of section 2 apply in relation to the function of the Children's Commissioner under subsection (1) above as in relation to his function under that section.

(3) In discharging his function under subsection (1) above the Children's Commissioner must take account of the views of, and any work undertaken by, the Children's Commissioner for Wales.

(4) Where the Children's Commissioner considers that the case of an individual child in Wales raises issues of public policy of relevance to other children, other than issues relating to a matter referred to in subsection (1) above, he may hold an inquiry into that case for the purpose of investigating and making recommendations about those issues.

(5) Subsections (2) to (8) of section 3 apply in relation to an inquiry under subsection (4) above.

(6) Where the Secretary of State considers that the case of an individual child in Wales raises issues of relevance to other children, other than issues relating to a matter referred to in subsection (1) above, he may direct the Children's Commissioner to hold an inquiry into that case.

(7) Subsections (2) to (7) of section 4 apply in relation to an inquiry under subsection (6) above.

. . .

8   Annual reports

(1) As soon as possible after the end of each financial year the Children's Commissioner must make a report on—

(a) the way in which he has discharged his functions under this Part, other than functions of holding inquiries;

(b) what he has found in the course of exercising those functions during the year; and

(c) the matters he intends to consider or research in the next financial year.

(2) The Children's Commissioner must in particular under subsection (1)(a) include an account of the steps taken by him to involve in the discharge of the functions referred to in that provision the children in relation to whom those functions are exercised.

(3) Where the Children's Commissioner makes a report under this section—

(a) he must send a copy to the Secretary of State; and

(b) the Secretary of State must as soon as possible lay a copy before each House of Parliament.

(4) The Children's Commissioner must publish a report under this section as soon as possible after the Secretary of State has laid it before each House of Parliament.

(5) The Children's Commissioner must also, to the extent that he considers appropriate, publish any report made under this section in a version which is suitable for children.

(6) In this section, 'financial year' has the same meaning as in paragraph 8 of Schedule 1.

9   Care leavers and young persons with learning disabilities

(1) This section applies for the purposes of this Part, other than section 2(11) and (12).

(2) Any reference to a child includes, in addition to a person under the age of 18, a person aged 18, 19 or 20 who—

(a) has been looked after by a local authority at any time after attaining the age of 16; or

(b) has a learning disability.

(3) For the purposes of subsection (2)—

a person is 'looked after by a local authority' if—

(a) for the purposes of the Children Act 1989 (c. 41), he is looked after by a local authority in England and Wales;

. . .

'learning disability' means a state of arrested or incomplete development of mind which induces significant impairment of intelligence and social functioning.

PART 2   CHILDREN'S SERVICES IN ENGLAND

General

10   Co-operation to improve well-being

(1) Each children's services authority in England must make arrangements to promote co-operation between—

(a) the authority;

(b) each of the authority's relevant partners; and

(c) such other persons or bodies as the authority consider appropriate, being persons or bodies of any nature who exercise functions or are engaged in activities in relation to children in the authority's area.

(2) The arrangements are to be made with a view to improving the well-being of children in the authority's area so far as relating to—

(a) physical and mental health and emotional well-being;

(b) protection from harm and neglect;

(c) education, training and recreation;

(d) the contribution made by them to society;

(e) social and economic well-being.

(3) In making arrangements under this section a children's services authority in England must have regard to the importance of parents and other persons caring for children in improving the well-being of children.

(4) For the purposes of this section each of the following is a relevant partner of a children's services authority in England—

(a) where the authority is a county council for an area for which there is also a district council, the district council;

(b) the police authority and the chief officer of police for a police area any part of which falls within the area of the children's services authority;

(c) a local probation board for an area any part of which falls within the area of the authority;

(d) a youth offending team for an area any part of which falls within the area of the authority;

(e) a Strategic Health Authority and Primary Care Trust for an area any part of which falls within the area of the authority;

(f) a person providing services under section 114 of the Learning and Skills Act 2000 (c. 21) in any part of the area of the authority;

(g) the Learning and Skills Council for England.

(5) The relevant partners of a children's services authority in England must co-operate with the authority in the making of arrangements under this section.

(6) A children's services authority in England and any of their relevant partners may for the purposes of arrangements under this section—

(a) provide staff, goods, services, accommodation or other resources;

(b) establish and maintain a pooled fund.

(7) For the purposes of subsection (6) a pooled fund is a fund—

(a) which is made up of contributions by the authority and the relevant partner or partners concerned; and

(b) out of which payments may be made towards expenditure incurred in the discharge of functions of the authority and functions of the relevant partner or partners.

(8) A children's services authority in England and each of their relevant partners must in exercising their functions under this section have regard to any guidance given to them for the purpose by the Secretary of State.

(9) Arrangements under this section may include arrangements relating to—

(a) persons aged 18 and 19;

(b) persons over the age of 19 who are receiving services under sections 23C to 24D of the Children Act 1989 (c. 41);

(c) persons over the age of 19 but under the age of 25 who have a learning difficulty, within the meaning of section 13 of the Learning and Skills Act 2000, and are receiving services under that Act.

11 Arrangements to safeguard and promote welfare

(1) This section applies to each of the following—

    (a) a children's services authority in England;

    (b) a district council which is not such an authority;

    (c) a Strategic Health Authority;

    (d) a Special Health Authority, so far as exercising functions in relation to England, designated by order made by the Secretary of State for the purposes of this section;

    (e) a Primary Care Trust;

    (f) an NHS trust all or most of whose hospitals, establishments and facilities are situated in England;

    (g) an NHS foundation trust;

    (h) the police authority and chief officer of police for a police area in England;

    (i) the British Transport Police Authority, so far as exercising functions in relation to England;

    (j) a local probation board for an area in England;

    (k) a youth offending team for an area in England;

    (l) the governor of a prison or secure training centre in England (or, in the case of a contracted out prison or secure training centre, its director);

    (m)any person to the extent that he is providing services under section 114 of the Learning and Skills Act 2000 (c. 21).

(2) Each person and body to whom this section applies must make arrangements for ensuring that—

    (a) their functions are discharged having regard to the need to safeguard and promote the welfare of children; and

    (b) any services provided by another person pursuant to arrangements made by the person or body in the discharge of their functions are provided having regard to that need.

(3) In the case of a children's services authority in England, the reference in subsection (2) to functions of the authority does not include functions to which section 175 of the Education Act 2002 (c. 32) applies.

(4) Each person and body to whom this section applies must in discharging their duty under this section have regard to any guidance given to them for the purpose by the Secretary of State.

12 Information databases

(1) The Secretary of State may for the purpose of arrangements under section 10 or 11 above or under section 175 of the Education Act 2002—

    (a) by regulations require children's services authorities in England to establish and operate databases containing information in respect of persons to whom such arrangements relate;

    (b) himself establish and operate, or make arrangements for the operation and establishment of, one or more databases containing such information.

(2) The Secretary of State may for the purposes of arrangements under subsection (1)(b) by regulations establish a body corporate to establish and operate one or more databases.

(3) A database under this section may only include information falling within subsection (4) in relation to a person to whom arrangements specified in subsection (1) relate.

(4) The information referred to in subsection (3) is information of the following descriptions in relation to a person—

    (a) his name, address, gender and date of birth;

    (b) a number identifying him;

(c) the name and contact details of any person with parental responsibility for him (within the meaning of section 3 of the Children Act 1989 (c. 41)) or who has care of him at any time;

(d) details of any education being received by him (including the name and contact details of any educational institution attended by him);

(e) the name and contact details of any person providing primary medical services in relation to him under Part 1 of the National Health Service Act 1977 (c. 49);

(f) the name and contact details of any person providing to him services of such description as the Secretary of State may by regulations specify;

(g) information as to the existence of any cause for concern in relation to him;

(h) information of such other description, not including medical records or other personal records, as the Secretary of State may by regulations specify.

(5) The Secretary of State may by regulations make provision in relation to the establishment and operation of any database or databases under this section.

(6) Regulations under subsection (5) may in particular make provision—

(a) as to the information which must or may be contained in any database under this section (subject to subsection (3));

(b) requiring a person or body specified in subsection (7) to disclose information for inclusion in the database;

(c) permitting a person or body specified in subsection (8) to disclose information for inclusion in the database;

(d) permitting or requiring the disclosure of information included in any such database;

(e) permitting or requiring any person to be given access to any such database for the purpose of adding or reading information;

(f) as to the conditions on which such access must or may be given;

(g) as to the length of time for which information must or may be retained;

(h) as to procedures for ensuring the accuracy of information included in any such database;

(i) in a case where a database is established by virtue of subsection (1)(b), requiring children's services authorities in England to participate in the operation of the database.

(7) The persons and bodies referred to in subsection (6)(b) are—

(a) the persons and bodies specified in section 11(1);

(b) the Learning and Skills Council for England;

(c) the governing body of a maintained school in England (within the meaning of section 175 of the Education Act 2002 (c. 32));

(d) the governing body of an institution in England within the further education sector (within the meaning of that section);

(e) the proprietor of an independent school in England (within the meaning of the Education Act 1996 (c. 56));

(f) a person or body of such other description as the Secretary of State may by regulations specify.

(8) The persons and bodies referred to in subsection (6)(c) are—

(a) a person registered in England for child minding or the provision of day care under Part 10A of the Children Act 1989 (c. 41);

(b) a voluntary organisation exercising functions or engaged in activities in relation to persons to whom arrangements specified in subsection (1) relate;

(c) the Commissioners of Inland Revenue;

(d) a registered social landlord;

(e) a person or body of such other description as the Secretary of State may by regulations specify.

(9) The Secretary of State may provide information for inclusion in a database under this section.

(10) The provision which may be made under subsection (6)(e) includes provision for a person of a description specified in the regulations to determine what must or may be done under the regulations.

(11) Regulations under subsection (5) may also provide that anything which may be done under regulations under subsection (6)(c) to (e) or (9) may be done notwithstanding any rule of common law which prohibits or restricts the disclosure of information.

(12) Any person or body establishing or operating a database under this section must in the establishment or operation of the database have regard to any guidance, and comply with any direction, given to that person or body by the Secretary of State.

(13) Guidance or directions under subsection (12) may in particular relate to—
    (a) the management of a database under this section;
    (b) the technical specifications for any such database;
    (c) the security of any such database;
    (d) the transfer and comparison of information between databases under this section;
    (e) the giving of advice in relation to rights under the Data Protection Act 1998 (c. 29).

Local Safeguarding Children Boards

13   Establishment of LSCBs

(1) Each children's services authority in England must establish a Local Safeguarding Children Board for their area.

(2) A Board established under this section must include such representative or representatives of—
    (a) the authority by which it is established, and
    (b) each Board partner of that authority,
as the Secretary of State may by regulations prescribe.

(3) For the purposes of this section each of the following is a Board partner of a children's services authority in England—
    (a) where the authority is a county council for an area for which there is also a district council, the district council;
    (b) the chief officer of police for a police area any part of which falls within the area of the authority;
    (c) a local probation board for an area any part of which falls within the area of the authority;
    (d) a youth offending team for an area any part of which falls within the area of the authority;
    (e) a Strategic Health Authority and a Primary Care Trust for an area any part of which falls within the area of the authority;
    (f) an NHS trust and an NHS foundation trust all or most of whose hospitals, establishments and facilities are situated in the area of the authority;
    (g) a person providing services under section 114 of the Learning and Skills Act 2000 (c. 21) in any part of the area of the authority;
    (h) the Children and Family Court Advisory and Support Service;
    (i) the governor of any secure training centre in the area of the authority (or, in the case of a contracted out secure training centre, its director);
    (j) the governor of any prison in the area of the authority which ordinarily detains children (or, in the case of a contracted out prison, its director).

(4) A children's services authority in England must take reasonable steps to ensure that the Local Safeguarding Children Board established by them includes representatives of

relevant persons and bodies of such descriptions as may be prescribed by the Secretary of State in regulations.

(5) A Local Safeguarding Children Board established under this section may also include representatives of such other relevant persons or bodies as the authority by which it is established consider, after consulting their Board partners, should be represented on it.

(6) For the purposes of subsections (4) and (5), relevant persons and bodies are persons and bodies of any nature exercising functions or engaged in activities relating to children in the area of the authority in question.

(7) In the establishment and operation of a Local Safeguarding Children Board under this section—

(a) the authority establishing it must co-operate with each of their Board partners; and

(b) each Board partner must co-operate with the authority.

(8) Two or more children's services authorities in England may discharge their respective duties under subsection (1) by establishing a Local Safeguarding Children Board for their combined area (and where they do so, any reference in this section or sections 14 to 16 to the authority establishing the Board shall be read as a reference to the authorities establishing it).

14 Functions and procedure of LSCBs

(1) The objective of a Local Safeguarding Children Board established under section 13 is—

(a) to co-ordinate what is done by each person or body represented on the Board for the purposes of safeguarding and promoting the welfare of children in the area of the authority by which it is established; and

(b) to ensure the effectiveness of what is done by each such person or body for those purposes.

(2) A Local Safeguarding Children Board established under section 13 is to have such functions in relation to its objective as the Secretary of State may by regulations prescribe (which may in particular include functions of review or investigation).

(3) The Secretary of State may by regulations make provision as to the procedures to be followed by a Local Safeguarding Children Board established under section 13.

15 Funding of LSCBs

(1) Any person or body specified in subsection (3) may make payments towards expenditure incurred by, or for purposes connected with, a Local Safeguarding Children Board established under section 13—

(a) by making the payments directly; or

(b) by contributing to a fund out of which the payments may be made.

(2) Any person or body specified in subsection (3) may provide staff, goods, services, accommodation or other resources for purposes connected with a Local Safeguarding Children Board established under section 13.

(3) The persons and bodies referred to in subsections (1) and (2) are—

(a) the children's services authority in England by which the Board is established;

(b) any person who is a Board partner of the authority under section 13(3)(a) to (h);

(c) in a case where the governor of a secure training centre or prison is a Board partner of the authority, the Secretary of State; and

(d) in a case where the director of a contracted out secure training centre or prison is a Board partner of the authority, the contractor.

16 LSCBs: supplementary

(1) The Secretary of State may by regulations make provision as to the functions of children's services authorities in England relating to Local Safeguarding Children Boards established by them.

(2) A children's services authority in England and each of their Board partners must, in exercising their functions relating to a Local Safeguarding Children Board, have regard to any guidance given to them for the purpose by the Secretary of State.

Local authority administration

17   Children and young people's plans

(1) The Secretary of State may by regulations require a children's services authority in England from time to time to prepare and publish a plan setting out the authority's strategy for discharging their functions in relation to children and relevant young persons.

(2) Regulations under this section may in particular make provision as to—

   (a) the matters to be dealt with in a plan under this section;

   (b) the period to which a plan under this section is to relate;

   (c) when and how a plan under this section must be published;

   (d) keeping a plan under this section under review;

   (e) consultation to be carried out during preparation of a plan under this section.

(3) The matters for which provision may be made under subsection (2)(a) include in particular—

   (a) the arrangements made or to be made under section 10 by a children's services authority in England;

   (b) the strategy or proposals in relation to children and relevant young persons of any person or body with whom a children's services authority in England makes or proposes to make such arrangements.

(4) The power to make regulations conferred by this section shall, for the purposes of subsection (1) of section 100 of the Local Government Act 2003 (c. 26), be regarded as included among the powers mentioned in subsection (2) of that section.

(5) In this section 'relevant young persons' means persons, other than children, in relation to whom arrangements under section 10 may be made.

18   Director of children's services

(1) A children's services authority in England may, and with effect from the appointed day must, appoint an officer for the purposes of—

   (a) the functions conferred on or exercisable by the authority which are specified in subsection (2); and

   (b) such other functions conferred on or exercisable by the authority as may be prescribed by the Secretary of State by regulations.

(2) The functions referred to in subsection (1)(a) are—

   (a) functions conferred on or exercisable by the authority in their capacity as a local education authority;

   (b) functions conferred on or exercisable by the authority which are social services functions (within the meaning of the Local Authority Social Services Act 1970 (c. 42)), so far as those functions relate to children;

   (c) the functions conferred on the authority under sections 23C to 24D of the Children Act 1989 (c. 41) (so far as not falling within paragraph (b));

   (d) the functions conferred on the authority under sections 10 to 12 and 17 of this Act; and

   (e) any functions exercisable by the authority under section 31 of the Health Act 1999 (c. 8) on behalf of an NHS body (within the meaning of that section), so far as those functions relate to children.

(3) Subsection (2)(a) does not include—

   (a) functions under section 120(3) of the Education Reform Act 1988 (c. 40) (functions of LEAs with respect to higher and further education);

   (b) functions under section 85(2) and (3) of the Further and Higher Education Act 1992 (c. 13) (finance and government of locally funded further and higher education);

(c) functions under section 15B of the Education Act 1996 (c. 56) or section 23 of the Learning and Skills Act 2000 (c. 21) (education for persons who have attained the age of 19);

(d) functions under section 22 of the Teaching and Higher Education Act 1998 (c. 30) (financial support to students);

(e) such other functions conferred on or exercisable by a children's services authority in England in their capacity as a local education authority as the Secretary of State may by regulations prescribe.

(4) An officer appointed by a children's services authority in England under this section is to be known as their 'director of children's services'.

(5) The director of children's services appointed by a children's services authority in England may also have responsibilities relating to such functions conferred on or exercisable by the authority, in addition to those specified in subsection (1), as the authority consider appropriate.

(6) The functions in relation to which a director of children's services may have responsibilities by virtue of subsection (5) include those referred to in subsection (3)(a) to (e).

(7) A children's services authority in England must have regard to any guidance given to them by the Secretary of State for the purposes of this section.

(8) Two or more children's services authorities in England may for the purposes of this section, if they consider that the same person can efficiently discharge, for both or all of them, the responsibilities of director of children's services, concur in the appointment of a person as director of children's services for both or all of them.

(9) The amendments in Schedule 2—

(a) have effect, in relation to any authority which appoint a director of children's services before the appointed day, from the day of his appointment; and

(b) on and after the appointed day have effect for all purposes.

(10) In this section, 'the appointed day' means such day as the Secretary of State may by order appoint.

19   Lead member for children's services

(1) A children's services authority in England must, in making arrangements for the discharge of—

(a) the functions conferred on or exercisable by the authority specified in section 18(1)(a) and (b), and

(b) such other functions conferred on or exercisable by the authority as the authority consider appropriate,

designate one of their members as their 'lead member for children's services'.

(2) A children's services authority in England must have regard to any guidance given to them by the Secretary of State for the purposes of subsection (1).

Inspections of children's services

20   Joint area reviews

(1) Any two or more of the persons and bodies to which this section applies must, at the request of the Secretary of State—

(a) conduct, in accordance with a timetable drawn up by them and approved by the Secretary of State, a review of children's services provided in—

(i)   the area of every children's services authority in England;

(ii) the areas of such children's services authorities in England as may be specified in the request;

(b) conduct a review of such children's services provided in the area of such children's services authority in England as may be specified in the request.

(2) Any two or more of the persons and bodies to which this section applies may conduct a review of any children's services provided in the area of a particular children's services authority in England.

(3) The purpose of a review under this section is to evaluate the extent to which, taken together, the children's services being reviewed improve the well-being of children and relevant young persons (and in particular to evaluate how those services work together to improve their well-being).

(4) The persons and bodies to which this section applies are—

(a) the Chief Inspector of Schools;

(b) the Adult Learning Inspectorate;

(c) the Commission for Social Care Inspection;

(d) the Commission for Healthcare Audit and Inspection;

(e) the Audit Commission for Local Authorities and the National Health Service in England and Wales;

(f) the chief inspector of constabulary;

(g) Her Majesty's Chief Inspector of the National Probation Service for England and Wales;

(h) Her Majesty's Chief Inspector of Court Administration; and

(i) the Chief Inspector of Prisons.

(5) Reviews under this section are to be conducted in accordance with arrangements made by the Chief Inspector of Schools.

(6) Before making arrangements for the purposes of reviews under this section the Chief Inspector of Schools must consult such of the other persons and bodies to which this section applies as he considers appropriate.

(7) The annual report of the Chief Inspector of Schools required by subsection (7)(a) of section 2 of the School Inspections Act 1996 (c. 57) to be made to the Secretary of State must include an account of reviews under this section; and the power conferred by subsection (7)(b) of that section to make other reports to the Secretary of State includes a power to make reports about such reviews.

(8) The Secretary of State may by regulations make provision for the purposes of reviews under this section and in particular provision—

(a) requiring or facilitating the sharing or production of information for the purposes of a review under this section (including provision for the creation of criminal offences);

(b) authorising any person or body conducting a review under this section to enter any premises for the purposes of the review (including provision for the creation of criminal offences);

(c) imposing requirements as to the making of a report on each review under this section;

(d) for the making by such persons as may be specified in or under the regulations of written statements of proposed action in the light of the report and the period within which any such action must or may be taken;

(e) for the provision to members of the public of copies of reports and statements made under paragraphs (c) and (d), and for charging in respect of any such provision;

(f) for the disapplication, in consequence of a requirement under this section, of any requirement under any other enactment to conduct an assessment or to do anything in connection with an assessment.

(9) Regulations under subsection (8) may in particular make provision by applying enactments falling within subsection (10), with or without modification, for the purposes of reviews under this section.

(10) The enactments falling within this subsection are enactments relating to the powers of persons and bodies to which this section applies for the purposes of assessments other than reviews under this section.

(11) Regulations under subsection (8) may make provision authorising or requiring the doing of anything by reference to the determination of a person of a description specified in the regulations.

21   Framework

(1) The Chief Inspector of Schools must devise a Framework for Inspection of Children's Services ('the Framework').

(2) The Framework must, for the purpose specified in subsection (3), set out principles to be applied by any person or body conducting a relevant assessment.

(3) The purpose referred to in subsection (2) is to ensure that relevant assessments properly evaluate and report on the extent to which children's services improve the well-being of children and relevant young persons.

(4) The principles in the Framework may—

    (a) include principles relating to the organisation of the results of any relevant assessment;

    (b) make different provision for different cases.

(5) For the purposes of subsections (2) to (4) a relevant assessment is an assessment conducted under any enactment in relation to any children's services.

(6) When devising the Framework, the Chief Inspector of Schools must consult the other persons and bodies to which section 20 applies.

(7) The Chief Inspector of Schools must publish the Framework, but before doing so must—

    (a) consult such persons and bodies, other than those referred to in subsection (6), as he thinks fit; and

    (b) obtain the consent of the Secretary of State.

(8) The Chief Inspector of Schools may at any time revise the Framework (and subsections (6) and (7) apply in relation to revisions to the Framework as to the original Framework).

22 Co-operation and delegation

(1) Each person or body with functions under any enactment of conducting assessments of children's services must for the purposes of those assessments co-operate with other persons or bodies with such functions.

(2) A person or body with functions under any enactment of conducting assessments of children's services may delegate any of those functions to any other person or body with such functions.

23 Sections 20 to 22: interpretation

(1) This section applies for the purposes of sections 20 to 22.

(2) 'Assessment' includes an inspection, review, investigation or study.

(3) 'Children's services' means—

    (a) anything done for or in relation to children and relevant young persons (alone or with other persons)—

        (i) in respect of which, apart from section 20, a person or body to which that section applies conducts any kind of assessment, or secures that any kind of assessment is conducted; and

        (ii) which is specified in, or is of a description prescribed by, regulations made by the Secretary of State;

    (b) any function under sections 10 and 13 to 19; and

    (c) any function conferred on a children's services authority under section 12.

(4) 'Relevant young persons' means persons, other than children, in relation to whom arrangements under section 10 may be made.

(5) 'The Chief Inspector of Schools' means Her Majesty's Chief Inspector of Schools in England.

. . .

PART 3   CHILDREN'S SERVICES IN WALES

General

25 Co-operation to improve well-being: Wales

(1) Each children's services authority in Wales must make arrangements to promote co-operation between—

    (a) the authority;

    (b) each of the authority's relevant partners; and

(c) such other persons or bodies as the authority consider appropriate, being persons or bodies of any nature who exercise functions or are engaged in activities in relation to children in the authority's area.

(2) The arrangements are to be made with a view to improving the well-being of children in the authority's area so far as relating to—

    (a) physical and mental health and emotional well-being;

    (b) protection from harm and neglect;

    (c) education, training and recreation;

    (d) the contribution made by them to society;

    (e) social and economic well-being.

(3) In making arrangements under this section a children's services authority in Wales must have regard to the importance of parents and other persons caring for children in improving the well-being of children.

(4) For the purposes of this section each of the following is the relevant partner of a children's services authority in Wales—

    (a) the police authority and the chief officer of police for a police area any part of which falls within the area of the children's services authority;

    (b) a local probation board for an area any part of which falls within the area of the authority;

    (c) a youth offending team for an area any part of which falls within the area of the authority;

    (d) a Local Health Board for an area any part of which falls within the area of the authority;

    (e) an NHS trust providing services in the area of the authority;

    (f) the Assembly to the extent that it is discharging functions under Part 2 of the Learning and Skills Act 2000.

(5) The relevant partners of a children's services authority in Wales must co-operate with the authority in the making of arrangements under this section.

(6) A children's services authority in Wales and any of their relevant partners may for the purposes of arrangements under this section—

    (a) provide staff, goods, services, accommodation or other resources;

    (b) establish and maintain a pooled fund.

(7) For the purposes of subsection (6) a pooled fund is a fund—

    (a) which is made up of contributions by the authority and the relevant partner or partners concerned; and

    (b) out of which payments may be made towards expenditure incurred in the discharge of functions of the authority and functions of the relevant partner or partners.

(8) A children's services authority in Wales and each of their relevant partners must in exercising their functions under this section have regard to any guidance given to them for the purpose by the Assembly.

(9) The Assembly must obtain the consent of the Secretary of State before giving guidance under subsection (8) at any time after the coming into force of any of paragraphs (a) to (c) of subsection (4).

(10) Arrangements under this section may include arrangements relating to—

    (a) persons aged 18 and 19;

    (b) persons over the age of 19 who are receiving—

        (i) services under sections 23C to 24D of the Children Act 1989 (c. 41); or

        (ii) youth support services (within the meaning of section 123 of the Learning and Skills Act 2000 (c. 21)).

26 Children and young people's plans: Wales

(1) The Assembly may by regulations require a children's services authority in Wales from time to time to prepare and publish a plan setting out the authority's strategy for discharging their functions in relation to children and relevant young persons.

(2) Regulations under this section may in particular make provision as to—
    (a) the matters to be dealt with in a plan under this section;
    (b) the period to which a plan under this section is to relate;
    (c) when and how a plan under this section must be published;
    (d) keeping a plan under this section under review;
    (e) consultation to be carried out before a plan under this section is published;
    (f) implementation of a plan under this section.

(3) The matters for which provision may be made under subsection (2)(a) include in particular—
    (a) the arrangements made or to be made under section 25 by a children's services authority in Wales;
    (b) the strategy or proposals in relation to children and relevant young persons of any person or body with whom a children's services authority in Wales makes or proposes to make such arrangements.

(4) Regulations under this section may require a children's services authority in Wales to obtain the Assembly's approval before publishing a plan under this section; and may provide that the Assembly may modify a plan before approving it.

(5) A children's services authority in Wales must have regard to any guidance given to them by the Assembly in relation to how they are to discharge their functions under regulations under this section.

(6) In this section 'relevant young persons' means the persons, in addition to children, in relation to whom arrangements under section 25 may be made.

27 Responsibility for functions under sections 25 and 26

(1) A children's services authority in Wales must—
    (a) appoint an officer, to be known as the 'lead director for children and young people's services', for the purposes of co-ordinating and overseeing arrangements made under sections 25 and 26; and
    (b) designate one of their members, to be known as the 'lead member for children and young people's services', to have as his special care the discharge of the authority's functions under those sections.

(2) A Local Health Board must—
    (a) appoint an officer, to be known as the Board's 'lead officer for children and young people's services', for the purposes of the Board's functions under section 25; and
    (b) designate one of the Board's members who is not an officer as its 'lead member for children and young people's services' to have the discharge of those functions as his special care.

(3) An NHS trust to which section 25 applies must—
    (a) appoint an executive director, to be known as the trust's 'lead executive director for children and young people's services', for the purposes of the trust's functions under that section; and
    (b) designate one of the trust's non-executive directors as its 'lead non-executive director for children and young people's services' to have the discharge of those functions as his special care.

(4) Each children's services authority in Wales, Local Health Board and NHS trust to which section 25 applies must have regard to any guidance given to them by the Assembly in relation to—
    (a) their functions under this section;
    (b) the responsibilities of the persons appointed or designated by them under this section.

28 Arrangements to safeguard and promote welfare: Wales

(1) This section applies to each of the following—

(a) a children's services authority in Wales;

(b) a Local Health Board;

(c) an NHS trust all or most of whose hospitals, establishments and facilities are situated in Wales;

(d) the police authority and chief officer of police for a police area in Wales;

(e) the British Transport Police Authority, so far as exercising functions in relation to Wales;

(f) a local probation board for an area in Wales;

(g) a youth offending team for an area in Wales;

(h) the governor of a prison or secure training centre in Wales (or, in the case of a contracted out prison or secure training centre, its director);

(i) any person to the extent that he is providing services pursuant to arrangements made by a children's services authority in Wales under section 123(1)(b) of the Learning and Skills Act 2000 (c. 21) (youth support services).

(2) Each person and body to whom this section applies must make arrangements for ensuring that—

(a) their functions are discharged having regard to the need to safeguard and promote the welfare of children; and

(b) any services provided by another person pursuant to arrangements made by the person or body in the discharge of their functions are provided having regard to that need.

(3) In the case of a children's services authority in Wales, the reference in subsection (2) to functions of the authority does not include functions to which section 175 of the Education Act 2002 (c. 32) applies.

(4) The persons and bodies referred to in subsection (1)(a) to (c) and (i) must in discharging their duty under this section have regard to any guidance given to them for the purpose by the Assembly.

(5) The persons and bodies referred to in subsection (1)(d) to (h) must in discharging their duty under this section have regard to any guidance given to them for the purpose by the Secretary of State after consultation with the Assembly.

29 Information databases: Wales

(1) The Assembly may for the purpose of arrangements under section 25 or 28 above or under section 175 of the Education Act 2002—

(a) by regulations require children's services authorities in Wales to establish and operate databases containing information in respect of persons to whom such arrangements relate;

(b) itself establish and operate, or make arrangements for the operation and establishment of, one or more databases containing such information.

(2) The Assembly may for the purposes of arrangements under subsection (1)(b) by regulations establish a body corporate to establish and operate one or more databases.

(3) A database under this section may only include information falling within subsection (4) in relation to a person to whom arrangements specified in subsection (1) relate.

(4) The information referred to in subsection (3) is information of the following descriptions in relation to a person—

(a) his name, address, gender and date of birth;

(b) a number identifying him;

(c) the name and contact details of any person with parental responsibility for him (within the meaning of section 3 of the Children Act 1989 (c. 41)) or who has care of him at any time;

(d) details of any education being received by him (including the name and contact details of any educational institution attended by him);

(e) the name and contact details of any person providing primary medical services in relation to him under Part 1 of the National Health Service Act 1977 (c. 49);

(f) the name and contact details of any person providing to him services of such description as the Assembly may by regulations specify;

(g) information as to the existence of any cause for concern in relation to him;

(h) information of such other description, not including medical records or other personal records, as the Assembly may by regulations specify.

(5) The Assembly may by regulations make provision in relation to the establishment and operation of any database or databases under this section.

(6) Regulations under subsection (5) may in particular make provision—

(a) as to the information which must or may be contained in any database under this section (subject to subsection (3));

(b) requiring a person or body specified in subsection (7) to disclose information for inclusion in the database;

(c) permitting a person or body specified in subsection (8) to disclose information for inclusion in the database;

(d) permitting or requiring the disclosure of information included in any such database;

(e) permitting or requiring any person to be given access to any such database for the purpose of adding or reading information;

(f) as to the conditions on which such access must or may be given;

(g) as to the length of time for which information must or may be retained;

(h) as to procedures for ensuring the accuracy of information included in any such database;

(i) in a case where a database is established by virtue of subsection (1)(b), requiring children's services authorities in Wales to participate in the operation of the database.

(7) The persons and bodies referred to in subsection (6)(b) are—

(a) the persons and bodies specified in section 28(1);

(b) the National Assembly for Wales to the extent that it is discharging its functions under Part 2 of the Learning and Skills Act 2000;

(c) the governing body of a maintained school in Wales (within the meaning of section 175 of the Education Act 2002 (c. 32));

(d) the governing body of an institution in Wales within the further education sector (within the meaning of that section);

(e) the proprietor of an independent school in Wales (within the meaning of the Education Act 1996 (c. 56));

(f) a person or body of such other description as the Assembly may by regulations specify.

(8) The persons and bodies referred to in subsection (6)(c) are—

(a) a person registered in Wales for child minding or the provision of day care under Part 10A of the Children Act 1989 (c. 41);

(b) a voluntary organisation exercising functions or engaged in activities in relation to persons to whom arrangements specified in subsection (1) relate;

(c) the Commissioners of Inland Revenue;

(d) a registered social landlord;

(e) a person or body of such other description as the Assembly may by regulations specify.

(9) The Assembly and the Secretary of State may provide information for inclusion in a database under this section.

(10) The provision which may be made under subsection (6)(e) includes provision for a person of a description specified in the regulations to determine what must or may be done under the regulations.

(11) Regulations under subsection (5) may also provide that anything which may be done under regulations under subsection (6)(c) to (e) or (9) may be done notwithstanding any rule of common law which prohibits or restricts the disclosure of information.

(12) Regulations under subsections (1)(a) and (5) may only be made with the consent of the Secretary of State.

(13) Any person or body establishing or operating a database under this section must in the establishment or operation of the database have regard to any guidance, and comply with any direction, given to that person by the Assembly.

(14) Guidance or directions under subsection (13) may in particular relate to—

(a) the management of a database under this section;
(b) the technical specifications for any such database;
(c) the security of any such database;
(d) the transfer and comparison of information between databases under this section;
(e) the giving of advice in relation to rights under the Data Protection Act 1998 (c. 29).

. . .

Local Safeguarding Children Boards

31 Establishment of LSCBs in Wales

(1) Each children's services authority in Wales must establish a Local Safeguarding Children Board for their area.

(2) A Board established under this section must include such representative or representatives of—

(a) the authority by which it is established, and
(b) each Board partner of that authority,

as the Assembly may by regulations prescribe.

(3) For the purposes of this section each of the following is a Board partner of a children's services authority in Wales—

(a) the chief officer of police for a police area any part of which falls within the area of the authority;
(b) a local probation board for an area any part of which falls within the area of the authority;
(c) a youth offending team for an area any part of which falls within the area of the authority;
(d) a Local Health Board for an area any part of which falls within the area of the authority;
(e) an NHS trust providing services in the area of the authority;
(f) the governor of any secure training centre within the area of the authority (or, in the case of a contracted out secure training centre, its director);
(g) the governor of any prison in the area of the authority which ordinarily detains children (or, in the case of a contracted out prison, its director).

(4) Regulations under subsection (2) that make provision in relation to a Board partner referred to in subsection (3)(a) to (c), (f) or (g) may only be made with the consent of the Secretary of State.

(5) A children's services authority in Wales must take reasonable steps to ensure that the Local Safeguarding Children Board established by them includes representatives of relevant persons and bodies of such descriptions as may be prescribed by the Assembly in regulations.

(6) A Local Safeguarding Children Board established under this section may also include representatives of such other relevant persons or bodies as the authority by which it is established consider, after consulting their Board partners, should be represented on it.

(7) For the purposes of subsections (5) and (6), relevant persons and bodies are persons and bodies of any nature exercising functions or engaged in activities relating to children in the area of the authority in question.

(8) In the establishment and operation of a Local Safeguarding Children Board under this section—

   (a) the authority establishing it must co-operate with each of their Board partners; and

   (b) each Board partner must co-operate with the authority.

(9) Two or more children's services authorities in Wales may discharge their respective duties under subsection (1) by establishing a Local Safeguarding Children Board for their combined area (and where they do so, any reference in this section and sections 32 to 34 to the authority establishing the Board shall be read as a reference to the authorities establishing it).

32   Functions and procedure of LSCBs in Wales

(1) The objective of a Local Safeguarding Children Board established under section 31 is—

   (a) to co-ordinate what is done by each person or body represented on the Board for the purposes of safeguarding and promoting the welfare of children in the area of the authority by which it is established; and

   (b) to ensure the effectiveness of what is done by each such person or body for those purposes.

(2) A Local Safeguarding Children Board established under section 31 is to have such functions in relation to its objective as the Assembly may by regulations prescribe (which may in particular include functions of review or investigation).

(3) The Assembly may by regulations make provision as to the procedures to be followed by a Local Safeguarding Children Board established under section 31.

33   Funding of LSCBs in Wales

(1) Any person or body specified in subsection (3) may make payments towards expenditure incurred by, or for purposes connected with, a Local Safeguarding Children Board established under section 31—

   (a) by making the payments directly; or

   (b) by contributing to a fund out of which the payments may be made.

(2) Any person or body specified in subsection (3) may provide staff, goods, services, accommodation or other resources for purposes connected with a Local Safeguarding Children Board established under section 31.

(3) The persons and bodies referred to in subsections (1) and (2) are—

   (a) the children's services authority in Wales by which the Board is established;

   (b) any person who is a Board partner of the authority under section 31(3)(a) to (e);

   (c) in a case where the governor of a secure training centre or prison is a Board partner of the authority, the Secretary of State; and

   (d) in a case where the director of a contracted out secure training centre or prison is a Board partner of the authority, the contractor.

34   LSCBs in Wales: supplementary

(1) The Assembly may by regulations make provision as to the functions of children's services authorities in Wales relating to Local Safeguarding Children Boards established by them.

(2) A children's services authority in Wales and each of their Board partners must, in exercising their functions relating to a Local Safeguarding Children Board, have regard to any guidance given to them for the purpose by the Assembly.

(3) The Assembly must obtain the consent of the Secretary of State before giving guidance under subsection (2) at any time after the coming into force of any of paragraphs (a) to (c), (f) or (g) of section 31(3).

PART 4   ADVISORY AND SUPPORT SERVICES FOR FAMILY PROCEEDINGS

CAFCASS functions in Wales

35   Functions of the Assembly relating to family proceedings

(1) In respect of family proceedings in which the welfare of children ordinarily resident in Wales is or may be in question, it is a function of the Assembly to—

(a) safeguard and promote the welfare of the children;

(b) give advice to any court about any application made to it in such proceedings;

(c) make provision for the children to be represented in such proceedings;

(d) provide information, advice and other support for the children and their families.

(2) The Assembly must also make provision for the performance of the functions conferred on Welsh family proceedings officers by virtue of any enactment (whether or not they are exercisable for the purposes of subsection (1)).

(3) In subsection (1), 'family proceedings' has the meaning given by section 12 of the Criminal Justice and Court Services Act 2000 (c. 43).

(4) In this Part, 'Welsh family proceedings officer' means—

(a) any member of the staff of the Assembly appointed to exercise the functions of a Welsh family proceedings officer; and

(b) any other individual exercising functions of a Welsh family proceedings officer by virtue of section 36(2) or (4).

36   Ancillary powers of the Assembly

(1) The Assembly may make arrangements with organisations under which the organisations perform the functions of the Assembly under section 35 on its behalf.

(2) Arrangements under subsection (1) may provide for the organisations to designate individuals who may perform functions of Welsh family proceedings officers.

(3) The Assembly may only make an arrangement under subsection (1) if it is of the opinion—

(a) that the functions in question will be performed efficiently and to the required standard; and

(b) that the arrangement represents good value for money.

(4) The Assembly may make arrangements with individuals under which they may perform functions of Welsh family proceedings officers.

(5) The Assembly may make arrangements with an organisation or individual under which staff of the Assembly engaged in the exercise of its functions under section 35 may work for the organisation or individual.

(6) The Assembly may make arrangements with an organisation or individual under which any services provided by the Assembly's staff to the Assembly in the exercise of its functions under section 35 are also made available to the organisation or individual.

(7) The Assembly may charge for anything done under arrangements under subsection (5) and (6).

(8) In this section, references to organisations include public bodies and private or voluntary organisations.

37   Welsh family proceedings officers

(1) The Assembly may authorise a Welsh family proceedings officer of a description prescribed in regulations made by the Secretary of State—

(a) to conduct litigation in relation to any proceedings in any court,

(b) to exercise a right of audience in any proceedings in any court,

in the exercise of his functions.

(2) A Welsh family proceedings officer exercising a right to conduct litigation by virtue of subsection (1)(a) who would otherwise have such a right by virtue of section 28(2)(a) of the Courts and Legal Services Act 1990 (c. 41) is to be treated as having acquired that right solely by virtue of this section.

(3) A Welsh family proceedings officer exercising a right of audience by virtue of sub-section (1)(b) who would otherwise have such a right by virtue of section 27(2)(a) of the Courts and Legal Services Act 1990 is to be treated as having acquired that right solely by virtue of this section.

(4) A Welsh family proceedings officer may, subject to rules of court, be cross-examined in any proceedings to the same extent as any witness.

(5) But a Welsh family proceedings officer may not be cross-examined merely because he is exercising a right to conduct litigation or a right of audience granted in accordance with this section.

(6) In this section, 'right to conduct litigation' and 'right of audience' have the same meanings as in section 119 of the Courts and Legal Services Act 1990.

38 Inspections

(1) Her Majesty's Inspectorate of Court Administration must at the request of the Assembly inspect, and report to the Assembly on—

(a) the discharge by the Assembly of its functions under this Part; and

(b) the discharge by Welsh family proceedings officers of their functions under this Part and any other enactment.

(2) The Assembly may only make a request under subsection (1) with the consent of the Secretary of State.

39 Protection of children

(1) The Protection of Children Act 1999 (c. 14) ('the 1999 Act') shall have effect as if the Assembly, in performing its functions under sections 35 and 36, were a child care organi-sation within the meaning of that Act.

(2) Arrangements which the Assembly makes with an organisation under section 36(1) must provide that, before selecting an individual to be employed under the arrangements in a child care position, the organisation—

(a) must ascertain whether the individual is included in any of the lists mentioned in section 7(1) of the 1999 Act, and

(b) if he is included in any of those lists, must not select him for that employment.

(3) Such arrangements must provide that, if at any time the organisation has power to refer an individual who is or has been employed in a child care position under the arrangements to the Secretary of State under section 2 of the 1999 Act (inclusion in list on reference following disciplinary actions etc), the organisation must so refer him.

(4) In this section, 'child care position' and 'employment' have the same meanings as in the 1999 Act.

40 Advisory and support services for family proceedings: supplementary

Schedule 3 (which makes supplementary and consequential provision relating to this Part, including provision relating to functions of Welsh family proceedings officers) has effect.

41 Sharing of information

(1) The Assembly and the Children and Family Court Advisory and Support Service may provide any information to each other for the purposes of their respective functions under this Part and Part 1 of the Criminal Justice and Court Services Act 2000 (c. 43).

(2) A Welsh family proceedings officer and an officer of the Service (within the meaning given by section 11(3) of that Act) may provide any information to each other for the pur-poses of any of their respective functions.

Transfers

42   Transfer of property from CAFCASS to Assembly

(1) For the purposes of the exercise of functions conferred on the Assembly by or under this Part, the Assembly and the Secretary of State may jointly by order make one or more schemes for the transfer to the Assembly of property, rights and liabilities of the Children and Family Court Advisory and Support Service (in this section, 'CAFCASS').

. . .

43   Transfer of staff from CAFCASS to Assembly

(1) For the purpose of the exercise of functions conferred on the Assembly by or under this Part, the Assembly and the Secretary of State may jointly by order make one or more schemes for the transfer of employees of CAFCASS to the Assembly.

. . .

PART 5   MISCELLANEOUS

Private fostering

. . .

45   Power to establish registration scheme in England

(1) The Secretary of State may by regulations require any person who fosters a child privately in the area of a children's services authority in England to be registered for private fostering by that authority in accordance with the regulations.

(2) Regulations under this section may make supplementary provision relating to the registration of persons for private fostering, including provision as to—

(a) how a person applies for registration and the procedure to be followed in considering an application;

(b) the requirements to be satisfied before a person may be registered;

(c) the circumstances in which a person is disqualified from being registered;

(d) the circumstances in which an application for registration may or must be granted or refused;

(e) the payment of a fee on the making or granting of an application for registration;

(f) the imposition of conditions on registration and the variation or cancellation of such conditions;

(g) the circumstances in which a person's registration may be, or be regarded as, cancelled;

(h) the making of appeals against any determination of a children's services authority in England in relation to a person's registration;

(i) temporary registration, or circumstances in which a person may be regarded as registered;

(j) requirements to be complied with by a children's services authority in England or a person registered under the regulations.

(3) The provision which may be made under subsection (2)(a) includes provision that any person who, in an application for registration under the regulations, knowingly makes a statement which is false or misleading in a material particular is guilty of an offence and liable on summary conviction to a fine not exceeding level 5 on the standard scale.

(4) The requirements for which provision may be made under subsection (2)(b) include requirements relating to—

(a) the suitability of the applicant to foster children privately;

(b) the suitability of the premises in which it is proposed to foster children privately (including their suitability by reference to any other person living there).

(5) The provision which may be made under subsection (2)(c) includes provision that a person may be disqualified where—

    (a) an order of a kind specified in the regulations has been made at any time with respect to him;

    (b) an order of a kind so specified has been made at any time with respect to any child who has been in his care;

    (c) a requirement of a kind so specified has been imposed at any time with respect to any such child, under or by virtue of any enactment;

    (d) he has been convicted of a criminal offence of a kind so specified, or a probation order has been made in respect of him for any such offence or he has been discharged absolutely or conditionally for any such offence;

    (e) a prohibition has been imposed on him under any specified enactment;

    (f) his rights and powers with respect to a child have at any time been vested in a specified authority under a specified enactment;

    (g) he lives in the same household as a person who is himself disqualified from being registered or in a household in which such a person is employed.

(6) The provision which may be made under subsection (2)(c) also includes provision for a children's services authority in England to determine whether a person is or is not to be disqualified.

(7) The conditions for which provision may be made under subsection (2)(f) include conditions relating to—

    (a) the maintenance of premises in which children are, or are proposed to be, privately fostered;

    (b) any other persons living at such premises.

(8) The provision which may be made under subsection (2)(j) includes—

    (a) a requirement that a person registered under the regulations obtain the consent of the children's services authority in England by whom he is registered before privately fostering a child;

    (b) provision relating to the giving of such consent (including provision as to the circumstances in which, or conditions subject to which, it may or must be given).

(9) The provision which may be made under subsection (2)(j) also includes—

    (a) a requirement for a children's services authority in England to undertake annual inspections in relation to persons registered under the regulations (whether in fact privately fostering children or not); and

    (b) provision for the payment of a fee by registered persons in respect of such inspections.

(10) Regulations under this section may—

    (a) authorise a children's services authority in England to issue a notice to any person whom they believe to be fostering a child privately in their area without being registered in accordance with the regulations; and

    (b) provide that a person who, without reasonable excuse, fosters a child privately without being registered in accordance with the regulations while such a notice is issued in respect of him is guilty of an offence and liable on summary conviction to a fine not exceeding level 5 on the standard scale.

(11) Regulations under this section may provide that a person registered under the regulations who without reasonable excuse contravenes or otherwise fails to comply with any requirement imposed on him in the regulations is guilty of an offence and liable on summary conviction to a fine not exceeding level 5 on the standard scale.

(12) Regulations under this section may provide that a person who fosters a child privately while he is disqualified from being registered is guilty of an offence unless—

    (a) he is disqualified by virtue of the fact that he lives in the same household as a person who is himself disqualified from being registered or in a household in which such a person is employed; and

(b) he did not know, and had no reasonable grounds for believing, that that person was so disqualified.

(13) Where regulations under this section make provision under subsection (12), they must provide that a person who is guilty of the offence referred to in that subsection is liable on summary conviction to—

(a) a fine not exceeding level 5 on the standard scale, or

(b) a term of imprisonment not exceeding 51 weeks (or, in the case of an offence committed before the commencement of section 281(5) of the Criminal Justice Act 2003 (c. 44), not exceeding six months), or

(c) both.

(14) Regulations under this section may—

(a) make consequential amendments (including repeals) to sections 67(2) to (6) and 68 to 70 of, and paragraphs 6 to 9 of Schedule 8 to, the Children Act 1989 (c. 41);

(b) amend Schedule 1 to the Local Authority Social Services Act 1970 (c. 42) (social services functions) as to add functions of a children's services authority in England under this section to the functions listed in that Schedule.

(15) Nothing in this section affects the scope of section 66(1).

(16) For the purposes of this section references to a person fostering a child privately have the same meaning as in the Children Act 1989.

46 Power to establish registration scheme in Wales

(1) The Assembly may by regulations require any person who fosters a child privately in the area of a children's services authority in Wales to be registered for private fostering by that authority in accordance with the regulations.

(2) Subsections (2) to (15) of section 45 apply in relation to regulations under this section as they apply in relation to regulations under that section with the substitution for references to a children's services authority in England of references to a children's services authority in Wales.

(3) Subsection (16) of that section applies for the purposes of this section.

47 Expiry of powers in sections 45 and 46

(1) If no regulations have been made under section 45 by the relevant time, that section shall (other than for the purposes of section 46(2) and (3)) cease to have effect at that time.

(2) If no regulations have been made under section 46 by the relevant time, that section shall cease to have effect at that time.

(3) In this section, the relevant time is the end of the period of four years beginning with the day on which this Act is passed.

. . .

Local authority services

49 Payments to foster parents

(1) The appropriate person may by order make provision as to the payments to be made—

(a) by a children's services authority in England or Wales or a person exercising functions on its behalf to a local authority foster parent with whom any child is placed by that authority or person under section 23(2)(a) of the Children Act 1989;

(b) by a voluntary organisation to any person with whom any child is placed by that organisation under section 59(1)(a) of that Act.

(2) In subsection (1)—

'appropriate person' means—

(a) the Secretary of State, in relation to a children's services authority in England;

(b) the Assembly, in relation to a children's services authority in Wales;

'local authority foster parent' and 'voluntary organisation' have the same meanings as in the Children Act 1989.

...

Other provisions

...

58 Reasonable punishment

(1) In relation to any offence specified in subsection (2), battery of a child cannot be justified on the ground that it constituted reasonable punishment.

(2) The offences referred to in subsection (1) are—

(a) an offence under section 18 or 20 of the Offences against the Person Act 1861 (c. 100) (wounding and causing grievous bodily harm);

(b) an offence under section 47 of that Act (assault occasioning actual bodily harm);

(c) an offence under section 1 of the Children and Young Persons Act 1933 (c. 12) (cruelty to persons under 16).

(3) Battery of a child causing actual bodily harm to the child cannot be justified in any civil proceedings on the ground that it constituted reasonable punishment.

(4) For the purposes of subsection (3) 'actual bodily harm' has the same meaning as it has for the purposes of section 47 of the Offences against the Person Act 1861.

...

PART 6   GENERAL

...

65 Interpretation

(1) In this Act—

'the Assembly' means the National Assembly for Wales;

'child' means, subject to section 9, a person under the age of eighteen (and 'children' is to be construed accordingly);

'children's services authority in England' means—

(a) a county council in England;

(b) a metropolitan district council;

(c) a non-metropolitan district council for an area for which there is no county council;

(d) a London borough council;

(e) the Common Council of the City of London;

(f) the Council of the Isles of Scilly;

'children's services authority in Wales' means a county council or county borough council in Wales.

...

SCHEDULES

SCHEDULE 1   CHILDREN'S COMMISSIONER

Status

1. (1) The Children's Commissioner is to be a corporation sole.

(2) The Children's Commissioner is not to be regarded as the servant or agent of the Crown or as enjoying any status, immunity or privilege of the Crown; and his property is not to be regarded as property of, or property held on behalf of, the Crown.

General powers

2. (1) The Children's Commissioner may do anything which appears to him to be necessary or expedient for the purpose of, or in connection with, the exercise of his functions.

(2) In particular he may—
  (a) co-operate with other public authorities in the United Kingdom;
  (b) enter into contracts; and
  (c) acquire, hold and dispose of any property.

Appointment and tenure of office

3. (1) The Children's Commissioner is to be appointed by the Secretary of State.

(2) The Secretary of State must, to such extent and in such manner as he thinks fit, involve children in the appointment of the Children's Commissioner.

(3) Subject to the provisions of this paragraph, a person shall hold and vacate office as the Children's Commissioner in accordance with the terms and conditions of his appointment as determined by the Secretary of State.

(4) An appointment as the Children's Commissioner shall be for a term not exceeding five years.

(5) A person who has held office as the Children's Commissioner is eligible for reappointment once only.

(6) The Children's Commissioner may at any time resign by notice in writing to the Secretary of State.

(7) The Secretary of State may remove the Children's Commissioner from office if he is satisfied that he has—
  (a) become unfit or unable properly to discharge his functions; or
  (b) behaved in a way that is not compatible with his continuing in office.

. . .

Civil Partnership Act 2004
(2004 c. 33)

PART 1   INTRODUCTION

1 Civil partnership
  (1) A civil partnership is a relationship between two people of the same sex ('civil partners')—
    (a) which is formed when they register as civil partners of each other—
      (i)   in England or Wales (under Part 2),

. . .

(2) Subsection (1) is subject to the provisions of this Act under or by virtue of which a civil partnership is void.

(3) A civil partnership ends only on death, dissolution or annulment.

(4) The references in subsection (3) to dissolution and annulment are to dissolution and annulment having effect under or recognised in accordance with this Act.

. . .

PART 2   CIVIL PARTNERSHIP: ENGLAND AND WALES

CHAPTER 1   REGISTRATION

Formation, eligibility and parental etc. consent

2 Formation of civil partnership by registration
  (1) For the purposes of section 1, two people are to be regarded as having registered as civil partners of each other once each of them has signed the civil partnership document—

(a) at the invitation of, and in the presence of, a civil partnership registrar, and

(b) in the presence of each other and two witnesses.

(2) Subsection (1) applies regardless of whether subsections (3) and (4) are complied with.

(3) After the civil partnership document has been signed under subsection (1), it must also be signed, in the presence of the civil partners and each other, by—

(a) each of the two witnesses, and

(b) the civil partnership registrar.

(4) After the witnesses and the civil partnership registrar have signed the civil partnership document, the relevant registration authority must ensure that—

(a) the fact that the two people have registered as civil partners of each other, and

(b) any other information prescribed by regulations,

is recorded in the register as soon as is practicable.

(5) No religious service is to be used while the civil partnership registrar is officiating at the signing of a civil partnership document.

(6) 'The civil partnership document' has the meaning given by section 7(1).

(7) 'The relevant registration authority' means the registration authority in whose area the registration takes place.

3 Eligibility

(1) Two people are not eligible to register as civil partners of each other if—

(a) they are not of the same sex,

(b) either of them is already a civil partner or lawfully married,

(c) either of them is under 16, or

(d) they are within prohibited degrees of relationship.

(2) Part 1 of Schedule 1 contains provisions for determining when two people are within prohibited degrees of relationship.

4 Parental etc. consent where proposed civil partner under 18

(1) The consent of the appropriate persons is required before a child and another person may register as civil partners of each other.

(2) Part 1 of Schedule 2 contains provisions for determining who are the appropriate persons for the purposes of this section.

(3) The requirement of consent under subsection (1) does not apply if the child is a surviving civil partner.

(4) Nothing in this section affects any need to obtain the consent of the High Court before a ward of court and another person may register as civil partners of each other.

(5) In this Part 'child', except where used to express a relationship, means a person who is under 18.

Registration procedure: general

5 Types of pre-registration procedure

(1) Two people may register as civil partners of each other under—

(a) the standard procedure;

(b) the procedure for house-bound persons;

(c) the procedure for detained persons;

(d) the special procedure (which is for cases where a person is seriously ill and not expected to recover).

(2) The procedures referred to in subsection (1)(a) to (c) are subject to—

(a) section 20 (modified procedures for certain non-residents);

(b) Schedule 3 (former spouses one of whom has changed sex).

(3) The procedures referred to in subsection (1) (including the procedures as modified by section 20 and Schedule 3) are subject to—

(a) Part 2 of Schedule 1 (provisions applicable in connection with prohibited degrees of relationship), and

(b) Parts 2 and 3 of Schedule 2 (provisions applicable where proposed civil partner is under 18).

(4) This section is also subject to section 249 and Schedule 23 (immigration control and formation of civil partnerships).

6 Place of registration

(1) The place at which two people may register as civil partners of each other—
   (a) must be in England or Wales,
   (b) must not be in religious premises, and
   (c) must be specified in the notices, or notice, of proposed civil partnership required by this Chapter.

(2) 'Religious premises' means premises which—
   (a) are used solely or mainly for religious purposes, or
   (b) have been so used and have not subsequently been used solely or mainly for other purposes.

(3) Subsections (3A) and (3B) apply in the case of registration under the standard procedure (including that procedure modified as mentioned in section 5).

(3A) The place must be—
   (a) on approved premises, or
   (b) in a register office.

(3B) If it is in a register office, the place must be open to any person wishing to attend the registration.

(3C) In this Chapter 'register office' means a register office provided under section 10 of the Registration Service Act 1953.

6A Power to approve premises

(1) The Chancellor of the Exchequer may by regulations make provision for and in connection with the approval by registration authorities of premises for the purposes of section 6(3A)(a).

7 The civil partnership document

(1) In this Part 'the civil partnership document' means—
   (a) in relation to the special procedure, a Registrar General's licence, and
   (b) in relation to any other procedure, a civil partnership schedule.

(2) Before two people are entitled to register as civil partners of each other—
   (a) the civil partnership document must be delivered to the civil partnership registrar, and
   (b) the civil partnership registrar may then ask them for any information required (under section 2(4)) to be recorded in the register.

The standard procedure

8 Notice of proposed civil partnership and declaration

(1) For two people to register as civil partners of each other under the standard procedure a notice of proposed civil partnership must be given—
   (a) if the proposed civil partners have resided in the area of the same registration authority for the period of 7 days immediately before the giving of the notice, by each of them to that registration authority;
   (b) if the proposed civil partners have not resided in the area of the same registration authority for that period, by each of them to the registration authority in whose area he or she has resided for that period.

(2) A notice of proposed civil partnership must contain such information as may be prescribed by regulations.

(3) A notice of proposed civil partnership must also include the necessary declaration, made and signed by the person giving the notice—

(a) at the time when the notice is given, and

(b) in the presence of an authorised person;

and the authorised person must attest the declaration by adding his name, description and place of residence.

(4) The necessary declaration is a solemn declaration in writing—

(a) that the proposed civil partner believes that there is no impediment of kindred or affinity or other lawful hindrance to the formation of the civil partnership;

(b) that the proposed civil partners have for the period of 7 days immediately before the giving of the notice had their usual places of residence in the area of the registration authority, or in the areas of the registration authorities, to which notice is given.

(5) Where a notice of proposed civil partnership is given to a registration authority in accordance with this section, the registration authority must ensure that the following information is recorded in the register as soon as possible—

(a) the fact that the notice has been given and the information in it;

(b) the fact that the authorised person has attested the declaration.

(6) 'Authorised person' means an employee or officer or other person provided by a registration authority who is authorised by that authority to attest notices of proposed civil partnership.

(7) For the purposes of this Chapter, a notice of proposed civil partnership is recorded when subsection (5) is complied with.

9 Power to require evidence of name etc.

(1) The registration authority to which a notice of proposed civil partnership is given may require the person giving the notice to provide it with specified evidence—

(a) relating to that person, or

(b) if the registration authority considers that the circumstances are exceptional, relating not only to that person but also to that person's proposed civil partner.

(2) Such a requirement may be imposed at any time before the registration authority issues the civil partnership schedule under section 14.

(3) 'Specified evidence', in relation to a person, means such evidence as may be specified in guidance issued by the Registrar General—

(a) of the person's name and surname,

(b) of the person's age,

(c) as to whether the person has previously formed a civil partnership or a marriage and, if so, as to the ending of the civil partnership or marriage, and

(d) of the person's nationality.

10 Proposed civil partnership to be publicised

(1) Where a notice of proposed civil partnership has been given to a registration authority, the registration authority must keep the relevant information on public display during the waiting period.

(2) 'The relevant information' means—

(a) the name of the person giving the notice,

(b) the name of that person's proposed civil partner, and

(c) such other information included in the notice of proposed civil partnership as may be prescribed by regulations.

(3) All information that a registration authority is required for the time being to keep on public display under subsection (1) must be kept on display by it at one register office provided for a district within its area.

11 Meaning of 'the waiting period'

In this Chapter 'the waiting period', in relation to a notice of proposed civil partnership, means the period—

(a) beginning the day after the notice is recorded, and

(b) subject to section 12, ending at the end of the period of 15 days beginning with that day.

12 Power to shorten the waiting period

(1) If the Registrar General, on an application being made to him, is satisfied that there are compelling reasons because of the exceptional circumstances of the case for shortening the period of 15 days mentioned in section 11(b), he may shorten it to such period as he considers appropriate.

(2) Regulations may make provision with respect to the making, and granting, of applications under subsection (1).

(3) Regulations under subsection (2) may provide for—

(a) the power conferred by subsection (1) to be exercised by a registration authority on behalf of the Registrar General in such classes of case as are prescribed by the regulations;

(b) the making of an appeal to the Registrar General against a decision taken by a registration authority in accordance with regulations made by virtue of paragraph (a).

13 Objection to proposed civil partnership

(1) Any person may object to the issue of a civil partnership schedule under section 14 by giving any registration authority notice of his objection.

(2) A notice of objection must—

(a) state the objector's place of residence and the ground of objection, and

(b) be signed by or on behalf of the objector.

(3) If a notice of objection is given to a registration authority, it must ensure that the fact that it has been given and the information in it are recorded in the register as soon as possible.

14 Issue of civil partnership schedule

(1) As soon as the waiting period in relation to each notice of proposed civil partnership has expired, the registration authority in whose area it is proposed that the registration take place is under a duty, at the request of one or both of the proposed civil partners, to issue a document to be known as a 'civil partnership schedule'.

(2) Regulations may make provision as to the contents of a civil partnership schedule.

(3) The duty in subsection (1) does not apply if the registration authority is not satisfied that there is no lawful impediment to the formation of the civil partnership.

(4) If an objection to the issue of the civil partnership schedule has been recorded in the register, no civil partnership schedule is to be issued until—

(a) the relevant registration authority has investigated the objection and is satisfied that the objection ought not to obstruct the issue of the civil partnership schedule, or

(b) the objection has been withdrawn by the person who made it.

(5) 'The relevant registration authority' means the authority which first records that a notice of proposed civil partnership has been given by one of the proposed civil partners.

15 Appeal against refusal to issue civil partnership schedule

(1) If the registration authority refuses to issue a civil partnership schedule—

(a) because an objection to its issue has been made under section 13, or

(b) in reliance on section 14(3),

either of the proposed civil partners may appeal to the Registrar General.

(2) On an appeal under this section the Registrar General must either confirm the refusal or direct that a civil partnership schedule be issued.

16 Frivolous objections and representations: liability for costs etc.

(1) Subsection (3) applies if—

(a) a person objects to the issue of a civil partnership schedule, but

(b) the Registrar General declares that the grounds on which the objection is made are frivolous and ought not to obstruct the issue of the civil partnership schedule.

(2) Subsection (3) also applies if—

(a) in reliance on section 14(3), the registration authority refuses to issue a civil partnership schedule as a result of a representation made to it, and

(b) on an appeal under section 15 against the refusal, the Registrar General declares that the representation is frivolous and ought not to obstruct the issue of the civil partnership schedule.

(3) The person who made the objection or representation is liable for—

(a) the costs of the proceedings before the Registrar General, and

(b) damages recoverable by the proposed civil partner to whom the objection or representation relates.

(4) For the purpose of enabling any person to recover any such costs and damages, a copy of a declaration of the Registrar General purporting to be sealed with the seal of the General Register Office is evidence that the Registrar General has made the declaration.

17 Period during which registration may take place

(1) The proposed civil partners may not register as civil partners of each other on the production of the civil partnership schedule until the waiting period in relation to each notice of proposed civil partnership has expired.

(2) Subject to subsection (1), under the standard procedure, they may register as civil partners by signing the civil partnership schedule on any day in the applicable period between 8 o'clock in the morning and 6 o'clock in the evening.

(3) If they do not register as civil partners by signing the civil partnership schedule before the end of the applicable period—

(a) the notices of proposed civil partnership and the civil partnership schedule are void, and

(b) no civil partnership registrar may officiate at the signing of the civil partnership schedule by them.

(4) The applicable period, in relation to two people registering as civil partners of each other, is the period of 12 months beginning with—

(a) the day on which the notices of proposed civil partnership are recorded, or

(b) if the notices are not recorded on the same day, the earlier of those days.

The procedures for house-bound and detained persons

18 House-bound persons

(1) This section applies if two people wish to register as civil partners of each other at the place where one of them is house-bound.

(2) A person is house-bound at any place if, in relation to that person, a statement is made by a registered medical practitioner that, in his opinion—

(a) because of illness or disability, that person ought not to move or be moved from the place where he is at the time when the statement is made, and

(b) it is likely to be the case for at least the following 3 months that because of the illness or disability that person ought not to move or be moved from that place.

(3) The procedure under which the two people concerned may register as civil partners of each other is the same as the standard procedure, except that—

(a) each notice of proposed civil partnership must be accompanied by a statement under subsection (2) ('a medical statement'), which must have been made not more than 14 days before the day on which the notice is recorded,

(b) the fact that the registration authority to whom the notice is given has received the medical statement must be recorded in the register, and

(c) the applicable period (for the purposes of section 17) is the period of 3 months beginning with—

(i) the day on which the notices of proposed civil partnership are recorded, or

(ii) if the notices are not recorded on the same day, the earlier of those days.

(4) A medical statement must contain such information and must be made in such manner as may be prescribed by regulations.

(5) A medical statement may not be made in relation to a person who is detained as described in section 19(2).

(6) For the purposes of this Chapter, a person in relation to whom a medical statement is made is to be treated, if he would not otherwise be so treated, as resident and usually resident at the place where he is for the time being.

19   Detained persons

(1) This section applies if two people wish to register as civil partners of each other at the place where one of them is detained.

(2) 'Detained' means detained—

    (a) as a patient in a hospital (but otherwise than by virtue of section 2, 4, 5, 35, 36 or 136 of the Mental Health Act 1983 (c. 20) (short term detentions)), or

    (b) in a prison or other place to which the Prison Act 1952 (c. 52) applies.

(3) The procedure under which the two people concerned may register as civil partners of each other is the same as the standard procedure, except that—

    (a) each notice of proposed civil partnership must be accompanied by a supporting statement, which must have been made not more than 21 days before the day on which the notice is recorded,

    (b) the fact that the registration authority to whom the notice is given has received the supporting statement must be recorded in the register, and

    (c) the applicable period (for the purposes of section 17) is the period of 3 months beginning with—

        (i)   the day on which the notices of proposed civil partnership are recorded, or

        (ii) if the notices are not recorded on the same day, the earlier of those days.

(4) A supporting statement, in relation to a detained person, is a statement made by the responsible authority which—

    (a) identifies the establishment where the person is detained, and

    (b) states that the responsible authority has no objection to that establishment being specified in a notice of proposed civil partnership as the place at which the person is to register as a civil partner.

(5) A supporting statement must contain such information and must be made in such manner as may be prescribed by regulations.

(6) 'The responsible authority' means—

    (a) if the person is detained in a hospital, the hospital's managers;

    (b) if the person is detained in a prison or other place to which the 1952 Act applies, the governor or other officer for the time being in charge of that prison or other place.

(7) 'Patient' and 'hospital' have the same meaning as in Part 2 of the 1983 Act and 'managers', in relation to a hospital, has the same meaning as in section 145(1) of the 1983 Act.

(8) For the purposes of this Chapter, a detained person is to be treated, if he would not otherwise be so treated, as resident and usually resident at the place where he is for the time being.

. . .

The special procedure

21   Notice of proposed civil partnership

(1) For two people to register as civil partners of each other under the special procedure, one of them must—

    (a) give a notice of proposed civil partnership to the registration authority for the area in which it is proposed that the registration take place, and

    (b) comply with any requirement made under section 22.

(2) The notice must contain such information as may be prescribed by regulations.

(3) Subsections (3) to (6) of section 8 (necessary declaration etc.), apart from paragraph (b) of subsection (4), apply for the purposes of this section as they apply for the purposes of that section.

22 Evidence to be produced

(1) The person giving a notice of proposed civil partnership to a registration authority under the special procedure must produce to the authority such evidence as the Registrar General may require to satisfy him—

(a) that there is no lawful impediment to the formation of the civil partnership,

(b) that the conditions in subsection (2) are met, and

(c) that there is sufficient reason why a licence should be granted.

(2) The conditions are that one of the proposed civil partners—

(a) is seriously ill and not expected to recover,

(b) cannot be moved to a place where they could be registered as civil partners of each other under the standard procedure, and

(c) understands the nature and purport of signing a Registrar General's licence.

(3) The certificate of a registered medical practitioner is sufficient evidence of any or all of the matters referred to in subsection (2).

23 Application to be reported to Registrar General

On receiving a notice of proposed civil partnership under section 21 and any evidence under section 22, the registration authority must—

(a) inform the Registrar General, and

(b) comply with any directions the Registrar General may give for verifying the evidence given.

24 Objection to issue of Registrar General's licence

(1) Any person may object to the Registrar General giving authority for the issue of his licence by giving the Registrar General or any registration authority notice of his objection.

(2) A notice of objection must—

(a) state the objector's place of residence and the ground of objection, and

(b) be signed by or on behalf of the objector.

(3) If a notice of objection is given to a registration authority, it must ensure that the fact that it has been given and the information in it are recorded in the register as soon as possible.

25 Issue of Registrar General's licence

(1) This section applies where a notice of proposed civil partnership is given to a registration authority under section 21.

(2) The registration authority may issue a Registrar General's licence if, and only if, given authority to do so by the Registrar General.

(3) The Registrar General—

(a) may not give his authority unless he is satisfied that one of the proposed civil partners is seriously ill and not expected to recover, but

(b) if so satisfied, must give his authority unless a lawful impediment to the issue of his licence has been shown to his satisfaction to exist.

(4) A licence under this section must state that it is issued on the authority of the Registrar General.

(5) Regulations may (subject to subsection (4)) make provision as to the contents of a licence under this section.

(6) If an objection has been made to the Registrar General giving authority for the issue of his licence, he is not to give that authority until—

(a) he has investigated the objection and decided whether it ought to obstruct the issue of his licence, or

(b) the objection has been withdrawn by the person who made it.

(7) Any decision of the Registrar General under subsection (6)(a) is final.

26   Frivolous objections: liability for costs

(1) This section applies if—

(a) a person objects to the Registrar General giving authority for the issue of his licence, but

(b) the Registrar General declares that the grounds on which the objection is made are frivolous and ought not to obstruct the issue of his licence.

(2) The person who made the objection is liable for—

(a) the costs of the proceedings before the Registrar General, and

(b) damages recoverable by the proposed civil partner to whom the objection relates.

(3) For the purpose of enabling any person to recover any such costs and damages, a copy of a declaration of the Registrar General purporting to be sealed with the seal of the General Register Office is evidence that the Registrar General has made the declaration.

27   Period during which registration may take place

(1) If a Registrar General's licence has been issued under section 25, the proposed civil partners may register as civil partners by signing it at any time within 1 month from the day on which the notice of proposed civil partnership was given.

(2) If they do not register as civil partners by signing the licence within the 1 month period—

(a) the notice of proposed civil partnership and the licence are void, and

(b) no civil partnership registrar may officiate at the signing of the licence by them.

Supplementary

28   Registration authorities

In this Chapter 'registration authority' means—

(a) in relation to England, a county council, the council of any district comprised in an area for which there is no county council, a London borough council, the Common Council of the City of London or the Council of the Isles of Scilly;

(b) in relation to Wales, a county council or a county borough council.

29   Civil partnership registrars

(1) A civil partnership registrar is an individual who is designated by a registration authority as a civil partnership registrar for its area.

(2) It is the duty of each registration authority to ensure that there is a sufficient number of civil partnership registrars for its area to carry out in that area the functions of civil partnership registrars.

(3) Each registration authority must inform the Registrar General as soon as is practicable—

(a) of any designation it has made of a person as a civil partnership registrar, and

(b) of the ending of any such designation.

30   The Registrar General and the register

(1) In this Chapter 'the Registrar General' means the Registrar General for England and Wales.

(2) The Registrar General must provide a system for keeping any records that relate to civil partnerships and are required by this Chapter to be made.

(3) The system may, in particular, enable those records to be kept together with other records kept by the Registrar General.

(4) In this Chapter 'the register' means the system for keeping records provided under subsection (2).

31   Offences relating to civil partnership schedule

(1) A person commits an offence if he issues a civil partnership schedule knowing that he does so—

(a) before the waiting period in relation to each notice of proposed civil partnership has expired,

    (b) after the end of the applicable period, or

    (c) at a time when its issue has been forbidden under Schedule 2 by a person entitled to forbid its issue.

(2) A person commits an offence if, in his actual or purported capacity as a civil partnership registrar, he officiates at the signing of a civil partnership schedule by proposed civil partners knowing that he does so—

    (a) at a place other than the place specified in the notices of proposed civil partnership and the civil partnership schedule,

    (aa) on premises that are not approved premises although the signing is purportedly in accordance with section 6(3A)(a),

    (ab) at any other time other than between 8 o'clock in the morning and 6 o'clock in the evening,

    (b) in the absence of a civil partnership registrar,

    (c) before the waiting period in relation to each notice of proposed civil partnership has expired, or

    (d) even though the civil partnership is void under section 49(b) or (c).

(3) A person guilty of an offence under subsection (1) or (2)(a), (aa), (b), (c) or (d) is liable on conviction on indictment to imprisonment for a term not exceeding 5 years or to a fine (or both).

(3A) A person guilty of an offence under subsection (2)(ab) is liable on conviction on indictment to imprisonment for a term not exceeding 14 years or to a fine or both.

(4) A prosecution under this section may not be commenced more than 3 years after the commission of the offence.

32   Offences relating to Registrar General's licence

(1) A person commits an offence if—

    (a) he gives information by way of evidence in response to a requirement under section 22(1), knowing that the information is false;

    (b) he gives a certificate as provided for by section 22(3), knowing that the certificate is false.

(2) A person commits an offence if, in his actual or purported capacity as a civil partnership registrar, he officiates at the signing of a Registrar General's licence by proposed civil partners knowing that he does so—

    (a) at a place other than the place specified in the licence,

    (b) in the absence of a civil partnership registrar,

    (c) after the end of 1 month from the day on which the notice of proposed civil partnership was given, or

    (d) even though the civil partnership is void under section 49(b) or (c).

(3) A person guilty of an offence under subsection (1) or (2) is liable—

    (a) on conviction on indictment, to imprisonment not exceeding 3 years or to a fine (or both);

    (b) on summary conviction, to a fine not exceeding the statutory maximum.

(4) A prosecution under this section may not be commenced more than 3 years after the commission of the offence.

33   Offences relating to the recording of civil partnerships

(1) A civil partnership registrar commits an offence if he refuses or fails to comply with the provisions of this Chapter or of any regulations made under section 36.

(2) A civil partnership registrar guilty of an offence under subsection (1) is liable—

    (a) on conviction on indictment, to imprisonment for a term not exceeding 2 years or to a fine (or both);

    (b) on summary conviction, to a fine not exceeding the statutory maximum;

and on conviction shall cease to be a civil partnership registrar.

(3) A person commits an offence if—

  (a) under arrangements made by a registration authority for the purposes of section 2(4), he is under a duty to record information required to be recorded under section 2(4), but

  (b) he refuses or without reasonable cause omits to do so.

(4) A person guilty of an offence under subsection (3) is liable on summary conviction to a fine not exceeding level 3 on the standard scale.

(5) A person commits an offence if he records in the register information relating to the formation of a civil partnership by the signing of a civil partnership schedule, knowing that the civil partnership is void under section 49(b) or (c).

(6) A person guilty of an offence under subsection (5) is liable on conviction on indictment, to imprisonment for a term not exceeding 5 years or to a fine (or both).

(7) A person commits an offence if he records in the register information relating to the formation of a civil partnership by the signing of a Registrar General's licence, knowing that the civil partnership is void under section 49(b) or (c).

(8) A person guilty of an offence under subsection (7) is liable—

  (a) on conviction on indictment, to imprisonment for a term not exceeding 3 years or to a fine (or both);

  (b) on summary conviction, to a fine not exceeding the statutory maximum.

(9) A prosecution under subsection (5) or (7) may not be commenced more than 3 years after the commission of the offence.

34　Fees

(1) The Chancellor of the Exchequer may by order provide for fees, of such amounts as may be specified in the order, to be payable to such persons as may be prescribed by the order in respect of—

  (a) the giving of a notice of proposed civil partnership and the attestation of the necessary declaration;

  (b) the making of an application under section 12(1) (application to reduce waiting period);

  (c) the issue of a Registrar General's licence;

  (d) the attendance of the civil partnership registrar when two people sign the civil partnership document;

  (e) such other services provided in connection with civil partnerships either by registration authorities or by or on behalf of the Registrar General as may be prescribed by the order.

(2) The Registrar General may remit the fee for the issue of his licence in whole or in part in any case where it appears to him that the payment of the fee would cause hardship to the proposed civil partners.

(3) Where a civil partnership registrar for any area attends when two people sign the civil partnership schedule on approved premises, in accordance with section 6(3A)(a)—

  (a) subsection (1)(d) does not apply, but

  (b) the registration authority for that area is entitled from those people a fee of an amount determined by the authority in accordance with regulations under section 6A.

35　Power to assimilate provisions relating to civil registration

(1) The Chancellor of the Exchequer may by order make—

  (a) such amendments of this Act as appear to him appropriate for the purpose of assimilating any provision connected with the formation or recording of civil partnerships in England and Wales to any provision made (whether or not under an order under section 1 of the Regulatory Reform Act 2001 (c. 6)) in relation to civil marriage in England and Wales, and

  (b) such amendments of other enactments and of subordinate legislation as appear to him appropriate in consequence of any amendments made under paragraph (a).

(2) 'Civil marriage' means marriage solemnised otherwise than according to the rites of the Church of England or any other religious usages.

(3) 'Amendment' includes repeal or revocation.

(4) 'Subordinate legislation' has the same meaning as in the Interpretation Act 1978 (c. 30).

36 Regulations and orders

(1) Regulations may make provision supplementing the provisions of this Chapter.

(2) Regulations may in particular make provision—

(a) relating to the use of Welsh in documents and records relating to civil partnerships;

(b) with respect to the retention of documents relating to civil partnerships;

(c) prescribing the duties of civil partnership registrars;

(d) prescribing the duties of persons in whose presence any declaration is made for the purposes of this Chapter;

(e) for the issue by the Registrar General of guidance supplementing any provision made by the regulations.

(f) for the issue by registration authorities or the Registrar General of certified copies of entries in the register and for such copies to be received in evidence.

(3) In this Chapter, except in subsection 6A, 'regulations' means regulations made by the Registrar General with the approval of the Chancellor of the Exchequer.

(4) Any power to make regulations or an order under this Chapter is exercisable by statutory instrument.

(5) A statutory instrument containing regulations under section 6A or an order under section 34 is subject to annulment in pursuance of a resolution of either House of Parliament.

(6) No order may be made under section 35 unless a draft of the statutory instrument containing the order has been laid before, and approved by a resolution of, each House of Parliament.

CHAPTER 2   DISSOLUTION, NULLITY AND
OTHER PROCEEDINGS

Introduction

37 Powers to make orders and effect of orders

(1) The court may, in accordance with this Chapter—

(a) make an order (a 'dissolution order') which dissolves a civil partnership on the ground that it has broken down irretrievably;

(b) make an order (a 'nullity order') which annuls a civil partnership which is void or voidable;

(c) make an order (a 'presumption of death order') which dissolves a civil partnership on the ground that one of the civil partners is presumed to be dead;

(d) make an order (a 'separation order') which provides for the separation of the civil partners.

(2) Every dissolution, nullity or presumption of death order—

(a) is, in the first instance, a conditional order, and

(b) may not be made final before the end of the prescribed period (see section 38); and any reference in this Chapter to a conditional order is to be read accordingly.

(3) A nullity order made where a civil partnership is voidable annuls the civil partnership only as respects any time after the order has been made final, and the civil partnership is to be treated (despite the order) as if it had existed up to that time.

(4) In this Chapter, other than in sections 58 to 61, 'the court' means—

(a) the High Court, or

(b) if a county court has jurisdiction by virtue of Part 5 of the Matrimonial and Family Proceedings Act 1984 (c. 42), a county court.

(5) This Chapter is subject to sections 219 to 224 (jurisdiction of the court).

38 The period before conditional orders may be made final

(1) Subject to subsections (2) to (4), the prescribed period for the purposes of section 37(2)(b) is—

(a) 6 weeks from the making of the conditional order, or

(b) if the 6 week period would end on a day on which the office or registry of the court dealing with the case is closed, the period of 6 weeks extended to the end of the first day on which the office or registry is next open.

(2) The Lord Chancellor may by order amend this section so as to substitute a different definition of the prescribed period for the purposes of section 37(2)(b).

(3) But the Lord Chancellor may not under subsection (2) provide for a period longer than 6 months to be the prescribed period.

(4) In a particular case the court dealing with the case may by order shorten the prescribed period.

(5) The power to make an order under subsection (2) is exercisable by statutory instrument.

(6) An instrument containing such an order is subject to annulment in pursuance of a resolution of either House of Parliament.

39 Intervention of the Queen's Proctor

(1) This section applies if an application has been made for a dissolution, nullity or presumption of death order.

(2) The court may, if it thinks fit, direct that all necessary papers in the matter are to be sent to the Queen's Proctor who must under the directions of the Attorney General instruct counsel to argue before the court any question in relation to the matter which the court considers it necessary or expedient to have fully argued.

(3) If any person at any time—

(a) during the progress of the proceedings, or

(b) before the conditional order is made final,

gives information to the Queen's Proctor on any matter material to the due decision of the case, the Queen's Proctor may take such steps as the Attorney General considers necessary or expedient.

(4) If the Queen's Proctor intervenes or shows cause against the making of the conditional order in any proceedings relating to its making, the court may make such order as may be just as to—

(a) the payment by other parties to the proceedings of the costs incurred by him in doing so, or

(b) the payment by the Queen's Proctor of any costs incurred by any of those parties because of his doing so.

(5) The Queen's Proctor is entitled to charge as part of the expenses of his office—

(a) the costs of any proceedings under subsection (2);

(b) if his reasonable costs of intervening or showing cause as mentioned in subsection (4) are not fully satisfied by an order under subsection (4)(a), the amount of the difference;

(c) if the Treasury so directs, any costs which he pays to any parties under an order made under subsection (4)(b).

40 Proceedings before order has been made final

(1) This section applies if—

(a) a conditional order has been made, and

(b) the Queen's Proctor, or any person who has not been a party to proceedings in which the order was made, shows cause why the order should not be made final on the ground that material facts have not been brought before the court.

(2) This section also applies if—
- (a) a conditional order has been made,
- (b) 3 months have elapsed since the earliest date on which an application could have been made for the order to be made final,
- (c) no such application has been made by the civil partner who applied for the conditional order, and
- (d) the other civil partner makes an application to the court under this subsection.

(3) The court may—
- (a) make the order final,
- (b) rescind the order,
- (c) require further inquiry, or
- (d) otherwise deal with the case as it thinks fit.

(4) Subsection (3)(a)—
- (a) applies despite section 37(2) (period before conditional orders may be made final), but
- (b) is subject to section 48(4) (protection for respondent in separation cases) and section 63 (restrictions on making of orders affecting children).

41 Time bar on applications for dissolution orders

(1) No application for a dissolution order may be made to the court before the end of the period of 1 year from the date of the formation of the civil partnership.

(2) Nothing in this section prevents the making of an application based on matters which occurred before the end of the 1 year period.

42 Attempts at reconciliation of civil partners

(1) This section applies in relation to cases where an application is made for a dissolution or separation order.

(2) Rules of court must make provision for requiring the solicitor acting for the applicant to certify whether he has—
- (a) discussed with the applicant the possibility of a reconciliation with the other civil partner, and
- (b) given the applicant the names and addresses of persons qualified to help effect a reconciliation between civil partners who have become estranged.

(3) If at any stage of proceedings for the order it appears to the court that there is a reasonable possibility of a reconciliation between the civil partners, the court may adjourn the proceedings for such period as it thinks fit to enable attempts to be made to effect a reconciliation between them.

(4) The power to adjourn under subsection (3) is additional to any other power of adjournment.

43 Consideration by the court of certain agreements or arrangements

(1) This section applies in relation to cases where—
- (a) proceedings for a dissolution or separation order are contemplated or have begun, and
- (b) an agreement or arrangement is made or proposed to be made between the civil partners which relates to, arises out of, or is connected with, the proceedings.

(2) Rules of court may make provision for enabling—
- (a) the civil partners, or either of them, to refer the agreement or arrangement to the court, and
- (b) the court—
    - (i) to express an opinion, if it thinks it desirable to do so, as to the reasonableness of the agreement or arrangement, and
    - (ii) to give such directions, if any, in the matter as it thinks fit.

Dissolution of civil partnership

44   Dissolution of civil partnership which has broken down irretrievably

(1) Subject to section 41, an application for a dissolution order may be made to the court by either civil partner on the ground that the civil partnership has broken down irretrievably.

(2) On an application for a dissolution order the court must inquire, so far as it reasonably can, into—

    (a) the facts alleged by the applicant, and

    (b) any facts alleged by the respondent.

(3) The court hearing an application for a dissolution order must not hold that the civil partnership has broken down irretrievably unless the applicant satisfies the court of one or more of the facts described in subsection (5)(a), (b), (c) or (d).

(4) But if the court is satisfied of any of those facts, it must make a dissolution order unless it is satisfied on all the evidence that the civil partnership has not broken down irretrievably.

(5) The facts referred to in subsections (3) and (4) are—

    (a) that the respondent has behaved in such a way that the applicant cannot reasonably be expected to live with the respondent;

    (b) that—

        (i) the applicant and the respondent have lived apart for a continuous period of at least 2 years immediately preceding the making of the application ('2 years' separation'), and

        (ii) the respondent consents to a dissolution order being made;

    (c) that the applicant and the respondent have lived apart for a continuous period of at least 5 years immediately preceding the making of the application ('5 years' separation');

    (d) that the respondent has deserted the applicant for a continuous period of at least 2 years immediately preceding the making of the application.

45   Supplemental provisions as to facts raising presumption of breakdown

(1) Subsection (2) applies if—

    (a) in any proceedings for a dissolution order the applicant alleges, in reliance on section 44(5)(a), that the respondent has behaved in such a way that the applicant cannot reasonably be expected to live with the respondent, but

    (b) after the date of the occurrence of the final incident relied on by the applicant and held by the court to support his allegation, the applicant and the respondent have lived together for a period (or periods) which does not, or which taken together do not, exceed 6 months.

(2) The fact that the applicant and respondent have lived together as mentioned in subsection (1)(b) must be disregarded in determining, for the purposes of section 44(5)(a), whether the applicant cannot reasonably be expected to live with the respondent.

(3) Subsection (4) applies in relation to cases where the applicant alleges, in reliance on section 44(5)(b), that the respondent consents to a dissolution order being made.

(4) Rules of court must make provision for the purpose of ensuring that the respondent has been given such information as will enable him to understand—

    (a) the consequences to him of consenting to the making of the order, and

    (b) the steps which he must take to indicate his consent.

(5) For the purposes of section 44(5)(d) the court may treat a period of desertion as having continued at a time when the deserting civil partner was incapable of continuing the necessary intention, if the evidence before the court is such that, had he not been so incapable, the court would have inferred that the desertion continued at that time.

(6) In considering for the purposes of section 44(5) whether the period for which the civil partners have lived apart or the period for which the respondent has deserted the applicant has been continuous, no account is to be taken of—

(a) any one period not exceeding 6 months, or

(b) any two or more periods not exceeding 6 months in all,

during which the civil partners resumed living with each other.

(7) But no period during which the civil partners have lived with each other counts as part of the period during which the civil partners have lived apart or as part of the period of desertion.

(8) For the purposes of section 44(5)(b) and (c) and this section civil partners are to be treated as living apart unless they are living with each other in the same household, and references in this section to civil partners living with each other are to be read as references to their living with each other in the same household.

46   Dissolution order not precluded by previous separation order etc.

(1) Subsections (2) and (3) apply if any of the following orders has been made in relation to a civil partnership—

(a) a separation order;

(b) an order under Schedule 6 (financial relief in magistrates' courts etc.);

(c) an order under section 33 of the Family Law Act 1996 (c. 27) (occupation orders);

(d) an order under section 37 of the 1996 Act (orders where neither civil partner entitled to occupy the home).

(2) Nothing prevents—

(a) either civil partner from applying for a dissolution order, or

(b) the court from making a dissolution order,

on the same facts, or substantially the same facts, as those proved in support of the making of the order referred to in subsection (1).

(3) On the application for the dissolution order, the court—

(a) may treat the order referred to in subsection (1) as sufficient proof of any desertion or other fact by reference to which it was made, but

(b) must not make the dissolution order without receiving evidence from the applicant.

(4) If—

(a) the application for the dissolution order follows a separation order or any order requiring the civil partners to live apart,

(b) there was a period of desertion immediately preceding the institution of the proceedings for the separation order, and

(c) the civil partners have not resumed living together and the separation order has been continuously in force since it was made,

the period of desertion is to be treated for the purposes of the application for the dissolution order as if it had immediately preceded the making of the application.

(5) For the purposes of section 44(5)(d) the court may treat as a period during which the respondent has deserted the applicant any period during which there is in force—

(a) an injunction granted by the High Court or a county court which excludes the respondent from the civil partnership home, or

(b) an order under section 33 or 37 of the 1996 Act which prohibits the respondent from occupying a dwelling-house in which the applicant and the respondent have, or at any time have had, a civil partnership home.

47   Refusal of dissolution in 5 year separation cases on ground of grave hardship

(1) The respondent to an application for a dissolution order in which the applicant alleges 5 years' separation may oppose the making of an order on the ground that—

(a) the dissolution of the civil partnership will result in grave financial or other hardship to him, and

(b) it would in all the circumstances be wrong to dissolve the civil partnership.

(2) Subsection (3) applies if—

(a) the making of a dissolution order is opposed under this section,

(b) the court finds that the applicant is entitled to rely in support of his application on the fact of 5 years' separation and makes no such finding as to any other fact mentioned in section 44(5), and

(c) apart from this section, the court would make a dissolution order.

(3) The court must—

(a) consider all the circumstances, including the conduct of the civil partners and the interests of the civil partners and of any children or other persons concerned, and

(b) if it is of the opinion that the ground mentioned in subsection (1) is made out, dismiss the application for the dissolution order.

(4) 'Hardship' includes the loss of the chance of acquiring any benefit which the respondent might acquire if the civil partnership were not dissolved.

48   Proceedings before order made final: protection for respondent in separation cases

(1) The court may, on an application made by the respondent, rescind a conditional dissolution order if—

(a) it made the order on the basis of a finding that the applicant was entitled to rely on the fact of 2 years' separation coupled with the respondent's consent to a dissolution order being made,

(b) it made no such finding as to any other fact mentioned in section 44(5), and

(c) it is satisfied that the applicant misled the respondent (whether intentionally or unintentionally) about any matter which the respondent took into account in deciding to give his consent.

(2) Subsections (3) to (5) apply if—

(a) the respondent to an application for a dissolution order in which the applicant alleged—

(i) 2 years' separation coupled with the respondent's consent to a dissolution order being made, or

(ii) 5 years' separation,

has applied to the court for consideration under subsection (3) of his financial position after the dissolution of the civil partnership, and

(b) the court—

(i) has made a conditional dissolution order on the basis of a finding that the applicant was entitled to rely in support of his application on the fact of 2 years' or 5 years' separation, and

(ii) has made no such finding as to any other fact mentioned in section 44(5).

(3) The court hearing an application by the respondent under subsection (2) must consider all the circumstances, including—

(a) the age, health, conduct, earning capacity, financial resources and financial obligations of each of the parties, and

(b) the financial position of the respondent as, having regard to the dissolution, it is likely to be after the death of the applicant should the applicant die first.

(4) Subject to subsection (5), the court must not make the order final unless it is satisfied that—

(a) the applicant should not be required to make any financial provision for the respondent, or

(b) the financial provision made by the applicant for the respondent is—

(i) reasonable and fair, or

(ii) the best that can be made in the circumstances.

(5) The court may if it thinks fit make the order final if—

(a) it appears that there are circumstances making it desirable that the order should be made final without delay, and

(b) it has obtained a satisfactory undertaking from the applicant that he will make such financial provision for the respondent as it may approve.

Nullity

49 Grounds on which civil partnership is void

Where two people register as civil partners of each other in England and Wales, the civil partnership is void if—

    (a) at the time when they do so, they are not eligible to register as civil partners of each other under Chapter 1 (see section 3),

    (b) at the time when they do so they both know—

        (i)   that due notice of proposed civil partnership has not been given,

        (ii) that the civil partnership document has not been duly issued,

        (iii) that the civil partnership document is void under section 17(3) or 27(2) (registration after end of time allowed for registering),

        (iv) that the place of registration is a place other than that specified in the notices (or notice) of proposed civil partnership and the civil partnership document,

        (v)   that a civil partnership registrar is not present, or

        (vi) that the place of registration is on premises that are not approved premises although the registration is purportedly in accordance with section 6(3A)(a), or

    (c) the civil partnership document is void under paragraph 6(5) of Schedule 2 (civil partnership between child and another person forbidden).

50 Grounds on which civil partnership is voidable

(1) Where two people register as civil partners of each other in England and Wales, the civil partnership is voidable if—

    (a) either of them did not validly consent to its formation (whether as a result of duress, mistake, unsoundness of mind or otherwise);

    (b) at the time of its formation either of them, though capable of giving a valid consent, was suffering (whether continuously or intermittently) from mental disorder of such a kind or to such an extent as to be unfitted for civil partnership;

    (c) at the time of its formation, the respondent was pregnant by some person other than the applicant;

    (d) an interim gender recognition certificate under the Gender Recognition Act 2004 (c. 7) has, after the time of its formation, been issued to either civil partner;

    (e) the respondent is a person whose gender at the time of its formation had become the acquired gender under the 2004 Act.

(2) In this section and section 51 'mental disorder' has the same meaning as in the Mental Health Act 1983 (c. 20).

51 Bars to relief where civil partnership is voidable

(1) The court must not make a nullity order on the ground that a civil partnership is voidable if the respondent satisfies the court—

    (a) that the applicant, with knowledge that it was open to him to obtain a nullity order, conducted himself in relation to the respondent in such a way as to lead the respondent reasonably to believe that he would not seek to do so, and

    (b) that it would be unjust to the respondent to make the order.

(2) Without prejudice to subsection (1), the court must not make a nullity order by virtue of section 50(1)(a), (b), (c) or (e) unless—

    (a) it is satisfied that proceedings were instituted within 3 years from the date of the formation of the civil partnership, or

    (b) leave for the institution of proceedings after the end of that 3 year period has been granted under subsection (3).

(3) A judge of the court may, on an application made to him, grant leave for the institution of proceedings if he—

(a) is satisfied that the applicant has at some time during the 3 year period suffered from mental disorder, and

(b) considers that in all the circumstances of the case it would be just to grant leave for the institution of proceedings.

(4) An application for leave under subsection (3) may be made after the end of the 3 year period.

(5) Without prejudice to subsection (1), the court must not make a nullity order by virtue of section 50(1)(d) unless it is satisfied that proceedings were instituted within the period of 6 months from the date of issue of the interim gender recognition certificate.

(6) Without prejudice to subsections (1) and (2), the court must not make a nullity order by virtue of section 50(1)(c) or (e) unless it is satisfied that the applicant was at the time of the formation of the civil partnership ignorant of the facts alleged.

52 Proof of certain matters not necessary to validity of civil partnership

(1) Where two people have registered as civil partners of each other in England and Wales, it is not necessary in support of the civil partnership to give any proof—

(a) that any person whose consent to the civil partnership was required by section 4 (parental etc. consent) had given his consent, or

(aa) that before the registration either of the civil partners resided, or resided for any period, in the area stated in the notices of proposed civil partnership to be the area of that person's place of residence.

(b) that the civil partnership registrar was designated as such by the registration authority in whose area the registration took place;

and no evidence is to be given to prove the contrary in any proceedings touching the validity of the civil partnership.

(2) Subsection (1)(a) is subject to section 49(c) (civil partnership void if forbidden).

53 Power to validate civil partnership

(1) Where two people have registered as civil partners of each other in England and Wales, the Lord Chancellor may by order validate the civil partnership if it appears to him that it is or may be void under section 49(b).

(2) An order under subsection (1) may include provisions for relieving a person from any liability under section 31(2), 32(2) or 33(5) or (7).

(3) The draft of an order under subsection (1) must be advertised, in such manner as the Lord Chancellor thinks fit, not less than one month before the order is made.

(4) The Lord Chancellor must—

(a) consider all objections to the order sent to him in writing during that month, and

(b) if it appears to him necessary, direct a local inquiry into the validity of any such objections.

(5) An order under subsection (1) is subject to special parliamentary procedure.

. . .

Presumption of death orders

55 Presumption of death orders

(1) The court may, on an application made by a civil partner, make a presumption of death order if it is satisfied that reasonable grounds exist for supposing that the other civil partner is dead.

(2) In any proceedings under this section the fact that—

(a) for a period of 7 years or more the other civil partner has been continually absent from the applicant, and

(b) the applicant has no reason to believe that the other civil partner has been living within that time,

is evidence that the other civil partner is dead until the contrary is proved.

Separation orders

56 Separation orders

(1) An application for a separation order may be made to the court by either civil partner on the ground that any such fact as is mentioned in section 44(5)(a), (b), (c) or (d) exists.

(2) On an application for a separation order the court must inquire, so far as it reasonably can, into—

(a) the facts alleged by the applicant, and

(b) any facts alleged by the respondent,

but whether the civil partnership has broken down irretrievably is irrelevant.

(3) If the court is satisfied on the evidence of any such fact as is mentioned in section 44(5)(a), (b), (c) or (d) it must, subject to section 63, make a separation order.

(4) Section 45 (supplemental provisions as to facts raising presumption of breakdown) applies for the purposes of an application for a separation order alleging any such fact as it applies in relation to an application for a dissolution order alleging that fact.

57 Effect of separation order

If either civil partner dies intestate as respects all or any of his or her real or personal property while—

(a) a separation order is in force, and

(b) the separation is continuing,

the property as respects which he or she died intestate devolves as if the other civil partner had then been dead.

Declarations

58 Declarations

(1) Any person may apply to the High Court or a county court for one or more of the following declarations in relation to a civil partnership specified in the application—

(a) a declaration that the civil partnership was at its inception a valid civil partnership;

(b) a declaration that the civil partnership subsisted on a date specified in the application;

(c) a declaration that the civil partnership did not subsist on a date so specified;

. . .

(2) Where an application under subsection (1) is made to a court by a person other than a civil partner in the civil partnership to which the application relates, the court must refuse to hear the application if it considers that the applicant does not have a sufficient interest in the determination of that application.

59 General provisions as to making and effect of declarations

(1) Where on an application for a declaration under section 58 the truth of the proposition to be declared is proved to the satisfaction of the court, the court must make the declaration unless to do so would be manifestly contrary to public policy.

(2) Any declaration under section 58 binds Her Majesty and all other persons.

(3) The court, on the dismissal of an application for a declaration under section 58, may not make any declaration for which an application has not been made.

(4) No declaration which may be applied for under section 58 may be made otherwise than under section 58 by any court.

(5) No declaration may be made by any court, whether under section 58 or otherwise, that a civil partnership was at its inception void.

(6) Nothing in this section affects the powers of any court to make a nullity order in respect of a civil partnership.

60 The Attorney General and proceedings for declarations

(1) On an application for a declaration under section 58 the court may at any stage of the proceedings, of its own motion or on the application of any party to the proceedings, direct that all necessary papers in the matter be sent to the Attorney General.

(2) The Attorney General, whether or not he is sent papers in relation to an application for a declaration under section 58, may—

    (a) intervene in the proceedings on that application in such manner as he thinks necessary or expedient, and

    (b) argue before the court dealing with the application any question in relation to the application which the court considers it necessary to have fully argued.

(3) Where any costs are incurred by the Attorney General in connection with any application for a declaration under section 58, the court may make such order as it considers just as to the payment of those costs by parties to the proceedings.

61 Supplementary provisions as to declarations

(1) Any declaration made under section 58, and any application for such a declaration, must be in the form prescribed by rules of court.

(2) Rules of court may make provision—

    (a) as to the information required to be given by any applicant for a declaration under section 58;

    (b) requiring notice of an application under section 58 to be served on the Attorney General and on persons who may be affected by any declaration applied for.

(3) No proceedings under section 58 affect any final judgment or order already pronounced or made by any court of competent jurisdiction.

(4) The court hearing an application under section 58 may direct that the whole or any part of the proceedings must be heard in private.

(5) An application for a direction under subsection (4) must be heard in private unless the court otherwise directs.

General provisions

62 Relief for respondent in dissolution proceedings

(1) If in any proceedings for a dissolution order the respondent alleges and proves any such fact as is mentioned in section 44(5)(a), (b), (c) or (d) the court may give to the respondent the relief to which he would have been entitled if he had made an application seeking that relief.

(2) When applying subsection (1), treat—

    (a) the respondent as the applicant, and

    (b) the applicant as the respondent,

for the purposes of section 44(5).

63 Restrictions on making of orders affecting children

(1) In any proceedings for a dissolution, nullity or separation order, the court must consider—

    (a) whether there are any children of the family to whom this section applies, and

    (b) if there are any such children, whether (in the light of the arrangements which have been, or are proposed to be, made for their upbringing and welfare) it should exercise any of its powers under the Children Act 1989 (c. 41) with respect to any of them.

(2) If, in the case of any child to whom this section applies, it appears to the court that—

    (a) the circumstances of the case require it, or are likely to require it, to exercise any of its powers under the 1989 Act with respect to any such child,

    (b) it is not in a position to exercise the power or (as the case may be) those powers without giving further consideration to the case, and

    (c) there are exceptional circumstances which make it desirable in the interests of the child that the court should give a direction under this section,

it may direct that the order is not to be made final, or (in the case of a separation order) is not to be made, until the court orders otherwise.

(3) This section applies to—

    (a) any child of the family who has not reached 16 at the date when the court considers the case in accordance with the requirements of this section, and

    (b) any child of the family who has reached 16 at that date and in relation to whom the court directs that this section shall apply.

64 Parties to proceedings under this Chapter

(1) Rules of court may make provision with respect to—

    (a) the joinder as parties to proceedings under sections 37 to 56 of persons involved in allegations of improper conduct made in those proceedings,

    (b) the dismissal from such proceedings of any parties so joined, and

    (c) the persons who are to be parties to proceedings on an application under section 58.

(2) Rules of court made under this section may make different provision for different cases.

(3) In every case in which the court considers, in the interest of a person not already a party to the proceedings, that the person should be made a party, the court may if it thinks fit allow the person to intervene upon such terms, if any, as the court thinks just.

CHAPTER 3   PROPERTY AND FINANCIAL ARRANGEMENTS

65 Contribution by civil partner to property improvement

(1) This section applies if—

    (a) a civil partner contributes in money or money's worth to the improvement of real or personal property in which or in the proceeds of sale of which either or both of the civil partners has or have a beneficial interest, and

    (b) the contribution is of a substantial nature.

(2) The contributing partner is to be treated as having acquired by virtue of the contribution a share or an enlarged share (as the case may be) in the beneficial interest of such an extent—

    (a) as may have been then agreed, or

    (b) in default of such agreement, as may seem in all the circumstances just to any court before which the question of the existence or extent of the beneficial interest of either of the civil partners arises (whether in proceedings between them or in any other proceedings).

(3) Subsection (2) is subject to any agreement (express or implied) between the civil partners to the contrary.

66 Disputes between civil partners about property

(1) In any question between the civil partners in a civil partnership as to title to or possession of property, either civil partner may apply to—

    (a) the High Court, or

    (b) such county court as may be prescribed by rules of court.

(2) On such an application, the court may make such order with respect to the property as it thinks fit (including an order for the sale of the property).

(3) Rules of court made for the purposes of this section may confer jurisdiction on county courts whatever the situation or value of the property in dispute.

67 Applications under section 66 where property not in possession etc.

(1) The right of a civil partner ('A') to make an application under section 66 includes the right to make such an application where A claims that the other civil partner ('B') has had in his possession or under his control—

    (a) money to which, or to a share of which, A was beneficially entitled, or

    (b) property (other than money) to which, or to an interest in which, A was beneficially entitled,

and that either the money or other property has ceased to be in B's possession or under B's control or that A does not know whether it is still in B's possession or under B's control.

(2) For the purposes of subsection (1)(a) it does not matter whether A is beneficially entitled to the money or share—

    (a) because it represents the proceeds of property to which, or to an interest in which, A was beneficially entitled, or

    (b) for any other reason.

(3) Subsections (4) and (5) apply if, on such an application being made, the court is satisfied that B—

    (a) has had in his possession or under his control money or other property as mentioned in subsection (1)(a) or (b), and

    (b) has not made to A, in respect of that money or other property, such payment or disposition as would have been appropriate in the circumstances.

(4) The power of the court to make orders under section 66 includes power to order B to pay to A—

    (a) in a case falling within subsection (1)(a), such sum in respect of the money to which the application relates, or A's s share of it, as the court considers appropriate, or

    (b) in a case falling within subsection (1)(b), such sum in respect of the value of the property to which the application relates, or A's interest in it, as the court considers appropriate.

(5) If it appears to the court that there is any property which—

    (a) represents the whole or part of the money or property, and

    (b) is property in respect of which an order could (apart from this section) have been made under section 66,

the court may (either instead of or as well as making an order in accordance with subsection (4)) make any order which it could (apart from this section) have made under section 66.

(6) Any power of the court which is exercisable on an application under section 66 is exercisable in relation to an application made under that section as extended by this section.

68 Applications under section 66 by former civil partners

(1) This section applies where a civil partnership has been dissolved or annulled.

(2) Subject to subsection (3), an application may be made under section 66 (including that section as extended by section 67) by either former civil partner despite the dissolution or annulment (and references in those sections to a civil partner are to be read accordingly).

(3) The application must be made within the period of 3 years beginning with the date of the dissolution or annulment.

69 Actions in tort between civil partners

(1) This section applies if an action in tort is brought by one civil partner against the other during the subsistence of the civil partnership.

(2) The court may stay the proceedings if it appears—

    (a) that no substantial benefit would accrue to either civil partner from the continuation of the proceedings, or

    (b) that the question or questions in issue could more conveniently be disposed of on an application under section 66.

(3) Without prejudice to subsection (2)(b), the court may in such an action—

    (a) exercise any power which could be exercised on an application under section 66, or

    (b) give such directions as it thinks fit for the disposal under that section of any question arising in the proceedings.

70 Assurance policy by civil partner for benefit of other civil partner etc.

Section 11 of the Married Women's Property Act 1882 (c. 75) (money payable under policy of assurance not to form part of the estate of the insured) applies in relation to a policy of assurance—

    (a) effected by a civil partner on his own life, and

(b) expressed to be for the benefit of his civil partner, or of his children, or of his civil partner and children, or any of them,

as it applies in relation to a policy of assurance effected by a husband and expressed to be for the benefit of his wife, or of his children, or of his wife and children, or of any of them.

71 Wills, administration of estates and family provision

Schedule 4 amends enactments relating to wills, administration of estates and family provision so that they apply in relation to civil partnerships as they apply in relation to marriage.

72 Financial relief for civil partners and children of family

(1) Schedule 5 makes provision for financial relief in connection with civil partnerships that corresponds to provision made for financial relief in connection with marriages by Part 2 of the Matrimonial Causes Act 1973 (c. 18).

(2) Any rule of law under which any provision of Part 2 of the 1973 Act is interpreted as applying to dissolution of a marriage on the ground of presumed death is to be treated as applying (with any necessary modifications) in relation to the corresponding provision of Schedule 5.

(3) Schedule 6 makes provision for financial relief in connection with civil partnerships that corresponds to provision made for financial relief in connection with marriages by the Domestic Proceedings and Magistrates' Courts Act 1978 (c. 22).

. . .

CHAPTER 4   CIVIL PARTNERSHIP AGREEMENTS

73 Civil partnership agreements unenforceable

(1) A civil partnership agreement does not under the law of England and Wales have effect as a contract giving rise to legal rights.

(2) No action lies in England and Wales for breach of a civil partnership agreement, whatever the law applicable to the agreement.

(3) In this section and section 74 'civil partnership agreement' means an agreement between two people—
(a) to register as civil partners of each other—
(i) in England and Wales (under this Part),

. . .

(4) This section applies in relation to civil partnership agreements whether entered into before or after this section comes into force, but does not affect any action commenced before it comes into force.

74 Property where civil partnership agreement is terminated

(1) This section applies if a civil partnership agreement is terminated.

(2) Section 65 (contributions by civil partner to property improvement) applies, in relation to any property in which either or both of the parties to the agreement had a beneficial interest while the agreement was in force, as it applies in relation to property in which a civil partner has a beneficial interest.

(3) Sections 66 and 67 (disputes between civil partners about property) apply to any dispute between or claim by one of the parties in relation to property in which either or both had a beneficial interest while the agreement was in force, as if the parties were civil partners of each other.

(4) An application made under section 66 or 67 by virtue of subsection (3) must be made within 3 years of the termination of the agreement.

(5) A party to a civil partnership agreement who makes a gift of property to the other party on the condition (express or implied) that it is to be returned if the agreement is terminated is not prevented from recovering the property merely because of his having terminated the agreement.

CHAPTER 6   MISCELLANEOUS

80   False statements etc. with reference to civil partnerships

(1) A person commits an offence if—

  (a) for the purpose of procuring the formation of a civil partnership, or a document mentioned in subsection (2), he—

    (i)   makes or signs a declaration required under this Part or Part 5, or

    (ii) gives a notice or certificate so required,

    knowing that the declaration, notice or certificate is false,

  (b) for the purpose of a record being made in any register relating to civil partnerships, he—

    (i)   makes a statement as to any information which is required to be registered under this Part or Part 5, or

    (ii) causes such a statement to be made,

    knowing that the statement is false,

  (c) he forbids the issue of a document mentioned in subsection (2)(a) or (b) by representing himself to be a person whose consent to a civil partnership between a child and another person is required under this Part or Part 5, knowing the representation to be false, or

  (d) with respect to a declaration made under paragraph 5(1) of Schedule 1 he makes a statement mentioned in paragraph 6 of that Schedule which he knows to be false in a material particular.

(2) The documents are—

  (a) a civil partnership schedule or a Registrar General's licence under Chapter 1;

  (b) a document required by an Order in Council under section 210 or 211 as an authority for two people to register as civil partners of each other;

  (c) a certificate of no impediment under section 240.

(3) A person guilty of an offence under subsection (1) is liable—

  (a) on conviction on indictment, to imprisonment for a term not exceeding 7 years or to a fine (or both);

  (b) on summary conviction, to a fine not exceeding the statutory maximum.

(4) The Perjury Act 1911 (c. 6) has effect as if this section were contained in it.

. . .

84   Evidence

(1) Any enactment or rule of law relating to the giving of evidence by a spouse applies in relation to a civil partner as it applies in relation to the spouse.

(2) Subsection (1) is subject to any specific amendment made by or under this Act which relates to the giving of evidence by a civil partner.

(3) For the avoidance of doubt, in any such amendment, references to a person's civil partner do not include a former civil partner.

(4) References in subsections (1) and (2) to giving evidence are to giving evidence in any way (whether by supplying information, making discovery, producing documents or otherwise).

(5) Any rule of law—

  (a) which is preserved by section 7(3) of the Civil Evidence Act 1995 (c. 38) or section 118(1) of the Criminal Justice Act 2003 (c. 44), and

  (b) under which in any proceedings evidence of reputation or family tradition is admissible for the purpose of proving or disproving the existence of a marriage,

is to be treated as applying in an equivalent way for the purpose of proving or disproving the existence of a civil partnership.

. . .

PART 6   RELATIONSHIPS ARISING THROUGH CIVIL PARTNERSHIP

246   Interpretation of statutory references to stepchildren etc.

(1) In any provision to which this section applies, references to a stepchild or step-parent of a person (here, 'A'), and cognate expressions, are to be read as follows—

A's stepchild includes a person who is the child of A's civil partner (but is not A's child);

A's step-parent includes a person who is the civil partner of A's parent (but is not A's parent);

A's stepdaughter includes a person who is the daughter of A's civil partner (but is not A's daughter);

A's stepson includes a person who is the son of A's civil partner (but is not A's son);

A's stepfather includes a person who is the civil partner of A's father (but is not A's parent);

A's stepmother includes a person who is the civil partner of A's mother (but is not A's parent);

A's stepbrother includes a person who is the son of the civil partner of A's parent (but is not the son of either of A's parents);

A's stepsister includes a person who is the daughter of the civil partner of A's parent (but is not the daughter of either of A's parents).

(2) For the purposes of any provision to which this section applies—

'brother-in-law' includes civil partner's brother,

'daughter-in-law' includes daughter's civil partner,

'father-in-law' includes civil partner's father,

'mother-in-law' includes civil partner's mother,

'parent-in-law' includes civil partner's parent,

'sister-in-law' includes civil partner's sister, and

'son-in-law' includes son's civil partner.

247   Provisions to which section 246 applies: Acts of Parliament etc.

(1) Section 246 applies to—

(a) any provision listed in Schedule 21 (references to stepchildren, in-laws etc. in existing Acts),

(b) except in so far as otherwise provided, any provision made by a future Act, and

(c) except in so far as otherwise provided, any provision made by future subordinate legislation.

(2) A Minister of the Crown may by order—

(a) amend Schedule 21 by adding to it any provision of an existing Act;

(b) provide for section 246 to apply to prescribed provisions of existing subordinate legislation.

. . .

SCHEDULES

SCHEDULE 1

PROHIBITED DEGREES OF RELATIONSHIP: ENGLAND AND WALES

PART 1   THE PROHIBITIONS

Absolute prohibitions

1. (1) Two people are within prohibited degrees of relationship if one falls within the list below in relation to the other.

Adoptive child	Grandchild
Adoptive parent	Parent
Child	Parent's sibling
Former adoptive child	Sibling
Former adoptive parent	Sibling's child
Grandparent	

(2) In the list 'sibling' means a brother, sister, half-brother or half-sister.

Qualified prohibitions

2. (1) Two people are within prohibited degrees of relationship if one of them falls within the list below in relation to the other, unless—

    (a) both of them have reached 21 at the time when they register as civil partners of each other, and

    (b) the younger has not at any time before reaching 18 been a child of the family in relation to the other.

Child of former civil partner	Former spouse of grandparent
Child of former spouse	Former spouse of parent
Former civil partner of grandparent	Grandchild of former civil partner
Former civil partner of parent	Grandchild of former spouse

(2) 'Child of the family', in relation to another person, means a person who—

    (a) has lived in the same household as that other person, and

    (b) has been treated by that other person as a child of his family.

3. Two people are within prohibited degrees of relationship if one falls within column 1 of the table below in relation to the other, unless—

    (a) both of them have reached 21 at the time when they register as civil partners of each other, and

    (b) the persons who fall within column 2 are dead.

Relationship	*Relevant deaths*
Former civil partner of child	The child
	The child's other parent
Former spouse of child	The child
	The child's other parent
Parent of former civil partner	The former civil partner
	The former civil partner's other parent
Parent of former spouse	The former spouse
	The former spouse's other parent

PART 2   SPECIAL PROVISIONS RELATING TO QUALIFIED PROHIBITIONS

Provisions relating to paragraph 2

4. Paragraphs 5 to 7 apply where two people are subject to paragraph 2 but intend to register as civil partners of each other by signing a civil partnership schedule.

5. (1) The fact that a notice of proposed civil partnership has been given must not be recorded in the register unless the registration authority—

    (a) is satisfied by the production of evidence that both the proposed civil partners have reached 21, and

    (b) has received a declaration made by each of the proposed civil partners—

(i)   specifying their affinal relationship, and

(ii)   declaring that the younger of them has not at any time before reaching 18 been a child of the family in relation to the other.

(2) Sub-paragraph (1) does not apply if a declaration is obtained under paragraph 7.

(3) A declaration under sub-paragraph (1)(b) must contain such information and must be signed and attested in such manner as may be prescribed by regulations.

(4) The fact that a registration authority has received a declaration under sub-paragraph (1)(b) must be recorded in the register.

(5) A declaration under sub-paragraph (1)(b) must be filed and kept by the registration authority.

6. (1) Sub-paragraph (2) applies if—

(a)   a registration authority receives from a person who is not one of the proposed civil partners a written statement signed by that person which alleges that a declaration made under paragraph 5 is false in a material particular, and

(b)   the register shows that such a statement has been received.

(2) The registration authority in whose area it is proposed that the registration take place must not issue a civil partnership schedule unless a High Court declaration is obtained under paragraph 7.

7. (1) Either of the proposed civil partners may apply to the High Court for a declaration that, given that—

(a)   both of them have reached 21, and

(b)   the younger of those persons has not at any time before reaching 18 been a child of the family in relation to the other,

there is no impediment of affinity to the formation of the civil partnership.

(2) Such an application may be made whether or not any statement has been received by the registration authority under paragraph 6.

8. Section 13 (objection to proposed civil partnership) does not apply in relation to a civil partnership to which paragraphs 5 to 7 apply, except so far as an objection to the issue of a civil partnership schedule is made under that section on a ground other than the affinity between the proposed civil partners.

Provisions relating to paragraph 3

9. (1) This paragraph applies where two people are subject to paragraph 3 but intend to register as civil partners of each other by signing a civil partnership schedule.

(2) The fact that a notice of proposed civil partnership has been given must not be recorded in the register unless the registration authority is satisfied by the production of evidence—

(a)   that both the proposed civil partners have reached 21, and

(b)   that the persons referred to in paragraph 3(b) are dead.

SCHEDULE 2

CIVIL PARTNERSHIPS OF PERSONS UNDER 18: ENGLAND AND WALES

PART 1   APPROPRIATE PERSONS

1. Column 2 of the table specifies the appropriate persons (or person) to give consent to a child whose circumstances fall within column 1 and who intends to register as the civil partner of another—

Case	Appropriate persons
1. The circumstances do not fall within any of items 2 to 8.	Each of the following— (a) any parent of the child who has parental responsibility for him, and (b) any guardian of the child.
2. A special guardianship order is in force with respect to the child and the circumstances do not fall within any of items 3 to 7.	Each of the child's special guardians.
3. A care order has effect with respect to the child and the circumstances do not fall within item 5.	Each of the following— (a) the local authority designated in the order, and (b) each parent, guardian or special guardian (in so far as their parental responsibility has not been restricted under section 33(3) of the 1989 Act).
4. A residence order has effect with respect to the child and the circumstances do not fall within item 5.	Each of the persons with whom the child lives, or is to live, as a result of the order.
5. An adoption agency is authorised to place the child for adoption under section 19 of the 2002 Act.	Either— (a) the adoption agency, or (b) if a care order has effect with respect to the child, the local authority designated in the order.
6. A placement order is in force with respect to the child.	The local authority authorised by the placement order to place the child for adoption.
7. The child has been placed for adoption with prospective adopters.	The prospective adopters (in so far as their parental responsibility has not been restricted under section 25(4) of the 2002 Act), in addition to any person specified in relation to item 5 or 6.
8. The circumstances do not fall within any of items 2 to 7, but a residence order was in force with respect to the child immediately before he reached 16.	The persons with whom the child lived, or was to live, as a result of the order.

2. In the table—

'the 1989 Act' means the Children Act 1989 (c. 41) and 'guardian of a child', 'parental responsibility', 'residence order', 'special guardian', 'special guardianship order' and 'care order' have the same meaning as in that Act;

'the 2002 Act' means the Adoption and Children Act 2002 (c. 38) and 'adoption agency', 'placed for adoption', 'placement order' and 'local authority' have the same meaning as in that Act;

'appropriate local authority' means the local authority authorised by the placement order to place the child for adoption.

PART 2   OBTAINING CONSENT: GENERAL

Consent of appropriate person unobtainable

3. (1) This paragraph applies if—
>   (a) a child and another person intend to register as civil partners of each other under any procedure other than the special procedure, and
>   (b) the registration authority to whom the child gives a notice of proposed civil partnership is satisfied that the consent of a person whose consent is required ('A') cannot be obtained because A is absent, inaccessible or under a disability.

(2) If there is any other person whose consent is also required, the registration authority must dispense with the need for A's consent.

(3) If no other person's consent is required—
>   (a) the Registrar General may dispense with the need for any consent, or
>   (b) the court may, on an application being made to it, consent to the child registering as the civil partner of the person mentioned in sub-paragraph (1)(a).

(4) The consent of the court under sub-paragraph (3)(b) has the same effect as if it had been given by A.

Consent of appropriate person refused

4. (1) This paragraph applies if—
>   (a) a child and another person intend to register as civil partners of each other under any procedure other than the special procedure, and
>   (b) any person whose consent is required refuses his consent.

(2) The court may, on an application being made to it, consent to the child registering as the civil partner of the person mentioned in sub-paragraph (1)(a).

(3) The consent of the court under sub-paragraph (2) has the same effect as if it had been given by the person who has refused his consent.

Declaration

5. If one of the proposed civil partners is a child and is not a surviving civil partner, the necessary declaration under section 8 must also—
>   (a) state in relation to each appropriate person—
>>   (i) that that person's consent has been obtained,
>>   (ii) that the need to obtain that person's consent has been dispensed with under paragraph 3, or
>>   (iii) that the court has given consent under paragraph 3 or 4, or
>   (b) state that no person exists whose consent is required to a civil partnership between the child and another person.

Forbidding proposed civil partnership

6. (1) This paragraph applies if it has been recorded in the register that a notice of proposed civil partnership between a child and another person has been given.

(2) Any person whose consent is required to a child and another person registering as civil partners of each other may forbid the issue of a civil partnership schedule by giving any registration authority written notice that he forbids it.

(3) A notice under sub-paragraph (2) must specify—
>   (a) the name of the person giving it,
>   (b) his place of residence, and
>   (c) the capacity, in relation to either of the proposed civil partners, in which he forbids the issue of the civil partnership schedule.

(4) On receiving the notice, the registration authority must as soon as is practicable record in the register the fact that the issue of a civil partnership schedule has been forbidden.

(5) If the issue of a civil partnership schedule has been forbidden under this paragraph, the notice of proposed civil partnership and all proceedings on it are void.

(6) Sub-paragraphs (2) and (5) do not apply if the court has given its consent under paragraph 3 or 4.

Evidence

7. (1) This paragraph applies if, for the purpose of obtaining a civil partnership schedule, a person declares that the consent of any person or persons whose consent is required under section 4 has been given.

(2) The registration authority may refuse to issue the civil partnership schedule unless satisfied by the production of written evidence that the consent of that person or those persons has in fact been given.

Issue of civil partnership schedule

8. The duty in section 14(1) to issue a civil partnership schedule does not apply if its issue has been forbidden under paragraph 6.

9. If a proposed civil partnership is between a child and another person, the civil partnership schedule must contain a statement that the issue of the civil partnership schedule has not been forbidden under paragraph 6.

PART 3   OBTAINING CONSENT: SPECIAL PROCEDURE

Consent of appropriate person unobtainable or refused

10. (1) Sub-paragraph (2) applies if—
   (a) a child and another person intend to register as civil partners of each other under the special procedure, and
   (b) the Registrar General is satisfied that the consent of a person ('A') whose consent is required cannot be obtained because A is absent, inaccessible, or under a disability.

(2) If this sub-paragraph applies—
   (a) the Registrar General may dispense with the need for A's consent (whether or not there is any other person whose consent is also required), or
   (b) the court may, on application being made, consent to the child registering as the civil partner of the person mentioned in sub-paragraph (1)(a).

(3) The consent of the court under sub-paragraph (2)(b) has the same effect as if it had been given by A.

(4) Sub-paragraph (5) applies if—
   (a) a child and another person intend to register as civil partners of each other under the special procedure, and
   (b) any person whose consent is required refuses his consent.

(5) The court may, on application being made, consent to the child registering as the civil partner of the person mentioned in sub-paragraph (4)(a).

(6) The consent of the court under sub-paragraph (5) has the same effect as if it had been given by the person who has refused his consent.

Declaration

11. If one of the proposed civil partners is a child and is not a surviving civil partner, the necessary declaration under section 8 must also—

   (a) state in relation to each appropriate person—
      (i)   that that person's consent has been obtained,
      (ii) that the need to obtain that person's consent has been dispensed with under
            paragraph 10(2), or
      (iii) that the court has given consent under paragraph 10(2) or (5), or
   (b) state that no person exists whose consent is required to a civil partnership
       between the child and another person.

Forbidding proposed civil partnership

   12. Paragraph 6 applies in relation to the special procedure as if—
      (a) any reference to forbidding the issue of a civil partnership schedule were a
          reference to forbidding the Registrar General to give authority for the issue of his
          licence, and
      (b) sub-paragraph (6) referred to the court giving its consent under paragraph 10(2)
          or (5).

Evidence

   13. (1) This paragraph applies—
      (a) if a child and another person intend to register as civil partners of each other
          under the special procedure, and
      (b) the consent of any person ('A') is required to the child registering as the civil
          partner of that person.
   (2) The person giving the notice (under section 21) of proposed civil partnership to the
registration authority must produce to the authority such evidence as the Registrar General
may require to satisfy him that A's consent has in fact been given.
   (3) The power to require evidence under sub-paragraph (2) is in addition to the power to
require evidence under section 22.

Issue of Registrar General's licence

   14. The duty of the Registrar General under section 25(3)(b) to give authority for the
issue of his licence does not apply if he has been forbidden to do so by virtue of paragraph 12.

PART 4   PROVISIONS RELATING TO THE COURT

   15. (1) For the purposes of Parts 2 and 3 of this Schedule, 'the court' means—
      (a) the High Court,
      (b) the county court of the district in which any applicant or respondent resides, or
      (c) a magistrates' court acting in the local justice area in which any applicant or
          respondent resides.
   (2) Rules of court may be made for enabling applications under Part 2 or 3 of this
Schedule—
      (a) if made to the High Court, to be heard in chambers;
      (b) if made to the county court, to be heard and determined by the district judge
          subject to appeal to the judge;
      (c) if made to a magistrates' court, to be heard and determined otherwise than in
          open court.
   (3) Rules of court must provide that, where an application is made in consequence of a
refusal to give consent, notice of the application is to be served on the person who has refused
consent.

SCHEDULE 3

REGISTRATION BY FORMER SPOUSES ONE OF WHOM HAS CHANGED SEX

Application of Schedule

1. This Schedule applies if—
    (a) a court—
        (i) makes absolute a decree of nullity granted on the ground that an interim gender recognition certificate has been issued to a party to the marriage, or
        . . .
        and, on doing so, issues a full gender recognition certificate (under section 5(1) of the Gender Recognition Act 2004 (c. 7)) to that party, and
    (b) the parties wish to register in England or Wales as civil partners of each other without being delayed by the waiting period.

The relevant period

2. For the purposes of this Schedule the relevant period is the period—
    (a) beginning with the issue of the full gender recognition certificate, and
    (b) ending at the end of 1 month from the day on which it is issued.

Modifications of standard procedure and procedures for house-bound and detained persons

3. If—
    (a) each of the parties gives a notice of proposed civil partnership during the relevant period, and
    (b) on doing so, each makes an election under this paragraph,
Chapter 1 of Part 2 applies with the modifications given in paragraphs 4 to 6.
4. (1) Omit—
    (a) section 10 (proposed civil partnership to be publicised);
    (b) section 11 (meaning of 'the waiting period');
    (c) section 12 (power to shorten the waiting period).
(2) In section 14 (issue of civil partnership schedule), for subsection (1) substitute—
'(1) As soon as the notices of proposed civil partnership have been given, the registration authority in whose area it is proposed that the registration take place must, at the request of one or both of the proposed civil partners, issue a document to be known as a "civil partnership schedule".'
(3) For section 17 (period during which registration may take place) substitute—

'17 Period during which registration may take place

(1) The proposed civil partners may register as civil partners by signing the civil partnership schedule at any time during the applicable period.
(2) If they do not register as civil partners by signing the civil partnership schedule before the end of the applicable period—
    (a) the notices of proposed civil partnership and the civil partnership schedule are void, and
    (b) no civil partnership registrar may officiate at the signing of the civil partnership schedule by them.
(3) The applicable period, in relation to two people registering as civil partners of each other, is the period of 1 month beginning with—
    (a) the day on which the notices of proposed civil partnership are given, or
    (b) if the notices are not given on the same day, the earlier of those days.'
5. In section 18 (house-bound persons), in subsection (3)—
    (a) treat the reference to the standard procedure as a reference to the standard procedure as modified by this Schedule, and

(b) omit paragraph (c) (which provides for a 3 month registration period).

6. In section 19 (detained persons), in subsection (3)—

(a) treat the reference to the standard procedure as a reference to the standard procedure as modified by this Schedule, and

(b) omit paragraph (c) (which provides for a 3 month registration period).

. . .

SCHEDULE 4

WILLS, ADMINISTRATION OF ESTATES AND FAMILY PROVISION

PART 1   WILLS

. . .

5. Except where a contrary intention is shown, it is presumed that if a testator—

(a) devises or bequeaths property to his civil partner in terms which in themselves would give an absolute interest to the civil partner, but

(b) by the same instrument purports to give his issue an interest in the same property,

the gift to the civil partner is absolute despite the purported gift to the issue.

. . .

SCHEDULE 5

FINANCIAL RELIEF IN THE HIGH COURT OR A COUNTY COURT ETC.

PART 1   FINANCIAL PROVISION IN CONNECTION WITH DISSOLUTION, NULLITY OR SEPARATION

Circumstances in which orders under this Part may be made

1. (1) The court may make any one or more of the orders set out in paragraph 2(1)—

(a) on making a dissolution, nullity or separation order, or

(b) at any time afterwards.

(2) The court may make any one or more of the orders set out in paragraph 2(1)(d), (e) and (f)—

(a) in proceedings for a dissolution, nullity or separation order, before making the order;

(b) if proceedings for a dissolution, nullity or separation order are dismissed after the beginning of the trial, either straightaway or within a reasonable period after the dismissal.

(3) The power of the court to make an order under sub-paragraph (1) or (2)(a) in favour of a child of the family is exercisable from time to time.

(4) If the court makes an order in favour of a child under sub-paragraph (2)(b), it may from time to time make a further order in the child's favour of any of the kinds set out in paragraph 2(1)(d), (e) or (f).

The orders: periodical and secured periodical payments and lump sums

2. (1) The orders are—

(a) an order that either civil partner must make to the other such periodical payments for such term as may be specified;

(b) an order that either civil partner must secure to the other, to the satisfaction of the court, such periodical payments for such term as may be specified;

(c) an order that either civil partner must pay to the other such lump sum or sums as may be specified;

(d) an order that one of the civil partners must make—
      (i)   to such person as may be specified for the benefit of a child of the family, or
      (ii) to a child of the family,
such periodical payments for such term as may be specified;
      (e) an order that one of the civil partners must secure—
      (i)   to such person as may be specified for the benefit of a child of the family, or
      (ii) to a child of the family,
to the satisfaction of the court, such periodical payments for such term as may be specified;
      (f) an order that one of the civil partners must pay such lump sum as may be specified—
      (i)   to such person as may be specified for the benefit of a child of the family, or
      (ii) to a child of the family.
  (2) 'Specified' means specified in the order.

Particular provision that may be made by lump sum orders

3. (1) An order under this Part requiring one civil partner to pay the other a lump sum may be made for the purpose of enabling the other civil partner to meet any liabilities or expenses reasonably incurred by the other in maintaining—
    (a) himself or herself, or
    (b) a child of the family,
before making an application for an order under this Part in his or her favour.

  (2) An order under this Part requiring a lump sum to be paid to or for the benefit of a child of the family may be made for the purpose of enabling any liabilities or expenses reasonably incurred by or for the benefit of the child before making an application for an order under this Part to be met.

  (3) An order under this Part for the payment of a lump sum may—
    (a) provide for its payment by instalments of such amount as may be specified, and
    (b) require the payment of the instalments to be secured to the satisfaction of the court.

  (4) Sub-paragraphs (1) to (3) do not restrict the powers to make the orders set out in paragraph 2(1)(c) and (f).

  (5) If the court—
    (a) makes an order under this Part for the payment of a lump sum, and
    (b) directs that—
      (i)   payment of the sum or any part of it is to be deferred, or
      (ii) the sum or any part of it is to be paid by instalments,
it may provide for the deferred amount or the instalments to carry interest at such rate as may be specified from such date as may be specified until the date when payment of it is due.

  (6) A date specified under sub-paragraph (5) must not be earlier than the date of the order.

  (7) 'Specified' means specified in the order.

When orders under this Part may take effect

4. (1) If an order is made under paragraph 2(1)(a), (b) or (c) on or after making a dissolution or nullity order, neither the order nor any settlement made in pursuance of it takes effect unless the dissolution or nullity order has been made final.

  (2) This paragraph does not affect the power of the court to give a direction under paragraph 76 (settlement of instrument by conveyancing counsel).

Restrictions on making of orders under this Part

5. The power to make an order under paragraph 2(1)(d), (e) or (f) is subject to paragraph 49(1) and (5) (restrictions on orders in favour of children who have reached 18).

PART 2   PROPERTY ADJUSTMENT ON OR AFTER DISSOLUTION,
NULLITY OR SEPARATION

Circumstances in which property adjustment orders may be made

6. (1) The court may make one or more property adjustment orders—
  (a) on making a dissolution, nullity or separation order, or
  (b) at any time afterwards.

(2) In this Schedule 'property adjustment order' means a property adjustment order under this Part.

Property adjustment orders

7. (1) The property adjustment orders are—
  (a) an order that one of the civil partners must transfer such property as may be specified, being property to which he is entitled—
    (i)   to the other civil partner,
    (ii) to a child of the family, or
    (iii) to such person as may be specified for the benefit of a child of the family;
  (b) an order that a settlement of such property as may be specified, being property to which one of the civil partners is entitled, be made to the satisfaction of the court for the benefit of—
    (i)   the other civil partner and the children of the family, or
    (ii) either or any of them;
  (c) an order varying for the benefit of—
    (i)   the civil partners and the children of the family, or
    (ii) either or any of them,
    a relevant settlement;
  (d) an order extinguishing or reducing the interest of either of the civil partners under a relevant settlement.

(2) The court may make a property adjustment order under sub-paragraph (1)(c) even though there are no children of the family.

(3) In this paragraph—
'entitled' means entitled in possession or reversion,
'relevant settlement' means, in relation to a civil partnership, a settlement made, during its subsistence or in anticipation of its formation, on the civil partners including one made by will or codicil, but not including one in the form of a pension arrangement (within the meaning of Part 4), and
'specified' means specified in the order.

When property adjustment orders may take effect

8. (1) If a property adjustment order is made on or after making a dissolution or nullity order, neither the property adjustment order nor any settlement made under it takes effect unless the dissolution or nullity order has been made final.

(2) This paragraph does not affect the power to give a direction under paragraph 76 (settlement of instrument by conveyancing counsel).

Restrictions on making property adjustment orders

9. The power to make a property adjustment order under paragraph 7(1)(a) is subject to paragraph 49(1) and (5) (restrictions on making orders in favour of children who have reached 18).

PART 3   SALE OF PROPERTY ORDERS

Circumstances in which sale of property orders may be made

10. (1) The court may make a sale of property order—
    (a) on making—
        (i)   under Part 1, a secured periodical payments order or an order for the payment of a lump sum, or
        (ii) a property adjustment order, or
    (b) at any time afterwards.
(2) In this Schedule 'sale of property order' means a sale of property order under this Part.

Sale of property orders

11. (1) A sale of property order is an order for the sale of such property as may be specified, being property in which, or in the proceeds of sale of which, either or both of the civil partners has or have a beneficial interest, either in possession or reversion.
(2) A sale of property order may contain such consequential or supplementary provisions as the court thinks fit.
(3) A sale of property order may in particular include—
    (a) provision requiring the making of a payment out of the proceeds of sale of the property to which the order relates, and
    (b) provision requiring any property to which the order relates to be offered for sale to a specified person, or class of persons.
(4) 'Specified' means specified in the order.

When sale of property orders may take effect

12. (1) If a sale of property order is made on or after the making of a dissolution or nullity order, it does not take effect unless the dissolution or nullity order has been made final.
(2) Where a sale of property order is made, the court may direct that—
    (a) the order, or
    (b) such provision of it as the court may specify,
is not to take effect until the occurrence of an event specified by the court or the end of a period so specified.

When sale of property orders cease to have effect

13. If a sale of property order contains a provision requiring the proceeds of sale of the property to which the order relates to be used to secure periodical payments to a civil partner, the order ceases to have effect—
    (a) on the death of the civil partner, or
    (b) on the formation of a subsequent civil partnership or marriage by the civil partner.

Protection of third parties

14. (1) Sub-paragraphs (2) and (3) apply if—
    (a) a civil partner has a beneficial interest in any property, or in the proceeds of sale of any property, and
    (b) another person ('A') who is not the other civil partner also has a beneficial interest in the property or the proceeds.
(2) Before deciding whether to make a sale of property order in relation to the property, the court must give A an opportunity to make representations with respect to the order.
(3) Any representations made by A are included among the circumstances to which the court is required to have regard under paragraph 20.

PART 4   PENSION SHARING ORDERS ON OR AFTER
DISSOLUTION OR NULLITY ORDER

Circumstances in which pension sharing orders may be made

15. (1) The court may make a pension sharing order—
   (a) on making a dissolution or nullity order, or
   (b) at any time afterwards.
(2) In this Schedule 'pension sharing order' means a pension sharing order under this Part.

Pension sharing orders

16. (1) A pension sharing order is an order which—
   (a) provides that one civil partner's—
      (i)   shareable rights under a specified pension arrangement, or
      (ii) shareable state scheme rights,
      are to be subject to pension sharing for the benefit of the other civil partner, and
   (b) specifies the percentage value to be transferred.
(2) Shareable rights under a pension arrangement are rights in relation to which pension sharing is available under—
   (a) Chapter 1 of Part 4 of the Welfare Reform and Pensions Act 1999 (c. 30), or
   (b) corresponding Northern Ireland legislation.
(3) Shareable state scheme rights are rights in relation to which pension sharing is available under—
   (a) Chapter 2 of Part 4 of the 1999 Act, or
   (b) corresponding Northern Ireland legislation.
(4) In this Part 'pension arrangement' means—
   (a) an occupational pension scheme,
   (b) a personal pension scheme,
   (c) a retirement annuity contract,
   (d) an annuity or insurance policy purchased, or transferred, for the purpose of giving effect to rights under—
      (i)   an occupational pension scheme, or
      (ii) a personal pension scheme, and
   (e) an annuity purchased, or entered into, for the purpose of discharging liability in respect of a pension credit under—
      (i)   section 29(1)(b) of the 1999 Act, or
      (ii) corresponding Northern Ireland legislation.
(5) In sub-paragraph (4)—
'occupational pension scheme' has the same meaning as in the Pension Schemes Act 1993 (c. 48);
'personal pension scheme' has the same meaning as in the 1993 Act;
'retirement annuity contract' means a contract or scheme approved under Chapter 3 of Part 14 of the Income and Corporation Taxes Act 1988 (c. 1).

Pension sharing orders: apportionment of charges

17. If a pension sharing order relates to rights under a pension arrangement, the court may include in the order provision about the apportionment between the civil partners of any charge under—
   (a) section 41 of the 1999 Act (charges in respect of pension sharing costs), or
   (b) corresponding Northern Ireland legislation.

Restrictions on making of pension sharing orders

18. (1) A pension sharing order may not be made in relation to a pension arrangement which—

    (a) is the subject of a pension sharing order in relation to the civil partnership, or

    (b) has been the subject of pension sharing between the civil partners.

(2) A pension sharing order may not be made in relation to shareable state scheme rights if—

    (a) such rights are the subject of a pension sharing order in relation to the civil partnership, or

    (b) such rights have been the subject of pension sharing between the civil partners.

(3) A pension sharing order may not be made in relation to the rights of a person under a pension arrangement if there is in force a requirement imposed by virtue of Part 6 which relates to benefits or future benefits to which that person is entitled under the pension arrangement.

When pension sharing orders may take effect

19. (1) A pension sharing order is not to take effect unless the dissolution or nullity order on or after which it is made has been made final.

(2) No pension sharing order may be made so as to take effect before the end of such period after the making of the order as may be prescribed by regulations made by the Lord Chancellor.

(3) The power to make regulations under sub-paragraph (2) is exercisable by statutory instrument which is subject to annulment in pursuance of a resolution of either House of Parliament.

PART 5   MATTERS TO WHICH COURT IS TO HAVE REGARD UNDER PARTS 1 TO 4

General

20. The court in deciding—

    (a) whether to exercise its powers under—

        (i) Part 1 (financial provision on dissolution etc.),

        (ii) Part 2 (property adjustment orders),

        (iii) Part 3 (sale of property orders), or

        (iv) any provision of Part 4 (pension sharing orders) other than paragraph 17 (apportionment of charges), and

    (b) if so, in what way,

must have regard to all the circumstances of the case, giving first consideration to the welfare, while under 18, of any child of the family who has not reached 18.

Particular matters to be taken into account when exercising powers in relation to civil partners

21. (1) This paragraph applies to the exercise by the court in relation to a civil partner of its powers under—

    (a) Part 1 (financial provision on dissolution etc.) by virtue of paragraph 2(1)(a), (b) or (c),

    (b) Part 2 (property adjustment orders),

    (c) Part 3 (sale of property orders), or

    (d) Part 4 (pension sharing orders).

(2) The court must in particular have regard to—

    (a) the income, earning capacity, property and other financial resources which each civil partner—

        (i) has, or

        (ii) is likely to have in the foreseeable future,

including, in the case of earning capacity, any increase in that capacity which it would in the opinion of the court be reasonable to expect a civil partner in the civil partnership to take steps to acquire;

(b) the financial needs, obligations and responsibilities which each civil partner has or is likely to have in the foreseeable future;

(c) the standard of living enjoyed by the family before the breakdown of the civil partnership;

(d) the age of each civil partner and the duration of the civil partnership;

(e) any physical or mental disability of either of the civil partners;

(f) the contributions which each civil partner has made or is likely in the foreseeable future to make to the welfare of the family, including any contribution by looking after the home or caring for the family;

(g) the conduct of each civil partner, if that conduct is such that it would in the opinion of the court be inequitable to disregard it;

(h) in the case of proceedings for a dissolution or nullity order, the value to each civil partner of any benefit which, because of the dissolution or annulment of the civil partnership, that civil partner will lose the chance of acquiring.

Particular matters to be taken into account when exercising powers in relation to children

22. (1) This paragraph applies to the exercise by the court in relation to a child of the family of its powers under—

(a) Part 1 (financial provision on dissolution etc.) by virtue of paragraph 2(1)(d), (e) or (f)),

(b) Part 2 (property adjustment orders), or

(c) Part 3 (sale of property orders).

(2) The court must in particular have regard to—

(a) the financial needs of the child;

(b) the income, earning capacity (if any), property and other financial resources of the child;

(c) any physical or mental disability of the child;

(d) the way in which the child was being and in which the civil partners expected the child to be educated or trained;

(e) the considerations mentioned in relation to the civil partners in paragraph 21(2)(a), (b), (c) and (e).

(3) In relation to the exercise of any of those powers against a civil partner ('A') in favour of a child of the family who is not A's child, the court must also have regard to—

(a) whether A has assumed any responsibility for the child's maintenance;

(b) if so, the extent to which, and the basis upon which, A assumed such responsibility and the length of time for which A discharged such responsibility;

(c) whether in assuming and discharging such responsibility A did so knowing that the child was not A's child;

(d) the liability of any other person to maintain the child.

Terminating financial obligations

23. (1) Sub-paragraphs (2) and (3) apply if, on or after the making of a dissolution or nullity order, the court decides to exercise its powers under—

(a) Part 1 (financial provision on dissolution etc.) by virtue of paragraph 2(1)(a), (b) or (c),

(b) Part 2 (property adjustment orders),

(c) Part 3 (sale of property orders), or

(d) Part 4 (pension sharing orders),

in favour of one of the civil partners.

(2) The court must consider whether it would be appropriate to exercise those powers in such a way that the financial obligations of each civil partner towards the other will be terminated as soon after the making of the dissolution or nullity order as the court considers just and reasonable.

(3) If the court decides to make—

(a) a periodical payments order, or

(b) a secured periodical payments order,

in favour of one of the civil partners ('A'), it must in particular consider whether it would be appropriate to require the payments to be made or secured only for such term as would in its opinion be sufficient to enable A to adjust without undue hardship to the termination of A's financial dependence on the other civil partner.

(4) If—

(a) on or after the making of a dissolution or nullity order, an application is made by one of the civil partners for a periodical payments or secured periodical payments order in that civil partner's favour, but

(b) the court considers that no continuing obligation should be imposed on either civil partner to make or secure periodical payments in favour of the other,

the court may dismiss the application with a direction that the applicant is not entitled to make any future application in relation to that civil partnership for an order under Part 1 by virtue of paragraph 2(1)(a) or (b).

PART 6   MAKING OF PART 1 ORDERS HAVING REGARD TO PENSION BENEFITS

Pension benefits to be included in matters to which court is to have regard

24. (1) The matters to which the court is to have regard under paragraph 21(2)(a) include any pension benefits under a pension arrangement or by way of pension which a civil partner has or is likely to have; and, accordingly, in relation to any pension benefits paragraph 21(2)(a)(ii) has effect as if 'in the foreseeable future' were omitted.

(2) The matters to which the court is to have regard under paragraph 21(2)(h) include any pension benefits which, because of the making of a dissolution or nullity order, a civil partner will lose the chance of acquiring.

(3) 'Pension benefits' means—

(a) benefits under a pension arrangement, or

(b) benefits by way of pension (whether under a pension arrangement or not).

Provisions applying where pension benefits taken into account in decision to make Part 1 order

25. (1) This paragraph applies if, having regard to any benefits under a pension arrangement, the court decides to make an order under Part 1.

(2) To the extent to which the Part 1 order is made having regard to any benefits under a pension arrangement, it may require the person responsible for the pension arrangement, if at any time any payment in respect of any benefits under the arrangement becomes due to the civil partner with pension rights, to make a payment for the benefit of the other civil partner.

(3) The Part 1 order must express the amount of any payment required to be made by virtue of sub-paragraph (2) as a percentage of the payment which becomes due to the civil partner with pension rights.

(4) Any such payment by the person responsible for the arrangement—

(a) discharges so much of his liability to the civil partner with pension rights as corresponds to the amount of the payment, and

(b) is to be treated for all purposes as a payment made by the civil partner with pension rights in or towards the discharge of that civil partner's liability under the order.

(5) If the civil partner with pension rights has a right of commutation under the arrangement, the Part 1 order may require that civil partner to exercise it to any extent.

(6) This paragraph applies to any payment due in consequence of commutation in pursuance of the Part 1 order as it applies to other payments in respect of benefits under the arrangement.

(7) The power conferred by sub-paragraph (5) may not be exercised for the purpose of commuting a benefit payable to the civil partner with pension rights to a benefit payable to the other civil partner.

(8) The powers conferred by sub-paragraphs (2) and (5) may not be exercised in relation to a pension arrangement which—

> (a) is the subject of a pension sharing order in relation to the civil partnership, or
> (b) has been the subject of pension sharing between the civil partners.

Pensions: lump sums

26. (1) This paragraph applies if the benefits which the civil partner with pension rights has or is likely to have under a pension arrangement include any lump sum payable in respect of that civil partner's death.

(2) The court's power under Part 1 to order a civil partner to pay a lump sum to the other civil partner includes the power to make by the order any provision in sub-paragraph (3) to (5).

(3) If the person responsible for the pension arrangement has power to determine the person to whom the sum, or any part of it, is to be paid, the court may require him to pay the whole or part of that sum, when it becomes due, to the other civil partner.

(4) If the civil partner with pension rights has power to nominate the person to whom the sum, or any part of it, is to be paid, the court may require the civil partner with pension rights to nominate the other civil partner in respect of the whole or part of that sum.

(5) In any other case, the court may require the person responsible for the pension arrangement in question to pay the whole or part of that sum, when it becomes due, for the benefit of the other civil partner instead of to the person to whom, apart from the order, it would be paid.

(6) Any payment by the person responsible for the arrangement under an order made under Part 1 made by virtue of this paragraph discharges so much of his liability in respect of the civil partner with pension rights as corresponds to the amount of the payment.

(7) The powers conferred by this paragraph may not be exercised in relation to a pension arrangement which—

> (a) is the subject of a pension sharing order in relation to the civil partnership, or
> (b) has been the subject of pension sharing between the civil partners.

Pensions: supplementary

27. If—

> (a) a Part 1 order made by virtue of paragraph 25 or 26 imposes any requirement on the person responsible for a pension arrangement ('the first arrangement'),
> (b) the civil partner with pension rights acquires rights under another pension arrangement ('the new arrangement') which are derived (directly or indirectly) from the whole of that civil partner's rights under the first arrangement, and
> (c) the person responsible for the new arrangement has been given notice in accordance with regulations made by the Lord Chancellor,

the Part 1 order has effect as if it had been made instead in respect of the person responsible for the new arrangement.

Regulations

28. (1) The Lord Chancellor may by regulations—

(a) make provision, in relation to any provision of paragraph 25 or 26 which authorises the court making a Part 1 order to require the person responsible for a pension arrangement to make a payment for the benefit of the other civil partner, as to—

(i) the person to whom, and

(ii) the terms on which,

the payment is to be made;

(b) make provision, in relation to payment under a mistaken belief as to the continuation in force of a provision included by virtue of paragraph 25 or 26 in a Part 1 order, about the rights or liabilities of the payer, the payee or the person to whom the payment was due;

(c) require notices to be given in respect of changes of circumstances relevant to Part 1 orders which include provision made by virtue of paragraphs 25 and 26;

(d) make provision for the person responsible for a pension arrangement to be discharged in prescribed circumstances from a requirement imposed by virtue of paragraph 25 or 26;

(e) make provision about calculation and verification in relation to the valuation of—

(i) benefits under a pension arrangement, or

(ii) shareable state scheme rights (within the meaning of paragraph 16(3)),

for the purposes of the court's functions in connection with the exercise of any of its powers under this Schedule.

(2) Regulations under sub-paragraph (1)(e) may include—

(a) provision for calculation or verification in accordance with guidance from time to time prepared by a prescribed person, and

(b) provision by reference to regulations under section 30 or 49(4) of the 1999 Act.

(3) The power to make regulations under paragraph 27 or this paragraph is exercisable by statutory instrument which is subject to annulment in pursuance of a resolution of either House of Parliament.

(4) 'Prescribed' means prescribed by regulations.

Interpretation of provisions relating to pensions

29. (1) In this Part 'the civil partner with pension rights' means the civil partner who has or is likely to have benefits under a pension arrangement.

(2) In this Part 'pension arrangement' has the same meaning as in Part 4.

(3) In this Part, references to the person responsible for a pension arrangement are to be read in accordance with section 26 of the Welfare Reform and Pensions Act 1999 (c. 30).

PART 7   PENSION PROTECTION FUND COMPENSATION ETC.

PPF compensation to be included in matters to which court is to have regard

30. (1) The matters to which a court is to have regard under paragraph 21(2)(a) include any PPF compensation to which a civil partner is or is likely to be entitled; and, accordingly, in relation to any PPF compensation paragraph 21(2)(a)(ii) has effect as if 'in the foreseeable future' were omitted.

(2) The matters to which a court is to have regard under paragraph 21(2)(h) include any PPF compensation which, because of the making of a dissolution or nullity order, a civil partner will lose the chance of acquiring entitlement to.

(3) In this Part 'PPF compensation' means compensation payable under—

(a) Chapter 3 of Part 2 of the Pensions Act 2004 (pension protection), or

. . .

Assumption of responsibility by PPF Board in paragraph 25(2) cases

31. (1) This paragraph applies to an order under Part 1 so far as it includes provision made by virtue of paragraph 25(2) which—
  (a) imposed requirements on the trustees or managers of an occupational pension scheme for which the Board has assumed responsibility, and
  (b) was made before the trustees or managers received the transfer notice.

(2) From the time the trustees or managers of the scheme receive the transfer notice, the order has effect—
  (a) except in descriptions of case prescribed by regulations, with the modifications set out in sub-paragraph (3), and
  (b) with such other modifications as may be prescribed by regulations.

(3) The modifications are that—
  (a) references in the order to the trustees or managers of the scheme have effect as references to the Board, and
  (b) references in the order to any pension or lump sum to which the civil partner with pension rights is or may become entitled under the scheme have effect as references to any PPF compensation to which that person is or may become entitled in respect of the pension or lump sum.

Assumption of responsibility by PPF Board in paragraph 25(5) cases

32. (1) This paragraph applies to an order under Part 1 if—
  (a) it includes provision made by virtue of paragraph 25(5) which requires the civil partner with pension rights to exercise his right of commutation under an occupational pension scheme to any extent, and
  (b) before the requirement is complied with the Board has assumed responsibility for the scheme.

(2) From the time the trustees or managers of the scheme receive the transfer notice, the order has effect with such modifications as may be prescribed by regulations.

Lump sums: power to modify paragraph 26 in respect of assessment period

33. Regulations may modify paragraph 26 in its application to an occupational pension scheme during an assessment period in relation to the scheme.

Assumption of responsibility by the Board not to affect power of court to vary order etc.

34. (1) This paragraph applies where the court makes, in relation to an occupational pension scheme—
  (a) a pension sharing order, or
  (b) an order including provision made by virtue of paragraph 25(2) or (5).

(2) If the Board subsequently assumes responsibility for the scheme, that does not affect—
  (a) the powers of the court under paragraph 51 to vary or discharge the order or to suspend or revive any provision of it;
  (b) on an appeal, the powers of the appeal court to affirm, reinstate, set aside or vary the order.

Regulations

35. Regulations may make such consequential modifications of any provision of, or made by virtue of, this Schedule as appear to the Lord Chancellor necessary or expedient to give effect to the provisions of this Part.

36. (1) In this Part 'regulations' means regulations made by the Lord Chancellor.

(2) A power to make regulations under this Part is exercisable by statutory instrument which is subject to annulment in pursuance of a resolution of either House of Parliament.

Interpretation

37. (1) In this Part—
'assessment period' means—
    (a) an assessment period within the meaning of Part 2 of the Pensions Act 2004 (pension protection),

. . .

'the Board' means the Board of the Pension Protection Fund;
'the civil partner with pension rights' has the meaning given by paragraph 29(1);
'occupational pension scheme' has the same meaning as in the Pension Schemes Act 1993 (c. 48);
'transfer notice' has the same meaning as in—
    (a) Chapter 3 of Part 2 of the 2004 Act,

. . .

(2) References in this Part to the Board assuming responsibility for a scheme are to the Board assuming responsibility for the scheme in accordance with—
    (a) Chapter 3 of Part 2 of the 2004 Act (pension protection),

. . .

PART 8   MAINTENANCE PENDING OUTCOME OF DISSOLUTION, NULLITY OR SEPARATION PROCEEDINGS

38. On an application for a dissolution, nullity or separation order, the court may make an order requiring either civil partner to make to the other for the other's maintenance such periodical payments for such term—
    (a) beginning no earlier than the date on which the application was made, and
    (b) ending with the date on which the proceedings are determined,
as the court thinks reasonable.

PART 9   FAILURE TO MAINTAIN: FINANCIAL PROVISION (AND INTERIM ORDERS)

Circumstances in which orders under this Part may be made

39. (1) Either civil partner in a subsisting civil partnership may apply to the court for an order under this Part on the ground that the other civil partner ('the respondent')—
    (a) has failed to provide reasonable maintenance for the applicant, or
    (b) has failed to provide, or to make a proper contribution towards, reasonable maintenance for any child of the family.
(2) The court must not entertain an application under this paragraph unless—
    (a) the applicant or the respondent is domiciled in England and Wales on the date of the application,
    (b) the applicant has been habitually resident there throughout the period of 1 year ending with that date, or
    (c) the respondent is resident there on that date.
(3) If, on an application under this paragraph, it appears to the court that—
    (a) the applicant or any child of the family to whom the application relates is in immediate need of financial assistance, but
    (b) it is not yet possible to determine what order, if any, should be made on the application,
the court may make an interim order.

(4) If, on an application under this paragraph, the applicant satisfies the court of a ground mentioned in sub-paragraph (1), the court may make one or more of the orders set out in paragraph 41.

Interim orders

40. An interim order is an order requiring the respondent to make to the applicant, until the determination of the application, such periodical payments as the court thinks reasonable.

Orders that may be made where failure to maintain established

41. (1) The orders are—
    (a) an order that the respondent must make to the applicant such periodical payments for such term as may be specified;
    (b) an order that the respondent must secure to the applicant, to the satisfaction of the court, such periodical payments for such term as may be specified;
    (c) an order that the respondent must pay to the applicant such lump sum as may be specified;
    (d) an order that the respondent must make such periodical payments for such term as may be specified—
        (i) to such person as may be specified, for the benefit of the child to whom the application relates, or
        (ii) to the child to whom the application relates;
    (e) an order that the respondent must secure—
        (i) to such person as may be specified for the benefit of the child to whom the application relates, or
        (ii) to the child to whom the application relates,
        to the satisfaction of the court, such periodical payments for such term as may be specified;
    (f) an order that the respondent must pay such lump sum as may be specified—
        (i) to such person as may be specified for the benefit of the child to whom the application relates, or
        (ii) to the child to whom the application relates.
    (2) In this Part 'specified' means specified in the order.

Particular provision that may be made by lump sum orders

42. (1) An order under this Part for the payment of a lump sum may be made for the purpose of enabling any liabilities or expenses reasonably incurred in maintaining the applicant or any child of the family to whom the application relates before the making of the application to be met.
    (2) An order under this Part for the payment of a lump sum may—
        (a) provide for its payment by instalments of such amount as may be specified, and
        (b) require the payment of the instalments to be secured to the satisfaction of the court.
    (3) Sub-paragraphs (1) and (2) do not restrict the power to make an order by virtue of paragraph 41(1)(c) or (f).

Matters to which the court is to have regard on application under paragraph 39(1)(a)

43. (1) This paragraph applies if an application under paragraph 39 is made on the ground mentioned in paragraph 39(1)(a).
    (2) In deciding—
        (a) whether the respondent has failed to provide reasonable maintenance for the applicant, and

(b) what order, if any, to make under this Part in favour of the applicant,
the court must have regard to all the circumstances of the case including the matters mentioned in paragraph 21(2).

(3) If an application is also made under paragraph 39 in respect of a child of the family who has not reached 18, the court must give first consideration to the welfare of the child while under 18.

(4) Paragraph 21(2)(c) has effect as if for the reference in it to the breakdown of the civil partnership there were substituted a reference to the failure to provide reasonable maintenance for the applicant.

Matters to which the court is to have regard on application under paragraph 39(1)(b)

44. (1) This paragraph applies if an application under paragraph 39 is made on the ground mentioned in paragraph 39(1)(b).

(2) In deciding—
    (a) whether the respondent has failed to provide, or to make a proper contribution towards, reasonable maintenance for the child of the family to whom the application relates, and
    (b) what order, if any, to make under this Part in favour of the child,
the court must have regard to all the circumstances of the case.

(3) Those circumstances include—
    (a) the matters mentioned in paragraph 22(2)(a) to (e), and
    (b) if the child of the family to whom the application relates is not the child of the respondent, the matters mentioned in paragraph 22(3).

(4) Paragraph 21(2)(c) (as it applies by virtue of paragraph 22(2)(e)) has effect as if for the reference in it to the breakdown of the civil partnership there were substituted a reference to—
    (a) the failure to provide, or
    (b) the failure to make a proper contribution towards,
reasonable maintenance for the child of the family to whom the application relates.

Restrictions on making orders under this Part

45. The power to make an order under paragraph 41(1)(d), (e) or (f) is subject to paragraph 49(1) and (5) (restrictions on orders in favour of children who have reached 18).

PART 10   COMMENCEMENT OF CERTAIN PROCEEDINGS AND DURATION OF CERTAIN ORDERS

Commencement of proceedings for ancillary relief, etc.

46. (1) Sub-paragraph (2) applies if an application for a dissolution, nullity or separation order has been made.

(2) Subject to sub-paragraph (3), proceedings for—
    (a) an order under Part 1 (financial provision on dissolution etc.),
    (b) a property adjustment order, or
    (c) an order under Part 8 (maintenance pending outcome of dissolution, nullity or separation proceedings),
may be begun (subject to and in accordance with rules of court) at any time after the presentation of the application.

(3) Rules of court may provide, in such cases as may be prescribed by the rules, that—
    (a) an application for any such relief as is mentioned in sub-paragraph (2) must be made in the application or response, and
    (b) an application for any such relief which—
        (i)   is not so made, or

      (ii) is not made until after the end of such period following the presentation of the application or filing of the response as may be so prescribed,

may be made only with the leave of the court.

Duration of periodical and secured periodical payments orders for a civil partner

47. (1) The court may specify in a periodical payments or secured periodical payments order in favour of a civil partner such term as it thinks fit, except that the term must not—

      (a) begin before the date of the making of an application for the order, or

      (b) extend beyond the limits given in sub-paragraphs (2) and (3).

(2) The limits in the case of a periodical payments order are—

      (a) the death of either civil partner;

      (b) where the order is made on or after the making of a dissolution or nullity order, the formation of a subsequent civil partnership or marriage by the civil partner in whose favour the order is made.

(3) The limits in the case of a secured periodical payments order are—

      (a) the death of the civil partner in whose favour the order is made;

      (b) where the order is made on or after the making of a dissolution or nullity order, the formation of a subsequent civil partnership or marriage by the civil partner in whose favour the order is made.

(4) In the case of an order made on or after the making of a dissolution or nullity order, sub-paragraphs (1) to (3) are subject to paragraphs 23(3) and 59(4).

(5) If a periodical payments or secured periodical payments order in favour of a civil partner is made on or after the making of a dissolution or nullity order, the court may direct that that civil partner is not entitled to apply under paragraph 51 for the extension of the term specified in the order.

(6) If—

      (a) a periodical payments or secured periodical payments order in favour of a civil partner is made otherwise than on or after the making of a dissolution or nullity order, and

      (b) the civil partnership is subsequently dissolved or annulled but the order continues in force,

the order ceases to have effect (regardless of anything in it) on the formation of a subsequent civil partnership or marriage by that civil partner, except in relation to any arrears due under it on the date of its formation.

Subsequent civil partnership or marriage

48. If after the making of a dissolution or nullity order one of the civil partners forms a subsequent civil partnership or marriage, that civil partner is not entitled to apply, by reference to the dissolution or nullity order, for—

      (a) an order under Part 1 in that civil partner's favour, or

      (b) a property adjustment order,

against the other civil partner in the dissolved or annulled civil partnership.

Duration of continuing orders in favour of children, and age limit on making certain orders in their favour

49. (1) Subject to sub-paragraph (5)—

      (a) no order under Part 1,

      (b) no property adjustment order made by virtue of paragraph 7(1)(a) (transfer of property), and

      (c) no order made under Part 9 (failure to maintain) by virtue of paragraph 41,

is to be made in favour of a child who has reached 18.

(2) The term to be specified in a periodical payments or secured periodical payments order in favour of a child may begin with—

(a) the date of the making of an application for the order or a later date, or

(b) a date ascertained in accordance with sub-paragraph (7) or (8).

(3) The term to be specified in such an order—

(a) must not in the first instance extend beyond the date of the birthday of the child next following the child's reaching the upper limit of the compulsory school age unless the court considers that in the circumstances of the case the welfare of the child requires that it should extend to a later date, and

(b) must not in any event, subject to sub-paragraph (5), extend beyond the date of the child's 18th birthday.

(4) Sub-paragraph (3)(a) must be read with section 8 of the Education Act 1996 (c. 56) (which applies to determine for the purposes of any enactment whether a person is of compulsory school age).

(5) Sub-paragraphs (1) and (3)(b) do not apply in the case of a child if it appears to the court that—

(a) the child is, or will be, or, if an order were made without complying with either or both of those provisions, would be—

(i)   receiving instruction at an educational establishment, or

(ii) undergoing training for a trade, profession or vocation,

whether or not the child also is, will be or would be in gainful employment, or

(b) there are special circumstances which justify the making of an order without complying with either or both of sub-paragraphs (1) and (3)(b).

(6) A periodical payments order in favour of a child, regardless of anything in the order, ceases to have effect on the death of the person liable to make payments under the order, except in relation to any arrears due under the order on the date of the death.

(7) If—

(a) a maintenance calculation ('the current calculation') is in force with respect to a child, and

(b) an application is made under this Schedule for a periodical payments or secured periodical payments order in favour of that child—

(i)   in accordance with section 8 of the Child Support Act 1991 (c. 48), and

(ii) before the end of 6 months beginning with the making of the current calculation,

the term to be specified in any such order made on that application may be expressed to begin on, or at any time after, the earliest permitted date.

(8) 'The earliest permitted date' is whichever is the later of—

(a) the date 6 months before the application is made, or

(b) the date on which the current calculation took effect or, where successive maintenance calculations have been continuously in force with respect to a child, on which the first of those calculations took effect.

(9) If—

(a) a maintenance calculation ceases to have effect by or under any provision of the 1991 Act, and

(b) an application is made, before the end of 6 months beginning with the relevant date, for a periodical payments or secured periodical payments order in favour of a child with respect to whom that maintenance calculation was in force immediately before it ceased to have effect,

the term to be specified in any such order made on that application may begin with the date on which that maintenance calculation ceased to have effect or any later date.

(10) 'The relevant date' means the date on which the maintenance calculation ceased to have effect.

(11) In this paragraph 'maintenance calculation' has the same meaning as it has in the 1991 Act by virtue of section 54 of the 1991 Act as read with any regulations in force under that section.

PART 11   VARIATION, DISCHARGE ETC. OF CERTAIN ORDERS
FOR FINANCIAL RELIEF

Orders etc. to which this Part applies

50. (1) This Part applies to the following orders—
   (a) a periodical payments order under Part 1 (financial provision on dissolution etc.) or Part 9 (failure to maintain);
   (b) a secured periodical payments order under Part 1 or 9;
   (c) an order under Part 8 (maintenance pending outcome of dissolution proceedings etc.);
   (d) an interim order under Part 9;
   (e) an order made under Part 1 by virtue of paragraph 3(3) or under Part 9 by virtue of paragraph 42(2) (lump sum by instalments);
   (f) a deferred order made under Part 1 by virtue of paragraph 2(1)(c) (lump sum for civil partner) which includes provision made by virtue of—
      (i) paragraph 25(2), or
      (ii) paragraph 26,
      (provision in respect of pension rights);
   (g) a property adjustment order made on or after the making of a separation order by virtue of paragraph 7(1)(b), (c) or (d) (order for settlement or variation of settlement);
   (h) a sale of property order;
   (i) a pension sharing order made before the dissolution or nullity order has been made final.

(2) If the court has made an order referred to in sub-paragraph (1)(f)(ii), this Part ceases to apply to the order on the death of either of the civil partners.

(3) The powers exercisable by the court under this Part in relation to an order are also exercisable in relation to any instrument executed in pursuance of the order.

Powers to vary, discharge, suspend or revive order

51. (1) If the court has made an order to which this Part applies, it may—
   (a) vary or discharge the order,
   (b) suspend any provision of it temporarily, or
   (c) revive the operation of any provision so suspended.

(2) Sub-paragraph (1) is subject to the provisions of this Part and paragraph 47(5).

Power to remit arrears

52. (1) If the court has made an order referred to in paragraph 50(1)(a), (b), (c) or (d), it may remit the payment of any arrears due under the order or under any part of the order.

(2) Sub-paragraph (1) is subject to the provisions of this Part.

Additional powers on discharging or varying a periodical or secured periodical payments order after dissolution of civil partnership

53. (1) Sub-paragraph (2) applies if, after the dissolution of a civil partnership, the court—
   (a) discharges a periodical payments order or secured periodical payments order made in favour of a civil partner, or
   (b) varies such an order so that payments under the order are required to be made or secured only for such further period as is determined by the court.

(2) The court may make supplemental provision consisting of any of the following—

    (a) an order for the payment of a lump sum in favour of one of the civil partners;

    (b) one or more property adjustment orders in favour of one of the civil partners;

    (c) one or more pension sharing orders;

    (d) a direction that the civil partner in whose favour the original order discharged or varied was made is not entitled to make any further application for—

        (i) a periodical payments or secured periodical payments order, or

        (ii) an extension of the period to which the original order is limited by any variation made by the court.

(3) The power under sub-paragraph (2) is in addition to any power the court has apart from that sub-paragraph.

54. (1) An order for the payment of a lump sum under paragraph 53 may—

    (a) provide for the payment of it by instalments of such amount as may be specified, and

    (b) require the payment of the instalments to be secured to the satisfaction of the court.

(2) Sub-paragraphs (5) and (6) of paragraph 3 (interest on deferred instalments) apply where the court makes an order for the payment of a lump sum under paragraph 53 as they apply where it makes such an order under Part 1.

(3) If under paragraph 53 the court makes more than one property adjustment order in favour of the same civil partner, each of those orders must fall within a different paragraph of paragraph 7(1) (types of property adjustment orders).

(4) Part 3 (orders for the sale of property) and paragraph 76 (direction for settlement of instrument) apply where the court makes a property adjustment order under paragraph 53 as they apply where it makes any other property adjustment order.

(5) Paragraph 18 (restrictions on making of pension sharing order) applies in relation to a pension sharing order under paragraph 53 as it applies in relation to any other pension sharing order.

Variation etc. of periodical or secured periodical payments orders made in cases of failure to maintain

55. (1) An application for the variation under paragraph 51 of a periodical payments order or secured periodical payments order made under Part 9 in favour of a child may, if the child has reached 16, be made by the child himself.

(2) Sub-paragraph (3) applies if a periodical payments order made in favour of a child under Part 9 ceases to have effect—

    (a) on the date on which the child reaches 16, or

    (b) at any time after that date but before or on the date on which the child reaches 18.

(3) If, on an application made to the court for an order under this sub-paragraph, it appears to the court that—

    (a) the child is, will be or, if an order were made under this sub-paragraph, would be—

        (i) receiving instruction at an educational establishment, or

        (ii) undergoing training for a trade, profession or vocation,

        whether or not the child also is, will be or would be in gainful employment, or

    (b) there are special circumstances which justify the making of an order under this sub-paragraph,

the court may by order revive the order mentioned in sub-paragraph (2) from such date as it may specify.

(4) A date specified under sub-paragraph (3) must not be earlier than the date of the application under that sub-paragraph.

(5) If under sub-paragraph (3) the court revives an order it may exercise its power under paragraph 51 in relation to the revived order.

Variation etc. of property adjustment and pension sharing orders

56. The court must not exercise the powers conferred by this Part in relation to a property adjustment order falling within paragraph 7(1)(b), (c) or (d) (order for settlement or for variation of settlement) except on an application made in proceedings—

   (a) for the rescission of the separation order by reference to which the property adjustment order was made, or

   (b) for a dissolution order in relation to the civil partnership.

57. (1) In relation to a pension sharing order which is made at a time before the dissolution or nullity order has been made final—

   (a) the powers conferred by this Part (by virtue of paragraph 50(1)(i)) may be exercised—

      (i) only on an application made before the pension sharing order has or, but for paragraph (b), would have taken effect, and

      (ii) only if, at the time when the application is made, the dissolution or nullity order has not been made final, and

   (b) an application made in accordance with paragraph (a) prevents the pension sharing order from taking effect before the application has been dealt with.

(2) No variation of a pension sharing order is to be made so as to take effect before the order is made final.

(3) The variation of a pension sharing order prevents the order taking effect before the end of such period after the making of the variation as may be prescribed by regulations made by the Lord Chancellor.

(4) The power to make regulations under sub-paragraph (3) is exercisable by statutory instrument which is subject to annulment in pursuance of a resolution of either House of Parliament.

58. (1) Sub-paragraphs (2) and (3)—

   (a) are subject to paragraphs 53 and 54, and

   (b) do not affect any power exercisable by virtue of paragraph 50(e), (f), (g) or (i) or otherwise than by virtue of this Part.

(2) No property adjustment order or pension sharing order may be made on an application for the variation of a periodical payments or secured periodical payments order made (whether in favour of a civil partner or in favour of a child of the family) under Part 1.

(3) No order for the payment of a lump sum may be made on an application for the variation of a periodical payments or secured periodical payments order in favour of a civil partner (whether made under Part 1 or 9).

Matters to which court is to have regard in exercising powers under this Part

59. (1) In exercising the powers conferred by this Part the court must have regard to all the circumstances of the case, giving first consideration to the welfare, while under 18, of any child of the family who has not reached 18.

(2) The circumstances of the case include, in particular, any change in any of the matters to which the court was required to have regard when making the order to which the application relates.

(3) Sub-paragraph (4) applies in the case of—

   (a) a periodical payments order, or

   (b) a secured periodical payments order,

made on or after the making of a dissolution or nullity order.

(4) The court must consider whether in all the circumstances, and after having regard to any such change, it would be appropriate to vary the order so that payments under the order are required—

   (a) to be made, or

   (b) to be secured,

only for such further period as will in the opinion of the court be sufficient to enable the civil partner in whose favour the order was made to adjust without undue hardship to the termination of those payments.

(5) In considering what further period will be sufficient, the court must, if the civil partnership has been dissolved, take into account any proposed exercise by it of its powers under paragraph 53.

(6) If the civil partner against whom the order was made has died, the circumstances of the case also include the changed circumstances resulting from that civil partner's death.

Variation of secured periodical payments order where person liable has died

60. (1) This paragraph applies if the person liable to make payments under a secured periodical payments order has died.

(2) Subject to sub-paragraph (3), an application under this Part relating to the order (and to any sale of property order which requires the proceeds of sale of property to be used for securing those payments) may be made by—

(a) the person entitled to payments under the periodical payments order, or

(b) the personal representatives of the deceased person.

(3) No such application may be made without the leave of the court after the end of 6 months from the date on which representation in regard to the estate of that person is first taken out.

(4) The personal representatives of the person who has died are not liable for having distributed any part of the estate of the deceased after the end of the 6 month period on the ground that they ought to have taken into account the possibility that the court might allow an application under this paragraph to be made after that period by the person entitled to payments under the order.

(5) Sub-paragraph (4) does not affect any power to recover any part of the estate so distributed arising by virtue of the making of an order in pursuance of this paragraph.

(6) In considering for the purposes of sub-paragraph (3) the question when representation was first taken out—

(a) a grant limited to settled land or to trust property is to be disregarded, and

(b) a grant limited to real estate or to personal estate is to be disregarded unless a grant limited to the remainder of the estate has previously been made or is made at the same time.

Power to direct when variation etc. is to take effect

61. (1) If the court, in exercise of its powers under this Part, decides—

(a) to vary, or

(b) to discharge,

a periodical payments or secured periodical payments order, it may direct that the variation or discharge is not to take effect until the end of such period as may be specified in the order.

(2) Sub-paragraph (1) is subject to paragraph 47(1) and (6).

62. (1) If—

(a) a periodical payments or secured periodical payments order in favour of more than one child ('the order') is in force,

(b) the order requires payments specified in it to be made to or for the benefit of more than one child without apportioning those payments between them,

(c) a maintenance calculation ('the calculation') is made with respect to one or more, but not all, of the children with respect to whom those payments are to be made, and

(d) an application is made, before the end of the period of 6 months beginning with the date on which the calculation was made, for the variation or discharge of the order, the court may, in exercise of its powers under this Part to vary or discharge the order, direct that the variation or discharge is to take effect from the date on which the calculation took effect or any later date.

(2) If—

    (a) an order ('the child order') of a kind prescribed for the purposes of section 10(1) of the Child Support Act 1991 (c. 48) is affected by a maintenance calculation,

    (b) on the date on which the child order became so affected there was in force a periodical payments or secured periodical payments order ('the civil partner's order') in favour of a civil partner having the care of the child in whose favour the child order was made, and

    (c) an application is made, before the end of the period of 6 months beginning with the date on which the maintenance calculation was made, for the civil partner's order to be varied or discharged,

the court may, in exercise of its powers under this Part to vary or discharge the civil partner's order, direct that the variation or discharge is to take effect from the date on which the child order became so affected or any later date.

(3) For the purposes of sub-paragraph (2), an order is affected if it ceases to have effect or is modified by or under section 10 of the 1991 Act.

(4) Sub-paragraphs (1) and (2) do not affect any other power of the court to direct that the variation of discharge of an order under this Part is to take effect from a date earlier than that on which the order for variation or discharge was made.

(5) In this paragraph 'maintenance calculation' has the same meaning as it has in the 1991 Act by virtue of section 54 of the 1991 Act as read with any regulations in force under that section.

PART 12   ARREARS AND REPAYMENTS

Payment of certain arrears unenforceable without the leave of the court

63. (1) This paragraph applies if any arrears are due under—

    (a) an order under Part 1 (financial provision on dissolution etc.),

    (b) an order under Part 8 (maintenance pending outcome of dissolution, nullity or separation proceedings), or

    (c) an order under Part 9 (failure to maintain),

and the arrears became due more than 12 months before proceedings to enforce the payment of them are begun.

(2) A person is not entitled to enforce through the High Court or any county court the payment of the arrears without the leave of that court.

(3) The court hearing an application for the grant of leave under this paragraph may—

    (a) refuse leave,

    (b) grant leave subject to such restrictions and conditions (including conditions as to the allowing of time for payment or the making of payment by instalments) as that court thinks proper, or

    (c) remit the payment of the arrears or of any part of them.

(4) An application for the grant of leave under this paragraph must be made in such manner as may be prescribed by rules of court.

Orders for repayment in certain cases of sums paid under certain orders

64. (1) This paragraph applies if—

    (a) a person ('R') is entitled to receive payments under an order listed in sub-paragraph (2), and

    (b) R's circumstances or the circumstances of the person ('P') liable to make payments under the order have changed since the order was made, or the circumstances have changed as a result of P's death.

(2) The orders are—

(a) any order under Part 8 (maintenance pending outcome of dissolution, nullity or separation proceedings);

(b) any interim order under Part 9;

(c) any periodical payments order;

(d) any secured periodical payments order.

(3) P or P's personal representatives may (subject to sub-paragraph (7)) apply for an order under this paragraph against R or R's personal representatives.

(4) If it appears to the court that, because of the changed circumstances or P's death, the amount received by R in respect of a relevant period exceeds the amount which P or P's personal representatives should have been required to pay, it may order the respondent to the application to pay to the applicant such sum, not exceeding the amount of the excess, as it thinks just.

(5) 'Relevant period' means a period after the circumstances changed or (as the case may be) after P's death.

(6) An order under this paragraph for the payment of any sum may provide for the payment of that sum by instalments of such amount as may be specified in the order.

(7) An application under this paragraph—

(a) may be made in proceedings in the High Court or a county court for—

(i) the variation or discharge of the order listed in sub-paragraph (2), or

(ii) leave to enforce, or the enforcement of, the payment of arrears under that order, but

(b) if not made in such proceedings, must be made to a county court;

and accordingly references in this paragraph to the court are references to the High Court or a county court, as the circumstances require.

(8) The jurisdiction conferred on a county court by this paragraph is exercisable even though, because of the amount claimed in the application, the jurisdiction would not but for this sub-paragraph be exercisable by a county court.

Orders for repayment after cessation of order because of subsequent civil partnership etc.

65. (1) Sub-paragraphs (3) and (4) apply if—

(a) a periodical payments or secured periodical payments order in favour of a civil partner ('R') has ceased to have effect because of the formation of a subsequent civil partnership or marriage by R, and

(b) the person liable to make payments under the order ('P') (or P's personal representatives) has made payments in accordance with it in respect of a relevant period in the mistaken belief that the order was still subsisting.

(2) 'Relevant period' means a period after the date of the formation of the subsequent civil partnership or marriage.

(3) P (or P's personal representatives) is not entitled to bring proceedings in respect of a cause of action arising out of the circumstances mentioned in sub-paragraph (1)(a) and (b) against R (or R's personal representatives).

(4) But, on an application under this paragraph by P (or P's personal representatives) against R (or R's personal representatives), the court—

(a) may order the respondent to pay to the applicant a sum equal to the amount of the payments made in respect of the relevant period, or

(b) if it appears to the court that it would be unjust to make that order, may—

(i) order the respondent to pay to the applicant such lesser sum as it thinks fit, or

(ii) dismiss the application.

(5) An order under this paragraph for the payment of any sum may provide for the payment of that sum by instalments of such amount as may be specified in the order.

(6) An application under this paragraph—

    (a) may be made in proceedings in the High Court or a county court for leave to enforce, or the enforcement of, payment of arrears under the order in question, but

    (b) if not made in such proceedings, must be made to a county court;

and accordingly references in this paragraph to the court are references to the High Court or a county court, as the circumstances require.

(7) The jurisdiction conferred on a county court by this paragraph is exercisable even though, because of the amount claimed in the application, the jurisdiction would not but for this sub-paragraph be exercisable by a county court.

(8) Subject to sub-paragraph (9)—

    (a) the designated officer for a magistrates' court to whom any payments under a payments order are required to be made is not liable for any act done by him in pursuance of the payments order after the date on which that order ceased to have effect because of the formation of a subsequent civil partnership or marriage by the person entitled to payments under it, and

    (b) the collecting officer under an attachment of earnings order made to secure payments under a payments order is not liable for any act done by him after that date in accordance with any enactment or rule of court specifying how payments made to him in compliance with the attachment of earnings order are to be dealt with.

(9) Sub-paragraph (8) applies if (and only if) the act—

    (a) was one which the officer would have been under a duty to do had the payments order not ceased to have effect, and

    (b) was done before notice in writing of the formation of the subsequent civil partnership or marriage was given to him by or on behalf of—

        (i)   the person entitled to payments under the payments order,

        (ii) the person liable to make payments under it, or

        (iii) the personal representatives of either of them.

(10) In sub-paragraphs (8) and (9) 'payments order' means a periodical payments order or secured periodical payments order and 'collecting officer', in relation to an attachment of earnings order, means—

    (a) the officer of the High Court,

    (b) the district judge of a county court, or

    (c) the designated officer for a magistrates' court,

to whom a person makes payments in compliance with the order.

PART 13   CONSENT ORDERS AND MAINTAINENCE AGREEMENTS

Consent orders for financial relief

66. (1) Regardless of anything in the preceding provisions of this Schedule, on an application for a consent order for financial relief, the court may, unless it has reason to think that there are other circumstances into which it ought to inquire, make an order in the terms agreed on the basis only of such information supplied with the application as is required by rules of court.

(2) Sub-paragraph (1) applies to an application for a consent order varying or discharging an order for financial relief as it applies to an application for an order for financial relief.

(3) In this paragraph—

'consent order', in relation to an application for an order, means an order in the terms applied for to which the respondent agrees;

'order for financial relief' means an order under any of Parts 1, 2, 3, 4 and 9.

Meaning of 'maintenance agreement' and 'financial arrangements'

67. (1) In this Part 'maintenance agreement' means any agreement in writing between the civil partners in a civil partnership which—

  (a) is made during the continuance or after the dissolution or annulment of the civil partnership and contains financial arrangements, or

  (b) is a separation agreement which contains no financial arrangements but is made in a case where no other agreement in writing between the civil partners contains financial arrangements.

(2) In this Part 'financial arrangements' means provisions governing the rights and liabilities towards one another when living separately of the civil partners in a civil partnership (including a civil partnership which has been dissolved or annulled) in respect of—

  (a) the making or securing of payments, or

  (b) the disposition or use of any property,

including such rights and liabilities with respect to the maintenance or education of a child (whether or not a child of the family).

(3) 'Education' includes training.

Validity of maintenance agreements

68. If a maintenance agreement includes a provision purporting to restrict any right to apply to a court for an order containing financial arrangements—

  (a) that provision is void, but

  (b) any other financial arrangements contained in the agreement—

    (i) are not void or unenforceable as a result, and

    (ii) unless void or unenforceable for any other reason, are (subject to paragraphs 69 and 73) binding on the parties to the agreement.

Alteration of agreements by court during lives of parties

69. (1) Either party to a maintenance agreement may apply to the court or, subject to sub-paragraph (6), to a magistrates' court for an order under this paragraph if—

  (a) the maintenance agreement is for the time being subsisting, and

  (b) each of the parties to the agreement is for the time being domiciled or resident in England and Wales.

(2) The court may make an order under this paragraph if it is satisfied that—

  (a) because of a change in the circumstances in the light of which—

    (i) any financial arrangements contained in the agreement were made, or

    (ii) financial arrangements were omitted from it,

    the agreement should be altered so as to make different financial arrangements or so as to contain financial arrangements, or

  (b) that the agreement does not contain proper financial arrangements with respect to any child of the family.

(3) In sub-paragraph (2)(a) the reference to a change in the circumstances includes a change foreseen by the parties when making the agreement.

(4) An order under this paragraph may make such alterations in the agreement—

  (a) by varying or revoking any financial arrangements contained in it, or

  (b) by inserting in it financial arrangements for the benefit of one of the parties to the agreement or of a child of the family,

as appear to the court to be just having regard to all the circumstances, including, if relevant, the matters mentioned in paragraph 22(3).

(5) The effect of the order is that the agreement is to be treated as if any alteration made by the order had been made by agreement between the partners and for valuable consideration.

(6) The power to make an order under this paragraph is subject to paragraphs 70 and 71.

Restrictions on applications to and orders by magistrates' courts under paragraph 69

70. (1) A magistrates' court must not entertain an application under paragraph 69(1) unless—
　　(a) both the parties to the agreement are resident in England and Wales, and
　　(b) the court acts in, or is authorised by the Lord Chancellor to act for, a local justice area in which at least one of the parties is resident.
　(2) A magistrates' court must not make any order on such an application other than—
　　(a) if the agreement includes no provision for periodical payments by either of the parties, an order inserting provision for the making by one of the parties of periodical payments for the maintenance of—
　　　(i)　the other party, or
　　　(ii)　any child of the family;
　　(b) if the agreement includes provision for the making by one of the parties of periodical payments, an order increasing or reducing the rate of, or terminating, any of those payments.

Provisions relating to periodical and secured periodical payments: duration

71. (1) If a court decides to make an order under paragraph 69 altering an agreement—
　　(a) by inserting provision for the making or securing by one of the parties to the agreement of periodical payments for the maintenance of the other party, or
　　(b) by increasing the rate of the periodical payments which the agreement provides shall be made by one of the parties for the maintenance of the other,
it may specify such term as it thinks fit as the term for which the payments or, as the case may be, the additional payments attributable to the increase are to be made under the altered agreement, except that the term must not extend beyond the limits in sub-paragraphs (2) and (3).
　(2) The limits if the payments are not to be secured are—
　　(a) the death of either of the parties to the agreement, or
　　(b) the formation of a subsequent civil partnership or marriage by the party to whom the payments are to be made.
　(3) The limits if the payments are to be secured are—
　　(a) the death of the party to whom the payments are to be made, or
　　(b) the formation of a subsequent civil partnership or marriage by that party.
　(4) Sub-paragraph (5) applies if a court decides to make an order under paragraph 69 altering an agreement by—
　　(a) inserting provision for the making or securing by one of the parties to the agreement of periodical payments for the maintenance of a child of the family, or
　　(b) increasing the rate of the periodical payments which the agreement provides shall be made or secured by one of the parties for the maintenance of such a child.
　(5) The court, in deciding the term for which under the agreement as altered by the order—
　　(a) the payments are to be made or secured for the benefit of the child, or
　　(b) the additional payments attributable to the increase are to be made or secured for the benefit of the child,
must apply paragraph 49(2) to (5) (age limits) as if the order in question were a periodical payments or secured periodical payments order in favour of the child.

Saving

72. Nothing in paragraphs 68 to 71 affects—
　　(a) any power of a court before which any proceedings between the parties to a maintenance agreement are brought under any other enactment (including a provision of this Schedule) to make an order containing financial arrangements, or
　　(b) any right of either party to apply for such an order in such proceedings.

Alteration of agreements by court after death of one party

73. (1) This paragraph applies if—
    (a) a maintenance agreement provides for the continuation of payments under the agreement after the death of one of the parties, and
    (b) that party ('A') dies domiciled in England and Wales.

(2) Subject to sub-paragraph (4), the surviving party or A's personal representatives may apply to the High Court or a county court for an order under paragraph 69.

(3) If a maintenance agreement is altered by a court on an application made under sub-paragraph (2), the same consequences follow as if the alteration had been made immediately before the death by agreement between the parties and for valuable consideration.

(4) An application under this paragraph may not, without the leave of the High Court or a county court, be made after the end of 6 months from the date on which representation in regard to A's estate is first taken out.

(5) A's personal representatives are not liable for having distributed any part of A's estate after the end of the 6 month period on the ground that they ought to have taken into account the possibility that a court might allow an application by virtue of this paragraph to be made by the surviving party after that period.

(6) Sub-paragraph (5) does not affect any power to recover any part of the estate so distributed arising by virtue of the making of an order in pursuance of this paragraph.

(7) Paragraph 60(6) applies for the purposes of sub-paragraph (4) as it applies for the purposes of paragraph 60(3).

PART 14   MISCELLANEOUS AND SUPPLEMENTARY

Avoidance of transactions intended to prevent or reduce financial relief

74. (1) This paragraph applies if proceedings for relief ('financial relief') are brought by one person ('A') against another ('B') under Part 1, 2, 4, 8, 9, or 11 (other than paragraph 60(2)), or paragraph 69.

(2) If the court is satisfied, on an application by A, that B is, with the intention of defeating A's claim for financial relief, about to—
    (a) make any disposition, or
    (b) transfer out of the jurisdiction or otherwise deal with any property,
it may make such order as it thinks fit for restraining B from doing so or otherwise for protecting the claim.

(3) If the court is satisfied, on an application by A, that—
    (a) B has, with the intention of defeating A's claim for financial relief, made a reviewable disposition, and
    (b) if the disposition were set aside, financial relief or different financial relief would be granted to A,
it make an order setting aside the disposition.

(4) If the court is satisfied, on an application by A in a case where an order has been obtained by A against B under any of the provisions mentioned in sub-paragraph (1), that B has, with the intention of defeating A's claim for financial relief, made a reviewable disposition, it may make an order setting aside the disposition.

(5) An application for the purposes of sub-paragraph (3) must be made in the proceedings for the financial relief in question.

(6) If the court makes an order under sub-paragraph (3) or (4) setting aside a disposition it must give such consequential directions as it thinks fit for giving effect to the order (including directions requiring the making of any payments or the disposal of any property).

75. (1) Any reference in paragraph 74 to defeating A's claim for financial relief is to—
    (a) preventing financial relief from being granted to A, or to A for the benefit of a child of the family,

(b) reducing the amount of any financial relief which might be so granted, or

(c) frustrating or impeding the enforcement of any order which might be or has been made at A's instance under any of those provisions.

(2) In paragraph 74 and this paragraph 'disposition'—

(a) does not include any provision contained in a will or codicil, but

(b) subject to paragraph (a), includes any conveyance, assurance or gift of property of any description (whether made by an instrument or otherwise).

(3) Any disposition made by B (whether before or after the commencement of the proceedings for financial relief) is a reviewable disposition for the purposes of paragraphs 74(3) and (4) unless it was made—

(a) for valuable consideration (other than formation of a civil partnership), and

(b) to a person who, at the time of the disposition, acted in relation to it in good faith and without notice of any intention on B's part to defeat A's claim for financial relief.

(4) If an application is made under paragraph 74 with respect to a disposition which took place less than 3 years before the date of the application or with respect to a disposition or other dealing with property which is about to take place and the court is satisfied—

(a) in a case falling within paragraph 74(2) or (3), that the disposition or other dealing would (apart from paragraph 74) have the consequence of defeating A's claim for financial relief, or

(b) in a case falling within paragraph 74(4), that the disposition has had the consequence of defeating A's claim for financial relief,

it is presumed, unless the contrary is shown, that the person who disposed of or is about to dispose of or deal with the property did so or, as the case may be, is about to do so, with the intention of defeating A's claim for financial relief.

Direction for settlement of instrument for securing payments or effecting property adjustment

76. (1) This paragraph applies if the court decides to make—

(a) an order under Part 1 or 9 requiring any payments to be secured, or

(b) a property adjustment order.

(2) The court may direct that the matter be referred to one of the conveyancing counsel of the court for him to settle a proper instrument to be executed by all necessary parties.

(3) If the order referred to in sub-paragraph (1) is to be made in proceedings for a dissolution, nullity or separation order, the court may, if it thinks fit, defer the making of the dissolution, nullity or separation order until the instrument has been duly executed.

Settlement, etc., made in compliance with a property adjustment order may be avoided on bankruptcy of settlor

77. The fact that—

(a) a settlement, or

(b) a transfer of property,

had to be made in order to comply with a property adjustment order does not prevent the settlement or transfer from being a transaction in respect of which an order may be made under section 339 or 340 of the Insolvency Act 1986 (c. 45) (transfers at an undervalue and preferences).

Payments etc., under order made in favour of person suffering from mental disorder

78. (1) This paragraph applies if—

(a) the court makes an order under this Schedule requiring—

(i) payments (including a lump sum payment) to be made, or

(ii) property to be transferred,

to a civil partner, and

(b) the court is satisfied that the person in whose favour the order is made is incapable, because of mental disorder, of managing and administering his or her property and affairs.

(2) 'Mental disorder' has the same meaning as in the Mental Health Act 1983 (c. 20).

(3) Subject to any order, direction or authority made or given in relation to that person under Part 8 of the 1983 Act, the court may order the payments to be made or, as the case may be, the property to be transferred to such persons having charge of that person as the court may direct.

Appeals relating to pension sharing orders which have taken effect

79. (1) Sub-paragraphs (2) and (3) apply if an appeal against a pension sharing order is begun on or after the day on which the order takes effect.

(2) If the pension sharing order relates to a person's rights under a pension arrangement, the appeal court may not set aside or vary the order if the person responsible for the pension arrangement has acted to his detriment in reliance on the order taking effect.

(3) If the pension sharing order relates to a person's shareable state scheme rights, the appeal court may not set aside or vary the order if the Secretary of State has acted to his detriment in reliance on the taking effect of the order.

(4) In determining for the purposes of sub-paragraph (2) or (3) whether a person has acted to his detriment in reliance on the taking effect of the order, the appeal court may disregard any detriment which in its opinion is insignificant.

(5) Where sub-paragraph (2) or (3) applies, the appeal court may make such further orders (including one or more pension sharing orders) as it thinks fit for the purpose of putting the parties in the position it considers appropriate.

(6) Paragraph 19 only applies to a pension sharing order under this paragraph if the decision of the appeal court can itself be the subject of an appeal.

(7) In sub-paragraph (2), the reference to the person responsible for the pension arrangement is to be read in accordance with paragraph 29(3).

Interpretation

80. (1) References in this Schedule to—
   (a) periodical payments orders,
   (b) secured periodical payments orders, and
   (c) orders for the payment of a lump sum,
are references to such of the orders that may be made under Parts 1 and 9 (other than interim orders) as are relevant in the context of the reference in question.

(2) In this Schedule 'child of the family', in relation to two people who are civil partners of each other, means—
   (a) a child of both of them, and
   (b) any other child, other than a child placed with them as foster parents by a local authority or voluntary organisation, who has been treated by both the civil partners as a child of their family.

(3) In this Schedule 'the court' (except where the context otherwise requires) means—
   (a) the High Court, or
   (b) where a county court has jurisdiction by virtue of Part 5 of the Matrimonial and Family Proceedings Act 1984 (c. 42), a county court.

(4) References in this Schedule to a subsequent civil partnership include a civil partnership which is by law void or voidable.

(5) References in this Schedule to a subsequent marriage include a marriage which is by law void or voidable.

SCHEDULE 6

FINANCIAL RELIEF IN MAGISTRATES' COURTS ETC.

PART 1   FAILURE TO MAINTAIN ETC.: FINANCIAL PROVISION

Circumstances in which orders under this Part may be made

1. (1) On an application to it by one of the civil partners, a magistrates' court may make any one or more of the orders set out in paragraph 2 if it is satisfied that the other civil partner—

    (a) has failed to provide reasonable maintenance for the applicant,

    (b) has failed to provide, or to make a proper contribution towards, reasonable maintenance for any child of the family,

    (c) has behaved in such a way that the applicant cannot reasonably be expected to live with the respondent, or

    (d) has deserted the applicant.

(2) The power of the court under sub-paragraph (1) is subject to the following provisions of this Schedule.

The orders: periodical and secured periodical payments and lump sums

2. (1) The orders are—

    (a) an order that the respondent must make to the applicant such periodical payments for such term as may be specified;

    (b) an order that the respondent must pay to the applicant such lump sum as may be specified;

    (c) an order that the respondent must make—

        (i) to the applicant for the benefit of a child of the family to whom the application relates, or

        (ii) to a child of the family to whom the application relates;

    such periodical payments for such term as may be specified;

    (d) an order that the respondent must pay such lump sum as may be specified—

        (i) to the applicant for the benefit of a child of the family to whom the application relates, or

        (ii) to such a child of the family to whom the application relates.

(2) The amount of a lump sum required to be paid under sub-paragraph (1)(b) or (d) must not exceed—

    (a) £1,000, or

    (b) such larger amount as the Lord Chancellor may from time to time by order fix for the purposes of this sub-paragraph.

(3) The power to make an order under sub-paragraph (2) is exercisable by statutory instrument which is subject to annulment in pursuance of a resolution of either House of Parliament.

(4) 'Specified' means specified in the order.

Particular provision that may be made by lump sum orders

3. (1) An order under this Part for the payment of a lump sum may be made for the purpose of enabling any liability or expenses reasonably incurred in maintaining the applicant or any child of the family to whom the application relates before the making of the order to be met.

(2) Sub-paragraph (1) does not restrict the power to make the orders set out in paragraph 2(1)(b) and (d).

Matters to which court is to have regard in exercising its powers under this Part- general

4. If an application is made for an order under this Part, the court, in deciding—
    (a) whether to exercise its powers under this Part, and
    (b) if so, in what way,
must have regard to all the circumstances of the case, giving first consideration to the welfare while under 18 of any child of the family who has not reached 18.

Particular matters to be taken into account when exercising powers in relation to civil partners

5. (1) This paragraph applies in relation to the exercise by the court of its power to make an order by virtue of paragraph 2(1)(a) or (b).
    (2) The court must in particular have regard to—
        (a) the income, earning capacity, property and other financial resources which each civil partner—
            (i) has, or
            (ii) is likely to have in the foreseeable future,
            including, in the case of earning capacity, any increase in that capacity which it would in the opinion of the court be reasonable to expect a civil partner in the civil partnership to take steps to acquire;
        (b) the financial needs, obligations and responsibilities which each civil partner has or is likely to have in the foreseeable future;
        (c) the standard of living enjoyed by the civil partners before the occurrence of the conduct which is alleged as the ground of the application;
        (d) the age of each civil partner and the duration of the civil partnership;
        (e) any physical or mental disability of either civil partner;
        (f) the contributions which each civil partner has made or is likely in the foreseeable future to make to the welfare of the family, including any contribution by looking after the home or caring for the family;
        (g) the conduct of each civil partner, if that conduct is such that it would in the opinion of the court be inequitable to disregard it.

Particular matters to be taken into account when exercising powers in relation to children

6. (1) This paragraph applies in relation to the exercise by the court of its power to make an order by virtue of paragraph 2(1)(c) or (d).
    (2) The court must in particular have regard to—
        (a) the financial needs of the child;
        (b) the income, earning capacity (if any), property and other financial resources of the child;
        (c) any physical or mental disability of the child;
        (d) the standard of living enjoyed by the family before the occurrence of the conduct which is alleged as the ground of the application;
        (e) the way in which the child was being and in which the civil partners expected the child to be educated or trained;
        (f) the considerations mentioned in relation to the civil partners in paragraph 5(2)(a) and (b).
    (3) In relation to the exercise of its power to make an order in favour of a child of the family who is not the respondent's child, the court must also have regard to—
        (a) whether the respondent has assumed any responsibility for the child's maintenance;
        (b) if so, the extent to which, and the basis on which, the respondent assumed that responsibility and the length of time during which the respondent discharged that responsibility;

(c) whether in assuming and discharging that responsibility the respondent did so knowing that the child was not the respondent's child;

(d) the liability of any other person to maintain the child.

Reconciliation

7. (1) If an application is made for an order under this Part—

(a) the court, before deciding whether to exercise its powers under this Part, must consider whether there is any possibility of reconciliation between the civil partners, and

(b) if at any stage of the proceedings on that application it appears to the court that there is a reasonable possibility of such a reconciliation, the court may adjourn the proceedings for such period as it thinks fit to enable attempts to be made to effect a reconciliation.

(2) If the court adjourns any proceedings under sub-paragraph (1), it may request—

(a) an officer of the Children and Family Court Advisory and Support Service, or

(b) any other person,

to attempt to effect a reconciliation between the civil partners.

(3) If any such request is made, the officer or other person—

(a) must report in writing to the court whether the attempt has been successful, but

(b) must not include in the report any other information.

Refusal of order in case more suitable for High Court

8. (1) If on hearing an application for an order under this Part a magistrates' court is of the opinion that any of the matters in question between the civil partners would be more conveniently dealt with by the High Court, the magistrates' court must refuse to make any order on the application.

(2) No appeal lies from a refusal under sub-paragraph (1).

(3) But, in any proceedings in the High Court relating to or comprising the same subject matter as an application in respect of which a magistrates' court has refused to make any order, the High Court may order the application to be reheard and determined by a magistrates' court acting for the same local justice area as the court which refused to make any order.

PART 2   ORDERS FOR AGREED FINANCIAL PROVISION

Orders for payments which have been agreed by the parties

9. (1) Either civil partner may apply to a magistrates' court for an order under this Part on the ground that that civil partner or the other civil partner has agreed to make such financial provision as may be specified in the application.

(2) On such an application, the court may order that the applicant or the respondent (as the case may be) is to make the financial provision specified in the application, if—

(a) it is satisfied that the applicant or the respondent (as the case may be) has agreed to make that provision, and

(b) it has no reason to think that it would be contrary to the interests of justice to do so.

(3) Sub-paragraph (2) is subject to paragraph 12.

Meaning of 'financial provision' and of references to specified financial provision

10. (1) In this Part 'financial provision' means any one or more of the following—

(a) the making of periodical payments by one civil partner to the other;

(b) the payment of a lump sum by one civil partner to the other;

(c) the making of periodical payments by one civil partner to a child of the family or to the other civil partner for the benefit of such a child;

(d) the payment by one party of a lump sum to a child of the family or to the other civil partner for the benefit of such a child.

(2) Any reference in this Part to the financial provision specified in an application or specified by the court is a reference—

(a) to the type of provision specified in the application or by the court,

(b) to the amount so specified as the amount of any payment to be made under the application or order, and

(c) in the case of periodical payments, to the term so specified as the term for which the payments are to be made.

Evidence to be produced where respondent not present etc.

11. (1) This paragraph applies if—

(a) the respondent is not present, or

(b) is not represented by counsel or a solicitor,

at the hearing of an application for an order under this Part.

(2) The court must not make an order under this Part unless there is produced to it such evidence as may be prescribed by rules of court of—

(a) the consent of the respondent to the making of the order,

(b) the financial resources of the respondent, and

(c) if the financial provision specified in the application includes or consists of provision in respect of a child of the family to be made by the applicant to the respondent for the benefit of the child or to the child, the financial resources of the child.

Exercise of powers in relation to children

12. (1) This paragraph applies if the financial provision specified in an application under this Part—

(a) includes, or

(b) consists of,

provision in respect of a child of the family.

(2) The court must not make an order under this Part unless it considers that the provision which the applicant or the respondent (as the case may be) has agreed to make in respect of the child provides for, or makes a proper contribution towards, the financial needs of the child.

Power to make alternative orders

13.(1) This paragraph applies if on an application under this Part the court decides—

(a) that it would be contrary to the interests of justice to make an order for the making of the financial provision specified in the application, or

(b) that any financial provision which the applicant or the respondent (as the case may be) has agreed to make in respect of a child of the family does not provide for, or make a proper contribution towards, the financial needs of that child.

(2) If the court is of the opinion—

(a) that it would not be contrary to the interests of justice to make an order for the making of some other financial provision specified by the court, and

(b) that, in so far as that other financial provision contains any provision for a child of the family, it provides for, or makes a proper contribution towards, the financial needs of that child,

then, if both the civil partners agree, the court may order that the applicant or the respondent (as the case may be) is to make that other financial provision.

Relationship between this Part and Part 1

14. (1) A civil partner who has applied for an order under Part 1 is not precluded at any time before the determination of the application from applying for an order under this Part.

(2) If—

(a) an order is made under this Part on the application of either civil partner, and

(b) either of them has also made an application for a Part 1 order,

the application for the Part 1 order is to be treated as if it had been withdrawn.

PART 3   ORDERS OF COURT WHERE CIVIL PARTNERS LIVING APART BY AGREEMENT

Powers of court where civil partners are living apart by agreement

15. (1) If—

(a) the civil partners have been living apart for a continuous period exceeding 3 months, neither civil partner having deserted the other, and

(b) one of the civil partners has been making periodical payments for the benefit of the other civil partner or of a child of the family,

the other civil partner may apply to a magistrates' court for an order under this Part.

(2) An application made under sub-paragraph (1) must specify the total amount of the payments made by the respondent during the period of 3 months immediately preceding the date of the making of the application.

(3) If on an application for an order under this Part the court is satisfied that the respondent has made the payments specified in the application, the court may make one or both of the orders set out in paragraph 16.

(4) Sub-paragraph (3) is subject to the provisions of this Schedule.

The orders that may be made under this Part

16. (1) The orders are—

(a) an order that the respondent is to make to the applicant such periodical payments for such term as may be specified;

(b) an order that the respondent is to make—

(i) to the applicant for the benefit of a child of the family to whom the application relates, or

(ii) to a child of the family to whom the application relates.

such periodical payments for such term as may be specified.

(2) 'Specified' means specified in the order.

Restrictions on orders under this Part

17. The court in the exercise of its powers under this Part must not require—

(a) the respondent to make payments whose total amount during any period of 3 months exceeds the total amount paid by him for the benefit of—

(i) the applicant, or

(ii) a child of the family,

during the period of 3 months immediately preceding the date of the making of the application;

(b) the respondent to make payments to or for the benefit of any person which exceed in amount the payments which the court considers that it would have required the respondent to make to or for the benefit of that person on an application under Part 1;

(c) payments to be made to or for the benefit of a child of the family who is not the respondent's child, unless the court considers that it would have made an order in favour of that child on an application under Part 1.

Relationship with powers under Part 1

18. (1) Sub-paragraph (2) applies if on an application under this Part the court considers that the orders which it has the power to make under this Part—

(a) would not provide reasonable maintenance for the applicant, or

(b) if the application relates to a child of the family, would not provide, or make a proper contribution towards, reasonable maintenance for that child.

(2) The court—

(a) must refuse to make an order under this Part, but

(b) may treat the application as if it were an application for an order under Part 1.

Matters to be taken into consideration

19. Paragraphs 4 to 6 apply in relation to an application for an order under this Part as they apply in relation to an application for an order under Part 1, subject to the modification that for the reference in paragraph 5(2)(c) to the occurrence of the conduct which is alleged as the ground of the application substitute a reference to the living apart of the civil partners.

PART 4   INTERIM ORDERS

Circumstances in which interim orders may be made

20. (1) This paragraph applies if an application has been made for an order under Part 1, 2 or 3.

(2) A magistrates' court may make an interim order—

(a) at any time before making a final order on, or dismissing, the application, or

(b) on refusing (under paragraph 8) to make on order on the application.

(3) The High Court may make an interim order on ordering the application to be reheard by a magistrates' court (either after the refusal of an order under paragraph 8 or on an appeal made by virtue of paragraph 46).

(4) Not more than one interim order may be made with respect to an application for an order under Part 1, 2 or 3.

(5) Sub-paragraph (4) does not affect the power of a court to make an interim order on a further application under Part 1, 2 or 3.

Meaning of interim order

21. (1) An interim order is an order requiring the respondent to make such periodical payments as the court thinks reasonable—

(a) to the applicant,

(b) to any child of the family who is under 18, or

(c) to the applicant for the benefit of such a child.

(2) In relation to an interim order in respect of an application for an order under Part 2 by the civil partner who has agreed to make the financial provision specified in the application, sub-paragraph (1) applies as if—

(a) the reference to the respondent were a reference to the applicant, and

(b) the references to the applicant were references to the respondent.

When interim order may start

22. (1) An interim order may provide for payments to be made from such date as the court may specify, except that the date must not be earlier than the date of the making of the application for an order under Part 1, 2 or 3.

(2) Sub-paragraph (1) is subject to paragraph 27(7) and (8).

Payments which can be treated as having been paid on account

23. (1) If an interim order made by the High Court on an appeal made by virtue of paragraph 46 provides for payments to be made from a date earlier than the date of the making of the order, the interim order may provide that payments made by the respondent under an order made by a magistrates' court are to be treated, to such extent and in such manner as may be provided by the interim order, as having been paid on account of any payment provided for by the interim order.

(2) In relation to an interim order in respect of an application for an order under Part 2 by the civil partner who has agreed to make the financial provision specified in the application, sub-paragraph (1) applies as if the reference to the respondent were a reference to the applicant.

When interim order ceases to have effect

24. (1) Subject to sub-paragraphs (2) and (3), an interim order made on an application for an order under Part 1, 2 or 3 ceases to have effect on the earliest of the following dates—
  (a) the date, if any, specified for the purpose in the interim order;
  (b) the date on which the period of 3 months beginning with the date of the making of the interim order ends;
  (c) the date on which a magistrates' court either makes a final order on, or dismisses, the application.

(2) If an interim order made under this Part would, but for this sub-paragraph, cease to have effect under sub-paragraph (1)(a) or (b)—
  (a) the magistrates' court which made the order, or
  (b) in the case of an interim order made by the High Court, the magistrates' court by which the application for an order under Part 1, 2 or 3 is to be reheard,
may by order provide that the interim order is to continue in force for a further period.

(3) An order continued in force under sub-paragraph (2) ceases to have effect on the earliest of the following dates—
  (a) the date, if any, specified for the purpose in the order continuing it;
  (b) the date on which ends the period of 3 months beginning with—
    (i) the date of the making of the order continuing it, or
    (ii) if more than one such order has been made with respect to the application, the date of the making of the first such order;
  (c) the date on which the court either makes a final order on, or dismisses, the application.

Supplementary

25. (1) An interim order made by the High Court under paragraph 20(3) on ordering an application to be reheard by a magistrates' court is to be treated for the purposes of—
  (a) its enforcement, and
  (b) Part 6 (variation etc. of orders),
as if it were an order of that magistrates' court (and not of the High Court).

(2) No appeal lies from the making of or refusal to make, the variation of or refusal to vary, or the revocation of or refusal to revoke, an interim order.

PART 5 COMMENCEMENT AND DURATION OF ORDERS UNDER PARTS 1, 2 AND 3

Duration of periodical payments order for a civil partner

26. (1) The court may specify in a periodical payments order made under paragraph 2(1)(a) or Part 3 in favour of a civil partner such term as it thinks fit, except that the term must not—
  (a) begin before the date of the making of the application for the order, or
  (b) extend beyond the death of either of the civil partners.

(2) If—

    (a) a periodical payments order is made under paragraph 2(1)(a) or Part 3 in favour of one of the civil partners, and

    (b) the civil partnership is subsequently dissolved or annulled but the order continues in force,

the periodical payments order ceases to have effect (regardless of anything in it) on the formation of a subsequent civil partnership or marriage by that civil partner, except in relation to any arrears due under the order on the date of that event.

Age limit on making orders for financial provision for children and duration of such orders

27. (1) Subject to sub-paragraph (5), no order is to be made under paragraph 2(1)(c) or (d) or Part 3 in favour of a child who has reached 18.

(2) The term to be specified in a periodical payments order made under paragraph 2(1)(c) or Part 3 in favour of a child may begin with—

    (a) the date of the making of an application for the order or a later date, or

    (b) a date ascertained in accordance with sub-paragraph (7) or (8).

(3) The term to be specified in such an order—

    (a) must not in the first instance extend beyond the date of the birthday of the child next following his reaching the upper limit of the compulsory school age unless the court considers that in the circumstances of the case the welfare of the child requires that it should extend to a later date, and

    (b) must not in any event, subject to sub-paragraph (5), extend beyond the date of the child's 18th birthday.

(4) Sub-paragraph (3)(a) must be read with section 8 of the Education Act 1996 (c. 56) (which applies to determine for the purposes of any enactment whether a person is of compulsory school age).

(5) Sub-paragraphs (1) and (3)(b) do not apply in the case of a child if it appears to the court that—

    (a) the child is, or will be, or, if such an order were made without complying with either or both of those provisions, would be—

      (i) receiving instruction at an educational establishment, or

      (ii) undergoing training for a trade, profession or vocation,

    whether or not also the child is, will be or would be, in gainful employment, or

    (b) there are special circumstances which justify the making of the order without complying with either or both of sub-paragraphs (1) and (3)(b).

(6) Any order made under paragraph 2(1)(c) or Part 3 in favour of a child, regardless of anything in the order, ceases to have effect on the death of the person liable to make payments under the order.

(7) If—

    (a) a maintenance calculation ('current calculation') is in force with respect to a child, and

    (b) an application is made for an order under paragraph 2(1)(c) or Part 3—

      (i) in accordance with section 8 of the Child Support Act 1991 (c. 48), and

      (ii) before the end of 6 months beginning with the making of the current calculation,

the term to be specified in any such order made on that application may be expressed to begin on, or at any time after, the earliest permitted date.

(8) 'The earliest permitted date' is whichever is the later of—

    (a) the date 6 months before the application is made, or

    (b) the date on which the current calculation took effect or, where successive maintenance calculations have been continuously in force with respect to a child, on which the first of those calculations took effect.

(9) If—
  (a) a maintenance calculation ceases to have effect by or under any provision of the 1991 Act, and
  (b) an application is made, before the end of 6 months beginning with the relevant date, for a periodical payments order under paragraph 2(1)(c) or Part 3 in favour of a child with respect to whom that maintenance calculation was in force immediately before it ceased to have effect,
the term to be specified in any such order, or in any interim order under Part 4, made on that application, may begin with the date on which that maintenance calculation ceased to have effect or any later date.

(10) 'The relevant date' means the date on which the maintenance calculation ceased to have effect.

(11) In this Schedule 'maintenance calculation' has the same meaning as it has in the 1991 Act by virtue of section 54 of the 1991 Act as read with any regulations in force under that section.

Application of paragraphs 26 and 27 to Part 2 orders

28. (1) Subject to sub-paragraph (3), paragraph 26 applies in relation to an order under Part 2 which requires periodical payments to be made to a civil partner for his own benefit as it applies in relation to an order under paragraph 2(1)(a).

(2) Subject to sub-paragraph (3), paragraph 27 applies in relation to an order under Part 2 for the making of financial provision in respect of a child of the family as it applies in relation to an order under paragraph 2(1)(c) or (d).

(3) If—
  (a) the court makes an order under Part 2 which contains provision for the making of periodical payments, and
  (b) by virtue of paragraph 14, an application for an order under Part 1 is treated as if it had been withdrawn,
the term which may be specified under Part 2 as the term for which the payments are to be made may begin with the date of the making of the application for the order under Part 1 or any later date.

Effect on certain orders of parties living together

29. (1) Sub-paragraph (2) applies if periodical payments are required to be made to a civil partner (whether for the civil partner's own benefit or for the benefit of a child of the family)—
  (a) by an order made under Part 1 or 2, or
  (b) by an interim order made under Part 4 (otherwise than on an application under Part 3).

(2) The order is enforceable even though—
  (a) the civil partners are living with each other at the date of the making of the order, or
  (b) if they are not living with each other at that date, they subsequently resume living with each other;
but the order ceases to have effect if after that date the parties continue to live with each other, or resume living with each other, for a continuous period exceeding 6 months.

(3) Sub-paragraph (4) applies if—
  (a) an order is made under Part 1 or 2 which requires periodical payments to be made to a child of the family, or
  (b) an interim order is made under Part 4 (otherwise than on an application under Part 3) which requires periodical payments to be made to a child of the family.

(4) Unless the court otherwise directs, the order continues to have effect and is enforceable even if—

(a) the civil partners are living with each other at the date of the making of the order, or

(b) if they are not living with each other at that date, they subsequently resume living with each other.

(5) An order made under Part 3, and any interim order made on an application for an order under that Part, ceases to have effect if the civil partners resume living with each other.

(6) If an order made under this Schedule ceases to have effect under—

(a) sub-paragraph (2) or (5), or

(b) a direction given under sub-paragraph (4),

a magistrates' court may, on an application made by either civil partner, make an order declaring that the order ceased to have effect from such date as the court may specify.

PART 6   VARIATION ETC. OF ORDERS

Power to vary, revoke, suspend or revive order

30. (1) If a magistrates' court has made an order for the making of periodical payments under Part 1, 2 or 3, the court may, on an application made under this Part—

(a) vary or revoke the order,

(b) suspend any provision of it temporarily, or

(c) revive any provision so suspended.

(2) If a magistrates' court has made an interim order under Part 4, the court may, on an application made under this Part—

(a) vary or revoke the order,

(b) suspend any provision of it temporarily, or

(c) revive any provision so suspended,

except that it may not by virtue of this sub-paragraph extend the period for which the order is in force.

Powers to order lump sum on variation

31. (1) If a magistrates' court has made an order under paragraph 2(1)(a) or (c) for the making of periodical payments, the court may, on an application made under this Part, make an order for the payment of a lump sum under paragraph 2(1)(b) or (d).

(2) If a magistrates' court has made an order under Part 2 for the making of periodical payments by a civil partner the court may, on an application made under this Part, make an order for the payment of a lump sum by that civil partner—

(a) to the other civil partner, or

(b) to a child of the family or to that other civil partner for the benefit of that child.

(3) Where the court has power by virtue of this paragraph to make an order for the payment of a lump sum—

(a) the amount of the lump sum must not exceed the maximum amount that may at that time be required to be paid under Part 1, but

(b) the court may make an order for the payment of a lump sum not exceeding that amount even if the person required to pay it was required to pay a lump sum by a previous order under this Schedule.

(4) Where—

(a) the court has power by virtue of this paragraph to make an order for the payment of a lump sum, and

(b) the respondent or the applicant (as the case may be) has agreed to pay a lump sum of an amount exceeding the maximum amount that may at that time be required to be paid under Part 1, the court may, regardless of sub-paragraph (3), make an order for the payment of a lump sum of that amount.

Power to specify when order as varied is to take effect

32. An order made under this Part which varies an order for the making of periodical payments may provide that the payments as so varied are to be made from such date as the court may specify, except that, subject to paragraph 33, the date must not be earlier than the date of the making of the application under this Part.

33. (1) If—
   (a) there is in force an order ('the order')—
      (i) under paragraph 2(1)(c),
      (ii) under Part 2 making provision of a kind set out in paragraph 10(1)(c) (regardless of whether it makes provision of any other kind mentioned in paragraph 10(1)(c)),
      (iii) under paragraph 16(1)(b), or
      (iv) which is an interim order under Part 4 under which the payments are to be made to a child or to the applicant for the benefit of a child,
   (b) the order requires payments specified in it to be made to or for the benefit of more than one child without apportioning those payments between them,
   (c) a maintenance calculation ('the calculation') is made with respect to one or more, but not all, of the children with respect to whom those payments are to be made, and
   (d) an application is made, before the end of 6 months beginning with the date on which the calculation was made, for the variation or revocation of the order,
the court may, in exercise of its powers under this Part to vary or revoke the order, direct that the variation or revocation is to take effect from the date on which the calculation took effect or any later date.

   (2) If—
   (a) an order ('the child order') of a kind prescribed for the purposes of section 10(1) of the Child Support Act 1991 is affected by a maintenance calculation,
   (b) on the date on which the child order became so affected there was in force an order ('the civil partner's order')—
      (i) under paragraph 2(1)(a),
      (ii) under Part 2 making provision of a kind set out in paragraph 10(1)(a) (regardless of whether it makes provision of any other kind mentioned in paragraph 10(1)(a)),
      (iii) under paragraph 16(1)(a), or
      (iv) which is an interim order under Part 4 under which the payments are to be made to the applicant (otherwise than for the benefit of a child), and
   (c) an application is made, before the end of 6 months beginning with the date on which the maintenance calculation was made, for the civil partner's order to be varied or revoked,
the court may, in exercise of its powers under this Part to vary or revoke the civil partner's order, direct that the variation or revocation is to take effect from the date on which the child order became so affected or any later date.

   (3) For the purposes of sub-paragraph (2), an order is affected if it ceases to have effect or is modified by or under section 10 of the 1991 Act.

Matters to which court is to have regard in exercising powers under this Part

34. (1) In exercising the powers conferred by this Part the court must, so far as it appears to the court just to do so, give effect to any agreement which has been reached between the civil partners in relation to the application.

(2) If—

    (a) there is no such agreement, or

    (b) if the court decides not to give effect to the agreement,

the court must have regard to all the circumstances of the case, giving first consideration to the welfare while under 18 of any child of the family who has not reached 18.

(3) Those circumstances include any change in any of the matters—

    (a) to which the court was required to have regard when making the order to which the application relates, or

    (b) in the case of an application for the variation or revocation of an order made under Part 2 or on an appeal made by virtue of paragraph 46, to which the court would have been required to have regard if that order had been made under Part 1.

Variation of orders for periodical payments: further provisions

35. (1) The power of the court under paragraphs 30 to 34 to vary an order for the making of periodical payments includes power, if the court is satisfied that payment has not been made in accordance with the order, to exercise one of its powers under section 59(3)(a) to (d) of the Magistrates' Courts Act 1980 (c. 43).

(2) Sub-paragraph (1) is subject to paragraph 37.

36. (1) If—

    (a) a magistrates' court has made an order under this Schedule for the making of periodical payments, and

    (b) payments under the order are required to be made by any method of payment falling within section 59(6) of the 1980 Act (standing order, etc.),

an application may be made under this sub-paragraph to the court for the order to be varied as mentioned in sub-paragraph (2).

(2) Subject to sub-paragraph (4), if an application is made under sub-paragraph (1), a justices' clerk, after—

    (a) giving written notice (by post or otherwise) of the application to the respondent, and

    (b) allowing the respondent, within the period of 14 days beginning with the date of the giving of that notice, an opportunity to make written representations,

may vary the order to provide that payments under the order are to be made to the designated officer for the court.

(3) The clerk may proceed with an application under sub-paragraph (1) even if the respondent has not received written notice of the application.

(4) If an application has been made under sub-paragraph (1), the clerk may, if he considers it inappropriate to exercise his power under sub-paragraph (2), refer the matter to the court which, subject to paragraph 37, may vary the order by exercising one of its powers under section 59(3)(a) to (d) of the 1980 Act.

37. (1) Before varying the order by exercising one of its powers under section 59(3)(a) to (d) of the 1980 Act, the court must have regard to any representations made by the parties to the application.

(2) If the court does not propose to exercise its power under section 59(3)(c), (cc) or (d) of the 1980 Act, the court must, unless upon representations expressly made in that behalf by the person to whom payments under the order are required to be made it is satisfied that it is undesirable to do so, exercise its power under section 59(3)(b).

38. (1) Section 59(4) of the 1980 Act (power of court to order that account be opened) applies for the purposes of paragraphs 35 and 36(4) as it applies for the purposes of section 59.

(2) None of the powers of the court, or of a justices' clerk, conferred by paragraphs 35 to 37 and sub-paragraph (1) is exercisable in relation to an order under this Schedule for the making of periodical payments which is not a qualifying maintenance order (within the meaning of section 59 of the 1980 Act).

Persons who may apply under this Part

39. An application under paragraph 30, 31 or 36 may be made—
    (a) if it is for the variation or revocation of an order under Part 1, 2, 3 or 4 for periodical payments, by either civil partner, and
    (b) if it is for the variation of an order under paragraph 2(1)(c) or Part 2 or 3 for periodical payments to or in respect of a child, also by the child himself, if he has reached 16.

Revival of orders for periodical payments

40. (1) If an order made by a magistrates' court under this Schedule for the making of periodical payments to or in respect of a child (other than an interim order) ceases to have effect—
    (a) on the date on which the child reaches 16, or
    (b) at any time after that date but before or on the date on which he reaches 18,
the child may apply to the court which made the order for an order for its revival.
    (2) If on such an application it appears to the court that—
    (a) the child is, will be or (if an order were made under this sub-paragraph) would be receiving instruction at an educational establishment or undergoing training for a trade, profession or vocation, whether or not while in gainful employment, or
    (b) there are special circumstances which justify the making of an order under this sub-paragraph,
the court may by order revive the order from such date as the court may specify, not being earlier than the date of the making of the application.
    (3) Any order revived under this paragraph may be varied or revoked under paragraphs 30 to 34 in the same way as it could have been varied or revoked had it continued in being.

Variation of instalments of lump sum

41. If in the exercise of its powers under section 75 of the 1980 Act a magistrates' court orders that a lump sum required to be paid under this Schedule is to be paid by instalments, the court, on an application made by either the person liable to pay or the person entitled to receive that sum, may vary that order by varying—
    (a) the number of instalments payable,
    (b) the amount of any instalment payable, and
    (c) the date on which any instalment becomes payable.

Supplementary provisions with respect to variation and revocation of orders

42. None of the following powers apply in relation to an order made under this Schedule—
    (a) the powers of a magistrates' court to revoke, revive or vary an order for the periodical payment of money and the power of a justices' clerk to vary such an order under section 60 of the 1980 Act;
    (b) the power of a magistrates' court to suspend or rescind certain other orders under section 63(2) of the 1980 Act.

PART 7 ARREARS AND REPAYMENTS

Enforcement etc. of orders for payment of money

43. Section 32 of the Domestic Proceedings and Magistrates' Courts Act 1978 (c. 22) applies in relation to orders under this Schedule as it applies in relation to orders under Part 1 of that Act.

Orders for repayment after cessation of order because of subsequent civil partnership etc.

44. (1) Sub-paragraphs (3) and (4) apply if—
  (a) an order made under paragraph 2(1)(a) or Part 2 or 3 has, under paragraph 26(2), ceased to have effect because of the formation of a subsequent civil partnership or marriage by the party ('R') in whose favour it was made, and
  (b) the person liable to make payments under the order ('P') made payments in accordance with it in respect of a relevant period in the mistaken belief that the order was still subsisting.

(2) 'Relevant period' means a period after the date of the formation of the subsequent civil partnership or marriage.

(3) No proceedings in respect of a cause of action arising out of the circumstances mentioned in sub-paragraph (1)(a) and (b) is maintainable by P (or P's personal representatives) against R (or R's personal representatives).

(4) But on an application made under this paragraph by P (or P's personal representatives) against R (or R's personal representatives) the court—
  (a) may order the respondent to pay to the applicant a sum equal to the amount of the payments made in respect of the relevant period, or
  (b) if it appears to the court that it would be unjust to make that order, may—
    (i) order the respondent to pay to the applicant such lesser sum as it thinks fit, or
    (ii) dismiss the application.

(5) An order under this paragraph for the payment of any sum may provide for the payment of that sum by instalments of such amount as may be specified in the order.

(6) An application under this paragraph—
  (a) may be made in proceedings in the High Court or a county court for leave to enforce, or the enforcement of, the payment of arrears under an order made under paragraph 2(1)(a) or Part 2 or 3, but
  (b) if not made in such proceedings, must be made to a county court,
and accordingly references in this paragraph to the court are references to the High Court or a county court, as the circumstances require.

(7) The jurisdiction conferred on a county court by this paragraph is exercisable by a county court even though, because of the amount claimed in an application under this paragraph, the jurisdiction would not but for this sub-paragraph be exercisable by a county court.

(8) Subject to sub-paragraph (9)—
  (a) the designated officer for a magistrates' court to whom any payments under an order made under paragraph 2(1)(a), or Part 2 or 3, are required to be made is not liable for any act done by him in pursuance of the order after the date on which that order ceased to have effect because of the formation of a subsequent civil partnership or marriage by the person entitled to payments under it, and
  (b) the collecting officer under an attachment of earnings order made to secure payments under the order under paragraph 2(1)(a), or Part 2 or 3, is not liable for any act done by him after that date in accordance with any enactment or rule of court specifying how payments made to him in compliance with the attachment of earnings order are to be dealt with.

(9) Sub-paragraph (8) applies if (but only if) the act—
  (a) was one which he would have been under a duty to do had the order under paragraph 2(1)(a) or Part 2 or 3 not ceased to have effect, and
  (b) was done before notice in writing of the formation of the subsequent civil partnership or marriage was given to him by or on behalf of—
    (i)   the person entitled to payments under the order,
    (ii) the person liable to make payments under it, or
    (iii) the personal representatives of either of them.

(10) In this paragraph 'collecting officer', in relation to an attachment of earnings order, means—

(a) the officer of the High Court, or

(b) the officer designated by the Lord Chancellor,

to whom a person makes payments in compliance with the order.

PART 8   SUPPLEMENTARY

Restrictions on making of orders under this Schedule: welfare of children

45. If—

(a) an application is made by a civil partner for an order under Part 1, 2 or 3, and

(b) there is a child of the family who is under 18,

the court must not dismiss or make a final order on the application until it has decided whether to exercise any of its powers under the Children Act 1989 (c. 41) with respect to the child.

Constitution of courts, powers of High Court and county court in relation to orders and appeals

46. The following provisions of the Domestic Proceedings and Magistrates' Courts Act 1978 (c. 22) apply in relation to an order under this Schedule relating to a civil partnership as they apply in relation to an order under Part 1 of that Act relating to a marriage—

(a) section 28 (powers of the High Court and a county court in relation to certain orders),

(b) section 29 (appeals), and

(c) section 31 (constitution of courts).

Provisions as to jurisdiction and procedure

47. (1) Subject to section 2 of the Family Law Act 1986 (c. 55) and section 70 of the Magistrates' Courts Act 1980 (c. 43) and any determination of the Lord Chancellor, a magistrates' court has jurisdiction to hear an application for an order under this Schedule if it acts in, or is authorised by the Lord Chancellor to act for, a local justice area in which either the applicant or the respondent ordinarily resides at the date of the making of the application.

(2) Any jurisdiction conferred on a magistrates' court by this Schedule is exercisable even if any party to the proceedings is not domiciled in England and Wales.

Meaning of 'child of the family'

48. In this Schedule 'child of the family', in relation to two people who are civil partners of each other, means—

(a) a child of both of them, and

(b) any other child, other than a child placed with them as foster parents by a local authority or voluntary organisation, who has been treated by both the civil partners as a child of their family.

SCHEDULE 21   REFERENCES TO STEPCHILDREN ETC. IN EXISTING ACTS

. . .

24. Section 113(2) of the Housing Act 1985 (c. 68) (members of a person's family).

. . .

33. The definition of 'relative' in section 105(1) of the Children Act 1989 (c. 41) (interpretation).

. . .

43. The definition of 'relative' in section 63(1) of the Family Law Act 1996 (c. 27) (interpretation of Part 4 of the 1996 Act).

...

45. Section 140(2) of [the Housing Act 1996 (c. 52)] (members of a person's family: Chapter 1).

...

47. The definition of 'relative' in section 178(3) of that Act (meaning of associated person).

...

Equality Act 2006
(2006 c. 3)

PART 1   THE COMMISSION FOR EQUALITY AND HUMAN RIGHTS

The Commission

1   Establishment
There shall be a body corporate known as the Commission for Equality and Human Rights.

...

3   General duty
The Commission shall exercise its functions under this Part with a view to encouraging and supporting the development of a society in which—
>   (a) people's ability to achieve their potential is not limited by prejudice or discrimination,
>   (b) there is respect for and protection of each individual's human rights,
>   (c) there is respect for the dignity and worth of each individual,
>   (d) each individual has an equal opportunity to participate in society, and
>   (e) there is mutual respect between groups based on understanding and valuing of diversity and on shared respect for equality and human rights.

...

Duties

8   Equality and diversity
(1) The Commission shall, by exercising the powers conferred by this Part—
>   (a) promote understanding of the importance of equality and diversity,
>   (b) encourage good practice in relation to equality and diversity,
>   (c) promote equality of opportunity,
>   (d) promote awareness and understanding of rights under the equality enactments,
>   (e) enforce the equality enactments,
>   (f) work towards the elimination of unlawful discrimination, and
>   (g) work towards the elimination of unlawful harassment.

(2) In subsection (1)—
'diversity' means the fact that individuals are different,
'equality' means equality between individuals, and
'unlawful' is to be construed in accordance with section 34.

(3) In promoting equality of opportunity between disabled persons and others, the Commission may, in particular, promote the favourable treatment of disabled persons.

(4) In this Part 'disabled person' means a person who—

(a) is a disabled person within the meaning of the Disability Discrimination Act 1995 (c. 50), or

(b) has been a disabled person within that meaning (whether or not at a time when that Act had effect).

9   Human rights

(1) The Commission shall, by exercising the powers conferred by this Part—

    (a) promote understanding of the importance of human rights,

    (b) encourage good practice in relation to human rights,

    (c) promote awareness, understanding and protection of human rights, and

    (d) encourage public authorities to comply with section 6 of the Human Rights Act 1998 (c. 42) (compliance with Convention rights).

(2) In this Part 'human rights' means—

    (a) the Convention rights within the meaning given by section 1 of the Human Rights Act 1998, and

    (b) other human rights.

(3) In determining what action to take in pursuance of this section the Commission shall have particular regard to the importance of exercising the powers conferred by this Part in relation to the Convention rights.

(4) In fulfilling a duty under section 8 or 10 the Commission shall take account of any relevant human rights.

(5) A reference in this Part (including this section) to human rights does not exclude any matter by reason only of its being a matter to which section 8 or 10 relates.

10   Groups

(1) The Commission shall, by exercising the powers conferred by this Part—

    (a) promote understanding of the importance of good relations—

        (i) between members of different groups, and

        (ii) between members of groups and others,

    (b) encourage good practice in relation to relations—

        (i) between members of different groups, and

        (ii) between members of groups and others,

    (c) work towards the elimination of prejudice against, hatred of and hostility towards members of groups, and

    (d) work towards enabling members of groups to participate in society.

(2) In this Part 'group' means a group or class of persons who share a common attribute in respect of any of the following matters—

    (a) age,

    (b) disability,

    (c) gender,

    (d) proposed, commenced or completed reassignment of gender (within the meaning given by section 82(1) of the Sex Discrimination Act 1975 (c. 65)),

    (e) race,

    (f) religion or belief, and

    (g) sexual orientation.

(3) For the purposes of this Part a reference to a group (as defined in subsection (2)) includes a reference to a smaller group or smaller class, within a group, of persons who share a common attribute (in addition to the attribute by reference to which the group is defined) in respect of any of the matters specified in subsection (2)(a) to (g).

(4) In determining what action to take in pursuance of this section the Commission shall have particular regard to the importance of exercising the powers conferred by this Part in relation to groups defined by reference to race, religion or belief.

. . .

PART 2   DISCRIMINATION ON GROUNDS OF
RELIGION OR BELIEF

General exceptions

61   Education, training and welfare

Nothing in this Part shall make it unlawful to do anything by way of—

(a) meeting special needs for education, training or welfare of persons of a religion or belief, or

(b) providing ancillary benefits in connection with meeting the needs mentioned in paragraph (a).

62   Care within family

Nothing in this Part shall make it unlawful for a person to take into his home, and treat in the same manner as a member of his family, a person who requires a special degree of care and attention (whether by reason of being a child or an elderly person or otherwise).

PART 3   DISCRIMINATION ON GROUNDS
OF SEXUAL ORIENTATION

81   Regulations

(1) The Secretary of State may by regulations make provision about discrimination or harassment on grounds of sexual orientation.

(2) In subsection (1) 'sexual orientation' has the meaning given by section 35.

(3) The regulations may, in particular—

(a) make provision of a kind similar to Part 2 of this Act;

(b) define discrimination;

(c) define harassment;

(d) make provision for enforcement (which may, in particular, include provision—

(i)   creating a criminal offence of a kind similar to, and with the same maximum penalties as, an offence created by an enactment relating to discrimination or equality;

(ii) about validity and revision of contracts;

(iii) about discriminatory advertisements;

(iv) about instructing or causing discrimination or harassment);

(e) provide for exceptions (whether or not of a kind similar to those provided for by Part 2 of this Act or any other enactment relating to discrimination or equality);

(f) make provision which applies generally or only in specified cases or circumstances;

(g) make different provision for different cases or circumstances;

(h) include incidental or consequential provision (which may include provision amending an enactment);

(i) include transitional provision.

(4) The regulations—

(a) shall be made by statutory instrument, and

(b) may not be made unless a draft has been laid before and approved by resolution of each House of Parliament.

Children and Adoption Act 2006
(2006 c. 20)

PART 1   ORDERS WITH RESPECT TO CHILDREN IN FAMILY PROCEEDINGS

. . .

Transitional provision

8   Transitional provision

(1) This section applies to any contact order under section 8 of the Children Act 1989 made before, and in force on, the relevant date.

(2) For so long as a contact order to which this section applies continues in force on and after the relevant date without being varied, the circumstances in which a notice under section 11I of the Children Act 1989 is to be attached to the contact order include—

    (a) where an application for such a notice to be attached to the contact order is made by a person who, as regards the order, falls within any of paragraphs (a) to (d) of section 11J(5) of the Children Act 1989;

    (b) where, in any family proceedings, a question arises with respect to the contact order.

(3) Where the person proposing to apply under subsection (2)(a) is the child with respect to whom the contact order was made, subsections (6) and (7) of section 11J have effect in relation to the application under subsection (2)(a) as they have effect in relation to an application under section 11J for an enforcement order.

(4) If a failure to comply with a contact order to which this section applies occurs while the contact order continues in force as described in subsection (2), each of sections 11K(1) and 11P(1) of the Children Act 1989 is to have effect, in relation to the failure, as if for paragraphs (a) and (b) there were substituted 'a notice under section 11I relating to the contact order'.

(5) In this section 'relevant date' means the day on which sections 3 to 5 come into force.

. . .

APPENDIX

International Conventions

The European Convention for the Protection of Human Rights and Fundamental Freedoms (1950)

...

Article 3

Prohibition of torture

No one shall be subjected to torture or to inhuman or degrading treatment or punishment.

...

Article 6

Right to a fair trial

1. In the determination of his civil rights and obligations or of any criminal charge against him, everyone is entitled to a fair and public hearing within a reasonable time by an independent and impartial tribunal established by law. Judgment shall be pronounced publicly but the press and public may be excluded from all or part of the trial in the interests of morals, public order or national security in a democratic society, where the interests of juveniles or the protection of the private life of the parties so require, or to the extent strictly necessary in the opinion of the court in special circumstances where publicity would prejudice the interests of justice.

2. Everyone charged with a criminal offence shall be presumed innocent until proved guilty according to law.

3. Everyone charged with a criminal offence has the following minimum rights:
    (a) to be informed promptly, in a language which he understands and in detail, of the nature and cause of the accusation against him;
    (b) to have adequate time and facilities for the preparation of his defence;
    (c) to defend himself in person or through legal assistance of his own choosing or, if he has not sufficient means to pay for legal assistance, to be given it free when the interests of justice so require;
    (d) to examine or have examined witnesses against him and to obtain the attendance and examination of witnesses on his behalf under the same conditions as witnesses against him;
    (e) to have the free assistance of an interpreter if he cannot understand or speak the language used in court.

...

Article 8

Right to respect for private and family life

1. Everyone has the right to respect for his private and family life, his home and his correspondence.

2. There shall be no interference by a public authority with the exercise of this right except such as is in accordance with the law and is necessary in a democratic society in the

interests of national security, public safety or the economic well-being of the country, for the prevention of disorder or crime, for the protection of health or morals, or for the protection of the rights and freedoms of others.

...

Article 12

Right to marry

Men and women of marriageable age have the right to marry and to found a family, according to the national laws governing the exercise of this right.

...

Article 14

Prohibition of discrimination

The enjoyment of the rights and freedoms set forth in this Convention shall be secured without discrimination on any ground such as sex, race, colour, language, religion, political or other opinion, national or social origin, association with a national minority, property, birth or other status.

...

The First Protocol

Article 1

Protection of property

Every natural or legal person is entitled to the peaceful enjoyment of his possessions. No one shall be deprived of his possessions except in the public interest and subject to the conditions provided for by law and by the general principles of international law.

The preceding provisions shall not, however, in any way impair the right of a State to enforce such laws as it deems necessary to control the use of property in accordance with the general interest or to secure the payment of taxes or other contributions or penalties.

Article 2

Right to education

No person shall be denied the right to education. In the exercise of any functions which it assumes in relation to education and to teaching, the State shall respect the right of parents to ensure such education and teaching in conformity with their own religious and philosophical convictions.

United Nations Convention on the Rights of the Child (1989)

Part I

Article 1

For the purposes of the present Convention, a child means every human being below the age of eighteen years unless, under the law applicable to the child, majority is attained earlier.

Article 2

1. States Parties shall respect and ensure the rights set forth in the present Convention to each child within their jurisdiction without discrimination of any kind, irrespective of the child's or his or her parent's or legal guardian's race, colour, sex, language, religion, political or other opinion, national, ethnic or social origin, property, disability, birth or other status.

2. States Parties shall take all appropriate measures to ensure that the child is protected against all forms of discrimination or punishment on the basis of the status, activities, expressed opinions, or beliefs of the child's parents, legal guardians, or family members.

Article 3

1. In all actions concerning children, whether undertaken by public or private social welfare institutions, courts of law, administrative authorities or legislative bodies, the best interests of the child shall be a primary consideration.

2. States Parties undertake to ensure the child such protection and care as is necessary for his or her well-being, taking into account the rights and duties of his or her parents, legal guardians, or other individuals legally responsible for him or her, and to this end, shall take all appropriate legislative and administrative measures.

3. States Parties shall ensure that the institutions, services and facilities responsible for the care or protection of children shall conform with the standards established by competent authorities, particularly in the areas of safety, health, in the number and suitability of their staff, as well as competent supervision.

. . .

Article 6

1. States Parties recognise that every child has the inherent right to life.

2. States Parties shall ensure to the maximum extent possible the survival and development of the child.

Article 7

1. The child shall be registered immediately after birth and shall have the right from birth to a name, the right to acquire a nationality and, as far as possible, the right to know and be cared for by his or her parents.

2. States Parties shall ensure the implementation of these rights in accordance with their national law and their obligations under the relevant international instruments in this field, in particular where the child would otherwise be stateless.

. . .

Article 9

1. States Parties shall ensure that a child shall not be separated from his or her parents against their will, except when competent authorities subject to judicial review determine, in accordance with applicable law and procedures, that such separation is necessary for the best interests of the child. Such determination may be necessary in a particular case such as one involving abuse or neglect of the child by the parents, or one where the parents are living separately and a decision must be made as to the child's place of residence.

2. In any proceedings pursuant to paragraph 1 of the present article, all interested parties shall be given the opportunity to participate in the proceedings and make their views known.

3. States Parties shall respect the right of the child who is separated from one or both parents to maintain personal relations and direct contact with both parents on a regular basis, except if it is contrary to the child's best interests.

4. Where such separation results from any action initiated by a State Party, such as the detention, imprisonment, exile, deportation or death (including death arising from any cause while the person is in the custody of the State) of one or both parents or of the child, that State Party shall, upon request, provide the parents, the child or, if appropriate, another member of the family with the essential information concerning the whereabouts of the absent member(s) of the family unless the provision of the information would be detrimental to the well-being of the child. States Parties shall further ensure that the submission of such a request shall of itself entail no adverse consequences for the person(s) concerned.

Article 10

1. In accordance with the obligation of States Parties under article 9, paragraph 1, applications by a child or his or her parents to enter or leave a State Party for the purposes of

family reunification shall be dealt with by States Parties in a positive, humane and expeditious manner. States Parties shall further ensure that the submission of such a request shall entail no adverse consequences for the applicants and for the members of their family.

2. A child whose parents reside in different States shall have the right to maintain on a regular basis, save in exceptional circumstances, personal relations and direct contacts with both parents. Towards that end and in accordance with the obligation of States Parties under article 9, paragraph 1, States Parties shall respect the right of the child and his or her parents to leave any country, including their own, and to enter their own country. The right to leave any country shall be subject only to such restrictions as are prescribed by law and which are necessary to protect the national security, public order (*ordre public*), public health or morals or the rights and freedoms of others and are consistent with the other rights recognised in the present Convention.

. . .

Article 12

1. States Parties shall assure to the child who is capable of forming his or her own views the right to express those views freely in all matters affecting the child, the views of the child being given due weight in accordance with the age and maturity of the child.

2. For this purpose, the child shall in particular be provided the opportunity to be heard in any judicial and administrative proceedings affecting the child, either directly, or through a representative or an appropriate body, in a manner consistent with the procedural rules of national law.

. . .

Article 18

1. States Parties shall use their best efforts to ensure recognition of the principle that both parents have common responsibilities for the upbringing and development of the child. Parents or, as the case may be, legal guardians, have the primary responsibility for the upbringing and development of the child. The best interests of the child will be their basic concern.

2. For the purpose of guaranteeing and promoting the rights set forth in the present Convention, States Parties shall render appropriate assistance to parents and legal guardians in the performance of their child-rearing responsibilities and shall ensure the development of institutions, facilities and services for the care of children.

3. States Parties shall take all appropriate measures to ensure that children of working parents have the right to benefit from child-care services and facilities for which they are eligible.

. . .

Article 22

1. States Parties shall take appropriate measures to ensure that a child who is seeking refugee status or who is considered a refugee in accordance with applicable international or domestic law and procedures shall, whether unaccompanied or accompanied by his or her parents or by any other person, receive appropriate protection and humanitarian assistance in the enjoyment of applicable rights set forth in the present convention and in other international human rights or humanitarian instruments to which the said States are Parties.

2. For this purpose, States Parties shall provide, as they consider appropriate, co-operation in any efforts by the United Nations and other competent intergovernmental organisations or non-governmental organisations co-operating with the United Nations to protect and assist such a child and to trace the parents or other members of the family of any refugee child in order to obtain information necessary for reunification with his or her family. In cases where no parents or other members of the family can be found, the child shall be accorded the same protection as any other child permanently or temporarily deprived of his or her family environment for any reason, as set forth in the present Convention.

. . .

Article 40

1. States Parties recognise the right of every child alleged as, accused of, or recognised as having infringed the penal law to be treated in a manner consistent with the promotion of the child's sense of dignity and worth, which reinforces the child's respect for the human rights and fundamental freedoms of others and which takes into account the child's age and the desirability of promoting the child's reintegration and the child's assuming a constructive role in society.

2. To this end, and having regard to the relevant provisions of international instruments, States Parties shall, in particular, ensure that:

   (a) No child shall be alleged as, be accused of, or recognised as having infringed the penal law by reason of acts or omissions that were not prohibited by national or international law at the time they were committed;

   (b) Every child alleged as or accused of having infringed the penal law has at least the following guarantees:

      (i)   To be presumed innocent until proven guilty according to law;

      (ii) To be informed promptly and directly of the charges against him or her, and, if appropriate, through his or her parents or legal guardians, and to have legal or other appropriate assistance in the preparation and presentation of his or her defence;

      (iii) To have the matter determined without delay by a competent, independent and impartial authority or judicial body in a fair hearing according to law, in the presence of legal or other appropriate assistance and, unless it is considered not to be in the best interest of the child, in particular, taking into account his or her age or situation, his or her parents or legal guardians;

      (iv) Not to be compelled to give testimony or to confess guilt; to examine or have examined adverse witnesses and to obtain the participation and examination of witnesses on his or her behalf under conditions of equality;

      (v)   If considered to have infringed the penal law, to have this decision and any measures imposed in consequence thereof reviewed by a higher competent, independent and impartial authority or judicial body according to law;

      (vi) To have the free assistance of an interpreter if the child cannot understand or speak the language used;

      (vii) To have his or her privacy fully respected at all stages of the proceedings.

3. States Parties shall seek to promote the establishment of laws, procedures, authorities and institutions specifically applicable to children alleged as, accused of, or recognised as having infringed the penal law, and, in particular:

   (a) The establishment of a minimum age below which children shall be presumed not to have the capacity to infringe the penal law;

   (b) Whenever appropriate and desirable, measures for dealing with such children without resorting to judicial proceedings, providing that human rights and legal safeguards are fully respected.

4. A variety of dispositions, such as care, guidance and supervision orders; counselling; probation; foster care; education and vocational training programmes and other alternatives to institutional care shall be available to ensure that children are dealt with in a manner appropriate to their well-being and proportionate both to their circumstances and the offence.

. . .

INDEX